Founding of Jamestown, Virginia
Landing of Pilgrims at Plymouth

Boston Massacre

Battles of Lexington and Concord
Declaration of Independence

Treaty of Paris

Constitutional Convention

George Washington

John Adams

Thomas Jefferson

Louisiana Purchase

James Madison

James Monroe

John Quincy Adams

Andrew Jackson

Independence of Texas

Martin Van Buren

William Henry Harrison, John Tyler

Annexation of Texas
Mexican War

James K. Polk

Zachary Taylor

Millard Fillmore

Franklin Pierce

James Buchanan

Civil War
Pacific Railroad Act

Abraham Lincoln

Pacific Railroad Act

Andrew Johnson

Ulysses S. Grant

(continued on back cover)

CALIFORNIA
AN INTERPRETIVE HISTORY

CALIFORNIA
AN INTERPRETIVE HISTORY
FOURTH EDITION

WALTON BEAN
Late Professor of History
University of California, Berkeley

JAMES J. RAWLS
Instructor of History
Diablo Valley College

McGRAW-HILL BOOK COMPANY
New York   St. Louis   San Francisco   Auckland   Bogotá   Hamburg
Johannesburg   London   Madrid   Mexico   Montreal   New Delhi
Panama   Paris   São Paulo   Singapore   Sydney   Tokyo   Toronto

CALIFORNIA: An Interpretive History

1 2 3 4 5 6 7 8 9 0   DOCDOC   8 9 8 7 6 5 4 3 2

ISBN 0-07-004206-3

This book was set in Palatino by University Graphics, Inc.
The editors were Marian D. Provenzano and Barry Benjamin;
the designer was Charles A. Carson;
the production supervisor was Rosann E. Raspini.
R. R. Donnelley & Sons Company was printer and binder.

Library of Congress Cataloging in Publication Data

Bean, Walton.
    California: An interpretive history.

    Includes bibliographies and index.
    1. California—History.   I. Rawls, James J.
II. Title.
F861.B4   1982   979.4   82-9959
ISBN 0-07-004206-3   AACR2

CONTENTS

Preface   xv

Chapter 1
Introduction: Geography and History   1

Chapter 2
The Original Californians   3

Food and population   3
Aspects of material culture   6
Location, linguistic groups, tribes   7
Social culture   9

Chapter 3
Discovery, Exploration, and Founding   11

The finding and naming of California   11
Cabrillo and the discovery of Alta California   12
Francis Drake and Nova Albion   13
The Manila galleon and the California coast   15
Vizcaíno and Monterey   16
Spain's Indian policies   17
The mission as a frontier institution   18
Gálvez and the plan for Alta California   19
The Franciscans and Father Serra   21
The sacred expedition   22

Chapter 4
Outposts of a Dying Empire   28

Bucareli, Anza, and the founding of San Francisco   28
Neve and the pueblos of San José and Los Angeles   32
The Yuma massacre   34
The impact of the missions   35
Attempts at reinforcement   38
Exploration of the Central Valley   40
The coming of the Russians   41
The last years under the Spanish flag   42

Chapter 5
A Marginal Province of a Troubled Republic 45

Government and politics in theory and practice 45
The secularization problem 47
From Echeandía to Figueroa 48
Figueroa and secularization 50
Alvarado and provincial autonomy 51
The heyday of the rancheros 53

Chapter 6
American Infiltration: Traders, Trappers, and Settlers 57

The Yankee traders 57
The beaver trappers 59
Early settlers 62
Covered wagons, 1841 to 1846 65

Chapter 7
The American Conquest 69

Overtures, diplomatic and undiplomatic 69
Plans of the Polk administration 71
John Charles Frémont 73
The Bear Flag Revolt 76
The Mexican War and California 78

Chapter 8
The Gold Rush 84

Marshall's discovery at Sutter's Mill 84
The forty-eighters 85
The forty-niners 88
The diggings 91
Early mining methods 92
Mining camp law 94
The historical significance of the gold rush 95

Chapter 9
A New State and Frontier Politics 98

Military governments 98
The constitutional convention and its problems 99
The first legislature 104
The compromise of 1850 and the admission of California to the Union 105
The feud between Broderick and Gwin 106
Movements for state division 109
California and the Civil War 110

Chapter 10
Crime and Punishment
113

The nature of vigilantism | 113
Early lynching in the mines | 115
The "Hounds" in San Francisco | 115
The San Francisco committee of 1851 | 116
Statewide vigilance | 118
The San Francisco committee of 1856 | 120

Chapter 11
Land-Title Troubles
126

Problems of the Mexican grants | 126
The reports of Halleck and Jones | 128
The act of 1851 and the land commission | 129
Some crucial cases | 130

Chapter 12
Racial Oppression
133

Treatment of Mexican miners | 133
Early discrimination against the Chinese | 134
The "Indian question" | 137
Episodes in extermination | 140
Decline and exploitation | 142
The "free" blacks | 142

Chapter 13
Culture and Anarchy
145

Newspapers and literary magazines | 145
Writers of the fifties | 147
Bret Harte | 149
Mark Twain | 151
Joaquin Miller and other poets | 153
Churches and schools | 154

Chapter 14
A Frontier Economy
157

Gold mining | 157
The beginnings of banking | 159
The first Comstock silver boom, 1859–1864 | 160
Agriculture | 162
Early manufactures | 163
Transportation | 163

Chapter 15
Building the Central Pacific Railroad 166

Early proposals 166
Judah and the conception of the Central Pacific 166
Enter the four "associates" 167
Federal and state support 169
Difficulties, and the death of Judah 171
Solving the problems of construction 172

Chapter 16
The "Terrible Seventies" 176

The onset of depression 176
Transporation monopoly 177
Land monopoly 180
The Comstock and overspeculation 184

Chapter 17
Political Turmoil and a New Constitution 188

The increase of anti-Chinese sentiment 188
The Workingmen's party of California 190
The constitution of 1879 194
The frustration of reform 196
Chinese exclusion 197

Chapter 18
Economic Growth 199

The wheat bonanza 199
Wines 200
The citrus industry 201
Boom in real estate 203
Water and land 206
Electric railways and urbanization 208

Chapter 19
Labor and Capital 212

Backgrounds of the California labor movement 212
The rise of unions in San Francisco 213
Triumph of the open shop in Los Angeles 216
Agricultural labor: unorganized and disfranchised 220
The IWW 221

Chapter 20
Culture and Oligarchy
225

Henry George 225
Ambrose Bierce 227
Frank Norris 229
Jack London 231
Historiography 232
Lords of the press 234
The arts and architecture 235
Schools, colleges, and universities 239

Chapter 21
Politics in the Era of Railroad Domination
245

The Colton letters 246
The Huntington-Stanford feud 247
Los Angeles fights for a free harbor 248
The funding bill 249
The Southern Pacific machine 251
William F. Herrin 253
Failure of nineteenth-century reform movements 254

Chapter 22
The Roots of Reform
257

Boss Ruef and the Union Labor party 257
The San Francisco graft prosecution 259
The Good Government movement in Los Angeles 262
The Lincoln-Roosevelt League 264

Chapter 23
The Republican Progressives in Power
270

Public utility regulation 271
Governmental efficiency and finance 271
"More democracy" 272
"Nonpartisanship" and cross-filing 273
Woman suffrage 274
Public morals 275
The progressives and labor 276
The progressives and the anti-Japanese movement 278
The decline of progressivism 281

Chapter 24
The Triumph of Conservatism
286

Rise and fall of the socialist movement 286
The Mooney case 288

The criminal syndicalism law 290
Decline of organized labor 292
Collapse of the Democratic party 293
The continuing decline of Republican progressivism 294
The "Federal Plan" of reapportionment 296

Chapter 25
Oil, Automobiles, and Movies 299

Origins of the oil industry 299
The black bonanza 300
The oil boom of the twenties 302
The automobile revolution 304
The movies discover California 307
Rise of "the industry" 308

Chapter 26
Conservation, Water, Power, and Politics 314

The Yosemite and John Muir 314
Pinchot and Roosevelt 316
The Hetch Hetchy controversy and San Francisco's water supply 317
The Owens Valley–Los Angeles Aqueduct 319
Origins of the Boulder Canyon project 321
Public or private power? 323
Hoover Dam 325
The Colorado River Aqueduct 327
The Central Valley Project 328

Chapter 27
The Great Depression and Politics 335

"Sunny Jim" 336
Social messiahs 337
Labor strife 338
Upton Sinclair and EPIC 341
From Merriam to Olson 344

Chapter 28
Cultural Trends 348

Robinson Jeffers 348
John Steinbeck 350
William Saroyan and other writers 354
William Randolph Hearst and other journalists 355
The arts 357
Architecture 359

Chapter 29
Wartime Growth and Problems

Wartime Growth and Problems 364

The impact of federal spending 364
Wartime shipyards 365
Rise of the aircraft industry 366
The "relocation" of the Japanese Americans 368

Chapter 30
Republican Ascendancy and Democratic Revival

Republican Ascendancy and Democratic Revival 377

"Nonpartisanship" favors the Republicans 377
The governorship of Earl Warren 378
The power of special interests 379
The spurious issue of "loyalty" 382
The governorship of Goodwin J. Knight 386
Rise of informal party organizations 387
The Democratic triumph of 1958 388
Brown's legislative program 389
The California water plan 390
Extremists, right and left 391

Chapter 31
Industrialized Agriculture and Disorganized Labor

Industrialized Agriculture and Disorganized Labor 396

Green gold 396
The empire of agribusiness 397
"Farm fascism" in the 1930s 399
The rise and fall of the bracero program 401
Unionization breaks through 403
"The equal protection of the laws" 407

Chapter 32
Diversity and Conflict

Diversity and Conflict 410

California Indians 410
Asians 413
Blacks 415
Mexican Americans 420
Women 423

Chapter 33
The Most Populous State

The Most Populous State 429

The growth rate: peak and slowdown 429
Transportation 432
Reapportionment 434
Education 435
Campus turmoil 436

The hippie movement   440
Black radicalism   441
The decline of radicalism   443

Chapter 34
Contemporary California Culture   446

Literature   446
Painting and sculpture   451
Architecture   456
Music   458

Chapter 35
Politics in the Reagan Years   463

The emergence of Reagan   463
"The creative society"   465
Reagan, Nixon, and 1968   468
Reagan and the elections of 1970   471
Welfare and taxation   472
Nixon and Watergate   474
Presidential politics, 1976   475

Chapter 36
The Era of Limits   478

The rise of Jerry Brown   478
Brown, Reagan, and the election of 1980   482
The tax revolt   486
The impact of Proposition 13   490

Chapter 37
The Environment and Energy   495

Regional protection   495
Growth control   497
Air pollution   499
Water resources   501
Pesticides and toxic wastes   504
The energy crisis   505
Nuclear power   506
Alternative sources   508

Index   513

One out of ten Americans today lives in California. For the past 15 years California has been the most populous state and, befitting its preeminence, it ranks first among the states in the number of college students, automobiles, and electoral votes. California is the nation's leading industrial *and* agricultural state, leading in almost every general manufacturing category and in the production of nearly 50 farm commodities. If California were a separate nation, it would be one of the world's major economic powers, ranking twelfth in the value of its international trade and seventh in gross national product.

The story of California's remarkable growth is an important part of modern history. In its Spanish and Mexican periods, California was a remote province, isolated and sparsely settled. Then came conquest by the United States and the gold rush, and California was on its way to becoming America's own new world, a land promising success and the realization of dreams. For generations "California" was virtually synonymous with "opportunity"—to Europeans and Asians as well as Americans—and from around the country and the world millions of would-be Californians arrived seeking something they had not been able to find at home. It was not, of course, always the same something, and whatever it was, the newcomers didn't always find it. Yet the allure of the Golden State remained.

The account offered here is an appraisal of the state's virtues and accomplishments—its expansion and prosperity, literature and art, energy and resourcefulness—as well as its faults and failures. Original interpretations are offered of California's most controversial and persistent problems, such as racism, vigilantism, the maltreatment of agricultural labor, and the sometimes violent struggle over control of the state's land and water resources.

Walton Bean, author of the earlier editions of this book, died in 1977. In preparing the current edition for publication I have been guided by an assumption that the main body of the text was sound and did not need major reworking. I have added new maps and illustrations throughout and updated the Selected Bibliographies at the end of each chapter. Substantial revisions were necessary in several of the later chapters, and three new chapters on recent events have been added. Ever since the book's first appearance in 1968 one of its strengths has been its comprehensive analysis of the vital developments of California in the twentieth century. Every effort has been made in the current edition to build upon that strength, extending the interpretive narrative to encompass the wide range of recent cultural, economic, social, and political developments in the state.

Grateful acknowledgment is made for permission to quote from the following previously published material: Richard Armour, "I Loved You, California," reprinted with permission of the author; Joan Didion, *Slouching Towards Bethlehem* (New York: Farrar, Straus & Giroux, 1968); John Kenneth Galbraith, "Two Pleas at Berkeley," *The New York Review of Books*, July 17, 1980; Maxine Hong Kingston, *The Woman Warrior: Memoirs of a Girlhood Among Ghosts* (New York: Knopf, 1976); Ishmael Reed, *Yellow Back Radio Broke-Down* (New York: Doubleday, 1969); and Edward Ruscha, in "The Art of the State: California," reprinted with permission from the January 1981 issue of *New West*, copyright 1981 *New West*.

I have benefited from the advice and assistance of many individuals in the preparation of this edition. I wish to acknowledge especially James D. Hart, James D. Houston, Gary F. Kurutz, Eugene C. Lee, Robert Ryal Miller, James J. Parsons, Donald H. Pflueger, Spencer C. Olin, Jr., Charles Wollenberg, and my colleagues and students at Diablo Valley College.

James J. Rawls

INTRODUCTION:
GEOGRAPHY AND HISTORY

California is a notoriously extraordinary place. Three elements in its geography have played especially crucial parts in its history: its extreme isolation, its extraordinary climate, and the great diversity among its various subregions.

The rise of a modern civilization began remarkably late in California because of its extreme geographical remoteness from Europe and Asia and even from the original Spanish and British colonial settlements in the western hemisphere. The Spanish founded their first settlement on the Pacific coast in 1519, at Panama. Not until 1769, two and a half centuries later, did they found their first settlement in Alta California at San Diego. Throughout the Spanish and Mexican periods the difficulty of getting to California prevented any substantial number of settlers from going there, and despite the American conquest and the tremendous lure of the gold discovery, California's isolation continued to retard its growth until, and even after, the opening of the first transcontinental railroad in 1869.

Once the barriers of geographical remoteness had been overcome, the unique and gentle climate of California became a greater attraction than gold had been. As James J. Parsons has pointed out, "It so happens that California's arbitrarily conceived boundaries outline the only area of winter rain and summer drought in North America." Except on the northwest coast, where the average annual precipitation ranges up to 109.43 inches (at Monumental in Del Norte County), rainfall in California ordinarily occurs only between late October and early May. In the state as a whole, the average yearly precipitation is 23.88 inches; however, throughout the late spring, the entire summer, and the early autumn there is very seldom any precipitation at all. California's climate is often called "Mediterranean," although its summers are more comparable to those of North Africa than to those of Italy, where occasional summer rainfall does occur.

For all but a few of the Indian tribes of California, the dry summers made agriculture impossible before the coming of the white man. But in the American period, when irrigation was developed on a vast scale, the uniqueness of

1

the climate gave California a virtual monopoly on the production of many highly valuable agricultural crops, and the invention of the refrigerated railway car made it possible to market them throughout the country. Climate was also a vital factor in the location of other major industries in California, notably the production of motion pictures and aircraft.

Within the common pattern of summer drought, California's climatic conditions vary widely, and it has many climates rather than one. General discussions of "the California climate" have usually described only the coastal or marine climate, with its relatively cool summers and warm winters and its relatively humid atmosphere throughout the year. In the great Central Valley, and other interior valleys, the variations in temperature are much wider, and in the vast desert areas they are extreme. The foothill climate, with its advantage of relative freedom from fog, also requires separate classification, and the mountain climate at some points in the Sierra Nevada is much like that of the Alps.

In many other respects, also, California's physiographic diversity is striking and historically significant. California is huge—the third-largest of the states, after Alaska and Texas. It extends over nearly 10° of latitude, with a coastline of 1264 miles, and its land surface is 158,693 square miles, or 99,898,880 acres. Within this vast area, the profusion of varying landscapes offers some of the world's most inspiring adventures in scenery and some of its finest opportunities for recreation. Altitudes vary from 14,495 feet at the top of Mt. Whitney, the highest point in the United States outside Alaska, to −282 feet at Badwater in Death Valley, although these two points are only 60 miles apart.

Among California's rich natural resources, its many varieties of forests and soils, its gold, oil, and other minerals have all contributed vitally to its economic development. So has water for irrigation and power, though getting the water from regions of excess to regions of shortage is one of the state's greatest problems.

SELECTED BIBLIOGRAPHY

James J. Parsons' "The Uniqueness of California," *American Quarterly*, VII (Spring 1955), pp. 45–55, is a good introduction to the effects of California's geography on its history. Geographical, historical, and political maps are contained in Michael W. Donley et al., *Atlas of California* (1979); Warren A. Beck and Ynez D. Haase, *Historical Atlas of California* (1974); and Robert D. Durrenberger, *Patterns on the Land* (1960).

THE ORIGINAL CALIFORNIANS

Before the coming of the white man, the way of life of the California Indians had remained virtually static for thousands of years. It was a survival of the stone age. But the causes and the meaning of this fact have been much misunderstood, largely because of the persistence of rather primitive ideas about the nature of primitive people, and particularly the persistence of racism—the belief that some races are biologically, morally, and intellectually inferior to others, and the use of this belief to justify the oppression of some races by others. Among competent ethnologists, the race theories underlying this pattern of thought have long been discredited.

The survival of a stone age culture in California was not the result of any hereditary biological limitations on the potential of the Indians as a race. They had been geographically and culturally isolated. The vast expanse of oceans, mountains, and deserts had sheltered California from foreign stimulation as well as from foreign conquest, and even within California the Indian groups were so settled that they had little contact with each other. On the positive side, there was something to be said for their culture just as it was. California supported a much larger number of Indians than did any other region of comparable size in North America north of Mexico. The California Indians had made a successful adaptation to their environment, and they had learned to live without destroying each other.

FOOD AND POPULATION

The nature and extent of the food supply deeply influenced the culture of the Indians of California, and determined the size of their population. Most of them lived entirely by hunting, fishing, and gathering. Agriculture was practiced only in the southernmost portion, particularly among the Cahuilla, and in the extreme southeastern portion along the lower Colorado River. But the natural sources of food were remarkably diverse and often ingeniously

3

obtained. The greatest staple was the acorn, which because of its high fat content has a higher caloric value than wheat. When washed free of tannic acid, acorn flour was made into porridge or bread. In many desert areas, mesquite pods took the place of acorns. Deer and small game were generally available. Insects were a widely accepted source of nutriment. Fish were abundant in the streams, notably salmon in the northwest. Fish and meat were often dried. Along the coast, shellfish were consumed in quantities, and many shell mounds as much as 30 feet high, which accumulated as heaps of kitchen refuse over periods of 3000 years, provide important archaeological clues to Indian life.

The term "Digger" as applied to the California Indians is a misnomer, based on the mistaken idea that they lived largely by grubbing up roots. American pioneer immigrants, seeing Indian women busy with digging sticks, were unaware that they wanted root fibers for basketmaking more often than for food. The diet of the California tribes did include certain roots and bulbs, but perhaps the real reason the Digger legend persisted was that it was easier to deprive the Indians of their lands and their lives if it could be believed that they were only miserable and subhuman creatures anyway.

The most distinctive method used in preparing food was the process of leaching the tannic acid from acorn flour. The flour produced by pounding husked acorns with a stone mortar and pestle was winnowed by tossing in a shallow basket. Then it was spread out in a sandy, shallow depression or basin and repeatedly doused with water to wash away the acid. Bread might then be baked in an earth oven, but much more commonly the flour was placed in a basket with water brought to a boil by dropping in hot stones. This produced a gruel or porridge, which was eaten either plain or flavored with berries, grass seeds, nuts, or bits of meat or fish.

The cooking basket might be caulked with pitch or tar, but it was often so tightly woven that it would hold boiling water without caulking. As this suggests, the California Indians were remarkably skilled in basketmaking. In this art they had no equals anywhere in the world, either in the utility of the product or in the beauty of the designs. They had developed basketry to such a point that pottery making was hardly necessary and was confined mainly to the southern region, which was influenced by southwestern Indian culture.

Hunting was mainly with the bow, which was often backed with sinew for extra strength. Arrows were cleverly feathered, and the heads were made of obsidian, which is sharper than flint and more readily shaped by flaking. Knives were also of obsidian. Fishing was done with nets or hooks; with harpoons, particularly for salmon; or by poisoning, accomplished by throwing buckeyes into small pools at the edge of a stream.

The ordinary tools of gaining a living, such as stones, arrows, harpoons, and knives, also served as the only weapons. Only the Colorado River Indians and a few of the northwest tribes had a weapon as such, the war club. The hunting and fishing were done mainly by men, the gathering of plant foods and the cooking by women. In general, everyone worked hard, and the divi-

A Pomo gift basket, decorated with shell disks and covered with yellow, green, blue, white, and red feathers in geometric design. (*Courtesy of the Smithsonian Institution.*)

sion of labor was fair and effective. The picture of the Indians as lazy is the result of the demoralization that set in after the coming of the white man, who treated Indians as if they were inferior beings and, seemingly, proved that they were.

The Mojaves and the Yumas practiced agriculture to the extent of dropping corn, bean, and pumpkin seeds in the mud left by the annual floodwaters along the lower Colorado; farther west, there is some evidence that agriculture existed among the Cahuilla. But with such partial exceptions, the Indian agriculture of the American southwest did not spread into California. One essential explanation of this is that the aboriginal California Indian population was in a Malthusian equilibrium. The natural food supply was moderately abundant and fairly well assured. The attempt to divert labor from hunting and gathering to the unfamiliar and risky techniques of agriculture would have produced a net loss from the disruption of the existing system.

The actual number of persons supported by this system in California, before the coming of the Spaniards, can never be precisely determined, but a reasonable estimate is that there were at least 300,000 Indians within the present boundaries of the state when the first Spanish settlement was founded in 1769. There have been extremely wide variations among the estimates of the aboriginal population of North America as a whole, but Indian population density in California before the coming of the white man was probably much greater than the average for other areas of North America north of Mexico.

ASPECTS OF MATERIAL CULTURE

Dwellings were generally simple, often conical or dome-shaped, except in the northwest, where they were often solid-frame structures built of redwood planks and in rectangular form. In central California, poles and brush were the most common building materials, and many houses were built partly underground or banked with earth for insulation.

The sweat house, or *temescal*, was a distinctive institution, and its use was generally confined to men. An open fire, not steam, was used to produce heat, and as the upper part of the *temescal* would fill with smoke, the men would lie on the floor. Then, while still perspiring freely, they would rush to a nearby stream or lake and plunge into the water. In central California this was done as a means of keeping clean as well as healthy, a ritually purifying act. Women and children were expected to do their bathing less ceremoniously, and in the early morning before the men were awake. The *temescal* also had some of the aspects of a men's club, and in some tribes the older boys and men customarily gambled, worked, and slept there.

The most common type of boat was the *tule balsa*, merely a raft made of rushes but often bound into a boatlike shape. Seagoing dugout canoes, carved from half of a redwood trunk, were used in the northwest; the Chumash of the Santa Barbara Channel region also made seaworthy canoes, though of plank rather than dugout construction.

Interior of a *temescal* in central California. *(Courtesy of the Bancroft Library.)*

Men ordinarily wore no clothing at all; the standard garment for women was a short skirt in two pieces, front and back. This was made of plant fibers or skins. In the latter case the lower part was slit into fringes for decoration and freedom of movement. When the weather forced a degree of protection from cold, both sexes wore blankets made of furs. The sea otter was most prized, but deer and rabbit skins were more common.

LOCATION, LINGUISTIC GROUPS, TRIBES

The pattern of availability of plant and animal foods, and the complete reliance upon them, tended to delimit not only the number of people but also their location. The California Indians lived in settled village communities of about 100 to 500 inhabitants, usually groups of kindred families; the location of these communities was determined very precisely by the availability of food.

Another culture-determining factor was the variety of languages. Language barriers combined with the localized nature of food supplies to discourage mobility and to intensify isolation and provincialism. Of the five main language stocks in California, four were common to other parts of North America, suggesting that there had been a vast jumble of migrations in very ancient times, before the mixture hardened. These five main stocks were subdivided into 21 language families, which in turn were subdivided into numerous dialects, most of which were mutually unintelligible. For example, the Indians of San Diego could not understand those of San Luis Rey, a few miles to the north, for the Diegueño spoke a dialect of the Yuman language family, while the Luiseño spoke one of the dialects of Shoshonean. Indian California was the region of greatest linguistic diversity in the world, excepting, according to some scholars, only the Sudan and New Guinea.

Typically, California Indians knew that they had been born and would die in a little town on the bank of a certain stream and that the land in the immediate vicinity belonged to their people. Just across certain hills, on another stream, were other people whom they might visit and with whom, if they could converse, they might intermarry, but on whose proprietary rights they should not infringe.

Anthropologists have attempted various definitions of the "tribe" in California. It may be considered as a body of people who shared a group name, a dialect, and a territory; on this basis there are over 100 such tribes. But many of the groups so defined had no known group name for themselves, so that names have been supplied by the Spaniards or by the anthropologists. Moreover, the tribe was usually merely a linguistic group. Politically it was likely to be a mere congeries of tribelets, each of them no more than a group of neighboring villages, perhaps with a principal village in a permanent location and three or four smaller ones that were periodically moved a short distance, when the houses had deteriorated.

CALIFORNIA INDIAN
TRIBAL TERRITORIES

Tribal boundaries changed over time. Boundaries depicted here are based on the earliest evidence available for each group. [From maps in Robert F. Heizer (ed.), *Handbook of North American Indians*, vol. 8: *California*, Smithsonian Institution, Washington, D.C., 1978.]

Elsewhere in North America a tribe was ordinarily a nation of several thousand people, having a strong and militant national consciousness. With the exception of the Mojaves and the Yumas on the southeastern margin, no such breadth of organization or political consciousness existed among the California Indians. The village community was usually the highest political unit. It is easy to see why the California Indians found it difficult to organize any widespread and effective resistance even to a handful of Spaniards, let alone to a horde of Anglo-Americans.

SOCIAL CULTURE

The most extraordinary diversity prevailed not only among the languages spoken but also in nearly all other aspects of culture. Elements of culture occurring only in part of California, most of them only in a small part, greatly outnumbered those that were universal. The northwest cultural province had many of the characteristics of the tribes to the north of it, and the culture patterns of southeastern California bore some resemblance to those of tribes to the east. The central cultural province was the most distinctively "Californian." Even within these broad subdivisions, there was great diversity. Meaningful generalizations can be made about California Indian culture only if it is understood that there were exceptions to almost every general statement.

The rudimentary nature of political organization, in fact its near absence, was interrelated with the very limited practice of warfare. Except for the tribes along the Colorado River, the California Indians generally were peaceable and unaggressive. The chief of a tribe was not necessarily the military leader, unless he had given some special evidence of military skill. Wars were seldom more than local feuds of revenge, more commonly involving persons and families than tribes. Murder was the prime cause, and ordinarily the victim's relatives could be propitiated by some sort of payment for their loss. Even when an intertribal offense led to a small battle, one side would often pay the other to prevent further attacks. If a series of reprisals occurred, it might end with each side compensating the other for the damages. Trespassing and food poaching were also occasional causes of war. Although there was no individual land ownership, the concept of tribal property was strongly developed.

Social classes hardly existed, except in the northwest, where there was the greatest interest in acquiring wealth and personal property and where slavery, based on debt, was commonly practiced. Indians in other areas were not uninterested in wealth, however. Gambling was widespread. Money was in the form of strings of beads made of dentalium shells or clam shells.

The family was by far the most important social institution, and in general a highly effective one. Marriage was by purchase, and polygamy was allowed if the husband could afford it. Adultery was regarded as an economic injury to the woman's husband, for which he might be paid; prostitution was unknown. In the central region a kinship taboo forbade conversation with one's mother-in-law. One interpretation sometimes placed on this custom, however, is erroneous: It actually resulted not from a fear of meddling by the spouse's parents, but rather from great respect for them. Most California tribes were exogamous; that is, marriage was outside the immediate clan within the tribe. The clan usually had a totem, a natural kind or class, especially of animals, conceived as being intimately related to that particular group of human beings; totemism was thus a convenient system of distinguishing such kinship groups, even though visible symbols, such as totem poles, were not used in California.

Religious leadership was combined with the medical profession in the person of the shaman, who was believed to be in direct communication with the supernatural world. Illness was thought to be caused by foreign disease objects in the body, and the shaman claimed the power both to introduce such objects and to remove them, usually by sucking them out.

There were widespread religious cults. The shamans did not usually dominate these loosely organized associations, although they might assume a certain degree of local leadership in explaining their rites. South of the Tehachapi Mountains the *toloache*, or jimson-weed cult, was prevalent. A drink made from the narcotic jimson weed was used to induce sacred visions as part of the initiation ceremonies. Among the Gabrielino and Juaneño this cult was much elaborated, and related to belief in a deity called Chinigchinich. In central California the Kuksu cult placed more emphasis on esoteric rites that included dancers impersonating several deities. The "world-renewal" cult was a major aspect of religious life on the northwest coast. Its rites were designed to renew abundant food supplies and to prevent calamities.

Ceremonial observances were everywhere associated with adolescence and with mourning, and there were many first-fruit, first-salmon, or acorn-harvest ceremonies, comparable to our own Thanksgiving. The religious ideas of some of the California Indians were more elaborate than commonly supposed. For example, the belief in a prehuman race, rather than an anthropomorphic creator, was an interesting foreshadowing of the idea of evolution. Some of the beliefs of the Spanish missionaries, such as the idea that human beings were sinful and fallen creatures, were essentially foreign to Indian religious beliefs.

The California Indians had no system of writing, beyond the use of designs and symbols in the decoration of rocks, or in groundpainting as a part of religious ceremony and instruction in the southern region. The highly stylized rock paintings of the Chumash were among the most spectacular and elaborate of any created in the United States. Yet the Indians of California were prehistoric in that they left no written records. In this sense, we speak of California as having been first "discovered" by the Spaniards, and of its "history" as having begun at that time.

SELECTED BIBLIOGRAPHY

For the general reader and student the best introductory volumes are Robert F. Heizer and Albert B. Elsasser, *The Natural World of the California Indians* (1980); Heizer and Mary Ann Whipple (eds.), *The California Indians, a Source Book* (1971); and Theodora Kroeber, *Ishi in Two Worlds* (1961). The most complete reference is Heizer (ed.), *California* (1978), a volume in the Smithsonian Institution's *Handbook of North American Indians*. An excellent summary account is Heizer, "The California Indians: Archaeology, Varieties of Culture, Arts of Life," *California Historical Society Quarterly*, XLI (March 1962), pp. 1–28.

The best estimate of the number of Indians in California before the coming of the Spaniards appears in Sherburne F. Cook, *The Population of the California Indians, 1769–1970* (1976). Other useful volumes include Lowell J. Bean, *Mukat's People: The Cahuilla Indians of Southern California* (1972) and Campbell Grant, *The Rock Paintings of the Chumash: A Study of California Indian Culture* (1965).

DISCOVERY, EXPLORATION, AND FOUNDING

The story of Spanish California is one of great color and fascination, even though the Spaniards themselves were disappointed in it and in general regarded it as one of the least important of their colonies.

THE FINDING AND NAMING OF CALIFORNIA

Hernán Cortés, the conqueror of the Aztec empire in central Mexico, was also chiefly responsible for discovering the lower part of what the Spanish ultimately called "the Californias." In his urge to explore northwestward from the lands of the Aztecs, Cortés was following the lure of various tales of magnificent wealth. Spaniards of his time put their trust in the ancient and medieval legends of the Terrestrial Paradise and the Amazon Island, and in such American Indian tales as those of the Seven Cities and of El Dorado, "the Gilded Man," a king whose subjects covered him with gold dust every morning and washed it off every night.

In 1533 Cortés dispatched the expedition that discovered lower California, first assumed to be an island rather than a peninsula. But the Indians were primitive and hostile, the desolate land itself seemed hostile, and navigation to and from it was treacherous because of the sudden and prolonged windstorms.

All the early Spanish exploring expeditions involved extreme hardships, and several ended in complete disaster. In some cases only fragmentary records of them exist. Many details are uncertain, and one of these is the identity of the explorer who first applied the name, California. The earliest authenticated record of the use of the name by explorers is in a journal of the Cabrillo expedition, but there it appears as a name already in common usage.

For centuries the derivation of the name was even more uncertain than the question of who first applied it. In 1862, however, Edward Everett Hale discovered what is undoubtedly the correct explanation. Hale was a Boston Unitarian minister and writer, otherwise best known for his story, "The Man without a Country." In the course of his wide readings he came across an old

11

Spanish novel, *Las Sergas de Esplandián (The Exploits of Esplandián)*, written about 1500 by Garcí Ordóñez de Montalvo. In it there were several references to an Amazon island called California.

Montalvo's *Sergas de Esplandián* was a sequel to his translation into Spanish of the Portuguese novel, *Amadís de Gaula*. It was an inferior sequel; as Hale remarked, the *Sergas* was deservedly forgotten for 300 years and its role as the source of the name of California was thus forgotten with it. In the early years of the sixteenth century, however, Montalvo's story went through several editions, and there can be little doubt that Cortés and his captains, if they had not read it, had at least heard it described. In 1524, in a letter to the king, Cortés reported his expectation of finding an island of Amazons a few days' sail to the northwest.

Amadís of Gaul had been the late-medieval ideal of the perfect knight. Montalvo's Esplandián was introduced as the son of Amadís. In the course of a siege of Constantinople in which father and son were leading the defense of the city against a motley army of pagans, there suddenly appeared among the besiegers a certain Calafía, queen of California. This, wrote Montalvo, was an island "on the right hand of the Indies" and "very near to the terrestrial paradise." It was inhabited by black women "without any men among them, because they were accustomed to live after the manner of Amazons." Their weapons were of gold, "for in all the island there is no other metal." In California "there were many griffins, on account of the great ruggedness of the country." When the griffins were young, "the women went out with traps to take them to their caves, and brought them up there. And being themselves quite a match for the griffins, they fed them with the men whom they took prisoners, and with the boys to whom they gave birth." For battle, these monstrous birds were trained to seize men from the ground and drop them from great heights. Later the Amazon queen became converted to Christianity, gained a proper respect for men, married a relative of Esplandián, and returned with him to California. "What happened after that," wrote Montalvo, "I must be excused from telling." The reader may doubt that the marriage was an entirely happy one.

It may have been in derision that Spanish explorers gave to a barren and hostile place the name of the fabled land of gold they had hoped to find. An alternative explanation is that to Spanish soldiers of the time of Cortés the "California" of contemporary parlance would in itself have been a highly opprobrious name, directly suitable for a land of desolation and terror—a land in which women were the soldiers and in which women despised men and set griffins on them.

Since California's actual history has so often resembled romantic fiction, it is not entirely inappropriate that it got its name from a novel.

CABRILLO AND THE DISCOVERY OF ALTA CALIFORNIA

The evidence that Spanish explorers first sighted Upper (or Alta) California by land, near its southeast corner, is not quite substantial enough to take the traditional honor of discovery away from Juan Rodríguez Cabrillo, who first sighted it from the sea in 1542. The main purpose of Cabrillo's expedition, sent out under the orders of the viceroy of New Spain, was to search for the long-rumored though mythical Strait of Anián, later sought by the English under the name of the northwest passage. For more than two centuries the dream of a water route to Asia through North America would continue to lure the explorers of several nations.

Cabrillo sailed from the port of Navidad on the west coast of Mexico on June 27, 1542. His two small ships, the *San Salvador* and the *Victoria*, were poorly built, manned by conscripts, and wretchedly provisioned. On September 28 he discovered and entered the fine harbor of San Diego. His name for it was San Miguel, but this and the names of all the other points he discovered were changed by later explorers, particularly by Vizcaíno.

After spending 6 days at San Diego, the little vessels made a series of anchorages at Catalina Island, San Pedro, and Santa Monica, and then at Ventura and several other points along the Santa Barbara Channel. They could make no landings north of Point Conception because of the powerful northwest winds. They next found refuge in a harbor on San Miguel Island, but there, unfortunately, Cabrillo fell and broke his arm. He insisted upon continuing the voyage, and for weeks his ships beat their way northward in the heavy seas, unable to find a safe landing place. He decided to spend the winter at San Miguel Island and there, in January of 1543, he died, apparently from an infection resulting from the broken arm which he had suffered on the same island 3 months earlier.

In obedience to Cabrillo's dying wish, and in spite of their pitiful hardships, his men agreed to continue their explorations under the leadership of the chief pilot, Bartolomé Ferrelo. Before they turned back on March 1, they had actually reached a point off the coast of southern Oregon, but again they could find no new anchorages. In April they reached their home port of Navidad, nearly starved and desperately sick with scurvy. They had found no straits and no rich cities, and they could hardly have appreciated the future value of what they did find. But it is clear that the discoverers of Upper California were men of admirable courage and extraordinary devotion to duty.

FRANCIS DRAKE AND NOVA ALBION

More than a generation elapsed between the Cabrillo expedition and the next landing by Europeans on the coast of Upper California. This was the visit of Francis Drake and the *Golden Hind* in 1579. It occurred by accident in the course of a 3-year voyage around the world, a voyage intended partly to open up English trade with the Moluccas and partly to "anoy" the king of Spain in "his Indyes" by engaging in what the English regarded as privateering and the Spaniards regarded as piracy. In this period Queen Elizabeth suspected King Philip of complicity in a series of plots on her life, and relations between England and Spain were seldom very far short of outright war. Another and incidental purpose of the voyage was a search for the northwest passage.

Nearly a year and a half after he sailed from England, Drake had to make an emergency landing on the coast of California to careen and repair his ship.

The *Golden Hind,* originally named the *Pelican,* was a vessel of only 100 tons burden, and by this time she was carrying about 30 tons of captured Spanish treasure, mostly silver. The seams in her hull had begun to open. On June 17, 1579, Drake found "a convenient and fit harborough" where he stayed for 5 weeks. It is probable that this was actually what is now called Drake's Bay, although the location of the landing has long been in dispute. The Indians were the feature of the visit that Drake's men found most interesting, and to which their accounts of it devoted the greatest detail. From the descriptions of the houses, the feathered baskets, the ceremonies, and the language of these Indians, anthropologists have clearly identified them as the Coast Miwok, whose country was present-day Marin County. Only Drake's Bay has the "white bancks and cliffes" whose resemblance to the cliffs on the English Channel contributed to Drake's naming the place Nova Albion, or New England.

In claiming the country for Queen Elizabeth, Drake erected a plate of brass with a chiseled inscription and a hole for a sixpence bearing Her Majesty's picture. In 1937 the University of California announced the finding of this plate and later placed it on display in the Bancroft Library. Experts at Columbia University made tests on the plate in 1938 and pronounced it genuine. However, new tests made in the mid 1970s at the Lawrence Berkeley Laboratory and at Oxford University used the far more sophisticated testing techniques developed in the interim, and the modern researchers concluded that it was "unreasonable to continue to believe in the authenticity of the plate." Analysis of the trace elements found in the metal corresponded to brass of the twentieth century rather than the sixteenth, and x-ray diffraction tests revealed that the brass was produced by a modern rolling process unknown at the time of Drake. Nevertheless the plate remains on display in the Bancroft, and the controversy over its authenticity continues.

Drake's landing on the California coast was a chance occurrence, and as an incidental result of it he "took possession" in case England should ever want the region. There is no sound evidence, however, that Drake or any other Englishmen of his time ever seriously intended to plant a colony there. This notion was largely created by the English more than two centuries later as a part of their claim to the Oregon country; it was revived by Americans, after they acquired California, as a kind of sentimental foreshadowing of Anglo-American possession. Drake's men did assume, incorrectly, that the Indians in placing a feathered crown on Drake's head were turning over the sovereignty of their country to him. The Indians also cried pitifully and tore their cheeks with their fingernails until the blood ran, and the English supposed this to be a kind of sacrifice to them as gods. The facts are that these were the mourning practices of the Coast Miwok and that the Indians undoubtedly regarded the Englishmen as relatives who had returned from the dead.

The main significance of the voyage of the *Golden Hind* was that she was the second ship to sail around the world, the first English ship to do so, and the first ship of any nation to make the entire voyage under one commander

An artist's conception of California Indians greeting Francis Drake in 1579. Note especially the central figures lacerating their cheeks and, in the background, the setting up of the plate of brass. *(Courtesy of the Bancroft Library.)*

(Magellan had been killed in the Philippines). Drake's title of knighthood, granted after his return, was a modest recognition of so great an achievement. The significance of his landing in California, however, has sometimes been misunderstood and exaggerated.

THE MANILA GALLEON AND THE CALIFORNIA COAST

The Philippine islands were added to the Spanish colonial empire by a gradual process of conquest beginning in 1565, and they were governed as a part of the viceroyalty of New Spain until the end of Spanish control in Mexico. By the time of the Drake expedition the Spaniards had already established a profitable trade route between Mexico and the Philippines, and for many decades Spanish interest in the coast of California was largely the result of the fact that the ships from Manila sailed past it, with their rich cargoes from the orient, on the last leg of their long trans-Pacific voyage to Acapulco.

Manila was a very convenient gathering point for luxury goods from many parts of east Asia, to be exchanged for silver and gold from the mines of Mexico, and the trade became so large that merchants in Spain were in danger of losing their Mexican markets. Under the prevailing mercantilistic system of discriminating against the colonies and in favor of the mother country, the king decreed in 1593 that the Manila galleons must be limited to one a year, and their cargoes to a value of 250,000 pesos. At the demand of the silk manufacturers of Seville, oriental silks were to be excluded entirely. Nevertheless the profits were extremely high, and since they were now concentrated in a single annual voyage, there was great temptation to crowd extra cargo into space that should have been reserved for food and water. The voyage from Manila usually took 6 or 7 months, during which the crews suffered horribly from starvation, thirst, and scurvy. They also had to fear English pirates, ever since the forays of Drake and, particularly, Thomas Cavendish, who captured one of the galleons off Lower California in 1587. There was, it seemed, a growing need for a port on the California coast where the annual Manila galleon could get fresh food and water and perhaps an escort vessel.

The Spanish authorities entrusted the galleon of 1595 to the Portuguese merchant-adventurer Sebastián Rodríguez Cermeño, on condition that the voyage should include an exploration of the California coast in search of the best site for a port of call. After an especially harrowing passage across the Pacific, Cermeño sighted land somewhere north of Cape Mendocino. There his ship, the *San Agustín*, was nearly wrecked by a storm, and several of the officers took every step short of mutiny in an effort to persuade him to give up the projected explorations. He refused, and on November 6, rounding Point Reyes, he anchored in Drake's Bay, which he called the Bay of San Francisco.

On shore, the Spaniards assembled a launch that had been brought along for use in exploring coastal areas. This little vessel was to be their salvation, for on November 30 a great gale from the southeast, the direction in which the bay is completely exposed, drove the *San Agustín* aground. The breakers pounded her to pieces in a few hours and strewed her cargo, provisions, and timbers along the beach. To the amazement and outrage of his crew, not even this disaster persuaded Cermeño to abandon his interest in exploration. With 70 men crowded into the open launch, the *San Buenaventura*, he found excuses for many landings, and although he sailed past the Golden Gate without seeing it, he described many other points with remarkable accuracy considering his difficulties.

VIZCAÍNO AND MONTEREY

Cermeño had found no new harbor that was safe, and the viceregal government doubted the throughness and accuracy of his charts. The further search for a good harbor in nórthern California was now entrusted, after long negotiations, to another *adelantado*, or merchant-adventurer, Sebastián Vizcaíno. On the understanding that he would be rewarded with various concessions including the future command of one of the Manila ships, Vizcaíno invested a considerable amount of his own capital in an elaborate expedition in 1602. Setting out from Acapulco with two ships and a launch, he permanently renamed many of the places along the California coast, and on December 16 he entered a bay that he named for the viceroy, the conde de Monterey. Vizcaíno announced himself as the discoverer of this bay, although he was not. Cermeño had seen it 7 years earlier, and his description of it, though not detailed, was actually far less misleading than that of Vizcaíno, who made absurdly exaggerated claims for its value as a harbor.

Vizcaíno seems to have feared that if he did not return with a favorable report, he would not receive the rewards he hoped for. The result was that he described the bay to the viceroy not only as having an abundance of fine timber for shipbuilding, but as being "sheltered from all winds"—a claim that can only be described as positively fraudulent, since the bay actually includes no proper harbor at all.

Viceroy Monterey, pleased with the idea that a fine port would bear his name, awarded Vizcaíno the command of the next Manila galleon. Shortly afterward, however, Monterey was promoted to the viceroyalty of Peru. His successor as viceroy of New Spain, the marqués de Montesclaros, completely distrusted Vizcaíno, revoked the award of the galleon, and went so far as to have the expedition's map maker convicted of forgery and hanged.

Montesclaros ridiculed and blocked the whole project of a California port of call. He pointed out, correctly, that when the galleons sighted California, they had only a few days' voyage left, since the strong prevailing winds and currents along the coast almost always bore them swiftly southward. In this judgment, history vindicated him, for even after Upper California was finally settled more than a century and a half later, the annual ships from Manila almost never stopped there.

The lapse of 60 years between Cabrillo and Vizcaíno, and of another 167 years between Vizcaíno and actual Spanish settlement of California, emphasizes the utter isolation of California and the low regard in which the Spaniards held it. California was a place that should have contained gold, but apparently did not; a place where a strait should have been, but was not; a barren and dangerous coast that a ship sailed past once a year. Getting to it from Mexico was far more trouble than it was worth. Just as the winds and currents made the southward voyage brief and easy, they made the northward voyage long, difficult, and sometimes impossible. Land travel seemed even more forbidding. Lower California was on the very rim of Christendom during the whole of the Spanish colonial period in America, which lasted more than three centuries, and for all but the last half-century of that period, Upper California remained beyond the rim.

SPAIN'S INDIAN POLICIES

New Spain lacked the manpower for the settlement of her remote and unprofitable northern frontiers. When the colonization of these areas finally came, it was largely through an ingenious plan intended to transform the Indians into colonists by the use of that remarkable institution, the Spanish mission.

The Spanish attitudes toward the Indians grew from an interesting blend of religious, economic, military, and political motives. The Indians were officially regarded not only as subjects of the Spanish monarchy with rights to its protection, but also as human beings with souls to be saved. Their Most Catholic Majesties, the Spanish monarchs, made frequent references to their duty of Christianization, and the missionaries were untiring in their efforts to carry it out. There were others, however, who were primarily interested in the Indians because they could be made to labor for the profit of their conquerors. In return for the salvation of their souls the Indians were required to contribute the labor of their bodies.

The most essential key to the Spanish colonial plan, however, was that Indians were to be made Spanish—in religion, in language, and in the gradual intermixture of blood. They were to be required to work; they were also to be permitted to live (if they survived the epidemics of smallpox and typhus). These views were quite different from those of the English colonists; there was no comparable plan for assimilating the Indian into the Anglo-American scheme of things, and displacement or extermination was almost the only alternative. As for racial intermarriage, the Anglo-Americans were usually intolerant of it. They were generally able to secure wives of English descent, whereas the Spanish American colonies were extremely unattractive to Spanish women.

THE MISSION AS A FRONTIER INSTITUTION

As a method of advancing and consolidating a frontier, the mission had its roots in the long struggle against the Mohammedan Moors in Spain. The cross and the sword had moved forward together, in forcible conversion of the infidel. In Spanish America, each mission had a small guard of soldiers, and there was usually a larger garrison at a *presidio*, or military post, nearby. Cooperation between padres and soldiers was seldom cordial, but it was always indispensable. The missionaries were typically men of tremendous courage and faith, but with the exception of those who actively sought martyrdom, they were usually aware that the strength of their own personalities had to be supplemented by the soldiers' weapons, even though they were constantly anxious lest the soldiers corrupt the Indian neophytes, or apprentices to Christianity.

The mission was not only a church but also an agricultural *pueblo*, or town, in which hundreds or even thousands of Indians were concentrated. There were cultivated fields, gardens, orchards, and vineyards, often fenced with nearly impenetrable hedges of prickly pear, and watered from irrigation ditches with stone dams. At a little distance, each mission had its *rancho*, and, eventually, large herds of cattle.

Theoretically every mission was temporary. If the plan had worked as the Spanish government hoped, each mission would have been "secularized" 10 years after its founding. That is, the pueblo would receive a grant of 4 square leagues of land; the fields, town lots, and other property would be parceled

out among the Indians; and community government would pass to native officials who had been trained for the purpose. The mission church would be
turned over to parish priests, known as "secular" clergy, as distinct from the
missionaries, who were called "regular" clergy because they were under the
regulations and vows of a particular order. The missionaries were then supposed to begin their work all over again farther on, in a continuous process of
frontier expansion.

In practice, however, the schedule was never met. Most missions continued for decades, and some for more than a century. Although the Laws of the
Indies provided that mission Indians should receive real training for self-government, in practice they received little or none. The missionary fathers made
the basic mistake of regarding the Indians as children whose minds were incapable of development beyond the child's level. They turned them into helpless dependents and kept them in that condition. Every detail of work, play,
clothing, and even the choice of a mate, was rigidly controlled. So far as possible the missionaries kept their charges from contact with any Europeans but
themselves and did not prepare them to take a place in any kind of society but
that of the mission. When secularization finally came, the whole community
simply disintegrated. There are many viewpoints concerning the effect of mission life itself on Indian morale. The Spanish missionaries often spoke of the
"temporal and spiritual conquest" of new provinces. The phrase is apt. Very
often, no real conversion took place after the Indians' own gods were
destroyed. Indians were spiritually as well as physically conquered, their spirit
broken.

Spain had entrusted the frontier regions of northwestern Mexico to the
black-robed missionaries of the Society of Jesus in 1591. A century later the
Jesuit frontier had been extended northwestward on the mainland as far as
the country of the Pimas, and Father Eusebio Kino had begun the building of
the missions in Pimería Alta—northern Sonora and southern Arizona. Kino
rediscovered the forgotten fact that Baja California was a peninsula and not an
island and persuaded his superiors to establish the first of the missions on the
peninsula in 1697. But in 1767 the king issued an order expelling the Jesuits
from all the Spanish dominions. Charles III of Spain had become convinced
that the Jesuits were involved in plots against the interests of the crown.

GÁLVEZ AND THE PLAN FOR ALTA CALIFORNIA

The expulsion of the Jesuits from New Spain was entrusted to Visitor-General
José de Gálvez, who turned the Baja California missions over to military
administrators under Captain Gaspar de Portolá, and then to the Franciscans
under Father Junípero Serra. The names of these three remarkable men soon
became important in the story of the founding of Alta California.

Gálvez was the most effective visitor-general in the history of New Spain,
though not the first. The *visita* was a distinctively Spanish administrative technique for investigations and reorganizations, and a *visitador-general* was a spe-

cial deputy of the king, with extraordinary powers overlapping and sometimes transcending those of the viceroy.

The *visita* of Gálvez, which began in 1765, was primarily intended to reform the finances and increase the revenues of New Spain as a part of the energetic attempts to reorganize the Spanish government under Charles III after the expensive and disastrous Seven Years War. The expulsion of the Jesuits was an added assignment. But the consolidation of the northwestern frontier and its extension to Alta California were Gálvez's own projects, and seem to have been the result of his intense personal ambitions. He had risen from rather humble origins, and although he was a brilliant, forceful, and generally successful administrator, he was also unusually vain, selfish, ruthless, deceitful, and unstable. It was, indeed, because of Gálvez's possession of this very combination of qualities that the occupation of San Diego and Monterey, long considered and periodically given up as hopeless, actually materialized. New Spain had been decaying, and he now made it appear to be flourishing and expanding. This was the sort of achievement which, along with others, later led to his being made Minister of the Indies.

Gálvez proposed a scheme for the consolidation and development of the whole of the far northwest under a vast new governmental unit to be called a *commandancy-general*, and to include the areas of Sinaloa, Sonora, Chihuahua, and the Californias. To justify this plan, he made use of the old and perennial fear that some other European power would establish itself on the Pacific coast and menace New Spain from the north. It was long believed that the Spanish colonization of Upper California occurred because of a diplomatic report that Russia was about to move in the direction of Monterey. The truth was that Gálvez's plan was already well-advanced when this absurdly exaggerated report reached him, and that he merely added it to the rumors he himself had been spreading about various alleged intentions of the English and the Dutch. Another argument used by Gálvez in support of his plans was that the development of Alta California would ultimately provide a great source of royal revenue, although, as it turned out, the result was an annual deficit during most of the period of Spanish rule.

Gálvez ordered the founding of the new port of San Blas on the coast of Mexico several hundred miles northwest of Acapulco as a naval and supply base for the Californias. In 1768 Gálvez sailed from San Blas for Baja California, where he completed the planning of the "sacred expedition" that would colonize Alta California in the following year. The various divisions of this expedition, two by land and three by sea, were to be launched from the peninsula.

The mainland approach was blocked by Indian rebellions in Sonora. These had been going on unchecked for many years, but Gálvez was sure that a determined military campaign could quickly suppress them. That campaign, however, proved to be as maddeningly unsuccessful and frustrating as a number of its predecessors had been. Once, while visiting Sonora, Gálvez actually suffered a temporary attack of insanity. He had been increasingly given to the belief that he received divine instructions, and now for a brief time he was convinced that he was God himself. At one moment he proposed to reduce the Indians to submission by importing 600 Guatemalan apes as soldiers.

From the viewpoint of the United States, it is fortunate that the Spaniards occupied Alta California when they did. Tenuous as that occupation was, it may ultimately have forestalled the acquisition of the territory by some nation strong enough to have delayed or even prevented its later acquisition by the United States. But at the time and under the circumstances in which it was undertaken, the Spanish occupation of Alta California was impractical and unnecessary, and largely a result of the mental instability of Gálvez, who conceived and ordered it.

THE FRANCISCANS AND FATHER SERRA

A handful of Spanish officers and missionaries and a scarcely larger number of mestizo and mulatto soldiers and sailors carried out the founding of the colony of Alta California under fantastic difficulties. The military men and the missionaries had quite different ideas of what they were doing and why, and they were often at cross-purposes. But their joint achievement is an impressive tribute to human courage in the face of adversity.

St. Francis of Assisi had founded the Order of Friars Minor, oldest and largest of his orders, in the thirteenth century. The Franciscans were the first missionaries in the new world, where their work began with Columbus's second voyage and continued vigorously in many parts of Spanish America through the later period when the Jesuits and other orders shared the missionary field. The name of Gray Friars was sometimes given to the Franciscans because their robes were woven of white and black wool; the color of their habit was still gray at the time of the founding of Alta California, though later it was changed to brown.

The decision to entrust the California missions to the Franciscans was the result of the belief that they were not only more obedient to the vows of poverty than were the Jesuits, but also less disposed to subordinate the interests of their country to those of their order. This had become the prevailing opinion in the Spanish government. It was inaccurate, and it was unfair to both the orders concerned. Certainly the relations between the Franciscans and the governmental officials in California were to include a long series of sharp disputes. Father Junípero Serra, in particular, vigorously subordinated everything to his conception of religious duty.

Father Junípero, the first and most famous of the missionaries in Alta California, was a Spanish farmer's son, born in the village of Petra on the island of Majorca in 1713. The family name Serra is the Catalonian form of the Castilian word *sierra*. Upon joining the Franciscan order, Miguel, as he was originally called, exercised the privilege of choosing a name by which he wished to be known "in religion." Junípero had been the name of one of St. Francis' closest companions, whose devotion was said to have inspired the founder to wish "that I had a whole forest of such Junipers."

Serra became a professor of philosophy at the University of Majorca, but at the age of 35 he determined to give up this quiet and relatively comfortable position for the strenuous life of a foreign missionary. He also hoped for martyrdom, as had St. Francis himself, although in neither case was this hope fulfilled. According to Father Francisco Palóu, Serra's former pupil and later companion, assistant, and biographer, Serra once spoke of martyrdom as the true "gold and silver of the Indies" for which they would search.

As prospective missionaries, Serra, Palóu, and Juan Crespí, another of Serra's former students, were first assigned to the apostolic College of San Fernando in Mexico City. This establishment was both a headquarters for Franciscan missionaries in New Spain and a special training center to accustom them to privation, fatigue, mortification, and penance.

In manifestations of zeal, no one excelled Serra. Upon his arrival in Mexico he had chosen to walk all the way from Vera Cruz to the capital. Early in the course of the journey he suffered an insect bite that became infected. He neglected medical care for it, and his leg and foot remained swollen and ulcerous for the rest of his life, a condition that he alternately ignored and regarded as a blessing. While delivering missionary sermons he would sometimes scourge his own shoulders with a chain, or, holding a cross in one hand, beat his breast with a stone held in the other, or burn his bared chest with lighted candles. He slept on a narrow bed made only of hard wooden boards. He kept a thong of sharp-pointed iron links hanging on the wall beside the bed for scourging himself when thoughts that he regarded as sinful came in the night. St. Francis had practiced mortification of the flesh, and it was not uncommon among the missionaries of Serra's time, although regulations of the apostolic college provided that it should never go so far as to be permanently incapacitating.

After an impressive record in missionary work in the Sierra Gorda and other parts of Mexico, Serra became father-president of the missions in Baja California, and then of the prospective new missions in Alta California. At the time of his appointment to the latter post, he was 55 years old. He held it until his death in 1784 at the age of 70. Throughout his life he was a vigorous, hard-driving man, never turning back from a task he had begun, always demanding the full measure of work from others as well as from himself. In physical stature, Serra was short, not more than 5 feet 2 or 3 inches in height—but in courage and determination, he was a giant.

THE SACRED EXPEDITION

Supplies and men for the first missions and presidios to be founded in Alta California came in part from the peninsula and in part from the mainland by way of San Blas. The Pious Fund of the Californias, transferred from the custody of the Jesuits to that of the Franciscans, was extended to the new ventures in the north, and Gálvez and Serra agreed that church furniture, ornaments, vestments, and utensils, as well as livestock and other supplies, were to be drawn from the Baja California missions.

It had always been proper to call upon old missions to contribute to the establishment of new ones, and any objection that might have arisen was obviated by the fact that at this time Father Serra was in charge of both. He had not been in Baja California long enough to become greatly attached to the missions there, and the plan provided that he would continue as father-president in the old California until the day he left it for the new, and then turn over the Baja missions to his faithful understudy, Father Francisco Palóu.

As was customary in founding new establishments, a number of Christianized Indians from the peninsula were taken along with the expedition in order to serve as, so to speak, bellwethers for the new flock. In addition to soldiers from the garrison at Loreto under Captain Fernando Rivera y Moncada, 25 Catalonian volunteers, light infantry under Lieutenant Pedro Fages, were detached from their previous assignment to the campaign in Sonora. There were also several blacksmiths, cooks, and carpenters, along with Miguel Costansó, military engineer and cartographer, and Dr. Pedro Prat, army surgeon of French ancestry.

The expedition as a whole was under the command of Capt. Gaspar de Portolá. When settlements had been established at San Diego and Monterey, Portolá and Rivera were to return to duty on the peninsula, leaving Lieutenant Fages in charge of the military and civil government of the new colony.

Three ships were provided for the expedition, the *San Carlos*, the *San Antonio*, and the *San José*, all less than 200 tons, and all hastily and imperfectly constructed under the difficulties that still hampered shipbuilding on the Pacific coast. All three vessels reached Baja California from San Blas in leaky condition, even before the beginning of the longer voyage, and all three had to be careened and repaired. Visitor-General Gálvez personally superintended the repairs and the loading of the flagship, the *San Carlos*, and carried some of the mission furniture on board with his own hands. When she sailed from La Paz, on January 9, 1769, he accompanied her in a launch to see her round Cape San Lucas. The *San Antonio*, a smaller supply ship, sailed from Cape San Lucas on February 15. The third vessel, the *San José*, was lost with all on board somewhere on her way toward San Diego.

Of the two land parties, the first was under Captain Rivera, with 27 *cuirassiers*. On the frontier the cuirass was a sleeveless jacket of tough leather, made by quilting several thicknesses of deerskin or sheepskin, and usually arrowproof. Father Crespí, chaplain and diarist of the expedition, noted quite accurately that these *soldados de cuera*, or leather-jacket soldiers, were the best light cavalry in the world and were equally skilled as cowboys. Driving a large herd of cattle, horses, and mules, this party set out from the northernmost Spanish outpost in Baja California on March 24.

The second land contingent, including Portolá and Serra, left the same point on May 15. Following the trail made by Rivera, and less encumbered with livestock, it could move somewhat more rapidly, but the journey over deserts and gullies was a hard one. When Serra's ulcerated leg threatened to disable him completely, he asked a muleteer to treat it as he would a sore foot on one of his animals. The muleteer's poultice of mud and herbs had an almost miraculous effect, and Serra was able to continue, much relieved.

The first objective of the whole expedition was the founding of a presidio and a mission at San Diego as a way station for the journey to Monterey. The *San Antonio* was first to arrive at San Diego, on April 11, after a relatively easy voyage of 54 days. The *San Carlos*, although she had started a month earlier, did not arrive until nearly 3 weeks later, after 110 days at sea. The effects of scurvy had advanced so far that no one was able to lower a boat, and the men on shore had to board her in order to do so. The first Spanish settlement in Alta California was a sail-tent hospital. Doctor Prat was himself so ill that he could be of little help to the others. He later became insane.

The first land party, under Rivera, arrived on May 14, and Rivera ordered the tents moved several miles northward to the foot of the hill where the presidio would later be built. Portolá rode in a little ahead of his men on June 29, and Serra and the others reached the stricken camp on July 1. Of about 300 men in the various branches of the sacred expedition of 1769, not more than half survived to reach San Diego, many died of scurvy there, and for months half the survivors were too sick to travel farther. All but a handful of the Christianized Indians who had been brought with the land contingents had died or deserted; the military officers had felt compelled to deny them rations from the dwindling food supplies.

Of the sailors, 38 had died. The *San Antonio*, with a truly skeleton crew of eight men, had to be sent back to San Blas to bring new supplies for the whole expedition and new crews for both ships. The *San Carlos* was left at anchor in the bay with two men on board to keep her from being stripped by the Indians. The whole situation was stark and desperate. Nevertheless, 2 weeks after his arrival at San Diego Portolá set out toward his main objective, the legendary harbor of Monterey, taking with him Rivera, Fages, Costansó, Father Crespí, and nearly all the others who were still able to travel, leaving Serra at San Diego to care for the more than 50 invalids.

On the way north the expedition felt several earthquakes near the river called the Santa Ana, or *Río de los Temblores*. Four days later the *Río de Porciúncula*, site of the future pueblo of Los Angeles, was named by Crespí for the day of its discovery and crossing, August 2. This was the day of the festival of Our Lady the Queen of the Angels, one of many titles of the Virgin Mary. For Franciscans, in particular, an important shrine of the Virgin was the chapel of Porciúncula, near Assisi, where St. Francis had worshiped.

Continuing northwestward on a route that would become El Camino Real (The King's Highway), remarkably close at most points to the route of the modern Highway 101, the expedition was delayed north of San Luis Obispo until a way could be found through the rugged Santa Lucias. After the group had found its way to what is now called the Salinas Valley, the going was much easier, but in following the Salinas River Portolá made the unfortunate mistake of supposing that it was the Carmel, which Vizcaíno had described. Thus when Portolá reached the shore of the Bay of Monterey, the peninsula and Point Pinos lay to the south, and not to the north as they should have. To add to the confusion he could see nothing resembling the fine harbor, praised by Vizcaíno and subjected in the interim to 167 years of idealized imagination. Moreover, Portolá and his half-starved men had managed to convince themselves that they would find the *San José*, with abundant food supplies, riding at anchor in that harbor.

After a few days' search the party pushed on northward along the coast. At the end of October they reached Point San Pedro and looked across the Gulf of the Farallons toward Point Reyes and Drake's Bay, which to them was Cermeño's Bay of San Francisco. Although Point Reyes was 40 miles away and they could not be sure of its identity from that distance, they saw enough to increase their fears that they must have passed Monterey without finding it. Sergeant José Ortega understood some Indians to be trying to tell him that a ship was anchored somewhere to the north. Heading a party of scouts, Ortega found his advance blocked by a vast and unknown bay, which he sighted, probably on November 1, 1769, from the top of the ridge between the present cities of Pacifica and Millbrae. Historians long supposed that he also found the Golden Gate at this time, but this is untrue. It was not until a year later that Pedro Fages, scouting northward along the east bay shore, became the first Spanish explorer to see the narrow gap between the peninsulas. Navigators had failed for centuries to see it from the ocean, assuming that Drake probably did not. Part of the explanation lies in the fogs that so often shroud the Golden Gate, and part in the fact that Angel Island and the Berkeley hills lie behind it in such a position as to give, from any distance at sea, the impression of a continuous coastline.

Neither Portolá nor anyone else in the expedition seems to have regarded the discovery of the great bay as anything but an obstacle, except for Father Crespí, who wrote in his diary: "It is a very large and fine harbor, such that not only all the navy of our Most Catholic Majesty but those of all Europe could take shelter in it."

Considering how long Spaniards had been searching for the Strait of Anián, it is surprising that no one speculated that it might now have been discovered, but for weeks the attention of these men had been desperately concentrated on the search for a harbor with a ship in it, and food on the ship. An attempt was made to get around the bay, and Ortega and his scouts got just around the southern end of it, but on November 11 the whole expedition gave up and turned back the way it had come. The group arrived back in San Diego on January 24, 1770.

Nothing encouraging had happened at San Diego during their absence. Serra had founded the mission of San Diego de Alcalá at a temporary location in a hut on Presidio Hill, on July 16, 1769, but there was not yet a single convert. The language barrier was at first impenetrable because the Baja California Indians were of no use as interpreters. The Diegueño were more than willing to come into the Spanish camp to receive presents. They were greatly attracted to any form of cloth, which had been unknown to them, and they soon took to stealing it, even from the bodies of the sick. Fortunately the Diegueño would not touch the food supplies of the Spaniards, to which, correctly in a way, they attributed the sickness. In August they had attacked the camp with a shower of arrows, but the killing of several of them by musket fire made them more respectful. At last one Indian baby was offered for baptism, but

Serra's joy turned to grief when the Indians suddenly snatched it from his arms and ran off before the ceremony could be completed. Yet nothing, it seemed, could discourage the indomitable father-president.

On February 10, 1770, Portolá sent Rivera and 40 men on the long journey back to Baja California for supplies. A month later, when there was still no sign of the *San José* or of the return of the *San Antonio*, Portolá announced that if no relief came by March 19, the feast of St. Joseph, the patron of the expedition, he and his men would march south the next morning. Serra and Crespí protested, refused to turn back, and arranged that they would be taken on board the *San Carlos*, still anchored in the bay, to await the coming of a supply ship. After 9 days of prayer, the *San Antonio* was sighted on the very afternoon of March 19. The danger of abandonment had passed.

In the admiring biography of Serra written years later by Francisco Palóu, who was not in San Diego to observe these events, the episode of the deadline is so dramatized that some historians have doubted that it ever really occurred. It seems to be confirmed in eyewitness accounts, however, including not only one by Crespí but also one by Portolá himself.

Portolá now sent the *San Antonio*, carrying Serra, Costansó, and Fages, on to Monterey. Portolá himself set out for the north again by land, with 12 soldiers, leaving 8 to guard San Diego. This time, at last, Portolá fully realized that what he had previously seen of the harbor of Monterey was all there was of it—at best a roadstead with no shelter from the north wind. But he had his orders, and so a presidio of poles and earth was constructed at Monterey under the direction of Costansó and a mission was built nearby under the direction of Serra. Both were formally established on June 3, 1770. Leaving Fages in charge of the government of Alta California, Portolá then sailed for Mexico.

There was great formal rejoicing in Mexico City over the establishment of the new province, even though the reports of Portolá to the visitor-general and the viceroy were more candid than they cared to hear. Portolá was of the opinion that if the Russians wanted Alta California, which he doubted, they should be allowed to have it as a punishment for their aggressive designs. The Spanish occupation of Monterey could never prevent the Russians from establishing themselves at some other point on the coast. It was impossible, Portolá wrote, "to send aid to Monterey by sea, and still more so by land, unless it was proposed to sacrifice thousands of men and huge sums of money." For example, he attributed the disappearance of the supply ship *San José* to the probability that at the end the scurvy had left not a single sailor able to steer her against the constant and terrible headwinds from the northwest.

SELECTED BIBLIOGRAPHY

Important works on the discovery and early exploration of California are Henry R. Wagner, *Spanish Voyages to the Northwest Coast of America in the Sixteenth Century* (1929) and *Cartography of the Northwest Coast of America to the Year 1800* (two volumes, 1937), and Maurice G. Holmes, *From New Spain by Sea to the Californias 1519–1668* (1963). See also Jack D. Forbes, "Melchor Díaz and the Discovery of Alta California," *Pacific Historical Review*, XXVII (November 1958), pp. 351–358; H. R. Wagner, *Juan Rodríguez Cabrillo, Discoverer of the Coast of California* (1941); and Harry Kelsey, "The California Armada of Juan Rodríguez Cabrillo," *Southern California Quarterly*, LXI (Winter 1979), pp. 313–336.

A translation of the parts of Montalvo's *Las Sergas de Esplandián* relating to Queen Califía, with commentary, may be found in Edward Everett Hale, *The Queen of California; the Origin of the Name of California* (first published in 1864; reprinted in 1945). See also Donald C. Cutter, "Sources of the Name 'California,'" *Arizona and the West*, III (Autumn 1961), pp. 233–243.

Warren L. Hanna, *Lost Harbour: The Controversy Over Drake's California Anchorage* (1979) is a convenient guide to the maze of arguments over Drake's landing spot. Hanna concludes that the evidence is insufficient to warrant a final judgment. See also N. B. Martin, "*Portus Novae Albionis*: Site of Drake's California Sojourn," *Pacific Historical Review*, XLVIII (August 1979), pp. 319–334. On the controversy over Drake's plate, see James D. Hart, *The Plate of Brass Reexamined: A Report Issued by the Bancroft Library* (1977) and the response by Robert H. Power, "A Plate of Brass 'By Me . . . C. G. Francis Drake,'" *California History*, LVII (Summer 1978), pp. 172–185, followed by Hart, *The Plate of Brass Reexamined: A Supplementary Report* (1979).

William L. Schurz chronicled *The Manila Galleon* (1939). On the Cermeño expedition, see Henry R. Wagner, "The Voyage to California of Sebastián Rodríguez Cermeño in 1595," *California Historical Society Quarterly*, III (April 1924), pp. 3–24, and Robert F. Heizer, "Archaeological Evidence of Sebastián Rodríguez Cermeño's California Visit," in the same journal, XX (December 1941), pp. 315–328. W. Michael Mathes, *Vizcaíno and Spanish Expansion in the Pacific Ocean, 1580–1630* (1968) considerably enhances Vizcaíno's reputation and the significance of his explorations.

The mission system appears in a very favorable light in Herbert E. Bolton, "The Mission as a Frontier Institution in the Spanish American Colonies," in his *Wider Horizons in American History* (1939). Clarence H. Haring, *The Spanish Empire in America* (1947) and Bailey W. Diffie, *Latin American Civilization, the Colonial Period* (1945) are somewhat more critical. For a survey of the literature see John Francis Bannon, "The Mission as a Frontier Institution: Sixty Years of Interest and Research," *Western Historical Quarterly*, X (July 1979), pp. 302–322. See also Francis Guest, "Mission Colonization and Political Control in Spanish California," *The Journal of San Diego History*, XXIV (Winter 1978), pp. 97–116.

Herbert I. Priestley, *José de Gálvez, Visitor-General of New Spain* (1916) and Charles E. Chapman, *The Founding of Spanish California; the Northwestward Expansion of New Spain, 1687–1783* (1916) deal with backgrounds of the colonization of Alta California.

Maynard J. Geiger, *The Life and Times of Fray Junípero Serra* (two volumes, 1959) is a work of urbane scholarship, in welcome contrast with the defensive tone of Zephyrin Engelhardt, *The Missions and Missionaries of California* (four volumes, 1908–1915).

Theodore E. Treutlein, *San Francisco Bay: Discovery and Colonization, 1769–1776* (1968) and Frank M. Stanger and Alan K. Brown, *Who Discovered the Golden Gate?* (1969) are illuminating. Accounts of the sacred expedition by Portolá, Costansó, Fages, and Vila are in the first two volumes of the *Publications* of the Academy of Pacific Coast History (1910–1911); see also Herbert E. Bolton, *Fray Juan Crespí, Missionary Explorer* (1927); H. I. Priestley, *A Historical, Political, and Natural Description of California by Pedro Fages* (1937); and Douglas S. Watson, *The Spanish Occupation of California* (1934).

CHAPTER 4

OUTPOSTS OF A DYING EMPIRE

The Spanish occupation of Alta California now consisted of two pinpoints on the coast, 450 miles apart. Differences of opinion between Serra and Fages deepened into a feud. In 1771 Serra moved the mission of San Carlos Borromeo from Monterey to the Carmel River, named long before by the Vizcaíno expedition in honor of its chaplains, three friars of the Order of Our Lady of Mount Carmel. This mission became Serra's headquarters for the arduous struggle to establish the others. Ultimately there would be 21 missions in Alta California, 9 of them founded during his lifetime, but at the beginning only Serra himself foresaw such a degree of success. Repeatedly Fages vetoed his requests for new missions because there were not enough soldiers to protect them. The earliest attempts at agriculture failed, and food supplies remained desperately low. In 1772 the California settlements were saved from starvation by the meat that Fages provided from a grizzly bear hunt in a valley north of San Luis Obispo.

BUCARELI, ANZA, AND THE FOUNDING OF SAN FRANCISCO

Visitor-General Gálvez returned to Spain in 1771, and a new viceroy, Antonio de Bucareli, arrived in the same year. At first Bucareli was too busy with other duties to take much interest in Gálvez's new colony. In 1773, however, he turned his attention to it, and for several years he gave it enough care and support to bring it through its precarious infancy. Again the fear of foreign encroachments reinforced Spanish interest in California, the English now rivaling the Russians as objects of concern. The voyages of Captain James Cook in the 1770s indicated a renewed English interest in the Pacific.

In 1773 Serra made a journey to Mexico City to plead for more support for new missions and the substitution of Sergeant Ortega for Lieutenant Fages as governor of Alta California. Instead, Bucareli replaced Fages with Captain Rivera, although this would soon involve Serra in more disputes with the new governor than with the old one.

About the same time, Captain Juan Bautista de Anza submitted a proposal for an expedition to open a land route from northern Sonora to Monterey. The land route from the peninsula was now useless because the impoverished Baja California missions had already contributed as much as they could, and besides they had just been turned over to the Dominicans. A mainland route from Sonora was now more practicable than before because recent mining discoveries and the subsequent increase in the population of that province had done more than all the military campaigns to overcome the Indian insurrections there.

With eager encouragement from Serra, Bucareli resolved not only to adopt Anza's project of a new land route to Monterey, but also to empower him to extend Spanish settlement to the strategic bay of San Francisco. Anza was an ideal leader for the project. Like his father and grandfather before him, he was a soldier of long experience on the northern Sonora frontier. The opening of a trail from Sonora to Alta Caifornia had been the dream of his family for three generations. He led two expeditions to California, one to explore the trail and the other to bring settlers, including some for the new San Francisco site.

On the first of these expeditions Anza rode out from Tubac, a presidio south of Tucson, in January of 1774. The party of 34 men was poorly mounted because the Apaches were constantly running off the best horses from the presidio herds. One of the men with Anza was Father Francisco Garcés. This remarkable Franciscan had already extended Kino's earlier explorations of the Colorado River region and had won the confidence of Salvador Palma, chief of the Yumas. The goodwill of the Yumas was a vital factor in the success of Anza's expeditions, and when that goodwill came to a tragic end a few years later, in the Yuma massacre of 1781, the trail to California which Anza blazed was to be cut off for nearly half a century.

Ferried across the Colorado River with the aid of the Yumas and their tule rafts, Anza and his men struck out westward across the sand dunes of the Colorado Desert, became lost, and finally struggled back to the river after 10 days. After leaving much of their baggage with Chief Palma, they traveled southward to get around the dunes, turned west again in the region of the present Mexican boundary, traversed what would later flourish as the Imperial Valley, moved northward along the eastern slopes of the mountains through the Anza Desert and the Borrego Valley, and crossed the mountains into the Cahuilla Valley by way of the Royal Pass of San Carlos.

On March 22, 1774, they reached the Mission of San Gabriel, founded 3 years earlier. Continuing to Monterey, and returning the way he had come, Anza reached Tubac in May, and a few months later went to Mexico City to make a full report to the viceroy. Encouraged by the opening of the new route from Sonora to California, Bucareli promoted Anza to the rank of lieutenant colonel, and planned new expeditions for 1775. An expedition to explore San Francisco Bay began under Captain Miguel Manrique, but this commander lost his mind a few days after leaving San Blas and had to be put ashore. He had left several loaded pistols about his cabin, and one of these accidentally exploded, wounding his successor, Lieutenant Juan Manuel de Ayala. The lateness of Spanish settlement of upper California can be vividly seen in the fact that this unfortunate pistol shot occurred within a few days of "the shot heard round the world," fired at Lexington, Massachusetts, on April 19, 1775, and signaling the beginning of the American Revolutionary War.

On August 5 a launch made at Monterey and piloted by Ayala's sailing master, José Cañizares, became the first Spanish vessel to enter the Golden Gate, known to the Spaniards merely as *La Boca*, or the mouth. Ayala's ship, the *San Carlos*, sailed through the next day. His wound confined him to his cabin, but the crew spent several weeks in making a thorough exploration of the arms of the bay with the launch. The names of Angel Island and of Alcatraz, the *Isla de los Alcatraces*, or island of the pelicans, date from the Ayala expedition, although the name of Alcatraz was then applied to the island now called Yerba Buena.

The second Anza expedition also began in 1775 and was responsible for the founding of the presidio and mission at San Francisco in the following year. Except for Anza's own small escort, this expedition consisted almost entirely of settlers who would remain in California as *pobladores*, or populators. There were about 30 soldier-colonists and their families and four civilian settlers and their families, recruited mainly in Sinaloa. The need for *married* soldiers in California came from both the need for future citizens for the province and the desire to reduce the difficulties with the Indians repeatedly caused by soldiers who were either unmarried or living far from their families in Mexico. In 1773, for example, three soldiers at San Diego had been accused of raping two Indian girls and murdering one of them. Sent to Mexico for trial, the soldiers were spared their lives but were sentenced to spend the rest of their lives as citizens of California, a somewhat paradoxical verdict reflecting the evil reputation the new colony had in Mexico.

The time when people would want to go to California was far in the future; only those in the direst poverty were willing to go, and then only on the promise of the government to outfit them completely and to pay all their expenses for years to come. Upon Anza's warning to Viceroy Bucareli, however, all such payments were in the form of clothing, food, equipment, and supplies, and not in cash, which might have been gambled away immediately. With the second Anza expedition went a large herd of cattle and horses to serve as breeding stock.

Following his previous route Anza reached San Gabriel with his second expedition in January 1776. There he learned that the Indians had attacked and destroyed the mission at San Diego in the previous November, killing Father Luis Jayme and two soldiers and mutilating the body of Father Jayme.

Governor Rivera had only 70 soldiers in the whole province, scattered among five missions and two presidios. He was on his way from Monterey to San Diego to punish the offenders, and Anza was induced to join forces with him for that purpose. Their arrival at San Diego, coinciding with those of a supply ship for San Blas and a small land force sent up from the peninsula, completely overawed the Indians; however, Rivera was excommunicated by the padres for entering the improvised church to seize an Indian chief who

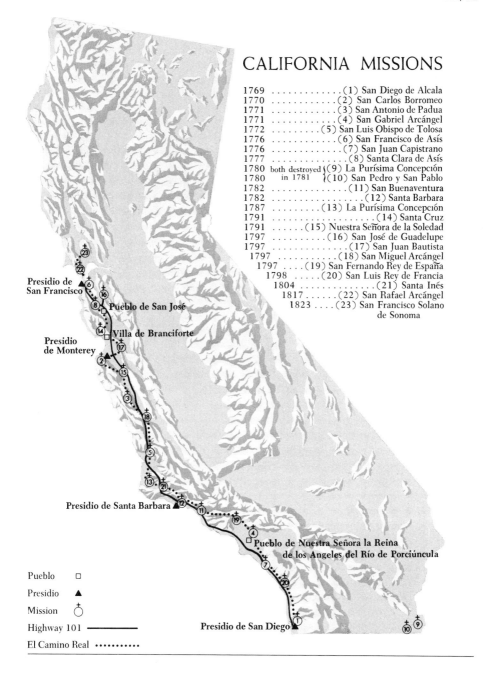

CALIFORNIA MISSIONS

1769	. . . .	(1) San Diego de Alcala
1770	. . . .	(2) San Carlos Borromeo
1771	. . . .	(3) San Antonio de Padua
1771	. . . .	(4) San Gabriel Arcángel
1772	. . . .	(5) San Luis Obispo de Tolosa
1776	. . . .	(6) San Francisco de Asís
1776	. . . .	(7) San Juan Capistrano
1777	. . . .	(8) Santa Clara de Asís
1780	both destroyed	(9) La Purísima Concepción
1780	in 1781	(10) San Pedro y San Pablo
1782	. . . .	(11) San Buenaventura
1782	. . . .	(12) Santa Barbara
1787	. . . .	(13) La Purísima Concepción
1791	. . . .	(14) Santa Cruz
1791	. . . . . .	(15) Nuestra Señora de la Soledad
1797	. . . .	(16) San José de Guadelupe
1797	. . . .	(17) San Juan Bautista
1797	. . . .	(18) San Miguel Arcángel
1797	. . . .	(19) San Fernando Rey de España
1798	. . . . .	(20) San Luis Rey de Francia
1804	. . . .	(21) Santa Inés
1817	. . . . . .	(22) San Rafael Arcángel
1823	. . . .	(23) San Francisco Solano de Sonoma

Presidio de San Francisco

Pueblo de San José

Presidio de Monterey

Villa de Branciforte

Presidio de Santa Barbara

Pueblo de Nuestra Señora la Reina de los Angeles del Río de Porciúncula

Presidio de San Diego

Pueblo □

Presidio ▲

Mission ⚥

Highway 101 ——————

El Camino Real • • • • • • • • • •

had sought the right of asylum, but who was suspected of being the main instigator of the revolt.

In March, Anza's party of colonists reached Monterey, and Anza himself proceeded to the San Francisco peninsula to choose the sites for the new presidio and mission. Governor Rivera, in spite of orders from the viceroy, had done nothing to prepare for the founding of San Francisco and was in fact bitterly opposed to it. He was now 65 years old and had repeatedly requested retirement. He was still a captain, and part of his irritation at this time was undoubtedly the result of his belief that Anza, who was only 41, had gained promotion to a higher rank for services no greater than his own. It was Rivera, after all, who had led the first overland party of Spanish colonists into California. A few years later, during the Yuma massacre, he would be killed while leading the last one, at the age of 70.

For the site of the new presidio, Anza chose a point near the northernmost tip of the San Francisco peninsula. The whole northern part of the peninsula consisted largely of sand dunes, but about 3 miles to the southeast of the presidio site Anza found a little oasis on a creek, and here, on March 29, 1776, he marked the site of the mission. He named the creek *Laguna de Nuestra Señora de los Dolores* because March 29 in the religious calendar was the Friday of Sorrows, referring to Our Lady of Sorrows, the Virgin Mary. From this there later arose the popular name of Mission Dolores for what was officially the Mission of San Francisco de Asís.

Various obstacles, including some set up by Governor Rivera, delayed the actual founding of the new establishments for several months. In the meantime Anza departed for Mexico and left Lt. José Moraga in charge of the new colonists. On June 27 a group of 193 persons, mostly soldier-settlers and their families, arrived at the site of the San Francisco mission. The presidio was formally established under the command of Moraga on September 17, and Father Palóu formally opened the mission on October 9.

NEVE AND THE PUEBLOS OF SAN JOSÉ AND LOS ANGELES

The new California was now regarded as more important than the old one, and this was reflected in the reorganization of their joint government in 1776. Felipe de Neve was now appointed governor of both the Californias, with headquarters at Monterey, where he arrived to replace Rivera early in 1777. Rivera's pleas for retirement were again denied, and he was again placed in charge of Baja California, this time as lieutenant governor under Neve's superior authority. Neve was another army officer, and probably the best administrator among the Spanish governors of California. In his *reglamento* of 1779, revising and enlarging an earlier decree of Viceroy Bucareli, Neve established the code of law that remained in effect until the end of Spanish rule.

Neve had been ordered to try to solve the food supply problems of the presidios by establishing agricultural towns or pueblos. The missions were beginning to be agriculturally self-supporting, but the padres protested against requisitions of their crops and herds to provide food for the garrisons. With the establishment of secular farming communities, one in the north and one in the south, Neve hoped that the military and civil establishment would no longer have to depend for food either upon the missions or upon the expensive and hazardous supply line from San Blas. In November 1777 he collected 14 men and their families from the presidios of Monterey and San Francisco and settled them at the new pueblo of San José de Guadalupe, the first town to be founded in Spanish Alta California.

In the same year Neve made a personal survey of possible locations for a southern pueblo. He chose a point near the *Río de Porciúncula*, not far from the site of the Indian village of Yang-Na, most of whose former inhabitants now resided in the mission of San Gabriel about 9 miles to the northeast. There was no harbor, and no navigable river, but that was of no importance for a small agricultural community. The place was on a plain extending 16 miles to the west, 60 miles to the east, and 25 miles to the south. Its name, the fullest of the versions in early official documents, was to be *El Pueblo de Nuestra Señora la Reina de los Angeles del Río de Porciúncula*, or the Town of Our Lady the Queen of the Angels by the River of Porciúncula. That this would soon be abbreviated was rather obviously inevitable, but the part of it to be chosen by popular usage was a matter of accident. It might have been *Pueblo*; or it might have been *Porciúncula*, which, since it means "little portion," would be more than a little incongruous today. It turned out to be *Los Angeles*, or rather, in the Spanish and Mexican periods, usually simply *Angeles*. The modern American expression, "the City of the Angels," often imagined to be a translation of the name, is inaccurate.

It is ironic that San Francisco and Los Angeles, hardly the least materialistic and self-indulgent of modern cities, were named, respectively, for the ascetic St. Francis of Assisi and for the Virgin Mary.

Like the San Francisco colonists, the Los Angeles *pobladores* were drawn from the poorest classes of Sinaloa, people to whom any change offered some hope of improvement. Neve asked for 24 experienced farmers, but it proved impossible to obtain that many. Early in 1781 12 settlers and their families, who had at last been brought together, were sent across the gulf and up the peninsula. One died of smallpox on the way. Rivera led another party, consisting of married soldiers for the California presidios, by way of the Anza Trail from Sonora.

The Los Angeles settlers and their dependents, 46 persons in all, arrived at San Gabriel mission in August. Their origins, as Hubert Howe Bancroft puts it, were a mixture of Indian and Negro with here and there a trace of Spanish. The San José colonists were ahead of them not only in priority of founding but also in educational matters. Of the nine heads of families now at San José, there was one who could read and write. This was José Tiburcio Vasquez, said to be the ancestor of the famous bandit.

After a few weeks under smallpox quarantine at some distance from San Gabriel, the *pobladores* moved to the spot Neve had chosen for them, about three-fourths of a mile west of the river of Porciúncula, and a little to the northwest of the present plaza. Neve set the date of September 4, 1781, for the founding of the pueblo, and it has served as the official birthday even though there were no ceremonies on that day, or indeed until 5 years later when the lands were formally allotted.

Although the government had undertaken to supply all the needs of the settlers and although Neve's regulations provided an extreme form of paternalistic control for the pueblos, the situation was far from that of a welfare state. Early in 1782, by order of the governor, three men were "sent away as useless to the pueblo and themselves," and their property was confiscated.

The padres considered the pueblo settlers to be a lazy and dissolute lot, good for nothing but drinking, gambling, and the pursuit of Indian women. Yet somehow, within a few years, irrigated agriculture and cattle raising at Los Angeles developed far enough to ensure the survival of the community, although its crops and herds could not yet rival those of San Gabriel, the "mother of agriculture in California" and the most productive of the missions.

Father-President Serra found Governor Neve even more determined than his predecessors to maintain the authority of the government over that of the missionaries. The governors had been so instructed, because it was the policy of the entire Spanish government at this time to treat the church as essentially an arm of the state. Of his many disputes with Neve, the one that disturbed the father-president most arose from Neve's insistence that there was a technical flaw in the papers authorizing Serra to administer the sacrament of confirmation. At the height of this long argument, Serra confided to Father Lasuén that he was suffering from insomnia, caused, he said, not by his bad leg but by the trouble given him by the governor.

THE YUMA MASSACRE

José de Gálvez, having become Minister of the Indies in the royal government at Madrid, was finally able to put into effect his earlier plan to reorganize the higher administration of the frontiers of New Spain. In 1776 the entire group of frontier provinces from Sinaloa, Sonora, and the Californias to New Mexico and Texas was detached from the control of the viceroy at Mexico City and placed under a commandant-general of the "Interior Provinces" with headquarters at Arispe in Sonora.

Teodoro de Croix, first commandant-general of the *Provincias Internas*, took little interest in the Californias, which he never visited. His attention was mainly on the defense of the frontiers to the east, where he hoped to crush the Apaches and end their perpetual raids. The Indians of Alta California, except for those at San Diego, had given very little trouble, and the concern of Croix with the California establishments was largely in reducing their expenses. Unfortunately he failed to realize that the Yumas, whose location on the Colorado River was so strategic, were much more capable of armed resistance than other Califormia tribes.

In 1780 two missions were founded in Yuma territory on the California side of the Colorado River, but, over the protests of the padres, both establishments were peculiar mixtures of mission, presidio, and pueblo. This novel economy measure failed dismally. In June 1781 Captain Rivera and his party of married soldiers reached the Colorado on their way to California. Some went ahead to San Gabriel, but about half of the party including Rivera camped on the eastern bank of the river to rest. Their cattle destroyed part of the Indians' supply of mesquite beans, and Rivera's men generally succeeded in antagonizing the Yumas even more than the Spaniards at the new missions had done. On July 17 the Yumas destroyed both missions and the next day crossed the river to surprise and kill Rivera and all his soldiers. The women and children with the Spaniards were captured. Altogether, 30 soldiers and 4 padres, including Garcés, were put to death. Captain Don Fernando Rivera y Moncada, the weary and irascible old veteran who had felt condemned to interminable service in some of the most difficult roles ever demanded of a soldier or a colonial administrator, was released from duty at last.

The Yuma massacre was one of the worst disasters in the whole history of the Spanish frontier. Some of the captives were later ransomed, but no serious attempt was made to punish the Yumas or to reopen the Colorado River route. The Anza Trail remained cut off until the 1820s, and in the meantime there was virtually no land communication at all between Mexico and California.

For the next 40 years, from the Yuma massacre in 1781 to the final collapse of Spanish rule over Mexico in 1821, New Spain made little effort to strengthen its outposts in Alta California. There, as elsewhere, the overextended Spanish colonial empire was on the defensive and crumbling. The mission system continued to expand, but it did not succeed in turning the Indians into genuine colonists. Other than the native Indians, there were about 600 persons in Alta California in 1781, and about five times as many in 1821, but the increase was almost entirely from the birth of descendants of the earlier colonists rather than from the arrival of new ones. The numbers of cattle and horses grew much more rapidly, and a fourth institution, the private rancho, began to develop along with the presidios, missions, and pueblos. Nellie Van de Grift Sánchez and other writers have called Spanish California an "Arcadia." Like that isolated mountain kingdom in ancient Greece, it was quiet, simple, and pastoral. But life in it was by no means as ideal as this analogy would imply.

THE IMPACT OF THE MISSIONS

Following Serra's death in 1784 his longtime companion Francisco Palóu served briefly as father-president. The following year Fermín Francisco de Lasuén became head of the Alta California missions and served as father-president from 1785 to 1803. It was Lasuén who supervised the building of the beautiful churches, several of which are extant, that replaced the rude structures of Serra's time. Under Lasuén each mission developed into a kind of polytechnical school, teaching the Indians to do fine leather work, operate tile factories and carpentry shops, and even do mural painting. During his tenure as father-president the number of missions doubled, from 9 to 18, and their Indian population more than doubled, rising to about 20,000, nearly as large as it ever became.

Indians at Mission San Carlos Borromeo in Carmel lined up in rigid formation for the visit of La Pérouse in 1786. From a 1791 watercolor copy of the lost original painting made at the occasion. *(Courtesy of the Museo Naval, Madrid.)*

Early visitors to Spanish California often described in detail the operations of the missions and their impact on the Indians. In 1786 the comte de La Pérouse, a European nobleman engaged in a global voyage of scientific exploration for the French government, visited Monterey. The two vessels under La Pérouse were the first ships, other than those of the Spanish themselves, to visit Alta California since the voyage of Drake more than two centuries earlier. The French visitor had the highest admiration for the character of the missionaries—"these men, truly apostolic, who have abandoned the idle life of a cloister to give themselves up to fatigues, cares, and anxieties of every kind." But he doubted that they were accomplishing anything of permanent value. Under their theocratic system the Indian was "too much a child, too much a slave, too little a man." In the resorting to stocks, irons, and the lash, and in the use of soldiers to hunt down those who tried to escape, La Pérouse found a distressing resemblance to the slave plantations he had seen in Santo Domingo.

Five years after La Pérouse's visit, Monterey welcomed another scientific exploring expedition, this time Spanish, under the command of Alejandro Malaspina. In the crew of one of Malaspina's ships, incidentally, was the first Anglo-American who came to California and stayed—one John Green, a sailor from Boston who died of dropsy a few hours after the expedition arrived at Monterey in 1791. Malaspina's impression of the mission system was in considerable contrast to that of La Pérouse. He denounced the "ridiculous inventions of many foreign authors, who, confusing at times the system with the abuses and ignoring always the primary object of such establishments, have painted all our missions in America as horrible and oppressive." There was no doubt in Malaspina's mind that the missionaries in California had accomplished a great good. The Spanish priests had brought to the Indians "the end of a thousand local wars that were destroying them, social beginnings, a pure and holy religion, safe and healthy foods," and a variety of other blessings.

The question of whether the Indians in the California missions were exploited and wretched or contented and appreciative will long remain a moot one. It has been said that "the preponderant testimony" describes the mission Indians as happy and well-adjusted, preferring mission life to their previous freedom and grateful for close supervision, hard work, colorful rituals, and the salvation of their souls. This is, to say the least, an extremely questionable conclusion. The bulk of the evidence has been the writings of the missionaries, who naturally tended to believe what they deeply yearned to believe about a matter so vital to their consciences. It is significant that the padres always applied the term "neophytes," or apprentices in Christianity, even to Indians who had been born in the missions and spent their entire lives there. The belief that any group of human adults could be happy under a system that treated them as if they were hopelessly retarded children was a very questionable one.

The best evidence of how the Indians actually felt about the missions would be the testimony of the Indians themselves, and unfortunately very few of them had any opportunity to get their testimony into the historical record. One who did was Victoria, an Indian girl who grew up in the Mission of San Gabriel and later married the "Scotch *paisano*," Hugo Reid. It should be noted that it was Reid who recorded his wife's recollections and that his non-Catholic background, along with his status as the recipient of a rancho grant carved out of San Gabriel mission lands, gave him a viewpoint that was particularly hostile to the missionaries. The Franciscan historian Father Zephyrin Englehardt described Hugo Reid as "that embittered Scotchman" who "lied about religious matters."

Nevertheless, it is clear that Victoria regarded life in the mission as a life of misery, humiliation, and terror. The alliance of the padres and the soldiers, she told her husband bitterly, had turned even Indian chieftains like her own father into humble, confused, awkward, and shamefaced men. She could not entirely understand why her people, the Gabrielino, who had once given good accounts of themselves in occasional battles with neighboring tribes, had offered so little resistance to the Spaniards; however, she remembered how the soldiers, armed with muskets, had come to her village when she was 6 years old and taken its people to the mission. At first the Indians had been filled with surprise and astonishment; then a strange lethargy set in. They were told to fear a hell that was lacking in their own religion. Corporal punishment, also, was something that had been unknown to them before.

One stark episode that Victoria remembered from her mission childhood occurred when an Indian woman who had a miscarriage was charged with infanticide and punished by having her head shaved, by being flogged every day for 15 days, by wearing irons on her feet for 3 months, and by "having to appear every Sunday in church, on the steps leading up to the altar, with a hideous painted wooden child in her arms." This took place while San Gabriel was under the regime of Father José María Zalvidea, a particularly stern disciplinarian. In Hugo Reid's opinion, Zalvidea "must ... have considered whipping as meat and drink to [the Indians], for they had it morning, noon and night."

Like Serra, Zalvidea was as stern with himself as with his Indian wards. He often lashed his own shoulders and back, and under his coarse robe he always wore a belt with iron points pressing into his flesh. He made San Gabriel "the Pride of the Missions," yet to a man of his faith, pride was the first of the seven deadly sins. Perhaps this conflict was one of the things that unbalanced his mind; he later suffered a nervous breakdown and was transferred to San Juan Capistrano for hospitalization.

The most revealing evidence of the impact of the missions on the California Indians was recorded in the mission registers. There one finds a terrifying death rate, caused primarily by diseases for which the Indians lacked immunity. Confinement within the adobe walls of the missions also deprived the Indians of the degree of sanitation they had enjoyed in their own villages from their *temescals* and their practice of occasionally burning their old dwellings and building new ones. Concentration of Indians in large numbers at the missions, the changes in diet, and the imposition of an alien discipline and regimentation all contributed to the high death rate. The mission registers also revealed a surprising variation in experience from mission to mission. Indians at the Santa Cruz mission, for example, survived an average of 8½ years after conversion, while those at San Luis Obispo survived more than twice as long. The infant mortality rate, also erratic, was generally high: more than half the Indians born in the missions died before their fifth birthday. During the entire mission period, the native population from San Francisco Bay to San Diego fell from 72,000 to 18,000—a decline of over 75 percent.

ATTEMPTS AT REINFORCEMENT

At the end of the eighteenth-century Spain began to experience a long series of international difficulties in which she would gradually drift from humiliation into utter disaster. In 1778 Captain James Cook had visited Nootka Sound, a harbor on Vancouver Island, and claimed the rights of discovery, although 4 years earlier Juan Pérez had discovered the place and claimed it for Spain. The publication of Captain Cook's account of the potential riches of the fur trade in the Nootka region led to an international race to exploit it. In 1789 Esteban José Martínez was sent to take possession of Nootka Sound for Spain, and to build a fort. Upon his arrival he found five ships anchored there—two American, one Portuguese, and two British. The British commander, Captain James Colnett, had also come with orders to take possession of the harbor and to build a fort and trading post. Martínez arrested Captain Colnett and seized his ships as prizes. The news of this act led England to threaten war. Spain appealed to France for help, but the French Revolution had begun and the National Assembly was not disposed to honor the Family Compact between the Bourbon monarchs. Thus in 1790, in the first Nootka Sound treaty, Spain was forced to give up its claims to exclusive rights on the Pacific coast north of California.

George Vancouver was appointed as a British commissioner to work out details of the application of the treaty, and in 1792 and the following year he visited several points in California, with special interest in the presidios. The fourth and last of these, at Santa Barbara, had been established in 1782. Vancouver was amazed at their weakness. At the time of his visits there were two cannon at the presidio of San Francisco, neither of them serviceable, and three at San Diego, none of them even mounted. Santa Barbara had two cannon, and Monterey eight. The Spanish authorities, worried because the extent of this weakness would now be known to the British government, made plans to try to strengthen their feeble hold on the province. Orders were given for the construction of new batteries, but there were only token results. Moreover, the guns installed in San Francisco, at what was later called Fort Point, were a few years later found to have been rendered unusable by exposure and neglect.

In 1796 the viceroy, the marqués de Branciforte, and the governor, Diego de Borica, made plans for a new type of pueblo to be colonized by retired soldiers and their families. These ex-soldiers not only would be self-supporting but would provide a ready reserve in case of foreign incursions. The attempt to carry out this project illustrated the able planning that so often characterized Spanish colonial administration, and the typical frustration of such planning by hopeless difficulties.

The site of the new pueblo, to be called the Villa de Branciforte, adjoined the lands of the Mission Santa Cruz—to the bitter objections of the padres. The funds available for founding the new town were sadly inadequate. Not a single ex-soldier could be found in Mexico who would go there voluntarily, and nearly all the colonists who finally arrived in 1797 were men convicted of petty crimes, now sentenced to live in a Spanish version of Botany Bay. It is not surprising that the Villa de Branciforte did not flourish, although it struggled along for many years as a collection of huts. Such was the last attempt under Spanish rule to found any new civil or military establishment in California, with the exception of a few cattle ranchos on lands granted mainly to noncommissioned officers retired from garrison duty.

A dismal impression of Spanish prospects in California must remain, even though Governor Diego de Borica, a jovial Basque who was an early California booster, did his best to brighten the picture in a number of his reports. "This is a great country," he wrote soon after his arrival at Monterey, "the most peaceful and quiet country in the world; one lives better here than in the most cultured court of Europe." The climate he described as "healthful, between cold and temperate," and in general "so good that all are getting to look like

Englishmen." There was "good bread, excellent meat, tolerable fish; and good humor which is worth all the rest. Plenty to eat, but the most astounding is the general fecundity, both of rationals and irrationals."

This last was a significant reference to the Spanish way of distinguishing the two main groups of the colonial population. The *gente de razón*, the people of reason, included all who were not full-blooded Indians. Literacy was much too rare to be a requisite. This idea of "civilized" or "rational" persons was also used interchangeably with "whites." Any admixture of white ancestry, mestizo or mulatto, was counted as white, and also qualified a person as rational. This distinction was itself irrational. In essence it was a distinction between human and subhuman. Among the rationals, the very few "pure-blooded Castilians," or rather those who could pass themselves off as such, were at the top of the colonial heap, and degrees of admixture often effectively determined social status.

Toward the end of his governorship (1794–1800), Borica was still inter-larding his reports with such glowing remarks as, "To live much, and without care, come to Monterey." But in view of the fact that ill health was causing him to beg for retirement, as Rivera and Neve had done before him, we must suspect that his continued praise of life in California may have been designed to help in finding a willing and competent replacement. This was not easy. The governorship of California was not one of the more desirable posts in the Spanish colonial service.

EXPLORATION OF THE CENTRAL VALLEY

Had the Spaniards chanced upon the treasure of the Sierra Nevada, the history of California and even of the modern world might be incalculably different. But it is not surprising that the very few Spanish explorers who traversed parts of the Central Valley as far as the foothills of the Sierra should have failed to notice bits of gold in the streambeds or in outcroppings of quartz. The Span-iards had no pressing reason to explore the vast range itself, and to have dis-covered the gold in its foothills they would have had to be a great deal luckier than the Spaniards generally were in California. In Mexico and Peru they had known that gold and silver were present because the Indians had already dis-covered them and learned to use them. The California Indians had not discov-ered precious metals; they had had no acquaintance with any metal whatever.

Spanish settlement in Alta California was confined to a thin coastal strip. Except for the two short-lived establishments on the Colorado which were wiped out by the Yuma, the farthest-inland Spanish settlement was Mission Soledad—only 30 miles from the sea. Following the discovery of the Central Valley by Pedro Fages during his exploration of the northeastern reaches of San Francisco Bay in 1772, there were periodic efforts to find places suitable for missions in various parts of the great interior region.

No missions were actually founded there, however, and the purposes of most of the Spanish expeditions into the valley were no more than those of pursuing escaped neophytes, punishing occasional raiders, and recovering stolen cattle and horses. The frequent raids on the livestock of the coastal settlements were carried on mainly by Indians who had once lived in the coastal areas but had fled to the interior to avoid missionization.

The outstanding figure among Spanish explorers of the Central Valley was Lt. Gabriel Moraga. His father, José, the first commandant of the Presidio of San Francisco, had brought Gabriel to California as a boy with the second Anza expedition. Between 1805 and 1817 the younger Moraga led a large number of expeditions into the great valley. He was responsible for such names as those of *El Río de Nuestra Señora de la Merced,* the River of Our Lady of Mercy; *El Río do Los Santos Reyes,* the River of the Holy Kings; the San Joaquin and Sacramento rivers; *Mariposa,* from the many butterflies seen there in 1806; and *Calaveras,* a place of skulls.

THE COMING OF THE RUSSIANS

In the early nineteenth century the Spanish claim of exclusive rights to settlement in California was challenged by the establishment of a Russian fur trading outpost north of San Francisco. Count Nikolai Petrovich Rezanov, an official of the Russian-American Fur Company, visited San Francisco in the spring of 1806. He came seeking supplies to relieve the danger of starvation in the Russian colony at Sitka, and incidentally investigating the possibilities of the fur trade in northern California itself. The Spaniards were aware that the Russian position in the Pacific northwest was almost as weak as their own, and they were concerned lest it be strengthened. Trade between Spanish colonies and foreigners was illegal. In the face of such difficulties, Rezanov's mission seemed doomed to failure.

At this point, "seeing that our situation was not getting better," he decided to improve it by a proposal of marriage to Doña Concepción Argüello, the 15-year-old daughter of the commandant of the San Francisco presidio.

Apart from the international political complications, there was a further impediment to granting Rezanov's request for the young woman's hand: he was of the Eastern Orthodox faith, whereas she was Roman Catholic. But her tender pleas moved the hearts of her father, the governor, and of the padres, and permission was given subject to ultimate approval in Rome. Rezanov then explained that he also would have to secure permission and that this would require him to consult the religious authorities in St. Petersburg, as well as the czar himself. Thus the wedding was postponed until his next visit to San Francisco, and in the meantime he was permitted to gather a cargo of supplies from the missions. Rezanov never returned to California, having died in the course of his journey to Russia. It was several years before the news of his death reached his fiancée.

Inevitably, accounts of this poignant episode have varied in their estimates of the sincerity of Rezanov's intentions. His own account suggests that he contemplated an honorable marriage, although one of diplomatic convenience. Interpretations of the lady's feelings have also varied. Bret Harte, in his poem "Concepción Argüello (Presidio de San Francisco, 1800) [sic]," invited his many readers to "listen to the simple story of a woman's love and trust." Others have pointed out that the story was not that simple. In fact it appears that Concepción's youthful love for Nikolai Petrovich, a man 35 years older than herself, was inspired in part by the contrast between the impoverished life of the presidio and her dreams of life at the court of St. Petersburg. As for Bret Harte's portrait of the lady in her later years as a "trembling, . . . wasted figure" who considered herself to have "died too" when Rezanov did, the actual evidence indicates that in middle age she became a stout and rather jolly woman who found much pleasure in acts of kindness and charity.

Rezanov had secured only a temporary trading concession. In 1812 the Russian-American Fur Company built a fortified village which they called Ross, a name derived from the same root as that of Russia. Located on the coast about 18 miles north of Bodega Bay, Fort Ross had several purposes. It was intended to produce food not only for itself but for the company's operations in Alaska, to serve as a headquarters for the hunting of sea otter in northern California waters, and also to serve as a station for the trade which the Russians hoped to open on a regular basis with the Spanish Californian settlements. Though such trade was still forbidden by the Spanish government, locally it was very much needed and wanted, and at this time Spain and Russia were on friendly terms. The Russians insisted that their new settlement carried no hostile intent and professed to have believed that San Francisco was the northernmost limit of Spain's legal possession of the coast. They knew that the Spaniards had no force available that could drive them out, and they politely disregarded the formal Spanish protests. On one occasion the garrison at San Francisco had to borrow powder from a visiting Russian ship in order to fire a salute from the only cannon in the presidio that could still be fired with any safety.

THE LAST YEARS UNDER THE SPANISH FLAG

Some of the little scenes that were being enacted in the frontier colony of California during this period were colorful and admirable; others were pitiful and drab. In any case, they received very little attention from the Spanish government, which was in an increasingly tragic situation. During most of the stormy era of the French Revolution and Napoleon, Spain was under the befuddled rule of Charles IV. It was characteristic of that monarch that he was almost the only person in Madrid who did not seem to know that his favorite adviser and chief minister, Manuel Godoy, a former captain of the royal guard, was the queen's lover. Partly as a result of Godoy's policies, Spain was in alliance with France and almost continuously at war with England from 1796 to 1808, and consequently trade between Spain and her American colonies was largely cut off by the British navy.

In 1807 Napoleon became impatient with the way the Spanish regime was being conducted. He lured Charles IV, the queen, and the crown prince, Ferdinand, to France for a visit, threw them into prison there, and announced that his brother, Joseph Bonaparte, would be the new king of Spain. In the spring of 1808 the Spanish people rebelled against this French regime, and for 5 years Spain was locked in one of the bitterest struggles in history, until the French armies were finally driven from the Iberian peninsula in 1813. Meanwhile Spain had little strength to spare for ruling her colonies, and their long and sporadic wars of independence set in. Amid the surging tides of world events, California remained a stagnant backwater.

The Mexican Revolution began in 1810 when the creole priest, Miguel de Hidalgo, published his famous outcry against tyranny from his parish in the village of Dolores. In all the years until the news of Mexico's final independence reached California in 1822, few people in that isolated colony other than the governors and a few of the padres had any understanding of the issues in the terrible internal strife that was taking place in Mexico and in Spain. Nor was there much interest in those struggles except for complaints that because of them the supply ships from San Blas came even less often than before, and for several years did not come at all. The people of the presidios and pueblos suffered not only from the absence of all the little extra comforts of life, but even from the absence of clothing other than the crude homemade articles. They became intensely jealous of the self-sustained and growing wealth of the missions. The padres were enjoying the fruits of choice lands and well-irrigated gardens—oranges and grapes, wines and brandies. Padres, as well as others, were increasingly inclined to engage in contraband trade with foreign vessels, exchanging cowhides and tallow for cloth and other luxuries.

The most sensational events of the period were the looting and burning of Monterey and San Juan Capistrano in 1818 by two privateering vessels sailing under the Argentine flag and commanded by the Frenchman Hippolyte de Bouchard. California was loyal to Spain, hence the military justification for these acts of pseudo patriotic piracy. Such was California's only participation in the wars of independence. Three years later the tattered flag of Spain was lowered for the last time at Monterey, and the new banner of Mexico, bearing an eagle and a snake, was raised in its place.

SELECTED BIBLIOGRAPHY

Bernard E. Bobb, *The Viceregency of Antonio Maria Bucareli in New Spain, 1771–1779* (1962) includes a description of Bucareli's policies toward California. Herbert E. Bolton, *Anza's California Expeditions* (five volumes, 1930) exhaustively chronicles the two expeditions and the founding of San Francisco; the first volume, also published separately as *Outpost of Empire* (1931), is Bolton's summary of the story; the other four volumes are documentary. Harlan Hague, *The Road to California: The Search for a Southern Overland Route, 1540–1848* (1978) sets the Anza expeditions in their broadest historical context. See also Theodore E. Treutlein, *San Francisco Bay: Discovery and Colonization* (1968). John Galvin (ed.), *The First Spanish Entry into San Francisco Bay, 1775* (1971) is a narrative of the Ayala expedition.

Edwin A. Beilharz, *Felipe de Neve, First Governor of California* (1971) is a valuable study. Documents on the founding of Los Angeles were included in the Historical Society of Southern California's annual Publication of 1931, the year of the sesquicentennial.

Two volumes of the *History of California*, volume I, 1542–1800, and volume II, 1801–1824, written by Henry L. Oak (also included as volumes XVIII [1884] and XIX [1885] of *The Works of Hubert Howe Bancroft*, binder's title *Bancroft's Works*), remain the most important books on the period of this chapter. Also useful are Edith Buckland Webb, *Indian Life at the Old Missions* (1952); Francis F. Guest, *Fermén Francisco de Lasuén, a Biography* (1973); and Sherburne F. Cook, *The Conflict between the California Indian and White Civilization*, Part II (1943). The many books that dwell on the romantic aspects include *California Pastoral* (1888), written actually as well as nominally by Bancroft; Nellie Van de Grift Sánchez, *Spanish Arcadia* (1929); Alberta Johnston Denis, *Spanish Alta California* (1927); and Irving B. Richman, *California under Spain and Mexico* (1911).

Leon G. Campbell, "The Spanish Presidio in Alta California during the Mission Period, 1769–1784," *Journal of the West*, XVI (October 1977), pp. 63–77, is a brief summary, while Max L. Moorhead, *The Presidio: Bastion of the Spanish Borderlands* (1975) offers a more extensive analysis but excludes the Californias.

"Spanish Explorations of California's Central Valley" is the subject of Donald C. Cutter's Ph.D. thesis, University of California, Berkeley (1950).

On the impact of the missions see Sherburne F. Cook, "Historical Demography," in Robert F. Heizer (ed.), *California* (1978), pp. 91–98, and Francis F. Guest, "An Examination of the Thesis of S. F. Cook on the Forced Conversion of Indians in the California Missions," *Southern California Quarterly*, LXI (Spring 1979), pp. 1–78. For an analysis of the importance of Indian labor, see the corresponding chapter in Robert Archibald, *The Economic Aspects of the California Missions* (1978). George Phillips suggests that the California Indians were far from passive in their response to the missions; see his essay in David J. Weber (ed.), *New Spain's Far Northern Frontier* (1979). For the views of foreign visitors see Jean Francois Galaup, comte de La Pérouse, *Voyage Round the World* (two volumes, translation, 1798–1799); Donald C. Cutter, *Malaspina in California* (1960); and Francis J. Weber, "The California Missions and Their Visitors," *The Americas*, XXIV (1968), pp. 319–336.

Accounts of the coming of the Russians include T. C. Russell (ed.), *The Rezanov Voyage to Nueva California in 1806* (1926); *Langsdorff's Narrative of the Rezanov Voyage to Nueva California in 1807* (1927); and "The Russians in California," *California Historical Society Quarterly*, XII (September 1933), a special issue. See also James R. Gibson, *Imperial Russia in Frontier America* (1976) and P. A. Tikhmenev, *A History of the Russian-American Company* (1978).

A MARGINAL PROVINCE
OF A TROUBLED REPUBLIC

As one of the most-isolated and least-valued of all the colonial possessions of Spain, California had grown used to being neglected. The independent nation of Mexico, periodically torn with revolutionary disturbances and established as a republic after a brief and tragic interlude under the "empire" of Agustín Iturbide, was even less able than Spain had been to concern itself seriously or effectively with the distant northern region.

GOVERNMENT AND POLITICS IN THEORY AND PRACTICE

The most influential framers of the Federal Constitution of the United Mexican States, adopted in 1824, were liberal idealists who modeled their country's new organic law in part on that of the United States of America. But there were great differences between the political, economic, and social backgrounds of the two countries. In Mexico, not even the upper class had acquired any substantial experience in self-government under Spanish colonial rule, and only a tiny fraction of the people were literate and prosperous enough to take an informed part in public affairs. Nevertheless, on paper the constitution of 1824 guaranteed both complete political equality and complete racial equality. Not only were Indians entitled to vote and to hold office, but like all other citizens they were supposed to enjoy full freedom of person and property. In this respect, indeed, the Mexican constitution went far beyond its American counterpart, to which the Thirteenth, Fourteenth, and Fifteenth Amendments, abolishing slavery and seeking to establish the civil rights of black people, had not yet been added.

The liberal Mexican constitution makers of 1824 dreamed of developing a civil society and a prosperous economy in which republican government and equal rights for all people could become more than empty phrases. As applied to the remote province of California, these vague hopes led to several new policies. Governors of California were now authorized to permit freer trade with foreigners, subject only to import duties, to move toward secularization of the missions, and to increase rancho land grants, including grants to foreigners willing to be naturalized and to accept Roman Catholicism.

Under the first Mexican constitution, California was only a territory, not a state, although it was promoted to the rank of a "department" under the constitution of 1836 and the laws of 1837. Governors were appointed by the government of Mexico. There was a provincial legislative branch, of sorts, in the form of an elected *diputación,* but in practice it functioned only occasionally when the governor chose to convene it, and then merely as an advisory rather than a legislative body. In effect, the governor not only acted as the civil and military executive but also controlled the provincial lawmaking process, and he exercised nearly all the judicial authority in the more important matters. In other words, there was no real separation of powers and no effective legal limitation of executive power. The general government of California remained what it had been under Spain, a petty military despotism. Control from Mexico City, however, was greatly weakened because the government could provide few soldiers of any sort, and none competent or reliable, for service in California; it lacked the money to pay them.

During California's Mexican period, one important substitute for a system of checks and balances did arise: the comic-opera "revolution," a political device characterized by bombastic "pronouncements," chesslike marches and countermarches, and noisy but bloodless artillery duels, just out of range, in which both sides retrieved each other's cannonballs and fired them back.

As the power of the Mexican governors and the Franciscan missionaries weakened, the real authority in California, insofar as there was any, gravitated into the hands of a small group of *ranchero* families, mostly California-born. The fact that these families were so closely intermarried was one reason that there was so little actual killing in battles between revolutionary factions. There was too much risk of killing a brother-in-law.

The main political motives of the leaders of this little ranchero oligarchy were, first, the hope of taking over from the missions their lands, their cattle, and their skillful cowboys and, second, the desire for political power and glory. In their struggles to achieve these objectives, the *californios* were badly divided by personal, factional, and sectional disputes. In the rivalry between *norteños* and *sureños,* such northern California leaders as Juan Bautista Alvarado, Mariano Guadalupe Vallejo, and José Castro were aligned against southern California politicos like José Antonio Carrillo, Pío Pico, and Juan Bandini. Confronted by the restless ambitions of these volatile native sons of California, governors sent up from Mexico had an increasingly difficult time.

Josiah Royce later maintained that the bloodless revolution, given the limitations of its social and historical context, was really a comparatively civilized method of settling internal political differences. In certain obvious respects it was infinitely preferable to the American Civil War, for example. The numerous California insurrections were, in part, merely a fairly harmless form of public entertainment. On the other hand, the Californians were capable of fighting with skill, courage, and deadly effectiveness when they thought it appropriate. They would prove this spectacularly against General Kearny's unfortunate American dragoons at the battle of San Pascual in 1846.

Government by mock revolution had serious defects, however, and one of these was that the resulting decisions were likely to be temporary. In one 5-year period, from 1831 to 1836, Mexican California had 11 distinct gubernatorial administrations, not counting 3 men who were appointed to the governorship by Mexico but whom the Californians did not permit to take office. By contrast, there had been only 10 governors in the whole period of more than half a century of Spanish rule.

THE SECULARIZATION PROBLEM

By far the most important political issue in the province during the 1820s and 1830s was the question of the secularization of the missions, or rather, and more realistically, the question of who was to profit from the acquisition of their lands and herds. This troublesome problem so far overshadowed all others that the whole story of the political and quasi-military events can best be understood in connection with it.

As early as 1749, by royal order, the Spanish government had made an attempt to secularize the missions of Mexico—that is, to turn the properties over to the Indians and to replace the missionaries with secular parish clergy. This attempt was abandoned largely because there were not enough secular priests available. In California, Governor Neve's *reglamento* of 1779 had tried to limit new missions to the purpose of religious instruction, given in the Indians' own native villages, but Father Serra succeeded in blocking this radical departure from the regular mission system.

When Mexico gained its independence, the California missionaries were alarmed. Most of the missionaries were Spaniards, and as such they were targets for the hostility of Mexican revolutionary nationalists. For centuries the creoles had hated the *gachupines*. A "creole," or *criollo*, was a person who had been born in the Spanish American colonies; sometimes the word meant a person of entirely European ancestry, sometimes it was used without regard to racial origin. The Mexican word *"gachupines,"* meaning men born in Spain, had originally meant "those who wear spurs," and it implied, usually correctly, that the Spanish-born regarded themselves as superior beings. That feeling was bitterly resented in Mexico, and ambitious people born in California were also beginning to feel the same kind of resentment, not only against Spaniards but against Mexicans, particularly officials.

For centuries the Spanish church had been an integral part of Spain's authoritarian system of colonial control. Inevitably, republican theories were often anticlerical. Such theories, however, were often rationalizations for avarice. There was rising criticism of the missions for their temporal wealth and for their exploitation of the Indians. Unfortunately these were the same privileges that many an eloquent anticlerical wanted to appropriate. Among the strongest critics of the mission system was Juan Bautista Alvarado. The missionaries, in his opinion, had "found the Indians in full enjoyment of their five senses, valiant in war . . . far-sighted in their own way"; but when the padres departed, "they left the Indian population half-stupefied, very much reduced in numbers, and duller than when they found them." As a native son of California who became one of its governors, Alvarado would secure extensive land grants for himself and his political followers.

The padres argued that the mission Indians were not ready for secularization, and this was certainly true. That the missions had failed to make them ready after more than a half a century, and showed no signs of ever making them ready, were facts that the missionaries blamed on the alleged inherent defects of the Indians rather than on the defects of the mission system or on their own desire to perpetuate it.

Meanwhile the Indians themselves were becoming increasingly restive. In 1824 during a concerted rebellion they briefly took over control of the missions at Santa Barbara, Santa Inés, and La Purísima Concepción, with some loss of life and much property damage. Soldiers crushed the insurrection after a battle in which there were many Indian casualties. In 1829 an Indian named Estanislao, after the Polish Saint Stanislaus, became the leader of a large band of Miwoks in the San Joaquin Valley. Near the river that was later named after him, "Stanislaus" and his followers fought a battle with 100 soldiers and militiamen under Lt. Mariano Vallejo. This and other campaigns completely failed to subjugate the Miwoks. Until the end of the Mexican period they would continue to block Mexican settlement of the San Joaquin Valley and to raid ranches in the coastal areas to obtain horses.

FROM ECHEANDÍA TO FIGUEROA

The first governor of California under the Mexican republican constitution, or more precisely and officially the first *jefe político superior* and *comandante general militar*, was José María Echeandía, a lieutenant colonel of engineers. He arrived in 1825 with instructions to proceed cautiously and gradually toward ultimate secularization; however, though he drafted various plans for this eventuality, a number of formidable difficulties stood in the way. The missions were still the chief source of supplies for the presidios. Cash revenues for the territorial government depended on duties levied on the goods imported in exchange for Californian cowhides and tallow, and the missions were still the chief producers of the hides and tallow.

To add to the governor's troubles, he was in poor health and spent much time in San Diego to escape the fogs of the north. In 1829 the unpaid soldiers at Monterey revolted under the leadership of an ex-convict who was living in California as a part of his sentence. The revolt was suppressed after a bloodless

"battle" near Santa Barbara, but later in the same year, in deep discourage-
ment, Echeandía submitted his resignation.

Early in 1830 a conservative and proclerical "centralist" faction gained
control of the government in Mexico. Its appointee as governor of California
was a reactionary politician and army officer, Lt. Col. Manuel Victoria, a vigorous opponent of secularization and a stern believer in the virtues of military
authority. Shortly before the centralist coup, the previous Mexican regime had
appointed the radical republican José María Padrés as governor, but before he
could take office his appointment was superseded by Victoria's. Padrés
remained in California in his earlier position of adjutant inspector of troops.
He despised both the personality and the ideas of the man who would now
hold the higher office. Padrés was not only a bitter critic of the missions, but
also a man of considerable ability and personal magnetism, and several young
Californians, including Vallejo and Alvarado, became his disciples. He taught
them, as Bancroft put it, "to theorize eloquently on the rights of man, the
wrongs of the neophytes, and the tyranny of the missionaries."

Shortly before Victoria arrived at Monterey, Padrés induced the outgoing
Governor Echeandía to issue an order for general secularization. When Victoria reached the capital early in 1831, he promptly suspended this decree and
soon afterward proclaimed a number of repressive measures. For opposition
to his policies he banished several prominent men, including Padrés, and
imprisoned several more. The result was an insurrection in southern California, led by José Antonio Carrillo and ex-Governor Echeandía.

When a small force under Governor Victoria met the rebels north of
Cahuenga Pass, near Los Angeles, on December 4, 1831, hostilities might have
been confined to the verbal level if the governor had not made a slurring
remark about the fighting qualities of his own men. One of his aides, Lt.
Romualdo Pacheco, was so goaded by this sarcasm that he drew his saber and
rode out ahead of the governor's troops. On the rebel side, young José María
Ávila was burning with resentment at having been imprisoned in Los Angeles
for sedition. He suddenly charged at Pacheco and killed him with a pistol,
then spurred toward Victoria and wounded him with a lance thrust. A soldier
shot Ávila with a musket, and Victoria, though badly wounded, killed Ávila
with his sword. Forty-three years later a son and namesake of Romualdo
Pacheco, born a month before his father's death, would become one of the
American governors of California.

By provoking actual bloodshed, Governor Victoria had violated the rules
of the California political game. He was packed off to Mexico on the next ship,
and there was a chaotic scramble for power. For about a year the south was
ruled by Echeandía and the north by Agustín Zamorano. (Zamorano is better
known for having imported California's first printing press, used mainly for
the publication of official documents.)

The ouster of Governor Victoria was a deathblow to the mission system.
Although the conservative faction was still precariously in power in Mexico

City, it recognized the need to conciliate the rebellious Californians by permitting secularization of the missions and by appointing a governor who could be trusted to carry it out in the fairest way possible. The man selected was Brevet Brigadier General José Figueroa, governor from early in 1833 until his death in 1835.

FIGUEROA AND SECULARIZATION

In terms of both ability and character, Figueroa was far the best of all the officials sent up by the Mexican republic. The tragedy was that no governor could have arranged the assignments of the mission lands to private ownership in an orderly and satisfactory manner under the conditions that existed.

In August 1833 the Mexican Congress adopted an immediate general secularization law which was extremely vague about procedures for carrying it out. It soon appeared, however, that this law was largely the work of that vocal champion of freedom for the Indians, José María Padrés, and that Padrés had also engineered the Mexican government's approval of an ambitious "colonization" scheme under which he and a group of his Mexican friends were to take over the lands of the missions. His close associate José María Híjar was to be not only the "director of colonization" but also the new governor of the territory.

A substantial number of colonists actually arrived from Mexico to occupy their new estates. Governor Figueroa, however, had already appointed the administrators, or *comisionados*, who were to supervise the disposal of mission lands, and his appointees were all Californians. A notable example was Mariano Guadalupe Vallejo, appointed by Figueroa as not only the administrator of the Solano mission and grantee of the Petaluma rancho, but also the military commander of the whole northern frontier district. When Vallejo, Alvarado, and other former Californian admirers of Padrés heard that among his colonists there were 21 prospective mission administrators from Mexico, and when they recalled that there were just 21 missions, their feelings toward their erstwhile intellectual leader underwent a sharp and sudden change. Fortunately, from their point of view, the credentials of Padrés and Híjar were canceled from Mexico City in another of the kaleidoscopic shifts of Mexican politics.

Figueroa's proclamation of August 9, 1834, defined the general terms under which the process of secularization was to be conducted over the next 2 years. Half the property was supposed to go to the Indians, and the law forbade them to dispose of it, but these provisions were not effectively carried out. Some Indians tried to make a living by farming their small allotments of land near the mission buildings, but none of them retained these lands more than a few years. Many never realized that they were supposed to have been given any land at all. The law attempted to limit the killing of cattle, but as the time of secularization approached, the missionaries slaughtered much of the stock in order to salvage, from the sale of the hides, as much wealth as possible for the Pious Fund. As a result, the missions were surrounded with thousands of skinned carcasses rotting in the sun.

For several years the morale of the padres had been declining. Many of them were old men who had lived so long in the missions that they regarded them as their only homes. Some, on the other hand, looked forward to relief from their responsibilities. Shortly before secularization one padre wrote that there was "hardly anything of the religious left in me. . . . I made the vows of a Friar Minor; instead I must manage temporalities, sow grain, raise sheep, horses, and cows. . . . These things are as disagreeable as thorns . . . , and they rob me of time, tranquility, and health both of soul and body."

Because there were no secular parish priests to replace them, the Franciscans remained at the mission churches to continue their religious duties. For a time many of the neophytes remained huddled around the padres, while some left the coastal area to find homes with alien tribes in the interior. Indians who had been trained as *vaqueros*, or cattle wranglers, became laborers on the private ranchos into which the mission lands were gradually subdivided. Still others were able to gain a living as laborers in the towns.

The padres had predicted accurately the fate that was in store for the mission Indians when secularization came. As Father-President Durán pointed out, the Indians living in the pueblo of Los Angeles were forced to labor for the merest pittances and were subjected to frightful punishments for their trivial misdeeds; they were given no security of any kind and were in every way "far more wretched and oppressed than those in the missions."

ALVARADO AND PROVINCIAL AUTONOMY

Figueroa was deeply disturbed by the failure of his secularization policies to protect the legal and moral rights of the Indians. In any event his efforts were cut short when, in the fall of 1835, he died of an apoplectic stroke. His passing removed a brake from the rapacity of the mission administrators and their friends and relatives, and again plunged California into noisy "revolutionary" struggles for control of the governorship. After the brief terms of José Castro and Nicolas Gutiérrez as acting governors, Mexico sent up a new champion of centralism, Colonel Mariano Chico, who repeated most of the blunders of Governor Victoria and lasted only 3 months before he too was expelled.

Juan Bautista Alvarado, the clever and eloquent young president of the *diputación*, now emerged as the hero of the Californians, particularly the northerners. With the aid of about 30 riflemen led by Isaac Graham, a Tennessee backwoodsman who had come to California to operate a whisky distillery, Alvarado seized control of Monterey and deported most of the Mexican officials. On November 7, 1836, California was proclaimed "a free and sovereign State," until Mexico should repudiate centralism and restore the principles of the federalist constitution of 1824. Alvarado became provisional governor, and

Vallejo, already in charge of the northern frontier, now became the military commander of the whole California department. Vallejo was Alvarado's uncle, though only 2 years his senior and also less than 30 years old.

An act of the Mexican Congress in 1835 had promoted Los Angeles from a pueblo to a city (*ciudad*) and ordered the capital transferred there. This federal law was a result of the efforts of California's congressional delegate, José Antonio Carrillo, a southern Californian and an expert in political intrigue. As one of his first official actions, Alvarado proclaimed that the capital would continue at his native Monterey, but he was forced to placate the southerners by permitting them to choose a subgovernor with considerable regional authority.

Even if Mexico had not had its hands full with the Texan War of Independence, it would probably have been disposed to compromise with Alvarado by appointing him as the legal governor of California under the Mexican republic. He accepted this arrangement in 1837 and continued to hold the office for 5 years.

In the period before the last fragments of the mission holdings passed into private hands at the end of 1845, the administration of these properties grew steadily more corrupt, incompetent, and generally disgraceful. In 1839 Alvarado made a belated and perfunctory effort at reform by appointing a visitor-general of missions, the naturalized Englishman, William E. P. Hartnell; however, Hartnell's efforts were futile, partly because mission administrators, such as Vallejo for San Rafael and Sonoma, and Pío Pico for San Luis Rey, had too much power in their respective districts. When Hartnell tried to make changes in some of Vallejo's plans for San Rafael, Vallejo actually arrested him.

Alvarado and Vallejo soon fell to quarreling with each other, and by 1842 they were both so disillusioned with the anarchic state of affairs in the province that they willingly turned over the political and military commands to the last governor from Mexico, Brigadier General Manuel Micheltorena. He was an amiable man, but his administration was no better than those of most of his predecessors. The army of 300 soldiers he brought with him consisted almost entirely of ex-convicts, and since as usual they failed to receive their pay, they obtained food and other items by a highly informal process of foraging, to the outrage of the local population. Alvarado and José Castro led still another revolt, and there was a new "battle of Cahuenga Pass" in February 1845. It was a repetition of the encounter on almost the same spot in 1830, except that this time the only casualties were a horse and a mule, but it was enough to induce Governor Micheltorena to follow the examples of Governors Victoria, Chico, and Gutiérrez by departing for Mexico, along with his ragged and thieving soldiers.

This marked the failure of the last attempt to reestablish any more than nominal Mexican control over California. Pío Pico assumed the governorship with Los Angeles as the capital, but having no influence much farther north than Santa Barbara he had to compromise with the *norteños* by recognizing José Castro as military commandant. This gave Castro the de facto control of the Monterey customs house and consequently of most of the governmental income. This arrangement, made on the eve of the Mexican War, left the province as weak and divided as it had ever been.

THE HEYDAY OF THE RANCHEROS

Throughout the Mexican period the potential resources of California remained not only undeveloped but largely unsuspected. The most substantial economic activity was cattle raising, and the chief commercial products were hides and tallow for export. The local processing of these commodities went no farther than the staking out of the hides to dry in the sun and rendering of the fat into tallow by melting it in kettles, after which it was poured for storage into bags called *botas*, made out of whole hides.

After the missions disintegrated, there was virtually no manufacturing. Rawhide was used as a local makeshift for all sorts of purposes, but the manufacture of hides into shoes and other leather products was done in New England. Even the simple processes of making soap and candles out of the tallow were done in Chile or Peru. The missions, for their own use, had made such things as coarse woolen blankets, crude shoes, the leather parts of saddles, soap, candles, and coarse pottery. They had also developed irrigated agriculture to the point of producing a remarkable variety of grains, vegetables, and fruits, and some wine and brandy. All these skills disappeared after secularization. The diet of the rancheros and their families consisted largely of fresh or dried beef. Not even milk was widely used, and little or no butter or flour was produced. Even such ordinary articles as brooms had to be imported.

There were about 20 private rancho land grants during the Spanish regime, and about 500 during the Mexican period, of which the great majority were made after secularization and especially by Governors Alvarado, Micheltorena, and Pico. Under the liberal Mexican colonization provisions of 1824 and 1828, the maximum legal limit for a private rancho grant in California was 11 square leagues—about 50,000 acres, or 76 square miles. Not even this generous limit was always applied, because in many cases several different grants were made to the same individuals.

In a ranching country where a dozen acres of grassland might be required to pasture a single cow through the long, dry summer season, such vast grants were not regarded as too large, and minor discrepancies in boundary measurements were of no importance. The boundaries were laid out without the aid of surveying instruments, and the methods of measuring distance ranged between pure guesswork and laying out lengths of a lasso from the back of a horse. As corners of the grant, the *diseño*, or map, might show markers no more permanent than a pile of stones or a clump of cactus. The whole process was accomplished with an easy informality which was very convenient at the time but which would later contribute to the maddening and almost endless confusion of efforts to establish land titles in American courts.

Except for a few grants in the Sacramento Valley, held mainly by naturalized foreigners, the ranchos were located where the missions had been, in a narrow strip along the coast. Cattle were driven on the hoof to the *matanzas*, or slaughterings, as near as possible to the coastal points where the hides and tallow were stored to await the foreign trading ships. Other than the horse and the mule, the only form of land transportation was the lumbering, spring-less, spine-jarring *carreta*, an oxcart with wheels sliced from a big log. Excellent horses, however, were so numerous that they were allowed to run and graze freely, dragging lassos for easy catching. Walking was a lost art. It was much easier to catch a passing horse, ride it where one wished to go, and turn it loose again. To Richard Henry Dana, all Californians in the 1830s seemed to be centaurs, and John Bidwell, in 1846, heard a local proverb to the effect that no Californian with a claim to any trace of Spanish blood would do any work that could not be done on horseback.

On the typical California rancho there were between 20 and several hundred Indian workers, perhaps 4000 in all. This work force included former mission Indians and new recruits gathered by the rancheros. In return for their labor, the Indians usually received nothing more than shelter, food, and clothing. Although the Indian laborers were nominally free, in practice they were bound in a state of peonage for as long as the ranchero cared to hold them. Rancho society was essentially feudal; the rancheros ruled as lords on their great landed estates, while the Indians who tended the fields and herds served as serfs.

The plentitude of cheap Indian labor also contributed to the ranchero's reluctance to work. A recurring phase in conversation was *"poco tiempo,"* or "too little time," meaning that there was not time enough today to do any-thing that could be done tomorrow. In the pursuit of pleasure, however, the Californians showed more vigor. There was prodigal hospitality in the enter-tainment of strangers, and singing and dancing were passions with Califor-nians of all ages. Favorite dances were the *fandango*, the *jota*, the *borrego*, the *jarabe*, the *bamba*, and the somewhat more dignified *contradanza*. The *bamba* required a señorita to perform its lively and intricate steps with a full glass of water on her head. In one of the easier variations, while constantly tapping the floor with her feet, she had to step into a silken hobble, raise it to her knees, lower it again, and give two or three whirls, all without spilling the water and all to the accompaniment of swift strumming of the guitar and many shouted comments intended to distract her.

Apart from weddings, which also occasioned 3-day celebrations, the chief social event was the annual *rodeo*, or roundup. Since there were no fences, the cattle that roamed over the thousand hills of several neighboring ranchos had to be annually segregated, and the calves branded. Then the families of the district would gather for days and nights of fiesta, with much dancing, bril-liant displays of horsemanship, cockfighting, gambling, and sometimes bull and bear baiting.

The absence of education was almost incredible. Only two of the Spanish governors, Borica and Solá, and only one Mexican governor, Figueroa, made any genuine efforts to establish schools, and the results were pitifully short-lived and ineffective. With few exceptions, the missionaries had opposed the

Fandango. A romanticized view of life on a California rancho, painted by Charles Christian Nahl in 1873. *(Courtesy of the Crocker Art Museum, Sacramento.)*

teaching of reading either to Indians or to others because it might increase unruliness and discontent. Now and then, for a few days or weeks, a retired soldier with almost no knowledge, and with no idea whatever of how to impart what little he had, would be given a pittance to try to operate a "school" at Monterey or at one of the other towns. Instruction was administered alternately with a cat-o'-nine-tails and a catechism. Vallejo, one of the few literate Californians, recalled with bitterness how one of these incompetent schoolmasters had nearly succeeded in destroying his boyhood interest in learning. In their adolescent years Vallejo and Alvarado had the good fortune to be protégés of Governor Solá, who taught them from books in his personal library. For about a year William E. P. Hartnell conducted a boy's school near Monterey under the patronage of Governor Figueroa, but it had to be closed soon after Figueroa's death for lack of funds and pupils. These few efforts, except for the teaching of manual arts and church music to the Indians in the missions, represented very nearly the entire history of formal education in California as a Spanish colony and a Mexican province.

California's population in 1845, other than the full-blooded native Indians, was only about 7000. Of these, less than 1000 were adult males. The number of native Californians who were literate, even by the loosest definition, was probably no more than 100. Many of the largest handholders could not write their own names.

Perhaps no period of history has ever been more extremely romanticized than have "the halcyon days of the dons" in California. The colorfulness of those days was sadly superficial, even for the landed ruling class, in spite of their gay costumes and their desperate attempts to live the good life.

SELECTED BIBLIOGRAPHY

Henry L. Oak's third and fourth volumes of "Bancroft's" *History of California* are indispensable for this period. Woodrow James Hansen, *The Search for Authority in California* (1960) offers a valuable analysis of political and social problems from about 1820 to 1849. On secularization, see David J. Weber, "Failure of a Frontier Institution: The Secular Church in the Borderlands under Independent Mexico, 1821–1846," *Western Historical Quarterly*, XII (April 1981), pp. 125–144. Gerald J. Geary, *The Secularization of the California Missions* (1934) is useful and enlightening even though consistently biased. See also C. Alan Hutchinson, "The Mexican Government and the Mission Indians of Upper California, 1821–1835," *The Americas*, XXI (1965), pp. 335–362.

Susanna Bryant Dakin, *A Scotch Paisano: Hugo Reid's Life in California, 1832–1853* (1939) and her volume on *The Lives of William Hartnell* (1949) add notably to the story of secularization and landholding. Other biographical treatments are Sheldon G. Jackson, *A British Ranchero in Old California: The Life and Times of Henry Dalton and the Rancho Azusa* (1977); Madie Brown Emparan, *The Vallejos of California* (1968); George Tays, "Mariano Guadalupe Vallejo and Sonoma—A Biography and a History," *California Historical Society Quarterly*, XVI–XVII (1937–1938), pp. 99–121, 216–255, 348–372, 50–73, 141–167, 219–242; and George L. Harding, *Don Agustín V. Zamorano* (1934). Robert G. Cleland, *The Cattle on a Thousand Hills* (1951) provides a good picture of the ranchos, of which a fairly typical example is described in Cleland's *The Irvine Ranch of Orange County* (1952). This was revised with an epilogue by Robert V. Hine (1962). See also David Hornbeck, "Land Tenure and Rancho Expansion in Alta California, 1784–1846," *Journal of Historical Geography*, IV (October 1978).

C. Alan Hutchinson, *Frontier Settlement in Mexican California: The Híjar-Padrés Colony and Its Origins, 1769–1835* (1969) is sympathetic with the colonization scheme and critical of Figueroa.

AMERICAN INFILTRATION: TRADERS, TRAPPERS, AND SETTLERS

The cosmopolitanism of modern California was notable even in the period of tenuous Mexican rule. Of the foreigners who came, the most important historically were the Americans. Very few of these, however, came with any original intention of Americanizing the province.

THE YANKEE TRADERS

American interest in California began in the late eighteenth century when New England merchants discovered that there was a lucrative market in China for the fur of the sea otter. These animals flourished, in what were thought to be inexhaustible numbers, along the Pacific coast from the Aleutian Islands to lower California, and particularly along the Alta California shores. The skin of a full-grown sea otter was 5 feet long and more than 2 feet wide, with a thick, black, glossy fur, and its value when shipped to the Chinese port of Canton was about $300. The fur seal was more numerous, but less valuable. Although the Spaniards forbade foreigners to obtain furs in California, they could not prevent them from doing so, and ships from New England gained the greatest share of the trade in competition with the British and the Russians.

The first recorded anchorage of an Amercan ship on the coast of California was the result of a bizarre incident in the sea otter trade. In 1796 the ship *Otter*, of Boston, stopped at Monterey on her way to the Hawaiian Islands and China with a cargo of sea otter pelts gathered along the Oregon coast. Her captain, Ebenezer Dorr, asked permission to obtain supplies, which Governor Borica granted. The Yankee captain also asked permission to leave in California several convicts who had escaped from the English penal colony in Australia. Borica refused this request, but Dorr put them ashore at night to get rid of them, even though they had paid him to take them to Boston. Ebenezer

Dorr could hardly have been a meaner man if his name had been Ebenezer Scrooge.

Seven years later another voyage for sea otter brought the *Lelia Byrd*, of Salem, into the bay of San Diego on the pretext of needing fresh food. Captain William Shaler and First Mate Richard Cleveland tried to make a clandestine agreement with the port commander for the acquisition of a stock of otter skins, but Cleveland was thrown into jail by the Spanish authorities and had to be forcibly rescued by his shipmates. The *Lelia Byrd* escaped from the harbor only after an exchange of shots with the little battery on Point Loma. Five years later Captain Shaler told his side of the story in an article published in the *American Register*. He regarded the violation of Spanish colonial trade restrictions as a kind of patriotic duty for enterprising Yankees, and his article not only advertised the possibilities of the California fur trade but also advocated American acquisition of the province. "It would be as easy to keep California in spite of the Spaniards," he wrote, "as it would be to win it from them in the first place."

By the end of the Spanish period both the sea otter and the fur seal had been almost exterminated along the coast of California. New England whalers began to pay increasingly frequent visits to the coast, but the main American trading interest in the region now shifted to cowhides and tallow. In 1821 the Mexican revolutionary regime opened the ports of Monterey and San Diego to foreigners, and the spring of 1822 saw the arrival of the *John Begg*, the first foreign ship to be openly welcomed by California port authorities. Among the passengers on this ship was William E. P. Hartnell, newly appointed resident manager at Monterey for the partnership of Hugh McCulloch and himself, California agents for the British trading firm of John Begg and Company. "Macala and Arnel," in the Hispanicized form of the partners' names, secured a 3-year contract to take all the hides the missions could furnish, at $1 each.

The advantage to the British was short-lived. Within a few weeks of Hartnell's coming, William A. Gale arrived on the *Sachem* from Boston with a cargo of notions. By bidding up the price of hides to $2, which was still a remarkable bargain, he seems to have persuaded some of the padres to evade their contract with the British agency. Gale became the resident agent of the Boston firm of Bryant and Sturgis, which soon had such a large share of the hide and tallow trade that for years the United States was commonly known in California as "Boston." During the Mexican period this one firm was responsible for the export of about half a million hides, or about four-fifths of the total. Hides were called "California banknotes," and were in fact the province's main form of currency.

Import duties were substantial, ranging at various times from about 25 percent to almost twice that figure. Often these duties were at least partially evaded. Customs officials were paid a commission for keeping their eyes open, but there were Yankee captains who were willing to pay them larger sums to keep their eyes closed. Even if duties were fully paid, however, the profits of bringing out a shipload of New England manufactured goods and returning to Boston with a cargo of hides were as high as 300 percent.

The classic description of the hide and tallow trade was written by Richard Henry Dana in *Two Years Before the Mast*. Though it is usually thought of as a portrayal of life at sea and as a tract intended to reform the working conditions of seamen, much of the book was devoted to Dana's observations ashore in California; the crew, in the employ of Bryant and Sturgis, spent most of the 2-year voyage in collecting hides along the California coast.

The Danas of Cambridge were one of the oldest and most distinguished families of New England. As a Harvard undergraduate, Richard Henry had suffered a temporary breakdown of his eyesight, attributed to a case of measles. At the age of 19, in 1834, he signed on as a common sailor for the long voyage to California in the hope that it would improve his health, a purpose which it seems to have accomplished remarkably well almost from the time the ship left Boston harbor.

The outward-bound cargo of "everything under the sun" was quickly disposed of at Monterey, where boatloads of eager purchasers were rowed out to the ship as if she were a floating department store. Dana's pride in his New England heritage was reinforced by what he saw of the Californians, "an idle, thriftless people" who could "make nothing for themselves." The country abounded in grapes, he wrote, "yet they buy, at a great price, bad wine made in Boston and brought round by us, and retail it among themselves at a real (12½ cents) by the small wine glass." Their cowhides, "which they value at two dollars in money, they barter for something which costs seventy-five cents in Boston; and buy shoes (as like as not made from their own hides, which have been carried twice around Cape Horn) at three and four dollars, and 'chicken-skin boots' at fifteen dollars a pair."

Loading the hides was a strenuous operation. Except for San Diego, none of the chief depositories of hides along the coast had an adequate harbor, and the ship had to be anchored as much as 3 miles offshore. A hide would spoil if it got wet, and each one, stiff and heavy and as broad as the arms could reach, had to be tossed up and balanced on the sailor's head so that he could wade through the surf and put it into a swaying small boat.

The hide and tallow trade was significant not only because it influenced the economic history of New England and of early California, but also because it increased the interest of Americans in a distant region with which for many years it formed almost their only contact. *Two Years Before the Mast*, published in 1840, brought Americans the same message that Captain Shaler's journal had carried more than three decades earlier, but Dana's message was more substantial and convincing. "In the hands of an enterprising people," he wrote, "what a country this might be!"

THE BEAVER TRAPPERS

Just as American seagoing commerce with California had begun in the quest for the skin of the sea otter, so the history of overland contact had its beginnings in the search for beaver pelts. The trapper was the spearhead of the

American landward advance, particularly in the far west; the first American overland expedition to California was conducted in 1826 by a young beaver hunter named Jedediah Strong Smith. It was he who deserved the title of "the Pathfinder," a title bestowed in later years upon a more publicized and less authentic hero, John C. Frémont. Smith set out with 17 men to traverse the unexplored desert region between the Great Salt Lake and California. His objectives were the opening of a virgin beaver country and the establishment of a place of deposit on the Pacific for the furs of this new empire. Traveling by way of the Sevier, Virgin, and Colorado rivers and then across the Mojave Desert and the San Bernardino Mountains, Smith and his men reached San Gabriel Mission on November 27, 1826. San Gabriel was then at the height of its temporal prosperity, and from Father José Bernardo Sánchez, the jovial successor of the gloomy Zalvidea, the Americans received a full measure of hospitality which they remained to enjoy for several weeks.

In the words of his biographer, Dale L. Morgan, Jedediah Smith was "an unlikely sort of hero for the brawling West of his time, that West about which it has been said that God took care to stay on his own side of the Missouri River." The "mountain men" have been portrayed in stereotype as murderous brawlers, given to drunken orgies at their periodic rendezvous. Actually, though there were many such men among them, the personalities and backgrounds of the trappers were remarkably diverse. Smith was a quiet young man who never used tobacco or profanity, partook of wine or brandy only sparingly, and was deeply imbued with a Calvinist religious faith. Harrison G. Rogers, the clerk of the expedition, was a staunch Presbyterian who on New Year's day in 1827 delivered a quite erudite "Address to the Rev. Father of San Gabriel Mission" on the early history and missionary activities of the Christian church. Sánchez listened with impeccable politeness to this effort to correct his theology and save his soul; and for thus allowing his guests "full liberty of conscience," as well as for setting a bountiful table and being generous with all sorts of supplies, Rogers recorded the good padre as "the greatest friend I ever met with in all my Travels," and as "worthy of being called a Christian." A few months later Smith gave the entire Sierra Nevada the name of "Mount Joseph" in honor of "old Father Sanchus."

In December, Smith journeyed to San Diego in the hope of securing Governor Echeandía's permission to travel in California, but the governor, lacking a full realization of the unlimited energies of American business enterprise, found it difficult to believe that Smith was not a spy. He was inclined to send Smith and his men to Mexico for trial, but he compromised and ordered them to leave California by the way they had come.

Smith chose to define "California" as being merely the coastal strip of missions and presidios. Thus he felt that he had complied with the governor's orders when he recrossed the San Bernardino Mountains in January 1827; instead of returning to the Colorado, he then moved northwestward across the Tehachapis into the San Joaquin Valley. This he found to be a trapper's paradise, and he had accumulated a large number of pelts by the time he reached the river known thereafter as the American. Late in May, apparently by way of the north fork of the Stanislaus River and Ebbetts Pass, Smith accomplished the first recorded crossing of the Sierra and reached his headquarters in northern Utah on July 3.

Within 10 days he was on his way back to California with 18 men, but his luck was worse than in the previous year. At the Colorado crossing the Mojaves attacked the party and killed 10 of its members. In September the survivors reached the camp of the first expedition in the northern San Joaquin Valley, but when Smith sought assistance at the Mission San José, about 15 miles north of the pueblo of the same name, Father Narciso Durán arrested him, and only released him to go to Monterey for another conference with Echeandía. The governor was even more disposed than before to make Smith stand trial for illegal entry into the province, but uncertainty about the consequences of such strong action led to a renewal of permission for the trappers to depart. Early in 1828 they made the first recorded journey by land up to the northwestern coast of California into Oregon. There the Umpquas killed most of the men. With only two others Smith finally reached the Hudson's Bay Company headquarters at Fort Vancouver. Three years later he was killed by Comanches on the Santa Fé Trail.

While Smith was pioneering the routes between the Great Salt Lake and California, other adventurous American trappers and traders had been making their way from Missouri into New Mexico. The most notable of these was James Ohio Pattie, who pressed on from Santa Fé to California by way of the Gila Valley. Pattie's father, Sylvester, was a product of the Kentucky and Missouri frontiers and had taken his son with him to the southwest. The younger Pattie proved to be a very enterprising but intensely conceited and hot-headed boy. In the fall of 1826 he and a party of other fur hunters trapped along the Gila River to the Colorado. Moving northward, they got into a quarrel and then a bloody battle with the Mojaves. In warfare with the Indians, Pattie and his companions committed atrocities as vicious as those of the "savages" themselves, and it is probable that the reason the Mojaves attacked the 1827 expedition of Jedediah Smith, although they had been peaceful during his previous journey through their country, was that they had had dealings with the Pattie expedition in the meantime.

When Pattie returned to Santa Fé, the governor of New Mexico confiscated all his furs because they had been gathered in Mexican territory without a license. Undaunted, he set out again along the Gila in the fall of 1827, this time in a group under the command of his father. At San Diego Governor Echeandía, already irritated by the unauthorized incursions of Jedediah Smith, put these new intruders in jail, where Sylvester Pattie died.

At this time an epidemic broke out in the northern missions. According to James Ohio Pattie's own account, he had fortunately brought along a supply of "smallpox vaccine," and he was released in order to undertake a vaccination tour, immunizing more than 20,000 persons, mostly Indians, as far north as Fort Ross. In historical fact the epidemic was of measles, not smallpox, and the "vaccination" fantasy was one of the many tall tales that later appeared in *The Personal Narrative of James O. Pattie.* The editor of that remarkable volume, and also, to an unknown extent, the writer of it, was Timothy Flint, an author of many works about the west in which fact and fiction were seldom clearly distinguishable. *The Personal Narrative,* first published in 1831, was the original "western," the prototype of uncounted thousands of writings that have since fed the public appetite for the vicarious enjoyment of adventure and violence.

Other trappers soon improved upon the routes of Smith and Pattie. The expeditions of Ewing Young and William Wolfskill blazed trails from Taos and Santa Fé to Los Angeles. In 1833 Joseph Reddeford Walker, a fur trapper from Tennessee and Missouri, made the first westward crossing through the center of the Sierra Nevada. Walker's expedition from the Rockies to California was a branch of the operations of Captain Benjamin Bonneville, who was on a 2-year furlough from the United States Army. Ostensibly, this leave was granted so that Bonneville could engage in the fur business, but one purpose of it may have been the encouragement of explorations, of potential military value, in Mexican territory. Walker's men discovered what was later the main wagon-train route through central Nevada, along the Humboldt River, which they called more appropriately the Barren. Though their trail over "the dark and deathlike wall" of the Sierra is partly a matter of speculation, it probably lay somewhere between the headwaters of the East Walker River and those of the Tuolumne. They have often been credited with being the first white people to see the Yosemite Valley. Cold, hunger, and exhaustion dulled their appreciation of it that day in the fall of 1833, and indeed some historians have maintained that what they really saw was Hetch Hetchy Valley.

EARLY SETTLERS

The first foreigners to settle permanently in Spanish California did so by accident. In 1814 John Gilroy, a Scotch sailor on an English ship, was left at Monterey because of sickness. He married a daughter of the Ortegas, acquired a part of their lands, and lived to see a flourishing American town, bearing his name, on the site of his rancho. Like so many holders of Mexican titles, however, he would finally lose his property to American land lawyers and squatters.

The first American settler in California, or rather the first one around whose name any substantial body of fact and legend has gathered, was Joseph Chapman, sometimes called "the unwilling pirate." A member of the Bouchard expedition, he was captured at Monterey in 1818 but claimed that Bouchard had shanghaied him in Honolulu. In any case, his skills as a millwright and boatbuilder soon made him a welcome and useful resident.

The next few years saw the arrival of several remarkable Yankees who came as traders and remained to gather a great share of the profits of merchandising into their own hands. William Goodwin Dana and Alfred Robinson at Santa Barbara and Abel Stearns at Los Angeles became the chief merchants of their communities and, partly by marriage, large landowners as well; Thomas O. Larkin became the most important merchant in Monterey.

William G. Dana arrived at Santa Barbara from Boston in 1826. Although he was a relative of the more famous Richard Henry, there was no direct reference to him in *Two Years Before the Mast,* and this has given rise to much interesting speculation. It was said that Richard refused to see William at the time of his visit to Santa Barbara. The reason, apparently, lay in the story of William's eager espousal of the Roman Catholic faith, of Mexican citizenship, and of young Josefa Carrillo of Santa Barbara, with no more regret than that the formalities of naturalization delayed the marriage for 2 years (by which time the bride was 16 years old). It seems probable that Richard, so much more bound to the Calvinist religion, the inherited patriotism, and the racial pride of the family, had his kinsman in mind when he wrote that certain Americans in California had "left their consciences at Cape Horn."

Don Abel Stearns was also the bearer of an old and distinguished Massachusetts family name. He went first to Mexico and had already become naturalized when he arrived in California in 1829, hoping for a land grant. Instead, Governor Victoria suspected him of some political plot and banished him. He returned in 1831 to join in the movement that overthrew Victoria and soon became a leading figure in the politics as well as the economy of Los Angeles. As a prosperous trader in hides and liquors he was as flagrant a smuggler as most of his competitors, yet in 1836 he was appointed *síndico,* or fiscal agent, of the village. Nicknamed *Cara de Caballo,* or Horseface, he was a homely man even before he acquired a scar about the mouth, left by the knife of a disgruntled customer in his store. Nevertheless, his appearance did not prevent his marriage to beautiful Doña Maria Francisca Paula Arcadia Bandini, and with the added influence of his wife's relatives he began to acquire the estates that soon made him the largest landowner and cattleman and the wealthiest citizen of southern California. He had no children, which was most unusual among those who married "native daughters." Don Guillermo and Doña Josefa Dana, for example, had 21.

The title of "don," derived from the Latin *dominus,* or "lord," was applied in Mexican California to almost any man of more or less substantial means, particularly a landowner. In baptism and naturalization a foreign first name was officially changed to its Spanish equivalent. In polite address this might also be done unofficially, as in the case of Don Thomás Larkin, one of the few foreign residents who managed to rise to positions of wealth and importance in California without embracing Roman Catholicism, Mexican nationality, and a native daughter.

Thomas Oliver Larkin, another Massachusetts Yankee, came to Monterey in 1832 at the suggestion of his half-brother, John Cooper, who was already engaged in trade there. One of Larkin's fellow passengers on the long voyage around the Horn was Rachel Hobson Holmes, on her way to join her husband at Hilo. There she discovered that she was a widow, and a few months later Larkin proposed to her by correspondence. A civil marriage ceremony between two non-Catholic foreigners would have been questioned by the Mexican authorities, and consequently the ceremony was performed on board a ship off the Santa Barbara coast. Mrs. Larkin was the first American woman to live in California.

Larkin opened a general store at Monterey, and his business as an intermediary between ranchers and traders was soon flourishing remarkably. Larkin had, as Bancroft put it, "no inconvenient veneration for the revenue laws," and he offered a tempting charge-account system. The chief officials of the province, among others, became heavily indebted to him. He did a thriving business in redwood lumber, largely for export to the Hawaiian Islands and Mexico. And in his designs for his own home, the customs house, and other buildings, he established the "Monterey style" of architecture.

All these early American immigrants had come by sea and taken up residence in the coastal strip. In addition, there were those who came overland and settled mainly in the interior; the term "pioneer" has sometimes been reserved, rather arbitrarily, for these overland settlers. Except for a number of men who came as beaver trappers and decided to stay, the first important settler in this American overload migration was "Dr." John Marsh. Still another son of Massachusetts, Marsh had graduated from Harvard with the class of 1823. Later he "read medicine" under an army surgeon stationed in Minnesota, but the surgeon died before Marsh had completed the program of study. Marsh then sold guns to the Sioux in violation of federal law, and in flight from a warrant for his arrest on this charge he emigrated to Los Angeles in 1836. He was destitute, and to earn money he secured permission to practice medicine. For credentials he offered his Harvard bachelor of arts diploma, correctly suspecting that he was the only person in the town who could read the Latin in which the diploma was printed. Because his fees were paid almost entirely in cowhides, his little adobe soon resembled a warehouse rather than a medical office. After a few months, in order to purchase a ranch, he sold his stock of hides for $500 and accepted Roman Catholicism and naturalization.

Marsh was now a morose and greedy man, determined to acquire wealth in compensation for his many disappointments. In 1837 he bought a huge tract near the Sacramento–San Joaquin delta at the foot of Mount Diablo. Marsh made it the first successful rancho in the great Central Valley. This he accomplished largely by taking payment in cattle for his medical services throughout the northern California settlements. He customarily exacted a fee of 50 head.

Two years after Marsh settled in the region of the San Joaquin delta, John Sutter arrived with his ambitious designs for the Sacramento Valley. Sutter, originally Johann August Suter, was a German Swiss, and in the history of the American movement overland into California he and his New Helvetia were to play a significant role.

Sutter, like Marsh, was a fugitive from tragedy and from justice. In Switzerland he had been married only 1 day before the birth of his first son, and the marriage was unhappy even though it finally produced five children. Sutter always lived extravagantly, and in 1834, faced with debtor's prison after the failure of his dry goods business, he deserted his family and absconded to America. After interludes in St. Louis and Santa Fé, he went with a trapping expedition to Oregon, and then by ship to Honolulu, Sitka, Yerba Buena, and Monterey, where he arrived in July 1839. In the meantime his powers of romantic imagination had made him "Captain" Sutter, formerly of "the Royal Swiss Guard of France." In Oregon he had heard of the Sacramento Valley,

Sutter's Fort. *(Courtesy of the Bancroft Library.)*

and there he now sought the wide-open spaces where people could plan things as they would like them to be.

The quarrel between Governor Alvarado and Comandante Vallejo was at its height, and Alvarado thought he saw a chance to use Sutter, and his grandiose colonization scheme, as a check upon Vallejo's power and pretensions. With the governor's blessing, Sutter selected a tract on the Sacramento River at its junction with the American. After 1 year, the minimum period of legal residence, the glamorous newcomer received not only Mexican citizenship and a grant of 11 square leagues but also the status of a regional official. He was authorized "to represent in the Establishment of New Helvetia all the laws of the country, to function as political authority and dispenser of justice, in order to prevent the robberies committed by adventurers from the United States, to stop the invasion of savage Indians and the hunting and trapping by companies from the Columbia."

Beginning with beaver pelts and wild-grape brandy, Sutter went on to establish a cattle ranch and farm, using the labor of Indians and vagabond foreigners and succeeding remarkably, for a time, in obtaining credit. In 1841, for example, when the Russian-American Fur Company abandoned Fort Ross, Sutter's note for $30,000 secured the purchase of its implements and livestock with only $2000 paid down. Several cannon from Ross strengthened the defenses of Sutter's own fort. That establishment would soon be a focal point for early American overland migration.

COVERED WAGONS, 1841 TO 1846

The first organized group to cross the Rockies for the purpose of settlement in California was the Bidwell-Bartleson party of 1841. The previous year, John Marsh had written a letter to some friends in the neighborhood of Independence, Missouri, praising the lands and climate of California and minimizing the difficulty of getting there. Lured by this and other rosy testimonials, more than 500 persons organized a Western Emigration Society and pledged to assemble near Independence in the following spring. During the winter, however, Missouri newspapers and merchants, interested in preventing an exodus of their readers and customers, circulated stories that painted a sharply different picture. One of these concerned the harsh treatment accorded some Americans at Monterey during the "Graham affair" in 1840.

Governor Alvarado had come to regret his shortsighted use of the help of Isaac Graham and his band of American riflemen in the little revolution of 1836. They complained that the governor was not sufficiently grateful to them. "I was insulted at every turn," Alvarado told Alfred Robinson, "by the drunken followers of Graham." It would be appropriate to call Isaac Graham a barefaced scoundrel, despite his unkempt beard, and the American ex-trappers and ex-sailors who hung around his distillery, though some of them made an honest living by cutting redwood for Larkin's lumber business, were no great credit to the country of their origin. Their alcoholic boasting led to rumors that they were plotting a Texan-style revolution. As a result, in April 1840 Graham and 38 other foreigners, mostly Americans, were arrested, packed into Monterey's one-celled jail, and then sent to Mexico. Later they were set free.

In Missouri, however, the news of the episode so discouraged the members of the Western Emigration Society that only one of the original signers appeared at the appointed place in May 1841. This was John Bidwell, a young former schoolteacher. In addition to Bidwell, 68 new prospects appeared. John Bartleson was elected captain, solely because he insisted that otherwise he would not go. As Bidwell later put it, very generously, Bartleson "was not the best man for the position," but "he had seven or eight men with him, and we did not want the party diminished."

No one in the group had ever been west, and their only maps were ridiculously inaccurate. By good luck they fell in with a party of missionaries and trappers bound for Oregon and guided by Thomas ("Broken Hand") Fitzpatrick, one of the best of the mountain men. When the time came to leave the Oregon Trail and strike out across the Great Basin for California, about half the emigrants prudently decided to go to Oregon with Fitzpatrick, and several others turned back toward Missouri. The rest managed to find the Humboldt River, but had to abandon their wagons. Near the Humboldt Sink, Bartleson and eight other men took the best horses, deserted the party, and rushed on ahead. They failed to find a pass and returned shamefacedly, begging a share of the little food that remained. Bidwell quietly readmitted them to the group. It did not need to be said that he and not Bartleson was now the captain. At the end of October, miraculously, they found their way over the Sierra and down to the Stanislaus, and on November 4, 1841, they arrived at Marsh's ranch.

The miserly Marsh demanded high prices for supplies. By contrast, when Bidwell visited Sutter's Fort a few weeks later, he was cordially welcomed, as nearly all newcomers were. Sutter was the emigrant's benefactor and friend.

New Helvetia was to be the headquarters for several rescue parties sent to help stranded travelers over the Sierra. On the other hand, legend has somewhat exaggerated Sutter's generosity. He saw the early American migrants as potential assets to his colonial establishment—as workers for his increasingly varied enterprises and as ultimate buyers of some of the vast lands he had received for the asking.

In the fall of 1841 an emigrant party including William Workman, John Rowland, and Benjamin D. Wilson traveled from Santa Fé to Los Angeles. In 1843 Lansford W. Hastings, a frontier lawyer with filibustering ambitions, led a group into California from Oregon. Several of its members, including Hastings, had the perverted desire to shoot down an Indian, and the unprovoked murders they committed in the upper Sacramento Valley stored up trouble for them and for future pioneers. The Stevens party, coming from Missouri in 1844, was the first to succeed in getting wagons over the Sierra, and also the first to make use of what would later be the main route, the Donner Pass, though that name was not acquired until the tragedy that was to follow 2 years later.

The year 1845 saw the beginning of a somewhat more substantial annual migration. Reports from Thomas O. Larkin, John Marsh, and John C. Frémont were stirring up interest in California. Lansford W. Hastings, through speech-making and the publication of his dangerously misleading *Emigrant's Guide*, was pursuing his dream of leading hordes of Americans to the western paradise, and hoping that their gratitude would make him a new Sam Houston, president of a Pacific republic or governor of a new American state. The largest emigrant party of 1845, the Grigsby-Ide group, had more than 100 members, and the total for the year was more than 250 persons.

More than twice as many came in 1846. In a sense they were in a new category, for although their plans were made before the outbreak of war between the United States and Mexico, California was under the American flag when they reached it.

The worse-than-worthless advice of Lansford W. Hastings was a cause of dangerous delays for many of them, and it led the Donner party into the worst disaster in the history of the California Trail. The Donner party was organized at Springfield, Illinois. It passed through Independence on time, in May, but instead of taking the established route by way of Fort Hall, north of the Great Salt Lake, it followed "Hastings' Cutoff" to the south of it. Winter set in early. On November 2 the main party decided to rest overnight only a few miles short of the Sierra summit. That night a snowstorm blocked the pass. Most of the party was snowed in near Donner Lake until February, and many survived only by eating the flesh of the dead. Of 87 persons in the original group, 40 perished. There was heroism as well as horror. When a rescue party arrived from Sutter's Fort, Tamsen Donner refused to leave her husband, George, who was too weak to travel. Their three daughters were saved, but George and Tamsen died.

Alfred Robinson had written to Larkin urging all possible efforts to publicize California, so that "the American population will be sufficiently large to play the Texas game." But California before the gold rush was less attractive to America settlers than either Texas or Oregon; the emigrants to California were primarily interested in trying to advance their own fortunes rather than their country's, and many were so discouraged that they drifted north to Oregon or back to "the States." Nevertheless, overland emigration would undoubtedly have made a change to American sovereignty inevitable in a few years. It had not yet accomplished this by 1846, but other, related historical forces had been in motion.

SELECTED BIBLIOGRAPHY

Adele Ogden's *The California Sea Otter Trade* (1937) is the best treatment of its subject. Significant memoirs are William Shaler, "Journal of a Voyage from China to the Northwestern Coast of America Made in 1804," *American Register . . . for 1808*, pp. 136–175, edited and with an introduction by Lindley Bynum (1935), and Richard Cleveland, *Narrative of Voyages and Commercial Enterprises* (1842). See also Magdalen Coughlin, "Boston Smugglers on the Coast (1797–1821): An Insight into the American Acquisition of California," *California Historical Society Quarterly*, XLVI (June 1967), pp. 99–120. The hide and tallow trade is best described in Richard Henry Dana, *Two Years Before the Mast* (1840, with many reprintings); Alfred Robinson, *Life in California* (1846); and Doyce B. Nunis, Jr. (ed.), *The California Diary of Faxon Dean Atherton, 1836–1839* (1964).

Robert G. Cleland, *This Reckless Breed of Men: The Trappers and Fur Traders of the Southwest* (1952) is readable and reliable. Dale L. Morgan, *Jedediah Smith and the Opening of the West* (1953) is a brilliant biography; the journal of Harrison Rogers is in Harrison C. Dale (ed.), *The Ashley Smith Explorations and the Discovery of a Central Route to the Pacific, 1822–1829* (1941). The Walker expedition was recorded in *The Adventures of Zenas Leonard*, edited by John C. Ewers (1959), and in *The Life and Adventures of George Nidever*, edited by William H. Ellison (1937). LeRoy R. Hafen (ed.), *The Mountain Men and the Fur Trade of the Far West* (10 volumes, 1971) provides 300 biographical sketches.

On American and other immigrants to California before 1849, both by sea and by land, an indispensable source is the "Pioneer Register," an alphabetical biographical dictionary appended to volumes II–V of the Bancroft *History of California*. The Larkin Papers, edited by George P. Hammond (10 volumes, 1951–1964), also has references to a remarkable number of persons. *John Marsh, Pioneer* (1930) and his biographer, George D. Lyman, were both medical men with far-ranging interests. James P. Zollinger, *Sutter, the Man and His Empire* (1939) and Richard Dillon, *Fool's Gold: The Decline and Fall of Captain John Sutter of California* (1967) are good biographies. *Sutter's Own Story*, edited by Erwin G. Gudde (1936), is his story as he told it orally to Bancroft.

Good accounts of the overland migration are in John D. Unruh, Jr., *The Plains Across: The Overland Emigrants and the Trans-Mississippi West, 1848–60* (1979); George R. Stewart, *The California Trail* (1962); and Irving Stone, *Men To Match My Mountains: The Opening of the Far West, 1840–1900* (1956). Rockwell D. Hunt, *John Bidwell, Prince of California Pioneers* (1942) is a useful biography. There were many memoirs, including Bidwell's *A Journey to California in 1841* (1842) and *Josiah Belden, 1841 California Pioneer*, edited by Doyce B. Nunis, Jr. (1962). On the Donner tragedy, see George R. Stewart, *Ordeal by Hunger* (1936). A well-balanced view of this period may be found in John A. Hawgood, "The Pattern of Yankee Infiltration in Mexican Alta California, 1821–1846," *Pacific Historical Review*, XXVII (February 1958), pp. 27–38.

THE AMERICAN CONQUEST

OVERTURES, DIPLOMATIC AND UNDIPLOMATIC

Official American efforts to acquire California had an inauspicious beginning in 1835, as an extension of President Andrew Jackson's plans for the purchase of Texas. These schemes originated largely in the fertile brain of Colonel Anthony Butler, an American speculator in Texas lands and an old friend of Jackson's, to whom the President had unwisely entrusted the ministry to Mexico. Butler disgraced himself and his government by letting it be known in Mexico City that he expected to purchase the republic's northern territories by buying some of its political leaders. When Butler later tried to implicate Jackson in his schemes for bribery, Old Hickory denounced him as a liar.

President Jackson was interested in California mainly because the acquisition of San Francisco Bay, as a port for American commerce and whaling in the Pacific, might reconcile the north to the annexation of Texas as a slave state. Early in 1837 General Santa Anna came to Washington, after his release by Sam Houston, to request American mediation between Texas and Mexico. Jackson then unsuccessfully offered $3.5 million for Mexican recognition of a southwestern boundary of the United States extending along the Rio Grande and thence westward to the Pacific along the 38th parallel. He was unaware that this line would have left the entrance to San Francisco Bay about 12 miles south of the border. He was equally unsuccessful in urging the Texans to bring California within their own boundaries, though Sam Houston dreamed of doing so.

Martin Van Buren of New York, Jackson's chosen successor in the presidency, privately deplored some of the more headlong tendencies of his illustrious old chief. He opposed the annexation of Texas and any territorial expansion of slavery. Moreover, the panic of 1837 began a few weeks after his inauguration, and his single term as President was one long period of depression in which the Treasury was in no condition to provide for purchasing new territory.

With economic recovery in the 1840s, the United States began to assert its manifest destiny to extend its borders to the Pacific. Early in the Tyler administration, Daniel Webster as Secretary of State and Waddy Thompson as minister to Mexico advocated a plan to secure California in exchange for cancellation of American financial claims against the Mexican government. But again, as in the Anthony Butler episode, an American blunder raised an outcry in Mexico City that made any peaceful cession of territory to the United States politically impossible. Early in September 1842, Commodore Thomas ap Catesby Jones, commander of the American Pacific squadron, received a false report at Callao, Peru, that the United States and Mexico were at war and that Mexico intended to cede California to Great Britain rather than see it fall into American hands. Admiral Thomas and his British Pacific squadron had just left Callao, reportedly under sealed orders from England. Jones, who had received instructions in Washington a year earlier to act quickly in just such an eventuality, promptly sailed for California in what he supposed to be a race with Thomas. He anchored at Monterey on October 18 and on the next day demanded the peaceful surrender of the port and the district. This was concluded on the 20th, the American flag was raised, and Jones proclaimed California under armed but courteous and benevolent American occupation. This proclamation remained in force only 1 day. On the 21st, when Jones landed in person and examined the latest official communications from Mexico, he realized that he had been completely and regrettably misinformed.

Commodore Jones sent a letter of explanation to Governor Micheltorena who was then in southern California. On receiving the news of the seizure, Micheltorena issued, for the record, a bombastic call to arms to repel the invader. With obvious relief, but well aware that the government in Mexico City would take a much more irritated view of the matter than did anyone in California, Micheltorena advised Jones to come to him at Los Angeles. There he received the commodore and his explanations with courtesy and hospitality, but sent reports to Mexico City in an entirely different tone. The Mexican government conveyed an angry protest to Washington demanding extreme punishment for Jones, but although the United States disavowed his actions, he suffered only a temporary removal from his command.

As the Jones incident clearly shows, American suspicions of the designs of Great Britain on California played a large part in American thinking, and incidentally provided a very useful rationalization of American designs. The fact was that Her Majesty's government had no intention whatever of trying to acquire California. Sir Robert Peel, prime minister from 1841 to 1846, was well aware that such an attempt would have involved a costly and hazardous war with the United States. It was not until the early twentieth century, when the British Foreign Office records were opened to historians, that the actual attitudes of the British government became known. In the years before the Mexican War, there were outward appearances of a designing nature, quite sufficient to provide fuel for American fears.

In 1839, for example, a London publisher brought out the first book in

English entirely devoted to California. This was Alexander Forbes's *History of Upper and Lower California* which advocated a plan for the British colonization of vast tracts of land in California. In 1841 Sir George Simpson of the Hudson's Bay Company visited California and concluded quite correctly that some native Californians were so afraid of American control that they would welcome a British protectorate. Sir George's enthusiasm for such a development was obvious, and Americans had no way of knowing that the British government did not support his views.

The French, also, had some degree of interest in California dating all the way back to the visit of the comte de La Pérouse. In 1842 the French agent Eugène Duflot de Mofras reported that California was certain to pass to some power other than Mexico, and soon. French hopes were faint, based on little more than the idea that Mexico might prefer to see California in the friendly hands of a Latin and Catholic nation, rather than under Anglo-Saxon Protestants. The weakness of Mexican control of California had been so apparent to any observer for so long that a spate of foreign designs was inevitable.

PLANS OF THE POLK ADMINISTRATION

James K. Polk of Tennessee was a political disciple of Andrew Jackson, who lived to congratulate him on his inauguration as President in March 1845. Polk, like his mentor, was always ready to believe any rumors of fell designs on the part of the British. Polk also shared some of the anti-British views of Senator Thomas Hart Benton of Missouri, powerful chairman of the Senate military affairs committee. Benton firmly though incorrectly believed that perfidious Albion had intended to acquire California ever since Drake claimed and named New Albion in 1579 and that she was now determined to have San Francisco Bay in order to strengthen her naval power in the Pacific.

On coming into office, President Polk confided to Secretary of the Navy George Bancroft that the acquisition of California would be one of his most cherished goals. Within the month of Polk's inauguration, Governor Micheltorena and his *cholo* troops were virtually deported from California, and this ended the last desperate effort to assert any effective control over the province from Mexico City. When the news of this development reached the east coast in June 1845, several American newspapers pointed out the ridiculous ease with which it had been accomplished, the apparent absence of any strong government at all in California, and the danger that Great Britain would take advantage of the situation. Before 1845, American newspaper references to California had been few. Now a chorus of editorials began to call for American acquisition.

During this same period, Polk received reports from Mexico City of the startling proposal of a young Irish priest named Eugene McNamara to bring 2000 families, 10,000 colonists altogether, to a grant of 3000 square leagues in California. McNamara gained the approval of the archbishop of Mexico, and addressed a burning appeal to the Mexican president in which he warned that "before another year the Californias will form a part of the American Nation. Their Catholic institutions will become the prey of the Methodist wolves; and the whole country will be inundated with these cruel invaders." The McNamara scheme was wildly impracticable, but many Americans regarded it with true alarm as being somehow simultaneously a British and a popish plot.

Having determined to acquire California, Polk would have preferred to purchase it. Duff Green, editor of the *United States Telegraph* in Washington, had reported a few months earlier that all the Mexican factions were so eager to ruin their opponents and confiscate their property that the slightest appearance of willingness to sell a foot of territory to the United States would cause any administration to be disgraced and overthrown as treasonable. Although this analysis would soon prove all too accurate, Polk nevertheless sent John Slidell on a special mission to Mexico with an offer of as much as $40 million for Upper California and New Mexico.

"Money," said Slidell's instructions, "would be no object when compared with the value of this acquisition." This was Polk's own view, but he was well aware that the prospects of success were dim, and therefore he put an alternative plan into operation simultaneously. This involved secret instructions to Thomas O. Larkin, consul at Monterey since the previous year, to try to persuade the Californians to secede from Mexico and seek American protection.

Larkin had been highly successful in his business pursuits in California, but he had not become a *californio*. He also took great pride in the fact that his were the first children born in California of parents who had both been born in the United States. He had been reporting to Washington every suspicion and rumor of sinister British intentions toward California, and in some instances he seems to have exaggerated his reports beyond what he himself believed, so great was his yearning for American annexation at this time. His letter of July 10, 1845, made a particularly strong impression on President Polk. In it he maintained that the recent appointment of a British vice consul for Upper California was extremely suspicious, and undoubtedly a cover for an appointment as a secret agent. On October 17, 1845, a secret dispatch signed by James Buchanan, the secretary of state, appointed Larkin "confidential agent in California." He was instructed to warn the Californians against any attempt to bring them under the jurisdiction of "Foreign Governments." Further, he was to "arouse in their bosoms that love of liberty and independence so natural to the American Continent." Should California assert and maintain her independence, Buchanan wrote to Larkin, "we shall render her all the kind offices in our power as a Sister Republic."

The plan had real possibilities. Larkin was on friendly terms with officials at Monterey, whom he had supplied for years with most of their provisions and merchandise. The government had reached a state of truly insufferable confusion, and almost everyone admitted the need for some decisive change. Since the departure of Micheltorena, the capital and the assembly had been at Los Angeles under Don Pío Pico as governor, while the customs and the treasury remained at Monterey, with Col. José Castro as military commander. Mariano Guadalupe Vallejo was frankly reconciled to American annexation because he considered it both inevitable and preferable to the alternatives. Colonel Castro, though he bristled at any suggestion of American military force, was confidentially circulating a plan for "declaring California independent in 1847–1848, as soon as a sufficient number of foreigners should arrive." Larkin also enlisted the cooperation of Jacob P. Leese of Sonoma, Don Abel Stearns of Los Angeles, and J. J. Warner from near San Diego, and all three became not only active in the scheme but also convinced that it would work.

The promising Polk-Larkin plan for winning the province by peaceful conciliation of the *paisanos* was impeded by resentment of the blustering actions of Capt. John C. Frémont in California in March 1846. A few weeks later the scheme was entirely nullified by the Bear Flag Revolt—in which Frémont also had a part—and by the outbreak of the Mexican War.

JOHN CHARLES FRÉMONT

Frémont was one of the most controversial figures not only in the history of California but in the history of the United States. His mother, the young wife of a wealthy and elderly citizen of Richmond, had run away with a young French émigré. In Virginia a divorce could only be obtained from the state legislature, which refused to pass the necessary act. Frémont's parents lived together as husband and wife until the death of the father, which occurred when John Charles was 5 years old. The circumstances of his birth seem to have given him, as in the analogous case of Alexander Hamilton, a feeling of extraordinary need to establish his place in the world. He was like the young Hamilton, too, in that his promising qualities attracted the sympathy of influential men who helped him to gain an education. But there was also a side of Frémont's personality that made him impulsive, unstable, and erratic throughout his life. He was ever the impatient opportunist and adventurer, and there was hardly a single action of his whole career that did not produce some troublesome set of complications, and interminable disagreement among biographers and historians about his motives and conduct.

As a lieutenant in the Corps of Topographical Engineers, Frémont met Senator Thomas Hart Benton, who inspired the younger man with his own fiery enthusiasm for the vast possibilities of westward exploration and expansion and with his dream of extending American territory to the Pacific. At Benton's home Frémont met the Senator's daughter Jessie, an extraordinary girl of 16 whose great intellectual gifts had been developed by her father's intensive and devoted tutoring. Frémont and Jessie were secretly married a few months later, and after stormy protests Benton was reconciled to the marriage. Frémont gained a brilliant and beautiful wife and a brilliant and influential father-in-law, and both became his invaluable though highly possessive allies.

John Charles Frémont. *(Courtesy of the Bancroft Library.)*

Frémont then led a series of western exploring and scientific expeditions, authorized by Congress at the prompting of Senator Benton. The first of these followed the Oregon Trail as far as South Pass in the Rockies. The final report of this expedition—combining Frémont's own genius for publicity with his wife's sparkling literary style, and also borrowing something of the flavor of Washington Irving's *Adventures of Captain Bonneville*—was widely circulated and established Frémont as a national hero.

His second expedition, in 1843 and 1844, proceeded to Oregon, then south along the eastern side of the Cascades and the Sierra Nevada, and across the Sierra into California by way of Carson Pass in the dead of winter. After a month's rest at Sutter's Fort, Frémont and his men traveled southward through the San Joaquin Valley and over Tehachapi Pass, then eastward by way of the Old Spanish Trail and Utah. The expedition's return was hailed with rejoicing since it had been gone so long that it was presumed lost.

There was a temporary flurry over Frémont's setting out with a howitzer, which the War Department had specifically ordered him not to take on the grounds that the expedition was supposed to be scientific and not military. It had to be explained that Jessie Frémont had intercepted this dispatch and had taken it upon herself to suppress it, but her father defended this action successfully in the Senate.

With the second expedition already well publicized, the Frémonts' collaborative prose soon described it in even more fascinating terms than the first. Understandably the report was another best-seller and became the most widely read description of the far west.

In Washington, D.C., in the spring of 1845, Frémont became convinced that war with Mexico was imminent, that his third expedition should be prepared for military rather than merely scientific activities, and that with it he should play an important role in conquering California. In this idea he received some private encouragement from Senator Benton and from Secretary of the Navy Bancroft. The senator, however, had no executive authority, nor was the secretary of the Navy Frémont's official superior.

There is no evidence that Frémont received authorization for military operations in Mexican territory either from President Polk or from the War Department. Nevertheless he recruited 60 armed men, all expert marksmen, and arrived in California in December 1845. Early in 1846 he appeared at Monterey. He had come, he said, merely to survey a route to the Pacific, and his men were not soldiers. Colonel Castro, however, peremptorily ordered Frémont and his armed force out of California. In angry and headstrong defiance, Frémont entrenched his men on Hawk's Peak (now Frémont Peak) in the Gabilán Mountains overlooking the Salinas Valley and raised the American flag. Castro called for volunteers and raised a force of about 200. Larkin mediated, and Frémont, after 3 days on his mountaintop, retreated to the Sacramento Valley. Obviously playing for time, he moved slowly northward—"slowly and growlingly," as he put it in a letter to his wife.

On May 9, 1846, he was overtaken near Klamath Lake in southern Oregon by Lieutenant Archibald H. Gillespie of the Marine Corps, who had come to California disguised as a merchant traveling for his health, under instructions from Polk and Buchanan to cooperate as a secret agent with Larkin in the plan of peaceful persuasion. Gillespie, like Frémont, was a rash and high-spirited young man. Arriving in California in April, he had heard reports that war with Mexico was imminent, and these reports he brought to Frémont along with a packet of letters from Senator Benton. The two young officers seem to have convinced each other that the plan for peaceful conciliation was now out of date, that British intervention was to be feared, that bold initiative was called for, and that Frémont's force should return to California prepared for military action.

Whether Gillespie brought Frémont any secret official authorization to proceed in this way has been hotly debated. There is no reliable documentary evidence for this claim. Frémont probably acted, as he had already acted several weeks earlier at Hawk's Peak, on his own imagination of what the interests of the United States required him to do under particular circumstances, and on his own guess at what orders he might have received from the War Department if it had been able to communicate with him at the time. Thus his own ambitions and impulses had free rein.

One event that illustrates Frémont's character occurred on the night after his talks with Gillespie; in his excitement Frémont forgot to post sentries, and more surprisingly, his guide, Kit Carson, failed to notice this oversight. A band of Klamath Indians attacked the camp and killed three men. Before the return to California there was a brief delay while Frémont and his party wiped out the adult male inhabitants of the nearest Indian village and destroyed its accumulated food supply. In encounters between whites and Indians, there were those on both sides who followed the dismal practice of taking revenge upon the innocent when the guilty were not readily available.

THE BEAR FLAG REVOLT

In the meantime, a crop of frightening rumors had circulated among the American immigrants recently settled in the Sacramento and Napa valleys. Frémont and his men had spread some of these rumors on their way northward. In particular, it was falsely reported that Colonel Castro would soon follow up his expulsion of Frémont with an expulsion of all the American settlers.

The origins of the Bear Flag Revolt were confused, and the evidence, especially on Frémont's part in it, is often contradictory. The American settlers in the area were a miscellaneous group of people in a very insecure situation. Nearly all of them were rough pioneers. Some were roving hunters and trappers, or runaway sailors. Most were squatters who probably believed the rumors that they would soon be attacked and driven out of California. Emboldened by the return of Frémont, on June 10 a group under the rough-and-ready Ezekiel Merritt began the revolt by seizing a herd of horses intended for Castro's militia. Some further and more formal action was needed, lest the rebels remain merely horse thieves. Thus on the morning of Sunday, June 14, a party of more than 30 armed settlers descended upon the village of Sonoma.

There were no longer any soldiers at this former military post, and Colonel Vallejo was no longer on active duty, but the filibusters surrounded his home and informed him that he was a prisoner of war. He invited the leaders in to explain what war he was a prisoner of, and when this proved a difficult question, he brought out bottles of *aguardiente* to aid in the discussion. Ezekiel Merritt, William Knight, and Robert Semple had entered first. The rest waited outside for several hours, then elected John Grigsby to go in and investigate. After another interval, they sent in William B. Ide, who, according to his own account, found the previous commissioners befuddled by Vallejo's brandy. Ide, a teetotaler, finally arranged the terms of capitulation, with Jacob P. Leese, Vallejo's brother-in-law, acting as translator.

Colonel Vallejo was probably the most widely respected citizen of California. He had no objection to being arrested because as an advocate of American annexation he was thus relieved of his embarrassing trust as a Mexican officer. The sensible course would now have been to parole him, and he was given some assurance that this would be done, but instead he was taken under arrest to Sutter's Fort. Frémont, who now placed the fort virtually under his own command, committed the foolish outrage of ordering Vallejo into a cell, where he was imprisoned for 2 months. Frémont, feeling that Castro had humiliated him, now acted as if it were Castro and not Vallejo who was his prisoner. He sternly reprimanded Sutter for trying to make Vallejo's bare cell more comfortable.

At Sonoma, Ide and his associates declared themselves a republic and devised a flag. It was a piece of white cotton cloth, with a star and a stripe. In the upper left-hand corner a large lone star, obviously suggesting an analogy with the history of Texas, was painted in red. To the right of the star, and facing it, was what was intended as a grizzly bear, passant. Under these emblems, "CALIFORNIA REPUBLIC" was lettered in black ink. A broad stripe of red flannel, made from an article of used clothing variously recalled as either a petticoat or a man's shirt, was sewn along the bottom of the cotton. This was the original of the banner which the California Legislature adopted in 1911 as the state flag and which since then must be flown over all state buildings.

Ide wrote a flowery and somewhat eccentric proclamation, solemnly though not deliberately misrepresenting most of the circumstances. He remained under the impression that he had "conquered California." In later years Ide and Frémont made rival claims, both considerably exaggerated, for credit in the matter of the Bear Flag Revolt. Frémont's connection with the beginning of it was highly equivocal and opportunistic. He helped to foment the rebellion by encouraging the American settlers to goad the *californios* into attacking them so that he and his men could come to their defense.

Castro sent about 50 men northward across the bay, under Joaquín de la Torre, to try to retake Sonoma. On June 24, there was a skirmish north of San Rafael, later magnified into the "battle of Olompali." In the entire "Bear Flag war," two Americans and five or six *californios* were killed. Torre's men soon evacuated the area north of the bay.

Frémont, having now assumed command of the Bear Flaggers and having informally merged his force with theirs, crossed from the Marin peninsula on July 1. Entering the long-ungarrisoned little ruin of the San Francisco presidio, he spiked its 10 old Spanish guns. This was a typically Frémontian act—dashing in appearance but superfluous in reality. Those venerable cannon had been cast in Lima about 1625. They had never been fired in anger, and for at least 40 years they had been incapable of firing so much as a salute.

In a more notable and enduring achievement, also described in his *Memoirs*, Frémont gave the entrance to the bay "the name of Chrysopylae, or Golden Gate, for the same reasons that the harbor of Constantinople was called Chryoceros, or Golden Horn."

Frémont joined a Fourth of July celebration at Sonoma, and the next day he more or less formally organized the "California battalion" of American volunteers, with himself in command and Lieutenant Gillespie as adjutant. On the 7th, however, Commodore Sloat raised the American flag at Monterey. It was raised at Yerba Buena and Sonoma on the 9th, and replaced the Bear Flag at Sutter's Fort on the 11th. The life of the Bear Flag "republic," a rather romantic and later fantastically romanticized period of a little less than a month, was thus ended. The revolt would probably have made a war between the United States and Mexico inevitable if that war had not already broken out on the disputed southern border of Texas.

By instigating the filibustering activities known as the Bear Flag Revolt, and by participating in them, Frémont actually accomplished only two things.

One was an unnecessary embitterment of feelings between Americans and *californios,* in violation of the United States government's policy and best interests. The other was an enhancement of his own somewhat spurious popular reputation as a patriot and hero.

THE MEXICAN WAR AND CALIFORNIA

The causes of the Mexican War were complex and are still disputed. Only a brief sketch of its general background is necessary here. In the 10 years since the establishment of the Republic of Texas in 1836, Mexico had never recognized it as independent. In February 1845 the American Congress passed a joint resolution inviting Texas to join the American Union, and President Tyler signed the resolution on March 1, 3 days before the inauguration of Polk. Mexico regarded the prospective American annexation of Texas as a hostile act and broke off diplomatic relations with the United States, threatening war but not declaring it. President Herrera prudently feared that a war would not only fail to regain Texas but also lose California and New Mexico. He hinted that he would receive an American minister. After Slidell had reached Mexico City, Herrera changed changed his mind, but the report that he had even considered receiving an American negotiator led to his overthrow by General Paredes.

Mexico was particularly bitter at the claim of Texas that its southern boundary was the Rio Grande, rather than the Nueces River, some distance to the north. On April 7, 1846, President Polk learned of Mexico's refusal to receive Slidell. The next day Gen. Zachary Taylor was ordered to cross the Nueces and occupy the disputed zone. Soon several Americans were killed in skirmishes with Mexican troops. With this news in hand, Polk asked Congress to declare that a state of war existed by hostile action of Mexico. Congress did so, and Polk signed the declaration on May 13, 1846.

Several months earlier, Secretary of the Navy Bancroft had instructed Commodore John D. Sloat of the Pacific squadron that in the event of war with Mexico he was to occupy such ports in California as he considered necessary for the establishment of American authority in the province. He was also to make every effort to establish friendly relations with the people and to avoid hostilities with them. In June, at Mazatlán, Sloat received definite but still unofficial reports that the United States and Mexico were at war. On July 2 he anchored at Monterey, but hesitated lest he repeat the embarrassing mistake of Commodore Jones. He offered to fire a salute to the Mexican flag, an honor which the port authorities declined because they lacked the powder to return it. The presidio at Monterey had three guns, all of different caliber, and the California navy consisted of one small vessel with no guns.

Larkin advised caution, but when Sloat learned of the operations of Frémont and the Bear Flaggers, he feared that complications might develop. After 5 days' delay, Sloat made up for his hesitancy on July 7 by issuing a proclamation which went so far as to declare that "henceforward California will be a portion of the United States." Although he came "in arms with a powerful force," it was not as an enemy to the people of California but "as their best friend." He painted a glowing picture of the benefits that would follow, including greater political freedom and stability, honest and efficient administration, and "a great increase in the value of real estate."

On July 23, Sloat, who had been in ill health for some time, turned over his command to Commodore Robert F. Stockton, and the tone of the occupation changed sharply. Stockton, like Frémont and Gillespie, was eager to distinguish himself by vigorous action. Like Frémont, Stockton had strong political ambitions, though these feelings had a somewhat different background. His grandfather, Richard Stockton, had been a signer of the Declaration of Independence, and his father had been a United States senator. The commodore himself had been offered the secretaryship of the Navy under Tyler.

As one of his first acts after assuming command, Stockton mustered the "California Battalion of Mounted Riflemen" into United States service (apparently the naval service, though this has never really been clear), commissioning Frémont as major and Gillespie as captain. Stockton then issued a new, bombastic, and offensive proclamation to the people, drawn up with the advice of Frémont and Gillespie. Colonel Castro at Santa Clara and Governor Pío Pico at Los Angeles announced that resistance was hopeless, and both left for Mexico. In August Los Angeles was occupied without resistance. Stockton was now able to announce that California was "entirely free from Mexican dominion," but he irritated the Angeleños by unnecessarily ordering martial law, and then made the further mistake of leaving Gillespie in charge with a small garrison.

The inhabitants of Los Angeles were not accustomed to strict maintenance of order, and Gillespie's rules were oppressive and arbitrary. The order for a curfew, for example, was highly unrealistic. When some of the more disorderly elements behaved with their customary exuberance, Gillespie began to treat them as rebels before they had actually thought of rebellion. They soon thought of it, and Capt. José María Flores and several other officers broke their paroles to lead a revolt that spread rapidly throughout southern California.

On September 24 Gillespie was besieged on Fort Hill near the Los Angeles plaza, but his courier managed to get through, and rode 500 miles in 5 days to inform Stockton at San Francisco. On the 27th the rebels captured a group of Americans about 25 miles east of Los Angeles. Soon afterward Gillespie surrendered under terms that permitted him to march his men to San Pedro for embarkation. At San Pedro, however, they met a relief force of marines and sailors who had arrived from San Francisco, and who now joined them for a march back toward Los Angeles. The march was hot and dusty and by foot since the rebels had rounded up all the horses in the region.

About 15 miles inland, at Domínguez Rancho on October 8, the Americans encountered a force led by José Antonio Carrillo, well-mounted and equipped with a surprisingly effective cannon. This had long been used to fire salutes at the Los Angeles plaza on festive occasions. Before the town's surrender to Stockton it had been buried in the garden of Señora Inocencia Reyes.

Dug up and lashed to the running gear of a wagon, fired with homemade powder and a cigarette, and moved rapidly about by skilled horsemen, it proved a deadly weapon, and the "battle of the Old Woman's Gun" was a brilliant little victory for the *californios*. The Americans, trying to pursue this mobile artillery on foot, suffered a number of casualties and withdrew to San Pedro.

Los Angeles remained in rebel hands for 3 months more, while Stockton went to San Diego for horses and supplies and Frémont moved down from the north with the California battalion, suppressing minor branches of the insurrection on the way. At this same time Gen. Stephen W. Kearny was crossing the desert from New Mexico.

In June, at Fort Leavenworth, General Kearny had received instructions from the secretary of war to occupy New Mexico and then proceed to California to organize a military and civil government there. Kearny occupied Santa Fé without resistance and set out for California with 300 dragoons. On the way, unfortunately, he met Kit Carson, whom Stockton had sent eastward in August with the premature news that California was peacefully and firmly in American hands. Kearny sent most of his force back and continued with only about 100 men. When they reached southern California, they had come 2000 miles in one of the longest and most difficult marches in American Army history. They were exhausted and half-starved, and most of their mounts had been worn out and replaced with mules or unbroken horses.

Several hours before dawn on December 6, Kearny was encamped near the Indian village of San Pascual, about 35 miles north-northeast of San Diego, when he learned that a rebel detachment was in the village. Kit Carson assured him that the Californians were cowards who would not and could not fight. Hoping to capture the rebels' horses, Kearny roused his men for an immediate advance in the darkness, cold, and fog. The wretched mounts of the dragoons moved with widely varying speeds, and the rebels, under Andrés Pico, lured them into a pursuit until they were widely strung out, then suddenly turned to attack them.

The American cavalry sabers were hopelessly ineffective against the Californian lances, wielded by men whom Kearny well described as "admirably mounted and the very best riders in the world; hardly one that is not fit for the circus." Practically all the casualties were on the American side—22 killed, including several officers, and 16 wounded, including Kearny himself. After 10 minutes of fighting, Don Andrés's men withdrew. On the basis of remaining in possession of the battlefield, Kearny reported the battle of San Pascual as a victory, and Army historians later certified it as "not . . . a defeat," but this verdict is open to question, to say the least. Stockton sent out a relief force, and with its help Kearny reached San Diego on December 12.

The rebel cause was weakened by the usual chronic dissensions, by a shortage of powder, and by the gradual abandonment of the hopes of Flores and others that they could hold out until Mexico should be victorious over the United States in the main theaters of war. A joint force under Stockton and Kearny recaptured Los Angeles on January 10, 1847, after minor skirmishes.

Flores now fled to Sonora, and Andrés Pico chose to surrender the rebel forces to Frémont, who had reached the San Fernando Valley from the north. Frémont was flattered at being the officer who now received the final surrender, and by the terms of the Capitulation of Cahuenga on January 13, 1847, he extended full pardon to all the rebels. The *californios* had acquitted themselves with honor. Kearny later reported to the adjutant general that they rebelled because they had been "most cruelly and shamefully abused by our people. Had they not resisted they would have been unworthy the name of men."

The surrender at Cahuenga ended organized resistance to the American occupation. It also marked the beginning of a series of bitter disputes between Kearny and Stockton, and between Kearny and Frémont, over the question of who was now in command and who was authorized to act as military and civil governor. Stockton's instructions from the Navy Department on this point were vague, while Kearny's instructions from the War Department were quite explicit. Nevertheless, Stockton still considered himself in charge. Before sailing for further operations on the west coast of Mexico, he appointed Frémont his successor as governor of California. Kearny refused to recognize this appointment and regarded Frémont, who had recently been promoted to lieutenant colonel, as under his own command. Frémont was able to persuade himself that authority he had received from a commodore in the Navy should prevail over the orders of a brigadier general in the Army who was now his own immediate superior. On this basis Frémont rashly assumed the powers of governor and repeatedly defied military orders from General Kearny. Further orders from Washington clearly sustained Kearny's side of the argument.

The question that now arose, as seen by Kearny and by nearly all the officers under his command except Frémont, was that of the effect on the discipline and morale of the Army if mutiny were to be condoned because the mutinous officer was a son-in-law of the chairman of the Senate Committee on Military Affairs. The feeling among most of Frémont's brother officers was such that if Kearny had ordered a court-martial in California, Frémont might have been shot. Instead the court-martial of Frémont was conducted in Washington, D.C. During the proceedings Frémont, and Benton as his counsel, did everything they could to impugn Kearny's integrity and destroy his reputation. Nevertheless, in January 1848 Frémont was found guilty of disobedience of orders and sentenced to dismissal from the service. President Polk approved the verdict but remitted the penalty. Bitterly, Frémont refused this executive clemency and resigned his commission. Popular opinion generally supported Frémont. In the eyes of the American people in the 1840s, insubordination was not a very serious offense.

Jessie Benton Frémont was of the opinion that "Our house—our library and my father's committee room—were the real war department. She seems to have done much to encourage her husband in this same view, and in other highly questionable opinions as well. One of these was that he was not sufficiently aggressive. In later years John Frémont was one of the first two senators from California, temporarily a millionaire from the mineral proceeds of his Mariposa land grant, the first candidate of the Republican party for the presidency in 1856, and temporarily a major general in the Civil War. Nevertheless Jessie once told one of his aides: "Oh, if my husband had only been more positive! But he never did assert himself enough. That was his great fault." She seems to have felt that if Frémont had only been as vigorous as she was, he and she would have been President of the United States and commander in chief of the Army and Navy.

The war with Mexico was concluded on February 3, 1848, with the signing of the Treaty of Guadalupe Hidalgo in which Mexico ceded California and other territories to the United States. Only 9 days earlier gold had been discovered in the foothills of the Sierra Nevada, an event unknown to the signers of the treaty. Knowledge of the discovery could have made little difference in the negotiations in any event. Mexico had been overrun by American troops and was in no position to quibble over terms of peace, even though California would now be considerably more valuable than it had yet appeared to be.

SELECTED BIBLIOGRAPHY

American projects for peaceful acquisition are described by Robert Glass Cleland in "The Early Sentiment for the Annexation of California," *Southwestern Historical Quarterly*, XVIII (1914–1915), pp. 40, 121–161, 231–260; George P. Hammond (ed.), *The Larkin Papers*, volumes III and IV; John A. Hawgood (ed.), *First and Last Consul: Thomas Oliver Larkin and the Americanization of California* (1970); Norman A. Graebner, *Empire on the Pacific* (1955); Charles G. Sellers, *James K. Polk, Continentalist* (1966); and Frederick Merk, *Manifest Destiny and Mission in American History* (1963). On rival aspirations, see Merk, *The Monroe Doctrine and American Expansionism, 1843–1849* (1966); E. D. Adams, "British Interest in California," *American Historical Review*, XIV (July 1909), pp. 744–763; George B. Brooke, "The Vest Pocket War of Commodore Jones," *Pacific Historical Review*, XXXI (August 1962), pp. 217–233; and Russell M. Posner, "A British Consular Agent in California: The Reports of James A. Forbes, 1843–1846," *Southern California Quarterly*, LIII (June 1971), pp. 101–112.

The campaign biographies of John C. Frémont that were published in 1856 were worshipful. Their judgments were sharply reversed in the 1880s by three important works: the second volume of Theodore H. Hittell's *History of California* (1885); Josiah Royce's *California, from the Conquest in 1846 to the Second Vigilance Committee in San Francisco, a Study of American Character* (1886; new edition with an excellent introduction by Earl S. Pomeroy, 1971); and Oak's fifth volume of "Bancroft's" *History of California* (1886). Among other criticisms, Royce, Oak, and Bancroft openly questioned Frémont's veracity, especially in his claim to have had secret authorization for his filibustering activities. Frémont's *Memoirs of My Life*, of which only the first volume was published (1887), reasserted the claim. Both Frémont and his wife were addicted to the human foible of deceiving themselves.

The first major biography of Frémont, by Allan Nevins, was generally sympathetic. The first edition of this work bore the title *Frémont, the West's Greatest Adventurer* (two volumes, 1928). Cardinal Goodwin, in *John Charles Frémont, an Explanation of his Career* (1930), asserted that Nevins had placed too much reliance on Frémont family papers. Nevins, in turn, complained that Goodwin's work, though able, was "studiously hostile" to its subject. In the later editions of Nevins's biography, some of its most favorable judgments were slightly modified, and the title was changed to *Frémont: Pathmarker of the West* (rather than "Pathfinder," which had been used in the long subtitle of the original edition). Bernard De Voto, in *The Year of Decision, 1846* (1942), deplored all adulation of Frémont, past, present, and future. But Irving Stone, with the license of the novelist, exalted Jessie and her husband in *Immortal Wife* (1944). Dwight L. Clarke, in *Stephen Watts Kearny, Soldier of the West* (1961), sought to rescue Kearny from the "historical eclipse" to which he was consigned by Frémont and his admirers. See also Kenneth M. Johnson, *The Frémont Court Martial* (1968). Ferol Egan, *Frémont, Explorer for a Restless Nation* (1977) is lively and engaging, and in general the best biography to date. Mary Lee Spence and Donald Jackson (ed.), *The Expeditions of John Charles Frémont*, vol. I: *Travels from 1838 to 1844* and *Map Portfolio* (1970) and volume II: *The Bear Flag Revolt and the Court Martial* with *Supplement: Proceedings of the Court Martial* (1973) make the original documents available.

A Biography of William B. Ide, by his brother Simeon, also appeared under the title *Who Conquered California?* (1880). See also Fred B. Rogers, *William Brown Ide, Bear Flagger* (1962); Werner H. Marti, *Messenger of Destiny* (1960), on Archibald Gillespie; and John A. Hawgood, "John C. Frémont and the Bear Flag Revolution: A Reappraisal," *Southern California Quarterly*, XLIX (June 1962), pp. 67–96. John A. Hussey, "The United States and the Bear Flag Revolt," Ph.D. thesis, University of California, Berkeley (1941) is substantial and well-balanced. Numerous articles and documents on the subject have appeared in various issues of the *California Historical Society Quarterly*. The chief engagement during the "conquest" is thoroughly described in Arthur Woodward, *Lances at San Pascual* (1948). On a less bloody but equally interesting conflict, see John Douglas Tanner, Jr., "The Campaign for Los Angeles—December 29, 1846, to January 10, 1847," *California Historical Society Quarterly*, XLVIII (September 1969), pp. 219–242.

THE GOLD RUSH

It is ironic but understandable that the Spaniards, who had found so much gold in other parts of the hemisphere, failed entirely to find the vast treasure of the Sierra Nevada. They had seen little reason to explore the approaches to the Sierra, and even less reason to settle there, and the local Indians, if they noticed any gold, had no interest in it. During the Mexican period a minor discovery was made in 1842 at Placerita Creek, about 35 miles northwest of Los Angeles. The first gold ever sent from California to the United States Mint came from that area, but the placers there were of trifling importance, received little attention, and were soon played out.

MARSHALL'S DISCOVERY AT SUTTER'S MILL

The crucial discovery was the result, although the accidental and indirect result, of an American's ingenuity. James Wilson Marshall was a moody and somewhat eccentric master carpenter who had come from Missouri to Oregon in 1844 and then south to California in 1845. His mechanical skills made him one of the most valued employees of John A. Sutter, but the scarcity of lumber in the Central Valley was frustrating to a carpenter and had discouraged a number of other Americans who had thought of making their homes there. In August 1847 Marshall contracted with Sutter to build a sawmill in the foot-hills in order to provide lumber both for Sutter's own use and for sale to immi-grants. Marshall chose a site on the south fork of the American River, where there was an abundance of timber and a flow of water that looked ideal for diversion into a millrace. The site was about 45 travel miles east-northeast of Sutter's Fort, at a place called Coloma from the Indian name Culloomah, or "beautiful vale." With a crew including several Mormons and a number of Indian laborers, construction proceeded remarkably well. In January it appeared that the tailrace needed to be further deepened and its bottom cleared of obstructions. It was while Marshall was inspecting the progress of this work that on January 24, 1848, he saw a glittering particle, caught behind a stone beneath the water. The tailrace was, in effect, a sluice cut through a sandbar at a bend of the river, and if Marshall had actually been searching for placer gold, he could hardly have hit upon a better way of finding it.

With his glittering discovery, Marshall rode down to New Helvetia. There, behind a locked door, Sutter put the samples to several tests in the light of what he knew of the properties of the metal and what he could learn from the *American Encyclopedia*. When Sutter concluded that "It's gold—at least twenty-three-carat gold," Marshall got into such a state of feverish excitement that he insisted on riding back to Coloma in the rain in the middle of the night—the first victim of the gold mania. Sutter's behavior was somewhat less erratic; his primary concern was that the discovery would endanger the completion of his sawmill. At Coloma he persuaded the workers to continue with their task and to confine their prospecting to Sundays.

Efforts to keep the news from spreading were in vain. For example, one of the children of Mrs. Wimmer, the cook at Coloma, talked of the discovery to a teamster; then, to save her boy from being ridiculed as a liar, the good woman showed the teamster some nuggets. Sutter himself, anxious as he was to keep the matter quiet, could not resist some boasting about it. He made an agreement with some Indians for a lease on the land around Coloma, and in dispatching a messenger to Col. Richard B. Mason, the military governor at Monterey, asking for validation of this agreement, Sutter not only revealed the discovery but sent along 6 ounces of gold to prove it.

Although the news leaked out quickly enough, it attracted very little attention for several months. There had been idle rumors of gold ever since the expeditions of Drake and Vizcaíno. None had actually been found until the trivial Placerita discovery of 1842, and this suggested that while there was some gold in California, there was not enough to make it worth digging. Brief news reports of gold near New Helvetia, written with obvious lack of conviction, appeared in the two little weekly newspapers of San Francisco—one item in the *Californian* on March 15, 1848, and another in the *California Star* 10 days later—without creating any notable excitement.

THE FORTY-EIGHTERS

The gold fever did not begin to be epidemic until May 12. On that day, in San Francisco, the mania that would eventually spread over the whole world was touched off deliberately and for purposes of revenue by the enterprising merchant, manipulator, real estate speculator, and Mormon elder, Samuel Brannan.

Brannan had arrived in 1846 as the leader of the California Mormons. A remarkably vigorous young man of Irish ancestry, articulate, ingenious, and highly opportunistic, he began his career as a molder of opinion and emotion by editing a journal published in New York for the Mormons of the Atlantic seaboard. When the leaders at Nauvoo, Illinois, determined in 1845 that the

View of San Francisco, 1847. *(Courtesy of the Bancroft Library.)*

Latter-Day Saints should "flee out of Babylon," Elder Brannan, then 26 years old, was delegated to lead a party of more than 200 by ship around the Horn to California. They sailed from New York in the ship *Brooklyn* on February 4, 1846, which happened to be the same day that the main body of Mormons set out from Nauvoo across the ice of the Mississippi River. As flights from the sovereignty of the United States, these migrations were frustrated by the Mexican War. When the *Brooklyn* anchored in San Francisco Bay, on July 31, 1846, she found herself alongside the U.S.S. *Portsmouth*, whose commander, Capt. John B. Montgomery, had landed on the 9th to raise the American flag over Yerba Buena.

The arrival of the Brannan party tripled the population of that village. The first buildings had been erected there in 1835 when William A. Richardson, an English deserter from a whaler, had put up a shanty of rough boards, and the American Jacob P. Leese had built a slightly more substantial structure out of redwood planks brought by boat from Monterey. Early in 1847, by his authority as *alcalde*, Lt. Washington Allon Bartlett of the *Portsmouth* changed the name of Yerba Buena to San Francisco. Otherwise, the town's history had not yet been very eventful. No one there was as yet especially prosperous, with the exception of Samuel Brannan, who was already its leading citizen.

Brannan engaged in an assortment of business activities and investments, flagrantly putting Mormon funds to his own use and profit. Charged with embezzlement, he was the defendant in one of the first jury trials ever held in California, but the jury disagreed. He continued to gather in the tithes and to decide what should be done with the proceeds. When Brigham Young sent down a deputation from Salt Lake City to bring back "the Lord's money," Brannan said that he would turn over the money when he got a receipt signed by the Lord. He repeatedly urged the Salt Lake Mormons to come to the paradise of California, and he never understood Brigham Young's decision that the Saints could maintain their integrity and solidarity only by concentrating in Utah. Finally Brannan's superiors "disfellowshipped," or excommunicated, him, though for some time he denied the validity of this proceeding.

One of Brannan's enterprises was a general store at Sutter's Fort. In March 1848, after customers at this store had begun to offer gold in payment for whisky and other commodities, Brannan became aware of the reality of the discovery and of the uses to which he could put it. He spent the next several weeks in quietly purchasing every article of merchandise he could get hold of in northern California that would be in demand by gold seekers, then moving these articles to his store at New Helvetia. Then, on May 12, he came down to San Francisco, waved a bottle of gold dust in one hand and his hat in the other, and shouted "Gold! Gold! Gold from the American River!" When samples of gold reached Monterey, on June 20, Alcalde Colton recorded that "the blacksmith dropped his hammer, the carpenter his plane, the mason his trowel, the baker his loaf, and the tapster his bottle. All were off for the mines, some on horses, some on carts, and some on crutches, and one went on a litter." Within a few days Governor Mason, Alcalde Colton, and the other officers were doing their own cooking.

The symptoms of the craze which the sight of gold now began to produce in many men have often been described, but perhaps never more vividly than by James H. Carson:

> I looked on for a moment; a frenzy seized my soul; unbidden my legs performed some entirely new movements of polka steps—I took several— houses were too small for me to stay in; I was soon in the street in search of necessary outfits; piles of gold rose up before me at every step; castles of marble, dazzling the eye with their rich appliances; thousands of slaves bowing to my beck and call; myriads of fair virgins contending with each other for my love—were among the fancies of my fevered imagination. The Rothschilds, Girards, and Astors appeared to be but poor people; in short, I had a very violent attack of the gold fever.

The most confirmed skeptics quickly succumbed. The editor of the *California Star*, Edward C. Kemble, a young man not yet out of his teens, continued to maintain as late as the issue of May 20 that the whole thing was a sham, "a supurb [sic] take-in as was ever got up to guzzle the gullible." The owner of the *Star* was none other than Brannan himself, and obviously he had not taken his young editor into his scheme. In any event, Kemble soon reversed himself and went off to join the gold rush.

Within a short time nearly every town in California lost a majority of its population. On May 29 the *San Francisco Californian* complained that "The whole country, from San Francisco to Los Angeles, and from the sea shore to the base of the Sierra Nevadas, resounds with the sordid cry of gold, GOLD, GOLD! while the field is left half-planted, the house half-built, and everything neglected but the manufacture of shovels and pickaxes." The paper also announced that it was suspending publication; it had no choice, in view of the departure of its staff, subscribers, and advertisers. A few days later the *California Star* also suspended for the same reason.

Even the California Indians did not remain immune to the lure of gold. Colonel Mason estimated in 1848 that more than half of the gold diggers in the California mines were Indians. At first many Indian miners worked as laborers for white Californians, often in a state of peonage similar to their status on the Mexican ranchos, while others labored as independent agents and traded their gold to white merchants for a variety of goods. As hostilities between Indians and whites increased, the number of Indian miners in the goldfields declined rapidly.

Soldiers and sailors deserted by the hundreds. Colonel Mason reported that he was powerless to stop desertions, especially after a soldier on a 3 weeks' furlough found $1500 worth of gold, more than his Army pay for 5 years. Mason toured the diggings in July. Some Mormon miners asked him whether they must turn over to Sam Brannan the tithes of their findings which he was soliciting from them, to which the governor replied that they were required to pay as long as they were fools enough to do so.

During the summer months the contagion began to spread to Hawaii, Oregon, and Utah, and in the fall to Mexico, Peru, and Chile. Altogether probably about 6000 good seekers came to California from these areas in 1848. The main gold rush from "the States" did not begin until the year of the discovery was almost over.

THE FORTY-NINERS

In September 1848 Lieutenant Edward F. Beale arrived in Washington with reports and also with some actual specimens of gold, sent by Larkin. This led to many newspaper comments and to fairly wide discussion, but as yet few planned to leave for California. The spread of the gold craze over the whole country came after the sending of President Polk's annual message to Congress on December 5. Polk welcomed the news as a justification of his policies in acquiring the Mexican cession. In evidence, the President appended Colonel Mason's report of his personal tour of the diggings, in which Mason asserted that there was enough gold "in the country drained by the Sacramento and San Joaquin Rivers" to pay the cost of the Mexican War "a hundred times over."

Two days later Lt. Lucien Loeser arrived at the capital with a tea caddy crammed with 230 ounces of gold. Placed on display at the War Department, this drew excited crowds, and the Philadelphia Mint soon announced that samples of it had a degree of fineness equal to the standard of United States gold coins.

The mania for sudden wealth now pervaded all classes, and the urge to be off to the goldfields stimulated many related industries. One of these was the marketing of fanciful devices for gold mining, pratically all of them destined to be junked. Another was the hasty publication of alleged guidebooks of varying degrees of fraudulence, most of them derived, at best, largely from Mason's report, along with some fragments of the writings of Larkin, Frémont, and Lansford W. Hastings. One such opus, published in New York in December 1848, was *The Emigrant's Guide to the Gold Mines . . .,* 30 pages long and selling for 25 cents, or 12½ cents without the map; the latter alternative was the better buy, since the map was entirely worthless. Another item, of 1849 vintage, was *The Digger's Handbook and Truth about California* by one D. L. Sydney. In penciled insertions on the title page of a surviving copy of this work, some disillusioned purchaser identified the author's initials, D. L., as "Damn Liar." Tin Pan Alley provided accompaniment, with "The Gold Digger's Waltz," "The San Francisco Waltz," "The Sacramento Gallop," and a pirated adaptation from Stephen Foster, which emerged as

> O Susanna! don't you cry for me!
> I'm going to California with my wash-bowl on my knee.

There were three main routes to the goldfields: by way of the Isthmus of Panama, around Cape Horn, or overland. The sea routes drew the heavy traffic in the first months of the great rush in the winter and early spring of 1849 because they were open all year round, although in the long run more than twice as many gold seekers would go to California by land as by sea. Before 1849 the Cape Horn route had been the most traveled one, but it covered a distance of about 18,000 nautical miles and took 5 to 8 months, and thus the Panama shortcut suddenly became attractive to thousands who feared that all the gold might be gone before they could arrive to claim their share of it.

Moreover, it happened that a new passenger service on the Panama route was just becoming available. Three 1000-ton paddle-wheel steamers were built for the run from Panama to California and Oregon. The first of these, the *California*, left New York in October 1848 with almost no passengers, on her way around the Horn toward the Pacific port of Panama. When she arrived there in January, she found 700 Americans clamoring to get aboard. They had traveled by ship to Chagres, by small boat up the fever-infested Chagres River, and by mule the rest of the way across the isthmus. The *California's* rated capacity was not more than 250, and she had taken on 69 Peruvians who refused to get off. Among the Americans waiting in Panama was Gen. Persifor F. Smith, on his way to relieve Colonel Mason as military commander in California. Hard-pressed by his angry compatriots, Smith issued a kind of proclamation, in which he asserted incorrectly that American law forbade foreigners to dig gold on American soil. The *Panama Star,* a newspaper founded by some of the Americans temporarily stranded for lack of transport, published the general's statement in its first issue, along with an equally ungenerous editorial: "If foreigners come [to California] let them till the soil and make roads, or do any other work that may suit them . . ., but the gold mines were reserved by nature for Americans only, who possess noble hearts." After days of intensive ticket scalping, the *California* sailed with about 400 on board. During most of 1849, because of delays at Panama, the average time from New York to San Francisco by this route was 3 to 5 months, though by 1850 increased service in the Pacific had reduced it to 6 to 8 weeks.

Of the Argonauts who chose to travel around the Horn, many were organized in joint stock companies, both for the voyage and in the expectation of working together in mining operations after their arrival. These companies usually purchased old ships, which they fondly supposed they could sell in California. Actually, most of these vessels joined the fleet of several hundred hulks that were abandoned to settle gradually into the mud along the San Francisco waterfront, and nearly all the companies disintegrated into smaller groups more suitable for prospecting. The removal from service of the hundreds of obsolete old vessels now consigned to the ghost fleet, at the same time that the gold rush was stimulating the building of the clipper ships, made the early 1850s the golden age of the American merchant marine. The new California clippers were twice as large as the China clippers designed in the 1840s, and with freight at $60 a ton, each of them paid for itself with its first cargo. The clippers were designed to carry premium freight at maximum speed. They were much less important for carrying passengers, who found them highly uncomfortable. In 1851 the maiden voyage of Donald McKay's *Flying Cloud* set a record of 89 days from New York to San Francisco, a record which no other sailing ship has ever excelled.

A majority of the forty-niners traveled overland, especially those from the Ohio and Mississippi valleys. The main route was the California Trail, by way of the Platte, South Pass, and Humboldt. This route was already well-established by the earlier emigrants, but for each person who followed it in 1848 there were 50 in 1849, some of them in wagon trains miles long. Between the Rockies and the Sierra the loss of oxen and the horses was dreadful because the great trek used up all the grass within easy reach of the trail. Men, women, and children had to walk in order to spare the strength of such animals as

Donald McKay's *Flying Cloud*. (Courtesy of the Bancroft Library.)

were still alive to draw the wagons, and some families had to fry the last of their bacon for axle grease. By the time they reached the 40 miles of unbroken desert southwest of the Humboldt Sink, many were no longer concerned to save their property, but only their lives, and the trail was littered with an almost incredible miscellany of discarded articles. There was very little danger from hostile Indians at this time, but there was a major epidemic of Asiatic cholera. The disease was not only agonizing and usually fatal but also peculiarly terrifying because medical science had not yet discovered that it was transmitted mainly through the contamination of drinking water, and those who tended the sick or came anywhere near them imagined that the ghastly affliction might be spread in various other ways.

Besides the three main arteries of travel, a number of alternate routes attracted smaller contingents. Some crossed the isthmus by way of Nicaragua rather than Panama. There were several fairly important southern trails, not only across Texas and New Mexico but also across old Mexico. A number of forty-niners branched off from the main California Trail by going southwest from Salt Lake to southern California, and for some who rashly attempted a shortcut from this route Death Valley earned its name. Others turned off from the Humboldt River into Black Rock Desert, to swing far north of the Sierra and into the upper end of the Sacramento Valley by way of the Pit River. This roundabout way, known as Lassen's Cutoff, was as outrageously misnamed as Hastings', and in general Peter Lassen and Lansford Hastings were about equally incompetent as guides. The majority chose a direct route through the central Sierra, though many were frightened by the reputation of Donner Pass and instead used Carson Pass about 20 miles south of Lake Tahoe.

THE DIGGINGS

Before the end of 1849, miners were swarming over the foothill region between the Yuba River in the north and Mariposa in the south, the region now appropriately traversed by California State Highway 49. Within this area lay the "mother lode," in a continuous belt extending about 120 miles from a point north of Coloma to a point near Mariposa, and varying in width from a few hundred feet to 2 miles. This network of thousands of veins of gold was formed when the cordilleran revolution produced the Sierra Nevada by cracking the earth's surface and thrusting up a great tilted block of the earth's crust. A long ribbon of molten gold ore flowed up into fissures in the granitic rock. Erosion then tore loose particles of gold and washed them into the rivers, where they lodged on sandbars, behind stones, or in "pot holes" in the banks or streambeds. These particles were known as *placer* gold, from a Spanish word meaning a place near the bank of a stream where alluvial gold could be found.

The miners spoke loosely of the "mother lode country" as including not only the great vein of ore still embedded in the rocks but also the larger area where placer gold had been deposited. The Mokelumne River, separating Amador and Calaveras counties, was the approximate boundary between the "northern mines" and the "southern mines." There were also some fairly important gold-bearing areas in other parts of California, particularly in the regions of Mt. Shasta and the Trinity and Klamath rivers, where a new rush began in 1850. Popular terminology lumped these with the northern mines, though they would be better described as in a separate "northwestern" group. Lesser discoveries were also made in several isolated parts of southern California.

EARLY MINING METHODS

Very few Americans had any previous experience in gold mining. New Spain had a major gold rush at Zacatecas in 1548, three full centuries earlier. Although the Spaniards in Mexico and Peru had at first sought gold largely with the sword from Indians who were already in possession of it, or with the whip through forced Indian labor in the mines, they had also developed a number of the more advanced techniques of the mining industry. In fact, there were dozens of Spanish-Mexican mining terms which had no English equivalents and which were soon put to use by the Americans in California. *Placer* was only the most familar of these; other examples included *bonanza*, or rich ore, and *borrasca*, or barren rock. In the United States, there was a gold mining industry of modest importance in Georgia and the Carolinas during the first half of the nineteenth century, and several veterans of these southern Appalachian diggings brought important knowledge of mining methods to California. The first was Isaac Humphrey, from Georgia, who was at Sutter's Fort at the time of the discovery. Arriving at Coloma a few weeks later and finding the early prospectors still using nothing more than their knives and spoons, he introduced them to the pan and then to the rocker or cradle.

Of the various devices for using the movement of water to separate particles of gold from sand, gravel, and clay, the simplest was a flat-bottomed pan made of iron or tin. A quantity of what was hoped to be "pay dirt," obtained with the pick and shovel, was tossed into the pan, throughly wetted and stirred, and the rocks or pebbles picked out of it. Then the miner held the pan under the surface of a pool or stream and swirled it about with a gently rotating motion for at least 10 minutes, one side of the pan held a little higher than the other, until the clay and nearly all of the sand were washed away. Gold being heavier, particles of it remained in the bottom.

The lure of the gold rush was the prospect of acquiring wealth quickly and easily—by lucky chance rather than hard work. But panning for gold turned out to be one of the most exhausting forms of manual labor ever devised. To the hard work with pick and shovel, panning added the necessity of squatting or stooping in the burning sun, either beside the icy water or in it, for hours, while moving the wrist, arm, and shoulder muscles and concentrating attention very carefully on the overflow.

The first improvement on the pan was the rocker, an oblong box without a top, several feet in length, mounted on rockers like a child's cradle and placed in a sloping position. It was open at the lower end, while above the upper end there was a hopper with a sieve. Three people usually worked together, one shoveling dirt into the hopper, another pouring buckets of water to wash the dirt down through the trough, and a third vigorously rocking the cradle. Thus the gold was trapped behind the cleats or "riffles" nailed at intervals along the bottom. No part of the operation of a rocker was as uncomfortable as panning, and some relief from the monotony of the labor could be had by exchanging jobs. Although much of the finer gold slid over the cleats and was lost, the average return was higher than in panning because a much larger quantity of dirt could be processed in a day.

Near the end of 1849 the "long tom" appeared as an enlargement and a considerable improvement of the rocker. The tom was usually about 12 feet long, stationary, and placed where a stream of water could be run through it from a ditch or a wooden flume. This eliminated both the pouring of water and the rocking of the cradle. About a year later the long tom evolved into a sluice, a whole series of riffle boxes fitted together into a continuous string, sometimes as much as several hundred feet in length. This device, though commonly employed even in ancient times, seems to have been reinvented in California. In an important related development, a wing dam was built part

A Primitive Outfit. After a sketch from life in 1850 by John W. Audubon. *(Courtesy of the Bancroft Library.)*

way across a stream to divert a flow of water into a sluice; sometimes an entire river was dammed and turned aside to expose the pay dirt in a section of the streambed. The reason such relatively efficient methods were so slow in appearing was that they required fairly large groups of men to work together, and in the first 2 years the miners were so intensely individualistic that the industry was still at most a small-business operation.

The final separation of gold from the sand and other dross was often accomplished by the use of mercury, or quicksilver, which has the property of amalgamating with gold. When this amalgam is heated in a closed vessel, the mercury vaporizes. Thus separated from the gold, the mercury can also be recovered, as soon as it cools again from vapor to liquid. Fortunately, quicksilver had been found in 1845 at New Almaden in the hills a few miles south of San José.

MINING CAMP LAW

The primary concern of the early California miners with legal problems was in the regulation of mining claims. Because the mining camps had sprung up beyond the reach of any established law, they had to adopt their own regulations. Practically none of the land in the gold region had passed into private hands, and the rights of the Indians were ignored. California was in the midst of a peculiarly awkward transition from Mexican to American sovereignty. Congress had not provided for the extension of American territorial government to any part of the Mexican cession, and even if it had, there was no federal mining law that would have been relevant to the California mining camps, because no precious metal had ever been discovered before on public lands of the United States.

In devising their own mining codes the Argonauts were acting in a tradition of American frontier self-government that went all the way back to the Mayflower Compact. In each camp there was a mass meeting to organize a "mining district" and elect a committee to draw up a set of regulations. Eventually more than 500 camps adopted such codes, so similar to each other as to rule out the possibility that they were separately and spontaneously invented. Spanish-Mexican mining codes and customs had a considerable influence, as did the experience of forty-niners from the lead and tin mines of Cornwall and other parts of England. Each code defined the permissible size of a claim and required that it be continuously worked if it was to remain valid. Thus the title was merely usufructuary, not a title to ownership of the land but merely to the use of it for mining purposes. Each district elected a recorder, variously called an alcalde, arbitrator, or chairman, and often its only officer. His duties were to keep the register of claims and to settle disputes arising from charges of claim jumping, sometimes with the assistance of a panel of arbitrators chosen by the contestants.

As described thus far, the plan was highly reasonable and highly democratic. A far less admirable aspect of the codes was that many of them included "restrictive covenants" barring Mexicans, Asians, or other foreigners. Still other problems of the mining camps arose from the extemporized administration of criminal justice, the resort to lynching and vigilantism. But racial oppression directed against foreigners and Indians in early American California and extralegal methods for the punishment of crime are the subjects of other chapters.

THE HISTORICAL SIGNIFICANCE OF THE GOLD RUSH

The traditional view of this remarkable migration describes it as the most fortunate as well as the most significant factor in the whole of California's history. It can be cogently argued, however, that in the long run the state would have been better off if it had contained no gold at all, that because of its other advantages it would eventually have become just as populous and prosperous, and that in the meantime its social evolution would have been not only more gradual but also far more orderly and civilized.

Obviously the lure of sudden wealth brought an early and rapid influx of population. At the end of 1848 about 6000 miners had obtained about $10 million worth of gold. In 1849 the amount produced was two or three times as large, but there were more than 40,000 miners to share in it, and thus the individual miner's average daily return declined radically. In 1852, the peak year, the output was about $80 million, and the number of miners about 100,000. During the 100 years after the beginning of the gold rush, the output of California gold totaled about $2 billion. All the gold produced in a century was worth less than the value of 1 year's agricultural output of the state in the 1960s, and much of the gold was ultimately destined to be put back into the ground, in the Treasury Department's hoard at Fort Knox.

It may be granted that if there had been no gold discovery, Oregon would probably have been ready for admission as a state before California was. The first transcontinental railroad might have been built to Oregon. But if California's first transcontinental railroad had been built later, it might have been in the hands of a somewhat less rapacious group of men and it might have obtained less of a stranglehold on the state's economy and politics.

What sort of people did the gold rush bring to California? Bancroft's famous description is interestingly balanced: " . . . the toiling farmer, whose mortgage loomed above the growing family, the briefless lawyer, the starving student, the quack, the idler, the harlot, the gambler, the hen-pecked husband, the disgraced; with many earnest, enterprising, honest men and devoted women." The women were few, however, and, in general, the notion that the Argonauts came to California as pioneers and commonwealth builders is a myth. The great majority of them came in the hope that they could quickly plunder California of her treasure and return to their homes. It is true that the penniless adventurer was excluded by the necessity of having an original stake of several hundred dollars for the expenses of the trip, and that many of the forty-niners were young married men hoping to make enough to return to their wives and children with financial security. But most of those who remained in California did so because they failed to accumulate even enough to get them back home. On the whole they were unsuccessful, disillusioned, embittered men.

The hard labor, the shockingly inflated prices of food, the badness and monotony of their own cooking, and the prevalence of sickness and of home-sickness all added to the widespread sense of desperation that so many of the diaries record. Hinton R. Helper, for example, took as dim a view of the gold rush as he later expressed concerning the institution of slavery and its impending crisis in his native south. Often there were efforts to find relief in a desperate kind of humor, as in the naming of such camps as Hell's Delight, Gouge Eye, Poker Flat, Devil's Retreat, Murderers' Bar, Poverty Hill, and Gomorrah, and in the organization of the Ancient and Honorable Order of E Clampus Vitus, or "the Clampers." The derivation of the name of this miner's fraternal society is unknown; there are no records of its early meetings, it is said, because they were devoted so largely to hard drinking that no one was ever in condition to keep minutes, or able the next day to recall what had happened. The constitution provided only that all members were officers and "of equal indignity," although some, such as the Clampatriarch and the Noble Grand Humbug, seem to have been more equal than others. The members were pledged to take care of widows and orphans, especially widows. In general, however, there was tragedy rather than humor or romance in the drinking, gambling, and vice in which many miners sought escape from the hardships and anxieties of "seeing the elephant," as the experience of mining came to be called.

The gold rush was the product of a kind of mass hysteria, and it set a tone and created a state of mind in which greed predominated and disorder and violence were all too frequent.

SELECTED BIBLIOGRAPHY

J. S. Holliday, *The World Rushed In: The California Gold Rush Experience* (1981) is a combination of biography and epic narrative. Other good general accounts include Donald Dale Jackson, *Gold Dust* (1980) and John W. Caughey, *Gold Is the Cornerstone* (1948), reissued as *The California Gold Rush* (1975). Rodman W. Paul, *California Gold* (1947) stresses the technological, economic, and legal aspects; see also his later work, *Mining Frontiers of the Far West, 1848–1880* (1963). Valeska Bari, *The Course of Empire* (1931) is a good collection of firsthand accounts. John W. Caughey (ed.), *Rushing for Gold* (1949, also published as the February 1949 issue of the *Pacific Historical Review* is a collection of excellent secondary studies.

California Gold Discovery: Centennial Papers of the Time, the Site and Artifacts (1947) includes a treatment of "Sutter's Sawmill" by Aubrey Neasham. See also Theressa Gay, *James Marshall, Discoverer of California Gold* (1967) and Rodman W. Paul (ed.), *The California Gold Discovery* (1966). Paul Bailey, *Sam Brannan and the California Mormons* (1953) deals with Brannan's role. Ralph P. Bieber, "California Gold Mania," *Mississippi Valley Historical Review*, XXXV (June 1948), pp. 3–28, describes the excitement in the east.

Hundreds of diaries or memoirs dealing with the gold rush have been published. E. Gould Buffum, *Six Months in the Gold Mines* (1850) and James H. Carson, *Early Recollections of the Mines* (1852) describe the days of '48.

John H. Kemble, *The Panama Route, 1848–1869* (1943) and Bayard Taylor, *El Dorado, or Adventures in the Path of Empire* (two volumes, 1850) deal with the isthmian approach. Oscar Lewis, *Sea Routes to the Gold Fields* (1949) also includes Cape Horn. Octavius T. Howe, *Argonauts of '49* (1923) is a history of the emigrant companies from Massachusetts. On the overland routes, see George R. Stewart, *The California Trail* (1962); Owen C. Coy, *The Great Trek* (1931); Irene D. Paden, *In the Wake of the Prairie Schooner* (1943); Walker D. Wyman (ed.), *California Emigrant Letters* (1952); Archer B. Hulbert, *The Forty-Niners* (1931), a synthetic diary; Alonzo Delano, *Life on the Plains and among the Diggings* (1854); and Ralph P. Bieber, *Southern Trails to California in 1849* (1937).

Some of the best descriptions of life in the diggings are in *The Shirley Letters from the California Mines, 1851–1852* (1949); Frank Marryat, *Mountains and Molehills* (1855, 1962); Sarah Royce, *A Frontier Lady* (1932); Josiah Royce, *California . . . a Study of American Character* (1886, 1948); and Charles H. Shinn, *Mining Camps* (1885, 1948). Hubert Howe Bancroft's social history of the gold rush, *California Inter Pocula* (1888), explains its title in its opening words: "Drunk! aye, drunk with avarice! Behold . . . California in her cups"—though an alternative translation might be "California between drinks," Views of the darker side include George Payson, *Golden Dreams and Leaden Realities* (1853) and Hinton R. Helper, *The Land of Gold; Reality Versus Fiction* (1855), also edited by Lucius Beebe and Charles M. Clegg under their title of *Dreadful California—Being a True & Scandalous Account of the Barbarous Civilization, Licentious Morals, Crude Manners and Depravities, Inclement Climate and Niggling Resources, together with Various Other Offensive & Calamitous Details of Life in the Golden State* (1948).

On mining camp law see John Umbeck, "The California Gold Rush: A Study of Emerging Property Rights," *Explorations in Economic History*, XIV (July 1977), pp. 197–226.

A NEW STATE AND FRONTIER POLITICS

The Congress of the United States, deadlocked over the future of slavery in new territories, provided no legal form of government whatever for California from the end of the Mexican War in 1848 until its admission into the Union on September 9, 1850. During this period the confused conditions of the gold rush intensified the confusion that resulted from California's undetermined and very peculiar legal and political status.

MILITARY GOVERNMENTS

From the outbreak of the war until the ratification of the treaty of peace, California was governed under the customs of international law which provided that in conquered territory under military occupation the previous system of local law remain in effect with such modifications as the military commander considered necessary. Thus the American commanders were also ex officio governors; however, there was much uncertainty about their legal status, powers, and responsibilities, both in Washington, D.C., and on the part of the commanders themselves.

Further confusion arose from the changes of personnel. When the "governorship" had passed from Commodore Sloat to Commodore Stockton to Colonel Frémont to General Kearny to Colonel Mason—five governors in the first 10 months—Captain DuPont of the U.S.S. *Cyane* wrote that "The Californians think . . . we cannot be much better than Mexico for they connect the appearance of every new commander-in-chief with the result of some new revolution."

The prevailing system of local government in Mexican California, which the American military governors necessarily adopted, was based on the powers of the alcalde, an office derived from the Arabian and Moorish *Al-Cadi*, or village judge. The duties of the alcalde were many and remarkably varied, and his jurisdiction was ill-defined and unclear. He performed the functions of mayor, sheriff, and judge, often arresting a person, presiding over the trial, passing sentence, and enforcing the sentence. He combined the judicial and executive powers, and he often exercised the legislative power as well—by extemporizing legislation, and by serving as the presiding and dominating officer of the town council or *ayuntamiento* if his town happened to have one.

The patriarchal aspects of the office and the absence of the separation of powers were shocking to many Americans. Walter Colton, appointed and later elected as the first American alcalde of Monterey in 1846, wrote that "such an absolute disposal of questions affecting property and personal liberty never ought to be confided to one man. There is not a judge on the bench in England or the United States whose power is so absolute as that of the alcalde of Monterey."

From the beginning the American military governors assumed that the ultimate annexation of California to the United States was a foregone conclusion, and this view was strengthened in March 1847 by the arrival of Colonel J. D. Stevenson's regiment of New York Volunteers, recruited with the understanding that they would be disbanded in California at the end of the war and would thus provide not merely a garrison but a body of permanent American settlers. Even before the end of the technical state of war, there were many protests against "the inefficient mongrel military rule," as a writer in the *California Star* described it, and against alcalde rule.

With the news of the ratification of the treaty, the question of how California was supposed to be governed became extraordinarily difficult and embarrassing. The situation was complicated both by the onset of the gold rush and by the fact that Congress failed to agree on any system of civil government. Congress provided for a territorial government in Oregon in the spring of 1848, but all such plans for New Mexico and California bogged down in the national political struggle which had raged since the introduction of Representative David Wilmot's proposal that slavery be forbidden in any territory acquired from Mexico.

The treaty signed at Guadalupe Hidalgo was ratified in May 1848, and the official news of the ratification reached California on August 6. Thereafter, military government had to be continued de facto, with no other legal basis than the law of necessity.

THE CONSTITUTIONAL CONVENTION AND ITS PROBLEMS

General Bennet Riley succeeded Colonel Mason as "civil" governor in April 1849. Late in May he received news that Congress had again adjourned without agreement on a territorial organization for California, and on June 3 he issued a call for a constitutional convention to meet at Monterey on September 1. He had no real authority to do this, but it was a wise and necessary solution of the problem. It was also consistent with the attitude of President Zachary Taylor, a southern Unionist who felt that California might help to break the congressional deadlock over the territorial expansion of slavery if it would confront the rest of the country with an accomplished fact, by drawing up a state constitution that would settle the explosive issue so far as California was concerned.

The President could make this suggestion only informally and unofficially because all the legal authority in the matter lay with Congress. Under the normal procedure, patterned roughly on that of the Northwest Ordinance, Congress would first have established a territorial government; then, when the territory had enough inhabitants, Congress would have passed an "enabling act," authorizing an elected convention (or sometimes the territorial legislature) to prepare a constitution and submit it for congressional approval with the admission of the state. All but four new states, since the original thirteen, had evolved through the territorial stage in this way. California would skip that stage entirely—as Vermont, Kentucky, Maine, and Texas had done—but under circumstances that differed from those prevailing in any of them.

President Taylor sent T. Butler King of Georgia as his personal and confidential emissary to California. In the sweltering summer of 1849, King traveled throughout the mining regions, urging the busy miners to take an interest in the forthcoming elections of delegates to the convention. The steamer on which King had arrived from Panama also carried another politician of even greater importance to California's future. This was William M. Gwin of Tennessee, a Democrat who had served one term in Congress and had been appointed to various minor federal offices by Presidents Jackson and Polk. Early in March 1849, as the presidency passed to a Whig, and after Congress had adjourned with no solution of the California tangle, Gwin realized that California would soon form its own state government. He left Washington with the announced intention of assisting in that process and then of returning as one of the first United States senators from the new state. He achieved both of these ambitions. Obviously, not all of California's golden opportunities were in its mines.

Early in September the convention assembled at Monterey, in Colton Hall, a substantial building that the first American alcalde had erected as a town hall and schoolhouse. Of the 48 delegates who attended, only 11 came from the southern districts: San Diego, 2; Los Angeles, 5; Santa Barbara, 2; San Luis Obispo, 2. From the northern districts 37 came: Monterey, 5; San José, 7; San Francisco, 8; Sonoma, 3; Sacramento, 8; and San Joaquin, 6. The newly populous mining districts of Sacramento and San Joaquin elected a number of other delegates who did not attend, primarily because they were unwilling to interrupt their search for gold.

The constitutional convention of 1849 was not mainly a convention of forty-niners, although they were now the bulk of the electorate. A large majority of the delegates at the convention had been in California more than 3 years—in contrast with Gwin "of San Francisco," who had been there only 3 months. About half the members were less than 35 years old. Eight were native Californians, of whom the most important were Mariano Guadalupe Vallejo of Sonoma and José Antonio Carrillo of Los Angeles. Of the Americans, a substantially larger number had come from northern states than from southern. The 14 lawyers formed the largest single occupational group. One delegate, B. F. Moore, from Florida and San Joaquin gave his occupation as "elegant leisure."

General Riley's proclamation had left open the question of whether the new government should be that of a state or of a territory, and this was one of the first questions the convention settled. On a motion introduced by Gwin, who could not become a senator from a territory, the vote was decisively for a state government, even though every southern California delegate who was present voted otherwise. The landowners of what would soon be the southern "cow counties" were well aware that the taxation of ranch land would be the main source of early state revenues, since the miners, though now a large majority of the citizens, generally owned no land on which to pay taxes. The administrative expenses of a territory, on the other hand, would have been paid by the federal government. Naturally the southern Californians would have preferred that alternative, but they were hopelessly outnumbered. Carrillo proposed a compromise by which the part of California north of San Luis Obispo would be a state and the southern part a territory, but the idea was not seriously considered.

To the surprise of many, the question of slavery was easily decided by a unanimous vote. However, the overwhelming sentiment for the exclusion of slavery from California was not based on humanitarian considerations. The question had come to a head in the mines when Col. Thomas Jefferson Green and a group of other Texans had appeared at Rose's Bar on the Yuba River with a number of black slaves. In Texas politics Green had been an unsuccessful rival of Sam Houston, who once maintained that Green had all the characteristics of a dog except fidelity. On the Yuba, Green and his fellow Texans appropriated a large number of claims and set their slaves to working them. The Argonauts, whether from the north or from the south, were sensitive on the matter of the dignity of hard manual labor, or rather of their particular form of it; they were outraged at the imputation that gold mining was work appropriate for black slaves. On Sunday, July 29, a mass meeting resolved "that no slave or Negro should own claims or even work in the mines," and served notice that the slaves must be out of the district by the next morning. Three days later the same miners elected William E. Shannon as their delegate to the convention at Monterey. It was Shannon who introduced the provision that "Neither slavery nor involuntary servitude, unless for the punishment of crimes, shall ever be tolerated in this state."

A few of the members of the convention held liberal views on racial matters, but the majority did not. This was clear in the debates on a proposal to exclude free blacks, as well as slaves, from California—debates that brought forth angry feelings. The proposal to exclude free blacks was introduced by M. M. McCarver from Kentucky and Sacramento. Many owners of slaves, he said, were planning to bring them to California and free them there on condition that they work in the mines as indentured servants. Moreover, McCarver asserted, free blacks were "idle in their habits, difficult to be governed by laws, thriftless and uneducated," and their presence in California would be an evil "greater than that of slavery itself." At one point the exclusion clause was actually adopted, and it would have remained in the document except for a growing fear that Congress might consider it in violation of the federal Constitution and therefore reject the California constitution as a whole. Blacks were citizens in some of the states in the north, and the federal Constitution declared that citizens of each state should be "entitled to all privileges and immunities of citizens in the several states." The overriding consideration was the fear of anything that might delay the full establishment of "a proper form of state government" and its full national recognition.

At this time the power to deny suffrage on the ground of race was still within the constitutional authority of a state. Here, the chief complication was that the former Mexican citizens of California had the right to become American citizens under the treaty of peace. Most Mexican Californians had some admixture of Indian ancestry, and Mexican law had not formally denied suffrage to Indians. In an uneasy compromise the California constitution extended the suffrage only to white male citizens, but authorized the state legislature by a two-thirds vote to extend it to Indians or the descendants of Indians. That the legislature would do this was most unlikely; the provision was mainly to prevent Congress from considering that the proposed constitution was in violation of the treaty with Mexico and thus find additional cause to delay California's admission as a state.

The problem that gave the convention most trouble was the question of the eastern boundary. Should this be based on the Sierra Nevada and the Colorado River, or should there be a much larger California extending several hundred miles farther east? Under Spain and Mexico, California had never had any definite eastern boundary at all, and each map maker had been forced to make a guess. On the maps in most common use at the time of the Mexican War, and notably on the one used in the official negotiation of the treaty, Mexican California had included not only the present area of Nevada but most of what are now Utah and Arizona as well. The convention's committee on boundaries proposed a Sierra–Colorado River line. Gwin, supported by Henry W. Halleck, secretary of state under Mason and Riley and delegate from Monterey, favored the much larger unit, with a boundary east of the Great Salt Lake. The convention, changing its mind repeatedly, almost broke up over this question.

A legend perpetuated by several historians, including Hubert Howe Bancroft and Josiah Royce, long maintained that the idea of an extreme eastern boundary was a plot to create a California so large that in a later division of the state the southern part would be opened to slavery. But in the convention at Monterey, the men from southern states more often voted for the smaller boundaries, and the men from northern states for the larger ones. As usual, the delegates were primarily concerned with the possible reactions in Washington, D.C. Some argued that Congress might reject the constitution and postpone the admission of California if its boundaries were too large. Others argued the opposite. Robert Semple quoted T. Butler King as saying, in his capacity as confidential agent of Present Taylor, "For God's sake leave us no territory to legislate upon in Congress." On the other hand, it was pointed out that the greater area was too large to be fairly represented in a state legislature, and that it would be particularly unfair and impractical to try to include the Mormons of the Salt Lake region when they were not represented in the convention. They had, in fact, already held a convention of their own in March 1849 and formulated a provisional constitution for a "State of Deseret."

In the end the decision was for the present boundaries of California: on the north, the 42d parallel; on the east, the 120th meridian southward to its juncture with the 39th parallel (a point in Lake Tahoe); thence in a straight southeasterly line to the intersection of the 35th parallel and the Colorado River; then down the middle of the channel of that river to the Mexican border, at the point where the Gila flows into the Colorado.

California was the first American state to include in its constitution a provision for the separate property of married women. All property of the wife, owned by her before marriage or acquired afterward by gift or otherwise, should remain her property. Such had been the law in Mexican California, and the Americans were under some obligation to preserve it—but an argument offered by Halleck was probably more effective. He advised all his fellow bachelors to vote for this section because it would attract not only prospective wives, but *wealthy* prospective wives, to California. In vain did some of the married delegates protest that nature had made men the protectors of women and that the constitution should not tamper with this relationship.

For public education, California made the usual provisions of a frontier state. That is, it announced its acceptance of the land grants that the federal government customarily made to new states for the support of public schools and for a "seminary of learning," or university. Robert Semple, president of the convention, exuberantly asked his colleagues: "Why should we send our sons to Europe to finish their education? If we have the means here we can procure the necessary talent; we can bring the President of Oxford University here by offering a sufficient salary." But even if Oxford had had an official with the title of president, the University of California could not easily have attracted him, even 20 years later when that institution was actually opened. Until the twentieth century it would remain small and isolated.

Some other uninformed statements were also made in the convention, as when a delegate objected to the phrase "a jury of his peers" on the ground that there was no house of peers in democratic America. But in general the convention did a fairly creditable job under difficult circumstances. It is true that not much of the constitution of 1849 was original. A majority of its provisions were taken from the constitution of Iowa, of which Gwin had arranged to have copies printed for the use of every delegate. Much of the rest of it came from the constitution of New York.

The design accepted for the state seal, on the other hand, was quite original and distinctive, if somewhat cluttered. Minerva, the Roman goddess of political wisdom and of handicrafts and the guardian of cities, appears in the foreground. At her feet crouches a grizzly bear feeding on bunches of grapes. A miner works with rocker and bowl, ships ply the Sacramento River, and the snowy peaks of the Sierra Nevada are seen in the distance. The Greek motto "Eureka" and 31 stars, the last one for the new state of California, are at the top of the design.

One point of dissension was raised: General Vallejo objected to the bear. It reminded him of the indignities he had suffered in the Bear Flag Revolt, and he proposed that it be removed from the seal unless it were shown as secured by a lasso in the hands of a *vaquero*. In the end he accepted the assurances of Anglo-American delegates that this particular bear signified no offense to the native Californians.

Another provision of the constitution forbade dueling. Yet Gwin, one of the leading advocates of this provision, would fight a duel himself in 1853, and a few years later another United States senator from California would be killed in one.

THE FIRST LEGISLATURE

A month after the convention adjourned, the first state officials were elected on November 13, 1849, the same day on which the constitution was ratified by a light vote, 12,061 in favor and 811 against. Peter H. Burnett was elected governor, and John McDougal lieutenant governor. On December 15 the legislature began to assemble at the first state capital, San José. In joint session of the two houses, it elected Frémont and Gwin as United States senators; Frémont had the larger number of votes, but a drawing by lot gave him the short term, ending March 3, 1851, while Gwin drew the term extending 4 years longer.

The permanent location of the state capital was left open to future bids from rival towns, in order to ensure that land and buildings would be provided without cost to the state government. The fact that California had not yet been admitted to the Union made the prospects of obtaining state funds uncertain, and because the first legislature failed to establish a permanent location, the capital was hawked about in a most undignified manner. Within 5 years the seat of government would be moved from San José to Vallejo, back to San José, back to Vallejo, to Sacramento, back to Vallejo, to Benicia, and at last, in 1854, permanently to Sacramento.

The first state legislature of California, though not a very distinguished body, did not entirely deserve the name that it acquired, "the legislature of a thousand drinks." The appellation seems to be grown out of a phrase repeatedly used by Thomas Jefferson Green. That irrepressible political adventurer from Texas, unabashed when the miners excluded him and his slaves from the Yuba diggings, had secured election as state senator from Sacramento. Moreover, he became chairman of the senate finance committee and was seeking election to one of the four new major-generalcies of the state militia. A number of the candidates for various offices to be filled by the legislature maintained bars from which they dispensed hospitality to the members in the hope of receiving their votes in return. At the end of each day's session, at least until the one that elected him as a militia commander, Green loudly invited the legislators to have "a thousand drinks" at his expense; journalists could not resist the temptation to apply the phrase as a description of the legislature generally.

THE COMPROMISE OF 1850 AND THE ADMISSION OF CALIFORNIA TO THE UNION

Congress nearly rejected the new government of California. The new state's admission would upset the equal balance in the number of free and slave states and in the number of their United States senators, a balance that had long given the south a veto against federal laws inimical to its "peculiar institution." In the great debates in the national capital, southern senators demanded an extension of the Missouri Compromise line of 36°30′ to the Pacific coast. This line would have bisected California just south of Monterey, and the portion of the south of it would have been organized as a territory open to slavery. The "great compromise" proposed, instead, that California be admitted as a free state, as its people desired, but that the territories of Utah and New Mexico be organized without the ban of the Wilmot Proviso against slavery. Daniel Webster, in his famous speech in the Senate on March 7, argued for this solution and tried to allay the protest of northern abolitionists and opponents of the expansion of slavery. Slavery, he said, had been perpetuated mainly for its usefulness in the production of cotton. Nature itself had excluded slavery from California and New Mexico by making their lands so arid that cotton could never be grown there, "and I would not take pains uselessly to reaffirm an ordinance of nature nor to re-enact the will of God." Webster could hardly have foreseen that with the help of irrigation California would one day produce more cotton than any other state but Texas.

At last, when the south had been further mollified by a stringent new law regulating the return of slaves who had escaped into northern states, the "omnibus" provisions of the great compromise were approved. The President signed the bill for the admission of California on September 9, 1850. The news reached San Francisco on October 18 and was celebrated with colorful parades, but the new state government had already been operating for nearly a year, exactly as if it had been authorized by Congress. Californians were showing a strong disposition to take things into their own hands.

THE FEUD BETWEEN BRODERICK AND GWIN

Most Californians of the 1850s were too busy searching for sudden private wealth to take a responsible interest in public affairs. Except for outbursts of privately organized "vigilance," they tended to leave the public business to a class of politicians who were themselves a rather peculiarly selected group of entrepreneurs. Theodore H. Hittell estimated that a tenth of the forty-niners were politicans who had failed in "the States." A large majority of these were Democrats, unemployed because of the Whig triumph in the election of the war hero General Zachary Taylor in 1848. This, coupled with the fact that the Whig party would soon be destroyed by its north-south split over slavery, ensured the Democratic domination of California politics until the coming of the Civil War. Under the constitution of 1849, elections of governors and other state officials were held every 2 years, in the odd-numbered years. The Democrats won virtually every important election in California in the 1850s except the state elections of 1855, which they lost to the Know-Nothings largely because of the bitter rivalry between the two main Democratic leaders—one of the most sensationally destructive rivalries in American political history.

Apart from the Democratic label, the chief resemblance between David C. Broderick of Tammany Hall and William M. Gwin of Tennessee was that both came to California in 1849 with the announced intention of being elected to the United States Senate. Broderick, who was only 29 at the time of his arrival at San Francisco, had received very little formal education. Gwin, 15 years older, had the advantages of formal training in both law and medicine and also of years of acquaintance with several of the country's leading political figures. Gwin was cool, dignified, and gracious, while Broderick was hotheaded, humorless, stubborn, and domineering.

The son of an immigrant Irish stonemason, Broderick had been a saloon-keeper in New York, a ward boss for Tammany Hall, and an unsuccessful candidate for Congress. Once in San Francisco, Broderick formed the nucleus of a Democratic political machine on the Tammany model with special attention to the use of volunteer fire-fighting companies as political clubs. Broderick also began the development of a personal fortune by joining a partnership in a private mint and by speculating in San Francisco waterfront lots; these speculations were greatly facilitated by the influence he acquired over city and state legislation. He became the first major political boss of San Francisco and soon gained control of the Democratic party machinery throughout the state.

Broderick entered the state senate in 1850 and the next year was elected its presiding officer. By forming an alliance with John Bigler, the speaker of the assembly, and by securing Bigler's election as governor in 1851 and again in 1853, Broderick gained control of the state patronage. He then felt ready to try to replace Gwin in the United States Senate. This, however, was a most formidable undertaking. California Democrats of southern origin, ridiculed by their opponents as the "Chivalry" or "Shiv" faction, almost unanimously preferred Gwin to Broderick, while by no means could all of Broderick's "Northern" or "Tammany" wing of the party be depended upon to support him against Gwin. As senior United States senator, Gwin controlled the federal patronage. Moreover, because California was still an isolated frontier state, it regarded its own interests as far more important than any national issues, and Gwin did much for California in securing federal legislation in its favor. As chairman of the Senate Committee on Naval Affairs, Gwin had introduced the bill to create the navy yard at Mare Island. Another of his bills provided for the San Francisco branch of the federal mint—an enormous improvement over Broderick's private mint.

In 1854 Broderick conceived the daring but unsuccessful scheme of trying to compel the state legislature of that year to elect him as Gwin's successor, even though the election would not normally have been held until a year later. In the legislative session of 1855, a deadlock between Gwin and Broderick prevented the election of either, or of anyone else. Consequently one of the United States senatorships remained vacant for 2 years, and the California Democrats were so bitterly divided that the pseudo-patriotic, nativist, self-styled "American" party, otherwise known as the Know-Nothings, gained control of the state government.

The Know-Nothing Order, nationally consolidated in 1852 out of several secret bodies, was first organized in California in May 1854. It took its name from the fact that originally it required its members to answer all questions by saying that they knew nothing about it, but it soon came partially into the open as a political movement and in the middle 1850s elected governors and legislatures in several states. The Whig party died in 1854, and the Republican party, born in the same year, was not yet strong enough to replace the Whigs. The Know-Nothing movement seemed, for a time, to offer an escape from the frightening national divisions over the slavery issue by promising to unite Americans against foreigners. As a national organization it was hostile to Roman Catholics because it assumed them to be under allegiance to a foreign power. In California, however, the nativist American movement was much influenced by the local hostility to foreign miners; in particular, racial antipathies were more important than religious or nationalistic ones, and there was much denunciation of the Chinese, while anti-Catholicism was soft-pedaled. In California, as elsewhere, the identification of candidates with the Know-Nothing party was almost entirely opportunistic. Under J. Neely Johnson, elected governor on the Know-Nothing ticket in 1855, the party offered no serious program of state legislation, nativist or otherwise.

The ambition of Broderick for a United States senatorship grew steadily more obsessive through repeated frustrations. At last, in 1857, he achieved his goal. Both of the Senate seats were to be filled, Gwin's having been vacant for 2 years. By the unscrupulous use of every trick which his fertile imagination could conceive, Broderick induced the legislature to elect him to the full 6-year term. Broderick forced Gwin to be content with the 4-year senatorial term, and under the threat of denying him even that, he compelled Gwin to write a letter promising to make no recommendations for the federal patronage. When President Buchanan learned what Broderick had done, he strongly disapproved of it and appointed followers of Gwin to the positions in the customs house, the branch mint, and the Indian agencies in California, and gave none of these appointments to Broderick's supporters.

Broderick was furious. In his one important speech in the United States Senate, and in many speeches after his return to California, he denounced Buchanan and Gwin in terms of the most violent personal vituperation. He did this, he said, because he was opposed to Buchanan's policy of encouraging the formation of a proslavery government in the territory of Kansas and because he had discovered that the Buchanan administration was corrupt. The depth and genuineness of Broderick's convictions on any matter of principle, however, must be very seriously questioned. The extent to which he was willing to injure his party and his friends in order to gratify his personal hatreds became so obvious that it shocked and alienated a number of his former supporters.

In the state elections of 1859 the Gwin group, now known as the Lecompton Democrats because they favored the admission of Kansas to statehood under the proslavery Lecompton constitution, won a sweeping victory over the Broderick men, who had to divide the anti-Lecompton vote with the Republicans. At this time the growth of the Republican party in California was impeded by the charge that it was friendly to the Negro, although its campaign orators denied this charge and sought to prove that the epithet of "Black Republicans" was undeserved. Leland Stanford, the unsuccessful Republican candidate for governor in 1859, said, in accepting the nomination, that his party stood for "the cause of the white man—the cause of free labor."

During the campaign, Chief Justice David S. Terry, a candidate for renomination to the state supreme court, made a speech in which he aligned himself with the Lecompton Democrats—hardly surprising in view of his background and his strongly prosouthern opinions. Broderick, while at breakfast in a hotel dining room in San Francisco, read a newspaper account of Terry's speech and was overheard in an outburst of angry denunciation. Whereas he had believed Terry to be the only honest member of the supreme court, it was now clear that the "d——d miserable wretch" was as corrupt as the other members. Terry waited for an apology until the end of the campaign. He had failed to win renomination, and only a few weeks remained in his term. On election day he resigned from the supreme court and shortly afterward challenged Broderick to a duel. This they fought on September 13, 1859, in a ravine near the ocean, just across the line in San Mateo County. Broderick nervously pulled the trigger of his pistol too soon, and his bullet went wild, but Terry's shot struck his opponent in the breast.

Admirers of Broderick came to believe that his dying words were: "They have killed me because I was opposed to a corrupt administration and the extension of slavery." Whether Broderick made this particular statement is doubtful, and in any case it was not an accurate description of the cause of the duel; however, the popular orator Edward D. Baker quoted it in a funeral eulogy and thus launched a myth that ultimately transformed Broderick into a kind of Pacific coast Lincoln.

MOVEMENTS FOR STATE DIVISION

The early historians who believed that Broderick's opposition to the territorial expansion of slavery, rather than his desire for political power, was his most significant motive were probably committing an error of emphasis. The same historians tended to see a proslavery conspiracy in the demands of southern California for separation from the rest of the state during the 1850s. This was simply and completely an error of fact, like the notion that the proposal for larger state boundaries in the constitutional convention of 1849 was a proslavery plot. It was true that the southern counties of California repeatedly sought permission to secede from the northern ones, but the slavery question did not have anything to do with these efforts except that many imagined that it did. The real cause of the movement was the grievance of southern California against too much taxation and too little representation.

The fears expressed by the southern California delegates in the convention of 1849, to the effect that their part of the state would have to pay an unfair share of taxes, proved to have been extremely well-founded. In 1852 Governor McDougal conceded that the 6 cow counties of southern California, with a population of 6000, paid $42,000 in property taxes, while the 12 mining counties, with a population of nearly 120,000, paid only $21,000. A state law exempted from taxation all mining claims on "United States lands," where the great majority of the claims were located. This was one of the innumerable statutes of the 1850s that conferred special favors on the mining interests. The transient population of the mining areas was counted in apportioning legislative districts, but 9 out of 10 miners neglected to pay their poll taxes.

Gradually the justice of southern California's grievance became recognized throughout the state, and in 1859 the legislature approved a plan introduced by Assemblyman Andrés Pico. This provided that the part of California south of 35°45′ (the northern boundary of San Luis Obispo County) should become the territory of Colorado. The voters of that region also approved the plan, but coming as it did on the eve of the Civil War, it had no chance of passage in the national capital. Most members of Congress, ignorant of affairs on the remote Pacific coast, could not be dissuaded from the belief that the measure was another dangerous aggravation of the slavery issue.

CALIFORNIA AND THE CIVIL WAR

The amount of pro-Confederate sentiment in California was grossly exaggerated during the war—by those who felt and cherished it, by those who feared it, and by those who for their own political and personal reasons wished to make it appear greater than it was. Most histories have reflected the contemporary exaggeration. Actually, less than 7 percent of the population of California in 1860 had come from the seceded states. There were many from the north who remained lukewarm in their support of the dreadful and distant conflict, and there were many from both the north and the south who detested it as fratricidal slaughter. But once the war had begun, there was never any genuine danger that California would desert the Union cause. Pro-Confederate opinion and activities were more colorful than significant.

Disloyal conspiracies did exist in California, but they were on a small scale. There were clandestine pro-Confederate societies like Knights of the Golden Circle, the Knights of the Columbian Star, and the Committee of Thirty, but they had only a fraction of the membership that wild rumor attributed to them. There were various dreams of seizing federal arsenals and gold shipments, and there was one romantic but futile attempt to put a conspiracy into actual operation. A group including Asbury Harpending, a young firebrand from Kentucky who had made a fortune in the California gold mines, secretly armed the small schooner *Chapman* at San Francisco in the hope of capturing a Pacific Mail steamer to use as a privateer under a Confederate letter of marque. Federal authorities knew of the plot almost from its beginning, and they seized the *Chapman* as she was weighing anchor.

The elections and the trends in party politics gave ample evidence that California was safe for the Union. In the state campaigns of 1861 the Republicans and the Union Democrats repudiated the right of secession and pledged the support of California for the war, and their candidates, running on these strongly Unionist platforms, polled together more than two-thirds of the votes. The Breckinridge Democrats favored the preservation of the Union on a basis of compromise with the southern states and opposed the policy of coercing them. In the previous year this same Democratic split had given the California electoral votes to Lincoln by only a very narrow plurality over the two Democratic candidates, Senators Douglas of Illinois and Breckinridge of Kentucky. In the California elections of 1861 the continuing Democratic schism enabled the Republicans to elect their first governor, Leland Stanford, by a substantial plurality. By 1864, although the Democrats were reunited in support of the Union, the Republicans had been very successful in branding all Democrats as disloyal, and consequently a large majority of Californians voted for the reelection of Lincoln. The Republicans called themselves the Union party from 1863 to 1867.

Since it was never necessary for anyone to "save California for the Union," it is absurd to say that anyone did; however, this honor has been variously claimed for Rev. Thomas Starr King, Col. Edward D. Baker, Governor Stanford, and others. King was a much beloved Unitarian minister, called to San Francisco from Boston in 1860. He was a captivating orator, and in several lecture tours he spoke for the Union and particularly for contributions to the work of the Sanitary Commission, the "Red Cross of the Civil War." Partly as a result of his efforts, California contributed more than a fourth of the amount that the commission received in the entire country. His death from diphtheria in 1864 was officially mourned throughout the state.

Colonel Baker was a close personal friend of Abraham Lincoln, whom he had first known when they were young lawyers in Springfield, Illinois. In the late 1850s Baker was one of the leading organizers of the Republican party in California. In 1860 the Republicans of the new state of Oregon invited him to come there as their leader and in the fall elected him United States senator. He had the honor of introducing Lincoln on the occasion of his inaugural address in 1861, and he became the President's chief adviser on matters concerning the Pacific coast. Impulsively he accepted the command of a regiment of Pennsylvania volunteers made up in part of men who had returned to Pennsylvania from California or Oregon. He was killed while leading his regiment at Ball's Bluff in October 1861.

California's military participation in the Civil War was very limited. The federal government did not favor the use of California volunteers in the main theaters of the war because their transportation was too expensive, and the draft was never enforced in California for the same reason. General Don Andrés Pico, victor of San Pasqual and signer of the Treaty of Cahuenga with Frémont, was deeply hurt by the rejection of his offer to raise a regiment of native Californian cavalry. About 500 young Californians, including several native ones, offered their services to Massachusetts if that state would pay the cost of their organization and transportation. It did so, and the "California Battalion," as part of the 2d Massachusetts Cavalry, took part in more than 50 engagements, mainly in Virginia. About 16,000 volunteers enlisted in California during the war, but they were used mainly for local garrison duty, for guarding the overland mail routes, or for policing Indians in the northwest. A "California Column" was sent to New Mexico in 1862 to repel a Confederate invasion of the territory, but the enemy withdrew before a battle could be fought, and many members of the column left it to join a local mining rush.

SELECTED BIBLIOGRAPHY

Theodore Grivas, *Military Governments in California, 1846–1850* (1962) does much to dispel the confusion that has surrounded its subject. The official *Report of the Debates in the Convention of California, on the Formation of the State Constitution* (1950) was well-prepared by J. Ross Browne. Cardinal Goodwin, *The Establishment of State Government in California, 1846–1850* (1914) is still a basic work on this period. Also valuable are William H. Ellison, *A Self-Governing Dominion: California, 1849–1860* (1950); Woodrow J. Hansen, *The*

Search for Authority in California (1960); James A. B. Scherer, *Thirty-First Star* (1942); and William E. Franklin, "Peter H. Burnett and the Provisional Government Movement," *California Historical Society Quarterly*, XL (June 1961), pp. 123–136. Donald C. Biggs, *Conquer and Colonize: Stevenson's Regiment and California* (1977) is a thorough account which emphasizes the positive contributions of Stevenson's men. Important memoirs are Walter Colton, *Three Years in California* (1850); Samuel H. Willey, *The Transition Period of California* (1901); William H. Ellison (ed.), "Memoirs of Hon. William M. Gwin," *California Historical Society Quarterly*, XXI (1940), pp. 1–26, 157–184, 256–277, 344–367; and Charles A. Barker (ed.), *Memoirs of Elisha Oscar Crosby* (1945). Robert G. Cowan, *The Admission of the 31st State by the 31st Contress* (1962) is an annotated bibliography of the congressional speeches.

In spite of the liberal property-rights provision of the 1849 constitution, California women still were restricted in their civil rights. See however Robert L. Griswold, "Apart But Not Adrift: Wives, Divorce, and Independence in California, 1850–1890," *Pacific Historical Review*, XLIX (May 1980), pp. 265–284.

The party politics of the era may be traced in Winfield J. Davis, *History of Political Conventions in California, 1849–1892* (1893). Earl Pomeroy, "California, 1846–1860: Politics of a Representative Frontier State," *California Historical Society Quarterly*, XXXII (December 1953), pp. 291–302, is a valuable commentary. Gwin's version is in William H. Ellison (ed.), "Memoirs of Hon. William M. Gwin," *California Historical Society Quarterly*, XIX (March, June, September, and December 1940). James O'Meara, *Broderick and Gwin* (1881) is realistic and balanced. Bancroft, following the lead of E. D. Baker's funeral oration, made Broderick a hero and martyr. Lately Thomas, *Between Two Empires . . . William McKendree Gwin* (1969) and David A. Williams, *David C. Broderick: A Political Portrait* (1969) make a pair of biographies. See also A. Russell Buchanan, *David S. Terry . . ., Dueling Judge* (1956). On the American party, see Peyton Hurt, "The Rise and Fall of the 'Know Nothings' in California," *California Historical Society Quarterly*, IX (March and June 1930), pp. 16–49, 99–128. Gerald Stanley explains "Racism and the Early Republican Party: The 1856 Presidential Election in California," *Pacific Historical Review*, XLIII (May 1974), pp. 171–187.

The state division movement is well-covered in William H. Ellison, *A Self-Governing Dominion*, and the Pacific Republic idea in Joseph Ellison, *California and the Nation*. The latter also has a good chapter on "Loyalty and Disloyalty."

Politics before, during, and after the war are described in Theodore H. Hittell, *History of California*, volume IV (1898); George T. Clark, *Leland Stanford* (1931); and Norman E. Tutorow, *Leland Stanford, Man of Many Careers* (1970). See also Royce D. Delmatier, Clarence F. McIntosh, and Earl G. Waters (eds.), *The Rumble of California Politics, 1848–1970* (1970), chaps. 1, 2; H. Brett Melendy and Benjamin F. Gilbert, *The Governors of California* (1965); Gerald Stanley, "Slavery and the Origins of the Republican Party in California," *Southern California Quarterly*, LX (Spring 1978), pp. 1–16; and Stanley, "The Slavery Issue and Election in California, 1860," *Mid-America*, LXII (January 1980), pp. 35–46.

Benjamin F. Gilbert, "California and the Civil War, a Bibliographical Essay," *California Historical Society Quarterly*, XL (December 1961), pp. 289–307, is very useful. See also his "The Confederate Minority in California," *California Historical Society Quarterly*, XX (June 1941), pp. 154–170. On California contributions to the war effort, see Milton H. Shutes, *Lincoln and California* (1943); Russell M. Posner, "Thomas Starr King and the Mercy Million," *California Historical Society Quarterly*, XLIII (December 1964), pp. 291–308; Aurora Hunt, *The Army of the Pacific* (1951); and Oscar Lewis, *The War in the Far West* (1961).

CRIME AND PUNISHMENT

One of the most striking and significant evidences of the chronic social disorganization in post-gold rush California was the outbreak of a rash of "vigilance committees." Most historical treatments of these bodies have condoned their actions, and many have even glorified them. The present account takes a different view.

THE NATURE OF VIGILANTISM

Richard Henry Dana, in the chapter that he added to his *Two Years Before the Mast* after his return visit to California in 1859, described San Francisco as having been rescued from

> its season of heaven-defying crime, violence, and blood . . . and handed back to soberness, morality, and good government, by that peculiar invention of Anglo-Saxon Republican America, the solemn awe-inspring Vigilance Committee of the most grave and responsible citizens, the last resort of the thinking and the good, taken to only when vice, fraud, and ruffianism have entrenched themselves behind the forms of law, suffrage, and the ballot.

Several historians, writing in the same tone of defensive righteousness, have perpetuated the racist notion that vigilantism was one of the evidences of Anglo-Saxon superiority, a proof of American ingenuity in adapting self-government to the special conditions of the frontier.

The truth is, first, that vigilantism was not a superior institution and second, that there was nothing exclusively Anglo-Saxon about it, except perhaps the use of the rope instead of the bullet. *Vigilante* is a Spanish word meaning lookout or a guard, and the first "committee of vigilance" in California was not in San Francisco in 1851. Rather it was the one described in a manuscript called *"Vigilantes de Los Angeles, 1836,"* by that committee's president, Victor

Prudon, a naturalized Mexican of French birth. This *"junta defensora de la seguridad pública"* seized a man and a woman from the custody of the alcaldes and shot them for the murder of the woman's husband.

The true and great contributions of "Anglo-Saxon" jurisprudence have been on the side of the due process of law, while the methods of the vigilance committees were parodies of due process. Their methods were generally more organized and elaborate than those of mere lynch mobs, but the "committees" did not hold their "trials" in open court. They acted in anger and in haste. They did not consider motions for change of venue. Witnesses for the defendants were usually afraid to testify, or even to appear. The committees often resorted to hanging because they had no way of enforcing a sentence of long-term imprisonment. And there was no provision for appeal or for executive clemency.

Taking the law into one's own hands, particularly after regular courts had been established, was itself a criminal action. Yet, remarkably enough, the early American historians of California almost unanimously applauded it. Even the idealistic philosopher Josiah Royce, in spite of his personal detestation of violence and bullying, strongly praised "popular justice" as exercised by the vigilance committees of San Francisco, although at the same time he condemned lynching in the mines as barbarous and futile. Hubert Howe Bancroft indulged in the most elaborate defenses and rationalizations of "popular tribunals" on such grounds as the sacred right of revolution. He maintained that the vigilantes were "the people," and that the people (especially the self-appointed "best" people) were above all law. These apologistic viewpoints have too often gone unchallenged.

People who form lynch mobs and vigilance committees, like all other people, are themselves inwardly tortured by assorted feelings of guilt. Samuel Brannan, who did more than anyone else to instigate vigilantism in San Francisco, was building the first great California fortune on money that he had diverted from church property and tithes to his personal use and profit, a practice not far from the robbing of alms boxes. Apostate though he was, he was not unaffected by the knowledge that his former church regarded him as the supreme example of the corrupting influence of money on the human soul. Clearly, Brannan was subconsciously seeking freedom from his own guilt in arrogating to himself the punishment of others.

The emotion of guilt is essentially the fear of punishment. Gratification in inflicting pain, humiliation, and even death and destruction upon someone else results from the subconscious, irrational feeling that thereby one somehow achieves escape from punishment, or even assures one's own survival. In varying degrees and circumstances the latent existence of this sadistic pattern is universal among human beings. Because it is the least admirable of human traits, and also because rational recognition of it defeats its hidden irrational purpose, people resort to extreme sanctimoniousness in order to disguise it, in their own minds most of all. This element accounts for the strange air of righteous solemnity often noted in a number of the public ceremonies sponsored by the San Francisco committees of vigilance. The rank and file of these organizations included a substantial contingent of the worst and most guilty, who joined for the conscious purpose of saving themselves from hanging. But the leadership included some of the "best" men, who joined for more subtle and obscure but not entirely different reasons. Vigilantism was a manifestation of moral self-delusion and righteous sadism.

EARLY LYNCHING IN THE MINES

During the summer and fall of 1848 there was very little crime in the mining camps because the great wave of gold seekers, with its large criminal element, had not yet arrived. Late in the fall, near the Calaveras River, a sailor who had deserted his ship was flogged, and his ears were cropped for a robbery. The miners who heard of the episode generally asserted that it had had a good effect on the conditions of public safety. At Sutter's Fort in December a merchant named C. E. Pickett killed a man in self-defense. Brannan, who had himself been the defendant in one of the first jury trials in American California and who was a business competitor of Pickett's, insisted that he be tried for murder. The first and second alcaldes and the sheriff resigned rather than conduct a trial. Because no one else was willing to serve as either prosecutor or judge, Brannan served in both capacities, but the jury balked and the prisoner was acquitted.

The first of the gold-rush mob actions that resulted in hanging occurred in the middle of January 1849 in a mining camp only 9 miles from the site of the discovery at Coloma. Thus Dry Diggings gained the name of Hangtown, later to be changed again to Placerville. Of five men who were whipped for robbery, three were then hanged by a mob that also threatened to hang E. Gould Buffum for trying to oppose the proceedings.

THE "HOUNDS" IN SAN FRANCISCO

Congress left California almost literally lawless from 1846 to 1850. Within this vacuum there began to appear, in San Francisco, a form of organized lawlessness and terrorism. When Colonel Stevenson's regiment of New York Volunteers was disbanded, a group of its members led by Lt. Sam Roberts formed an organization called the Regulators, or more commonly, the Hounds, allegedly dedicated to maintaining public order, and especially devoted to hounding Spanish Americans and other "foreigners" out of California. Alcalde Leavenworth tried to use them as deputy policemen, but he could not control them. They held drunken parades and levied tribute, bullied merchants by day and looted foreign settlements by night. In the evening of July 15, 1849, they paraded to an attack upon Little Chile, a tent community at the foot of Telegraph Hill, where some of them murdered a mother and criminally assaulted her daughter.

The next morning Sam Brannan addressed a crowd from the roof of the

"Hounds" attacking Chileans. *(Courtesy of the Bancroft Library.)*

alcalde's little office on the Plaza. A counterorganization called the Law and Order party was formed and its members deputized, a charitable fund for the Chileans was collected, and by sunset Roberts and 18 other Hounds had been caught and imprisoned in a ship in the bay.

Nine men were more or less legally convicted of crimes, but the penalty was banishment, and this proved unenforceable. Many of the Hounds continued their depredations, though no longer openly. In such activities they were joined by some of the "Sydney Ducks," ex-convicts or escaped convicts from Australia. The Australian immigrants were thus given a bad name that most of them did not deserve.

THE SAN FRANCISCO COMMITTEE OF 1851

The beating and robbery of C. J. Jansen, a prominent merchant, in his shop in the heart of town on February 19, 1851, produced another outburst of popular excitement. Two Australians, Berdue and Windred, were arrested and mistakenly identified by Jansen as the men who had assaulted and robbed him. Berdue was wrongly believed to be James ("English Jim") Stuart, another Australian who had escaped from jail at Marysville while awaiting trial for the murder of a sheriff. A mob incited by Brannan was preparing to seize and hang the two prisoners without a trial when a young merchant named William Tell Coleman managed to catch the ear of the crowd and to persuade it to organize a "people's court." This procedure, with Coleman acting as prosecutor, resulted in a hung jury. The two men were then returned to the jurisdiction of the regular authorities.

On May 4, 1851, there occurred the fifth and greatest in a series of fires that had repeatedly devastated the city. The fact that this fifth fire occurred on the anniversary of the second one intensified the growing suspicion that all the fires were incendiary, set by Hounds and Sydney Ducks in revenge and defiance and to facilitate looting. Loot was found hidden in the "Sydney Town" district and criminals were thought to be emboldened by the failure to hang the supposed robbers of Jansen. A volunteer night patrol was organized, and on Sunday, June 8, the *Alta California* published a proposal for a "committee of safety" or "committee of vigilance." That afternoon a meeting in Sam Brannan's office determined to call a larger meeting of other responsible citizens, and on June 9, in Brannan's building, that meeting adopted a constitution for the first San Francisco "Committee of Vigilance."

The very next evening, taps on a fire bell summoned the committee to pass judgment on John Jenkins, who had been caught stealing a small safe and was dragged to the committee's headquarters instead of the police station. Jenkins was insolent and threatened that his friends were organizing to rescue him and destroy the committee. The decisive moment came when William A. Howard, a sea captain, cried, "Gentlemen, as I understand it, we came here to

The execution of John Jenkins. *(Courtesy of the Bancroft Library.)*

hang somebody." Coleman opposed hanging a man at night and suggested waiting until dawn, when Jenkins would "rise with the sun." But Brannan secured the approval of the crowd in the Plaza, and there, from a beam at the south end of the "Old Adobe," Jenkins was hanged by moonlight. Thus the committee began its work by hanging the first criminal it apprehended, within a few hours after his crime, and for a rather petty robbery rather than a murder. The death penalty for robbery and grand larceny had been adopted by the California Legislature early in 1851 and remained in effect until 1856. But hanging a person for stealing meant that there was no greater penalty for murder, and over the state as a whole it had the net effect of greatly increasing the number of murders committed by robbers to prevent identification or pursuit.

A coroner's inquest into the death of Jenkins identified nine vigilantes as parties to it, but the committee made their arrest impractical by releasing the names of all its members. In July the committee chanced to apprehend the real James Stuart, and thus secured the exoneration of the innocent Berdue, who was then awaiting execution by action of the legally constituted courts. This episode, though the result of mere accident, won the committee many admirers whom it would not otherwise have gained. After securing a highly picaresque confession from Stuart, the committee hanged him, and in August it also hanged two other Sydney Ducks, McKenzie and Whittaker, whom Stuart's confessions had implicated in various robberies.

In the meantime the executive committee had deposed Sam Brannan as its president and replaced him with the less impulsive and less erratic Stephen Payran. The roster shows that along with Brannan the founders and early members of the vigilance committee of 1851 were predominantly commission merchants and sea captains—two groups who disliked government, courts, lawyers, and politicians as forces that threatened interference with their own freedom of action. It was a peculiar base on which to rest a claim that the leading vigilantes were "the best citizens" of the community, but this claim was made, and has been periodically repeated ever since. It is significant that no lawyers whatever were members of the Committee of Vigilance. The committee would not have welcomed their membership, even had they wished to join it.

Before its extrajudicial activities ended in September, the vigilance committee of 1851 had made nearly 90 arrests. Besides its four hangings, it had whipped 1 man, sentenced 28 to deportation, remanded 15 to the authorities for trial, and released 41.

STATEWIDE VIGILANCE

San Francisco's example inspired the formation of several local vigilance committees in other towns and a further increase of less formal lynching in the mining communities. Of dozens of such cases, perhaps the most infamous was the hanging of the Mexican woman Juanita by a mob of miners at Downieville on July 5, 1851. They had gathered to hear a Fourth of July oration by United States Senator John B. Weller and afterward had celebrated far into the night. In the early hours of the morning Juanita killed one of them with a knife. The friends of her victim, one Joseph Cannon, asserted the theory that he had not intended to harm her and that his purpose in entering her cabin was only to apologize to her for having broken her door down, which had happened only because he was intoxicated.

Within a few hours Juanita was brought to "trial" by what one observer, David P. Barstow, called "the hungriest, craziest, wildest mob that ever I saw anywhere." After saying that she would defend herself again in the same way under the same circumstances, Juanita adjusted her own noose and stepped from the improvised scaffold. Barstow was certain that "the hanging of the woman was murder. No jury in the world, on any principle of self-defense or protection of life and property, would ever have convicted her."

At Napa in May of 1851 a group of citizens lynched Hamilton McCauley, largely as a matter of local pride and as an incident in their political feud with neighboring Benicia. Napa was a town of northerners, Benicia a town of southern Chivalry Democrats. McCauley, of Benicia, had tried to chastise a freed black man on the street in Napa. The black not only struck back but beat McCauley severely in a fight that followed. The local justice of the peace taunted McCauley, who stabbed him to death. For this crime McCauley was legally sentenced to execution. His friends persuaded Governor John McDougal to commute the sentence to life imprisonment, but residents of Napa hanged the prisoner before the sheriff could arrive from Benicia to deliver the commutation paper.

In the riotous cow town of Los Angeles in the 1850s there were more executions, both legal and extralegal, than in the much larger city of San Francisco. It was sometimes difficult to distinguish the legal executions from the lynchings in Los Angeles because of the tendency of the constituted authorities to authorize vigilantism. In 1851, the mayor and the city council created a vigilance committee by formal action. Among those it hanged were three men charged with the murder of Major General J. H. Bean of the California militia. One of the men hanged was later proved innocent. In 1854, Mayor Stephen C. Foster dispersed a mob bent on lynching the gambler and killer Dave Brown by promising that if the regular authorities did not succeed in convicting and executing him, he would resign as mayor and join the vigilantes. When Brown's lawyers secured a stay of execution, Mayor Foster kept his promise, directed the lynching, and resumed his office after it was over.

The most famous case in the southern mines occurred at Columbia on October 10, 1855. This was the hanging of John S. Barclay for killing an intoxicated man who had laid violent hands on Barclay's wife. There was a mock trial in which only the prosecutor, a local political idol who had just been elected to the state senate, was permitted to speak at any length. The drunken viciousness of the mob, the extreme courage of the sheriff in risking his life to try to take the prisoner away from it, and the fact that by that time the legal courts in the area were well-organized produced some local reaction against lynching in general.

THE SAN FRANCISCO COMMITTEE OF 1856

The revival of the vigilance committee in San Francisco in 1856 was in part a result of the subconscious and irrational motivations that were characteristic of vigilante behavior in general. Interacting with these psychological aspects, however, were economic, political, and even ethnic and religious factors. The committee of 1856 was dominated by the city's leading merchants, who wished to bring about great reductions in their taxes by discrediting the city government as corrupt and wasteful and by taking control of it themselves. The city had been governed mainly by the Democratic organization headed by David C. Broderick. Many of Broderick's followers were Irish Catholics, and many of them were particular objects of vigilante hostility.

The immediate cause of the revival of the vigilance movement was the shooting of James King of William, the anti-Catholic editor of the *Daily Evening Bulletin,* by the politician James P. Casey, on May 14, 1856. James King had added the name of William, his father, to distinguish him from other James Kings in the Dictrict of Columbia, where he was born. He came to San Francisco in 1848, and in the early 1850s became wealthy as a banker. The sudden loss of his fortune, however, embittered him, and he became a newspaper editor in order to attack the various men upon whom he blamed his own troubles and those of the city. His editorship of the *Bulletin* was a sort of journalistic vigilantism. The pen, he felt, could be mightier than the rope or the whip; the printing press, a mightier punisher of evil than the gallows. He denounced the Tammany-style political machine of David C. Broderick and accused him of having imported James P. Casey from New York City as an expert ballot-box stuffer. Casey was elected a county supervisor in an election widely denounced as corrupt. King published in the *Bulletin* the fact that Casey had served a term in the New York state penitentiary at Sing Sing.

A great many people had come from the older parts of the country to escape their pasts, so many that it was often considered a necessary convention in California that a person's past was nobody's business. A popular song of the period was

> Oh, what was your name in the States?
> Was it Thompson or Johnson or Bates?
> Did you murder your wife and flee for your life?
> Oh, what was your name in the States?

King's exposure of his prison record deeply disturbed Casey and made him almost incoherent. He threatened King in the *Bulletin* office and shot him on the street an hour later.

The shooting of King became interrelated in the public mind with the earlier killing of General William H. Richardson by the gambler Charles Cora. Richardson, then serving as United States marshal, had become extremely angry when Cora and his mistress, the wealthy Arabella Ryan, keeper of a notorious house of prostitution, attracted attention by sitting directly behind Richardson and his wife in a box at the opeining of a new theater. The next evening Richardson, clearly intoxicated, accosted Cora on the street and drew a derringer pistol. Cora drew his own derringer and fired a fatal shot. Arabella Ryan, who called herself Belle Cora, then secured the services of Colonel Edward D. Baker, and in the subsequent trial Baker's forceful plea on the ground of self-defense led to a hung jury. Cora was in jail awaiting a second trial when the shooting of James King of William occurred.

Among the objects of King's journalistic crusades had been gambling houses and prostitution, which he alleged to have been protected by politicians and the police. Many San Francisco women, including particularly the wives of several vigilante leaders, now added their voices to those that were demanding strong measures.

On the evening of the day that King was shot, a group of former members of the vigilance committee of 1851 determined to reactivate the movement, under the leadership of William Tell Coleman, now the most respected of the group. Coleman was a man of handsome and commanding appearance who had come to Sacramento in 1849 at the age of 25. The early lynchings in the region had impressed him as demonstrations of the great value of "prompt and summary punishment." He was consistently successful in business from his first transaction, in which he found one merchant who promised to buy as many bottles of a certain patent medicine as he could deliver at $5 a bottle, and another who sold him nearly 300 bottles at $3 each. Since then, William T. Coleman & Company, with headquarters in San Francisco, had become one of the country's leading mercantile firms.

The committee began to collect arms and to form a military unit. On the other hand, a number of prominent citizens formed the Law and Order party, denouncing the vigilantes and adopting the name of the organization of 1849, which had taken all its actions against the Hounds in full cooperation with the legal authorities. Among the Law and Order leaders were Mayor Van Ness, Sheriff Scannell, and General William Tecumseh Sherman, whom the governor of the state had recently appointed commander of the San Francisco district of the California militia.

On May 16 Governor J. Neely Johnson came down from Sacramento to confer with Coleman. Few state executives have ever been more bitterly denounced than Johnson was for his role in these conferences and in the events that followed them. He was only 28 years old at the time—California in the 1850s was a young man's country—and he was in an extremely explosive situation. Having been swept into office only the year before, in the sudden and brief triumph of the American or Know-Nothing party in California, he was painfully inexperienced. In his discussion with Coleman he believed that he had secured a promise that the vigilantes would not attack the jail to seize Cora and Casey. Coleman later maintained that he had merely promised to give notice before moving to seize the two men and that a condition even of this promise was that the governor guarantee *"an immediate trial and instant execution"* by the public authorities. Four days after the shooting, 2500 armed vigilantes advanced on the county jail and removed Cora and Casey to the committee's headquarters. The sheriff's 150 deputies made no attempt to resist, and thus a self-appointed committee had virtually taken over the government of San Francisco at a time of almost hysterical public excitement.

Two days later, on the 20th, while Cora was being tried before the vigilance tribunal, word came that James King of William had died. The emotional effect of this announcement ensured the hanging not only of Casey but also of Cora, although Cora was condemned by a bare majority of the vigilante tribunal while Casey was condemned unanimously.

Both men were hanged with great public ceremony on the 22d, the day of King's funeral. Cora had just been quietly married to Arabella Ryan. He died with outward composure and without comment. Casey made a brief and excited speech, denying that he was guilty of murder.

The Law and Order leaders had hoped that the committee, having "hanged somebody," would now disband. Instead it made further arrests and strengthened the defenses of its headquarters building, known as Fort Gunnybags. A Law and Order committee urged Governor Johnson to call out the state militia to suppress insurrection. One leader of this Law and Order group was John McDougal, governor in 1851, whose popularity and reputation in

Published by the *NOISY CARRIER'S BOOK AND STATIONERY CO.*, 87 *Battery Street, San Francisco.*

Fort Gunnybags. From a contemporary letter sheet. *(Courtesy of the California Historical Society.)*

the state had been destroyed when he had issued proclamations criticizing the earlier Committee of Vigilance.

Before calling out the militia, Governor Johnson and General Sherman secured a promise of arms from General John E. Wool, commandant of the federal Army on the Pacific coast and of the federal arsenal at Benicia. Justice David S. Terry of the state supreme court issued a writ of habeas corpus for the release of Deputy Sheriff William Mulligan, keeper of the county jail, who was being held prisoner by the vigilance committee. The committee defied the writ. Sheriff Scannell telegraphed the governor that a large body of armed men was defying the authority of county and state government and asked for help from the militia. On June 2 Governor Johnson ordered General Sherman to call upon "such numbers" of the militia as he considered necessary, and 2 days later the governor proclaimed San Francisco to be in a state of insurrection.

At this point General Wool reneged on his promise of arms. Response to the call to militia duty had been sparse, and Sherman was unwilling to command men whom he could not arm. He resigned as militia commander and was succeeded by Volney E. Howard, a former attorney general of Texas.

Justice Terry, a close friend of Howard and like him a former Texan, now became the chief adviser of the Law and Order faction, taking time out from his regular judicial duties. He unearthed a statute requiring the federal government to furnish a certain allotment of arms to the state militia, and General Wool released 113 muskets. When this shipment was dispatched to San Francisco in a small schooner, the vigilantes intercepted it. On June 21, J. R. Maloney, one of the militiamen who had been in charge of the shipment, gave an account of the affair to a group of Law and Order men including Judge Terry. Vigilante policeman Sterling A. Hopkins, who had served as hangman in the execution of Cora and Casey, tried to arrest Maloney, obviously in order to prevent him from testifying against the vigilantes on a piracy charge. In the ensuing scuffle a vigilante accidentally fired a pistol, and Justice Terry stabbed Hopkins with a bowie knife. When Terry sought refuge in a militia armory, a large body of vigilantes forced their way into the building and arrested him. Shortly afterward they confiscated the last of the arms remaining in possession of militia units anywhere in the city.

As one of its members put it, the vigilance committee had organized to hunt coyotes, but in Supreme Court Justice Terry it had a grizzly bear by the tail. Nevertheless it conducted a trial, in which Terry brilliantly conducted his own defense. Fortunately, Hopkins did not die. Though Terry was "convicted" of assault with intent to kill, he was released on August 7 after a bitter disagreement among the vigilance leaders.

The next day the executive committee decided that although it would remain in existence, the vigilance committee as a whole should disband. It did so after a great parade of 6000 armed men on August 18. Fort Gunnybags was kept open for several months as a museum, and attracted large crowds. There, after the hangings of Cora and Casey, the alleged murderers Brace and Hetherington had also been tried and hanged; Francis Murray, alias "Yankee" Sullivan, ex-pugilist and accused ballot-box stuffer, had committed suicide in his cell; and 30 men had been sentenced to deportation with orders not to return to San Francisco on pain of death. It was claimed that several hundred other bad characters had left the city in fear of the vigilantes.

The San Francisco Committee of Vigilance of 1856 was, as Josiah Royce described it, "a Business Man's Revolution." It was an application of private enterprise to the administration of justice. The philosophy of the vigilante leadership clearly reflected a set of attitudes characteristic of most early California businesspeople and some later ones—their dislike and distrust of government and of public officeholders, their resentment of taxation, and their contempt for politicians as an inferior class. These feelings were peculiarly accentuated in a new community in which all business was highly speculative, and in which so many people—entrepreneurs and politicians alike—were hoping to make large fortunes quickly.

After the disbandment of the vigilance committee its leaders formed the People's party, which swept the city elections of November 1856 and won most of the city offices for the next 10 years. Its primary objective was drastic tax reduction; the leadership of both the vigilance committee and the People's party included many of the city's most chronic tax evaders, and their charges of city government extravagance in the period just before they took control were simply false. In 1855 city expenditures had actually been reduced to the point where the police and the teachers had gone unpaid for several months. Early in 1856 the state legislature's Consolidation Act had produced further economies by combining the city and county governments of San Francisco, after breaking off the southern part into the new county of San Mateo. In 1857, under the People's party administration, San Francisco taxes were further slashed, so extremely that several of the schools had to be closed and the city could not afford to buy hoses for the volunteer fire companies.

Study of the crime rate before and after the vigilance movement of 1856 does not support the claim of any actual reduction in crime after the vigilantes took over. The charges that the legally constituted courts had been corrupt were in general not true, so far as the judges were concerned, and the abuses of the jury system were mainly the result of the general evasion of jury duty by otherwise respectable citizens. As for vigilante jurisprudence, its record of violations of due process was appalling.

The leaders of the vigilance committees would have served California far better if they had confined their activities to legal methods and to genuine reforms. It is doubtful that they accomplished anything whatever of real value, and they left a vicious, dangerous, and persistent tradition of contempt for the normal processes of democratic government.

SELECTED BIBLIOGRAPHY

An account of the first formal organization of vigilantes in California (1836) is in Robert W. Blew, "Vigilantism in Los Angeles, 1835–1874," *Southern California Quarterly*, LIV (Spring 1972), pp. 11–30.

The tone of most historical treatments of the vigilantes was set by three important and influential accounts, all written about the same time. Charles H. Shinn, in his *Mining Camps, a Study in American Frontier Government* (1885), accepted very uncritically the reminiscences of the participants whom he interviewed. Josiah Royce, in *California, from the Conquest in 1846 to the Second Vigilance Committee in San Francisco, a Study of American Character* (1886; new edition, 1948), was more critical of the miners, but praised the San Francisco committees. Hubert Howe Bancroft, in *Popular Tribunals* (two volumes, 1887), defended some of the rural tribunals and was positively worshipful of the urban ones; his views reflected the feelings of most San Francisco businesspeople, of whom Bancroft was one.

Mary Floyd Williams edited the *Papers of the San Francisco Committee of Vigilance of 1851* (1919). Her *History of the San Francisco Committee of Vigilance of 1851* (1921) is scholarly in details but generally very admiring. George R. Stewart, *Committee of Vigilance, Revolution in San Francisco, 1851* (1964) is also sympathetic. The highly laudatory spirit of *"The Lion of the Vigilantes," William T. Coleman and the Life of Old San Francisco* (1939), by James A. B. Scherer, is well-suggested by its title, taken from Robert Louis Stevenson. Also generally favorable is Roger Olmsted, "San Francisco and the Vigilante Style," *The American West*, VII (January and March 1972).

Essential early accounts were by James O'Meara, William Tecumseh Sherman, and William T. Coleman, all reprinted in Doyce B. Nunis, Jr. (ed.), *The San Francisco Vigilance Committee of 1856; Three Views* (1971), with an excellent historical introduction and bibliographical essay.

Critical treatments of vigilantism are in Ethel May Tinneman, "The Opposition to the San Francisco Vigilance Committee in 1856," M.A. thesis, University of California, Berkeley (1941); William H. Ellison, *A Self-Governing Dominion, California, 1849–1860* (1950); A. Russell Buchanan, *David S. Terry of California, Dueling Judge* (1959); John W. Caughey, *Their Majesties, the Mob* (1960), its title taken from one of the letters of Dame Shirley; Richard Maxwell Brown, "Pivot of American Vigilantism: The San Francisco Vigilance Committee of 1856," in *Reflections of Western Historians* (1969), edited by John A. Carroll; and Roger W. Lotchin, *San Francisco, 1846–1856: From Hamlet to Modern City* (1974).

Peter R. Decker, *Fortunes and Failures: White-Collar Mobility in Nineteenth Century San Francisco* (1978) includes an analysis of merchant involvement in the vigilance movements.

LAND-TITLE TROUBLES

Among the circumstances that made for demoralization, lawlessness, and violence in early American California, one of the most important was the confused condition of the ownership of land. Not until 1851 did the United States government determine its general policy toward the confirmation of titles to the vast lands that had been granted under Mexico, and after the determination of the policy, many more years were required to secure actual approval of claims. In the meantime the titles remained in dispute, and the development of the state was held back accordingly.

PROBLEMS OF THE MEXICAN GRANTS

American laws required that land titles be defined exactly and clearly, and by American standards the Mexican system was incredibly lax and vague. In California, not even the relatively loose requirements of Mexican law had been effectively or consistently observed. Land had been abundant and of very little value, and Mexican-Californian officialdom was somewhat lackadaisical and frequently disrupted by sudden changes of personnel. The authorities failed to provide the grantees with adequate evidence of their titles or to keep adequate records in the archives. Maps, when there were any, were absurdly sketchy, for professional surveyors were seldom available. The whole of the Pomona Valley, for example, was breezily described as "the place being vacant which is known by the name of [Rancho] San José, distant some six leagues, more or less, from the Ex-Mission of San Gabriel, a map of which place we will lay before your Excellency as soon as possible." The frequent use of the expression "a little more or less" (*poco más ó menos*) after any measure of distance was typical of the Mexican grant system. There were several legal requirements, such as that a grant had to have been approved by the territorial assembly and to have been occupied; very seldom, however, had all of the requirements been fulfilled.

There were more than 500 ranchos in Alta California in 1846, but more than 800 claims were filed in the American courts, many of them covering portions of ranchos. The claims covered nearly all the valley lands of the coastal region as far north as the Russian River and a number of large tracts in the Sacramento and northern San Joaquin valleys.

The treaty of Guadalupe Hidalgo promised that "property of every kind" belonging to Mexicans in the ceded territories should be "inviolably respected," but American settlers generally believed that all the lands in California were now, or ought to be, United States public lands by right of conquest. Under the preemption system, made general by the act of 1841, Americans were accustomed to occupy tracts on the federal public lands before they were surveyed and opened to settlement, and then to be permitted to buy the land at the minimum price.

The American settlers of California could not believe that a few hundred Mexican grantees would be permitted to monopolize some 13 million acres of land, little of it visibly improved and much of it entirely unoccupied. Most of the claims did not represent lands that had been long in the possession of old

LAND GRANTS

in

CALIFORNIA

to 1846

The dark areas on the map show the grants that were later confirmed by the United States. From W. W. Robinson, *Land in California*, University of California Press, Berkeley, California, 1948.

California families as their homes. In fact a majority of the grants were dated within the last 5 years before the American conquest, and it was accurately suspected that some of those claimed to have been made under Governors Micheltorena and Pico had been signed by them after the forced expirations of their terms of office, and antedated. There were many multiple grants. The various claims of the Pico family totaled 532,000 acres, and those of the De la Guerra and Carrillo families more than 300,000 each. Moreover, large-scale speculation had begun. Thomas Larkin, for example, had purchased several claims totaling nearly 200,000 acres.

THE REPORTS OF HALLECK AND JONES

Governor Mason had instructed his secretary of state, Captain Henry W. Halleck (later General Halleck, Union chief of staff during the Civil War), to make a study of California land titles. In a report completed early in 1849, Halleck pointed out that most of the Mexican claims were imperfect and asserted that many of them were fraudulent. This report had the effect of encouraging the views of those who were known to themselves as "settlers" and less favorably described as "squatters." Their vigorous opinions produced several episodes of violence, of which the most tragic was the "squatter riot" at Sacramento in the summer of 1850.

The town was located on land granted to Sutter by Alvarado, a grant that would eventually be upheld. Several thousand settlers, refusing to recognize the validity of this title, had squatted on vacant lots owned by purchasers from Sutter. After sheriff's deputies began to destroy the squatter's houses and fences, there was a meeting to collect money for a legal defense fund. James McClatchy, later the founder of the city's leading journalistic family, told this meeting that "If the speculators want to fight, I am for giving them battle. . . . Let us put up all the fences pulled down and also put up [hang] all the men who pull them down." He was arrested for trying to carry out at least a part of his threat. On August 13, when an armed band moved to rescue McClatchy from the riverboat that served as a jail. Mayor Harden Bigelow gathered a crowd of citizens, and in a clash at 4th and J Streets the city assessor and three squatters were killed and the mayor was wounded. The next day another battle led to the death of Sheriff Joseph McKinney and several others on both sides.

In the meantime the secretary of the interior had appointed a brilliant young attorney, William Carey Jones, to make another investigation. Jones had married a sister of Jessie Benton Frémont, and the views of California land titles that he embodied in his report in March 1850 coincided with the opinions of his father-in-law, Senator Benton, and also with those of John C. Frémont, his brother-in-law and client, who had had the good fortune to purchase the only Mexican grant on which large amounts of gold were subsequently discovered. The Jones report maintained that the grants were mostly "perfect titles. . . ., and those which were not perfect—that is, which lack some formality, or some *evidence* of completeness, have the same *equity* as those which are perfect." Thus Jones recommended a very liberal policy toward the Mexican grants. Naturally the claimants praised this report and the settlers denounced it.

THE ACT OF 1851 AND THE LAND COMMISSION

The act that determined the policy of the United States toward the land claims in California was introduced by Senator William M. Gwin, chief political spokesman for the American settlers. His bill provided for the appointment by the President of a board of three commissioners. This board was to decide the validity of all claims to land under Mexican titles. All the lands of the rejected claims were to be regarded as public lands. Both the claimant and the United States had the right of appeal to the federal district court and then to the United States Supreme Court. Critics of this plan argued that it would have the effect of confiscating the lands of the grantees in California, and thus of violating the treaty with Mexico; every title would be treated as a fraud against the United States until its holder had established it in three different courts, one of them the Supreme Court, located 3000 miles away.

The land commission held its hearings from January 1852 to March 1856. All its sessions were held in San Francisco except for one brief term at Los Angeles. Of the more than 800 cases presented to it, all but a few were appealed to the district court, and 99 were appealed to the Supreme Court. Ultimately 604 claims, involving nearly 9 million acres, were confirmed, while 209 claims, involving about 4 million acres, were rejected. Some of the cases dragged on in the courts for several decades, and the *average* length of time required to secure evidence of ownership was *17 years* from the time of submitting a claim to the board.

By the time a grant was confirmed, its original holder was usually bankrupt. Even before 1851 most of the grantees had been in financial straits from such troubles as droughts, taxes, careless management, and disputes among heirs. The litigation required for an American title under the system established by the Gwin act was long and ruinously expensive. Although the alleged excessiveness of the lawyers' fees has often been exaggerated, there were dozens of instances in which grantees were ruined while their attorneys became rich, especially by taking part of the fees in land, holding the land as a speculation, and ultimately winning the case. If grantees tried to sell part of their land to pay the costs of litigation, they could get only a low price because they did not yet have a secure title. Mortgages, to which most of the grantees had to resort, were available only at catastrophic rates of compound interest ranging as high as 8 percent a month in the early 1850s. If grantees finally managed to establish their title in court, they often found their land occupied by settlers who refused to get off.

The most important effect of land-title troubles on the history of California was not in the hardships of the Mexican grantees, but rather in the damage done to the early development of American agriculture in the state. John S. Hittell estimated that during the 1850s a quarter of a million Americans who would otherwise have settled in California did not do so because of the insecurity of land titles; including all family members the net loss to California was probably a full million potential residents.

SOME CRUCIAL CASES

The commission, in its earliest decisions, set precedents for liberal interpretation and for deciding the cases on "broad principles of equity." During the first several years, much to the disgust of the settlers, the federal courts also tended to view the claims in what the Supreme Court called a "large and liberal spirit." Judicial liberality toward the grant holder was particularly striking in the case of Frémont's claim to Las Mariposas, the only Mexican grant in the mother lode region. Consisting of a sizable part of the present Mariposa County, this grant had been made to Juan B. Alvarado by Governor Micheltorena in 1844. Far from having fulfilled the requirement of occupancy, Alvarado had not even seen the place when in 1847 he sold it to Frémont for $3000. Gold was discovered on it in the spring of 1849—so much gold, in fact, that it became known as the "$10 million" grant. The district court ruled the claim invalid on the ground that the original recipient of the grant had never fulfilled a single one of the several conditions attached to it. The Supreme Court, however, in a majority opinion delivered by Chief Justice Roger B. Taney, confirmed Frémont's claim, and a patent was issued to him in February 1856, a few months before he became the first Republican nominee for the presidency. Among its many defects, Las Mariposas was an example of the "floating" grant, that is, one in which the total area was stated but the boundaries were not specified. When the official survey was made, the boundaries were swung about in such a way as to include three rich mining districts that Frémont had not previously claimed. Several lives were then lost in attempts to evict miners who had been working in these districts.

In San Francisco, titles were at least as chaotic as in any other part of the state. The pueblo grant of 4 square leagues was not confirmed until 1866, and there were several conflicting claims of private grants, widely and correctly believed to be fraudulent but covering large parts of the area of the city. In this situation squatterism was inevitable and rampant, and many a fortune in San Francisco real estate was founded on "shot-gun titles." Squatters fortified the lots they occupied, and one of them tried to fence off Union Square. Landowners had to hire private police.

Several fantastic claims were at first confirmed by the land commission and later detected as fraudulent. In the early years the United States district attorney for northern California was overwhelmed with work, while the services of many brilliant lawyers were available to the claimants. In the single year of 1859 the Supreme Court rejected claims containing nearly 2.5 million acres. Attorney General Jeremiah Black reported to Congress that the production of fabricated land-grant documents had become an organized industry and that ex-Governors Micheltorena and Pico and several officials who had served under them had become professional forgers and perjurers. William Carey Jones, however, denounced Black's report as "reckless and mischievous."

The entire cities of Oakland, Berkeley, and Alameda were built on the land of a single grant, the Rancho San Antonio, conveyed to Sergeant Luís Peralta in 1820 as a reward for long service in the Spanish army in northern California. Don Luís divided the ranch among his four sons in 1842. For years after 1846 Vicente Peralta stubbornly insisted that he wished no town to be built on his land, and refused to sell parts of it for that purpose. Consequently in 1850 the original street plan of Oakland was laid out as a squatter enterprise. The Peralta grant was recognized in the courts, and several decades passed before the taints of squatterism were finally cleared from Oakland titles. It is not surprising that in the twentieth century the services of title insurance companies have been more widely required and used in California than in any other state.

Los Angeles anticipated its later expansive tendencies by claiming that its pueblo grant had been 4 leagues square rather than 4 square leagues. This claim, which would have given the municipality 16 square leagues, was finally reduced to the usual 4.

Many writers have blamed the act of 1851 for the tragic difficulties of early American land problems in California, and Bancroft went so far as to assert that it would have been practically impossible to have devised a worse plan for dealing with them. Yet, even with the advantages of hindsight, no one has convincingly suggested a better one. Henry George and others maintained that the government should have confirmed the small claims after brief examination, and tested only the large and suspicious ones in the courts. When a large claim was declared valid, George thought the claimant should have been allowed only a small part of it and that the government should have bought the remainder from him at the low prices prevailing in 1848. Most of the area of the large grants would then have become public land. But this would have been a high-handed violation of the Treaty of Guadalupe Hidalgo and irreconcilable with any system of law then prevailing in the United States.

SELECTED BIBLIOGRAPHY

Ogden Hoffman, *Report of Land Cases Determined in the United States District Court of the Northern District of California* (1862) and the "specimen cases" in Hubert Howe Bancroft, *History of California*, vol. VI (1888), pp. 548–560, are excellent descriptions. The district court records are now in the Bancroft Library. See Also Robert H. Becker, *Diseños of California Ranchos* (1964) and *Designs on the Land* (1969), and the relevant maps in Warren A. Beck and Ynez D. Haase, *Historical Atlas of California* (1974).

Most nineteenth-century writers were very critical of the American government's policies toward the Mexican grants. These included Bancroft and his staff; Theodore H. Hittell, *History of California*, vol. III (1898); John S. Hittell, *The Resources of California* (1863 and later editions); Josiah Royce, "The Squatter Riot of '50 in Sacramento," *The Overland Monthly*, VI (September 1885), pp. 225–246, and his *California, . . . a Study of American Character* (1886); and Henry George, *Our Land Policy, National and State* (1874).

Joseph Ellison, *California and the Nation, 1850–1869* (1927); W. W. Robinson, *Land in California* (1948); and William H. Ellison, *A Self-Governing Dominion; California, 1849–1860* (1950) included well-balanced treatments of the Mexican-grant problems. Paul W. Gates, in "The Adjudication of Spanish-Mexican Land Claims in California," *Huntington Library Quarterly*, XXI (May 1958), pp. 213–236, and "California's Embattled Settlers," *California Historical Society Quarterly*, XLI (June 1962), pp. 99–130, concluded that it was the settlers, rather than the grantees, who were most unfairly treated. See also his "Pre-Henry George Land Warfare in California," *California Historical Society Quarterly*, XLVI (June 1967), pp. 121–148; "The Suscol Principle, Preemption, and California Latifundia," *Pacific Historical Review*, XXXIX (November 1870), pp. 453–472; "The California Land Act of 1851," *California Historical Quarterly*, L (December 1971), pp. 395–430; and "Carpetbaggers Join the Rush for California Land," *California Historical Quarterly*, LVI (Summer 1977), pp. 98–127.

RACIAL OPPRESSION

In the years after the gold rush a large majority of the American citizens of California, whether they had come from northern or southern states, cherished a fixed belief in the innate superiority of "whites" over other races. They also believed that Protestant Christians were better people than the followers of other religious faiths and that persons of Anglo-American nativity were innately superior to those of other national origins.

Of the fears, the hatreds, and the various kinds of intolerance that accompanied this set of opinions, the deepest were probably associated with the idea of racial superiority. In part, this was because that idea was very closely associated with economic group interest; equally important, however, were the essentially irrational aspects of racial fears and hatreds.

TREATMENT OF MEXICAN MINERS

As Americans poured into the mining districts of California in 1849 and 1850, they found themselves in competition with substantial numbers of foreigners. The most numerous of these were Mexicans from the state of Sonora, as the naming of one of the largest towns in the southern mines attested. Feelings of hostility left over from the Mexican War were intensified because many of the Sonorans were experienced miners, skillful in locating good claims, while others were peons brought to California in labor gangs to work the claims of their wealthier Mexican masters. Americans feared that foreigners were removing too much of the readily available gold and that there would soon be none left. Mining camp codes, enforced by vigilance committees and soon ratified by the state legislature, excluded Mexicans and Asians from many of the diggings.

Further evidence of antiforeign sentiment appeared when the California Legislature of 1850 enacted a foreign miners' license tax. Introduced by Senator Thomas Jefferson Green, the act required miners who were not citizens of the United States to pay a fee of $20 a month. This levy was so high that the Mexicans, upon whom most of the burden would fall, were unable or unwilling to pay it, and a mass meeting in the town of Sonora announced their refusal. Hundreds of armed American miners, including many veterans wearing their old Mexican War uniforms, then gathered at Sonora to aid the collectors of the tax and to prevent Mexicans from mining without a license.

At this time there were about 15,000 Mexicans in the "southern mines"—Calaveras, Tuolumne, and Mariposa counties. Under the pressures of the tax and of threats of violence, about 10,000 left the region in the summer of 1850, most of them to return to Mexico. Although the Treaty of Guadalupe Hidalgo provided that Mexican citizens of California who chose to remain there for a year became American citizens automatically, many Americans, in ignorance or defiance of this provision, lumped all "Mexicans" together, and many native Californians were driven from the mines along with the Mexican nationals, in fear of their lives and with bitterness in their hearts. Their protests had little or no political effect. On the other hand, the protests of American merchants in the mining districts, who had lost so many customers, were strong enough to carry considerable weight in the legislature, especially when it became clear that the nearly prohibitive tax was bringing in only a small amount of revenue. The tax was repealed in 1851, but it was soon reenacted in more moderate form.

In the troubles at Sonora in 1850 several hundred Frenchmen had been involved on the side of the Mexicans, to such a degree that the episode was sometimes called "the French Revolution." Mob violence between French and American miners was again narrowly averted in the summer of 1851 near Mokelumne Hill. The earliest discrimination by American Californians against foreigners, however, was directed mainly against Mexicans and other Spanish Americans. Beginning in 1852, the prime target of xenophobia became the Chinese, who had replaced the Mexicans as the most numerous and the most obviously "alien" of the various foreign groups. The California Indians, not easily classified as foreigners, were in a separate and peculiar category.

EARLY DISCRIMINATION AGAINST THE CHINESE

At the end of 1849 only a few hundred Chinese had come to seek the gold of California. In 1851, however, the outbreak of the great Taiping Rebellion against the Manchu dynasty plunged China into 15 years of civil war and general disorder that further deepened the poverty of most of its people. For more than two centuries, periods of extraordinary economic depression had induced many thousands of Chinese to emigrate, particularly from south China to several parts of southeast Asia. Now rumors of easy wealth brought a great stream of Chinese emigrants to "the Golden Mountains," their name for California. Nearly all of them, like most of the American Argonauts, were young men who dreamed of acquiring a fortune and returning home to enjoy it with the families they had left behind. But whereas most of those Americans who were disappointed in this hope eventually reconciled themselves to becoming permanent residents of California, the Chinese tended to cling for the rest of their lives to the dream of returning to their homeland, even though pitifully few of them were ever able to do so. Having no desire to become a part of a foreign country, most of the early Chinese immigrants remained alien by their own choice as much as by that of the Americans.

Even worse than the discrimination that the Chinese suffered at American hands was their oppression by creditors and other exploiters among their own race. Following a pattern long established in Chinese overseas migration, impoverished young men from Canton, Hong Kong, or the neighboring rural areas made contracts for the payment of their passage under the "credit-ticket" system. In California their labor was sold, through Chinese subcontractors, to Chinese mining companies which paid them very low wages. The American miners permitted these companies to acquire and to work only the claims which they themselves had abandoned, or those which had never contained enough gold to produce a sizable profit. The hapless Chinese workers were kept in a state of debt bondage enforced by a Chinese creditor-employer network. This system operated without reference to American courts or other legal authorities and was reenforced by various types of associations. The most important of these were the district companies, based on the several districts of southeastern China from which nearly all the California Chinese had come.

Indentured servitude, in which men labored for a period of years to repay the cost of their passage, was nothing new in American history. Indentured servants from England had made up more than half of the white population of several of the 13 English colonies on the Atlantic seaboard in the seventeenth century and the first half of the eighteenth. As one observer put it, the progenitor of many a proud American family had originally come to colonial America because his person could be advantageously exchanged there for a quantity of tobacco or sassafras root. But most of the Chinese immigrants, harried both by Americans and by greedy and powerful men of their own race, found it far more difficult to rise out of debt bondage and extreme poverty.

In 1852 the number of Chinese in California rose to about 25,000. Concentrated in the mining regions and in San Francisco, they were now by far the largest of the foreign minorities. They formed a tenth of the state's population other than Indians, and nearly a third of the population in several of the mining counties. An outburst of agitation against them began when a bill was introduced in the state senate to legalize the enforcement in California of labor contracts made in China. Throughout the mining camps there was such a rash of mass meetings and resolutions denouncing this "coolie bill" that the measure was decisively defeated. Later in the legislative session of 1852 the foreign miners' license tax was reenacted with the clear understanding that it would be enforced primarily upon the Chinese. The tax was set at $3 per month, later raised to $4.

Much to the irritation of the white miners, but greatly to the benefit of the state treasury, the tax failed to discourage the Chinese, who paid it willingly in the hope that it would reconcile the whites to their continued presence in the mines. Until 1870 when the state supreme court belatedly declared it unconstitutional, this tax, paid by the Chinese almost exclusively, brought in nearly a fourth of the state's entire revenue, even though thieving tax collectors, dissatisfied with the commissions allowed them, often let the Chinese miner off with a payment of $2 if he agreed not to demand a receipt. In addition, many Chinese were victimized by Americans impersonating tax collectors.

The Chinese almost always considered it useless and unwise to try to defend themselves against any action, even including violence and robbery, directed against them by Americans. This was true even before a peculiar decision of the state supreme court rendered them still more helpless. A state law of 1850 forbade blacks and Indians to testify in court, either "in favor of, or against a white man." In *People v. Hall* in 1854, Chief Justice Hugh C. Murray (who was 29 years old) pronounced the doctrine that the Chinese were legally Indians, since both were probably descended from the same Asiatic ancestors. Thus nonwhites (and whites also) were denied legal protection from any outrage at the hands of a white person if the only witnesses were black, Chinese, or Indian.

In the meantime another legal weapon against the Chinese had been found in the federal law which had provided since 1790 that only "free white persons" could be naturalized. This provision was a deep flaw in the application of American ideas of democracy. As for the Chinese immigrants in particular, it happened that most of them had no desire for the privilege of American naturalization. Hence they would not have suffered greatly from the denial of it, if that denial had not come to be used in a remarkable number of California laws as an excuse for other forms of discrimination. This shabby device would continue to be employed for nearly 100 years. Turned primarily against land ownership by Japanese immigrants in California in the twentieth century, its use would end only when discrimination on the ground of race as such was finally stricken from the federal naturalization statutes in 1952. In California, state laws directed against "aliens ineligible to citizenship," as a euphemism for aliens of nonwhite ancestry, began to appear in 1855 when the legislature sought to impose a head tax of $50 on all immigrants "who cannot become citizens." This was soon declared unconstitutional because the state could not tax immigration, but another state law of 1855 made ineligibility for citizenship the main definition of those to whom the foreign miners' license tax applied, and thus ensured the enforcement of the tax more specifically against the Chinese. The latter law remained in effect for many years.

Fortunately, the Chinese were a people who had developed a remarkable combination of fatalism and adaptability during many centuries of oppression in China itself. Their sufferings, however, and those of all the other racial minorities, were overshadowed by the disasters that befell the California Indians.

THE "INDIAN QUESTION"

Since the 1820s the federal government had followed a "removal policy" as its general solution of "the Indian problem." A "permanent Indian frontier" had been created along the eastern edge of the Great Plains. That region, which extended from Texas to the Canadian border, was then regarded as a "Great American Desert" where whites would never want to live. By a long series of treaties the Indian "nations" or tribes of the eastern and central parts of the country had been induced to move west of this line to new lands which the American government promised to reserve for them in perpetuity. But this process had scarcely been completed when in the 1840s the extension of the American boundary to the Pacific made the line obsolete.

In California, where it was no longer possible to remove the Indians to lands farther west, many American settlers argued that the only solution was to remove them from the face of the earth. Governor Burnett told the legislature that a "war of extermination will continue to be waged between the races until the Indian race becomes extinct," and that it was "beyond the power or wisdom of man" to avert the "inevitable destiny of this race." Among the American Californians this was the predominating view, and the overwhelming barbarousness of it was at the root of the tragic futility of all attempts to solve the "Indian question."

Units loosely organized as state militia went on ineffectual and expensive Indian-hunting expeditions in 1850. In 1851 Governor John McDougal asserted in a letter to President Millard Fillmore that 100,000 Indian warriors were in a state of armed rebellion, and the following year one of California's United States senators, John B. Weller, claimed that only a "master spirit" was needed to "confederate the tribes in a bloody and devastating war."

These statements were fantastically false. By this time there were less than 100,000 Indians of all ages and both sexes left in the whole state, and because of their inability to understand each other's languages and their lack of tribal organization, they were no more capable of "confederating" for war or for any other purpose than they had ever been. Yet the most terrifying assertions about them were widely believed in California.

The state's politicians demanded that the federal government provide the funds to pay the expenses of campaigns conducted against the Indians by state militia volunteers. This, at first, the federal authorities refused to do. Secretary of War C. M. Conrad wrote to Governor McDougal that the pay of California's volunteer Indian fighters was "exorbitant and beyond anything ever known in this country" and that it offered "inducement to perpetual collisions with the Indians." Secretary Conrad maintained that the troubles resulted far more often from the aggressive behavior of the whites than from that of the Indians and that there was no genuine need for a perpetual war between them.

The policies of the federal government toward the California Indians, though very different from the policies of the state, were equally unsuccessful in providing any effective solution. In 1850 Congress passed an act authorizing three Indian agents, or commissioners, to negotiate a series of treaties. The commissioners were Redick McKee of Virginia, George W. Barbour of Kentucky, and Dr. Oliver M. Wozencraft, a practicing physician from Louisiana, who had been a member of the constitutional convention at Monterey. The three commissioners were men of some humanitarian feelings, and they were shocked and alarmed by the belligerent attitude of the state government.

Placing their hope of ensuring peace in the idea of segregating the Indians from the whites as completely as possible, the commissioners negotiated 18 treaties affecting 139 tribes or bands. These treaties would have removed the Indians from the mining districts and other areas of white settlement and concentrated them on large reservations totaling 11,700 square miles, or 7,488,000 acres. This was about 7½ percent of the entire land area of the state. Moreover, although Congress had appropriated only $50,000 for the work of the commissioners, they let contracts totaling nearly $1 million for provisions and beef cattle for the reservations, on the theory that, as they reported to Washington, "it is *cheaper* to feed the whole flock for a *year* than to fight them for a *week.*"

The federal commissioners overreached themselves, and, unfortunately, their plan failed. Only a small fraction of the California Indians moved even temporarily to the proposed reservations. Opponents of the plan believed it intolerable that vast tracts of rich land within the state should be made the exclusive domain of Indians, and the state legislature recommended that the federal government continue its traditional policy of removing the Indians entirely outside the boundaries of the state. The legislature was careful to distinguish, however, between the "wild" or "hostile" Indians which it wanted removed and those which it regarded as "tame" or "useful." In the latter category were the Indians who had been influenced by the missions and were now an important source of labor for white farmers and ranchers. The legislature objected to these Indians being placed on the proposed reservations because it would deprive whites of their Indian workers.

When the treaties came up for ratification in 1852, California's United States senators, Gwin and Weller, opposed them so vigorously that the Senate rejected all of them. The vast reservations proposed by McKee, Barbour, and Wozencraft thus were never created. The size of the reservations and the amount of food and supplies the commissioners promised the Indians far exceeded the intentions of Congress, but had their grand design been successful, the history of Indian and white relations in California surely would have been less bloody.

There was widespread fear that the rejection of the treaties would lead the Indians to outbreaks of violence. Thus in 1853, as a palliative, Congress adopted a much more modest plan suggested by Edward F. Beale, the new superintendent of Indian affairs for California. Beale recommended a system of smaller reservations that would also serve as military posts for the United States Army. The Indians would be taught to engage in agriculture and handicrafts, much in the manner of the Spanish missions though without the religious emphasis. Ultimately, it was hoped, the Indians on these reservations

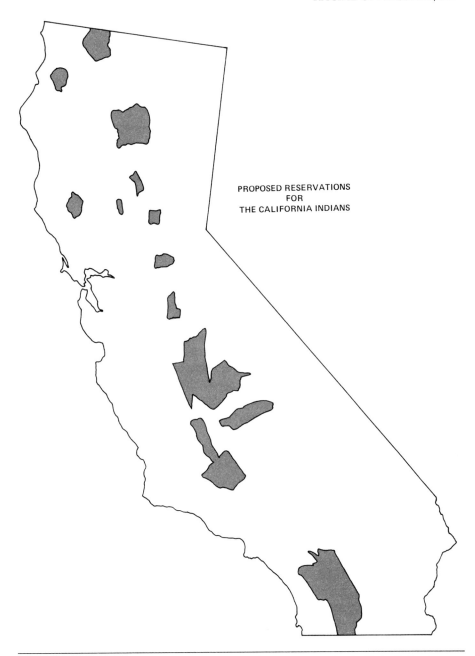

PROPOSED RESERVATIONS
FOR
THE CALIFORNIA INDIANS

The dark areas represent the large reservations proposed in treaties negotiated with the California Indians and rejected by the United States Senate in 1852.

might become self-sustaining. Five such establishments, of 25,000 acres each, were authorized under the act of 1853. The first, at Tejon in the Tehachapi foothills, attracted about 2500 Indians. Other reservations were soon established, notably the Nome Lackee in Colusa County, the Klamath on the Klamath River, and the Mendocino on the Pacific coast.

Beale pushed his experiment with enthusiasm and vigor, but it had scarcely begun when he was removed from office in 1854, partly because of his inefficiency in business matters and partly through the efforts of political enemies. The Office of Indian Affairs in Washington was peculiarly vulnerable to the abuses of the spoils system, and its personnel rotated with every new administration. In general, Beale's successors and their subordinates were incompetent and venal political appointees. In 1858 a federal investigator reported that the reservations were a lamentable failure—mere almshouses for a trifling number of Indians.

Unsuccessful as this pitiful system was, however, the federal government failed to devise a better one, and Beale's plan became the model for federal Indian reservations all over the west for many decades afterward. In 1870, Indian agents began to be appointed on the recommendation of Christian churches, and the California Indians were placed under the care of the Methodists. But little or no improvement was possible within the limitations of the small-reservation system.

EPISODES IN EXTERMINATION

The two decades after the gold rush produced dozens of wretched episodes that can best be described as massacres, the great majority of them perpetrated on the Indians by the whites. As the incoming tide of whites drove the Indians from their traditional food-producing areas, many Indians were able to survive only by seizing horses and other livestock belonging to whites, and this led to instant and violent retaliation.

Miners and ranchers banded together to kill Indians, fulfilling the early prophecy of Governor Burnett that a "war of extermination" would be waged on the California frontier. Thousands of Indians were killed. Typical of the extreme anti-Indian sentiment was the demand by the Chico *Courant* in 1866 for vigorous armed action against the Indians. "It has become a question of extermination now," the *Courant* explained. "The man who takes a prisoner should himself be shot. It is a mercy to the red devils to exterminate them, and a saving of many white lives. Treaties are played out. There is only one kind of treaty that is effective— cold lead."

Many of the punitive expeditions launched against the Indians were financed by the state government, and during the 1850s more than $1 million worth of state bonds was issued to pay the expenses of local volunteer campaigns for "the suppression of Indian hostilities." The federal government, overcoming its earlier reluctance, reimbursed the state for most of these expenditures under congressional appropriation acts of 1854 and 1861, although federal auditors disallowed some of the most obviously exaggerated claims. Thus the actions of the frontier bands took on the aspect of legalized and subsidized murder.

Few of the California Indians were able to offer effective resistance to the military and quasi-military campaigns against them. The main exceptions came in the mountainous northern part of the state. The most famous conflict in that region occurred after a band of Modocs left the reservation which they had been forced to share with the Oregon Klamaths and returned without permission to their former country on Lost River. The conflict could have been prevented by allowing the Modocs to occupy a bit of land which was of very little value to the whites, and which would have been only a tiny fragment of the lands that had once been Modoc territory. In 1873 a force of 400 soldiers, mostly of the regular Army, drove the Modocs to take refuge in the lava beds. There, although heavily outnumbered and fighting only with old muzzle-loaders and pistols against rifles and artillery, the Modocs fortified themselves so well that they inflicted many casualties while suffering very few of their own. At a peace conference where they were offered no better terms than a return to the reservation in Oregon, their chief, Kientepoos ("Captain Jack"), was goaded by some of his warriors into a plot in which they murdered General E. R. S. Canby and a Methodist missionary and wounded an Indian Agent. Ultimately the Modocs were defeated and Kientepoos was hanged, but not until the war had cost the lives of about 75 whites and half a million dollars.

Some of the most geographically isolated of the California tribes, such as the Yahi, tried to continue their ancient manner of life and to avoid all contact with white society. The country of the Yahi was in the Mill Creek region south of Mount Lassen, a district of barren hills whose chief vegetation was scrub oak and poison oak. The gold seekers of the 1850s hunted the Yahi as if they were wild animals, and by 1870 it was supposed that they were extinct. But in 1911 a man who was apparently the last survivor of the tribe was found in a slaughterhouse near Oroville,where he had come in search of food. Prof. Alfred L. Kroeber of the University of California called him Ishi, the Yahi word for *man*. *Yahi* meant simply *the people*.

Professor Kroeber and Prof. Thomas T. Waterman also of the University of California brought Ishi to the university's museum of anthropology, then in San Francisco. There the "last wild Indian in North America" lived for several years until his death. Middle-aged and in reasonably good health at the time of his "capture" by the sheriff at Oroville, Ishi caught his first cold in San Francisco, and later succumbed to tuberculosis. But in the meantime this stone-age man had adapted himself remarkably well to a twentieth-century environment. Alfred Kroeber believed that Ishi had made the transition from one culture to another more effectively and more quickly than he himself could have done, and the episode became an important example of the kind of evidence that led virtually every competent anthropologist in the world to reject the idea of the biological inferiority of so-called primitive races.

DECLINE AND EXPLOITATION

During the Spanish and Mexican periods there had been no more than a few dozen Spaniards, a few thousand Mexicans, and a few hundred Anglo-Americans in California, and yet the California Indian population had dropped from at least 300,000 to no more than 150,000 by 1845.

With the coming of hundreds of thousands of whites following the American conquest, the Indian death rate tragically accelerated. By 1870 there were only about 30,000 Indians left. In 1900 there were less than 16,000. Disease continued to take the largest toll, probably accounting for about 60 percent of the deaths during the second half of the nineteenth century. Starvation and malnutrition probably added about 30 percent of the death toll. Less than 10 percent resulted from purely physical assault through formal military campaigns, informal expeditions, and various other forms of homicide.

Some Indians adapted to the new order by working for whites, often in a state of peonage comparable to that which had existed on the Mexican ranchos. Indian labor was especially prized during the early years of the American period when all other available laborers were making for the goldfields. In those flush times it was often difficult to procure white labor at any price, and the Indians of California filled the gap. Americans adopted various regulations which continued the Mexican system of Indian labor exploitation. Under a military order of 1847 and an act of the state legislature in 1850, any unemployed Indian could be declared a vagrant and forced to labor on public works, while those not needed for this purpose could be auctioned off to the highest bidder as indentured servants. The flourishing illegal business of kidnapping Indians, especially children, for sale as household and farm servants was continued. A white person could mistreat and even murder an Indian with virtual impunity. J. Ross Browne wrote that "If ever an Indian was fully and honestly paid for his labor by a white settler, it was not my luck to hear it." The treatment of Indian laborers was in general so oppressive that it contributed more to their extinction than to their support, and particularly in agriculture the feeling that the landowner had a right to a supply of cheap labor drawn from the people of some supposedly inferior race set an evil precedent for future generations.

As for the alternative of assimilating the Indians into the general population this was made impossible in the early American period not only by the prejudices of the whites against the Indians but also by the deep resentment which the Indians felt against the whites.

THE "FREE" BLACKS

Although the efforts of Governor Burnett to secure legislation excluding free blacks from California were no more successful than the similar efforts in the constitutional convention, the coming of "persons of color" was effectively discouraged in less direct ways, and in the late 1850s there were only about

2500 of them in California. Several state laws, such as the ban against their testimony in legal proceedings, infringed their civil rights and treated them as an inferior people. In 1852 the state adopted a harsh fugitive-slave law reflecting the odious federal statute that had been a part of the compromise under which California was admitted to the Union. Only one actual fugitive slave is known to have reached California, but the law was enforced against a number of blacks whose masters had brought them there and later wished to return them to the south. The last and most famous of these cases, that of Archy Lee, was tried in 1858. Peter H. Burnett was then on the state supreme court. With the concurrence of the ex-Texan Justice David S. Terry, he ruled that although the master had forfeited his right to the slave by bringing him to a free state after its admission to the Union, and by remaining for a substantial time, an exception should be made in this instance because the master was young and in poor health and in need of his slave's services. This decision was widely ridiculed, and Lee was freed shortly afterward by a United States commissioner in San Francisco.

The law which most threatened the property and safety of California blacks was the ban on legal testimony. In 1852 blacks in San Francisco organized a Franchise League to petition the legislature to grant them equal civil rights. Three years later a statewide California Colored Convention was formed in Sacramento, and the petition campaign for the right to testify became more vigorous. In 1863 the testimony law was finally changed, extending the right of legal testimony to blacks, but Chinese and Indians remained under the ban until 1872 when the testimony law was dropped from the California code in deference to the federal civil rights act. The Colored Convention also actively campaigned for black voting rights, but the legislature refused to extend the franchise to blacks until 1870 when the Fifteenth Amendment to the United States Constitution was ratified.

SELECTED BIBLIOGRAPHY

On public policy toward racial minorities, see R. F. Heizer and A. F. Almquist, *The Other Californians* (1971); Lucile Eaves, *A History of California Labor Legislation* (1910); and William C. Fankhauser, *A Financial History of California* (1913), on the foreign miners' license tax. On the Mexicans, see Leonard M. Pitt, *The Decline of the Californios: A Social History of the Spanish-Speaking Californians, 1846–1890* (1966); M. Colette Standart, "The Sonoran Migration to California, 1848–1856," *Southern California Quarterly*, LVIII (Fall 1976), pp. 333–358; and R. H. Morefield, "Mexicans in the California Mines, 1848–53," *California Historical Society Quarterly*, XXXV (1956), pp. 37–46. See also Richard H. Peterson, "Anti-Mexican Nativism in California, 1848–1853: A Study of Cultural Conflict," *Southern California Quarterly*, LXII (Winter 1980), pp. 309–328. On the Chinese, see Gunther Barth, *Bitter Strength* (1964) and "The Chinese in California," *California History*, LVII (Spring 1978), special issue; S. C. Miller, *The Unwelcome Immigrant* (1970); A. P. Saxton, *The Indispensable Enemy* (1971); D. V. DuFault, "The Chinese in the Mining Camps," *Southern California Quarterly*, XLI (1959), pp. 155–170; Mary R. Coolidge, *Chinese Immigration* (1939); Rodman W. Paul, "The Origin of the Chinese Issue in California,"

Mississippi Valley Historical Review, XXV (1938), pp. 181-196; and Stanford M. Lyman, *The Asian in the West* (1970).

On the Indians see James J. Rawls, "Images of the California Indians: American Attitudes toward the Indians of California, 1808-1873," Ph.D. thesis, University of California, Berkeley (1975), and "Gold Diggers: Indian Miners in the California Gold Rush," *California Historical Quarterly*, LV (Spring 1976), pp. 28-45; Theodora Kroeber, *Ishi in Two Worlds* (1962); chapters in Joseph Ellison's *California and the Nation* and William H. Ellison's *A Self-Governing Dominion*; Benjamin D. Wilson's report in John W. Caughey (ed.), *The Indians of Southern California in 1852* (1952); J. Ross Browne, *The Indians of California* (1864; 1944); Stephen Bonsal, *Edward Fitzgerald Beale* (1912); Richard Dillon, *Burnt-Out Fires: California's Modoc Indian War* (1973); and George H. Phillips, *Chiefs and Challengers; Indian Resistance and Cooperation in Southern California* (1975), "Indians in Los Angeles, 1781-1875; Economic Integration, Social Disintegration," *Pacific Historical Review*, XLIX (August 1980), pp. 427-452, and *The Enduring Struggle: Indians in California History* (1981). *The Population of the California Indians, 1769-1970* (1976), by Sherburne F. Cook, deals with the decline in numbers.

The best account of blacks in the period is Rudolph M. Lapp, *Blacks in Gold Rush California* (1977). See also the same author's *Archy Lee* (1969), "Negro Rights Activities in Gold Rush California," *California Historical Society Quarterly*, XLV (1966), pp. 3-20, and "The Negro in Gold Rush California," *Journal of Negro History*, XLIX (1964), pp. 81-98. Other accounts include William E. Franklin, "The Archy Case," *Pacific Historical Review*, XXXII (1963), pp. 137-154 and J. A. Fisher, "The Struggle for Negro Testimony," *Southern California Quarterly*, LI (1969), pp. 313-324.

CULTURE AND ANARCHY

The society that the gold rush produced in California was not the typical society of the older American agrarian frontier. Rather, the California mining districts and the towns that served them became, in the words of Franklin Walker, "the acme of all frontiers, the most concentrated of quickly flourishing societies," whose people "lived through a condensed version of the world's economic growth." A metropolitan and cosmopolitan city sprang up at San Francisco, a city that telescoped half a century's growth into a year, as Bayard Taylor put it, and within 5 years was a financial rival of New York and, in some respects, a cultural rival of Boston. The fact that California became rich even before it became a state, and the fact that San Francisco's per capita wealth, though far from being evenly distributed, was suddenly the highest in the nation, meant that there were many who could afford the good things of life. The demand was primarily for material luxuries, but it included cultural satisfactions as well, for the gold rush had drawn a remarkable number of educated men. Moreover, the great distance from the eastern sources of cultural amenities had a hothouse effect on their local production.

On the other hand, the new culture, being so precocious, was inevitably awkward and crude. The new Californians themselves were predominantly youthful, and overwhelmingly male. Half the forty-niners were between the ages of 20 and 30, and a man of 45 was likely to be described as "the old gentleman." The female contingent, one-twelfth of the population of California according to the census of 1850, would increase only to one-third in 1880 and would not equal the number of males until about 1900. This society made up so largely of young men without women was peculiarly rough and boisterous.

NEWSPAPERS AND LITERARY MAGAZINES

The most immediate demand of most Americans for the printed word, after, perhaps, their Bibles, was in the form of the newspaper, and the attempt to meet this need had begun soon after the American occupation. The first issue of California's first newspaper, the weekly *Californian,* appeared at Monterey on August 15, 1846, about 5 weeks after Commodore Sloat's landing. To publish it, the naval chaplain Walter Colton went into partnership with the tall frontiersman Robert Semple, whom Colton described as "true with the rifle, ready with his pen and quick at the type case." In a dusty storeroom they found a battered Ramage press, made in Boston many years earlier. Agustín V. Zamorano, a Mexican official, had imported it to Monterey in 1834, and it had been used intermittently, mainly for proclamations by the governors. "The press was old enough to be preserved as a curiosity," Colton recalled, and "the types were all rusty. . . . It was only by scouring that the letters could be made to show their faces." There was a barrel of ink but no paper, and the early issues came out on sheets intended for cigar wrappings, about 12 inches by 8 inches. Half in English and half in Spanish, the *Californian* appeared each week until May of 1847 when Semple moved it to San Francisco and sold it. Its first rival, established by Sam Brannan, was the weekly *California Star,* which had been appearing regularly at San Francisco since January 9, 1847. It was printed in a loft above a gristmill.

At that stage in the development of California journalism, it was not surprising that 4 months passed between the great gold discovery and the recognition of its importance by the two tiny newspapers, and that Edward C. Kemble, the young editor of the *Star* in 1848, missed one of the greatest news stories of the century and had to spend the rest of his life trying to explain his oversight. After the suspension of the two little San Francisco weeklies during the early months of the gold mania, Kemble became the owner of both of them. The result of this merger was the *Alta California.* First published under that title in January 1849, it became the first California daily a year later, and survived for 41 years more. In many respects it was the most important of all of California's early newspapers.

There were soon literally hundreds of newspapers. Throughout the mining districts almost every boomtown had its paper, some with such names as the *Nevada City Miner's Spy Glass* and the *Downieville Old Oaken Bucket* (though in picturesqueness of title none could match *Satan's Bassoon,* published briefly in San Francisco). Most of the mining-district papers, of course, were ephemeral, partly because of the mobility of their subscribers.

The gold that poured into San Francisco multiplied the wealth of "the city" in many other forms. John Russ Stevenson's regiment bought two town lots in Yerba Buena for $30 in 1847 and sold them a decade later for enough to build the Russ House, the city's largest hotel. No one made a fortune in journalism in this period, but that was largely because so many tried. In the 10 years after the gold discovery 132 periodicals were started in San Francisco alone, and the total number of their proprietors, editors, and reporters was more than 1000. Though most of these papers survived less than a year, their total per capita circulation and their variety were greater than in New York, London, or anywhere else. They were printed in six different languages, represented eight religious denominations and seven political parties, and, as Kemble said, "devoted themselves to the interests of religion, politics, morals, law, medicine, literature, commerce, agriculture, news and slander." In 1859 there were 12 San Francisco dailies, most notably the *Alta*, the *Herald*, the *Call*, and the *Bulletin*.

Poetry, short stories, and other literary pieces often appeared in the early newspapers, for no other frontier has ever inspired so many of its people to write. The scenes of California, and the experiences of getting there and living there, were so often extraordinary and dramatic that they cried out for description. A literary weekly, the *Golden Era*, flourished from the first day of its publication in 1852 and soon had more subscribers than any other paper on the Pacific coast. Much of its success was due to the enthusiasm of one of its young editors, Rollin M. Daggett, who traveled through the mining districts to sell subscriptions and also wrote many of the sketches describing the miners' life. Though it paid nothing for poetry and only $5 a column for prose, nearly every writer who achieved any reputation in early American California found in it the opportunity for literary apprenticeship. Bret Harte worked on its staff, first as a typesetter and then as a columnist, and it was in the *Era* that he published his first successful story, "M'liss."

The tone of the *Golden Era* was informal to the point of breeziness, and this gave it a popular appeal that enabled it to outlast a number of competitors, including several that aspired to higher literary levels. One of these was *Hutchings's Illustrated California Magazine*, published for 5 years beginning in 1856. Its founder, James M. Hutchings, was an Englishman who had worked in the mines before establishing himself as a writer with his *Miner's Ten Commandments* (leading off with "Thou shalt have no other claim than one"). Printed on a single sheet, this new decalogue sold nearly 100,000 copies. Hutchings asserted that the intelligence and good taste of the reading public of California, and particularly of the mining population, had been underrated and that his magazine would correct this error. Illustrated with woodcuts, it is best known for early writings in praise of California's mountain scenery, with which its publisher was so entranced that he spent his later years as the first hotelkeeper in the Yosemite Valley.

WRITERS OF THE FIFTIES

Of all the nearly innumerable accounts of life in the mining camps of the gold-rush period, the best were the letters written by a remarkably observant young woman, Louise Amelia Knapp Smith Clapp, who signed herself "Dame Shirley." Her husband, Dr. Fayette Clapp, practiced medicine in 1851 and 1852 at Rich Bar and then at Indian Bar on the north fork of the Feather River, and while living with him there she wrote 23 letters to her sister in the east. "I take pains to describe things as I see them," she wrote, "hoping that thus you will obtain an idea of life in the mines *as it is.*" During much of her sojourn she was the only woman in camp, and she invited her sister to imagine spending a winter in a place where there were "no fresh books, no shopping, calling, nor gossiping little tea-drinkings . . . no latest fashions, no daily mail (we have an express once a month), no promenades, no rides or drives; no vegetables but potatoes and onions, no milk, no eggs, no *nothing.*" When the gold began to play out, and fear, hate, and brutality became chronic, a lynching and incidents of persecution of Mexicans evoked some of her most vivid and sensitive passages. Yet, taken as a whole, her experiences in the diggings were so fascinating that when the camp broke up she left it with regret.

The "Shirley letters" were first published in 1854 in *The Pioneer,* a lively but unfortunately short-lived San Francisco literary monthly. This same journal also served to popularize the writings of the first of the far-western humorists, Lt. George H. Derby of the U.S. Army topographical engineers, otherwise known as "John Phoenix." Derby was a brilliant young West Pointer who had graduated seventh in a class of 59, in spite of the difficulty he usually found in taking anything seriously. It was said, for example, that he answered an examination question on what to do if besieged in a fort with provisions running low by saying that he would abandon the fort and besiege the enemy. Assigned to duty in California, he wrote some humorous sketches for the *Alta* under his alternate pseudonym of "Squibob" ("a Hebrew word, signifying 'There you go, with your eye out'"); however, his first really important literary opportunity came when he was sent to San Diego in 1853 to build a dam on the San Diego River. His boredom with the sleepy little town ended when his friend Judge John J. Ames, editor of the weekly *San Diego Herald,* the Democratic organ in the district, went north to solicit more funds from the state Democratic campaign chest. "Phoenix," left in charge of the paper for several weeks, burlesqued everything in its news and editorial columns, and among other delightful outrages switched its political support to the Whigs. Then he described editorially, and in advance, the fight that might be expected to occur when the powerfully built and vengeful Ames should return to San Diego: "We held [him] down over the press by our nose (which we had inserted between his teeth for that purpose)" and, "while our hair was engaged in holding one of his hands," struck off a fair copy of the *Herald's* advertisements on the back of his shirt. Actually, Ames appreciated this most famous joke of early California as much as anyone did, and a few years later he edited the first collection of his friend's *Phoenixiana* in book form. Almost as important as Derby's own writings in the history of American humor were the many stories that were told about him, one being that before introducing his bride to his mother he told each that the other was deaf and then let them shout at each other for half an hour.

Alonzo Delano, or "Old Block," also wrote many humorous sketches, collected into a book called *Chips from the Old Block,* which sold nearly 15,000 copies in California. He was famous for his prodigious nose; in fact he once asked a passing stranger to brush a mosquito from the end of that protuberance, because "You are nearer to it than I am." For eastern readers, on the other hand, he wrote one of the most realistic accounts of the gold rush, *Life on the Plains and among the Diggings.*

It is significant that the best writers of the far west in these years of hazard and hardship were people who had suffered intense personal tragedies in their earlier lives. Shirley was an orphan, Phoenix's father was an eccentric who deserted the family, and Old Block's wife died young, leaving him to care for two invalid children. That Phoenix and Block were humorists may be explained in considerable part by the fact that people often laugh because they are afraid they will cry. Mark Twain would write in his old age that "Everything human is pathetic. The secret source of humor is not joy but sorrow."

Tragedy also haunted the life of John Rollin Ridge, or "Yellow Bird." That he was half Indian might not in itself have made his life too difficult, for his father was a wealthy Cherokee chief who married the daughter of the principal of the private academy in Connecticut where he had received his education. But when John was 12 years old, he witnessed the bloody knife murder of his father by a group of Cherokees who hated him for signing the treaty under which they had given up their lands in Georgia and moved across the Mississippi. A decade later Ridge appeared in gold-rush San Francisco and began to write poems under the name of Yellow Bird, a literal translation of his Indian name.

Ridge's main literary achievement was the creation of California's greatest legend in his book called *The Life and Adventures of Joaquín Murieta, Celebrated California Bandit*, published in 1854. Bandits flourished in the early fifties. Many of them were Mexicans, and some of these probably considered themselves to have been driven to lives of crime by mistreatment at the hands of Americans. Of the many cattle thefts and other robberies committed in various parts of the state, some of the most notorious were attributed to five men, all known as "Joaquín," though they had five different surnames, one of which was Murieta. In 1853 the state legislature passed an act authorizing Capt. Harry Love, a former Texan, to recruit a band of mounted rangers at state expense for the capture of any or all of the five Joaquíns; Governor Bigler, about to seek reelection, personally offered $1000 reward for any of them. The rangers returned from their forays with a head pickled in a jar of alcohol and collected the reward, although there was no reliable identification, and one of the rangers later boasted in a saloon that one pickled head was as good as another.

Such was the vague and dubious factual background from which John Rollin Ridge constructed his narrative. One of the threads he wove into it was the Robin Hood legend. Another thread was obviously suggested by one of the Shirley letters, describing the whipping of a Mexican by the vigilance committee of Indian Bar and the victim's oath of deadly vengeance against his tormentors. This man now became "Joaquín Murieta", and as Joaquín carried out his oath of revenge, always with his knife, Yellow Bird may have been vicariously avenging himself against the murderers of his father. Through Joaquín's guerrilla attacks upon the *gringos*, Ridge may also have vicariously redressed some of the grievances of his own people.

BRET HARTE

Francis Brett Harte had been sending poems to the papers under the name of "Bret" for several years before he came to California as a boy of 17, in 1854. Legend has exaggerated his subsequent experience and knowledge of the California mining camps, just as his famous stories created a romanticized picture of mining life which came to be accepted as more genuine than the reality. On the other hand, it is not true that, as Josiah Royce later asserted, Harte was never anywhere near the mines. He taught school for a few months in a Sierra mining town which was probably La Grange, and which probably became the village of Smith's Pocket in "M'liss." He may have prospected for a short time, very amateurishly and unsuccessfully. The novels of Dickens, which Harte had read and reread voraciously during his adolescent years, seem to have had as much influence on his writing as any actual experiences of his own.

Having followed a married sister to the town of Union, now Arcata, Harte became the printer's devil and then the junior editor of the town's weekly paper, the *Northern Californian*. In February 1860 a gang of local scoundrels sneaked into the Indian village on Gunther's Island in Humboldt Bay one morning before dawn and perpetrated the most contemptible racist massacre in the history of the state. With hatchets and axes they killed 60 Indians, mostly women and children, for no better reason than that some other tribe a hundred miles back in the mountains had been causing trouble. Harte bitterly denounced the murders in an article headed "Indiscriminate Massacre of Indians—Women and Children Butchered." Threats against his life soon became so menacing that he left Arcata by steamer for San Francisco, but he had already demonstrated his personal courage beyond question.

In San Francisco, not long after this episode, Jessie Benton Frémont read some of Harte's work in the *Golden Era,* invited him to her home, and introduced him to her literary and political friends. Becoming active in Republican circles, he wrote many Unionist poems and worked vigorously for the Unionist cause in close friendship and cooperation with Edward Dickinson Baker and Thomas Starr King. Later Jessie Frémont used her influence to get him a federal patronage appointment as a clerk in the surveyor general's office, and then a better position in the branch mint. These jobs allowed him time for writing while assuring him of an income. For several years his poems and stories about California were mostly romantic tales of Spanish colonial days.

The writing that gave Harte an enduring place in the history of literature was done in less than 3 years while he served as the first editor and the most important contributor of *The Overland Monthly,* founded in 1868 by the San Francisco bookseller and publisher Anton Roman. Up to this time Harte had regarded the American period in California with a kind of genteel contempt. In one of his early articles he had called the 1850s "a hard, ugly, unwashed, vulgar, and lawless era." Roman seems to have persuaded him in 1868, however, that the time had come to enshrine the gold rush in romantic fiction, and for the early issues of *The Overland* Harte wrote his best stories. "The Luck of Roaring Camp" is concerned with the death of the camp prostitute in childbirth and the adoption of the baby by the miners. In "The Outcasts of Poker Flat" a gambler and a prostitute sacrifice their own lives in attempts to save their companions, trapped by a snowstorm. In "Tennessee's Partner," after a miner has gone to the dogs and been hanged for robbery (Harte called the lynching a "weak and foolish deed"), his partner claims the body for burial and soon afterward dies of grief and loneliness.

Harte's most famous poem, usually known as "The Heathen Chinee" though its original title was "Plain Language from Truthful James," appeared in *The Overland* in 1870 and hilariously tells of how a pair of gamblers were outcheated in a card game by the bland and wily Ah Sin. Harte was unhappy when this poem, which he regarded as a trifling little burlesque, became the most widely known of all his writings, and because he detested racial persecution, he was further troubled when the climactic line, "We are ruined by Chinese cheap labor," had the serious side effect of popularizing an anti-Chinese slogan. Unintentionally, he had made a major contribution to the antioriental stereotype in America.

The editors of *The Atlantic Monthly* lured Harte to the east coast in 1871 with a large advance against future writings. For the rest of his life his work was largely repetitive and of poorer quality. His most successful theme, redemption through self-sacrifice, became almost a trademark of his later stories. American editors tired of them, but in England there seemed to be an insatiable demand for "more like 'The Luck,'" and it was in England that he lived and wrote during his last years.

MARK TWAIN

The greatest and the most original literary product of the American west was undoubtedly Mark Twain. Although his writing career began in Virginia City, Nevada, that beginning is a part of the literary history of California, just as the whole history of the Comstock lode was closely interwoven with the economic and social history of San Francisco.

Samuel L. Clemens came to Nevada in 1861, at the age of 25. His brother Orion was secretary to the Nevada territorial governor, and Sam was secretary to Orion. In this capacity he had neither salary nor duties, but he was badly in need of some new field of adventure. The outbreak of the Civil War had put an end to steamboating on the Mississippi River, and 2 miserable weeks in a home guard unit at Hannibal had given him a permanent detestation of war, even though the unit had seen no action and was not even entirely sure which side it was on. After trying his hand at mining, in which he was enthusiastic but unsuccessful, he became a reporter for the Virginia City *Territorial Enterprise* in 1862. Early in the following year he began to sign his articles with what would later be the best known of all American pseudonyms, "Mark Twain," a riverboat leadsman's term meaning 2 fathoms deep.

The *Territorial Enterprise* was an offshoot of the San Francisco *Golden Era*. As San Francisco provided most of the financing for the operation of the Comstock silver mines, so it also furnished most of the early Comstock writers. But the journalistic atmosphere of Virginia City was even freer than that of the larger metropolis. It specialized in burlesques and hoaxes, and in this school Mark Twain learned the writing trade. The editor of local news and mining for the *Enterprise* was William Wright, a master of comic invention whose pseudonyms included "Ebenezer Queerkutt," "Picaroon Pax," and, finally and

Mark Twain as a young man in San Francisco, 1864–65. *(Courtesy of the Bancroft Library.)*

most appropriately, "Dan De Quille." To the great amusement of the readers of the *Enterprise*, Mark Twain and Dan De Quille soon became inveterate rivals, each trying to outdo the other with hilarious tall tales. The most popular of Mark Twain's early "scoops" was an account of the discovery of a petrified man—petrified in the stance of thumbing his nose at posterity. In 1864 Mark Twain moved to San Francisco, met Bret Harte, and wrote sketches for the *Era*. He spent a visit to the mother lode country mainly in loafing in a saloon at Angel's Camp, listening to tall tales. One of these grew into the story of the celebrated jumping frog of Calaveras County, so larcenously deprived of the laurels of victory when it was weighted down with a belly full of birdshot. Published in a New York paper and promptly reprinted in newspapers all over the country, this story made Twain nationally famous.

In 1867 the *Alta California* sent him on a cruise to the Mediterranean and the Holy Land with a party of culture-hungry American tourists. Two years later he gathered his reports to the *Alta* into *The Innocents Abroad*. Except for a brief visit to San Francisco to arrange for the release of copyright so that this volume could be published in New York, he never returned to California, and instead made his home in Hartford, Connecticut. He had had enough of life in the wild west, but in 1872, before turning to other literary themes, he published *Roughing It*, an autobiographical narrative of his western experiences, full of such episodes as his visit to Mono Lake, where, he alleged, it got so cold that the only way to serve a brandy toddy was to chop it off and wrap in in a paper.

JOAQUIN MILLER AND OTHER POETS

The factual details of the life of Cincinnatus H. Miller are often difficult to determine because of the romantic imaginativeness of much of his autobiographical writing. It is probable that he was born in Indiana in 1837, that the family moved to Oregon in 1852, and that he ran away to California in 1854 when he was 17. But whereas according to his own version, while living near Mount Shasta, he loved an Indian princess who saved his life, another account of the same circumstances had it that he cohabited with an Indian woman who helped him break out of jail when he was arrested for borrowing a horse. In any case, his Indian mistress bore him a daughter named Cali-Shasta.

During the early part of the Civil War, Miller edited a pacifist newspaper in Oregon. In 1863 he came to San Francisco with plans for a writing career combined with a honeymoon. His bride was the daughter of a fisherman on the southern Oregon coast. She shared Miller's admiration for Byron and wrote poems under the name of Minnie Myrtle. The young couple failed to make a living by writing in San Francisco, and their marriage ended in separation. Miller explained that Byron had never amounted to anything as a poet until after he left his wife.

Back in Oregon, Miller bacame a country lawyer and a judge, with no more equipment, it is said, than one law book and two six-shooters. In 1869 he published a long and very bad poem, "Joaquin," further glorifying the Murieta legend and describing the bandit's sweetheart as a lineal descendant of Montezuma. Miller's friends, in affection, and his critics, in derision, began to call him "Joaquin," and he adopted this as his pen name. In 1870 he went to England, where he was soon accepted with enthusiasm as "the poet of the Sierras." Always a skillful showman, and quite willing to take advantage of the need of many of the English to regard Americans as eccentric and uncouth, he appeared in London in a red shirt, high boots, and broad sombrero, trying to look as much as possible as if he had stepped straight out of Roaring Camp. Ocasionally he went so far as to smoke two cigars at once or, on being introduced to a debutante in a Mayfair drawing room, to express his appreciation of her charms by getting down and biting her on the ankle, evoking squeals of delight. His poems were always melodramatic and often erotic. Their crudities (he once rhymed "Goethe" with "teeth") were accepted as proof of their genuine frontier origin.

In 1886 he bought a tract of land called "The Hights" (as he usually spelled it), on the hills above Oakland, on which he planted thousands of trees and built monuments to Moses, Frémont, and Browning, along with a funeral pyre for himself. There, for more than a quarter of a century, he was a California landmark, and his hospitality was a joy to droves of clubwomen.

Some of Miller's poems were not entirely without literary merit. This is the most that can reasonably be said for them, but they were probably as important as the poetic efforts of any of his contemporaries on the Pacific coast, even though aspiring poets were very numerous. When Bret Harte compiled an anthology of California poetry in 1866, there were so many outraged protests from poets whose work had not been included that he felt compelled to bring out another volume.

Many of the aspirants were women, and the most talented of these was Ina Coolbrith. She had had a miserable early life, which she seldom talked about. Born Josephine Smith, she was the daughter of a younger brother of the Prophet of the Mormon church. Her father died when she was a child, and her mother left the church when the Prophet announced the doctrine of polygamy. Ina suffered through an unhappy early marriage and a deeply distressing divorce in Los Angeles, and came to San Francisco about 1865. Harte engaged her as one of his coeditors of *The Overland Monthly*, and she became a good friend of several of California's male writers, though the thought of remarriage was too painful for her to consider. Her gentle verses were an escape from sadness through pleasure in such things as flowers, birds, and the wind. For more than 20 years she was a librarian in the Oakland public library, and some of the happiest moments of her life began when a ragged boy named Jack London asked her whether she could suggest anything for him to read. She was also a foster mother, in the more literal sense, to Joaquin Miller's daughter Cali-Shasta, and to two nieces.

Quite a different sort of poet was Adah Isaacs Menken, who bared her emotions in her passionate poems as she bared her body on the stage, in flesh colored tights and strapped onto the back of a horse, in a more or less dramatized version of Byron's "Mazeppa."

CHURCHES AND SCHOOLS

Many a Yankee about to depart for the goldfields had listened to a special sermon in which he was exhorted to "Take your Bible in one hand and your New England civilization in the other" and bring light to California. The first Protestant congregation in San Francisco had been organized in November 1848, when it was necessary to include Methodists, Baptists, Presbyterians, Congregationalists, Episcopalians, and Mormons in a community church in order to pay the salary of one chaplain, Timothy Dwight Hunt. "There was sweet pleasure in our unity in diversity," Hunt recalled, with a twinge of regret that the unity could not endure. As wealth rapidly increased and the city's population gradually became a little more settled, eight major Protestant denominations were soon going their separate ways to heaven. By 1852 San Francisco had at least 30 places of worship, including 22 Protestant, 6 Roman Catholic, and 2 Jewish. William Speer, a Presbyterian missionary formerly stationed in Canton, worked heroically but with limited success to convert the Chinese in San Francisco. Throughout the mining camp towns, earnest evangelists were spreading the gospel, though unfortunately their ministrations were usually least successful with those most obviously in need of redemption.

The Roman Catholic church in California, which had fallen into utter decay during the last years under Mexico, experienced a remarkable development as a result of the gold rush. In 1846 there were only 13 priests in the whole of Alta California, most of them almost starving. By the early '50s there were more than 100, and their work was being very generously supported. In 1852 it became appropriate to appoint the first archbishop of San Francisco, Joseph S. Alemany.

In contrast with the earnest concern for religious education on the part of the churches, the state government failed miserably to make adequate provision for public schools. Governor Burnett's first message to the legislature in December 1849 did not even mention the subject of education. Not until 1851 did the legislature pass a law authorizing local communities to establish public schools at their own expense, and not until the following year did it provide any state financial support, even though the state was receiving the larger share of the taxes on real property. California's first public high schools, in San Francisco and Sacramento, were not established until 1856. Superintendent of Public Instruction Andrew Jackson Moulder reported that in the 5 years before 1858 California had spent $754,000 on its prisons, and little more than a third of that amount for public education—an expenditure of nearly $2000 for each convict, and $9 for each child. Scarcely more than a fourth of the children of school age were attending public schools, usually for less than 6 months of the year.

The gross dereliction on the part of the state government, reflecting the selfishness and irresponsibility of the majority of its citizens and their elected representatives, afforded a special opportunity for the private efforts of a devoted few. Various private schools and academies came into existence, most of them church-supported, but it is doubtful that any real collegiate instruction began before the sixties. By 1866, largely through the efforts of John Swett as state superintendent, several new laws had been passed expanding educational opportunity. For white children, though not for others, something like a decent public elementary school system was established, but even this existed only in the larger towns. Such was the limited state of educational progress a full 20 years after the American occupation of California.

SELECTED BIBLIOGRAPHY

Any account of the subject of this chapter must be indebted to Franklin Walker's excellent volume, *San Francisco's Literary Frontier* (1939). Also useful are Gunther Barth, *Instant Cities: Urbanization and the Rise of San Francisco and Denver* (1975); Kevin Starr, *Americans and the California Dream* (1973); Roger W. Lotchin, *San Francisco, 1846-1856* (1974); and the chapter on "Culture and Anarchy on the Pacific Coast: The Age of Gold," in Louis B. Wright's *Culture on the Moving Frontier* (1955).

A History of California Newspapers, 1846-1858, by Edward C. Kemble, first published as an extensive supplement to the *Sacramento Union* of Dec. 25, 1858, and edited by Helen Harding Bretnor (1962), is still the basic work on the rowdy and individualistic journalism of its period. *The Annals of San Francisco* (1854), by Frank Soulé, John H. Gihon, and James Nisbet, is a historical treasure-house drawn almost entirely from the newspapers. See also John P. Young, *Journalism in California* (1915); John Bruce, *Gaudy Century* (1948); Emerson Daggett (ed.) *Frontier Journalism* (vol. II, 1939), in the WPA *History of Journalism in San Francisco;* John D. Carter, "The San Francisco *Bulletin,* 1855–1865," Ph.D. thesis, University of California, Berkeley (1941); and William B. Rice, *The Los Angeles Star, 1851–1864; the Beginnings of Journalism in Southern California* (1947). F. P. Weisenburger, *Idol of the West* (1966) is a biography of Rollin M. Daggett.

The best edition of *The Shirley Letters from the California Mines* is by Carl I. Wheat (1949); see also Rodman W. Paul, "In Search of 'Dame Shirley,'" *Pacific Historical Review,* XXXIII (May 1964), pp. 127–146. George R. Stewart, *John Phoenix, Esq.: The Veritable Squibob* (1937) is an engaging biography.

George R. Stewart, *Bret Harte, Argonaut and Exile* (1931) is thorough and critical. See also Richard O'Connor, *Bret Harte, a Biography* (1966). Materials on Mark Twain's western period include Edgar M. Branch, *The Literary Apprenticeship of Mark Twain* (1950); Ivan Benson, *Mark Twain's Western Years* (1938); Henry Nash Smith (ed.), *Mark Twain of the Enterprise* (1957); and Bernard Taper (ed.), *Mark Twain's San Francisco* (1963). James J. Rawls (ed.), *Dan De Quille of the Big Bonanza* (1980) includes an account of the rivalry of Mark Twain and De Quille. Martin S. Peterson, *Joaquin Miller, Literary Frontiersman* (1937) deals with the poet's life, work, and literary reputation. See also M. M. Marberry, *Splendid Poseur:Joaquin Miller—American Poet* (1953). Josephine D. Rhodehamel and Raymund F. Wood, *Ina Coolbrith: Librarian and Laureate of California* (1973) is a biography of California's first poet laureate.

On the churches, see William W. Ferrier, *Pioneer Church Beginnings and Educational Movements in California* (1927); William Hanchett, "The Question of Religion and the Taming of California, 1849–1854," *California Historical Society Quarterly,* XXXII (March and June 1953), pp. 49–56, 119–144; John B. McGloin, "The California Catholic Church in Transition, 1846–1850," *California Historical Society Quarterly,* XLII (March 1963), pp. 39–48, and *California's First Archbishop: The Life of Joseph Sadoc Alemany, O. P., 1814–1888* (1966); and Francis J. Weber, *California's Reluctant Prelate: The Life and Times of Right Reverend Thaddeus Amat, C. M. (1811–1878)* (1964), a biography of the first bishop of Los Angeles. On the schools, see Irving G. Hendrick, *California Education: A Brief History* (1980); W. W. Ferrier, *Ninety Years of Education in California, 1846–1936* (1937); John Swett, *History of the Public School System of California* (1876) and his *Public Education in California* (1911); David F. Ferris, *Judge Marvin and the Founding of the California Public School System* (1962); James E. Myers, "The Educational Work of Andrew Jackson Moulder," Ph.D. thesis, University of California, Berkeley (1961); Nicholas C. Polos, "A Yankee Patriot: John Swett, the Horace Mann of the Pacific," *History of Education Quarterly,* IV (March 1964), pp. 17–32, and *John Swett: California's Frontier Schoolmaster* (1978).

A FRONTIER ECONOMY

Early in 1848 California's population other than Indians was less than 15,000. According to the federal census of 1850 it was about 93,000, but this census had a number of notorious defects, the most glaring of which was that all the returns for San Francisco, Contra Costa, and Santa Clara counties were lost. The state took its own census in 1852 and counted 223,856. For 1860 the regular census figure was more than 380,000, and for 1870 more than 560,000. Since the small proportion of women made California's birthrate lower than its death rate, immigration was obviously responsible for the remarkable growth in population. And in these years the search for economic opportunity was by far the most important force in bringing newcomers to California.

Throughout the period between the gold rush of '49 and the completion of the transcontinental railroad 20 years later, the mining of precious metal continued to dominate the economy, for although the gold output gradually declined after the peak years of the early 1850s, the rich silver mines of the Comstock lode in western Nevada began to produce enormous new wealth in 1859, and the development of the Comstock was essentially a California enterprise.

GOLD MINING

"The miners are beginning to discover," said the *Alta California* in the autumn of 1851, "that they are engaged in a science and a profession, and not in a mere adventure." Within a few years the gold in the beds and banks of the streams and in surface outcroppings of quartz was inevitably depleted. Rich deposits of the metal lay far below the surface in solid rock or deep in the gravelly hillsides, but mining them required the use of engineering techniques that demanded heavy equipment and substantial amounts of capital.

In extracting gold from solid rock, through processes variously described as quartz, vein, or lode mining, the auriferous rock taken from a mine shaft or tunnel had to be crushed to a fine powder. After an assortment of ingenious contraptions had proved worthless, better results were obtained with more traditional devices, of which the most important was the stamp mill. Dating at least as far back as the sixteenth century in Europe, this was essentially a large mechanized version of the mortar and pestle.

Another machine important in quartz mining was a mule-powered contrivance developed in Spanish America and called an *arrastre*, usually anglicized as "arrastra." A mule, plodding around a circular track, moved a horizontal shaft extending from a central post that served as a pivot, and heavy abrasive stones attached to the shaft were thus dragged over the gold-bearing material.

It was difficult to grind the ore fine enough, and often less than half the gold actually contained in the crushed rock could be separated from it by quicksilver amalgamation. Part of the loss occurred because some of the gold was encased in metallic sulfides on which the mercury would not act. After about 1860, treatment of the heated mixture by chlorine gas to break down the sulfides increased the yield considerably. Sometimes the pulverized rock, mixed with water, was made to flow over coarse blankets so that fine particles of gold were caught in the cloth. The legend of the golden fleece had probably originated in the application of this method to sheepskin in ancient times.

Another major source of gold lay in the "Tertiary gravels." During the Tertiary geologic era a great river flowed through the region of the northern mines, laying down an immense bed of gravel containing scattered flakes of gold. Later when the whole region was thrust up to become part of the Sierra Nevada, new rivers—the Feather, the Yuba, the Bear, and the American—began to flow transversely through the bed of the older one. Much of that bed, however, was now on hilltops and hillsides which had since been gradually covered over with debris. When the gravel hills were first discovered, attempts to mine them took the form of shafts and tunnels called "coyote holes." But working in these burrows, on hands and knees, by candlelight and in fetid air, was miserable and dangerous. The solution came with the introduction of hydraulic mining, in which an entire hillside could be washed loose by directing powerful streams of water against it. For this purpose, in 1853, a former sailmaker named Anthony Chabot constructed a canvas hose, and a Connecticut Yankee named Edward E. Matteson invented a tapered nozzle of sheet iron. Thus "hydraulicking" was born. As the stream placers gave out and the river-mining communities declined, hydraulic towns like Dutch Flat, Iowa Hill, and Gold Run sprang up and flourished. In 1861 the development of the "crinoline hose," a double-strength canvas hose bound with iron loops, made it possible to throw a stream of water several hundred feet. Large amounts of water, accumulated at points considerably higher than the nozzle of the hose, had to be supplied through ditches and wooden flumes, and thousands of miles of these were constructed.

Part of the financing required by the expensive quartz and hydraulic operations came from joint-stock companies organized by working miners, but for men of small capital the chances for profit steadily declined. Many of those who remained in the industry were employed by increasingly large corpora-

Hydraulicking. *(Courtesy of the Bancroft Library.)*

tions, which tended to hire Americans as specialists in management and the handling of equipment and machinery, while employing Chinese and Mexicans for less-skilled labor. According to John S. Hittell, about 100,000 men were still engaged in gold mining in California in 1861, but by 1873 there were less than 30,000, of whom three-fifths were Chinese.

Whatever techniques might be devised, the supply of gold was not inexhaustible. After hitting a record level of more than $80 million for 1852, the state's gold production decreased year by year until 1865, when it was less than $18 million. At that point it became stabilized, continuing to average about $17 million a year until the turn of the century.

THE BEGINNINGS OF BANKING

Few of the citizens of California in the early American period understood the nature and importance of banks as institutions for the lending and investment of money in business and industrial enterprise. To most Californians, as to most Americans in the years since the disastrous nationwide panic of 1837, "bank" was a hated word, for it seemed to mean primarily a corporation enjoying the special legal privilege of printing and issuing notes that circulated as paper money.

This privilege had, indeed, been much abused in the older states. Most of the paper money in circulation throughout the country had been issued by hundred of separate banking corporations chartered by special acts of state legislatures. The notes of these so-called state banks were unregulated either by government or by specie reserves, and many people had been swindled by receiving payment in such depreciated paper.

William M. Gwin was one of these, and in the tradition of Jacksonian democracy he had led the crusade against paper money in the California constitutional convention of 1849. The result was a provision similar to those included in nearly every other new state constitution adopted between the panic of 1837 and the Civil War: "The Legislature shall have no power to pass any act granting any charter for banking purposes." In California the presence of gold in great quantities made possible its use as the dominant medium of exchange, and for many decades even large financial transactions in California were likely to be conducted in piles of gold coins, especially the $20 gold pieces known as double eagles.

Thus the state's constitutional ban against the issuance of bank notes as paper money caused relatively little trouble. But in a growing economy the need for savings, lending, and investment institutions was so great that their existence was inevitable. The main effect of the state's provisions against chartering banks was simply to confine the banking business to entirely private concerns, without any particular legal sanction and without any public regulation. In the early mining camps banking arrangements were often very simple. At the "bank" of G. D. Dickerson at Mokelumne Hill, according to Ira B. Cross, "the vault . . . was an excavation a yard square, under the bed occupied by himself and Mrs. Dickerson; its compartments were buckskin bags, and the time-lock was a revolver of large caliber." Saloonkeepers often doubled as bankers. For many years after the gold rush a great deal of the banking was done as a sideline by firms engaged in other businesses, notably express companies, real estate brokers, and merchandisers of all sorts.

Under the circumstances, the wonder is that banking failures and defalcations were not more frequent than they were. In the early 1850s, flush times and fantastic rates of interest made the lending of money immediately profitable. But a panic began in 1855, touched off by the collapse of the San Francisco branch of a St. Louis express and banking concern. Partly because the drop in the state's gold output had already contracted the money market, the panic spread quickly, bringing ruin to several other banking agencies. Adams & Company had been weakened by ruthless competition from Wells, Fargo, the western branch of the powerful American Express. When Adams & Company went down in the California panic of 1855, there was such a run on the offices of Wells, Fargo that even this giant of early western finance had to resort to a temporary suspension of payments. Economic revival came slowly, until the great treasure of the Comstock lode brought a new era of financial growth.

THE FIRST COMSTOCK SILVER BOOM, 1859-1864

Between the Washoe and Carson Valleys, a little less than 40 miles due east of Donner Pass and about 20 miles east of the California state line, stood a barren-looking mountain known in the 1850s as Sun Peak. Deep in the mountain, later named Mount Davidson, and coming to the surface on its eastern side, lay the world's richest deposits of silver, mixed with lesser deposits of gold.

Eventually $400 million worth of the two metals, largely silver, would be taken from this great lode before its permanent decline in the early 1880s, and for a time the city that mushroomed around the entrances to the mine shafts would be larger than any in the far west except San Francisco and Salt Lake City.

Beginning as early as 1850, placers in a canyon at the base of the mountain yielded moderate amounts of gold, but the flakes were hard to separate from a wretched "blue stuff." This the prospectors threw aside, cursing it because it clogged the riffle bars in their gold rockers. First to establish that the blue stuff was silver ore and to discover some of the outcroppings of the lode far up near the head of the canyon were Ethan Allen Grosh and Hoseah Ballou Grosh, sons of a Pennsylvania minister.

In 1857 both of the Grosh brothers died and their secret was temporarily lost. However, a sheepherder and prospector named Henry Tompkins Paige Comstock, known as "Old Pancake" from his chief article of diet, had learned enough from the Groshes to suspect that they had made some great strike. His frantic efforts to locate it for himself were unsuccessful, and in 1859 the lode was discovered anew by the Irish prospectors Patrick McLaughlin and Peter O'Riley. Comstock was in no sense the real discoverer, but by means of bluster and bluff he was able to fool McLaughlin, O'Riley, and the other miners then in the district into believing that he had established some sort of title to the land. Thus for no better reason than his capacity for bragging and deceit, his name became immortalized in the name of the lode.

Another local prospector was James Fennimore, a drunken teamster who had fled from a murder charge in California and changed his name to Finney and who was known in the Washoe regions as "Old Virginia" from his habit of boasting about the state of his birth. One night, the story goes, he fell and broke a whiskey bottle. Rising unsteadily to his knee, he said, "I baptize this ground Virginia Town." For a time the place was known as Virginia, and later as Virginia City.

The circumstances of the naming of the Comstock lode and of its local metropolis are not inappropriate to the general tenor of their history—a fantastic narrative in which the dissolute, selfish, and dishonest aspects of human nature were all too apparent. These qualities, on the other hand, were alloyed with considerable amounts of ingenuity, courage, and hard work.

Interest continued to center in the gold content of the lode until July 1859, when some ore samples taken over the Sierra to Nevada City were assayed at nearly $3200 a ton in silver, and about half as much in gold. Soon the great rush of fifty-niners from California to Washoe was on, reversing the direction of the rush of '49. To the amazement of the Comstock miners, one of the hardest problems came from the unprecedented size of the veins. Removal of the ore created chambers too vast to be supported by any known method of timbering, and disastrous cave-ins threatened to shut down one of the richest mines until a young German engineer, Philip Deidesheimer, saved the situation by inventing the process of "square sets." These were made of timbers 4 to 6 feet long framed together in a series of interlocked cribs resembling a honeycomb.

The Comstock soon demanded large aggregations of capital for its mines and ore-processing mills, and San Francisco bankers, along with thousands of small investors, rushed to outbid each other for shares in the bonanza. Virginia City saloons provided not only whisky but great quantities of oysters and champagne, and tickets to see such visiting luminaries as Adah Isaacs Menken were sold for as much as $100.

Several mines paid huge returns for several years, but there were many fraudulent sales of stock in properties with no real access to the lode, and the richer mines became entangled in a maze of litigation. In 1864, when a number of the largest ones had run into *borrascas* and were levying assessments on their stockholders instead of paying dividends, the inflated market for silver stocks collapsed and their total value shrank by more than half. The Comstock had come to the end of its first boom, though it was destined for another and larger one a few years later.

AGRICULTURE

As in several other parts of the American far west, cattle ranching was second to mining in the economic life of the frontier period. But agriculture in the sense of the cultivation of the soil, as distinct from grazing, was far less important. The California missions had once produced a variety of grains and fruits for local consumption, but after the missions were secularized, these activities had almost disappeared except for a little grape growing for the purpose of making wine or brandy. Cultivation can barely be said to have existed at all in California during the last years under Mexico, and even after the gold rush its advance was slow and sparse. The insecurity of land titles, the lure of quicker wealth in other activities, and the unfamiliarity of such peculiar farming conditions as the rainless summers all served to retard agricultural development. The food supply of the Argonauts was largely imported; the main exception was California beef, salted or driven to the mining camps on the hoof.

In 1846 there had been about 400,000 cattle in Alta California, worth about $4 a head. At the end of 1849 the price reached $500 a head at Sacramento, and for years afterward it was more than $50. Large herds were driven overland from the lower Mississippi valley and the southwest, thus increasing the stock and, to a degree, improving the breeds. Most of the native Californian rancheros, though suddenly and temporarily prosperous, were ruined by land litigation, interest, taxes, and inexperience in business and financial matters and lost their ranches to Americans or Europeans.

In 1860 the number of cattle in the state was more than 3 million, but 2 years of disastrous drought, from 1862 to 1864, nearly wiped out the herds and the industry. The great drought marked the transition from the "age of grass" to an age of grain, and wheat now replaced beef as the state's most important agricultural product. In the early years the growing of wheat was largely concentrated in the Sacramento Valley, where Sutter had begun to raise it.

Fruit and vegetable production in the early American era were significant mainly in confirming some of the extraordinary potentialities of California soils and climate, and thus foreshadowing the tremendous developments of the future. One of the most important pioneers in the dissemination of knowledge in this field was not a farmer, but a Yankee merchant who became the state's leading agricultural publicist and lobbyist. This was James Lloyd LaFayette Warren, who came to Sacramento from Boston in 1849, engaged in general merchandising, and then specialized in seeds, nursery stock, and agricultural implements. He sponsored the exhibitions that grew directly into the California state fair, and in 1854 he secured the establishment of the State Agricultural Society and even a small annual appropriation for it. He also founded the *California Farmer*, the state's first agricultural periodical.

EARLY MANUFACTURES

The needs of the miners for great quantities of lumber made sawmills the foremost branch of manufacturing in the early period of statehood. Wooden sluices and flumes were indispensable in the more advanced stages of placer and hydraulic mining, as were heavy timbers in the underground operations of the quartz and silver mines. Moreover, construction in the towns was generally of wood, as was fencing in the rural areas. To meet these demands a raw material of spendid quality and supposedly inexhaustible quantity was available in the redwoods. In 1860 Mendocino County produced 35 million feet of lumber, mostly redwood, and Humboldt and Santa Cruz counties milled 30 and 10 million feet, respectively.

Flour milling grew and flourished along with the increasing production of wheat. The development of mills for the making of coarse woolen cloth was similarly interrelated with the spread of sheep raising, while tanneries and the making of heavy leather goods were encouraged by the plentiful supply of cowhides. Another important infant industry was the making of wagons and carriages, of which the outstanding shops were those of John Studebaker at Placerville and Phineas Banning at Wilmington. Claus Spreckels and William T. Coleman emerged as leaders in the refining of sugarcane from the Pacific islands. In iron manufactures the leading establishment was the Union Iron Works at San Francisco, founded in 1849 and using imported iron. The absence of any important deposits of either iron or coal in California, shortages of labor and capital, and the lack of a regional population large enough to make an adequate market were among deterrents to the growth of manufacturing in the state.

TRANSPORTATION

Before the railroads came, the movement of freight and passengers by water was considerably easier than their movement by land. Consequently the first major arteries of inland trade and transportation in American California were the routes of the paddlewheel steamers on San Francisco Bay and on the larger rivers of the Central Valley—between San Francisco and the most important commercial towns of the interior, Sacramento, Stockton, and Marysville. After dozens of small companies had entered the business, overcompetition and rate wars led in 1854 to the consolidation of most of them into the California Steam Navigation Company, which came to enjoy a virtual monopoly of the bay and river traffic. On land, the development of stagecoach lines soon replaced the "pack mule express," and in 1854 five-sixths of the local stage lines were integrated into the California Stage Company, which could then offer regular service over routes totaling more than 1500 miles.

The Overland California Mail Act, passed by Congress in 1857, provided subsidies in the form of mail contracts and thus made possible the opening of overland stagecoach service between St. Louis and San Francisco in the following year. The postmaster general awarded the contract to the Overland Mail Company, headed by John Butterfield of New York, which was able to establish within 12 months a stage line 2800 miles long, employing nearly 1000 people, and providing 24-day service between San Francisco and the Mississippi River. In the meantime there had been spectacular but unsuccessful experiments with camel caravans over the southern route to California and with the pony express over the central one. The pony express, though highly colorful, failed to make any substantial profits during its 18 months of operation and came to an end with the opening of the transcontinental telegraph line in October 1861.

SELECTED BIBLIOGRAPHY

Doris M. Wright "The Making of Cosmopolitan California ... 1848–1870," *California Historical Society Quarterly*, XIX–XX (December 1940 and March 1941), pp 65–79, 323–343, is a detailed study of the varied components in the growth of population. Georges Sabagh, "A Critical Analysis of California Population Statistics ... 1850–1870," M.A. thesis, University of California, Berkeley (1943), points out the defects of the census figures. See also Ralph Mann, "The Decade After the Gold Rush: Social Structure in Grass Valley and Nevada City, 1850–1860," *Pacific Historical Review*, XLI (November 1972), pp. 484–504.

Gold mining in the 1850s and 1860s is described in Rodman W. Paul, *California Gold* (1947) and John W. Caughey, *Gold Is the Cornerstone* (1948), reissued as *The California Gold Rush* (1975). The rise of the hydraulic method is the subject of the first chapter of Robert L. Kelley, *Gold vs. Grain* (1959).

Ira B. Cross, in *Financing an Empire: History of Banking in California* (four volumes, 1927) and in "Californians and Hard Money," *California Folklore Quarterly*, IV (July 1945), pp. 270–277, treats these complex matters with clarity.

The most widely read account of the early years of the Comstock lode was in Mark Twain's *Roughing It*. More serious treatments include Eliot Lord, *Comstock Mines and Miners* (1883); Charles H. Shinn, *The Story of the Mine* (1896); George D. Lyman, *The Saga of the Comstock* (1934); and Grant H. Smith, *History of the Comstock Lode* (1943). California and Nevada mining are placed in broader context in Rodman W. Paul, *Mining Frontiers of the Far West, 1848–1880* (1963); Richard H. Peterson, *The Bonanza Kings: The Social*

Origins and Business Behavior of Western Mining Entrepreneurs, 1870–1900 (1977); and Mark Wyman, *Hard-Rock Epic: Western Miners and the Industrial Revolution, 1860–1910* (1979).

On cattle ranching, see Robert G. Cleland, *The Cattle on a Thousand Hills* (1941); John W. Caughey, "Don Benito Wilson," *Huntington Library Quarterly*, II (April 1939), pp. 285–300; and James M. Jensen, "Cattle Drives from the Ranchos to the Gold Fields of California," *Arizona and the West*, II (Winter 1960), pp. 341–352. On the development of California agriculture: Lawrence J. Jelinek, *Harvest Empire: A History of California Agriculture* (1979); Frank Adams, "The Historical Background," in *California Agriculture* (1946), edited by Claude B. Hutchison; Robert G. Cleland and Osgood Hardy, *The March of Industry* (1929); John S. Hittell, *Resources of California* (1863, 1874, etc); Titus F. Cronise, *The Natural Wealth of California* (1868); Walton Bean, "James Warren and the Beginnings of Agricultural Institutions in California," *Pacific Historical Review*, XIII (December 1944), pp. 361–375; Paul W. Gates, *California Ranchos and Farms, 1846–1862* (1947); Nelson Klose, "California's Experimentation in Sericulture," *Pacific Historical Review*, XXX (August 1961), pp. 213–228; and Gerald L. Prescott, "Farm Gentry vs. the Grangers: Conflict in Rural America," *California Historical Quarterly*, LVI (Winter 1977/78), pp. 328–345. Especially useful is Richard J. Orsi (compiler), *A List of References for the History of Agriculture in California* (1974).

The economic material in the *History of California*, volume VII, 1860–1890, by Frances Fuller Victor and William Nemos (*Bancroft's Works*, volume XXIV, 1890), is fairly comprehensive, though undigested. A valuable study of lumbering is H. Brett Melendy, "One Hundred Years of the Redwood Lumber Industry, 1850–1950," Ph.D. thesis, Stanford University (1952).

On transportation within the state, see Jerry MacMullen, *Paddlewheel Days in California* (1944); Ernest A. Wiltsee, *The Pioneer Miner and the Pack Mule Express* (1931); William and George H. Banning, *Six Horses* (1930); and Oscar O. Winther, *Express and Stagecoach Days in California* (1936). On the overland operations: LeRoy R. Hafen, *The Overland Mail, 1849–1869* (1926); Roscoe P. Conkling and Margaret B. Conkling, *The Butterfield Overland Mail, 1857–1869* (three volumes, 1948); Edward Hungerford, *Wells, Fargo: Advancing the American Frontier* (1949); J. V. Frederick, *Ben Holladay, the Stagecoach King* (1940); W. Turrentine Jackson, *Wagon Roads West* (1952) and "Wells, Fargo Staging over the Sierra," *California Historical Society Quarterly*, XLIX (June 1970), pp. 99–134; Harlan D. Fowler, *Camels to California* (1950); and Raymond W. Settle and Mary Settle, *Saddle and Spurs: The Pony Express Saga* (1955).

BUILDING THE CENTRAL PACIFIC RAILROAD

For 20 years after the gold rush, Americans in California felt extremely remote from the people of the older states, as indeed they were. For many, the dream of a transcontinental railroad symbolized all sorts of hopes for better things.

EARLY PROPOSALS

In the older parts of the country, talk of a transcontinental railroad had begun at least as early as 1832. The first proposal to receive a serious hearing before Congress came in 1845 from Asa Whitney, a New York merchant who had made a large fortune in trade with China and who saw a Pacific railroad as a great new artery of American and European trade with the orient.

Throughout the 1850s, with the intensification of sectional bitterness, southerners feared that a northern or central railroad would develop new free states, and argued that a southern route, which did not have to cross the great barriers of the Rockies and the Sierra Nevada, could be built much more economically and quickly. Northerners, on the other hand, were adamant against a railroad that would aid the expansion of slaveholding. Congress could agree only on a provision for surveys of all the possible routes. These surveys, published in 1855 in 13 fat volumes of *Pacific Railroad Reports*, concluded only that five different transcontinental routes were feasible.

JUDAH AND THE CONCEPTION OF THE CENTRAL PACIFIC

Credit for the specific plan that led to the building of the first transcontinental railroad belongs mainly to Theodore D. Judah, a brilliant young construction engineer. Judah in his twenties had established a reputation as an engineering genius through such feats as the building of the Niagara Gorge Railroad in New York. In 1854, when he was 28, the promoters of the Sacramento Valley

Railroad brought him to California to build their line from Sacramento to Folsom, the first railroad on the Pacific coast.

Judah soon became so fanatically devoted to the idea of a central route for the first transcontinental railroad that a number of his listeners questioned his sanity on the subject, particularly those who had had the experience of crossing the Sierra Nevada. But the idea, with its promise of an end to California's isolation, became increasingly popular, and in 1859 the state legislature approved a Pacific Railroad Convention to drum up interest in the railroad project. When this body met in San Francisco, it delegated Judah to carry its views to Washington, D.C.; however, although he lobbied skillfully and impressively, the sectional deadlock still prevented action.

In 1860 Judah made an intensive search for the best crossing of the Sierra. Daniel W. Strong, a druggist in the prosperous hydraulic-mining town of Dutch Flat, pointed out that Dutch Flat was located on a natural ramp, a long and unbroken ridge extending upward toward Emigrant Gap and Donner Pass. Judah observed that because the slope of this ridge was so gradual and continuous, it would be possible for a railroad to reach the summit elevation of about 7000 feet in a distance of little more than 70 miles from the valley floor with a maximum grade of only 105 feet to a mile. Tremendously excited by this discovery, Judah sat at the counter of Strong's drugstore and drew up tentative articles of association for the Central Pacific Railroad of California.

Judah, Strong, and a number of citizens of Dutch Flat and the neighboring towns were able to muster about a third of the money that would have to be paid down in order to form a corporation. Full of confidence, Judah hurried to San Francisco to secure the remainder, but to his disappointment and disgust not one of the large capitalists in the city would invest in the project. Until Congress acted, they said, construction of the railroad could not begin, and they estimated that after its beginning, 12 to 20 years would pass before its completion. Their money was bringing large and immediate returns in far safer enterprises.

ENTER THE FOUR "ASSOCIATES"

In his appeals to the San Francisco financiers Judah had made the tactical error of including an appeal to their public spirit and long-range vision. He turned next to the merchants of Sacramento, and with them he made no such blunder. Instead he planned his arguments in order to put all the emphasis on the possibilities of large and early returns on very modest initial investments: with a concrete proposal before it, Congress would offer cash subsidies that would pay for the construction; operating income need not wait for completion of the transcontinental line, or even of the line within California; the profitable freighting business between Sacramento and the Comstock could very soon be captured for the Dutch Flat route, simply by building a good wagon road over Donner Pass to the head of construction of the Central Pacific as it advanced into the mountains.

One evening in the autumn of 1860, in a room over the hardware store of Huntington & Hopkins in Sacramento, a group of merchants assembled to hear Judah's plea. Among those present were Collis P. Huntington, Leland Stanford, Charles Crocker, and Mark Hopkins. Since these men were destined to be the "big four," the "railroad kings," of California and of most of the American far west, and thus to acquire not only fantastic wealth but also enormous economic and political power, their backgrounds are of considerable interest.

All of them had come from middle- or lower-middle-class families, and though all were prosperous by 1860, none, as yet, was rich. Collis P. Huntington, the son of a miserly tinker in a small town in Connecticut, had become self-supporting at the age of 14 and a successful traveling salesman a year later. At 21 he was operating his own store at Oneonta, New York. In 1849, with a capital of $1200, he joined the gold rush. Buying and selling food and other supplies while waiting for steamer connections in Panama, he tripled his capital. In California, one day's work in the mines convinced him that mining was not his occupation, and instead he opened a store in Sacramento. Leland Stanford, son of an innkeeper in rural New York, had studied law in an office in Albany and practiced in Wisconsin before coming to California to enter the grocery business in partnership with his brothers. He had been the unsuccessful Republican candidate for state treasurer in 1857 and for governor in 1859. Charles Crocker had been a peddler, iron maker, and gold miner, and was now a Sacramento dry goods merchant. Mark Hopkins, Huntington's partner in the hardware business, was a shrewd and industrious storekeeper, the quietest and least aggressive member of the group; like the rest of them, however, he could be extraordinarily stubborn when he wished to be.

These four—"the associates," as they soon began to call themselves— were tentatively interested in Judah's plan, but cautious. In the spring of 1861, however, the outbreak of the Civil War convinced them that Congress would soon approve the project and subsidize it, and on June 28 the Central Pacific Railroad of California was formally incorporated. Stanford, who had again received the Republican nomination for governor, was elected president of the company, Huntington vice president, and Hopkins treasurer.

Judah was one of the directors and the chief engineer. He was not yet aware of the extent to which he had now lost control of the enterprise or of the difficulties he would soon have with the company's officers. His contributions to the project had thus far been much greater than theirs in every sense except the financial, and their original financial investment was almost incredibly small. The state's railroad incorporation law required stock subscriptions of $1000 per mile of track proposed, in this case $115,000 for 115 miles of track between Sacramento and the state line, but only 10 percent of this amount had to be paid down. Huntington, Stanford, Crocker, Hopkins, and Judah each subscribed for 150 shares of stock at $100 a share; other individuals, most of whom would soon drop out, subscribed for 830 shares more, a total of 1580 shares. But since only 10 percent was paid down, the company started with a mere $15,800 in cash.

In sworn statements made in a legal document filed a few months later,

Mark Hopkins, Collis P. Huntington, Theodore Judah, Leland Stanford, Charles Crocker. *(Courtesy of the Bancroft Library.)*

the not-yet-very-big four reported that their combined personal assets, mostly tied up in their business firms, totaled about $100,000. This figure is interesting and significant in comparison with the personal fortunes totaling about $200 million which they would ultimately gain from Theodore Judah's project.

FEDERAL AND STATE SUPPORT

Judah's next contribution was to secure the indispensable aid of the federal government. In the fall of 1861 he traveled to Washington in the company of the new congressman Aaron A. Sargent, who agreed to sponsor the cause of the Central Pacific in the House of Representatives. Through Senator James A.

McDougall of California, Judah also guided the drafting of the corresponding measure in the Senate. Moreover, he was made clerk of the key railroad committees of both houses and was thus in an ideal position to provide arguments for the project at every point in the debates.

In more recent years, for Congress to permit a lobbyist to hold such a position would be grossly improper. In that era, however, the concept of conflict of interest had scarcely begun to develop in the government service. Judah had little difficulty in persuading Congress that the project was of extraordinary importance. He described it as a military necessity in a war that would continue for many years. A railroad would strengthen the bonds that held the far west in the Union and would hasten the flow of much-needed gold from California and silver from Nevada. The withdrawal of the southern senators and representatives from Congress had removed the main opposition to a central route, and Judah's surveys gave assurance that a route directly across the Sierra was entirely feasible.

The result was the Pacific Railroad Act of 1862, which President Lincoln signed on July 1. It was amended 2 years later to make its terms more generous to the railroads, and thus one can conveniently summarize the acts of 1862 and 1864 together. The Central Pacific, a California corporation, was to build eastward from Sacramento. The Union Pacific, a corporation chartered by Congress, was to build westward from Omaha, Nebraska. The federal government would furnish very extensive loans and land grants to both of these companies.

The loans were in the form of United States 6 percent 30-year bonds, to be issued at the basic rate of $16,000 per mile of track. In the Sierra Nevada and the Rocky Mountains, however, the amount would be $48,000 per mile; for the region between the Sierra and the Rockies it would be $32,000. As security the act of 1862 gave the government a first mortgage on all property of the railroads. This was changed to a second mortgage in 1864 to enable the companies to market their own bonds more effectively by offering the first-mortgage lien to private investors. But it is entirely clear that the government still expected its loans to be repaid—in spite of the later arguments of the railroads in their efforts to escape this obligation.

In addition to loans, United States public lands were granted to the railroad companies in alternate sections, checkerboard fashion, on both sides of the right-of-way. The practice of making gifts of federal land to encourage the development of railroads had been in use since 1850. Under the act of 1864, the Central Pacific and the Union Pacific were given 10 alternate sections (square miles) on each side of the line—that is, half of the land in a strip totaling 40 miles in width. Most of this land would have little value until the railroad was built through it, but its value would then be much increased. The purpose of retaining ownership of the alternate sections for the government was to allow the public treasury to share in the benefits of this increase and at the same time to provide some check on the prices which the railroads could eventually have demanded if they had been allowed a monopoly on all the lands in the 40-mile strip.

Leland Sanford was elected governor in September 1861 and took office in January 1862. He did not scruple to advance his own interests as president of the Central Pacific Railroad by using all his influence as governor. In 1863 he induced the state to add further subsidies to those promised by the federal government. The legislature also authorized several counties to issue bonds enabling them to subscribe for large amounts of Central Pacific stock. The constitutionality of some of this legislation was disputed, but in general the state courts upheld it. When a vacancy occurred in the state supreme court, Governor Stanford appointed Charles Crocker's brother, Edwin B. Crocker, to the unexpired term. The new judge was also the Central Pacific's chief legal counsel, and he did not resign from that position while he was serving as a supreme court justice.

DIFFICULTIES, AND THE DEATH OF JUDAH

Actual construction of the railroad began on January 8, 1863, after Governor (and railroad president) Stanford had thrown the first shovelful of earth in the presence of a crowd assembled near the levee at the foot of K Street in Sacramento. But in spite of the support already promised by the federal government, a tangle of problems held back the early progress of construction and threatened the very life of the project. Costs were heavy. Iron rails and locomotives had to be bought in the east at wartime prices and transported to Sacramento by sea at wartime freight rates. Cash was short, for each 40-mile unit of construction had to be completed before the federal subsidy on it was forthcoming, and interests hostile to the railroad did everything they could to discourage private investors from lending it money. The Pacific Mail Steamship Company, the California Steam Navigation Company, Wells, Fargo & Company, the California Stage Company, and the Sacramento Valley Railroad, as well as all the California bankers who had money invested in one or more of these enterprises, naturally anticipated that the building of the Central Pacific would injure them, and they joined in denouncing it. A pamphlet called *The Great Dutch Flat Swindle* charged that the promoters were not genuinely interested in a transcontinental railroad at all, but merely in the profits of a wagon road to Washoe, and in the collection of subsidies.

The Central Pacific's own chief engineer had reason to know that these charges were not entirely unfounded as they applied to the motives of the "associates" at this time. Feeling that his own personal honor was involved, Judah was now bitterly at odds with the four men who were in control. The differences were those between a man primarily interested in the construction of a great railroad and four men primarily concerned with making enormous profits. When these four awarded the construction contracts to Charles Crocker and Company, a dummy concern owned by themselves, Judah protested as strongly as he could. At last he broke with them completely. In October 1863 he sailed for New York, having accepted $100,000 for his interest in the Central Pacific, but taking with him options to buy out Huntington, Stanford, Crocker, and Hopkins for $100,000 each if he could persuade the Vanderbilts or other eastern capitalists to back him.

At this point the Sacramento four were discouraged and willing, as Charles Crocker put it, to "take a clean shirt and get out," but Judah contracted yellow fever in Panama and died on November 2, shortly after his arrival in New York. His death was a major tragedy. If he had lived and if his hopes for a reorganization of the Central Pacific under his own leadership had been fulfilled, the history of California might have been very different.

In order to begin collecting the larger subsidies for building in the Sierra Nevada, the big four maintained that the "western base" of the mountains was located only 7 miles east of Sacramento. On the plea that without the higher initial subsidies the whole project might have to be abandoned—and with the aid of some ingenious testimony by the California state geologist and the state surveyor general—the federal government was persuaded to accept this remarkable claim, and the base of the Sierra Nevada was thus moved a considerable distance westward into the Sacramento Valley. The big four were now men who could move mountains. They felt no gratitude toward Judah and did not even name a crossroads station in his honor. When at last something like a suitable monument to Judah was erected at Sacramento in 1930, the initiative came not from the railroad's management but from the American Society of Civil Engineers.

SOLVING THE PROBLEMS OF CONSTRUCTION

By 1865 the initial shortage of cash had been overcome. Federal, state, and county subsidies had built up the Central Pacific's treasury, and freight and passenger revenues began to come in with the completion of the early sections of track. Moreover, the money paid out for construction was being paid to Charles Crocker and Company on terms that assured very generous profits to that company's backers, the big four. At the outset Crocker knew nothing whatever about the building of a railroad, but in view of the remarkable profits to be gained from that activity, under contracts made without the inconvenience of competitive bidding, he was more than willing to learn.

A shortage of labor now replaced the shortage of cash as the most chronic problem holding back the rate of construction. California white workers demanded high wages, and many of them accepted jobs only in order to get a free ride for part of the way to the Washoe mines; then they would work on the railroad only long enough to earn the price of a stage ticket for the remainder of the distance to Virginia City. In desperation Stanford suggested an experiment with Chinese laborers, even though in his inaugural address as governor in 1862 he had vigorously denounced the immigration of Asians. J. H. Strobridge, superintendent of construction under Crocker, ridiculed the idea on the ground that men whose average weight was only about 110 pounds would be useless for such heavy labor, but Charles Crocker was not

Chinese workers replacing a trestle with earth fill. *(Courtesy of the Bancroft Library.)*

so sure, and he decided to give the Chinese a trial. The first experiment, with a crew of 50 Chinese in 1865, was so phenomenally successful that agents were soon recruiting them by the thousands, first in California and then in South China. At the peak of its construction work, the Central Pacific would employ more than 10,000 Chinese laborers, largely brought from China for the purpose.

Labor unions in San Francisco protested, but as the railroad advanced into the mountains and construction continued throughout the year, white workers lost all interest in jobs that required the performance of hard and dangerous labor under the conditions of winter in the Sierra. The Chinese, on the other hand, would work under any conditions at all, for long hours, and at low wages, and they made only one brief effort to strike. Near Cisco in July 1867 about 3500 of them demanded a 12-hour day and $40 a month instead of $30. They gave up even these modest demands when the company threatened to discharge them. Crocker was becoming a hard-driving manager. Roaring up and down the line "like a bull," as he put it, he constantly urged the Chinese to greater efforts. Astonishing quantities of earth were moved with no more equipment than wheelbarrows and one-horse dump carts.

With its labor problem solved, the Central Pacific next confronted some of the world's most extraordinary physical obstacles to the building of a railroad. To get around "Cape Horn," a huge and almost vertical cliff, Chinese workers were suspended along its granite face in wicker baskets, chipping away at the rock with hammers and chisels to create a ledge. Much greater were the difficulties in the building of Summit Tunnel, which had to be drilled through a quarter of a mile of granite so hard that blasts of the black powder then in use merely spurted back through the drill holes. The steam powered drill had recently been invented, and Stanford purchased one and sent it up the railhead. Strobridge refused to use it, however, even though Stanford furiously pointed out that the daily progress of the Union Pacific was being measured in miles, and that of the Central Pacific in inches. Summit Tunnel took more than a year to complete, beginning in the summer of 1866. It was the last major tunnel in the world to be built with hand tools. On the other hand, the construction of 37 miles of snowsheds did much to redeem the Central Pacific from the charge of backwardness in methods of mountain railroad building.

Charles Crocker and Company did nearly all the original construction work between Sacramento and the Nevada line. To build the remainder of the road the big four organized a new corporation in 1867. This was the Contract and Finance Company, in which Huntington, Stanford, Crocker, and Hopkins were practically the only stockholders. In fairness to them it must be said that the Central Pacific was not the only railroad in this period whose chief stockholders were following the practice of letting contracts to themselves. The Union Pacific, for example, was doing the same thing through its dummy, the Crédit Mobilier. Because the books of Charles Crocker and Company and the Contract and Finance Company mysteriously disappeared, it has never been possible to determine exactly how large their profits were. But from evidence gathered in later investigations by the federal government, the big four probably received twice as much as they had to pay out for the actual costs of construction.

As the tracks advanced across Nevada and into Utah, a spectacular race developed between Crocker's Chinese and the Union Pacific's Irish Americans. At its climax, "Crocker's pets" established the record of 10 miles of track laid in a single day, and although the Union Pacific's chief construction engineer, Grenville M. Dodge, pointed out that "they took a week preparing for it, and embedded all their ties beforehand," he could not entirely conceal his admiration. Before Congress fully realized that it had neglected to specify the point where the two railroads should meet, they were building side by side, both anxious to garner the subsidy for every possible mile.

Promontory, Utah, was finally designated as the meeting point, and there in a famous and colorful ceremony on May 10, 1869, the joining of the rails officially took place. Telegraphers reported each step over wires kept open throughout the nation. A polished laurel tie was laid down, the last rail was put in place, and several spikes were presented, including one of Comstock silver and two of California gold. A telegraph line was attached to the last spike and another to a silver sledgehammer; Stanford swung to complete the circuit, and missed, but a telegrapher simulated the blow with his key, and church bells, fire bells, factory whistles, and cannon announced the news in cities all over the country. Exactly a century after the founding of the first Spanish settlement in Alta California in 1769, iron rails linked American California to her kindred states.

SELECTED BIBLIOGRAPHY

The apparently deliberate destruction of many of the most significant documents by officials of the Central Pacific and its subsidiary companies, and the destruction of the entire central depository of records of the Southern Pacific by the San Francisco earthquake and fire of 1906, have placed most unfortunate limits on detailed historical knowledge of the building and development of "the railroad." Nevertheless, several important works have been written. Oscar Lewis, *The Big Four* (1938) is highly readable. Helen H. Jones, *Theodore D. Judah* (1969) is a biography; Carl I. Wheat, "A Sketch of the Life of Theodore D. Judah," *California Historical Society Quarterly*, IV (September 1925), pp. 219–271, is more than a mere sketch. Stuart Daggett, *Chapters on the History of the Southern Pacific* (1922) is an intensely critical study by a professor of transportation economics. Wesley S. Griswold, *A Work of Giants: Building the First Transcontinental Railroad* (1963) and Robert West Howard, *The Great Iron Trail: The Story of the First Transcontinental Railroad* (1963) are useful accounts of the construction of both the Central Pacific and the Union Pacific. See also Harry J. Carman and Charles H. Muller, "The Contract and Finance Company and the Central Pacific Railroad," *Mississippi Valley Historical Review*, XIV (December 1927), pp. 326–341.

George T. Clark, *Leland Stanford* (1931); Norman E. Tutorow, *Leland Stanford: Man of Many Careers* (1970); and David S. Lavender, *The Great Persuader* (1970), on C. P. Huntington, are sympathetic biographies. Cerinda W. Evans, *Collis Potter Huntington* (two volumes, 1954) is extremely, earnestly, and naïvely apologistic. The recent availability of *The Collis P. Huntington Papers, 1856–1901* (1978) on microfilm is likely to stimulate additional research.

THE ''TERRIBLE SEVENTIES''

By a cruel paradox, the completion of the first transcontinental railroad not only failed to bring California the expected surge of prosperity, but marked instead the beginning of a deep and general depression that continued through the whole of the next decade. A frustrated and embittered populace blamed its disappointments and sufferings on the railroad and on the Chinese. Thus the difficulties of a long period of economic distress were aggravated by racial antagonism and political upheaval.

THE ONSET OF DEPRESSION

One of the many unexpected and unfavorable effects that the completion of the Pacific railroad had on the economy of California was that it suddenly exposed its merchants and manufacturers to intense competition from those of the eastern cities. Until 1869 the bulk of the commerce of California and of most other parts of the far west had come by water to San Francisco. Now the San Francisco merchants, already overstocked in anticipation of new demand, instead found the market glutted with new goods shipped in by rail. Months before the opening of the transcontinental line, hundreds of agents of the mercantile houses of Chicago, in particular, had invaded the far west, busily writing orders and capturing the customers of San Francisco firms. As for the hope that the goods exchanged between Europe and the orient would be transshipped by rail across North America and thus help to enrich California's great seaport, most of that trade now passed instead through the Suez Canal, opened in the same year as the Pacific railroad.

California speculators had so overinflated the prices of land in anticipation of a boom that the actual completion of the Central Pacific caused a reaction and a decline in real estate values, rather than an advance. Though the railroad brought in thousands of new residents, most of them could not afford to buy land at high prices, and many could not afford it at any price.

After many years of labor shortage there was now an oversupply and chronic unemployment. In 1868 various labor organizations had been strong enough to secure the passage of a state law providing for an 8-hour day in public works contracts, and unions had been able to persuade many private employers to agree to the same policy. In order to roll back this advance on the part of labor, certain employers in San Francisco established a California Labor and Employment Exchange and an Immigrant Aid Association, through which they carried on a nationwide propaganda campaign designed to bring as many new workers as possible to California and thus to weaken labor's bargaining power. At the same time, Chinese immigration increased sharply, encouraged by the Burlingame Treaty of 1868, and the completion of the railroad released about 12,000 Chinese construction workers, nearly all of whom drifted back to crowd the California labor market.

When the panic of 1873 struck the national economy as a whole, it intensified the depression that had begun in California 4 years earlier.

TRANSPORTATION MONOPOLY

When the first transcontinental railroad was opened, the big four did not believe that freight and passenger revenues would ever provide the large and guaranteed profits that they had received from construction subsidies. Thus they made efforts to retire from railroading with the fortunes they had already accumulated, but for several reasons they did not carry out their plans. The original reason was that they could find no buyers on terms they regarded as favorable, but there were other and more positive factors, which reconciled them to continuing in the railroad business. There were more land grants to be had, from further construction within California and from a new transcontinental line to be built on the southern route. Even more important, there was the prospect of being able to control rates and ensure profits by establishing throughout most of the far west a monopoly—of unprecedented degree and scope—over transportation, the life's blood of the regional economy.

To ensure its control over the main seaport area, the Central Pacific put together a network of local rail lines around San Francisco Bay and also gained virtually complete domination of the bay's strategic waterfronts.

In 1852 the ownership of all the waterfront and tidelands of Oakland had been granted to that infant community by the state. Oakland, in turn, had promptly granted the whole of these lands to one of its leading citizens, Horace W. Carpentier, in return for his promise to build three wharves and a schoolhouse. In 1868 Carpentier offered the railroad a controlling interest in the waterfront if it would make Oakland its main terminus on the east side of the bay. Ownership of the lands then passed to the Oakland Waterfront Company, a new corporation in which Carpentier and Leland Stanford were the main stockholders. Not until the early twentieth century would the monopoly of Oakland's waterfront be broken.

San Francisco, though it put up a bitter fight, was hardly more successful in escaping from decades of railroad domination. Most of its tidelands had remained under state ownership. In 1868, at the suggestion of ex-Governor Stanford, a state senate committee recommended that several miles of the San Francisco waterfront, including all of it that was suitable for railroad terminal facilities, be sold at nominal prices to corporations controlled by the big four. The *Bulletin* led other newspapers in denouncing this proposal as a breathtaking outrage, and the railroad had to be content with a mere 60 acres. But this was enough for a terminal; the Central Pacific had other means of assuring that no competing railroad would approach San Francisco for a long time to come, and it had already established political control of the state board of harbor commissioners.

While they were completing their stranglehold on the bay, the big four were also making plans to capture the rest of California. They bought out the promoters of the California and Oregon Railroad and began construction of the "Shasta route," extending up the Sacramento Valley and eventually to Portland. A line to run southward from the San Francisco Bay region through the coastal counties to Los Angeles and San Diego had been proposed in 1865 as the announced purpose of a Southern Pacific Railroad Company incorporated by a group of San Francisco capitalists. The big four acquired control of the Southern Pacific in the late sixties. In the meantime, in 1866, Congress had provided for the first southern transcontinental railroad and authorized the Southern Pacific to build its western link. Thus by gaining control of the original Southern Pacific, the chief owners of the Central Pacific not only gained control of southern California but also guaranteed themselves a long period of freedom from competition with another transcontinental route.

In 1870 the big four were ready to begin construction of the line to southern California—the contracts, of course, being awarded to the Contract and Finance Company. They had already decided not to build along the coast, but rather through the San Joaquin Valley, because the usable lands in the coastal counties were under private ownership, while the San Joaquin Valley was still largely government land where the railroad could locate its grants along its right-of-way.

In its dealings with cities and towns the railroad was equally ruthless in putting its own interests ahead of the public's. Los Angeles, though it had only about 6000 people, was the largest town in southern California and already had rail connections with the coast at San Pedro and Santa Monica. Crocker threatened to ruin Los Angeles by leaving it off the main line unless it would make the Southern Pacific a present of the Los Angeles and San Pedro Railroad, and pay a further subsidy of $600,000. In an effort to make San Bernardino an example of what could happen to towns that resisted this kind of extortion, the Southern Pacific built its division point a few miles away, thus creating the new town of Colton. For similar reasons the Central Pacific had created the "spite towns" of Lathrop, near Stockton, and Goshen, near Visalia.

By 1882 the Southern Pacific had gained full domination of the southern transcontinental line; its "Sunset Route" extended all the way from southern California to New Orleans. For many years the big four sought to maintain the fiction that the Central Pacific, the Southern Pacific, and a number of other lines were under separate control, but the newspapers and the public became well-aware that "the railroad" was a single entity. They began to call it "the Octopus" and to think of its tracks as tentacles reaching from Oregon to Louisiana. Officially, the name Southern Pacific emerged as the name of the whole system in 1884, when the Southern Pacific Company of Kentucky was incorporated and took a lease on all property of the Central Pacific. Kentucky was chosen for the legal corporate headquarters of the system, not because the big four had plans for operating there, but simply because the railroad incorporation laws of that state were among the laxest in the Union.

Monopoly of California rails would not have provided so effective a monopoly of transportation if there had been extensive competition by water. But in 1869 the big four bought the California Steam Navigation Company, and with it the control of the bulk of the river traffic. As for ocean commerce, they first made a series of rate-fixing agreements with the Pacific Mail Steamship Company and then, in 1874, organized their own steamship line, the Occidental and Oriental. By 1880 they had so weakened the formerly dominant Pacific Mail that they were able to control it also.

In no other region of the United States did a railroad enjoy such a degree of freedom from competition. Thus entrenched, the big four were free to adopt a system of setting freight rates according to the highest charge that the traffic would bear without completely bankrupting the shipper and thus depriving the railroad of his future business. The railroad could also favor one shipper and ruin another by quoting different rates for the same service. Often its agents would demand to examine the shipper's books and then set the rate according to what they thought the shipper could afford to pay. No railroad system in the world had a greater variety of rates—some high, some low, some published, some secret.

The more modern idea is that an impartial public regulatory body should determine freight and passenger rates that give the railroad a fair profit, according to the costs of providing the transportation. The big four regarded such notions as radical and dangerous nonsense. They firmly believed that in selling transportation they should act just as they would in selling anything else. When Huntington had sold shovels or when Stanford had sold barrels of flour in the Sacramento of the 1850s, they had charged as much as they could get. As late as 1900, Collis P. Huntington would still operate the Southern Pacific according to the ethical principles and the economic and social ideas of a Yankee trader in the gold rush.

The railroad's power to make or break almost anyone engaged in agriculture, mining, manufacturing, or commerce, through its discriminatory freight rates, was effectively used in interrelation with the development of its control over politics. Through its rates it could reward its friends and punish its enemies. If politicians did not have economic interests of their own which could be favored or ruined by rate manipulation, their constituents did. The railroad also corrupted politics in a variety of ways and at all levels of government, federal, state, and local. Money was paid to politicians under an assortment of

The Curse of California. A cartoon from a San Francisco weekly magazine, *The Wasp,* Aug. 19, 1882. *(Courtesy of the Bancroft Library.)*

disguises. An officeholder or candidate who was a lawyer might receive a secret fee or salary for unspecified "legal services." For others, there were contributions for "campaign expenses." The Southern Pacific developed a political machine far more powerful than any other in the state. California's government, as well as its economy, became a prisoner of "the railroad."

LAND MONOPOLY

Further public resentment against the railroad grew out of the fact that it had become by far the largest private landowner in the state. Railroads that became parts of the Southern Pacific system received from the federal government a total of 11,588,000 acres in California, about one-fifth of all the land that is now in private ownership. These railroad land grants, added to various other factors, made the ownership of California's arable land more concentrated than in any other part of the nation. "Land monopoly" was a burning issue.

We have already seen the problems of land tenure that were left over from the Mexican grant system. These had the effect of concentrating much land in the coastal region in large units owned by American speculators. Mexican grants totaling 8,850,000 acres had been confirmed in the American courts. True, the rest of the land in the state had become part of the United States public domain, and the general policy of the federal government, under such laws as the Pre-emption Act of 1841 and the Homestead Act of 1862, encouraged the ownership of this land in small farm units. But in California the operation of that policy was almost entirely thwarted. Both before and after the railroad land-grant acts of the 1860s, public lands that were usable generally passed into the hands of large holders and speculators. If land was fertile or potentially fertile and located where transportation facilities would make it possible to market its produce, such land was usually engrossed by speculators before a genuine homesteader had a chance to file on it.

According to the theory pronounced in 1893 by Frederick Jackson Turner, then a young professor of American history at the University of Wisconsin, "the existence of an area of free land, its continuous recession, and the advance of American settlement westward, explain American development." This "Turner hypothesis" was an oversimplification and exaggeration even as applied to the upper Mississippi valley, the region Turner knew best. As applied to the development of California, the Turner theory of the significance of the frontier is worse than worthless.

The Homestead Act did not put an end to cash sales at auction of public lands that had more than minimum value. This was particularly true of arable public lands within the limits of railroad land grants. The government's retention of the alternate sections in checkerboard pattern often failed to help the early settler, for by the time they were surveyed and opened the settler typically found himself outbid by the speculator. Government surveyors, private surveyors working under government contracts, and officials of the federal and state land offices acquired advance knowledge of the lands and used this knowledge for speculation on their own behalf or in collusion with others. Many of the most successful California land brokers were also surveying contractors, and thus laid the foundations of their prosperous careers.

The federal government granted more than 8 million acres of land to the state—2 million acres as "swamp and overflow" land under the act of 1850 and more than 6 million acres for educational purposes. The state's disposition of these lands was careless, improvident, and in many cases riddled with fraud. Lands in California that had the appearance of swamps in the rainy season might actually be among the richest lands, but they were sold, mostly to large operators, at $1.25 per acre, which was refunded to the purchasers if they swore that they had spent a like amount in reclamation.

The possibilities for building up huge land holdings were spectacularly illustrated in the story of Henry Miller, who became the state's leading cattle baron. Born Heinrich Alfred Kreiser, he had arrived in New York from Germany at 19, in 1847, with no resources except his boyhood training in the care of livestock and the cutting of meat. In 1849, with the savings from his wages as a butcher's helper, he bought a ticket to California. From operating a butcher shop in San Francisco, Miller quickly branched out, buying cattle and

Miller Lux holdings in the north San Joaquin Valley. From Wallace Smith, *Garden of the Sun,* Lymanhouse, Los Angeles, 1939. *(Courtesy of the Bancroft Library.)*

then buying lands for pasturage. In the modern San Joaquin Valley, for example, he was so skillful in acquiring swamp and overflow lands that eventually he owned both banks of the San Joaquin River in a solid strip more than 100 miles long, from the area west of Modesto to the region of Madera. Through water monopoly he was able to control much of the land surrounding his own. He formed an effective partnership with Charles Lux, a tall Alsatian who was somewhat more polished than Miller and had a slightly better command of English, and who often represented the firm's interests in San Francisco while Miller was looking after its ranches in the interior. Ultimately Miller & Lux owned more than a million acres in California, Nevada, and Oregon, and Miller liked to boast that he could ride from Mexico to Oregon and sleep every night in a ranch house of his own.

The engrossment of arable land in advance of agricultural settlement and development was a chronic problem in California, and would long have remained so, even if it had not been increased and complicated by the railroad land grants. In general, the question of the wisdom and necessity of granting public lands to railroads in the American west has remained highly debatable. The legal purpose of the grants was to aid the construction of the lines, but the railroads derived their returns from them after the lines were built—often many years afterward. In California, in particular, the grants clearly proved to have been an unwise and unsound policy. They added greatly to the wealth and power of the owners of the Southern Pacific at a time when their wealth and power had already become far too great for the public good.

The expansion of the railroad network in the 1870s did have the desirable effect of encouraging the spread of agricultural settlement in the great Central Valley, but it also created a special set of land-tenure problems. Some of these may be seen in poignantly human terms in the tragic experiences of the settlers of the district of Mussel Slough, near Hanford in what is now Kings County.

The Southern Pacific had published a number of pamphlets inviting settlers to occupy lands within the limits of its grant in the southern counties of the San Joaquin Valley. The railroad had not yet acquired full legal ownership of these lands from the federal government, but its pamphlets promised that as soon as it did so, the settlers would be assured the right to buy the land they had occupied. Prices were predicted in vague and misleading terms, such as "from $2.50 upward" per acre; however, it was very clearly stated that the prices would not include the value of the settler's improvements. Mussel Slough, which carried part of the waters of the Kings River into Tulare Lake, offered possibilities for irrigation, and between 1872 and 1875 the settlers pooled their labor and constructed an elaborate system of irrigation works.

Congress repeatedly failed to appropriate enough money for the effective administration of the land offices, and this delayed the sale of the lands for many years. In 1878, after the railroad had at last acquired the titles, it addressed letters to all settlers informing them of the price of the land they occupied and that it was now for sale "to anyone." These prices ranged from $17 to $40 per acre, and the settlers charged that they included the value of their improvements, in violation of the railroad's published promises. But the federal courts upheld the railroad's contention that it was violating no specific legal contract. The settlers tried to negotiate a compromise price scale, and here, as in a number of other matters, there is some evidence that Stanford would have liked to compromise in the interest of public relations and good-will. Huntington, however, was adamant. His demand for "what the land is worth" resembles his demand for what the traffic would bear.

Walter J. Crow and Mills D. Hart now purchased occupied lands from the Southern Pacific at about $25 per acre. The settlers charged that Crow and Hart, whom they described as "Buzzard and Gizzard," were dummy purchasers hired by the railroad, although this assumption was based only on the fact that they were willing to pay the railroad's price for the land. The two men were not complete newcomers to the region as several accounts have mistakenly assumed; Crow's family were themselves pioneer settlers of the San Joaquin Valley, and his grandfather was the founder of Crow's Landing, west of Modesto.

On the morning of May 11, 1880, United States Marshal Alonzo W. Poole, acting under federal court orders from San Francisco, drove out in a buggy with Crow and Hart to put them in possession of the lands they had purchased and to evict the occupants. When a group of more than 20 settlers appeared, mounted and armed, the result was the "battle of Mussel Slough," at a point about 5 miles northwest of Hanford. The marshal did not participate in the shooting, and it is impossible to determine who fired first. Seven men were killed, including Crow and Hart. Later five of the settlers were convicted of resisting a federal officer and served 8-month jail sentences. But since much of the public believed that the railroad had cruelly deceived and robbed the settlers, the prisoners were widely regarded as heroes rather than convicts. More than any other single development, the tragedy at Mussel Slough dramatized the intense popular resentment against large landholders in general and the railroad in particular.

THE COMSTOCK AND OVERSPECULATION

During the 1870s the mining industry proved to be as great a disappointment as the railroad. In this period the Comstock lode experienced its greatest boom. It produced about three times as much silver as in the previous decade, because of the unparalleled richness of the ore at the deeper levels. Yet the effect on California was not to relieve the depressed conditions of the 1870s but to make them worse. The capital of the region, badly needed in other fields, became concentrated in the speculative market for Nevada mining stocks, and the gyrations of these stocks on the San Francisco exchange infected the public with a gambling mania that became one of the most unhappy characteristics of the times. The new bonanza created enormous fortunes for a few men who controlled the richest mines and thus had inside knowledge to use in manipulating the stock market—but by this process they impoverished thousands of other investors. The "bonanza kings" also engaged in a number of spectacular struggles with each other, in which the investing public and the general welfare usually suffered.

The first group to attain a degree of power that justified the title of "kings of the Comstock" were certain officials of the Bank of California, who became known as the "bank ring" or "Ralston's ring." A state law of 1862 had permitted the incorporation of banks, and under this law William Chapman Ralston had organized the Bank of California in San Francisco in 1864, just as the first Comstock boom was ending. Most of the mines were in *borrasca*, and several of them were flooded. Many of the owners were in financial difficulties, and William Sharon, who Ralston had chosen as the bank's agent in Virginia City, tempted them into heavy borrowing. Then, after a series of foreclosures, the bank came into control of a major portion of the mines and mills. These were consolidated under Sharon's management and new machinery was installed; deeper deposits of rich ore were discovered, and millions of dollars began to pour into the vaults of the bank and the personal accounts of its officials.

With so much of the Comstock's silver behind it, the Bank of California now became and remained for several years the most highly regarded financial institution in the far west, and William Chapman Ralston was generally rocognized as the leading citizen of San Francisco. Toward that city, in his own mind, his relationship became that of Lorenzo de Medici to Florence. He sponsored and controlled a panoply of enterprises—carriage, watch, and furniture factories, woolen mills, foundries, and sugar refineries, a theater, and urban and rural real estate. In his villa at Belmont he provided lavish hospitality for every famous personage who came to San Francisco. For the distinguished tourist in California an invitation to Belmont became more essential than a trip to Yosemite. When Ambassador Anson Burlingame passed through on his way to China, Ralston named a townsite after him and sold him one of its attractive lots for a future home.

It is interesting to compare the occasion when Ralston had the opportunity to have a town named after himself. The directors of the Central Pacific, in the process of creating a new community on their line in the northern San Joaquin Valley, offered to name it Ralston, partly in gratitude for a loan he had once made to Stanford. Ralston politely declined the honor—but the railroad directors insisted on bestowing it upon him less directly. They named the town Modesto. The idea that modesty was actually one of Ralston's prominent traits can only be regarded, as the directors regarded it, with some hilarity. They were well-aware that it was San Francisco, and not a raw new village, which he wished to be considered as his monument.

About the time of the organization of the Bank of California, a self-trained mining engineer named Adolph Sutro conceived a brilliant and daring plan for a revolutionary method of mining the Comstock lode. This was to build a tunnel 4 miles long, beginning at a point near the Carson River and extending into the heart of Mount Davidson to strike the center of the lode at a depth of about 1650 feet, directly under Virginia City. At that time the mines had reached levels of only about 500 feet, but many geologists believed that the lode was a true fissure vein, thousands of feet deep. A tunnel, Sutro thought, was the only effective solution. This was a magnificent plan, but Ralston and Sharon opposed it. If the mines became dependent on the use of his tunnel, then Sutro, not Ralston and Sharon, would rule the Comstock. Other capitalists, following the lead of the mighty Bank of California, refused to invest in the tunnel or to lend money to its promoter.

Not even a beginning was made in the actual construction of the Sutro tunnel until the autumn of 1869. In the meantime the supremacy of Ralston and Sharon was being challenged from another quarter, by the rising fortunes of a group of four Irishmen who would eventually be the wealthiest of the Comstock's kings. John W. Mackay, James G. Fair, James C. Flood, and William S. O'Brien had all been sons of poor Irish immigrants. Mackay and Fair achieved their first successes as Comstock mine superintendents. Flood and O'Brien began their careers as partners in the ownership of a San Francisco saloon, where for several years they had the benefit of informative conversation with the leading stockbrokers who were their best customers. Then, having established a stock brokerage firm of their own, they met Mackay and Fair, with whom they formed a remarkably effective combination. Mackay and Fair were experts on the mines; Flood and O'Brien knew the San Francisco stock market. With inside information, shrewd guesses, and good luck, their fortunes increased steadily, and in 1873 they struck the big bonanza, the very "heart of the Comstock," underlying a group of neglected mines which they had bought up and merged under the name of the Consolidated Virginia.

Ralston, whose preeminence was thus threatened, had been overextending himself in imaginative but unsound investments, such as silk mills and a large tobacco plantation near Gilroy. In 1872 he began construction of the Palace Hotel, intended to be the largest and most lavish in the world. With its tier-on-tier balconies around a central garden court, it required 3 years to complete and cost nearly $7 million. The Palace was a larger luxury hotel than the city could then support, and for many years most of its hundreds of rooms were usually unoccupied.

In the attempt to replenish his wealth, dangerously depleted by such prodigal ventures, Ralston resorted to a desperate gamble. Believing that the Consolidated Virginia's big bonanza must extend into the property of the neighboring Ophir mine, he set out to gain control of the Ophir by buying up a majority of its stock. This drove prices on the San Francisco exchange to ridiculous and unprecedented heights. Elias Jackson Baldwin, then the Ophir's largest stockholder, sold out to Ralston at the very peak, and was known ever after as "Lucky" Baldwin. In January 1875, information that the great bonanza did not actually extend to the Ophir led to the collapse of its stock.

On August 26, 1875, a run on the Bank of California forced Ralston to close the bank's doors. Next morning the directors asked for and received his resignation; then he went for his accustomed swim in the waters of the bay, from which his body was recovered a few hours later. Whether he died by accident or suicide is unknown.

The "Irish four" made Ralston's calamity their own opportunity. Mackay, Fair, Flood, and O'Brien took over several of the bank's mines and mills, consolidated them with their own combine, and established a degree of control over the Comstock that exceeded anything the bank ring had achieved. Not content with the profits of mining the greatest silver strikes of all time, they took full advantage of their power to "milk" the stock market. A suit by an outraged minority stockholder provided documentation of some of their methods; periodically they sold their stocks at the highest levels, then bought them back at low prices after deliberately giving out bearish information to break the market, thus ruining many of the smaller holders. They also did everything they could to obstruct the completion of Sutro's tunnel, just as Ralston and Sharon had done. By the time the tunnel was completed, in 1879, the richest ore bodies had already been exhausted and the great days of the Comstock were over.

SELECTED BIBLIOGRAPHY

"The Terrible Seventies" is the title of a chapter in Gertrude Atherton's *California, an Intimate History* (1914). The volumes by Lewis, Daggett, Tutorow, and Lavender, cited for the previous chapter, are also useful here. See also Henry George, "What the Railroad Will Bring Us," *The Overland Monthly*, I (October 1868), pp. 297–304, and John H. Kemble, "The Big Four at Sea; the History of the Occidental and Oriental Steamship Company," *Huntington Library Quarterly*, III (April 1940), pp. 339–358.

On land monopoly, see Chapter 6, "California Latifundia," in Carey McWilliams, *California: The Great Exception* (1949) and Paul W. Gates, "The Homestead Law in an Incongruous Land System," *American Historical Review*, XLI (July 1936), pp. 652–681. Gates, "California's Agricultural College Lands," *Pacific Historical Review*, XXX (May 1961), pp. 103–122, shows the extent to which the Morrill Act facilitated land speculation. Lloyd J. Mercer, "Land Grants to American Railroads: Social Cost or Social Benefit?" *Business History Review*, XLIII (Summer 1969), pp. 134–151, defends the grants. The largest speculator's defense of his own activities may be found in "Henry George Reexamined: William S. Chapman's Views on Land Speculation in Nineteenth Century California," by Gerald D. Nash, in *Agricultural History*, XXXIII (July 1959), pp. 133–137.

Edward F. Treadwell, *The Cattle King* (1931) is a laudatory "dramatized biography" of Henry Miller by a Miller & Lux attorney. James L. Brown, *The Mussel Slough Tragedy* (1958) is a balanced account, as is the chapter on the same subject in Wallace Smith, *Garden of the Sun; a History of the San Joaquin Valley, 1772–1939* (1939); see also John A. Larimore, "Legal Questions Arising from the Mussel Slough Land Dispute," *Southern California Quarterly*, LVIII (Spring 1976), pp. 75–94.

George D. Lyman, *Ralston's Ring; California Plunders the Comstock Lode* (1937) covers the period from 1864 to 1875. See also David Lavender, *Nothing Seemed Impossible: William C. Ralston and Early San Francisco* (1975); Dan De Quille (William Wright), *The Big Bonanza* (1876, 1947); C. B. Glasscock, *The Big Bonanza* (1931); the works by Lord and Smith cited for Chapter 14; and Robert E. Stewart, Jr., and Mary F. Stewart, *Adolph Sutro, A Biography* (1962). Oscar Lewis, *Silver Kings; the Lives and Times of Mackay, Fair, Flood, and O'Brien* (1947) deals largely with their personal lives and those of their families.

POLITICAL TURMOIL AND A NEW CONSTITUTION

THE INCREASE OF ANTI-CHINESE SENTIMENT

During most of the 1860s, when jobs were plentiful in California, the flow of Chinese immigration was slight; indeed, there were years in the middle sixties in which the Chinese who returned from California to China actually outnumbered those who came. At the end of that decade, however, when the beginning of a long period of hard times and unemployment coincided with a renewed upsurge of Oriental immigration, many Californians and particularly workers demanded ever stronger measures designed not merely to exclude any further Chinese immigrants but to drive out those who had already arrived. At the same time, the federal government—through the Burlingame Treaty, the Fourteenth Amendment, and the Civil Rights Act of 1870—positively encouraged Chinese immigration and blocked various efforts of state and local authorities to discourage it.

Anson Burlingame was American minister to China under Presidents Lincoln, Johnson, and Grant. As an enlightened Boston Republican, he prided himself on freedom from race prejudice. As American minister, he formed a strong admiration for the Chinese and a strong sympathy for the Chinese imperial government. The Burlingame Treaty of 1868 provided for the right of free immigration. The United States agreed to it with only one amendment, which continued the denial of the right of naturalization. The Fourteenth Amendment to the federal Constitution, ratified in the same year, forbade any state to "deprive any person of life, liberty, or property, without due process of law" or to "deny to any person within its jurisdiction the equal protection of the laws." The federal Civil Rights Act of 1870 prohibited discrimination in the courts and discriminatory taxes against any particular group of immigrants.

Under these measures the federal courts struck down most of the varied and ingenious anti-Chinese weapons in the arsenals of California state and municipal law. For example, in 1870 when the flow of new arrivals had made the tenements of San Francisco's Chinatown even more than usually over-crowded, a new ordinance made it a misdemeanor to maintain or occupy any sleeping room with less than 500 cubic feet of air per person. But the attempt to enforce this provision soon overcrowded the jails to such a degree that the city was grossly violating its own ordinance. In some of the most important opinions that invalidated this and various other anti-Chinese statutes, Justice Stephen J. Field of the United States Supreme Court wrote masterpieces of refined but scathing sarcasm.

Much of the anti-Chinese feeling was based on essentially irrational fears, directed against an alien people who worshiped strange gods, ate strange foods, and were thought to suffer from strange diseases. But there were more substantial grounds for anxiety about the enormous numbers of the Chinese who might swarm into the state if they were freely permitted to do so, not the least of which was that their willingness to accept low wages tended to depress the wages of American workers. It is significant that Irish Americans were in the vanguard of most of the attacks on the Chinese. A generation earlier, when large numbers of Irish had migrated to the United States after the potato fam-ine of the 1840s, it was they who had been denounced as a menace to the living standards of American labor. Now they could enjoy the position of being the denouncers. In the 1870s the Irish and the Chinese were the two largest foreign-born groups in California, each forming more than a tenth of the population of the state. In San Francisco more than a fifth of the popula-tion was Chinese, while the Irish formed almost as large a proportion. The Irish, being white and thus eligible for naturalized citizenship, now formed a large bloc of voters, while the Chinese had no votes.

"Anti-coolie clubs" joined with labor unions and "eight hour leagues" in organizing anti-Chinese parades and other public demonstrations in San Fran-cisco. "Coolie" was a word around which a great deal of emotion and confu-sion revolved. It was not, as most Americans assumed, a word of Chinese ori-gin, or a word peculiarly descriptive of a Chinese labor system. Its probable derivation was from *kuli,* meaning "muscle" in Tamil, a language of the Coro-mandel coast of southern India. The British, using it to mean a hired unskilled laborer or servant, introduced the word into China, where it was approxi-mated by two Chinese characters meaning "bitter strength." In the middle of the nineteenth century a flourishing traffic in the importation of laborers from China into Cuba and South America became known as the "coolie trade." Many of these laborers had been kidnapped and were held under "labor con-tracts" that amounted to slavery; consequently the American, British, and Chinese governments made the vicious traffic illegal and sought to stamp it out.

It was often charged that the bulk of Chinese immigration to California was a part of this same infamous coolie system, enforced by the Chinese Six Companies in San Francisco. On the other hand, these companies earnestly denied that any Chinese had come to California involuntarily and earnestly asserted that their own purposes in helping their compatriots to find jobs were wholly benevolent. The truth was somewhere between these two opposite claims. It was true that the Six Companies performed many of the functions of benevolent fraternal societies. But even if they did not enforce any particular labor contracts and even though the credit-ticket system theoretically permitted immigrants to choose their own jobs, the enforcement of that system by the companies nevertheless involved a degree and kind of exploitation and debt peonage that deepened and prolonged the poverty of most of the immigrants involved.

The strongest defenders of the Chinese, apart from Christian missionary groups, were California employers, whose most common argument was that the Chinese did no harm to American labor because they performed only the hard or menial tasks that white workers did not want, such as the reclaiming of tule swamps, seasonal agricultural labor, domestic service, or laundering. But opponents of Chinese immigration argued that the Chinese were monopolizing a number of such occupations because their availability as cheap labor had depressed the wages paid in them. Moreover the Chinese were being employed in a growing list of industries in which they were clearly in competition with whites, especially the manufacturing of clothing, cigars, and tinware. When Chinese began to be not merely workers in such factories but also owners of them, thus threatening to put white manufacturers out of business, a number of white employers suddenly became as anti-Chinese as the white workers had ever been.

There were several outbreaks of mob violence. The worst occurred in Los Angeles on the evening of October 24, 1871, after a white man had been killed in the course of a police attempt to intervene in a dispute between two Chinese companies. With complete inpunity a mob of about 500 people looted and burned the local Chinatown and killed 18 or 19 Chinese, leaving 15 of them hanging from makeshift gallows. Lesser incidents occurred sporadically throughout the 1870s in towns all the way from Chico to San Diego. California newspapers deplored these outbreaks, largely on the ground that they gave California a bad name in the eastern states and made eastern newspapers unsympathetic toward California's demands for Chinese exclusion.

THE WORKINGMEN'S PARTY OF CALIFORNIA

Unemployment, discontent with economic, social, and political conditions in general, and the idea that the Chinese were the prime cause of all difficulties combined to bring about a crisis of unrest in San Francisco in the summer and fall of 1877. The number of Chinese immigrants arriving at San Francisco in the previous year, more than 22,000, had broken all records, and the resulting situation may be compared not to a melting pot but to a pressure cooker. A severe drought in the winter of 1876–1877 had sharply reduced both agricultural production and the hydraulic mining of gold. Moreover, the final decline of the Comstock lode had begun. Even the Consolidated Virginia, richest of all the Comstock mines, suspended dividend payments in January 1877, and the values of stocks in the leading mines, mostly owned in San Francisco, shrank by $150 million within a few months.

For several years the unemployed of the whole state had flocked into "the city," where they gathered on street corners and vacant lots to discuss their grievances and to grow bitter at the lavish displays of wealth by some of their more fortunate fellow citizens. In the evening of July 23, 1877, there was a mass meeting on the "sand lots" in front of the San Francisco city hall. The reasons for this particular meeting had nothing to do with the anti-Chinese movement. Rather, it was called to express sympathy with the workers in the great railroad strike against reduction of wages, then going on in the eastern states, and to protest against the use of troops in the recent labor riots in Pittsburgh. The meeting itself was entirely orderly, but before it was over an anti-coolie club with a band and banners pushed its way into the crowd and called for a resolution against the Chinese. After this demand had been refused, a mob of hoodlums left the outskirts of the meeting, gathered recruits, and wrecked or burned a score of Chinese laundries.

The next day a meeting of business owners organized a Committe of Public Safety, with William T. Coleman, the head of the viligance committee of 1856, as president. Nearly 6000 men enrolled in this "merchants' militia" within a few hours, and the federal authorities responded to Coleman's requests for aid by sending five armed naval vessels from Mare Island to San Francisco and placing 1700 rifles from the Benicia arsenal at his personal disposal. Fearing the consequences of the use of firearms, however, Coleman did not issue all of the rifles, and armed most of his force with hickory pick handles.

In the evening of July 25 a mob tried to burn the docks of the Pacific Mail Steamship Company. Some such action had been suggested periodically for years, because the Pacific Mail was said to be the largest importer of coolies. The "pick handle brigade" and the police were able to disperse the mob and prevent the burning of the docks, but a neighboring lumberyard was burned, and in the melee four men were killed and a number wounded. This marked the end of the rioting, and a few days later the Committee of Public Safety was almost entirely disbanded. Some of the money that had been subscribed for it by frightened property owners was given to the city government for the hiring of 150 special police officers.

From these events many of the city's thousands of unemployed formed the impression that the forces of government were in alliance with the propertied classes against the "workingmen." Thus they were prepared to welcome the idea of a new workers' party that would try to end this injustice by gaining control of the government. Oddly enough, the man who now emerged as the leader of such a movement, a young Irish American named Denis Kearney, was the proprietor of a small business and had himself been a member of the pick handle brigade. A completely adequate explanation of his motives is probably impossible, but he soon acquired a large following, mainly through his emotional and melodramatic style of oratory.

Denis Kearney addressing the Workingmen's party on Nob Hill, Oct. 29, 1877. *(Courtesy of the Bancroft Library.)*

Kearney had been born in the county of Cork in Ireland, had received no formal education at all, and at the age of 11, after the death of his father, had been sent to sea as a cabin boy. In the next 10 years he rose to the rank of first mate, then settled in San Francisco and worked as a drayman. With hard work, thrift, and temperate habits he saved enough to establish a small draying concern of his own. His maritime experiences had given him the power to command people, and when the Workingmen's Party of California took form, between August and October of 1877, he begun as its secretary but soon became its "president." To audiences gathered on the sandlots, Kearney said that workers had as much right as the property owners to be armed and to form militia companies, and to emphasize his point he shouted that "every workingman should have a musket."

In the evening of October 29 Kearney held one of the most dramatic and successful of his meetings. He gathered more than 1000 of his followers at the top of Nob Hill where Crocker, Stanford, and Hopkins had built their mansions, and where Crocker had built his famous "spite fence." Crocker had wished to occupy the entire block between California and Sacramento streets, but a man who owned one small lot with a house on it had refused to sell. Crocker had then surrounded the lot on three sides with a board fence 40 feet high, almost entirely shutting out the view and the sunshine from the little home. Pointing to the fence, Kearney cried that if it was not soon taken down, the working people should tear it down. Then he went on to other remarks about the outrages committed by large capitalists, the corruption of incumbent politicians, and the need for his new political party.

Fearing that Kearney's speeches would lead to more riots like those of July, the city government hastily adopted an ordinance against addressing any meeting of more than 25 persons in language suggesting violence or destruction of property. This promptly became known as the "gag law," and served mainly to increase the pressure of the discontent that it sought to repress. Under this ordinance Kearney was arrested, but in his trial in January 1878 he was acquitted on the ground that no violence had actually resulted from his words. In fact, Kearney's speeches and the hope of successful political action through his new party seem to have offered a kind of safety valve. His speeches were generally extemporaneous, and accounts of them differed widely. For example, he was charged with having said that his followers should hold a Thanksgiving day parade if they had to march "up to their knees in blood", but it was established in court that he had said not "blood" but "mud." The *Chronicle* and the *Call*, which were then engaged in a circulation war for dominance of the morning field, often made his speeches sound more incendiary than they were. By giving a maximum of sensational publicity to his movement, the newspapers presented it with thousands of new

The Wasp's view of the Workingmen's party parade in San Francisco on Thanksgiving day, 1877. *(Courtesy of the Bancroft Library.)*

recruits. These were attracted most of all by Kearney's denunciations of the Chinese. Whatever else he may have said, it is certain that he formed the habit of ending his speeches with: "And whatever happens, the Chinese must go!"

THE CONSTITUTION OF 1879

Demands for a new state constitution had been heard periodically since the 1850s and had increased in volume as the great depression of the 1870s lengthened and deepened. After several defeats at the polls, the calling of a new constitutional convention was finally approved by the voters in the state elections of September 5, 1877. At that time the Workingmen's Party of California was still only in its inceptive stage in San Francisco. By the following April, however, when the legislature passed an enabling act setting the elections of delegates to the convention for June 18, 1878, the party under Kearney's leadership was sufficiently well-organized to nominate a full ticket of delegates in every part of the state. Fear that the Workingmen might actually control the convention became so great among conservatives that in most districts the Republican and Democratic nominations were fused, under the label of "Nonpartisan."

The convention whose delegates were elected in June of 1878 and which met at Sacramento in September was more than three times as large as the Monterey convention of 1849, with 152 delegates as compared with 48. It was in session nearly 6 months, as compared with 6 weeks. In place of an imitative, short, and concise document, it produced one that was much more original, extraordinarily long, and extremely detailed. Yet California's second constitutional convention achieved remarkably little net improvement over the first, and virtually every hope of effective reform was ultimately disappointed.

Of the 152 delegates 78 were Non-partisans, 51 Workingmen, 11 Republicans, 10 Democrats, and 2 independents. Of the Workingmen, 30 were from San Francisco, and thus the Workingmen carried the city but not the state. By occupation, 57 delegates were lawyers, mostly conservatives; 39 were farmers; 8 were merchants; and the others were scattered over a wide range reflecting the diverse skilled trades of the San Francisco work force. The conservative delegates, including some of the shrewdest lawyers and politicians in the state, could have controlled the convention easily had it not been that some of the reforms demanded by the Workingmen were also demanded by the farmers, and that, on the issues where these two groups could unite, they commanded a majority. In Los Angeles County two delegates had even been elected on a joint farmer-worker ticket.

The economic and political discontent of the farmers in the 1870s was expressed largely through the Grange movement, or The Patrons of Husbandry. Founded in Washington, D.C., in 1867 as a social and educational organization for farmers and their wives, with local lodge units known as Granges, the movement became so active in politics after the national panic of 1873 that it gained control of several legislatures in the middle west and secured the passage of state laws for the regulation of railroad rates. More than a fourth of the delegates in the California convention were in effect representatives of the Grange movement, though they had no separate party denomination and included men elected under all five of the official labels.

Railroad regulation was one objective that attracted not only the joint support of workers and farmers but the support of many business organizations as well. A law of 1876 had defined and prohibited extortion and unjust discrimination in rates and had created a state board of three transportation commissioners. The railroad executives had rendered this body powerless simply by refusing to make reports to it, and the legislature of 1878 had reduced the membership to one commissioner, who did nothing more than gather statistics. In an effort to make regulation a reality, the new constitution provided for a state railroad commission of three members elected to 4-year terms, with power to establish rates and to set fines and imprisonments for violations.

The farmers also demanded changes in the tax structure to decrease their excessive tax burden. With the help of the workers they secured a provision that mortgage holders must pay the tax on their portion of the equity in a farm. In the hope of fairer assessments of taxes on land, which had fallen very heavily on the farmers and very lightly on the railroad under the system of independent county assessors, a state board of equalization was created.

Corporations and especially banks were the targets of much invective in the convention. Dr. Charles C. O'Donnell, a San Francisco physician who was one of the most vociferous of the Workingmen delegates, defined a corporation as "a corrupt combination of individuals, formed together for the purpose of escaping individual responsibility for their acts." The new constitution included a number of provisions that sought to increase the accountability of bank and other corporation directors and stockholders.

The anti-Chinese article was long, elaborate, and emotional. It authorized the legislature to protect the state from "aliens, who are, or may become . . . dangerous or detrimental"; it forbade the employment of Chinese by corporations, or on public works "except in punishment for crime"; it authorized cities to restrict the occupancy of Chinese to certain districts or even to forbid their residence within city limits; and it denounced and prohibited "Asiatic coolieism" as "a form of human slavery."

Many of the delegates to the constitutional convention regarded themselves as more truly the representatives of the people than were the members of the legislature, in whom they had very little confidence. They wrote into the constitution of the state a mass of details that would normally have been left to legislative action. The result was almost the longest written constitution in the world, several times as long as the Constitution of the United States; it was ultimately exceeded in length and verbosity only by the constitutions of Louisiana and India.

Virtually no one was entirely satisfied with the convention's massive product, and the public debate over its ratification was confused. Conservatives denounced it as communistic and malicious. Workers, on the other hand, were angered because it did so little that was directly in the interest of labor.

The provision that "eight hours shall constitute a legal day's work on all public works" added nothing whatever to the law of 1868, which had proved to be merely a recommendation without any provision for enforcement. The strongest sentiment for ratification came from the farming areas, where the Grangers cherished dreams of lower freight rates and lower taxes. On May 7, 1879, the new constitution was adopted by a majority of less than 11,000 out of a total vote of 145,000.

THE FRUSTRATION OF REFORM

The general failure of the constitution of 1879 to produce major improvements in the state's government was most glaringly exemplified in the story of the railroad commission. The first elected members were Charles J. Beerstecher, a San Francisco lawyer who had been one of the Workingmen's party delegates in the convention; Joseph S. Cone of Red Bluff, a wealthy farmer; and George B. Stoneman, a future Democratic governor of the state and the only member of the commission who made a serious attempt to carry out his duties, or even to examine the railroad companies' books. These he found incomprehensible, and he had no authority to employ an expert.

Instead of establishing new rates, the commission generally adopted the existing ones, except for a lowering of freight rates on certain agricultural products of the northern Sacramento Valley, where Cone's farm was located. A legislative investigation revealed that Beerstecher suddenly acquired a fortune for which he could not account and that Cone was permitted to buy lands which he then sold to the treasurer of the Southern Pacific at a profit of $100,000. Largely by means of such corrupt methods, the railroad's power to control the state would continue to exceed the state's power to regulate the railroad for three decades more.

The constitutional requirement that the creditor rather than the debtor must pay the tax on the mortgaged portion of property was soon easily and almost universally evaded by raising the interest to a rate large enough to include the tax. Equally disappointing to the farmers was the general ineffectiveness of the state board of equalization. The railroad was usually able to escape from higher assessments by contesting them in the courts.

The Workingmen's party began to disintegrate soon after it reached the zenith of its power in the elections of September 3, 1879, in which the Workingmen elected the chief justice of the supreme court, 5 of the 6 associate justices, 11 senators, and 16 members of the assembly. In addition they elected the Rev. Isaac S. Kalloch, a Baptist minister and sensational pulpit orator, as mayor of San Francisco. His administration, however, was stormy, unsuccessful, and discredited. In the course of a long-continued exchange of personal insults, Kalloch was shot and wounded by Charles de Young, publisher of the *Chronicle*. Kalloch's son later shot and killed de Young and was acquitted of murder. Kearney himself was constantly involved in dissensions with other leaders or would-be leaders of the movement. Within a year after the adoption of the new constitution the Workingmen's party had virtually disappeared.

The constitution, though without substantial reason, was given some of the credit for the upturn in economic conditions in California in 1880, and the return of prosperity reduced the intensity of demands for political and social change.

CHINESE EXCLUSION

Another development that reduced public discontent in California was the surrender of the federal government to the state's demands for a ban on Chinese immigration. This occurred because the anti-Chinese vote in California actually came to hold the balance of power between the parties in national as well as in state politics. Within the state, no party won the governorship in more than two consecutive elections during the half century from 1849 to 1899, and often the majorities were less than 1000 votes. Chinese immigration to the United States was so concentrated on the Pacific coast that the other states could not understand California's concern about the problem, but it became clear that her electoral votes, along with those of Washington and Oregon, could swing the presidency to the party that made the strongest promises to exclude the Chinese.

The presidential elections of 1876 and 1888 were so close that the majorities in the electoral college went to the candidates who had received the minorities of the popular votes. The popular majorities for James A. Garfield in 1880 and Grover Cleveland in 1884 were less than 25,000. In this situation the national Republican and Democratic platforms began to rival each other in echoing Californian anti-Chinese slogans.

Though the federal courts nullified the main provisions of the California constitution with respect to the Chinese, new treaties with China permitted Congress to provide for their exclusion. A federal law in 1882 prohibited Chinese immigration for 10 years, in 1892 this was extended for 10 years more, and in 1902 the ban was made permanent.

SELECTED BIBLIOGRAPHY

Mary Roberts Coolidge, *Chinese Immigration* (1909), the work of a sociologist very sympathetic to the Chinese, tends to assume that unreasoning race prejudice and political opportunism were the only real causes of opposition to Chinese immigration. Elmer C. Sandmeyer, *The Anti-Chinese Movement in California* (1939) presented a more balanced view. Important records of testimony taken in 1876 are the *Report of the Joint Special Committee to Investigate Chinese Immigration*, 44th Cong., 2d Sess. (1877) and the report of the special committee of the California State Senate on *Chinese Immigration; Its Social, Moral, and Political Effect* (1878). Barth, *Bitter Strength*, cited in Chapter 12, is also important here. Other studies include Stuart C. Miller, *The Unwelcome Immigrant: The American Image of the Chinese, 1785-1882* (1970) and Ping Chiu, *Chinese Labor in California, 1850-1880: An Economic Study* (1963), a defense of the Chinese which generally coincides with the employers' arguments. On the Los Angeles riot of 1871, consult the articles by Paul M.De Falla, *Historical Society of Southern California Quarterly*, XLII (March and June 1960), pp. 57-88, 161-185, and William R. Locklear, *Historical Society of Southern California Quarterly*, XLII (September 1960), pp. 239-256.

Alexander P. Saxton, *The Indispensable Enemy: Labor and the Anti-Chinese Movement in California* (1971) throws new light not only on the movement in general but also on its interrelations with the rise of organized labor. See also Stanford M. Lyman, *The Asian in the West* (1970) and Howard Brett Melendy, *The Oriental Americans* (1972).

A good account of the Workingmen's movement is Ralph Kauer, "The Workingmen's Party of California," *Pacific Historical Review*, XII (September 1944), pp. 278-291. Important contemporary treatment includes J. C. Stedman and R. A. Leonard, *The Workingmen's Party of California* (1878), an impassioned defense of Kearney and of the party, and Henry George, "The Kearney Agitation in California," *Popular Science Monthly*, XVII (August 1880), pp. 433-453. The chapter on "Kearneyism in California" in James Bryce, *The American Commonwealth*, vol. II (1889; new edition, 1910) is very critical. Valuable accounts may be found in Ira B. Cross, *A History of the Labor Movement in California* (1935); Cross's edition of the autobiography of *Frank B. Roney: Irish Rebel and California Labor Leader* (1931); Lucile Eaves, *A History of California Labor Legislation* (1910); Winfield J. Davis, *History of Political Conventions in California, 1849-1892* (1893); and Neil L. Shumsky, "San Francisco's Workingmen Respond to the Modern City" *California Historical Quarterly*, LV (Spring 1976), pp. 46-57.

Davis's work is also useful on the history of the constitutional convention, of which the *Debates and Proceedings* were published in three volumes (1880). The best study is Carl B. Swisher, *Motivation and Political Technique in the California Constitutional Convention, 1878-1879* (1930). See also Dudley T. Moorehead, "Sectionalism and the California Constitution of 1879," *Pacific Historical Review*, XII (September 1943), pp. 287-294.

ECONOMIC GROWTH

The increase of wealth in California in the late nineteenth and the early twentieth centuries was substantial, but it was far from being an orderly process. Neither the people of California nor those of the United States had yet learned to exert any significant degree of control over the violent fluctuations of the regional and national economies. The 1880s were relatively prosperous, but the panic of 1893 led to another depression so severe that the growth of California's population in the 1890s was a mere 22.4 percent—the lowest rate for any decade between the 1830s and the 1930s.

The turn of the century, however, coincided with the beginning of a new cycle in which the growth of northern California was impressive and that of southern California truly phenomenal.

THE WHEAT BONANZA

The droughts that had ruined the cattle industry in the early 1860s were followed by a series of rainy winters, and beginning with the crop year 1866–1867 the generous rainfall made possible a full discovery of the potentialities of the Sacramento and San Joaquin valleys for the growing of wheat without irrigation. It was an ideal crop for the wide, flat valley lands in a time of distant markets and a sparse rural population with limited capital, and for about 30 years, from the early 1860s until the panic of 1893, wheat was California's largest and most profitable agricultural commodity.

The largest wheat grower in the state was Dr. Hugh J. Glenn, who had a medical degree from the University of Missouri but who occupied himself after 1867 with buying land on credit until he had 55,000 acres, extending for 20 miles along the west bank of the Sacramento River, where he ultimately produced more than half a million bushels a year. His mammoth wheat ranch was in Colusa County; in 1891, after his death, his achievements were memorialized in the creation of Glenn County.

Wheat ranching was a highly speculative enterprise. It also became increasingly mechanized, and one of the most significant aspects of the age of wheat in the great Central Valley of California lay in its contributions to the development of agricultural machinery. The old walking plow known as the "foot burner," with its single plowshare, was replaced by the "Stockton gang plow," which had several shares attached to a beam, moved on wheels, and was adjustable in width and depth. In the scene made famous in Frank Norris's *Octopus*, there were 35 such plows in echelon formation, each with 5 plow-shares and drawn by 10 horses. At the Glenn Ranch plowing was often done with as many as 100 gang plows at once, each drawn by an eight-mule team. The Central Valley also produced new machines for planting, pulverizing the earth, and spreading it over the seed in one operation, as well as improvements of the earlier machines to combine the cutting and threshing of the grain. The flat land and dry summers of the valley made it possible to use the largest steam-powered "combined harvesters" in the world, machines so large and heavy that they required 36 horses to move them. The need for mechanical motive power led directly to the invention of the tractor, first used in the San Joaquin Valley with steam power in 1886. Later Benjamin Holt of Stockton and others would adapt the tractor to the internal combustion engine and develop the "caterpillar" track.

The dry farming of wheat had the peculiar disadvantages of a one-crop agricultural economy. It was a kind of soil mining, ruthlessly carried on year after year without fertilizer or rotation, and inevitably the soil was exhausted and the yields declined. The average farm was large, bleak, and ugly. Fruit and vegetables came only from cans, purchased along with other food supplies at the grocery store in town. Wheat as a dominant crop began to decline in the middle 1880s under competition from the Mississippi valley and from Russia, and it collapsed in the depression of the 1890s. The spread of irrigation had also begun to make wheat less profitable than other California farm products.

One partial compensation for the decline of wheat growing in the 1890s was the rise of sugar-beet production in the same decade, led by Claus Spreckels with his beet fields and refining plants in the Watsonville and Salinas areas and by the Oxnard brothers, Robert and Henry, in southern California.

WINES

The growing of grapes and the manufacture of the fermented juice into wine had their beginnings in California at the missions, for sacramental purposes and for the personal use of the mission fathers, but though the vines were hardy, the mission grapes and the processes of manufacture were of poor quality. Commercial production also began in southern California. Jean Louis Vignes, a most appropriately named vintner from the region of Bordeaux, brought cuttings from France to a vineyard in Los Angeles in the early 1830s, and William Wolfskill established another vineyard nearby a few years later.

After the discovery of gold the center of grape and wine production shifted to the valleys around San Francisco Bay, and in the 1850s the Hungarian exile Agoston Haraszthy began the work that made him the father of the modern California wine industry, especially at his Buena Vista estate in the Sonoma Valley. In 1861 the state legislature appointed him a commissioner to report on means of improving the industry, and in this capacity he toured the wine regions of Europe and returned with 200,000 cuttings and rooted vines, representing 1400 varieties. Meanwhile, the success of the cooperative community at Anaheim, a German wine colony southeast of Los Angeles founded in 1857, had also become an important factor in the industry's growth.

In the 1870s and 1880s the California vineyards were nearly wiped out by *Phylloxera*, a genus of tiny insects resembling aphids, and the ravages of this pest were brought under control only by gradually replanting the vineyards with resistant stocks. In spite of this and other temporary setbacks the industry flourished, largely by a process of fusing a great number of varieties of European vines and wine-making skills. Vineyards spread through the Sonoma, Napa, Santa Clara, and Livermore valleys. The climate and soils of the Central Valley were also found to be highly favorable, particularly for dessert wines, table grapes, and raisins; ultimately the greatest of all concentrations of vineyards in California would be in Fresno County. In 1900 California produced 19 million gallons of wine, more than 80 percent of the nation's output.

THE CITRUS INDUSTRY

Like the mission grape, the mission orange was not of very good quality. It was thick-skinned, pithy, and often sour. William Wolfskill and a few others operated orange groves in the Los Angeles area in the 1850s and 1860s with mission stock and a few slightly better varieties from Hawaii and Sicily, but production was small and the market even smaller. The more significant beginnings of the California orange industry came with three new developments of the 1870s. These were the discovery that oranges grew better on lands that were slightly higher and out of the coastal fog belt, the introduction of the navel orange from Brazil, and the advent of the railroad.

In 1870 J. W. North and his associates purchased the lands of a defunct silk colony on the Rancho Jurupa near what would soon be the town of Riverside, began an irrigation canal from the Santa Ana River, and planted orange groves. Three years later members of the Riverside group obtained two of the dozen budded trees which the first American Protestant missionary at Bahia, Brazil, had sent to the Department of Agriculture at Washington. Within a remarkably short time the large, sweet, seedless Bahia navels were in production under the name of "Riverside navels." But the growers who established a number of new communities in emulation of Riverside, and with stock obtained from it, did not wish to contribute to its advertising; they again changed the popular name, this time to the "Washington navel." Substantial rail shipments to St. Louis and Chicago were under way before the end of the

1870s and in the next decade, with the development of refrigerator cars, rail shipments were increased in volume and extended to the Atlantic coast. The great citrus belt of southern California was in process of rapid formation.

Use of the summer-ripening Valencia orange, along with the winter-ripening Brazilian navels, made possible a year-round output. Moreover the Valencias flourished nearer the coast, and with their increasing introduction in the early twentieth century the citrus belt extended from Santa Barbara to San Diego and from Pasadena to Riverside. Southern California became responsible for more than two-thirds of the nation's production of oranges and more than 90 percent of its lemons.

The early development of the marketing of citrus fruits involved many difficulties. The period from 1869 to the end of the century was one of serious decline in American agricultural prices because of expanding production, deflated currency, and the farmer's weak position in bargaining. Farmers seldom had enough information about the market to know what a fair price would be, and speculators took every possible advantage of their ignorance. The markets for citrus fruits and other California specialty crops were from 2000 to 3000 miles away, and they were developing only gradually. With many growers and packers sending haphazard shipments, prices were so erratic that the commission merchants demanded the use of the consignment system, under which the growers bore all the risk. Sometimes the anxious shipper of a carload of fruit would receive nothing but a bill and the information that the arrival of other shipments on the same day had so glutted the market that the price received was insufficient to pay the freight and handling charges. It was often suspected and frequently established that the commission handlers reported the eastern prices falsely, and California citrus growers formed the opinion that the commission merchant was a greater menace to their prosperity than frost. The answer was the cooperative marketing organization, in which the California fruit growers eventually achieved considerable success.

In an effort to combat the speculators who controlled the citrus market in the early years, an Orange Growers' Protective Union of Southern California was formed in 1885. Another orange growers' union was formed in 1891 and reorganized as the Southern California Fruit Exchange in 1893. After oranges had begun to be grown in important quantities as far north as Oroville and Chico, central California growers joined the organization, and in 1905 the new name of California Fruit Growers' Exchange reflected this broadened membership. The organization was so successful that its brand name, "Sunkist," finally became almost synonymous with "California oranges and lemons" in popular usage, and in 1952 its name was officially changed to Sunkist Growers, Inc.

The nonprofit methods of the grower-owned cooperative exposed it to specious charges of being anticapitalistic. As the cooperative system took root in several other fields of agriculture, including deciduous fruits, raisins, walnuts, and dairy and poultry products, many of the private wholesalers frantically denounced the whole cooperative marketing idea as sheer communism.

On the other hand, one of the ablest leaders of the California Fruit Growers' Exchange, Charles C. Teague of Santa Paula, described it as a "federated democracy." The growers were organized in local packing associations; these elected the directors of district exchanges, who in turn elected the directors of the central board.

The democracy, of course, extended only to the growers, not to the unorganized and disfranchised people who did the physical work. The citrus industry was built on cheap alien labor, in the beginning mainly Chinese and later Japanese and Mexican.

The remarkable economic achievements of the citrus growers were due in part to the fact that many of them were "gentlemen farmers," individuals who had acquired considerable capital before they were attracted to California to enter this particular industry, and therefore could generate sufficient money and credit to ensure success. They called themselves "growers" to dissociate themselves from the rustic clumsiness and ignorance which they felt to be implied by the word "farmer." In later decades California agriculture in general would become so successfully commercialized that the word "agriculture" itself would begin to be replaced by the new term "agribusiness."

BOOM IN REAL ESTATE

Through the 1870s the main movement of population into California was confined to its northcentral parts. From the next decade onward, however, southern California grew at a more rapid rate then did the north.

The first southern California real estate boom, a very modest one, occurred between 1868 and 1876. After the droughts that wiped out the livestock of the region, Abel Stearns narrowly escaped the sale of his 200,000 acres of land in the San Gabriel and Santa Ana valleys for $4000 in delinquent taxes. He was saved from utter financial ruin when a group of San Francisco capitalists led by Sam Brannan purchased his ranches and began in 1868 to subdivide them into 40-acre tracts. Having bought the land at distress prices, the Brannan syndicate netted more than $2 million from this investment.

Along with the spread of the citrus industry, a special factor in this early boom was the "health rush" to southern California which began about 1870. That the climate of the area was helpful in curing tuberculosis was actually a sad delusion, but the physicians of the time encouraged thousands of invalids and their families to believe it, and southern California newspaper editors and other boosters proclaimed its truth. By 1900, after medical theory had generally abandoned the idea, its influence declined, though a myriad of other health fads continued to flourish.

The alleged health-giving properties of California's climate led one observer to assert that California was fast becoming "the land of handsome men," while David Starr Jordan pronounced with the scientific authority of a recognized biologist and educator that "California college girls, of the same age, are larger by almost every dimension than are the college girls of Massachusetts. They are taller, broader-shouldered, thicker-chested (with ten cubic inches more lung capacity), have larger biceps and calves, and a superiority of tested strength."

The superior potential of California for agriculture was also widely advertised, though the reports of squashes and melons so large they had to be picked on horseback led to counterpropaganda from other parts of the country to the effect that California farmers spent more time in exaggeration than in cultivation. A newspaper editor in Jackson, Mississippi, wrote that "California is a state of mind—exaltation is in the atmosphere. Birds of gorgeous plumage flit through the trees but they have no song. Flowers astound in size, gorgeous color, and infinite variety, but they have little perfume." If this writer had also asserted that the grapes, though beautiful, were sour, it could scarcely have been more obvious that envy was mixed with his derision.

The Southern Pacific Railroad had a vast amount of land to sell, and it took a leading part in the great campaign of advertising California. The railroad's publicity bureau had a number of able popular writers on its payroll, and in a flood of books, both fiction and nonfiction, and of magazine articles and stories, they described California's charms and embellished its romantic heritage. It was the Southern Pacific that began the publication of the phenomenally popular *Sunset*, a magazine of western travel and living.

Many independent writers contributed to this flood of publicity. The transplanted New Englander Charles F. Lummis, editor of the monthly magazine *Land of Sunshine*, later renamed *Out West*, went so far in romanticizing southern California's past and present that for a time he was the leading cultural chauvinist of the region. Throughout the country the lure of California was becoming so strong that there was an eager market for almost anything that was written or said about it, even though some of the excesses of boosterism sometimes repelled the more sensitive. For example, tourist Mina Halsey, in her memoir called *A Tenderfoot in Southern California*, reported hearing the assurance that "if the Pilgrim fathers had landed on the Pacific Coast instead of the Atlantic, little old New York wouldn't be on the map."

When the Santa Fe Railroad reached Los Angeles in 1885, it began a rate war with the Southern Pacific. For a brief time a ticket from Kansas City to Los Angeles could be bought for $1, and the low rates, along with the attendant advertising, launched southern California as a major tourist attraction and contributed to the real estate boom that reached a climax in 1887. Real estate sales in Los Angeles County exceeded $200 million during that year, subdivisions sprang up in deserts, and the classic story of the Mississippi Bubble was surpassed in the record of incredible paper profits—and sudden crash. In the long run, however, no amount of greedy and excessive speculation could destroy the inevitable rise of California real estate values as lands were settled and brought into profitable use.

The Southern Pacific also played a part in the advertising of California agricultural products, particularly oranges, as a highly successful method of increasing both the railroad's freight business and its land sales at the same time. In 1907 the California Fruit Growers' Exchange, in spite of its constant

A promotional brochure published by the Southern Pacific Railroad in 1907, "boosting" the attractions of California. (*Courtesy of the California State Library, Sacramento.*)

and bitter denunciations of the Southern Pacific's freight rates, made an agreement with the railroad for a joint advertising experiment which used Iowa as a laboratory, billboarding that state with the slogan "Oranges for Health— California for Wealth." The results led the exchange to adopt a large and permanent program of advertising in the same vein, and during the next 7 years orange acreage in California increased by more than 70 percent, mostly in the southern part of the state.

In the early twentieth century, however, the great growth of southern California became increasingly urban rather than rural. In 1920 the population of the Los Angeles metropolitan areas was five times as large as in 1900. During the same period the urban population of the San Francisco Bay area did not quite double, and thus by 1920 the populations of the two metropolitan regions were approximately equal, at about a million each.

WATER AND LAND

The peculiar importance of water in the economy of California and the peculiar patterns of its seasonal and regional distribution have made it not only a vital but a perpetually controversial factor in the state's history. Two of the major controversies came to a head in the 1880s, one a struggle of Sacramento Valley against the hydraulic mining industry, and the other a battle of farmers against "water monopolists" over the control of water for irrigation. Both quarrels were so bitter and destructive that they could be settled only when laissez faire gave way to the intervention of government.

Since the 1850s the hydraulickers had been dumping floods of mud, sand, and gravel into the Yuba, Bear, American, and Feather Rivers. Farms were buried by mining debris; Marysville, Yuba City, and other towns were repeatedly flooded; and the rivers, eventually including most of the Sacramento itself, were rendered unnavigable. After many inconclusive legal skirmishes, a decision of the United States circuit court in 1884 outlawed the dumping of debris into rivers, but the hydraulickers had been producing $10 million worth of gold a year, and they did not give up easily. Clandestine operations continued, harried by the "spies" of the farmers' Anti-Debris Association. After many tempestuous and inconclusive wrangles in the state legislature, a federal law in 1893, introduced by Congressman Anthony J. Caminetti of Amador County, finally solved the problem by creating a federal regulatory agency, the California Debris Commission.

The development of irrigation in California in the nineteenth century was slow, in large part because early state policy not only failed to prevent the monopolization of water rights but actually encouraged it. California water law was extremely confused and inadequate during nearly the whole first 40 years of statehood. In 1850 the first legislature simplified its tasks by adopting the common law of England for California. Members of the legislature were not particularly aware that this system included the doctrine of water law known as "riparian rights," an expression derived from the Latin *ripa*, the bank of a river, and signifying that the owner of land bordering a stream had full rights to a reasonable use of water while the owners of land not contiguous to the stream had no rights to it. Even while the first legislature was in session, the customs and regulations of the mining camps were crystallizing into an opposing system based on the doctrine of "prior appropriation," which had been used for centuries in Spain, France, and Italy—countries which, like most of California, were considerably drier than England. This concept gave the first user of water the unrestrained right to divert it from the stream and to sell this right to others.

In California the conflicting interests of the advocates of these two legal doctrines led them to fight each other to a political standstill, and consequently California lagged behind almost every other state in the American southwest in adopting a coherent system of water law giving clear preference to the doctrine of appropriation.

Of the innumerable court battles during this long period of confusion, the most important was fought between two giants, the Miller & Lux Land and Cattle Company and the firm of James B. Haggin and Lloyd Tevis, over water rights in the San Joaquin Valley. Miller and Lux were among the state's most hated water monopolists because of their success in making strategic acquisitions of riverbank lands with an eye to riparian rights. In spite of their assertions that they were cattle raisers and not land speculators, they used their riparian rights in a variety of antisocial ways. They forced landowners to sell out to them; they accumulated enormous underdeveloped and unused holdings; and they delayed the process of subdivision and resale to ensure huge speculative profits for themselves. To the land holdings that gave them control of much of the San Joaquin River area they had added a 50-mile stretch along the Kern. Haggin and Tevis acquired rights of appropriation farther up the Kern with the intention of diverting water through irrigation canals to lands at some distance from the river. The state supreme court ruled in *Lux v. Haggin* in 1886 that the riparian rights of Miller and Lux made such appropriation illegal.

This decision was reached only by a bare majority, and only after one of the judges had reversed himself. Moreover it was hotly denounced as a triumph of the English common law over American common sense, and as a victory for monopoly and speculation over the farmer and agricultural progress. Its intense unpopularity contributed to the calling of a stormy special session of the legislature in the summer of 1886, and finally to the passage of an important new law in the next regular session.

This was the Wright Irrigation Act of 1887, which authorized the establishment of irrigation districts, special units of local government to be formed by more than 50 persons or by a majority of the landowners in the area. These districts were to have the power of eminent domain, the power to overcome riparian rights by condemnation suits, and the right to sell bonds to finance the purchase of water rights and the construction of dams, canals, and other irrigation works. The bill's author was C. C. Wright, state senator from Modesto, where unsuccessful efforts to form such a district had been going on for some time. Within the year following the passage of the law 10 irrigation districts covering more than a million acres were in existence, most notably those in the regions of Modesto and Turlock. The early projects developed under this law had great difficulties—economic, engineering, legal, and political. Most of the larger landowners opposed them, and state supervision was as yet inadequate. But by 1911, when the fiftieth district was formed, the system had clearly established its vital role in the creation of California's modern agriculture.

The most colorful figure in the history of California irrigation development was Canadian-born George Chaffey, a self-educated engineering genius. After studying irrigation at Riverside, Chaffey created the highly successful communities of Etiwanda and Ontario in the 1880s. There he developed the idea of mutual water companies with one share of water company stock attached to each acre of land, built the first commercial hydroelectric plant in California and the first electrically lighted house west of the Rockies, and founded a college.

The greatest of all Chaffey's accomplishments, however, was his development of irrigation in the lower Colorado River area. The region was one of the dreariest desert wastes in the world, though the soil potential was extraordinary. In 1896 the California Development Company was organized, and in 1900 it secured Chaffey's services. Below the Mexican border he found some ancient dry watercourses through which very economical canals could be built, and within a year he had completed a 70-mile canal through Mexican territory, entering California at the twin border townsites which he called Mexicali and Calexico.

One of his greatest inspirations was a new name for the Colorado Desert: the Imperial Valley. This dramatic change of name did much to change the image that had repelled settlers from the area. They began to move into it in substantial numbers, and the desert did in fact begin to turn into a kind of agricultural empire.

Chaffey left the company in 1905. Not long afterward his successors built a risky bypass canal around the diversion headgate. After torrential rains the river burst through at this weak point and poured northwestward into the Imperial Valley, turning the dry Salton Sink into the Salton Sea, covering 40 miles of the Southern Pacific's roadbed, and threatening eventually to inundate the whole region. The federal government did not intervene because the break was in Mexican territory, and the flooding continued unchecked for nearly 2 years. The Southern Pacific, after taking the opportunity to acquire control of the California Development Company, finally brought the flood under control in 1907 by dumping thousands of carloads of rock and gravel, and the development of the Imperial Valley was resumed.

ELECTRIC RAILWAYS AND URBANIZATION

The years before and after the turn of the century were the era of the street and interurban electric railway—a development that played a vital part in the urbanization and particularly in the suburbanization of American society. The building of electric railway lines tremendously facilitated the growth of metropolitan areas by making it possible for those who worked in the center of a city to live in its outskirts or suburbs in more comfortable homes built on less expensive land. Few workers were willing to spend more than a total of an hour a day in commuting; therefore, in the horse-and-buggy and horsecar era the practical maximum size of a city was little more than 12 square miles, that is, the area within a radius of 2 miles, the distance that could be traveled in 30 minutes. The trolley car, which could travel at least 5 miles in the same length of time, made it possible for the main residential area of a city to be nearly seven times as large as before—nearly 80 square miles. The interurban electric railway also did much to increase mobility, and tended to consolidate neighboring towns into a single metropolis.

The cable car had provided a colorful interlude. It was invented in San Francisco by Andrew S. Hallidie, a manufacturer of wire rope, and after the first cable line was built in 1873, on Clay Street, the idea spread to other cities. But the electric trolley introduced in Richmond, Virginia, in 1888 was obviously so much more efficient and economical even on steep hills that cable lines soon disappeared everywhere except in San Francisco, where a few have been retained, largely as tourist attractions and for reasons of local nostalgia.

Street and interurban electric railways reached the height of their importance between the 1890s and the beginning of the automobile age in 1919. The chief opportunities for profits for the promoters of these lines came not from operating revenues but from simultaneous speculation in the real estate which a new line could make suddenly and enormously more valuable.

San Francisco, "the city" of American California's first half century, was confined to a mere thumbnail of land only 7 miles square at the tip of a peninsula. Most of the space eventually to be occupied by the metropolis of the San Francisco Bay region was in the East Bay. These facts made a strong impression on Francis Marion "Borax" Smith, a capitalist of large imagination. In 1893, Smith began to reinvest the fortune that he had acquired in the borax business in Death Valley in a great scheme to consolidate and expand the street railway lines of the East Bay cities into the Key System, and to connect this network with San Francisco by an expanded and consolidated ferry service.

In the southern part of the state, Henry Edwards Huntington was the leading figure in interurban transportation development. Henry was the nephew of Collis P. Huntington, who had no son and who hoped that his nephew would succeed him in the leadership of the Southern Pacific Railroad. This dynastic plan was strengthened when Collis arranged the marriage of Henry to a sister of Collis's adopted daughter. After serving an apprenticeship in the management of several of his uncle's smaller enterprises in the east and south, Henry Huntington came to California in 1892. On his way to San Francisco he stopped at Los Angeles, was entertained at the San Marino ranch near Pasadena, and formed such a favorable impression of southern California that he later bought the San Marino property and there, eventually, made his home. In San Francisco in the 1890s he became vice president of the Southern Pacific, but after the death of his uncle in 1900 the hopes for his succession to the presidency of the railroad were frustrated when Edward H. Harriman of New York, who already controlled the Union Pacific, gained control of the Southern Pacific as well. This virtual merger continued until 1913 when the federal government dissolved it.

Henry Huntington faced the new century by moving most of his own investments and operations to southern California. For several years part of his attention had been devoted to street railway companies in both San Francisco and Los Angeles. But now, after selling his Southern Pacific stock to Harriman, he disposed of his interests in the Market Street and other San Francisco lines to a new syndicate of trolley promoters called the United Railroads. In 1902 he invested most of his funds in a consolidation and expansion of the street and interurban railways of the region in and around Los Angeles under the name of the Pacific Electric Railway Company.

Within a few years the Pacific Electric (PE) and its big red cars welded 42 incorporated cities within a 35-mile radius of Los Angeles into the fastest-growing body in America. The PE became by far the largest network of its kind, with more cars than any five other interurban electric systems, and its transportation of freight as well as passengers cut so heavily into the business of the Southern Pacific in the region that after many efforts Harriman finally succeeded in buying Huntington out, at an enormous price, in 1910.

In less than a decade Huntington became wealthier than his uncle had ever been, mainly by buying great tracts of land in southern California just before announcing that new branches of the Pacific Electric would be built through them. He had separated from his first wife in the year his uncle died. He was divorced in 1906, and a few years later married his uncle's widow, thus consolidating the entire family fortune. After 1910 he retired from the more active aspects of business and devoted himself to filling his mansion at San Marino with his collection of manuscripts and rare books in the fields of English, colonial, and southwestern American literature and history. After his death in 1927 this was opened to scholars as the Huntington Library. The magnificent grounds of his estate, and his great collection of paintings, were opened to the public.

Henry Huntington shaped the system of transportation which, along with other forces, launched the entire region from Santa Monica to Redlands, and from San Fernando to Santa Ana, on the road to becoming the great City of Southern California.

SELECTED BIBLIOGRAPHY

Various aspects of economic development are treated in Robert G. Cleland and Osgood Hardy, *The March of Industry* (1929); Claude B. Hutchison (ed.), *California Agriculture* (1946); and Gerald D. Nash, *State Government and Economic Development: A History of Administrative Policies in California, 1849–1933* (1964).

Accounts of wheat ranching are in Wallace Smith, *Garden of the Sun: A History of the San Joaquin Valley—1772–1939* (1939) and Joseph A. McGowan, *History of the Sacramento Valley*, vols. I,II (1961). On marketing problems see Rodman W. Paul, "The Great California Grain War; the Granger Challenges the Wheat King," *Pacific Historical Review*, XXVII (November 1958), pp. 331–350, and "The Wheat Trade between California and the United Kingdom," *Mississippi Valley Historical Review*, XLV (December 1958), pp. 391–412. On sugar, see Thomas J. Osborne, "Claus Spreckels and the Oxnard Brothers: Pioneer Developers in California's Beet Sugar Industry, 1890–1900," *Southern California Quarterly*, LIV (Summer 1972), pp. 117–126.

On wine production, see Vincent P. Carosso, *The California Wine Industry, 1830–1895; a Study of the Formative Years* (1951); Joan M. Donohue, "Agostin Haraszthy: A Study in

Creativity," *California Historical Society Quarterly*, XLVIII (June 1969), pp. 153–163; and Ralph B. Hutchinson, "The California Wine Industry," Ph.D. thesis, University of California, Los Angeles (1969).

The rise of the citrus and related industries and of cooperative marketing can be traced in Walter Reuther, H. J. Webber, and L. D. Batchelor (eds.) *The Citrus Industry* (1967); Rahno Mabel MacCurdy, *The History of the California Fruit Growers' Exchange* (1925); Erich O. Kraemer and Henry E. Erdman, *History of Coöperation in the Marketing of Fresh Deciduous Fruits* (1933); H. E. Erdman, "The Development and Significance of California Coöperatives, 1900–1915," *Agricultural History*, XXXII (July 1958), pp. 179–184; Charles C. Teague, *Fifty Years a Rancher* (1944); Richard J. Orsi, "The Octopus Reconsidered: The Southern Pacific and Agricultural Modernization in California, 1865–1915," *California Historical Quarterly*, LIV (Fall 1975), pp. 197–220; and a novel, Sidney H. Burchell, *Jacob Peek, Orange Grower; a Tale of Southern California* (1915).

On real estate booms and the rise of southern California, see Remi A. Nadeau, *Citymakers . . .*, 1868–1876 (1948); John E. Baur, *Health Seekers of Southern California* (1959); Glenn S. Dumke, *The Boom of the Eighties in Southern California* (1944); T. S. Van Dyke, *Millionaires of a Day* (1890), a genial satire; Harris Newmark, *Sixty Years in Southern California* (1916); James M. Guinn, *A History of California and . . . of Los Angeles and Environs* (three volumes, 1915); W. W. Robinson *Ranchos become Cities* (1939); Richard F. Pourade, *The Glory Years* (1964), vol. IV of his *History of San Diego*; Carey McWilliams, *Southern California Country* (1946); and Franklin Walker, *Literary History of Southern California* (1950). Examples of the promotional literature include Charles Nordhoff, *California for Health, Pleasure, and Residence* (1872); Ben C. Truman, *Homes and Happiness in the Golden State* (1883); and Charles Dudley Warner, *Our Italy* (1891). Frank L. Beach, "The Transformation of California, 1900–1920," Ph.D. thesis, University of California, Berkeley (1963), analyzes the great acceleration of the westward movement from the older states to California in the early twentieth century. See also Warren Thompson, *Growth and Changes in California's Population* (1955).

Irrigation developments are described in Frank Adams, *Life of George Chaffey* (1928); Frederick D. Kershner, "George Chaffey and the Irrigation Frontier," *Agricultural History*, XXVII (October 1953), pp. 115–122; William Smythe, *The Conquest of Arid America* (1905); Lawrence B. Lee, "William Smythe and the Irrigation Movement: A Reconsideration" *Pacific Historical Review*, XLI (August 1972), pp. 289–311; and David O. Woodbury, *The Colorado Conquest* (1941). The early Imperial Valley was the locale of Harold Bell Wright's bestselling novel, *The Winning of Barbara Worth* (1911).

George W. Hilton, *The Cable Car in America* (1971) traces the cable car's rise and decline. On the great era of street and interurban electric railways, see John Anderson Miller, *Fares, Please: From Horse Cars to Streamliners* (1940); George H. Hilton and John F. Due, *The Electric Interurban Railways in America* (1960); William D. Middleton, *The Interurban Era* (1961); Spencer Crump, *Ride the Big Red Cars; How Trolleys Helped Build Southern California* (1962); Laurence R. Veysey, "The Pacific Electric Railway Company" (1953, typescript on microfilm Bancroft Library), and Robert M. Fogelson, *The Fragmented Metropolis: Los Angeles, 1850–1930* (1967). John E. Pomfret, *The Henry E. Huntington Library and Art Gallery* (1969) begins with a good sketch of Huntington's career.

LABOR AND CAPITAL

BACKGROUNDS OF THE CALIFORNIA LABOR MOVEMENT

Organized relationships between workers and employers in California began to enter their modern phase in San Francisco in the 1880s. There had been labor unions in the city since the early 1850s, but none of them had been large, and most had been short-lived. The first large-scale labor movement in the state, the Workingmen's party of 1877 to 1880, had contributed very little to the development of modern labor organization. Kearney was ignorant of the principles of trade unionism. His followers came mainly from the ranks of the unorganized and the unemployed, and with minor exceptions the Workingmen's party received no support from the few small unions then in existence in California. The Workingmen's party put its faith entirely in political action, and in that sphere its chief accomplishment was its role in the movement that led to the exclusion of the Chinese by federal law. California legislation in the interest of labor remained very limited. A state bureau of labor statistics was established in 1883, but laws providing on paper for the mechanics' lien and for an 8-hour day on government work lacked provisions essential for their enforcement.

Throughout the country attempts at effective labor organization suffered from labor's chronic disunity and confusion of aims. One great dispute was over the question of whether labor should avoid organized political action and confine itself to "pure and simple" or "bread and butter" unionism, that is, to collective bargaining with employers for strictly economic goals. Another basic disagreement concerned the form of organization. The oldest and most conservative plan was that of craft unionism, in which each skilled trade in a city had its own local union, reaching out toward federation with other locals in the same craft on a state and national basis, and also toward city, state, and national federations of the unions of the various crafts. This idea produced the body that would ultimately evolve into American labor's most important one. Founded in a small convention at Pittsburgh in 1881, it was reorganized under the name of the American Federation of Labor in 1886.

The Noble Order of the Knights of Labor, on the other hand, stood for a single national union capable of including workers of all crafts or of none. It advocated producers' cooperatives, to be owned by the workers and to take over as many industries as possible, and at times it allied itself with the Greenback Labor party, a movement that combined currency inflation and socialism in proposals to convert the national debt into ready money which would be lent to workers' cooperatives so that they could put private manufacturers out of business.

To the left of the Knights of Labor and the Greenbackers were the Marxists, not yet clearly divided on the issue of peaceful socialism versus communist violence; the anarchists, advocates of the abolition of government; and the syndicalists, who believed that a mighty labor organization should in effect become the government.

Among these alternatives, American labor made an overwhelming choice in favor of craft unionism—collective bargaining for higher wages, shorter hours, and other improved conditions, with political action limited to objectives closely related to these. In other words, American labor decided to seek a fairer share of the benefits of the private system of economic enterprise rather than a replacement of that system by socialized public ownership of the means of production. While British labor moved toward a new political party, based directly on the trade unions and advocating nationalization of ownership by peaceful means and through the democratic process, American organized labor in general rejected not only socialism but also the idea of forming any major political party of its own. This happened essentially because the per capita resources of the United States and the relative opportunity for the individual to rise in society were greater than in England or in any other country.

THE RISE OF UNIONS IN SAN FRANCISCO

It is true that some of the most important leaders of the labor movement in San Francisco in the 1880s were socialists. In 1881 Frank Roney, a member of the Iron Moulders' Union and a former Irish revolutionary, became president of the San Francisco Trades Assembly, then the only citywide federation of unions. A year later Burnette G. Haskell began a lively career as a radical labor organizer.

Haskell was a native Californian, the son of a wealthy pioneer family. Though trained as a lawyer, he was too erratic and visionary to be happy or successful in a routine law practice and instead became the editor of *Truth*, a small weekly paper that his father had founded. One evening in 1882, in search of news, he attended a meeting of the Trades Assembly. Until then he had taken no interest in labor's problems, but from that time onward he threw himself into the cause of socialism. It was typical of him that he tried to reconcile socialism and anarchism, an effort in which, needless to say, he failed. The International Workmen's Association which he organized in San Francisco in 1882 should not be confused, though it often has been, with two other organizations: the International Workingmen's Association, or "First International" or "red international," formed by Karl Marx and others in England in 1864 and dissolved in 1876; and the International Working People's Association, or "black international," formed by anarchist followers of Bakunin in London in 1881.

Haskell also took part in the organization of new labor unions in several trades, in several of the smaller northern California cities as well as in San Francisco. By far the most enduring contribution of his life was his leadership in the founding of the Coast Seamen's Union.

San Francisco's position as the leading seaport of the Pacific coast made it inevitable that the labor problems of the waterfront would play a central part in the history of the city's labor relations as a whole. Moreover, working conditions in the maritime industry were peculiarly atrocious before the development of effective unions. Other workers had the legal right to quit work, but for the sailor this was "desertion," and under United States law until 1915 it led to arrest and imprisonment. Until 1898 corporal punishment was permitted at sea for "justifiable cause" as interpreted by the captain of the ship, under the theory formulated in a court decision of 1806 that "the simple and somewhat rude character of seamen" required extraordinary discipline. Flogging had been abolished by federal law in 1850 after a long campaign led by Richard Henry Dana and others, but this had merely meant that other forms of physical torture were substituted; the officer corps of the merchant marine continued to be a refuge for sadists—"bucko mates." The food was vile, and the sleeping quarters were cramped and ill-ventilated "dogholes."

The chief method of hiring seamen which prevailed throughout the world in the nineteenth century was the infamous crimping system. The "crimps," keepers of sailors' boarding houses on the waterfront, served also as the main employment agencies. While in port the sailor lived on credit advances from the crimp for food, clothing, and liquor, until the crimp arranged his next voyage. No sailor could get a ship in any other way, and no master could get a crew except by negotiating with the crimp to pay the sailor's wage advance. The master often had to pay the crimp an additional fee, known as "blood money" because drugged and slugged men were frequently shanghaied aboard covered with blood.

Union organization to escape from such conditions began in the coasting trade because the sailors in it were a relatively homogeneous group, more often in port and more likely to be acquainted with each other than were the "deepwater" sailors. In particular, the Pacific coast lumber schooners were specialized vessels, and their crews had to be skilled in handling lumber as well as in seamanship. It was a group of such men whom Burnette Haskell persuaded to organize the Coast Seamen's Union in 1885.

In the same year Haskell formed the Kaweah colony, a utopian cooperative enterprise for timb   utting in what would later be Sequoia National Park. On the theory that this scheme would provide employment for sailors out of work, Haskell gained the support of many union members for the colony, and even the investment of some of the union's funds. The Kaweah experiment was unsuccessful, however, and the sailors, perceiving that Haskell was eccentric and undependable, rejected his leadership and with it the socialistic influence in their union. Instead, after merging with a separate union of steamship sailors to form the Sailors' Union of the Pacific in 1891, the coast sailors found their greatest leader for decades to come in Andrew Furuseth, a man who was proud of the sailor's craft and devoted to the philosophy and methods of craft unionism. Furuseth, more than any other individual, was ultimately responsible for the reforms of the La Follette Seamen's Act of 1915, which abolished imprisonment for desertion, regulated working conditions, and finally broke the power of the crimps.

In their dark and difficult early years in the 1880s and 1890s, however, the main achievement of the sailors' unions was mere survival. Their strikes led the employers to form a Shipowners' Association which, in periods of crisis, temporarily established central hiring offices. These would have been an improvement over the crimping system except that they introduced a new evil, the hiring hall controlled by the employers and run primarily for the purpose of weeding out union members.

In many other industries, also, harsh working conditions still prevailed in the late nineteenth century. San Francisco bakers, for example, worked from 12 to 18 hours a day for 7 days a week, except Sundays, when they worked 6 hours; they were compelled to board at "homes" provided by the employers. Conditions showed the greatest improvements in the few occupations in which the bulk of the workers were unionized before 1900, notably the building trades. The carpenters and other building trades unions tended to regard themselves as a skilled aristocracy of labor. In the 1890s their separate federation, the Building Trades Council, seceded from the main citywide body, the San Francisco Labor Council, and even held separate Labor Day parades, marching in opposite directions on Market Street. In general, only a small minority of wage earners were union members, and in many occupations there were no unions at all. Formal agreements between employers and unions were rare, and in most cases the employer set the terms and could change them without notice.

In the relatively prosperous years of the early twentieth century, unionism in San Francisco made a remarkable surge forward. There was a great increase in membership, and new unions were successfully established in a number of occupations that had been considered unorganizable in other communities. The often-repeated statement that San Francisco in this period became "the first closed-shop city in the United States" was an exaggeration, however, for except in the building trades the closed-shop contract, under which the employer agreed to hire only members of the union, was actually adopted in very few instances. Indeed, most bargaining agreements were still entirely informal. But in comparison with other American cities, San Francisco did become a stronghold of unionism about 1900, and remained so until the early 1920s.

In the summer of 1901 the teamsters joined with the sailors and the longshoremen in a waterfront strike that tied up the port for several weeks. Violence between strikers on the one hand and strikebreakers and the police on the other led to hundreds of injuries and four deaths. Again, as in 1877 when the apparent use of the police on the side of the business community had led the "workingmen" to form a new political party, so in 1901 the assignment of the police to protect strikebreakers led to the organization of the new Union Labor party of San Francisco. For a time that party actually gained control of the city government. During its first 6 years of existence, however, it was controlled by an opportunistic and corrupt political boss, Abraham Ruef, and thus it became significant mainly for its part in the extreme corruption of California party politics, which would at last produce major attempts at political reform in the city and the state.

TRIUMPH OF THE OPEN SHOP IN LOS ANGELES

In the same turn-of-the-century period when the idea of the closed shop was coming as near to acceptance in San Francisco as anywhere else in America, Los Angeles was becoming the country's leading citadel of the open shop, based on precisely the opposite principle, under which employers not only refused to make agreements requiring union membership of their employees but even refused to bargain with unions at all.

This remarkable polarization of institutional patterns in the two cities was one of the many extreme contrasts between them. The population of the "cow counties," as southern California was long derisively described in the north, remained relatively sparse and rural before 1900, and because industry was still on a trifling scale in Los Angeles several decades after it had begun to flourish in San Francisco, unions in Los Angeles were less deeply rooted. But of all the factors impeding union growth in southern California the most remarkable and effective was the personality of Harrison Gray Otis, publisher of the *Los Angeles Times*. With a great fortune built on a highly profitable newspaper and on vast real estate investments in California and Mexico, Otis made himself the leader of the most intransigent group of organized employers to be found anywhere in the United States.

He was named for that earlier Harrison Gray Otis, a distant relative, who had been one of the most distinguished political leaders of New England, and although the two Harrison Gray Otises flourished at opposite ends of the nineteenth century as well as of the country, their social philosophies were remarkably alike. The Massachusetts senator had been a leader of the Federalists, whom one of their associates described as the party of "the wise, the good, and the rich." The southern California publisher, three generations later, was equally convinced that men of wealth, in their wisdom and genius, were the only men to be trusted with economic or political power.

A related part of Otis's thinking was the result of his military experiences, as a young officer in an Ohio regiment during the Civil War and later as a general in the California National Guard. The military plan of social organization impressed him as an excellent system. The good soldier never struck and never boycotted. This feeling provided much of the emotional force behind Otis's crusade for the open shop, which he rationalized as "industrial freedom"—the freedom of workers not to join a union and the freedom of employers to discharge them if they did. Otis often said that he favored the "closed shop," by what he regarded as the only proper definition of it: closed to union members.

In 1890 Otis precipitated the first major conflict between employers and unions in Los Angeles, with the intention of destroying the printers' union, the oldest union in the city. Printers, as Otis pointed out, were the only workers in southern California who were still getting boom-time wages. The boom of the 1880s having collapsed, a wage cut was in order. But instead of negotiating a new agreement Otis announced a 20 percent cut, locked his union printers out, and refused to discuss a compromise. Before doing this he had formed an association with the publishers of the other three Los Angeles dailies, and had arranged to bring in nonunion printers from San Diego and elsewhere. He paid these strikebreakers the previous union wages—until the strike collapsed. Other unions helped the printers by contributing funds and by joining in a boycott of the *Times* and its advertisers. This boycott was a failure, but it tended to solidify the Los Angeles labor movement for the years of struggle that lay ahead.

The employers who were most antagonistic to unions formed an Employers' Association under the leadership of Otis and A. Hamburger, proprietor of the People's Store and one of Otis's largest advertisers. They also established an Independent Labor Bureau to carry on a wide campaign of advertising in the east, promising jobs at high wages for nonunion workers. The Merchants' and Manufacturers' Association of Los Angeles, originally formed in the 1890s to promote commercial and industrial enterprise, was at first outwardly neutral in Otis's war with the unions, but in 1903 the M&M announced that it would unite with employers injured by boycotts, which it branded as "unAmerican, unjust, unwarranted, and illegal." Soon afterward, however, it launched a boycott policy of its own—against employers who negotiated with unions. Bank loans were withheld and orders were transferred to other companies. The M&M's boycott was more effective than any that union labor ever attempted.

At this time the drive for the open shop was becoming a national movement. A major slogan of this movement was "The Right to Work," the title of a widely discussed article by Ray Stannard Baker which expressed sympathy for the "scab" miners in a recent Pennsylvania coal strike. The National Association of Manufacturers declared against recognition of labor unions in 1903, and its president founded a Citizens' Industrial Association of America. This body, in turn, fostered local Citizens' Alliances in which the public was invited to join with employers in fighting organized labor. In Los Angeles the Citizens' Alliance soon recruited the country's largest per capita membership, with heavy financial support from Otis, Henry E. Huntington, and others.

Labor was not entirely without allies in the struggle for the support of public opinion. Edward W. Scripp's *Los Angeles Record*, an evening daily, was a voice for organized labor and against Otis from its founding in 1895. And in

1903 William Randolph Hearst, then a Democrat seeking labor's support for his ambition to be President of the United States, established the *Los Angeles Examiner* as a morning daily in direct competition with the *Times*. In an editorial in the first issue the *Examiner* promised to "support with its whole power the proposition that labor is justified in demanding a fair share of the wealth it produces." By 1906, however, Hearst's paper had begun to recede from its original prolabor stand, and the unions became disillusioned with him.

The struggle reached a crisis in 1910, when organized labor took the offensive in a drive for effective unionization of the Los Angeles metal trades. In the spring the metal trades employers of San Francisco agreed to an 8-hour day but warned that they could not long continue it unless their competitors in Los Angeles were unionized and forced to accept the same terms. Consequently, union organizers and funds from San Francisco suddenly strengthened the metal trades unions of Los Angeles to such a degree that they were able to begin a strike of 1500 workers on June 1, 1910, the largest strike the city had ever witnessed. The employers refused to negotiate, and the battle attracted national attention because the whole future of the open shop was clearly at stake in the city where it was strongest. The *Times* outdid itself in denouncing the assault on "the cradle of industrial freedom," and organized labor and its sympathizers throughout the country denounced the *Times* as the nation's leading symbol of union smashing.

Before dawn on the morning of October 1, while the strike was still in full swing, a tremendous explosion destroyed the *Times* building, killed 20 men, and injured 17 others. Immediately the open-shop forces attributed this "crime of the century," as the *Times* called it, to a dynamite bomb planted by union labor's agents. Labor's partisans, on the other hand, charged that the cause was a leaking gas main, typical of the "fire-trap" in which Otis had compelled his employees to work. Unhappily the truth was that a dynamite bomb had been used and that certain individual union officials were guilty of planning the outrage.

The tragedy of the *Times* was a part of a nationwide struggle between the International Association of Bridge and Structural Iron Workers and the National Erectors' Association, a group which included most of the large employers in the field and which was dominated by United States Steel, the largest corporation in the country. In 1906 the National Erectors' Association began a belligerent campaign to destroy the power of the Iron Workers and succeeded in establishing the open shop throughout the industry in all large cities except Chicago and San Francisco. Driven to desperation, the union's national leaders secretly resorted to terrorism, and over a period of several years dozens of nonunion construction projects in a number of cities were damaged by explosions of dynamite, though until the *Times* bombing none of these had resulted in loss of life.

William J. Burns, head of a private detective agency, was already investigating some of the lesser incidents when he was employed by the mayor of Los Angeles to investigate the *Times* disaster. In April 1911 Burns arrested Ortie McManigal, a professional dynamiter, who confessed his own part in the

The *Los Angeles Times* building following the dynamite bombing of Oct. 1, 1910. *(Courtesy of the Bancroft Library.)*

bombing campaign and described its planning by officials of the union at their national headquarters in Indianapolis. Union secretary John J. McNamara, his brother James B. McNamara, and McManigal were then brought to Los Angeles to be tried for complicity in the bombing of the *Times*.

Samuel Gompers, president of the American Federation of Labor (AFL), staked his prestige and that of the AFL on the belief that the charges against the McNamara brothers were a frame-up, and Clarence Darrow, one of the country's ablest trial lawyers, was employed for the defense. In 1907 Darrow had secured the acquittal of three officials of the Western Federation of Miners who were charged with hiring a dynamiter to murder a former governor of Idaho. That American courts and communities were capable of the hysterical punishment of scapegoats had been apparent in the Haymarket Square bombing in Chicago in 1886. For that crime, four men had been convicted and executed essentially becasue they were anarchists, even though no shred of evidence connected them with the person who threw the bomb.

But on December 1, 1911, the millions of Americans who had believed the McNamara brothers to be the innocent victims of an employer conspiracy were stunned by their confession of guilt. The evidence against them was overwhelming, and Darrow advised his clients to plead guilty in order to save their lives.

Lincoln Steffens had conducted personal negotiations with Darrow, the prosecution, the judge, the mayor, labor, employers, Otis, and various other newspaper publishers and community leaders. Steffens saw the *Times* disaster as a proof of the dangerousness, the cruelty, and the futility of extremism in industrial relations. He proposed that the agreement to save the McNamaras from the death penalty be followed by a great series of peace conferences to end the warfare between capital and labor in the United States. But Steffens alone seems to have taken this idea seriously. Instead, the McNamaras' confession demoralized American labor, emboldened employers, and intensified the bitterness between the two sides. In Los Angeles the result was 30 more years of dominance for the open shop.

AGRICULTURAL LABOR: UNORGANIZED AND DISFRANCHISED

Historically, the family farm has been the institution most typical of American agriculture. Only a fourth of those gainfully employed in farming in the United States have been wage workers, and these have been "hired men" attached more or less permanently to one farm and living with the family that owned it. In California, however, more than two-thirds of the total number of persons engaged in agriculture have been wage laborers, the majority of them alien, nonwhite, and migratory. California's "peculiar institution," comparable in some ways to Southern black slavery, has been seasonal migratory agricultural labor in which the worker lacked the protection offered in other fields by labor unions and by the right to vote.

Several circumstances contributed to this situation: the persistence of large units of land ownership in California, specialization in a particular seasonal crop, as opposed to the year-round operations of the "general farm" more common in the middle west, and the availability, in each successive generation, of some new supply of cheap labor drawn from some supposedly inferior race—first the Indians, then the Chinese, and later the Japanese, Hindustanis, Mexicans, and Filipinos.

Union organization would have been peculiarly difficult under these circumstances, even if the agricultural employers had not been violently opposed to it. California trade unions were not merely indifferent to the welfare of alien nonwhite workers, but sternly hostile to their presence in the United States. Groups of migratory laborers, white or nonwhite, usually disbanded at the end of the local harvest season, and wages were too low to have permitted the payment of union dues. Even the minority who were citizens of the United States were seldom in any one place long enough to qualify as voters, and because agricultural employers had great influence in the election and reelection of county supervisors and sheriffs, while migratory workers had no such influence, local lawmaking and law enforcement weighed heavily on the employer's side.

In the 1880s the majority of seasonal and casual laborers in California agriculture were Chinese, whom the large growers regarded as an ideal labor force. Many of the Chinese immigrants were skilled and experienced farmers with much to teach their American employers about agricultural efficiency, but the exclusion act of 1882 and a steady drift of Chinese from the rural areas to the cities and towns began to deplete this source of labor supply. Moreover, during the depression after the panic of 1893, unemployed whites from the cities, seeking work as "fruit tramps," participated in riots that drove thousands of Chinese laborers from the fields. A few blacks were brought from the southern states, but agricultural wages were so low that they soon found better pay in unskilled labor or domestic service in the cities.

For about a decade, beginning in the late 1890s, the growers found another temporary solution in the Japanese, particularly as field workers in the sugar-beet industry that sprang up after the Dingley tariff of 1897 put a heavy duty on imported sugar. But the Gentlemen's Agreement of 1907 restricted Japanese immigration, and moreover the Japanese were quick to escape from the role of cheap and docile laborers. Through clubs or associations with members of their own race as "secretaries," they began to engage in collective bargaining, and to the pained surprise of the growers they conducted the first successful strikes in the history of California agriculture. When they began to acquire land, by purchase or lease, white farmers soon joined with city labor unions in anti-Japanese agitation. In the second decade of the century the growers turned to the Hindustanis, especially for labor in the Imperial Valley, and to the Mexicans, particularly during and after World War I.

THE IWW

Not even a serious attempt to organize a conventional labor union among California agricultural workers was made until 1903, when a Fruit Workers' Union affiliated with the AFL was formed at San Jose. Its existence was brief. The growers dealt with it by ignoring it, and it attracted little attention of any sort except for a few contemptuous newspaper editorials. By default, the attempt to organize the migratory workers fell into the hands of the new and radical movement called the Industrial Workers of the World.

The IWW was an anarcho-syndicalist organization formed in Chicago in 1905. The preamble of its constitution denounced craft unionism and called instead for "one great union" made up largely of unskilled workers. The IWW did not exclude any worker because of race, and it condemned the AFL for practicing racial discrimination. The IWW manifesto adopted as its "revolutionary watchword" the "historic mission of the working class to do away with capitalism." Sabotage, sympathetic strikes for the purpose of paralyzing an industry, and "any and all tactics that will get the results sought with the least expenditure of time and energy" were regarded as justified.

The doctrine of the IWW appealed to those whose condition seemed utterly hopeless. Its numerical strength was often absurdly exaggerated by the newspapers, and the degree of notoriety it achieved was largely the result of the frightened manner in which many employers and public authorities reacted to it. One tactic of the IWW was the demand for the right of free speech, and when the police and other officials would deny this right, the IWW attracted wide public sympathy. Street-corner gatherings to hear political or religious exhortations were then common occurrences in American cities, and in the early twentieth century many cities adopted ordinances against street speaking—ordinances which were enforced against political radicals but not against such meetings as those of the Salvation Army.

In 1910, when the IWW launched a drive to organize farm laborers in the region of Fresno, several of its members were arrested for speaking on the streets of the town. More than a hundred other members then arrived on freight trains for the purpose of filling the jail, where they attracted so much outraged attention by the mass singing of radical songs that police and fire fighters resorted to drenching them with firehoses. A mob burned the organization tent and talked of storming the jail to lynch the prisoners. Chester H. Rowell, progressive editor of the *Fresno Republican*, excoriated the IWW but also denounced the methods being used against it. Instead of giving way to hysterical repression, he advised, Fresno should undercut the IWW by encouraging the growth of normal labor unions and by following the example of Porterville, where the threat of a similar IWW "invasion" had been dissolved by the simple announcement that there would be no arrests for street speaking. In Fresno, after a stalemate of several months, a compromise freed the men from jail and permitted them to speak in designated areas of the city.

Another and greater free speech fight occurred in 1912 in San Diego, following the adoption of an ordinance that forbade street-corner speaking in the downtown district. This ordinance had been approved after Harrison Gray Otis made a speech to a group of San Diego business people recommending strong measures to suppress radical propaganda. Dozens of the "Wobblies"— a nickname which Otis was the first to use in print—then came from other parts of the state to repeat their strategy of overflowing the jails. Business owners formed a vigilance committee, and some of its members inflicted cruel beatings on a number of Wobblies without interference from the police and with open encouragement from the San Diego newspapers, the *Union* and the *Tribune*, both owned by the beet-sugar capitalist, John D. Spreckels. Only the police and the vigilantes, not the IWW, resorted to violence. The *San Francisco Bulletin* asked whether it was the "radicals" or the self-styled "good citizens" who had acted as the real anarchists and who had done more to violate the principles of the Constitution of the United States.

In its effort to organize farm labor the IWW developed methods especially adapted to the conditions of the migratory workers. Giving up the idea of local organizations with permanent dues-paying members, the Wobblies traveled about among the seasonal labor camps, formed temporary organizations "on the job," and asked either very small dues or none at all. These tactics were employed among the workers involved in the tragic incident known as the "Wheatland riot" of August 3, 1913, which occurred on the Durst ranch near the town of Wheatland in Yuba County a few miles southeast of Marysville.

Ralph Durst, one of the state's largest employers of migratory labor, had collected a surplus of workers for the hop-picking season through alluring advertisements in newspapers in several parts of California and southern Oregon. Needing about 1500 workers, he advertised for 2700, and attracted 2800, mostly aliens. Conditions in his work camp were barbaric. As housing, a few tents were available for rental, but most of the workers built their own rude shelters of gunnysacks and poles, or slept in the open. For 2800 men, women, and children there were eight outdoor toilets, which also had to serve as the only garbage disposal facilities. The temperature was more than 100°F in the shade. Durst not only refused to provide drinking water in the fields, but refused the workers permission to rent a water wagon and haul it themselves; a cousin of Durst's had a concession to sell "lemonade," made with citric acid. The "bonus" wage that had been advertised turned out to be nothing more than a device for holding back part of the workers' wages if they left before the end of the picking season.

A mass meeting elected a committee to demand better conditions, with Richard Ford, a member of the IWW better known as "Blackie" Ford, as spokesman. Durst slapped Ford, and the next day, August 3, a posse arrived from Marysville to arrest the agitators. Ford was then addressing another mass meeting, and a deputy fired a shot in the air "to sober the mob." This led to a general melee in which the district attorney, a deputy sheriff, and two workers were killed and many were injured. Governor Johnson sent five companies of the National Guard to Wheatland, and in a trial at Marysville early in 1914, Ford and Herman Suhr, another IWW member, were convicted of second-degree murder on the theory that by leading the strike that resulted in the shooting they were guilty of conspiracy to murder the district attorney. Durst, who was as responsible for the tragedy as any other individual, received no punishment.

SELECTED BIBLIOGRAPHY

Ira B. Cross made basic contributions in his *History of the Labor Movement in California* (1935) and his edition of the autobiography of *Frank B. Roney, Irish Rebel and California Labor Leader* (1931). David F. Selvin, *Sky Full of Storm* (1966) is a survey of the history of union organization in California. See also Alexander P. Saxton, *The Indispensable Enemy: Labor and the Anti-Chinese Movement in California* (1971) and Philip Taft, *Labor Politics American Style: The California State Federation of Labor* (1968).

Aspects of the rise of unionism in San Francisco are treated in Lucille Eaves, *A History of California Labor Legislation with an Introductory Sketch of the San Francisco Labor Movement* (1910); Robert E. L. Knight, *Industrial Relations in the San Francisco Bay Area, 1900–1918* (1960); Paul S. Taylor, *The Sailors' Union of the Pacific* (1923); and Hyman G. Weintraub, *Andrew Furuseth: Emancipator of the Seamen* (1959).

Grace. H. Stimson, *Rise of the Labor Movement in Los Angeles* (1955) and its sequel, Louis B. Perry and Richard S. Perry, *A History of the Los Angeles Labor Movement, 1911–1941* (1963), formed the first inclusive account of the history of organized labor in any large American city. Richard C. Miller, "Otis and His *Times*," Ph.D. thesis, University of California, Berkeley (1961), is penetrating and critical. For the *Times*'s viewpoint see

The Forty-Year War for a Free City: A History of the Open Shop in Los Angeles (1929). On the McNamara case see also William J. Burns, *The Masked War* (1913); Louis Adamic, *Dynamite* (1931); Clarence Darrow, *The Story of My Life* (1932); *The Autobiography of Lincoln Steffens* (1931); and Graham Adams, Jr., *The Age of Industrial Violence, 1910–1915* (1966).

On agricultural labor see Carey McWilliams, *Factories in the Field* (1939); Varden Fuller, "The Supply of Agricultural Labor as a Factor in the Evolution of Farm Organization in California," in United States Congress, Senate Committee on Education and Labor, *Violations of Free Speech and Rights of Labor. Hearings . . .* , part 54 (1940); and Paul S. Taylor, "Foundations of California Rural Society," *California Historical Society Quarterly*, XXIV (September 1945), pp. 193–228.

Hyman Weintraub, "The I.W.W. in California, 1905–1931," M.A.thesis, University of California, Los Angeles (1947), is the most detailed account of its subject. Others may be found in Ronald Genini, "Industrial Workers of the World and Their Fresno Free Speech Fight, 1910–1911," *California Historical Quarterly*, LIII (Summer 1974), pp. 100–114; Grace L. Miller, "The I.W.W. Free Speech Fight: San Diego, 1912," *Southern California Quarterly*, LIV (Fall 1972), pp. 211–238; Rosalie Shanks, "The I.W.W. Free Speech Movement, San Diego, 1912," *Journal of San Diego History*, XIX (Winter 1973), pp. 25–33; Cletus E. Daniel, "In Defense of the Wheatland Wobblies: A Critical Analysis of the IWW in California," *Labor History*, XIX (Fall 1978), pp. 485–509; Woodrow C. Whitten, "The Wheatland Episode," *Pacific Historical Review*, XVII (February, 1948), pp. 37–42; Paul F. Brissenden, *The I.W.W., a Study of American Syndicalism* (1919,1957); and Carleton H. Parker, *The Casual Laborer in America* (1920). General accounts of the IWW are Patrick Renshaw, *The Wobblies* (1967); Melvyn Dubofsky, *We Shall Be All* (1969); and Joseph R. Conlin, *Bread and Roses Too: Studies of the Wobblies* (1969).

Mitchell Slobodek, *A Selective Bibliography of California Labor History* (1964) is thorough and well-annotated.

CULTURE AND OLIGARCHY

In the late nineteenth century a few men with great fortunes dominated California to a degree that justifies the description of its social and political systems as oligarchic. Several of the state's major writers devoted their work largely to protests against this situation. For this as well as other reasons California was producing a remarkable portion of the country's most significant writing.

HENRY GEORGE

In the writings of Henry George, California made a striking contribution to the history of ideas. George's theories grew directly out of his personal observation of the California social environment in the late 1860s and the 1870s, and his beliefs were the responses of a sensitive man to conditions and problems that were then more particularly apparent in California than in any other part of the world. He concluded that monopoly in land, above all, had given oligarchical power to such men as the big four, "who a few years ago were selling coal-oil or retailing dry goods, but who now count their fortunes by the scores of millions." George's denunciation of the "unearned increment" from the increase in the value of land and his remedy, a single tax that would confiscate private land ownership, formed a major chapter in the history of native American radicalism.

George was born in 1839 in Philadelphia. His formal education ended early, and throughout his life he insisted that formal education had little importance or value. He worked for several years as a printer before he came to San Francisco at the age of 19. There he was soon married, and his efforts to keep his wife and children from outright starvation gave him a burning personal knowledge of the meaning of poverty. His writing career began with a series of jobs as reporter or editor for newspapers in San Francisco, Oakland, and Sacramento. When George was sent to New York by the *San Francisco Her-*

ald, he was struck by "the shocking contrast between monstrous wealth and debasing want." He felt a call to seek an understanding of this paradoxical and baffling condition, and to do something to ameliorate it. A year later, back in California, an answer suddenly occurred to him.

One day in 1870, when he was editing the *Oakland Transcript*, he sought relaxation in a ride through the foothills overlooking the bay. A passing teamster told him that the land they were crossing, part of a large unused tract, was being held for a price of $1000 per acre. "Like a flash it came upon me," he recalled in later years; here was the answer to the enigma of why progress had its twin in poverty, of why when wealth increased, poverty increased with it. As land values rose with the growth of population, the person who worked the land had to pay too much for the privilege. The noblest form of labor, the production of food, was robbed to pay a huge unearned increment to the land speculator.

George denounced the railroad as the state's largest private landowner and as the beneficiary of vast subsidies in both land and cash. In a pamphlet on *The Subsidy Question* (1871), he turned laissez faire theories against big business, reversing the usual line of argument. Since the publication of Darwin's *Origin of Species* in 1859, followed by Herbert Spencer's efforts to apply the Darwinian theory of natural selection to the evolution of social institutions, it had become the fashion to indulge in pseudoscientific attempts to transfer Darwin's ideas directly from biology to sociology, economics, and politics. Thus social Darwinist defenders of private business argued that government regulation was a dangerous tinkering with the process of natural selection and the survival of the fittest in free competition. But George pointed out that the railroad, which dominated business in California, had grown not by free competition but by monopoly; that it had been built mainly with government money; and that subsidies were a tremendous form of governmental intervention in the workings of a free economy.

In 1871, also, George published *Our Land and Land Policy*, a pamphlet of about 100 pages in which he first outlined his general doctrine. Stressing the enormous withdrawals of public lands as grants to the railroads, he proposed that the ownership of these and all other lands should be returned to the people, by means of a single massive tax on land that would equal its rental value and thus have the effect of appropriating its ownership and income to the government. George argued that the earning power of all wealth consisted of wages, interest, and rent; that with the increasing productive power of labor and capital, rent tended to increase even more; and that this forced down both wages and interest. An end to private rent and to speculation in land would bring an end to industrial depressions and the maldistribution of wealth, would free business from all other forms of taxation, and indeed would cure virtually all the ills of society.

George opposed the ratifying of the new California constitution. It provided in Article XVII, section 2, that "The holding of large tracts of land, uncultivated and unimproved, by individuals or corporations is against the public interest and should be discouraged," but this provision went on to say "by all means not inconsistent with the rights of private property." The last clause, George felt, would block the only reform that was truly essential. In his view, "private property in land is robbery."

George's doctrine appeared in elaborated form in 1879 in his *Progress and Poverty*, which became one of the phenomenal bestsellers of all time. By the turn of the century there were more than 5 million copies of his writings in circulation, and their influence abroad, particularly in England, was at least as great as in the United States. In 1886 George was nearly elected mayor of New York in a three-cornered race in which he received more votes than did Theodore Roosevelt. Both the devotion of his own followers and the tolerance accorded his ideas by the majority who disagreed with them were remarkable. He wrote with a personal sincerity and an intense love of humanity which no one could doubt, and he popularized what had been well-called the dismal science of economics in words that often had not only the qualities of poetry but the fervor of religion. The single tax, he wrote, would bring "the Golden Age ... , the culmination of Christianity—the city of God with its walls of jasper and its gates of pearl."

By later standards some of his ideas were illiberal. One of his early editorials justified lynching; he was opposed to labor organizations and to strikes; and he was extremely hostile to the Chinese. On the other hand, he criticized the Kearneyites for overemphasizing Chinese exclusion and thus losing sight of the need for more fundamental social change. George's own dogma, of course, was open to the criticism that it exaggerated a single factor and offered a simple remedy.

The single tax was a naïve and emotional panacea. It has never been put into practice anywhere, partly because there have been too many landowners. Yet the idea and the man who advanced it still command respect for their part in stimulating popular thought about the problems of society.

AMBROSE BIERCE

Another major literary product of California journalism was Ambrose Gwinett ("Almighty God") Bierce, also known as "Bitter Bierce" and "The Wickedest Man in San Francisco." Though quite as vigorous as Henry George in criticizing things as they were, Bierce claimed to despise reform and reformers—one of the many paradoxes that characterized his personality.

The son of Marcus Aurelius Bierce, an unprosperous farmer who fathered 13 children and gave every one of them a name beginning with "A," Ambrose was born in a backwoods portion of southeastern Ohio. The economic and emotional hardships of his early life contributed much to his permanent embitterment. In Bierce's parody, the saccharine opening lines of "The Old Oaken Bucket,"

> How dear to this heart are the scenes of my childhood,
> When fond recollection presents them to view . . . ,

were soured into

> With what anguish of mind I remember my childhood,
> Recalled in the light of a knowledge since gained;
> The malarious farm, the wet, fungus-grown wildwood,
> The chills then contracted that since have remained.

Bierce welcomed the Civil War as an escape from his family, but 4 years of bloody action did nothing to sweeten his temperament. After the war he came to the far west, and in 1868 he took over the writing of a column called "The Town Crier" in the *San Francisco News Letter,* published by Frederick Marriott, an Englishman who was prosperously gratifying the western reader's taste for satire, scandal, and the macabre. Bierce was ideally qualified for this kind of assignment, and his success in it encouraged him to write in the same ironic vein for the rest of his life.

In 1872 Bierce married Mollie Day, the beautiful daughter of a wealthy San Francisco family, and the bride's father paid for a honeymoon trip to England. Bierce remained there for 4 years and would have liked to remain permanently, but his wife was so intensely homesick that she returned to San Francisco, and eventually persuaded him to join her. He returned with the greatest resentment and reluctance and soon became the much-feared literary dictator of the Pacific coast with his columns in the San Francisco *Argonaut,* then in the *Wasp,* and finally, after 1887, in young William Randolph Hearst's *Examiner.*

Bierce's short stories have often been compared to those of Edgar Allan Poe, but where Poe often resorted to the supernatural, the weird events in Bierce's narratives always had some sardonic but ostensibly rational explanation at the end. His best stories were those collected in *Tales of Soldiers and Civilians,* later published as *In the Midst of Life.*

Bierce's experiences as a husband and father were disastrous and tragic failures. Toward women, who both frightened and enchanted him, he was outwardly contemptuous and patronizing. Two women writers were among his most perceptive critics. Gertrude Atherton, who sought his advice, said that his scorn for almost all novels grew out of his inability to write a novel of his own. Mary Austin's opinion was that he was "a man secretly embittered by failure to achieve direct creation" and that in his need for worshipful young protégés he was "seeking to make good in some other's gift what he had missed."

In *The Devil's Dictionary,* Bierce defined "birth" as "The first and direst of all disasters," and he often argued that suicide was not only a right but almost a duty. And although the circumstances of Bierce's own demise have remained a mystery, it is clear that in 1913 when he planned to join the army of Pancho

Villa as an "observer," he was seeking a death which he did not quite wish to inflict by his own hand. "Goodbye," he wrote to his niece, "if you hear of my being stood up against a Mexican stone wall and shot to rags please know that I think it a pretty good way to depart this life. It beats old age, disease, or falling down the cellar stairs. To be a Gringo in Mexico—ah, that is euthanasia!" Bierce was a deeply tortured man, never fully aware of the causes of his misery.

FRANK NORRIS

In contrast with Bierce, who regarded childhood as a disaster and the rest of life as not much better, Frank Norris attributed to his childhood much of his great enthusiasm for both real and fictional experience. The gifted novelist, Norris once wrote, was the man who retained the dramatizing imagination of a boy.

Benjamin Franklin Norris, Jr., was born in Chicago in 1870 of able and energetic parents. His father was a successful and wealthy jeweler who wanted his oldest son to join him in business, while his mother, who had been a successful actress before her marriage, wanted her sons to have artistic careers. When Frank was 14 the family moved to San Francisco. At 17 he was sent to Paris to study art, but when he began to write stories instead, his father maintained that he was wasting his time and summoned him home. At 20 he enrolled in the University of California and spent 4 years there. Having disliked the stylistic conformity which his English professors at Berkeley demanded, he spent a fifth collegiate year in a creative writing course at Harvard, where he worked on two stories of San Francisco, *McTeague* and *Vandover and the Brute.*

Much influenced by the works of Emile Zola, *McTeague* was the first important contribution to naturalism by an American writer. Its hero is a charlatan dentist, McTeague, who marries Trina, a girl who has won $5000 in a lottery; however, her cousin and jilted suitor takes revenge by informing the authorities that the dentist is practicing without a license. The novel became a study of the degeneration of Trina into miserliness and of McTeague into sadistic brutality. At last the ex-dentist murders his wife, and her cousin pursues him into Death Valley where the two men die handcuffed together.

Vandover and the Brute has the same basic theme—a man's deterioration into the beast within him. A talented young artist, the story goes, neglects his gift and gives way to what Norris regarded as his own most dangerous vices, idleness and dissipation. In the end, Vandover's downward path goes so far that he actually becomes a victim of lycanthropy, the delusion that he is a wolf.

Norris soon discovered that the naturalism of these works was too undiluted to permit the publication of either of them as a first novel at a time when the American reading public still demanded that fiction be highly romanticized. In search of further training and experience as a writer he joined the editorial staff of the San Francisco *Wave*. His next novel, a rousing sea story called *Moran of the Lady Letty*, was deliberately constructed as a potboiler and brought out serially in the *Wave* in the hope that some New York publisher might recognize its popular appeal. The hope was fulfilled. S. S. McClure, who kept an eye on the San Francisco journals for new writers, telegraphed an offer to publish *Moran* as a book and to employ Norris as a regular writer. The publication of *McTeague* followed a few months later, in 1899.

Much encouraged, Norris conceived one of the most ambitious projects in the history of American literature, a trilogy to be called the *Epic of the Wheat*. The first part would describe the growing of the wheat in California, the second its distribution by the board of trade or "pit" in Chicago, and the third its consumption in a famine-stricken village in Europe. Each of the three novels would have a central episode based on an actual occurrence, and the first, *The Octopus, a Story of California*, would center upon the battle of Mussel Slough. But Norris was not concerned with precise accuracy of historical detail; his intention was to tell the truth in what he regarded as a larger sense, including the greatest possible element of dramatic impact. Although in the course of his research he did apparently visit the town of Tulare, the Bonneville of *The Octopus*, he spent much more time on a 10,000-acre wheat ranch near Hollister, so that the locale described in the novel was not actually that of the San Joaquin Valley in 1880 but rather of a coastal valley in 1899, and the wheat growers were not the small farmers of the actual episode, but large ranchers. Consolidating his Californiana, Norris also transplanted a mission and a sleepy old Mexican town, based on San Juan Bautista, across the Coast Range and into a story in which they had had no actual part.

The Octopus also included a number of more basic inconsistencies. As a "novel with a purpose," *The Octopus* departed from Norris's goal of naturalistic objectivity and became in many of its passages a propagandistic tract for reform of the trusts. Norris was perceptibly influenced by the writers whom he met in the offices of *McClure's Magazine* and who would soon launch the muckraking movement. Theodore Roosevelt read *The Octopus* as a tract and remarked to a friend that apparently "conditions were worse in California than elsewhere." Although *The Octopus* was a work of greater social and historical interest than *McTeague*, as a piece of writing it was less carefully constructed and less finished. Yet it was and will remain one of the most important of American novels.

Although Norris often wrote mystical praises of "the People," that is, the lower and lower-middle classes, he was a snob, with strong biases of both class and race. He was anti-Oriental and anti-Semitic, and an admirer of Kipling's Anglo-Saxonism as well as of his literary style. Like most major writers, Norris was as contradictory and complicated as life itself, and he loved life to a degree that made his early death at 32, of appendicitis, peculiarly sad. *The Pit*, based on an actual attempt to corner the wheat market at Chicago, had degenerated into a conventional love story, and was appearing serially in the *Saturday Evening Post* when he died. He had not begun the writing of *The Wolf*, the projected third volume.

JACK LONDON

Few men have risen to success through greater difficulties than did Jack London. He was an unwanted and illegitimate child, born in San Francisco in 1876, presumably the son of William H. Chaney, an itinerant Irish astrologer who denied paternity and whom he never saw. His mother secured a name for him by marrying John London, a kindly widower who gave his stepson what little feeling of stability there was in his earliest years. The boy grew up on the Oakland waterfront. At 15 he was an oyster pirate, at 17 he went to sea on one of the last seal-hunting voyages out of San Francisco Bay, and at 18, in 1894, he traveled to the east coast and back as a member of the California contingent of Coxey's army of unemployed. One of his hobo acquaintances introduced him to the *Communist Manifesto,* and his left-wing socialist opinions solidified after he returned to Oakland and experienced a series of cruelly hard and low-paying jobs, in which he worked for 60 hours a week in a jute mill, in a hand laundry, and at shoveling coal. For years he signed many of his letters "Yours for the Revolution."

After a few months at Oakland High School and a semester at the University of California, he joined the Klondike gold rush in 1897 and spent a year and a half in Alaska, where he discovered no gold but a great deal of material for the stories through which he hoped to make a living. His first publisher, the *Overland Monthly,* offered him $5 for a story of 5000 words, and when even this small payment was slow in coming, he visited the office of the magazine and collected the amount in small change from the pockets of the assistant editor and the business manager, by threat of physical violence. But success came soon afterward. In 1900 S. S. McClure discovered London, as he had discovered Norris, and published London's first book, a collection of stories called *Son of the Wolf.* Within a few years London was the highest-paid, best-known, and most popular writer in the world, displacing his hero Rudyard Kipling in the possession of these honors.

The Call of the Wild (1903), the most famous of London's many stories of the far north, concerned a dog that was kidnapped in California and taken to Alaska where he reverted to savagery and ran with a wolf pack. There were several partly autobiographical novels, including *Martin Eden* (1909) and *John Barleycorn* (1913). And there were several novels or other works of socialist propaganda, the most important of which was *The Iron Heel* (1907). This story was especially striking in that it predicted the rise of fascism. On the whole, however, London's social and political ideas were little more than a jumble of Darwin, Spencer, Marx, and Nietzsche.

As his attempt to cross Marx's proletarianism with Nietzsche's Superman suggests, London's professions of socialism were out of tune with his own strongest feelings. His best writing was concerned not with hopes of an idealized collectivist society, but rather with the opposite theme of the triumph of some individual man or beast over more ordinary members of the respective species in some contest of wild and primordial violence. London's racism, moreover, was more extreme than either Kipling's or Norris's.

London was too emotionally insecure to be capable of happy marriage or of any other stable personal relationship. His second wife, Charmian Kittredge, lived in mortal terror that some other woman would take him away from her as easily as she had seduced him from his first wife, Bessie Maddern. Hoping to find security in a magnificent house, London spent more than $90,000 on a mansion of stone near Glen Ellen, but shortly before he was to have moved into it the interior of the house was destroyed by fire. There could be no doubt that the fire had been set deliberately, and the loss was intensified by the pain of speculating on the identity of the person who had hated him enough to do such a devilish thing to him. The alcoholism that had endangered his health for many years became progressively worse, and in 1916, at 40 and in great pain from uremia, he ended his life, perhaps inadvertently, with an overdose of morphine. His career had symbolized the elemental power of humanity to struggle against tragedy and heartbreak, a struggle that was no less admirable because in his case the odds were too heavy to be overcome.

HISTORIOGRAPHY

Well before the end of the nineteenth century, California witnessed the carrying out of a truly remarkable project for the writing of its history, a project which in its unbounded ambitiousness was characteristic of the state itself. One day in 1859 Hubert Howe Bancroft, the most successful bookseller in San Francisco and in the whole of the west, happened to place together all the items in his store that dealt with the Pacific coast. Such was the nucleus of the incomparable Bancroft Library. From collecting books, and later manuscripts, Bancroft progressed to the idea of bringing together the history that was in them. Calculating at one point that it would take him 400 years to read the whole of his collection, let alone to write a history from it, and being of a practical turn of mind, he employed a staff of assistants when the actual research and writing project began in 1871. The ablest of these was Henry L. Oak, a young graduate of Dartmouth College who was originally employed as librarian and who had no more formal training as a historian or experience as a writer than did Bancroft himself.

Few things even in California have grown as the Bancroft project grew. *Bancroft's Works*, published between 1882 and 1890, filled 39 fat and closely packed volumes. The native races of the Pacific states received five volumes, Central America three, and Mexico six; on California there were seven general chronological volumes and four others on special subjects; and the rest of the set covered the other parts of western North America. Bancroft himself was substantially the author of about one-fourth of these books. The others were written, as well as researched, by his assistants.

In all these *Works*, however, Bancroft most unwisely and unfortunately represented himself as the sole author; the assistants received no credit except in the thirty-ninth volume, called *Literary Industries*, in which Bancroft described the process of authorship in a most inadequate and misleading way. In the process of marketing the mammoth series, also, Bancroft resorted to devices that were highly questionable, though he himself did not consider them so. He secured a great claque of favorable reviews for the early volumes by making personal calls on dozens of famous authors in the east, and many purchasers whom his canvassers signed up at the beginning were not told what a large number of volumes they were contracting to buy. Finally, when the *Works* were followed in the early 1890s by the *Chronicles of the Builders of the Commonwealth,* originally projected as the *Chronicles of the Kings,* and when it became known that in these enormously expensive vanity publications the length and tone of each biography was determined by the number of thousands of dollars subscribed by the biographee, there was a blast of public criticism that damaged Bancroft's reputation.

It came to be the general impression that what Collis P. Huntington was to California's economy, Hubert Howe Bancroft was to its historiography. They were, indeed, men of very similar outlook. For example, both felt that labor unions and the income tax were communistic devices by which those who did not accumulate anything were trying to obtain some of the savings of those who did. Huntington subscribed a large sum for the glowing 110-page biography of him that appeared in the *Chronicles of the Builders.* On the other hand, the biography of Leland Stanford, which had been fully prepared for publication, was omitted from the set because Stanford refused to make payment. When the *Works* had first begun to appear, Stanford had generously subscribed for 40 sets, under the impression that a full set would consist of five or six volumes. But after receiving and paying for 40 copies of each volume of the *Works* through the twenty-third one, he canceled his subscription in an acid letter.

The five volumes on the general history of California to 1848 were written by Henry L. Oak. As a whole they were superior to the two volumes on the period 1848 to 1890 written mainly by two of Bancroft's other assistants, William Nemos and Frances Fuller Victor. And a comparison of Oak's writings with the volumes on California that were actually written by Bancroft (*California Pastoral, California Inter Pocula,* and *Popular Tribunals*) makes it clear that Oak was a better historian than his employer. Much in Oak's early volumes was ill-organized, overdetailed, and tedious, but especially in his volume on the period of the "conquest," 1846 to 1848, there were many passages of shrewd analysis and brilliant narrative. Bancroft's own historical style was florid, windy, and pontifical.

The great value of Bancroft's services to the history of western North American lay not in his own contributions as a writer, but in the collection of materials and in the basic organization of a vast research project. These latter services were enormous and unique, and if he had tried to do much more of the research and writing himself the huge enterprise could never have been completed.

The failure to give credit to his writers was another matter. When Henry Oak, having become a brooding invalid after 20 years of hard and anonymous labor, wrote an ineffectual protest, Bancroft replied: "I doubt that authors are in the habit of giving their employees any credit at all." In making this statement Bancroft was quite unaware of its impropriety and irrelevance. Why later historians have failed to give proper credit to Oak for the authorship of the best volumes in the Bancroft history of California is harder to explain.

When the wealthy land-title lawyer Theodore H. Hittell wrote his own *History of California,* which was published in four volumes between 1885 and 1897, the extreme public criticisms of a number of Bancroft's methods had misled Hittell into supposing that there could be no value in any of *Bancroft's Works,* and he refused to consult them. Hittell's history was a good one; it could have been still better if he had not made this unfortunate misjudgement. John S. Hittell, brother of Theodore, was also an important pioneer of California historiography, especially in the documentation of the state's resources and economic development.

Not long after Josiah Royce had become a junior member of the philosophy department at Harvard, the publisher of a projected series of volumes on "American Commonwealths" selected him, as one of the most promising young men who had come to the east out of California, to write a volume on his native state. Royce obtained permission to use the Bancroft library, already by far the largest and best collection of sources in the west. He also received much helpful advice from Oak. Royce's *California, from the Conquest in 1846 to the Second Vigilance Committee in San Francisco, a Study of American Character* (1886) took the form of an effort to establish the validity of the Hegelian dialectic of order and disorder, authority and freedom. In his later years at Harvard, Royce went on to become one of the leading American defenders of philosophical idealism.

LORDS OF THE PRESS

In the later decades of the nineteenth century and the early years of the twentieth, journalism in California's metropolis of San Francisco differed from that of the frontier days in that there came to be a smaller number of larger newspapers, owned and controlled by a few wealthy men.

Of the major San Francisco dailies destined to survive into the twentieth century the oldest were the *Evening Bulletin,* founded in 1855, and the *Morning Call,* which dated from 1856. But these were ultimately outstripped in circulation and influence by two morning papers: the *Examiner,* which began as the weekly *Democratic Press* in 1863, and the *Chronicle,* founded as the *Daily Dramatic Chronicle* in 1865 by the brothers Charles and M. H. de Young.

One of the most striking developments in the whole colorful history of American newspapers was the rise of William Randolph Hearst, who was born in San Francisco in 1863 and took over the ownership and control of the *Examiner* in 1887, when he was less than 24 years old. George Hearst, his father, had bought the paper a few years earlier to advance his political ambitions. The elder Hearst was a self-trained mining engineer who had risen from poverty to a great fortune. Beginning with a tiny investment in the Ophir mine in Virginia City, he had gone on to develop the Homestake mine in South Dakota and the Anaconda silver and copper mines in Montana, and to expand his wealth still further with several huge ranches. In January 1887, a Democratic majority in the California legislature elected him to the United States Senate, and it was on March 4, the day he took his seat in Washington, that he made the gift of the *San Francisco Examiner* to his son.

A few months earlier, William Randolph Hearst had been expelled from Harvard at the end of his junior year for indulging in an obscene expression of contempt for his professors. Since then he had worked as a reporter for Joseph Pulitzer's *New York World* in order to study Pulitzer's methods. These he would soon apply to the moribund little *Examiner* with many elaborations of his own and with spectacular results. Young Hearst quickly expanded the *Examiner* from four pages to eight, banished advertising from the front page in favor of headlines followed by sensational stories of crime and corruption, and brought in many special features for the reader's amusement. The term "yellow journalism" has its origin when Hearst hired away from Pulitzer the cartoonist of a popular early comic strip called "the Yellow Kid."

Hearst invested heavily in new printing equipment, especially for printing illustrations, and he went to unusual lengths with the "arranged story." If the news that actually happened was not lively enough, Hearst manufactured news that was. At the *Examiner's* expense a young couple were married in a balloon, and even, according to the *Examiner*, spent their honeymoon there—"up in the clouds." The real secret of Hearst's success was in his genius for spectacular entertainment. "The public," he wrote in an editorial in 1896, "is even more fond of entertainment than it is of information," and this philosophy of journali. n became increasingly important in later years when he acquired an unprecedented number of newspapers in many cities, including the largest cities in the country. He maintained extraordinarily close control over the news and editorial policies of all his papers, and thus he had a greater influence on what was printed and read in America than any other man before or since.

No other California newspaper publisher acquired national influence comparable to Hearst's but within the state there were several figures of regional importance. In Sacramento the history of the *Bee* became synonymous with that of the McClatchy family, from the time when James McClatchy became editor in 1857, the year the *Bee* was founded. McClatchy had come from Ireland as a boy, and he brought an Irishman's hatred of land monopoly to his leadership of the squatters in the gold-rush period and then to the *Bee's* editorial columns. At his death in 1883 the control of the paper passed to his son Charles ("C.K."), who was its fighting editor for nearly 50 years.

THE ARTS AND ARCHITECTURE

The outstanding painter of pioneer life in California was Charles Christian Nahl. Born into a family that had achieved artistic distinction in Germany for six generations, Nahl came to California in 1850 and was soon the leading

Sunday Morning in the Mines. Painted by Charles Christian Nahl in 1872. *(Courtesy of the Crocker Art Museum, Sacramento.)*

producer of lithographs for letter sheets, the famous souvenir stationery on which the miners wrote home the news from the goldfields. After Judge E. B. Crocker became his patron in 1867, Nahl was able to devote the greater part of his time to his work in oils, and a number of his paintings were included in the Crocker Art Gallery in Sacramento. Probably the best of these, and certainly the best known, was his *Sunday Morning in the Mines*, which appears badly overcrowded with figures and detail in small reproductions, but less so in the original, a canvas 9 feet long and 6 feet high.

Thomas A. Ayres became famous as the first artist to portray Yosemite Valley. In 1855 Ayers was a member of the first tourist party ever to enter the valley; in five days he produced five drawings, one of which, *The High Falls*, has scarcely been excelled among the thousands of later efforts. Albert Bierstadt and Thomas Hill were among the many who later painted the Yosemite and other California landscapes.

The most intriguing work of Hill, however, was his attempt to provide the ultimate commemoration of the transcontinental railroad in his *Driving the Last Spike*. Leland Stanford had commissioned this painting and promised $50,000 for it; such, at least, was Hill's impression, but after the artist had spent 4 years at work on the huge and elaborate canvas, Stanford refused to buy it and denied that he had ordered it. His most vocal objection was that some 70 officials of the Union and Central Pacific railroads were in the massive picture, very few of whom had actually been present at the scene; even Judah, who had died 6 years previously, was included. In somewhat the same mood in which he broke relations with Hubert Howe Bancroft, Stanford stood foursquare against contractual imposture, and in favor of historical accuracy. It was also true, however, that relatives of Charles Crocker strongly objected to the

Driving the Last Spike. This controversial canvas, painted by Thomas Hill between 1887 and 1891, contains over 400 figures, including 70 recognizable portraits. *(Courtesy of the Bancroft Library.)*

prominent position occupied by Stanford at the center of Hill's picture, and that Stanford's repudiation of the painting tended to restore the peace in the railroad family.

Scottish-born William Keith, whose active career extended from the 1860s until his death in 1911, attained greater prestige than any other California art-

A photograph of the scene at Promontory, Utah, May 10, 1869. Note the contrast with Hill's idealized painting. *(Courtesy of the Bancroft Library.)*

ist. His early paintings of the Sierra country were done with almost photographic realism, but his maturity and his success came when, much to the disappointment of his close friend John Muir, he turned from the high mountains to pastoral landscapes of the foothills, done with a highly mystical quality.

The best California sculptor of the period was probably Ralph Stackpole, whose busts of several well-known San Franciscans were excellent portraits in stone. Greater popular acclaim, however, went to the attitudinized athletic figures by Douglas Tilden, such as the five men operating an antique drill press in the sculpture created for the "Mechanics' Monument" at Market and Bush Streets in San Francisco.

In the field of music, San Francisco had heard its first grand opera as early as February 12, 1851, when the Pellegrini opera troupe presented Bellini's *La Sonnambula* at the Adelphi Theater. But throughout the nineteenth century, traveling performers from the east continued to outshine the local talent, both in music and in drama.

In architecture, regional developments were somewhat more distinctive. "California mission architecture" has as much interest for the history of myth-making as for the history of architecture. Charming legends to the contrary, the roof tiles were not shaped on the thighs of Indian women, and the designs for the California mission buildings added little to the older Mexican models. As for the so-called Monterey colonial style, introduced by Thomas Larkin in the 1830s, it was adapted from buildings he had seen in Massachusetts and North Carolina, and nothing about it was either Spanish-colonial or Mexican-republican except the use of adobe as the handiest material for the walls. Nevertheless, in the early twentieth century, "mission revival" and Monterey

Postcard showing California Street cable car and Stanford and Hopkins mansions on Nob Hill. *(Courtesy of the Bancroft Library.)*

colonial buildings formed the basis of an important regional architectural tradition.

The availability of redwood in the American period gave San Francisco in the late nineteenth century a larger proportion of wood frame residential buildings than any other city in the nation. Redwood became so common that there were many attempts to use paint to disguise it as stone, and the wooden house of David D. Colton on Nob Hill was even painted to simulate an Italian marble palace. Even so, the Colton house was a less offensive monument to conspicuous and meretricious waste than were the neighboring mansions of Crocker, Stanford, and the rest. Beauty was regarded as deriving from ornamentation rather than from any genuine architectural function, and there was a profusion of jigsaw carpentry on porches and of ironwork on mansard roofs. In the construction of public buildings the era is notorious for the tendency of architects to try to build monuments to themselves rather than design structures that would effectively serve the purposes for which they were intended.

SCHOOLS, COLLEGES, AND UNIVERSITIES

The development of a sense of public responsibility for education in California in the nineteenth century was slow, lagging far behind the growth of the state's economic resources and population. Not until 1874, when the legislature passed "an act to enforce the educational rights of children," did the state adopt compulsory education, and even then, although it applied only to the elementary level, the law was bitterly opposed on the grounds that it was un-American, that it interfered with the liberty of parents, and that it was an arrogation of new power by the government. As for public secondary education, there were only 16 high schools in the state in 1879, and several of them were wiped out by the provision of the new constitution that denied state tax funds to high schools on the ground that the primary and grammar schools were still inadequately supported—which was all too true. When Kate Douglas Wiggin taught the first free kindergarten in California in a slum district of San Francisco in 1878, she had to raise money for it herself, partly through the income from her own short stories and novels.

In its provisions for elementary school textbooks, California was somewhat more enterprising. In 1875, as a result of charges of corruption and collusion between local school board members and booksellers, an act of the legislature forbade excessively frequent changes in the books required. And by a constitutional amendment approved by the voters in 1884, California became the first state to provide that a uniform series of elementary school textbooks approved by the state board of education should be published by the state printing office. At first these books were sold, though at a very considerable saving in price; beginning in 1912, by state constitutional amendment, they would be distributed free.

Slow development of high schools made it inevitable that the growth of an effective demand for colleges would be even slower. For many years after colleges were opened they would have to maintain "preparatory departments," in which most of their very limited numbers of students were enrolled.

Twenty years elapsed between the enthusiastic predictions of Robert Semple in the constitutional convention at Monterey and the actual opening of the University of California, with 38 students, in the fall of 1869. In the meantime, the private enterprise of religious leaders had taken the responsibility for lighting the torch of higher education. Even before the Monterey convention adjourned in the fall of 1849, a group of Congregational and Presbyterian ministers had held a meeting in San Francisco to plan a New England–style college in California. This project first took shape as the Contra Costa Academy, a "family boarding school for boys," opened in Oakland in 1853. The institution was incorporated as the College of California in 1855, though it continued to function only as a preparatory school until 1860, when it enrolled its first freshman class. In the history of higher education, as this example indicates, chronology is not an exact science, for there is often a lack of agreement as to which step constituted the "founding" of a college.

Had it not been for the Morrill Act of 1862, in which the federal government offered land-grant endowments to the states for agricultural colleges, California would have delayed even longer than it did in establishing a state university. It was in order to secure the federal land-grant endowment that the California Legislature in 1866 issued a charter for an "Agricultural, Mining, and Mechanic Arts College." The trustees of the College of California then offered to turn over their entire property to the state, to be merged with the proposed agricultural college into a state university. That the private college was dangerously mired in debt was a factor in the trustees' decision, but their offer included a magnificent tract of land north of Oakland to which they had acquired title and to which they had planned to move their own institution. There they had already laid out the adjoining town lots and named the future community for Bishop George Berkeley, the Irish philosopher whose hopes of founding a college in colonial New England had once led him to write a poem "On the Prospect of Planting Arts and Learning in America," a poem including the words "Westward the course of empire takes its way. . . ." John W. Dwinelle, a scholarly land-title lawyer and one of the college's trustees, was elected to the state legislature and introduced the bill that became the charter of the University of California on March 23, 1868, superseding the agricultural college's charter adopted 2 years earlier.

Throughout the nineteenth century it was difficult to attract eminent scholars to the faculty of any institution in the far west, including the University of California. Daniel Coit Gilman remained as president for only 3 years before Johns Hopkins lured him back to the east. But a few able men did come to stay. Joseph LeConte, biologist and philosopher, won admiration with his writings and lectures on "evolutionary idealism," in which he reconciled Darwinian theory with belief in God. Eugene W. Hilgard began the process of building the college of agriculture into a great institution of applied scientific research. Through his ability to convince the farmers of the practical value of that research, he succeeded in quieting some of their chronic suspicions that the Morrill Act endowment was being frittered away on a merely literary college. In 1899 the regents brought Benjamin Ide Wheeler to the presidency from a professorship of Greek at Cornell, and for nearly 20 years, in the heyday of the "strong president" system in American higher education, Wheeler was the university's benevolent despot. During this period Henry Morse Stephens popularized history not only to a generation of students but also in many public lectures throughout the state, and Charles Mills Gayley and his "great books" course drew classes so large that they sometimes had to be held outdoors in the Greek Theater, a gift of William Randolph Hearst.

Leland Stanford, from the time of his rise to affluence, periodically contemplated the making of some generous gift to the people of California. Leland and Jane Lathrop Stanford had been childless for the first 18 years of their marriage, until the birth of Leland, Junior; their son occupied a very central place in their lives, and in 1885, when he was less than 16 years old, he died. Within the same year, the parents who had lost their only child founded a university which would bear his name, and in which, as they put it, the children of California would become the foster children of their love. For the Leland Stanford, Junior, University they promised not only their large and beautiful stock farm at Palo Alto, as a campus, but also the bulk of their fortune.

During their long and careful search for a president, Daniel Coit Gilman told them of a distinguished biologist, David Starr Jordan, then president of Indiana University. Although Jordan had recently stated the opinion that the future of American higher education lay with the state universities, he agreed to come to Stanford, and he set it on its course toward the point at which loyal alumni would describe Stanford as "the Harvard of the West"—and Harvard as "the Stanford of the East."

At the outset there were many expressions of doubt that California needed or could successfully maintain two universities within 50 miles of each other, but in 1891 when Stanford opened the enrollment was 559 (including a young man named Herbert Hoover), and there were nearly twice as many at Berkeley. Ten years later the enrollments at both institutions had more than doubled, and nearly 10 percent were graduate students. The 1890s were a turning point. One vital factor was the state law of 1891 which authorized the establishment of a high school by approval of the voters of any city or incorporated town of more than 1500 people, and of a union high school by any two or more districts, the curricula to be such as to prepare the students for the university.

Of the colleges founded by the various Protestant denominations, the majority began as "church controlled" and were later described as "church related and supported"; several of them eventually became independent. The University of the Pacific, begun by the Methodists as an academy at San Jose in 1851, was moved to Santa Clara and ultimately reestablished at Stockton in

1924. The Methodists also founded the University of Southern California in 1879. Occidental College was established by the Presbyterians in 1887, and Pomona College by the Congregationalists in the same year. The Quakers founded Whittier College in 1901, and the Baptists established Redlands in 1909.

Of the Catholic institutions, the Jesuit universities of Santa Clara and San Francisco date from schools opened in the 1850s, and St. Vincent's College in Los Angeles, chartered in 1869, became Loyola University. St. Mary's College, growing out of a school established by Archbishop Alemany in San Francisco in 1863, was placed under the administration of the Christian Brothers, moved to Oakland, and relocated in 1928 in Moraga Valley.

The charter of the University of California required it to admit women, following the lead of several midwestern state universities founded in the previous two decades. California's "normal schools," beginning in San Francisco in 1862, were at first devoted almost entirely to the postsecondary training of women as elementary teachers. In 1900 these institutions enrolled about half the women then pursuing higher education. Most of the collegiate institutions other than the Catholic ones were coeducational. The oldest women's college in the west was opened as a young ladies' seminary in Oakland in 1871 by Dr. and Mrs. Cyrus T. Mills and chartered as Mills College in 1885 on a nonsectarian basis.

SELECTED BIBLIOGRAPHY

On several aspects of this chapter see Kevin Starr, *Americans and the California Dream, 1850–1915* (1973).

Charles A. Barker, *Henry George* (1955) is the standard work; the earlier biography by Henry George, Jr. (two volumes, 1911) retains some interest. The best treatment of Bierce is Paul Fatout, *Ambrose Bierce, the Devil's Lexicographer* (1951). Important writings on Frank Norris include the biography by Franklin Walker (1932); the studies by Ernest L. Marchand (1942), Warren French (1962), and Donald Pizer (1966); and Robert D. Lundy, "The Making of *McTeague* and *The Octopus*," Ph.D. thesis, University of California, Berkely (1956). See also the special issue of *American Literary Realism, 1870-1910*, XI (Autumn 1978). On the treatment of the battle of Mussel Slough by Norris and others, see the articles by Irving McKee, *Pacific Historical Review*, XVII (February 1948), pp. 19–28, and James Lorin Brown, ibid., XXVI (November 1957), pp. 373–376. Joan London, *Jack London and His Times* (1939); Irving Stone, *Jack London: Sailor on Horseback* (1938); and Richard O'Connor, *Jack London* (1964) are biographies. More recent works on London include Andrew Sinclair, *Jack: A Biography of Jack London* (1977); Richard Etulain (ed.), *Jack London on the Road* (1979); Ray Ownbey, *Jack London: Essays in Criticism* (1980); and the special issue of *Pacific Historian* XXI (Summer 1977).

On historiography see John W. Caughey, *Hubert Howe Bancroft* (1946) and Harry Clark, *A Venture in History* (1973); Earl Pomeroy, "Josiah Royce, Historian in Search of Community," *Pacific Historical Review*, XL (February 1971), pp. 1–20; Robert W. Righter, "Theodore H. Hittell and Hubert H. Bancroft," *California Historical Quarterly*, L. (June

1971), pp. 101–110; and Claude R. Petty, "John S. Hittell and the Gospel of California," *Pacific Historical Review*, XXIV (February 1955), pp. 1–16.

Robert Louis Stevenson left some lively vignettes of his sojourn in California; all are included in James D. Hart (ed.), *From Scotland to Silverado* (1966).

Much information on both major and minor literary figures may be found in Gertrude Atherton, *Adventures of a Novelist* (1932); Mary Austin, *Earth Horizon* (1932); Franklin Walker, *San Francisco's Literary Frontier* (1939); *A Literary History of Southern California* (1950), and *The Seacoast of Bohemia* (1966); and Lawrence Clark Powell, *California Classics; the Creative Literature of the Golden State* (1971).

Journalism in California (1915), by John P. Young, managing editor of the *San Francisco Chronicle* for more than 40 years, was originally written to celebrate the fiftieth anniversary of that newspaper. John Roberts Bruce, *Gaudy Century; the Story of San Francisco's Hundred Years of Robust Journalism* (1948) is gaudier and less useful on the later than on the early period. The *History of Journalism in San Francisco* (seven volumes, 1939–1941, mimeographed), by the California Writers' Program of the WPA, though not actually a general history of its subject and not always accurate in details, includes much information on a number of special aspects. Of the several biographies of Hearst, those by Cora B. Older (1936) and John K. Winkler (1928, 1955) were almost as indulgent toward their subject as were his own parents; Edmond D. Coblentz, *William Randolph Hearst, a Portrait in His Own Words* (1952) is a useful anthology; the best general treatment to date is W. A. Swanberg, *Citizen Hearst* (1961), its title suggested by Orson Welles's remarkable film *Citizen Kane* (1940). James R. Wotherspoon, "The San Francisco *Argonaut*, 1877–1097," Ph.D. thesis, University of California, Berkeley (1962), deals with the most important of the weeklies. Robert Davenport, "San Francisco Journalism in the Time of Fremont Older," Ph.D. thesis, University of California, Los Angeles (1969), is valuable, as are Fremont Older, *My Own Story* (1926) and Jerome A. Hart, *In Our Second Century* (1931). On Los Angeles journalism, see Richard Connelly Miller, "Otis and His *Times*," PhD. thesis, University of California, Berkeley (1961); Edwin Bingham, *Charles F. Lummis, Editor of the Southwest* (1955); and the autiobiography of *William Andrew Spalding, Los Angeles Newspaperman* (1961), edited by Robert V. Hine.

Art in California (1916), including essays by Bruce Porter, Porter Garnet, Bernard Maybeck, and others, is an illustrated survey of California painting, sculpture, and architecture as represented at the Panama-Pacific International Exposition. The *Monographs* of the California Art Research Project (20 volumes, mimeographed, 1937) include accounts of about 50 California artists, mostly painters, who made their residence chiefly in San Francisco; though far from being an adequate history of art in California, this series was an interesting preliminary effort in that direction. Other useful works include Jeanne Van Nostrand, *The First Hundred Years of Painting in California, 1775–1875* (1980); the *California Centennials Exhibition of Art* (1949); Carl O. Borg and Millard Sheets, *Cross, Sword, and Gold Pan* (1936); "Thomas A. Ayres, Artist-Argonaut of California," *California Historical Society Quarterly*, XX (September 1941), pp. 275–279, by Jeanne S. Van Nostrand; "Charles Christian Nahl, the Painter of California Pioneer Life," *California Historical Society Quarterly*, XV (December 1936), pp. 295–305, by Eugen Neuhaus, himself a distinguished painter and teacher of art; and, also by Neuhaus, *William Keith, the Man and the Artist* (1938). Brother Fidelis Cornelius, *Keith, Old Master of California* (two volumes, 1941–1956) includes hundreds of reproductions.

Edmond M. Gagey, *The San Francisco Stage, a History* (1950) is based on annals compiled by the research department of the San Francisco Federal Theatre. Constance Rourke, *Troupers of the Gold Coast* (1928) is concerned mainly with Lotta Crabtree.

Harold Kirker, *California's Architectural Frontier: Style and Tradition in the Nineteenth Century* (1960) is an important social history. See also Porter Garnett, *Stately Homes of California* (1915).

William Warren Ferrier, *Ninety Years of Education in California, 1846–1936* (1937) is valuable for the early decades, though less so for the period after 1900. See also Irving G. Hendrick, *California Education: A Brief History* (1980) and Doyce B. Nunis, Jr., "Kate Douglas Wiggin: Pioneer in California Kindergarten Education," *California Historical Society Quarterly* (December 1962) pp. 291–307. On university founding see John R. Thelin, "California and the Colleges." *California Historical Quarterly*, LVI (Summer and Fall, 1977), pp. 140–163, 230–249; Verne A. Stadtman, *The University of California, 1868–1968* (1970) and Edward M. Burns, *David Starr Jordan, Prophet of Freedom* (1953).

POLITICS
IN THE ERA OF
RAILROAD DOMINATION

The last third of the nineteenth century was an age of unparalleled corruption in American public life. As an English historian once put it, the names of several presidents of railroads were of greater importance in that era of American history than the names of several presidents of the United States. The leaders of huge corporations dominated not only the American economy but American politics as well; and they tended not only to despise the politicians, many of whom they easily corrupted, but also to feel contempt for government itself.

In that period it was said that the Standard Oil Company had done everything to the legislature of Pennsylvania except to refine it, but in no state was politics more subservient to big business than in California, for in no other state, as James Bryce remarked, were politics and the economy "so much at the mercy of one powerful corporation." In California the Southern Pacific represented the greatest accumulation of wealth. It was the largest landowner and the largest employer of labor. Its rail system was the longest in the nation, extending from Portland to New Orleans and from Ogden to San Francisco. The building of the Santa Fe to Los Angeles in the 1880s brought some temporary competition in southern California, but this was soon nullified by rate agreements, and the Southern Pacific acquired partial control of the Santa Fe by buying stock.

In the 1890s a group of San Francisco capitalists including Adolph Sutro, Claus and John D. Spreckels, and James D. Phelan built a "People's Railroad" through the San Joaquin Valley, but they were soon coerced into selling it to the Santa Fe. Not until 1910, when the Western Pacific reached Oakland, did the Southern Pacific begin to meet serious competition. By coincidence, that was also the year in which its influence over the state's politics was broken at last.

The degree of railroad domination in California has sometimes been exaggerated, and this has led some historians to minimize it to the extent of calling it a mere legend. It is true, of course, that railroad control could not have been complete in every instance, but in general it was highly effective. The power of the Southern Pacific was not a monolith, but it was not a myth.

When the government of California began its attempts to regulate the Southern Pacific in the 1870s, the railroad responded by intensifying its control of the state government. The more corrupt methods by which the railroad intervened in politics were kept as secret as possible, but the workings of the Southern Pacific's "invisible government" could not always be kept invisible, and they were starkly revealed in such episodes as the publication of the "Colton letters" and the "Dear Pard" letters, the struggle of Los Angeles for a free harbor, and the railroad's attempt to escape from the payment of its debt to the United States.

THE COLTON LETTERS

For 4 years before his sudden death in 1878, David D. Colton had been the confidential manager of the railroad's political interests in California, while Collis P. Huntington was serving the same function in Washington, D.C. Having received his early training as a young political lieutenant of David C. Broderick, Colton was highly skilled in the shadier methods of influencing politicians. He amassed a fortune by performing this type of confidential service in exchange for opportunities to share in the profits of enterprises which would benefit from the special political privileges he could obtain.

Colton first attracted the attention of the big four by establishing a friendship with Charles Crocker, his neighbor on Nob Hill. Though Stanford and Hopkins disliked and distrusted Colton, Collis P. Huntington saw the potential value of his special talents and persuaded the others to approve an agreement in 1874 under which Colton was permitted to acquire a large amount of railroad stock on credit. The new associate often used the expression "we five" in his letters to Huntington, though some of the newspapers described the group more accurately as "the Big Four and a Half."

When Colton died, his widow received only a little more than half a million dollars in the settlement of his estate. Not long afterward when some of the details of the estate of Mark Hopkins were made public and Mrs. Colton noticed that some of Hopkins's shares of stock were quoted as having a far higher cash value than she had been allowed for her husband's identical shares, she concluded that the railroad leaders had cheated her. When they coldly refused a more favorable settlement and countered with charges that her husband had embezzled railroad funds, she sued them for $4 million. In 1883, in the course of the trial, her attorneys suddenly introduced as evidence several hundred letters that had been exchanged between Colton and Huntington in the years between 1874 and 1878.

In explicit detail these letters revealed Colton's activities in influencing the elections, reelections, and votes of members of the California Legislature and the California congressional delegation, and Huntington's similar activities with members of Congress in the east. There were innumerable references to payments of money without vouchers and discussions of the amounts which particular legislators and legislative measures might be expected to cost. In one letter, for example, Huntington had written that "It costs money to fix things. . . . I believe with $200,000 I can pass our bill, but that it is not worth this much to us." In another instance he wrote that "the boys are very hungry, and it will cost us considerable to be saved."

The state supreme court, in the case of *Ellen M. Colton v. Leland Stanford et al.*, refused to award Mrs. Colton a larger settlement, on the ground that she had formally signed and accepted the railroad's original terms. But the damage to the Southern Pacific's reputation was far greater than the value of the widow's highest demands. For decades afterward the railroad's opponents could and did cite the Colton letters whenever they wished to denounce the Southern Pacific for corrupting politics. Moreover, a widespread public reaction was that the big four were men who would defraud a partner's widow—a more serious moral offense to some people than the payment of money for the votes of politicians.

THE HUNTINGTON-STANFORD FEUD

Collis P. Huntington's contempt for people who sought public office, which was extremely apparent throughout his letters to Colton, bore a significant relation to his feelings toward Leland Stanford. For many years Huntington had resented the degree to which Stanford received the lion's share of public attention while he, Huntington, did most of the hard work of managing the railroad's affairs. In 1885, when Stanford secured election to the United States Senate, Huntington was deeply angered. The honor had been promised, as a new term, to former Senator Aaron A. Sargent, a close friend of Huntington's who had rendered many years of faithful service to the railroad's interests in both houses of Congress.

When the founding of a memorial university was announced, Huntington felt that Stanford's vanity had become completely unendurable, and he made plans to deflate it. At an annual meeting of stockholders in 1890 Huntington announced that he would support Stanford's election to a second term as senator only on condition that he himself be elected to the presidency of the railroad, which Stanford had held for 30 years. Then, after assuming the presidency, Huntington publicly stated that unlike his predecessor he would never "use this great corporation to advance my personal ambition at the expense of its owners, or put my hands in the treasury to defeat the people's choice, and thereby put myself into positions that should be filled by others."

Enemies of the Southern Pacific had often charged that large amounts of railroad money were spent by the railroad to secure Stanford's election and reelection by the California Legislature as United States senator. Now the charge was directly corroborated by the president of the railroad itself. Huntington threw his open denunciation in Stanford's face with no more warning than either of them had had from Ellen Colton. In fact, Huntington deliberately violated a promise, given as one of the conditions of the change of presidency, that there would be no such public attack. In the next few hours Stanford's friends saw him age 10 years, and his death in 1893 was undoubtedly hastened by Huntington's carefully laid plan to destroy him.

Beginning in 1892 and continuing for several years afterward, Stanford's former private secretary, J. M. Bassett, published in the *San Francisco Report* at weekly intervals a series of letters which he addressed to Huntington. These letters opening with the salutation "Dear Pard," were at least partly intended to injure Huntington as Stanford had been injured. They were filled with charges of the wholesale corruption of national, state, and local officials by the railroad, and though they had little effect in penetrating the thick skin of Collis P. Huntington, they added significantly to a growing mass of public evidence.

LOS ANGELES FIGHTS FOR A FREE HARBOR

In another of his early actions as the new president of the Southern Pacific, Huntington reversed Stanford's policy toward the location of a modern deepwater harbor for Los Angeles. Senator Stanford had been supporting proposals for federal aid in the construction of a breakwater at San Pedro. Huntington decided that the harbor must be built at Santa Monica because he was able to purchase enough land there to ensure that the Southern Pacific could dominate the harbor by preventing any competing railroad from gaining access to it.

Huntington saw no reason that the railroad should have less control over the future port of Los Angeles than it had long exerted over the port of San Francisco, where for more than 40 years, as Governor Hiram Johnson would tell the legislature in 1913, the Southern Pacific through its control of the state harbor commission "practically owned and operated the waterfront." But Los Angeles, though it had only 50,000 people in the early 1890s, felt the stirrings of its future growth and power and determined to fight for a harbor that would be at least relatively free of Southern Pacific control.

In 1891 a board of Army engineers appointed with the approval of Senator Stanford reported that San Pedro Bay was the best site in the region for the construction of a breakwater and thus for the creation of a great harbor adequate for the largest oceangoing ships. But the next year, while an appropriation for this purpose was under consideration by the Senate Commerce Committee, Huntington served blunt notice that he would use all his influence in Congress to block any appropriation for the San Pedro project. Los Angeles rebelled, and its chamber of commerce was able to enlist some powerful allies in the fight. Harrison Gray Otis and the *Times*, the St. Louis capitalists who had built a terminal railroad from Los Angeles to San Pedro, and Democratic United States Senator Stephen M. White, a Los Angeles attorney, joined the rebellion. Huntington's supporters in Congress argued that the government should not spend money for a harbor at San Pedro when "private enterprise"—that is, Mr. Huntington—was willing to undertake the cost of construction nearby; however, it was well known that Huntington expected to persuade Congress to pay for a still larger breakwater at Santa Monica.

In 1896 Congress passed an appropriation for whatever site a new board of engineers should approve. When this report again favored San Pedro, Huntington secured 2 more years of delay. But at last, in April 1899, the first barge-load of rock was dumped to begin construction of the breakwater at San Pedro. In later years the people of the Los Angeles Harbor District would join with the federal government, private interests, and the city of Long Beach in providing funds; the breakwater would be extended eastward to protect the combined harbor of San Pedro and Long Beach; and Los Angeles would become one of the world's great seaports, as well as one of its great cities.

THE FUNDING BILL

The original construction of the Central Pacific had been made possible by federal loans of nearly $28 million payable in 30 years. No payment of interest was required until the full maturity of the loans. Simple interest at 6 percent added more than $50 million to the total obligation that was legally payable by the year 1899. In the 1870s, though the big four began to vote themselves huge dividends, they set aside nothing for the ultimate payment of the railroad's debt to the government and instead propounded a long series of ingenious and specious arguments for its cancellation.

Congress in 1878 passed a law requiring the Central Pacific to create a sinking fund of 25 percent of the net earnings of the parts of its rail network that had been built with federal aid. Huntington, in a letter to Colton, described the legislators who voted for the new law as "communists," and Colton replied that "this Congress is simply a band of robbers." But the railroad, by manipulating both traffic and bookkeeping so as to credit as little as possible of the net earnings to the original "bond-aided" portions of the lines and as much as possible to other parts of the system, kept the sinking fund to a small fraction of its total debt to the government, and in the 1890s Huntington advanced a series of proposals for a funding plan to delay payment for 50 or 100 years, at the extremely low interest rate of ½ of 1 percent. In California this aroused more opposition than any other measure in the long history of public resentment against the railroad, and Adolph Sutro and William Randolph Hearst led a chorus of denunciation of it as a plot to escape the debt entirely.

Adolph Sutro had sold all his stock in his Comstock tunnel as soon as it was completed. With the million dollars salvaged from that venture, he had moved to San Francisco, and there, by buying land whenever the local market for it reached the bottom of one of its periodic depressions, had become the owner of one-twelfth of the city's entire area. Seal Rocks, the Cliff House, the gardens of his home, and other adjoining portions of his great estate were opened to the public as a park. When the Market Street Railway Company, a

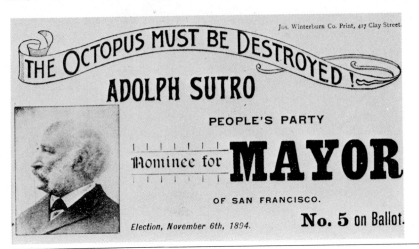

A handbill from Adolph Sutro's anti-railroad mayoral campaign in 1894. *(Courtesy of the Sutro Library, San Francisco.)*

Southern Pacific subsidiary, took over the trolley line to this park and refused to continue a low round-trip fare, Sutro built his own parallel line and declared himself the defender of the people against the greed of the Octopus.

In 1894 Sutro was elected mayor of San Francisco on the Populist ticket. The Populist movement, the radical third party that originated among the farmers of the middle west, was at the height of its influence during the aftermath of the panic of 1893. Sutro won the Populist nomination and the election, partly because his many philanthropies had made him a popular figure, but also because he organized a series of mass meetings to denounce Huntington's funding plan. At these meetings Sutro promised to urge the state of Kentucky to repeal the charter of the Southern Pacific Company.

William Randolph Hearst also threw the full weight of the *San Francisco Examiner* into the battle against the funding plan, and in 1894 the *Examiner* obtained more than 200,000 signatures on petitions against it. In 1896, when the crucial vote in Congress was approaching, Hearst sent Ambrose Bierce and the cartoonist Homer Davenport to Washington, D.C. For more than 20 years Bierce's opinions of the Southern Pacific leadership had been typified by his frequent printed references to "£eland $tanford," and his articles on the funding bill were as merciless as anything in his long career of journalistic mayhem. His most effective dispatch reported a conversation on the steps of the national Capitol in which Huntington asked him to name his price for stopping his attacks and Bierce replied that his price was the railroad's full debt to the government, payable to the United States Treasury. At the same time, Davenport was making Huntington the villain of some of his most famous cartoons.

In the face of Huntington's claim that failure to adopt his funding plan would bankrupt the whole Southern Pacific system and that no one would then be willing to buy it, the rebellious California Legislature adopted a resolution urging the federal government not only to foreclose but to assume the ownership and operation of the railroad if necessary. When the funding bill was finally voted down in Congress in January 1897, popular opinion in California was so overjoyed that Democratic Governor James H. Budd proclaimed Saturday, January 16, a public holiday in celebration. Two years later a compromise agreement was reached, and under its terms the railroad completed the payment of its entire debt to the federal government by 1909.

THE SOUTHERN PACIFIC MACHINE

The Los Angeles harbor fight and the funding battle were almost the only major political defeats that the railroad suffered before 1910. These two defeats occurred during the hard times of the 1890s, when public discontent was at a maximum, and they were in considerable part the results of personality conflicts in which the increasing tactlessness and ruthlessness of the aging Collis P. Huntington infuriated other large operators. Moreover, these two issues involved the national government. In purely state and local matters, attempts to break the grip of the railroad's political machine brought only a long succession of humiliating failures for nearly half a century.

In 1862, when a state constitutional amendment increased the term of the governor from 2 years to 4, it was argued that the longer term would attract better people to the gubernatorial office. But it failed to do so, largely because the corrupting influence of the railroad in state politics had already begun and steadily continued to grow.

By the 1890s the head of the railroad's political department, who was also its chief legal counsel, had become a much more important official than the governor; in fact he usually had the power to name the governor, or any other public officer in California. Under his direction there was a railroad political manager in every county in the state. This manager might be the Republican boss in a Republican county or the Democratic boss in a Democratic county; in important or doubtful counties he was merely the railroad boss, with whom both Republican and Democratic bosses had to deal.

A system of political alliance with the other public utility corporations was an important factor in the railroad's power over local political bosses. The railroad itself was then the only statewide public utility, but the political interests of local street railway, gas, light, and telephone companies were similar to its own, if on a smaller scale. The railroad and other public utilities were the private business corporations that could profit most directly from special favors granted by state and local government agencies, and consequently they joined in furnishing the bulk of the money that corrupted state and local politics. This alliance came to be known in California as "the associated villainies."

To place all the blame upon the railroad and other utility corporations, however, ignores the fact that they could not have corrupted the state if so many of its citizens had not been corruptible. Leland Stanford's biographer,

George T. Clark, argued that such charges must be false because, "in Edmund Burke's notable phrase, 'I do not know the method of drawing up an indictment against an whole people.'" Actually, of course, it was neither possible nor necessary for the railroad to corrupt everyone. Influence over a few thousand strategically placed individuals was sufficient.

When lawyers who were not already on the railroad's payroll were elected to the state legislature, they were likely to receive a letter from the law department of the Southern Pacific stating that the railroad wished to retain an outstanding attorney from their region during a period which happened to coincide with that of the coming session at Sacramento. A retainer fee was enclosed, and the privileged nature of the attorney-client relationship protected the secrecy of the transaction.

Of all the agencies of state government, the railroad was most careful to control the bank commission, which it allowed to be created ostensibly as a reform measure in 1878. Bankers who gave aid and comfort to the railroad's enemies could suddenly find themselves in disastrous trouble with this board of commissioners. Consequently, business people or farmers who displeased the railroad by denouncing its rates, or by voting against its candidates while serving as delegates to a party convention, would suddenly find themselves unable to obtain further loans from their bank.

Another effective form of influence was the free pass. It cost relatively little, and it reached people who would have resisted more obvious forms of bribery. Instead of being considered a bribe, the railroad pass was a status symbol. The person who held it felt allied with the successful and powerful leaders of society against the ignorant and envious rabble. The constitution of 1879 specifically forbade free passes for state officeholders, but the provision was never enforced.

Many of the smaller newspapers were subsidized not only with advertising contracts but with regular and secret monthly stipends. Larger publishers such as Harrison Gray Otis, M. H. de Young, and John D. Spreckels were far too wealthy to be influenced by trifling financial considerations. But each of these three men had perennial hopes of going to the United States Senate, and though they often joined in attacks on the railroad, there were also many occasions when each of them tempered his criticism of the Southern Pacific because of his own political ambitions.

Not even the courts were immune from the railroad's influence. Justices of the federal and state supreme courts traveled on passes. Most of the judges of the federal district and circuit courts in San Francisco were appointed at the instance of California senators who spoke with the railroad's voice. Justice Stephen J. Field, great and brilliant "craftsman of the law," was a personal associate of the big four, owed his position in the United States Supreme Court to their influence, and rendered them invaluable service by writing many of the opinions through which the highest court long protected the railroad and other corporations from effective government regulation.

As for the judiciary at the state level, the machine controlled the election of judges, and one of the regular duties of a county boss was to provide the railroad with secret annotated lists of veniremen to aid its attorneys in impaneling sympathetic juries.

WILLIAM F. HERRIN

Among the important sources of the railroad's power was its ability to enlist the most talented lawyers in its service. One such person was William F. Herrin, who headed the Southern Pacific's legal and political departments from 1893 to 1910. It was under Herrin that the railroad's political machine in California reached its highest level of efficiency.

Herrin was a product of pioneer life. Born on a farm in Oregon, he worked his way through a small college and a small law school and within a few years after beginning his practice in San Francisco had become the chief attorney for the Sharon estate, Miller & Lux, and the Spring Valley Water Company. In 1889 he won a national reputation when, as special counsel, he aided a United States attorney in defending a federal marshal, David Neagle, against a murder charge.

The case grew out of the earlier and equally sensational legal battle in which Sarah Althea Hill had claimed that she was the legal wife of Senator William Sharon under the terms of a "contract marriage," and that she was thus entitled to a large part of his enormous fortune. During the court proceedings Sharon died, and his alleged widow married one of her attorneys, David S. Terry, former chief justice of the California Supreme Court, who had killed Senator Broderick in their famous duel. United States Justice Stephen J. Field, while on federal circuit court duty in San Francisco, ruled that Mrs. Terry had not been Sharon's wife and had no valid claim on the Sharon estate. Both the Terrys had brought weapons into the courtroom, and both of them threatened Field's life.

At the time of Justice Field's next visit to California, United States Marshal Neagle was assigned as his bodyguard, and when, in a railway station in Lathrop Terry approached Field and struck him, Neagle shot Terry dead. *In re Neagle* became one of the great cases in the history of American federal-state relations. Because Neagle was a federal officer who had presumably acted in the line of duty, the United States government wished to protect him from prosecution for murder under the laws of California. But no federal law authorized either his assignment as bodyguard or his action in killing Terry; the United States Supreme Court ruled that these had been "fairly and properly inferable" from the Constitution. It was one of the broadest interpretations yet given to the implied powers of the national government.

Herrin was the attorney who contributed most to the preparation of the case for Neagle in the circuit court proceedings at San Francisco. At the same time, he was also distinguishing himself more privately in his capacity as attorney for Henry Miller by persuading the railroad to grant special secret rates and rebates on Miller's shipments of cattle and wheat. Collis P. Hunting-ton, deeply impressed with Herrin's talents, chose him, as he had once chosen David D. Colton, to be the railroad's western political manager.

From his office in the Southern Pacific's headquarters at Fourth and Townsend streets in San Francisco, Herrin not only directed all the company's manifold political activities, but grappled with all its complex legal problems as well. Comparison of Herrin with Colton suggests the evolution that occurred between the railroad's first generation and its second in the development of its political techniques.

FAILURE OF NINETEENTH-CENTURY REFORM MOVEMENTS

A significant factor in the perpetuation of the railroad's control of California was the often-repeated argument of railroad apologists that reasonable persons should put their abilities to work, and find their rewards, within the established order of things. The effectiveness of such appeals was closely related to the widespread sense of futility that followed the many disheartening failures of reform. The railroad always devoted special care to its efforts to gain control of reform movements and leaders. A classic example was Newton Booth, a Republican who was elected governor in 1871 on a platform opposing further state and local subsidies to the railroad. In the panic year of 1873, insurgent Republicans with strong support from the Grange movement put forward a third party called the Independent Taxpayers and gained a majority in the state legislature in a three-cornered race with the regular Republicans and the Democrats. Governor Booth assumed the leadership of the Independent Taxpayers' reform party of California and echoed its promises to force the railroad's fares and freight rates down and its tax payments up. But somehow nothing substantial was done toward accomplishing these objectives. The new party secured Booth's election to the United States Senate. A few months later he was listed in one of Huntington's secret letters to Colton as among the railroad's most important friends.

The last decades of the century in California did bring some valiant struggles for reform. One such crusade induced the state legislature to adopt the Australian or secret ballot in 1891. But this applied only to general elections and not to the nominating process. Candidates for state, county, and city offices were nominated by party conventions. There was no effective legal regulation of the party primaries in which the delegates to these conventions were elected. State law still regarded the political party as a kind of private enterprise, or private club. A state constitutional amendment in 1901 sought to regulate primaries, but succeeded in modifying only the forms rather than the substance of boss control over the selection of convention delegates.

Usually the railroad placed more reliance on Republican candidates and officeholders than upon Democrats, but the Democratic party failed dismally to provide an effective vehicle for reform. The railroad was quite willing to make use of Democrats whenever they happened to have a better chance of election, and it often supported the candidates and machines of both parties at once. The California Democrats suffered from a shortage of inspiring leadership. Senator George Hearst was no reformer, and he was in close political alliance with Chris Buckley, the Democratic boss of San Francisco, who often received money from the railroad and from anyone else who was willing to pay. Senator Stephen M. White, whose father had been a Workingmen's candidate for governor, opposed the railroad only when it was politically safe and expedient to do so. James H. Budd, the Democratic governor elected in 1894, could accomplish little in the face of Republican majorities in the legislature.

The economic distress of the 1890s intensified a growing belief that both major parties were morally bankrupt, and this led to a new flourishing of support for third-party movements. The Nationalist party had a brief but striking career in 1890. Formed by enthusiastic readers of Edward Bellamy's utopian romance, *Looking Backward, 2000-1887*, this movement advocated a gradualist, nonviolent Christian socialism. But its appeal was mainly to urban discontent, and nearly all of its following in California was in San Francisco and Los Angeles.

The Nationalist party soon was overshadowed by the rise of the People's or Populist party. The Populist movement was based mainly on the increasingly bitter discontent of the farmers, but it hoped to gain support from city workers as well. At the heart of populism was a distrust of political parties and a firm belief that no important reform could be accomplished until control of the machinery of government was taken out of the hands of party bosses and party conventions and given to the people. Thus the most enduring contribution of the Populists in California was the spread of public interest in their demands for the direct primary, the initiative, the referendum, and the recall. A few years later this part of the Populist program would play a major role in the progressive movement, the California reform movement which at last brought to an end the era of railroad domination.

SELECTED BIBLIOGRAPHY

Aspects of the railroad's political activities are described in Daggett, *Chapters on the History of the Southern Pacific;* Lewis, *The Big Four;* the chapter on politics in Treadwell, *The Cattle King;* Ralph N. Traxler, "Collis P. Huntington and the Texas and Pacific Railroad Land Grants," *New Mexico Historical Review*, XXIV (April 1959), pp. 117-133; and Jack W. Bates, "The Southern Pacific Railroad in California Politics," M.A. thesis, University of the Pacific (1942).

Important works on state politics are Winfield J. Davis, *History of Political Conventions in California, 1849-1892* (1893) and Theodore H. Hittell, *History of California*, vol. IV (1898), mainly a history of gubernatorial administrations from 1849 to 1887.

Biographical treatments include Edith Dobie, *The Political Career of Stephen Mallory White, a Study of Party Activities under the Convention System* (1927); Curtis E. Grassman, "Prologue to Progressivism: Senator Stephen M. White and the California Reform Impulse, 1875-1905," Ph.D. thesis, University of California, Los Angeles (1970); Carl B. Swisher, *Stephen J. Field, Craftsman of the Law* (1930); Oscar T. Shuck, *History of the Bench and Bar of California* (1901); and J. Edward Johnson, *History of the Supreme Court Justices of California*, vol. I: *1850–1900* (1963).

On the harbor fight, see Charles Dwight Willard, *The Free Harbor Contest at Los Angeles* (1899); Ella A. Ludwig, *History of the Harbor District of Los Angeles* (1928); Clarence H. Matson, *Building a World Gateway: The Story of Los Angeles Harbor* (1945); and Anthony F. Turhollow, *A History of the Los Angeles District, U.S. Army Corps of Engineers, 1898–1965* (1975). Most of the railroad's arguments for cancellation of its debt were brought together by its counsel Creed Haymond in *The Central Pacific Railroad and the United States* (three parts, 1887–1889).

The first volume of the memoirs of Franklin Hichborn, "California Politics, 1891–1939" (reproduced typewriting, copies in several libraries including that of the University of California, Los Angeles), provides many insights into the structure and functioning of the Southern Pacific machine. See also Alexander Callow, Jr., "San Francisco's Blind Boss," *Pacific Historical Review*, XXV (August 1956), pp. 261–280, and William A. Bullough, *The Blind Boss and His City: Christopher Augustine Buckley and Nineteenth Century San Francisco* (1979). Attempts at state regulation are discussed in Gerald D. Nash, "The California Railroad Commission, 1876–1911," *Southern California Quarterly*, XLIV (December 1962), pp. 287–306, and Ward M. McAfee, *California's Railroad Era, 1850–1911* (1973).

R. Hal Williams, *The Democratic Party and California Politics, 1880–1896* (1973) argues that railroad domination of California politics has been so exaggerated that it has become "a legend." Richard J. Orsi, "The Octopus Reconsidered: The Southern Pacific and Agricultural Modernization in California, 1865–1915," *California Historical Quarterly*, LIV (Fall 1975), pp. 197–220, stresses the positive contributions of the railroad.

On late nineteenth-century reform efforts, see Curtis E. Grassman, "Prologue to California Reform: The Democratic Impulse, 1886–1898," *Pacific Historical Review*, XLII (November 1973), pp. 518–536, and Eric F. Petersen, "The Struggle for the Australian Ballot in California," *California Historical Quarterly*, LI (Fall 1972), pp. 227–243.

On the case of Sarah Althea Hill and William Sharon, see Robert H. Kroninger, *Sarah and the Senator* (1964), and Gary L. Roberts, "In Pursuit of Duty," *The American West*, VII (September 1970), pp. 27–33, 62–63, on Neagle's shooting of Terry.

California populism is discussed in Donald E. Walters, "Populism in California, 1889–1900," Ph.D. thesis, University of California, Berkeley (1952), and "The Feud between California Populist T. V. Cator and Democrats James Maguire and James Barry," *Pacific Historical Review*, XXVII (August 1958), pp. 281–298; Eric F. Petersen, "The End of an Era: California's Gubernatorial Election of 1894," in the same journal, XXXVIII (May 1969), pp. 141–156; David B. Griffiths, "Anti-Monopoly Movements in California, 1873–1898," *Southern California Quarterly*, LII (June 1970), pp. 93–121; and Michael P. Rogin and John L. Shover, *Political Change in California* (1970).

THE
ROOTS
OF REFORM

The forces that contributed to the reform impulse in California in the early twentieth century were many and varied, but the statewide reform coalition that finally achieved a breakthrough in the state elections of 1910 had its immediate origins in developments in the cities of San Francisco and Los Angeles.

BOSS RUEF AND THE UNION LABOR PARTY

For several decades before the great earthquake and fire of 1906, about a fourth of the people of California lived in San Francisco. Among the sources of the prevailing corruption in California's politics, the deep-seated habit of corruption in the government of its major city was second only to the malign influence of the railroad. There was far too much truth in the statement of the *San Francisco Call* in 1887 that "To hold one of the principal city offices for two years is equivalent to obtaining a large fortune."

Throughout the United States, as Lord Bryce remarked in *The American Commonwealth*, the government of cities was a conspicuous failure of American democracy. This had been true in varying degrees since the early days of New York's Tammany Hall under Aaron Burr, but the problem had become worse in the age of industrialization and urbanization between the Civil War and the rise of the progressive movement in the early twentieth century. Cities, corporations, and labor unions grew so rapidly that government and law could not keep up with them. One result was an increase in the importance of the city boss as an extralegal figure who could furnish a bridge between the lagging institutions of politics and the urgent demands of the expanding conglomerations of economic power. The boss served as a broker in a corrupt system of alliances between big business and politics that menaced democracy in cities throughout the nation.

Cosmopolitan San Francisco might have been expected to produce as the most famous of its bosses a figure as colorful as the city itself. Abraham Ruef was the only son of a moderately wealthy San Francisco family of French Jewish origin. He was a man of unusual culture and brilliant intelligence, heightened by a good university and legal education. After graduating in the middle 1880s from the University of California in Berkeley and from its law school in San Francisco, he entered politics as an idealistic young reformer. But his ideals began to decline when he attended his first Republican county convention, an experience that impressed him with the apparently hopeless realities of machine rule. Surrendering to opportunism, he became the Republican sub-boss for the district in the northern part of the city then known as the Latin Quarter. There, at the grass roots level, he learned to bestow the many services and favors that typical nineteenth-century American city bosses and their machines exchanged for the gratitude and the votes of poor and immigrant families—from gifts of turkeys at Christmas to help with naturalization papers.

At the turn of the century the mayor of San Francisco was the reform Democrat James D. Phelan, the most politically promising leader among the very large number of San Franciscans of Irish Catholic descent. A son of one of the city's leading bankers, Phelan was also a millionaire banker in his own right, and as a public officeholder he was above the temptations to corruption that afflicted persons of lesser integrity and inferior financial independence. Ordinarily Phelan held fairly liberal views on a number of economic and social issues, including the rights of organized labor, but during the great strike in the summer of 1901 his wealthy friends persuaded him to order city police to ride on the drays beside "scab" teamsters, thus using the police themselves as virtual strikebreakers.

This led to an angry outcry that if the power of government was thus to be used for the destruction of unions, then union members must enter politics and elect a government of their own; with this intention a group calling itself the Union Labor Party of San Francisco was organized in September. The philosophy and strategy of American craft unionism were generally opposed to any such movement, and not a single important official of any of the larger San Francisco unions would associate with the new party. It might have died at birth had it not acquired a foster father: Abraham Ruef perceived that he could use it for his own purposes, though he had no genuine interest whatever in labor unions except his interest in their members' votes for candidates he controlled.

Because Mayor Phelan had angered conservatives by refusing to call for state troops to put down the strike almost as much as he had angered labor by his use of city police, his renomination was impossible. The Democratic and Republican nominees for mayor were colorless men. For the Union Labor candidacy, on the other hand, Ruef chose his friend Eugene E. Schmitz, president of the musicians' union. Schmitz was of German-Irish descent and of Roman Catholic faith, and in San Francisco this combination of ethnic and religious factors appealed to such an extraordinarily high percentage of the electorate that it was an essential source of Schmitz's political success, and consequently of Ruef's as well. But the votes that Ruef could deliver from his Republican machine in his own district were also important, along with the votes of labor union members and the ones that were drawn by Schmitz's appearance and the sound of his voice. He was a tall, handsome, distinguished-looking, commanding figure of a man, and also a model husband and father. "The psychology of the mass of the voters," Ruef told Schmitz, "is like that of a crowd of small boys," to whom such qualities had a deep emotional appeal.

Schmitz was elected mayor in 1901, 1903, and 1905. In the first two of these elections the Union Labor ticket gained only a few seats on the 18-member board of supervisors, the legislative branch of the city-and-county government. But in 1905, to Ruef's own surprise, every one of his 18 Union Labor nominees for the board of supervisors was elected. Voting machines were used for the first time, and nearly all of Schmitz's admirers, fearing to invalidate their votes among the complicated battery of levers, took the easy course of pulling down one lever for the straight party ticket.

Most of the new city fathers were obscure men who knew little about the nature of their office except the popular belief that supervisors customarily received bribes. They suspected, quite accurately, that Ruef received large payments from public utility corporations. In vain he pointed out to them that as a lawyer who held no public office he could quite legally receive such payments as attorney's fees, but that payments to them, as public officials, would be bribery. The new supervisors concluded that although this fine distinction might be law, it was not justice. They demanded that Ruef share his fees with them if he expected them to vote for the measures his corporate clients desired.

Several transactions of this kind were carried out in 1906. For example, the United Railroads of San Francisco, the largest street railway company, asked for a special ordinance permitting it to convert all its remaining cable car lines to overhead electric trolleys. The company paid an attorney's fee of $200,000 to Ruef; he divided $85,000 among the supervisors, and the ordinance was passed. The Pacific Gas and Electric Company paid Ruef $20,000; of this sum he paid $13,250 to the supervisors and thereby persuaded them not to make a drastic reduction in the gas rate. There were other corrupt arrangements involving telephone and water companies.

THE SAN FRANCISCO GRAFT PROSECUTION

Such instances of corruption were by no means unprecedented, either in San Francisco or in other large American cities of the time. What was really extraordinary about them was that through some very unusual circumstances they became known to the public in complete detail: The year 1906 brought two crucial events in San Francisco's history. One was the disastrous earthquake and fire, in April, and the other, in October, was the announcement of the beginning of what turned out to be the most persistent graft prosecution in the history of any city in the United States.

San Francisco after the 1906 earthquake and fire. The dome is that of the ruined city hall. *(Courtesy of the Bancroft Library.)*

The earthquake which rocked San Francisco at 5:14 in the morning of April 18 was so severe that it caused a number of deaths and injuries within the first few moments. But San Franciscans, anxious to counteract the idea that a similar catastrophe could ever destroy their city again, have always correctly insisted that the greatest damage was done not by the earthquake—over which human beings had no conceivable control—but rather by the subsequent fire, whose recurrence a better-planned water system could render impossible. The initial shock, which started more than 50 separate fires almost immediately by breaking gas connections and chimneys and overturning stoves, also shattered most of the flimsy water mains and left the fire fighters helpless. The fires, merging into one vast, continuous conflagration and raging for 3 days and 2 nights, destroyed the greater part of the city; 452 lives were lost.

The painful difficulties of the struggle to build a new city on the ruins of the old made San Franciscans less tolerant of corruption in their city government and prepared them to welcome an investigation which a small group of reformers had begun to plan, in close secrecy, before the earthquake.

The originator of this plan was Fremont Older, editor of the *San Francisco Bulletin*. Older secured a promise of cooperation from the district attorney, and he induced the reform-minded millionaire capitalist Rudolph Spreckels, to pledge his financial support. Spreckels ultimately contributed nearly $250,000 to the prosecution fund, mostly for hiring special detectives. Ex-Mayor Phelan also contributed. Older persuaded President Theodore Roosevelt to lend the services of the federal government's ablest special prosecutor, Francis J.

Heney, and also of its star detective, William J. Burns, who was then head of the Secret Service of the Treasury Department. Heney was appointed assistant district attorney of San Francisco.

The prosecution's first major move was to secure indictments charging that Ruef and Schmitz had extorted money from the proprietors of several French restaurants under the threat of blocking the renewals of their liquor licenses. The term "French restaurant" then had a special connotation in San Francisco. On the first floor there was a conventional restaurant serving excellent food at moderate prices, but on the second floor there were private supper bedrooms, and the upper floors were houses of prostitution.

The charge that the boss and the mayor had taken money from these establishments was a charge of reprehensible but relatively petty graft, and based on as yet limited evidence. The real breakthrough came when Burns trapped one of the supervisors, Thomas Lonergan, into taking a planted bribe. Heney then offered Lonergan immunity from all prosecution in return for a complete disclosure of every bribery in which he and his colleagues had participated. The other supervisors, confronted with Lonergan's testimony, were also granted immunity and also made complete confessions. With this overwhelming mass of evidence Heney then obtained a full confession from Ruef himself, after promising not to prosecute him if he would testify against the "higher-ups"—the corporation executives who had made the payments to him as their "attorney." Heney then secured indictments for bribery against Patrick Calhoun, president of the United Railroads, nationally known financier, and grandson of the great statesman John C. Calhoun; against Tirey L. Ford, chief counsel of the United Railroads and former attorney general of California; and against several of the highest executives of the gas and telephone companies.

Heney's strategy was based in part on the ideas of his close friend Lincoln Steffens, the nation's leading journalistic authority on municipal corruption. Both Steffens and Heney had been born in San Francisco, and they shared a deep interest in the future of the city and the state. Steffens's boyhood home was the house in Sacramento that had since become the governor's mansion.

Steffens had written a famous series of articles originally published in *McClure's* and brought together in 1904 in his book called *The Shame of the Cities*. The more important source of the massive graft system in America, Steffens concluded, was not the weak little politician who took bribes, but the wealthy and powerful captain of industry who paid them. "The typical businessman," Steffens had written, "is a bad citizen. If he is a 'big businessman' he is twice as bad." By 1906, however, Steffens had come to feel that because the blame for corruption was shared by so many, the punishment of individuals was useless and inappropriate. Instead he advocated that after the full shock of publicity of the mass of offenses in San Francisco, there should be a general amnesty, so that all could join in the building of a sounder social fabric.

Heney, on the other hand, had no faith in this particular aspect of Steffens's views. Rather, Heney believed that only the exemplary punishment of the greatest offenders could accomplish anything of permanent value. He confided to Steffens that if he should succeed in convicting the general counsel and the president of the United Railroads, Ford and Calhoun, he would then reach for the top and try to send to prison, for bribery, not only the general counsel of the Southern Pacific, William F. Herrin, but also its president, the mighty Edward H. Harriman himself.

But the prosecution fell far short of these objectives. In a series of long trials of Ford and Calhoun, in which thousands of veniremen were examined and rejected in the attempt to find supposedly impartial jurors, the results were either hung juries or acquittals. To convict the United Railroads executives of bribery, Ruef would have had to testify that they had paid him his attorney's fee in full knowledge that he would use part of the money to bribe public officeholders. Ruef refused to give such testimony. In bitter anger and frustration, Heney revoked the immunity agreement he had made with Ruef and brought him to trial for the trolley bribery. The result was that of all the defendants, Ruef alone was ultimately forced to serve a term in the state prison at San Quentin.

Mayor Schmitz was convicted of extortion in one of the French restaurant cases in June 1907 and automatically removed from office, but his conviction was invalidated by the higher courts.

The San Francisco business community had enthusiastically supported the prosecution at its beginning, when it had appeared to be directed against corrupt politicians, especially "Union Labor" politicians, but when these men were promised immunity as a reward for furnishing the evidence on which a number of the city's best-known business executives were indicted, the business community's enthusiasm for the prosecution rapidly cooled. In the city elections of 1909 the prosecution was voted out of office in favor of an administration that would discontinue the graft cases. Heney, running for district attorney, was badly defeated by Charles M. Fickert, a former Stanford football hero.

The San Francisco graft prosecution aroused a deeper and more sustained indignation in the rest of the state than it did in "the city" itself, and thus it contributed to the growing statewide demands for political reform.

THE GOOD GOVERNMENT MOVEMENT IN LOS ANGELES

Many San Franciscans liked to regard their city as pleasure-loving and even as romantically wicked. P.H. McCarthy, president of the San Francisco Building Trades Council and Union Labor nominee for mayor in 1909, was elected on his promise to replace the graft prosecution with a campaign to make San Francisco "the Paris of America." By contrast, Los Angeles regarded itself as a highly moral community in these years before the advent of Hollywood. Saloons were closed on Sundays, and there were more churches than in any other city of comparable size in the United States. The Southern Pacific machine dominated Los Angeles politics, but opposition to it was building up in almost every sector of political opinion from the right to the left.

Charles Dwight Willard, as secretary of the Los Angeles Chamber of Commerce in the 1890s, had been one of the most effective leaders in the fight against the railroad's control of the harbor. So had Harrison Gray Otis, leader of the city's conservative employers. In Otis's view no general political or social plan could possibly contribute as much to the growth, improvement, and prosperity of the community as did the leadership of vigorous individuals like himself. Therefore, as he saw it, the general welfare required that there be no unnecessary restraints upon such persons in the free exercise of their talents for acquiring the wealth that was their incentive and reward. But the railroad had become just such a restraint upon free enterprise, and Otis opposed its bureaucratic power almost as much as he feared and detested labor unions, or even socialism.

As distinct from the conservatives, like Otis, who had a chronic distrust of government and feared that any political change would open the door to unionism and radicalism, there were various groups of reformers who placed their faith in the improvement and strengthening of government. These groups were divided into political and moral reformers on the one hand, and social and economic reformers on the other.

The political and moral reformers included prominent business people, lawyers, and journalists who shared the conservatives' belief in the supreme importance of business enterprise, but also believed that much could be accomplished by bringing "business efficiency" and "business integrity" into politics. The social and economic reformers believed that government should not merely become more honest and more efficient, but that it should be used to effect deeper and broader improvements in the workings of society. They included socialists and persons impressed by the writings of Henry George and Edward Bellamy or by the social gospel then being preached in many churches. To an extraordinary degree, union labor in Los Angeles had also been driven into alliance with such groups, as a result of the extreme tactics of Otis and his associates.

In the face of this diversity among the opponents of the railroad machine in Los Angeles, it was very difficult to assemble a strong coalition of reformers, but this was accomplished, largely through the remarkable talents of Dr. John Randolph Haynes. Since his arrival in 1887 with doctorates in both medicine and philosophy from the University of Pennsylvania, Haynes had combined the most successful medical practice in Los Angeles with the building of a large fortune in real estate—a combination of achievements that won the respect of some of the most conservative of the business community and led them to retain their trust in him even though at one point he had also organized the city's first Christian Socialist club. His socialism was not very strong; he opposed strikes and boycotts and favored private property. He was the personal physician of several leading business people, including Otis himself. Largely through Haynes's charm and prestige, and through a Direct Legislation League that he headed, Los Angeles was persuaded to adopt the initiative, the referendum, and the recall in its new charter of 1903.

This was the first provision for the recall in any governmental unit in the world and the first adoption of the initiative and the referendum by a city. In 1904, moreover, Los Angeles put the recall to use for the first time in history. A Good Government League, in which Dr. Haynes was prominent, organized a successful campaign to recall City Councilman J. R. Davenport for voting to award the public printing contracts to the *Los Angeles Times* when several other bids had been much lower.

This episode ended any possibility of support from Otis for the political reformers, and thereafter the *Times* never spoke of the Good Government League except to denounce and ridicule its leaders as "the Goo-Goos." But the opposition of the *Times* served to increase the support for reform on the part of Otis's newspaper rival and personal enemy, Edwin T. Earl, publisher of the *Los Angeles Express*. Earl was not only a publisher but also the state's largest lemon grower and consequently an opponent of the Southern Pacific, whose freight rates on lemons were among its most piratical exactions.

In the spring of 1906 Earl hired a young journalist named Edward A. Dickson and authorized him to begin a series of editorials in the *Express* denouncing the railroad machine for its control of the Los Angeles city council. Soon afterward Dickson joined with three young lawyers, Meyer Lissner, Russ Avery, and Marshall Stimson, in organizing a Non-Partisan Committee of One Hundred, and in the city election of 1906 the reform candidates nominated by this group won almost every important office except the mayoralty.

THE LINCOLN-ROOSEVELT LEAGUE

The composition and the political orientation of the Los Angeles Non-Partisan Committee of 1906 had special significance because the people who organized it were also to play an important part in the following year in the original organization of the statewide reform movement known as the Lincoln-Roosevelt Republican League.

All the leaders and nearly all the members of the Los Angeles "Non-Partisan" group were in fact Republicans. Many were business people who favored political and moral as distinct from social and economic reform. Neither Dr. Haynes, nor any other community leader strongly identified with "social reform" ideas, nor any representative of organized labor was included in the Los Angeles Non-Partisan Committee. The leaders of this group were far from agreeing with Lincoln Steffens that business as such was the source of political corruption. Rather, as reformers like Dickson and Lissner saw it, the corruptionist executives and minions of the Southern Pacific were traitors not only to the ideals of American government but to the ideals of American business itself; good men, who embodied these ideals, should drive the traitors from political power; leadership by "the businessmen who are interested in good government" was the country's best, and indeed, its only hope.

For decades most people in business had been Republicans, while city workers had usually been Democrats. In the early twentieth century, reform-minded Republicans in California were deeply concerned lest the Democrats gain leadership of the reform movement in general and thus capture the state government. Indeed, reform Democrats would almost certainly have won the governorship both in 1902 and in 1906 had their chances not been sabotaged by the ambitious machinations of William Randolph Hearst in his attempts to gain the Democratic nomination for the presidency. In 1902 Hearst had refused to support Franklin K. Lane of San Francisco, the Democratic candidate for governor of California, because he feared Lane as a potential rival for Democratic leadership. This had caused Lane's defeat by the Republican candidate, Dr. George C. Pardee of Oakland, in a close election.

Governor Pardee had made some reform proposals which, though very limited and generally unsuccessful, were enough to cause the railroad to oppose his renomination, and the Republican state convention at Santa Cruz in September 1906 made it even more obvious than usual that the California Republican party machinery was subservient to the railroad and its allies. Abe Ruef, who had just reached the height of his power, controlled every member of the large San Francisco delegation and could thus choose the nominee for governor. To secure the nomination of the railroad's candidate, James N. Gillett, William F. Herrin gave Ruef $14,000 "to pay the expenses of the delegates." On the evening after the convention adjourned there was a testimonial banquet at which a photograph was taken, showing Ruef seated at the center of a long table with Gillett standing behind him, his hand on Ruef's shoulder in a gesture of affectionate gratitude. Justices of the state supreme and appellate courts, indebted to Ruef for their renominations, were included in the group, along with such machine stalwarts as Walter Parker, Herrin's lieutenant in Los Angeles. For years afterward this picture was widely reprinted with such captions as "The Shame of California" and "Herrin's Cabinet."

The announcement of the beginning of the San Francisco graft prosecution in October 1906, discrediting Ruef and the nominees of the Santa Cruz convention along with him, gave the Democrats an extraordinary opportunity

The Shame of California. Photograph from the San Francisco *Call,* Sept. 10, 1906. Abe Ruef is seated in the center. The future governor, James N. Gillett, stands behind him. Justice Frederick W. Henshaw of the state supreme court stands at the far left, Congressman Joseph R. Knowland at the far right.

to win the governorship and most of the other state offices. They had a strong antirailroad platform, and their candidate for governor, Theodore A. Bell, was a vigorous young man with a good reform record as district attorney of Napa County. Once more, however, Hearst ruined the chances of the California Democrats. In an effort to show the national Democratic party that it could not do without him, Hearst in 1906 was sponsoring a third-party movement called the Independence League, in New York, California, and a few other states. The league's ticket in California, with San Francisco district attorney William H. Langdon as the candidate for governor, took enough votes from Bell and the Democrats to give the election to Gillett and the Republicans.

In December 1906 Dr. Haynes again displayed his talent for encouraging broad coalition among reformers by organizing a dinner at the California Club in Los Angeles with Lincoln Steffens as the principal speaker and Dickson and Lissner among the guests. Steffens made it clear that he was no longer inclined to blame corruption upon all business as a class, and he urged the Los Angeles reformers to extend to the state level the efforts that had brought important successes in the recent city elections.

A few weeks later Dickson went to Sacramento as correspondent for the *Los Angeles Express* at the session of the state legislature beginning in January 1907, and the accident that assigned adjoining desks in the press row to Dickson and to Chester H. Rowell, editor of the *Fresno Morning Republican*, became one of the most important circumstances leading to the movement that would free the Republican party and the state government from the Southern Pacific Railroad.

Rowell was destined to be the outstanding intellectual leader of that movement. He was the son of Jonathan H. Rowell, a Republican congressman from central Illinois. When his father was chairman of the House committee on elections, Chester Rowell had served as clerk of that committee and thus had gained some valuable insights into the workings of practical politics.

Dickson and Rowell had never met before, but as they exchanged impressions of the 1907 legislature, which was hardly less subservient to the railroad than the Santa Cruz convention had been, the two journalists discovered that they shared a burning disgust with the condition of California politics. They agreed to join in an attempt to organize a reform movement and sent out the call for a new organization in letters to reform-minded Republicans, especially newspaper publishers and editors, throughout the state.

A southern California group met in Los Angeles on May 21, 1907, adopted Dickson's suggestion of the name of "Lincoln Republicans," and drew up an "emancipation proclamation," which announced as its first objective "the emancipation of the Republican Party in California from domination by the Political Bureau of the Southern Pacific Railroad Company and allied interests." Other proposals were the direct primary; the initiative, referendum, and recall; effective regulation of railroad and other utility rates; the outlawing of racetrack gambling; conservation of forests; a workmen's compensation act; a minimum wage law for women; and woman suffrage.

On August 1 a larger statewide group met in Oakland and adopted the official name of "the League of Lincoln-Roosevelt Republican Clubs." This hyphenated title was the result of a significant compromise with the desire of Francis J. Heney to change the name to "the Roosevelt League." Heney was an intense admirer of Theodore Roosevelt and particularly of that aspect of his views which led the President to denounce as "malefactors of great wealth" such men as E. H. Harriman, head of the Southern Pacific. Roosevelt's national leadership was an important source of inspiration to progressive Republicans in California, as in other states, but at Dickson's insistence the name of Lincoln was also retained and included to appeal to Republicans of more traditional views.

In 1908 the reformers were able to elect enough members of the legislature to make possible the enactment of a direct primary law in the 1909 session, and it became clear that in 1910, with the nominations of party candidates taken away from machine-controlled conventions and given directly to the voters, the league might gain control not only of the state Republican party organization but of the entire state government, particularly if it could find a very strong candidate for governor to head its ticket.

At first it was supposed that the candidate would be Heney, whose leadership of the San Francisco graft prosecution was making him the state's best-known reformer. But in November 1908, early in the trial of Ruef, Heney was shot and almost fatally wounded by a man whose earlier criminal record Heney had exposed while questioning him as a prospective juror. Whether Heney would make a full recovery was uncertain for several months, and when he did return to the fray, his personality was more extreme and irascible than ever. Many Republicans regarded Heney as "too radical" and particularly resented his open dislike and distrust of all businessmen. Moreover, Heney was a registered Democrat.

During Heney's convalescence his place was taken by Hiram W. Johnson, who had been one of his special assistants in the district attorney's office. Thus Hiram Johnson became chief prosecutor in the trial that ended in the conviction of Ruef, and thus he first attracted wide attention as a young man with a potential future as a leader of political reform. In one of those unpredictable circumstances that are such vital ingredients in history, one obscure and demented man had made Theodore Roosevelt President of the United States by pulling the trigger of a pistol. Another, by a similar act, launched Hiram Johnson into state and national politics.

As a courtroom and a platform orator, Johnson rivaled or exceeded the powers of Heney in denouncing evil and in arousing support for reform, and Johnson could appeal to a broader cross section of voters. He did not share Heney's extreme antibusiness bias and would not alienate the votes of so many conservative Republicans; at the same time he could gain support from organized labor. Johnson had been an attorney for the San Francisco teamsters' union for 8 years.

He was reluctant to run for governor, however. His father, Grove L. Johnson, an assemblyman from Sacramento, had long been the principal leader of the Southern Pacific machine in the state legislature. Hiram had first practiced law in partnership with his father in Sacramento, and it was largely to escape their bitter quarreling over differences of political opinion that he had moved to San Francisco. There he had developed a highly lucrative legal practice and had built a delightful home at the top of Russian Hill. To give up these amenities for a return to the scene of his abrasive and torturing conflicts with his father seemed to him, and to his wife, a very poor exchange. He did not consent to run until February 1910, when Heney finally removed himself from the race and joined with Rowell and others in urging Johnson to become the League's candidate, on the ground that he was the only one who could win and thus free the state from its bondage.

In August, in the first and perhaps the most important statewide direct primary elections in California's history, Johnson won the Republican nomination for governor, and the league won control of the Republican party. Johnson's campaign was unique, colorful, and literally hard-driving. He toured the state in an open automobile, and in the smaller towns announced his arrival by ringing a cowbell. Everywhere he stressed a single theme, his famous "promise to kick the Southern Pacific Railroad out of politics." Among his variations on the theme of the railroad's villainy, he described its practice of secretly charging bribery expenses to operating costs and then charging still higher rates to cover the expenses. "Get us coming and going?" he cried in a speech at Los Angeles. "Why they get us every way, and we foot the bill—we pick our own pockets to bribe ourselves with our own money!" In citrus-producing areas Johnson reminded the growers how long they had struggled for tariff protection against ruinous imports of cheap foreign lemons, and how, when at last they had gained a favorable rate in the Payne-Aldrich Tariff of 1909, the railroad had promptly raised its freight rates on lemons in the exact amount of the price increase that the new tariff made possible.

Actually, in the election in November 1910 the railroad was no longer a genuine issue. The Democratic nominee for governor, Theodore Bell, vied with Johnson in denouncing it. Moreover, he discussed a wider range of reform issues than Johnson did. Anticipating the slogans of future Democrats, Bell said that "California needs a New Deal, a Fair Deal." Unfortunately for the Democrats, and much to their disgust, William F. Herrin concluded that Bell would be the less effective and less dangerous reformer and ordered the railroad's subbosses to support him. The support of the railroad, once so crucial in California politics, now cost Bell the votes of thousands who would not credit his outraged disavowals. It was a major factor in giving the governorship to Johnson, who received 177,191 votes to Bell's 154,835. Another factor was the substantial vote of 47,819 for the Socialist candidate, J. Stitt Wilson of Berkeley.

SELECTED BIBLIOGRAPHY

The memoirs of Abraham Ruef, "The Road I Traveled; an Autobiographic Account of My Career from University to Prison, with an Intimate Recital of the Corrupt Alliance between Big Business and Politics in San Francisco," *San Francisco Bulletin*, Apr. 6 to Sep. 5, 1912, were written while Ruef was in San Quentin. Other accounts of this period are in Fremont Older, *My Own Story* (1926); Franklin Hichborn, *"The System" as Uncovered by the San Francisco Graft Prosecution* (1915); *The Autobiography of Lincoln Steffens* (1931); and Walton Bean, *Boss Ruef's San Francisco* (1952). John B. McGloin includes in his panorama of *San Francisco: The Story of a City* (1978) a portrait of Eugene Schmitz as politically naive and only technically guilty of any wrongdoing.

On other roots of reform see William Issel, "Class and Ethnic Conflict in San Francisco Political History: The Reform Charter of 1898," *Labor History*, XVIII (Summer 1977), pp. 341–359; Albert H. Clodius, "The Quest for Good Government in Los Angeles, 1890–1910," Ph.D. thesis, Claremont Graduate School (1953); Donald R. Culton, "Charles Dwight Willard, Los Angeles City Booster and Professional Reformer, 1888–1914," Ph.D. thesis, University of Southern California (1971); W. H. Hutchinson, *Oil, Land, and Politics* (two volumes, 1965), a biography of Senator Thomas R. Bard; Keith W. Olson, *Biography of a Progressive: Franklin K. Lane, 1864–1921* (1979); Edward F. Staniford, "Governor in the Middle," on George C. Pardee, governor from 1903 to 1907, Ph.D. thesis, University of California, Berkeley (1955); and Martin J. Schiesl, "Progressive Reform in Los Angeles under Mayor Alexander, 1909–1913," *California Historical Quarterly*, LIV (Spring 1975), pp. 37–56.

On the rise of the Lincoln-Roosevelt League and its triumph in 1910, see George E. Mowry, *The California Progressives* (1951); J. Gregg Layne, "The Lincoln-Roosevelt League," *Historical Society of Southern California Quarterly*, XXV (September 1943), pp. 79–101; Grace L. Miller, "The Origins of the San Diego Lincoln-Roosevelt League, 1905–1909," *Southern California Quarterly*, LX (Winter 1978), pp. 421–444; Irving McKee, "The Background and Early Career of Hiram Warren Johnson, 1866–1910," *Pacific Historical Review*, XIX (February 1950), pp. 17–30; Alice M. Rose, "The Rise of California Insurgency: Origins of the League of Lincoln-Roosevelt Republican Clubs, 1900–1907," Ph.D. thesis, Stanford University (1942); Spencer C. Olin, Jr., *California's Prodigal Sons: Hiram Johnson and the Progressives, 1911–1917* (1968); and Miles C. Everett, "Chester Harvey Rowell, Pragmatic Humanist and California Progressive," Ph.D. thesis, University of California, Berkeley (1965).

THE REPUBLICAN PROGRESSIVES IN POWER

The men who organized the Lincoln-Roosevelt Republican movement, which gained control of the government of California in the elections of 1910, were primarily individualists. Most of them were young men from the urban upper middle class—lawyers, editors, or independent business enterprisers. They were highly literate, and three out of four were college-educated. Eager to participate in public affairs, and finding that to do so under the old system of machine control would mean the sacrifice of their integrity, they overthrew the old system. In January 1911, in full control of both houses of the state legislature, the progressives confidently set out to establish a new order of politics in California. They were not, of course, solely responsible for progressive reform in the state. Although the progressives often denounced "the interests," many diverse interest groups and organizations, economic and social as well as political, also played significant parts in the reform process.

The extent of public support for the work of the legislature of 1911 became clear in the special election of October 10, when the 23 of its measures that required constitutional amendments were submitted to the voters and all but one passed. Theodore Roosevelt described the California program of 1911 as "the beginning of a new era in popular government" and as "the greatest advance ever made by any state for the benefit of its people." That assessment was not without political motivation, and it was somewhat exaggerated. For example, the reforms adopted in Wisconsin after the election of Robert M. La Follette as governor in 1900 were at least as advanced. La Follette, however, was now a rival of Roosevelt for the national leadership of Republican progressivism and for the presidency, while T.R. was already looking toward Hiram Johnson as a vice presidential running mate.

The reforms achieved in California in the single year of 1911 were remarkable, but this was partly because no other major state was more critically in need of reform.

PUBLIC UTILITY REGULATION

In the regulation of railroads and other public utilities the progressives achieved their most unquestionable success. An act drafted largely by John M. Eshleman, who had been elected to the railroad commission in 1910, gave the commission full and effective power to set uniform rates and to end the extortionate and discriminatory practices in which the Southern Pacific had indulged for so many decades. In the vanguard of the demand for this reform were groups of shippers and merchants, who wanted to stabilize their businesses. Another measure assigned the commission the power to regulate the rates charged by all other public utilities, except those that were municipally owned. The graft prosecution in San Francisco had more than demonstrated the inadequacy of local regulation of utilities, and officials of several utility corporations favored the new law. The two 1911 laws provided California with what was probably the most comprehensive system of public utility regulation in the country.

Both measures passed by unanimous votes in both houses. Railroad regulation, in particular, was so long overdue in 1911 that not even the railroad attorneys and lobbyists tried to oppose it. Officials of the Southern Pacific found themselves glad to escape from such costly nuisances as the payment of secret rebates to favored shippers within the state, notably several oil companies. After the new system had been in operation a few months, William F. Herrin made a remarkable address to the California Bar Association in which he concluded that "I think no railroad manager would agree to dispense with government regulation at the cost of returning to the old conditions."

GOVERNMENTAL EFFICIENCY AND FINANCE

Many progressive reformers believed that the principles of scientific management, then in vogue in private enterprise, must be introduced into government. They proceeded to develop California's first coherent system of supervision over state finances, largely under the leadership of John Francis Neylan, a dynamic young newspaper reporter who had attracted Johnson's attention while covering the 1910 campaign for the *San Francisco Bulletin*. Neylan proposed the creation of a new agency to be called the State Board of Control, and at the age of 26 he was appointed its first chairman. Under this board California had its first comprehensive budget and its first general inventory of state property. The board exposed graft, regained embezzled money, and secured the removal of 16 corrupt officials.

Taxation in California had undergone a major reorganization in 1910, mainly as a result of the desire of business leaders for a more orderly system. Since 1879 all property taxes had been collected by county boards of assessment under the loose supervision of a state board of equalization. Under the act of 1910 a state tax on the gross incomes of corporations was created, and property taxes were to be paid only to county and local governments. The new state taxes on corporation incomes were set at very moderate levels. Progressive legislatures raised them in 1913 and 1915, but only slightly and against stiff resistance from corporation representatives.

The Bank Act of 1909 was another example of the influence of private economic groups on reform in the progressive era and of the desire of many such groups to use the power of government to bring greater orderliness into their own activities and thus increase their profits and reduce their losses. The act was drawn up mainly by a committee of the California Bankers Association and remained the state's fundamental banking law until the 1930s. It created the office of state superintendent of banks, whose duties would include periodic examination of the financial soundness of the banks. The act also allowed savings banks to continue making loans, provided they maintained separate departments for the savings and loan functions and segregated the funds of each. A proposal by some progressive legislators for an assessment on banks to provide the insurance of their deposits was denounced and blocked by the bankers as "socialism, thinly disguised."

"MORE DEMOCRACY"

The progressives' view of human nature reflected an Emersonian optimism about humanity's innate capacity for good, and therefore they had a strong faith in the political abilities of "the people." Most of the leading California Republican progressives, though they regarded themselves as patrician reformers, also had a strong faith in democracy as against the conservative emphasis on "representative" government. Thus the heart of their reform program lay in a group of devices for increasing the power of the voters.

Foremost among these devices was a state constitutional amendment providing two methods of direct participation by the people in the lawmaking process: The initiative enabled the voters to enact laws or constitutional amendments that had presumably been blocked by legislators' unresponsiveness to popular demands; the referendum empowered the people to veto acts of the legislature. A petition signed by 8 percent of the number of voters in an immediately preceding gubernatorial election could place an initiative proposal on the ballot; a referendum required 5 percent. Some of the progressives would have preferred a fixed number of signatures, perhaps 30,000. They pointed out that under the percentage system, with future increases in the state's population, the gathering of an ever-increasing number of signatures would become too difficult and expensive for reform groups and practicable only for large special interests. But this warning, which would prove distressingly valid in later years, went unheeded in 1911. The initiative and referendum amendment was approved unanimously in the assembly and with only one dissenting vote in the state senate.

The recall of public officials, the second major proposal that Governor Johnson urged upon the legislature, was much more hotly contested, especially because it included the recall of judges. The conservative minority argued that this would interfere with the impartiality of court decisions by requiring judges to "keep their ears to the ground," but Johnson replied that this was better than keeping their ears to the railroad tracks. The recall was approved by large majorities in both houses.

Several other measures were also designed to give more power to the voters and to decrease the power of "party bosses." For example, the "party column" and the "party circle," which had encouraged voting a straight party ticket, were eliminated from the ballot.

"NONPARTISANSHIP" AND CROSS-FILING

The corruption of political parties in California by machine rule had been so extreme that the Johnson progressives mistakenly blamed much of the evil on the party system itself. Consequently, they tried to bring about the virtual destruction of political parties in the state, and although they did not quite succeed in doing this, their efforts had the effect of ensuring that party organization, party responsibility, and the two-party system would remain extraordinarily weak in California for almost half a century to come.

The idea of nonpartisan elections was first applied at the level of city government, when the state legislature ratified a new city charter for Berkeley in 1909. Elections of judges and school officials throughout the state were made nonpartisan in 1911, and elections of county officials in 1913.

For state elections, the "cross-filing" system was adopted in an amendment of 1913, permitting a candidate to become the nominee of more than one political party for the same office. Under this provision, not only could the name of a candidate appear on the primary election ballot of more than one party, but the candidates' own party affiliations were not identified on the primary ballots.

In arguing that cross-filing was in the interest of the general welfare, the Johnson progressives were rationalizing their need to use it for their own special convenience. In 1912, when the national Progressive or "Bull Moose" party split off from the Republicans, no Progressive party was formally organized in California even though Governor Johnson was the national third party's nominee for Vice President. In 1913 Johnson wished to form a Progressive party in the state, but many of his supporters in the legislature, elected with the Republican label, feared for their reelections if they had to forfeit it. Cross-filing was the solution. It enabled the Progressive party of California to be formed, in December 1913 and in the following year many of the state legislators received both the Republican and the Progressive nominations.

The originators of cross-filing had not realized the full extent of its ultimate effects on the party system. These began to be apparent when one legislator was reelected in the primaries by receiving the nominations of all five parties, the Progressives, the Republicans, the Democrats, the Prohibitionists, and the Socialists.

In 1915, having thus reduced the political party system to a shambles and finding that the results had given them firmer control of the legislature than ever before, the Johnson progressives tried to carry the nonpartisan idea to its logical conclusion. The legislature adopted an amendment providing that all state officers must be elected without party designation. But this proposal, the most extreme measure of its kind ever enacted in an American state, never went into effect. Conservative Republicans allied with Democrats to block it by turning the Progressives' own weapon, the referendum, against them. Johnson argued that state government "has become now a matter of efficient business management," which "may best be obtained without politics." Coming from as consummate a politician as Johnson this argument was highly disingenuous, and to his bitter disappointment the California voters rejected it. In a light turnout in the special referendum election of October 1915 they vetoed his "state nonpartisan elections" law. The cross-filing system, however, would remain in effect for decades, favoring incumbents, encouraging candidates to masquerade as members of parties other than their own, and enabling them to deceive thousands of ill-informed voters.

WOMAN SUFFRAGE

In 1911 California became the sixth state to adopt woman suffrage, although the all-male voters approved it by less than 2 percent, the smallest margin for any of the state constitutional amendments adopted that year. Hiram Johnson was emotionally opposed to it, though he took no public stand on the issue. Its adoption owed less to support from the progressives as a whole than to the efforts of a number of able and determined women.

For decades such women had struggled against sex discrimination in various fields. The first women to practice law in California, for example, were Clara Shortridge Foltz and Laura De Force Gordon, whose vigorous lobbying induced the legislature in 1877 to repeal the law that had denied them admission to the bar. Not until 1890 did the San Francisco Medical Society admit its first woman member, Lucy Maria Field Wanzer. The organized suffrage movement in California began in 1869. An early leader of it was Ellen Clark Sargent, whose husband Senator Aaron A. Sargent first introduced in Congress the measure that would become the Nineteenth Amendment in 1920.

Suffrage for American women had made its first breakthrough in the mountainous areas of the west, where its principal advocates had been women in small towns. Wyoming Territory adopted it first, in 1869. Colorado, Utah, and Idaho followed suit in the 1890s. Except for Washington, in 1910, California was the first state outside the Rocky Mountain area to grant women the vote. The California suffragists had mounted a strong campaign in the 1890s, and the legislature had approved an amendment for submission to the voters, but they rejected it by a wide margin in 1896. The Woman's Christian Temperance Union supported the measure, and many voters feared that woman suffrage would bring prohibition. Overwhelming opposition to votes for women in San Francisco and Oakland outweighed the favorable sentiment in other parts of the state.

In the progressive era, on the other hand, upper-middle-class clubwomen from the cities, including San Francisco and its surrounding towns, as well as Los Angeles, were in the forefront of the campaign. Their statewide organization was called the California Equal Suffrage League, but its most effective subsidiary was the College Equal Suffrage League, an elite intellectual phalanx. These leaders of the suffrage movement formed a coalition with the Republican progressives. Katherine Philips Edson, the most politically active of Los Angeles clubwomen, was credited with having induced the Lincoln-Roosevelt League at its first meeting to endorse woman suffrage. Elizabeth Thacker Kent led the California equal suffrage campaign in Marin County and later played a larger role in the nationwide movement when her husband William went to Congress.

PUBLIC MORALS

One factor in the success of equal suffrage in 1911, in contrast with its defeat in 1896, was that temperance was becoming more widely accepted as an important social reform. Much of the support for the Lincoln-Roosevelt League had come from religious and other organizations interested in suppressing the evils of drinking, gambling, and vice. When the league's "emancipation proclamation" of 1907 had promised to free the state from control by the Southern Pacific "and allied interests," many assumed that this expression referred mainly to the various public utility corporations; however, in the eyes of others, it was the liquor, gambling, and prostitution contingents of the "associated villainies" which seemed the most powerful and dangerous of all. Those interests had, in fact, played a strong part in corrupt machine politics because they feared stricter law enforcement and were interested in preventing it. As the "moral reformers" pointed out, Abe Ruef had been the attorney for the California Liquor Dealers' Association as well as for the United Railroads of San Francisco.

The Lincoln-Roosevelt candidate for lieutenant governor in 1910 was A. J. Wallace, a Los Angeles Methodist Minister and oilman who was for many years the president of the Anti-Saloon League of California. Although Johnson privately detested his running mate, Wallace was easily elected and received nearly as many votes as Johnson himself in almost all parts of the state except San Francisco and the wine-producing counties of the bay region.

The leaders of the temperance organizations, though many of them were actually prohibitionists, recognized that outright prohibition was still unacceptable to most of the voters. Therefore they concentrated their attack on the saloon and argued that it was often a center of prostitution as well as of excessive drinking. Since 1874 state law had permitted local areas, at the option of their voters, to ban saloons. In 1911 the legislature passed a much stronger local-option law, based on the county supervisorial district as the unit and eliminating various earlier legal handicaps to adoption and enforcement of such laws at the local level. In the next 5 years, under this legislation more than half the districts in the state voted to close all the saloons within their borders.

Under another act of 1911, racetrack gambling was outlawed and remained so for 20 years. Still another measure made slot machines illegal, after a debate in which the decisive factor was the reading of manufacturers' catalogs explaining how easily the machines could be adjusted to guarantee the owner a heavy profit. A Red Light Abatement Act, declaring houses of prostitution to be public nuisances, was defeated in 1911 but passed in the session of 1913.

THE PROGRESSIVES AND LABOR

Paradoxically, the Republican progressive leaders had a strong group consciousness along with their feelings of individualism. Their letters to each other often included proud references to "our sort," but they feared and detested "class government" by any class other than themselves, and many of them, especially those from Los Angeles, feared the power of organized labor more than the power of big business. In their view it was the state government, under their own enlightened and humanitarian progressive leadership, that could best protect and guarantee the true interests of labor, and when this had been accomplished, the temporary evil of labor unionism would wither away. Fortunately for the unions, Governor Hiram Johnson was more sympathetic toward organized labor. His earlier services as attorney for the teamsters' union led many union leaders to support him in 1910, and he appointed several of them to state administrative positions. Studies of voting in San Francisco working-class districts suggest that many union members who had voted Democratic or Socialist in 1910 were persuaded to vote for Johnson in 1914. Organized labor was not unaware that the basic philosophy of many Republican progressives was hostile to important union goals. Yet—and again paradoxically—labor had an important role in California progressivism. By later standards the labor legislation of the Johnson years was not very advanced, but it was more than labor had ever received from Sacramento before.

Workmen's compensation, or employers' liability for industrial accidents, was one area in which the goals and ideas of the progressives and the labor unions coincided, and new laws on this subject formed a solid achievement of labor legislation in the progressive years. Some archaic doctrines of common law had long permitted employers to evade financial responsibility for accidental injuries or deaths of their employees in the course of their work. In 1911 a compromise plan removed these limits on the employer's legal responsibility and created an industrial accident board to administer the law, but this act included only a voluntary insurance provision. In 1913 a new and broader law made employer participation in the state-operated workmen's insurance system compulsory, except in agriculture.

The desire of the progressives to protect the interests of "the people" as a whole by curbing the power of both labor unions and employers was clearly evident in the struggle in 1911 over the Weinstock arbitration bill. Harris Weinstock, the author of this proposal, was a merchant prince of Sacramento whom the Lincoln-Roosevelt League had considered among its possible condidates for governor. His bill would have forbade both strikes and lockouts in public utilities until after an impartial board appointed by the governor had recommended terms of settlement. The State Federation of Labor fought this measure bitterly, charging that it was an entering wedge for total compulsory arbitration and the ultimate abolition of the right to strike, and although all five of the Los Angeles progressive senators voted for it, the bill was finally defeated.

A similar battle in 1911 attended the defeat of an anti-injunction bill that labor unions favored and that would greatly have strengthened their position in collective bargaining. Introduced by a Democratic state senator, Anthony Caminetti, this measure would not only have limited the use of court injunctions against strikes; it would also have outlawed the blacklist and the "yellow dog" contract, in which the employee agreed not to join a union; it also would have legalized secondary boycotts and peaceful picketing. This last provision would have invalidated an extreme antipicketing ordinance that the Good Government administration in Los Angeles had adopted the year before.

In the state minimum wage law for women and children, the progressives gave a degree of substance to their claim that they were better protectors of the interests of labor than were the unions themselves. Organized labor at first opposed any minimum wage laws whatever, for the same reason that it opposed compulsory arbitration—that the setting of terms by government boards might weaken and even replace union bargaining. The minimum wage, labor feared, would become the maximum. The 1911 legislature adopted an 8-hour day for women, excluding farm labor and the canning and packing industries, but it did not seriously consider a minimum wage. No state had such a law until Massachusetts adopted the first one in 1912. Katherine Philips Edson of Los Angeles, president of the California Federation of Women's Clubs, led the movement that secured the passage of a California minimum wage law for women and children in 1913.

Records of the bureau of labor statistics showed that a third of the women workers in California were being paid less than 15 cents an hour, and Katherine Edson and other advocates of the new law argued that this condition was a menace to the women's health and morals. An industrial welfare commission was to administer the act, and Governor Johnson, who had joined in pressing for passage of the law, appointed Mrs. Edson as the commission's executive officer.

In August 1913 the Wheatland riot suddenly and dramatically awakened public consciousness, and to some extent the public conscience, to the vile and disgraceful conditions in many farm labor camps. (See Chapter 19.) A state-sponsored investigation revealed that the conditions at Durst's hop ranch were typical of those inflicted on migratory workers by many other large agricultural employers throughout the state. The Commission of Immigration and Housing, created by the legislature a few months before, assumed the authority to inspect farm labor camps, and of the 641 that it investigated in 1914, only 195 met its minimum standards, and 188 were branded as dangerously unsanitary. The next year the legislature passed a new labor camp sanitation and housing act, to be enforced by the commission, but though it made admirable efforts at enforcement, its efforts were stubbornly resisted and were never fully effective. The man who had most to do with planning this legislation and who served as the commission's first chairman was the distinguished social worker–businessman Simon Lubin, a son of David Lubin, the half brother and partner of Harris Weinstock. Another act, also a product of the Wheatland tragedy, required all employers to provide their workers with drinking water.

THE PROGRESSIVES AND THE ANTI-JAPANESE MOVEMENT

An important area of agreement between organized labor and the California progressives was their shared hostility toward the Japanese. The immigration of Japanese to California had been insignificant until the late 1890s, but it steadily increased in the early twentieth century, and in 1905 San Francisco labor union leaders formed an Asiatic Exclusion League to combat it. Under pressure from this league the Union Labor city government announced its intention of segregating Japanese public school children along with the Chinese.

California had almost completely excluded Chinese children from its public schools until a court ruling had forbade this practice in 1885. In San Francisco, a separate public school had then been provided for them in Chinatown. When this Chinese school was rebuilt after the earthquake and fire, its name was changed to the Oriental School, and on October 11, 1906, the board of education adopted an order requiring Japanese public school children to attend it.

Protests from the Japanese government led to a diplomatic crisis between Japan and the United States, and President Roosevelt ordered an investigation by his secretary of commerce and labor, Victor H. Metcalf, a resident of Oakland and the only Californian in the cabinet. Metcalf reported that there had been only 93 Japanese pupils in the 23 public schools in San Francisco and that many of them had been born in the city. However, 27 had been alien teenagers placed in the elementary grades because of their lack of previous schooling in English. White racists, including Sacramento Assemblyman Grove L. Johnson, declaimed upon the menace to little American schoolgirls who were seated beside older boys with evil oriental thoughts.

Early in 1907 President Roosevelt invited Mayor Schmitz and the members of the San Francisco Board of Education to Washington, D.C., where they agreed to a compromise. Only overage pupils and those not having facility in

English might be placed in separate schools, and the new regulations would apply to all children of alien birth, not to Japanese as such.

In return President Roosevelt promised limits on Japanese immigration and negotiated the Gentlemen's Agreement in which Japan promised not to issue passports good for the continental United States to laborers, whether skilled or unskilled. But parents, wives, or children of Japanese already resident in the United States were not covered by this agreement, and through proxy marriages, arranged quite legally and in the traditional fashion by parents or other go-betweens in Japan, thousands of earlier Japanese immigrants brought "picture brides" to America. Many Californians denounced this as oriental duplicity, and demanded complete Japanese exclusion.

Chester Rowell, as the leading philosopher of the California Republican progressives, sought to formulate the argument for exclusion in terms of idealism tempered by realistic historical reflection. Democracy, he believed, was possible only in a homogeneous society, without extreme differences in economic and social status or even in physical appearance. If experiments in interracial democracy were to be tried anywhere, Rowell wrote, it should not be in a country with a record of spectacular failure in such efforts. America already had two great unsolved problems with the blacks in the south and the Chinese in California, and after these experiences it should have the foresight to prevent the growth of another problem of the same kind.

Many Californians now portrayed the Japanese with the same racial stereotypes that had been used against the Chinese in earlier decades, particularly the charges that they were unassimilable and that their low standard of living depressed wages. Soon, however, the Japanese became the object of a new complaint—that their standard of living rapidly became too high. Brought to California to replace the Chinese as cheap farm laborers, some of them began acquiring farm land of their own. Much of this was land that they reclaimed in the Sacramento and San Joaquin valleys and in the San Joaquin delta. They were the first to demonstrate that rice could be grown successfully in California and that potatoes could be grown on a commercial scale. George Shima, known as the "potato king," produced the bulk of the state's crop on his large farm in the delta region.

Bills intended to halt the expansion of the Japanese in California agriculture began to be introduced in every legislative session, and were frequently protested by the Japanese ambassador in Washington. James D. Phelan, in a statement as near to tolerance of the Japanese as he ever came, once suggested that the United States should say "diplomatically" that it regarded "the unassimilable Japanese as efficient human machines," but that "as such, they are a menace to our prosperity and happiness. Then the more sensitive citizens of Japan may find some consolation in our confession of economic inferiority." But while a wealthy urban politician might make such a statement, the small farmers of California, who feared the competition of Japanese, reacted with increased resentment and fury to the idea of making any such humiliating confession.

White supremacy and yellow peril were the doctrines of the overwhelming majority of California voters—progressives and conservatives, Republicans, Democrats, and even Socialists. The leaders of the Republican progressives, as their historian George E. Mowry had pointed out, were with very few exceptions white Anglo-Saxon Protestants of old American stock, a fact that was particularly striking in view of the generally polyglot and immigrant character of the state's population. The Irish and the southern Europeans had tended to become Democrats. Italian Americans joined Irish Americans in the front ranks of the anti-Japanese movement.

For several years state Senator Caminetti and other Democrats in the legislature embarrassed the Republican state and national adminstrations by repeatedly pressing for a law against Japanese land ownership. But a remarkable reversal occurred in March 1913, in the middle of that year's session of the legislature, when control of the national government passed to the Democrats, and with it the responsibility for conducting diplomatic relations with Japan. Governor Johnson and the California progressive Republicans were now free to take their turn at exploiting the anti-Japanese weapon.

In the spring of 1913 Johnson joined with Francis J. Heney and California Attorney General Ulysses S. Webb in drafting an act which provided that aliens ineligible for American citizenship could not own land in the state or lease it for more than 3 years. Under federal law, all Asians were ineligible for naturalization, but there had been no legal immigrants from China since the federal Exclusion Act of 1882. Thus the newly passed California law applied almost exlusively to Japanese aliens, without openly saying so.

The device was transparent, and Japan protested so strongly that President Wilson sent Secretary of State William Jennings Bryan to Sacramento to lobby against the bill. Bryan asked that the bill be made applicable to all aliens, but this led to protests from European-owned land and mining interests. Officials of the Panama Pacific International Exposition, to be held in San Francisco, opposed the bill in fear that Japan would boycott the enterprise. Others criticized the bill as unnecessary because the land owned or leased by Japanese was only a tiny fraction of the total acreage, but Chester Rowell replied that the "menace of Japanese ownership" was "not a present fact, but a fear of the future."

Actually, as Johnson was quite aware, the chief effects of the new law were more emotional and political than economic. Although it did have some deterrent effect on Japanese land ownership, it also had loopholes. Some Japanese aliens transferred their land titles or leases to their American-born children or to corporations with a majority of the stock entrusted to American-born Japanese.

Hiram Johnson's anti-Oriental views were almost as vigorous as those of his father, but his reasons for acting as the behind-the-scenes manager of what was usually called the Heney-Webb alien land bill were primarily reasons of political strategy. The legislature was determined to pass some bill of this kind, and to oppose a measure that was so popular with the state's electorate would have lost him many of his followers. Instead he won many new ones, particularly in northern California. The alien land measure also served to distract attention from the growing disunity among the progressives and from their increasing disagreements over the nature and limits of reform.

THE DECLINE OF PROGRESSIVISM

In California, as well as in national politics, the extremely individualistic temperaments of the Progressive leaders were sources of weakness as well as of strength. They led inevitably to a series of personal quarrels that played a major part in the disintegration of the progressive movement.

The personality of Hiram Johnson bore some resemblance to that of Theodore Roosevelt, and in the early years of their association Johnson exploited this resemblance to the point of imitating Roosevelt's gestures and exclamations. Both were extraordinarily intelligent and courageous political fighters, but both also had in extraordinary degree the human failings of self-centeredness. It might have been said of Johnson, as it was said of T. R., that he disliked attending weddings and funerals because at a wedding he was not the groom and at a funeral he was not the corpse. Both men were prone to impute dishonest motives to anyone who disagreed with them and to attribute to any

Roosevelt and Johnson

"*For there is neither East nor West,*
Border nor Breed nor Birth,
When two strong men stand face to face
Though they come from the ends of the earth."
—Kipling

The Bull Moose ticket. A 1912 campaign poster. *(Courtesy of the Library of Congress.)*

rival the egotism that was characteristic of themselves. And both were masters of invective.

Johnson's personal letters often included vitriolic opinions of other politicians, including his friends, and when he lost his temper with an enemy, he was capable of using the most extreme language, even in a public speech. During the primary campaign of 1910, Harrison Gray Otis's *Los Angeles Times* had touched one of Johnson's most sensitive nerves by referring to his father's record of support for the railroad. Speaking in Los Angeles that evening, Johnson described Otis as "vile, infamous, degraded, and putrescent. Here he sits in senile dementia, with gangrened heart and rotting brain, grimacing at every reform and chattering in impotent rage against decency and morality."

In 1914 Johnson wished to run for the United States Senate and had chosen John M. Eshleman to succeed him as governor, but Francis J. Heney made it known that he would run either for governor or for for senator, whichever of the two offices Johnson did not seek. Johnson now regarded Heney as a dangerous rival and Heney's supporters as mutineers against his own leadership. He could not break openly with Heney without a disastrous split in the Progressive party, but he solved the problem by running for governor himself, by backing Eshleman for lieutenant governor, and by giving Heney virtually no support in his campaign for senator.

The result was that James D. Phelan, the Democratic candidate, was elected senator over the Progressive nominee, Heney, and the conservative Republican nominee, Congressman Joseph R. Knowland. In sharp contrast, the votes for Johnson for governor and Eshleman for lieutenant governor were overwhelming. Johnson became the first governor of California to be reelected since 1853. He planned to run for the other Senate seat in 1916 and then turn over the governorship to Eshleman.

In June 1916 the Progressive national convention, at Johnson's urging, again nominated Roosevelt for the presidency, but Roosevelt declined the nomination and thus virtually scuttled the national Progressive party. Returning to the Republican fold, he announced his support for Charles Evans Hughes. In California the old-guard Republicans headed by William H. Crocker, son of Charles Crocker and leader of San Francisco's propertied aristocracy, gleefully assumed that the influence of Hiram Johnson was dead. Hughes made the same miscalculation. In his campaign visit to California in August, Hughes permitted Crocker and his associate, Francis V. Keesling, to plan all his speaking arrangements. They excluded Johnson from every platform where Hughes appeared and did not even arrange a meeting between the two. By chance, both stopped at the Virginia Hotel in Long Beach on the afternoon of August 20, but Hughes left for Los Angeles without being informed that Johnson was in the hotel. When he learned of it that evening, instead of telephoning Johnson personally he sent his campaign manager, accompanied by Johnson's enemy Keesling to make the explanation, and this irritated Johnson even more.

The California primaries were held 9 days later. Johnson was still a registered Progressive, but he had cross-filed for the Republican nomination for

United States senator. To the horror of the old guard, he won the Republican nomination over their candidate, and the Johnson progressives, most of whom had now returned to the Republican party, recaptured control of the Republican state organization.

Under the circumstances, Johnson could hardly have been expected to support Hughes very enthusiastically, and he did not. Hughes lost any chance for labor votes when Crocker, a leader of open-shop forces in San Francisco, arranged a luncheon for him in a restaurant where he was served by scab waiters during a strike. Other votes went to Wilson because he had kept the country out of war. For these and other reasons, Hughes lost California, by less than 4000 votes, and the presidency of the United States by losing California. But Johnson, with both Republican and Progressive nominations, won the senatorship by a margin of nearly 300,000.

Once again the California Republican progressives seemed to have triumphed, but the untimely death of Lieutenant Governor Eshleman in February 1916 had reopened the problem of succession and created further disunity. Having the power to fill the vacant lieutenant governorship by appointment, Johnson wished to choose another man whose personal loyalty to Johnson himself would be as complete as Eshleman's had been, but the southern California leaders insisted on the appointment of Congressman William D. Stephens, a successful wholesale grocer who had been president of the Los Angeles Chamber of Commerce. Johnson regarded Stephens as "a Taft" who would betray the cause of progressivism. He was not merely something less than a thoroughgoing Johnson man; rather, Johnson charged, Stephens would belong "body and soul" to Edwin T. Earl and Edward A. Dickson with whom Johnson's relations had become embittered.

Johnson was so reluctant to have Stephens succeed him that he delayed resigning the governorship until after the beginning of his term as senator and actually held both offices for 2 weeks in March 1917. He might have held them both for months longer if President Woodrow Wilson had not called Congress into special session in the war emergency.

Johnson had almost come to believe that he *was* the California progressive movement, and it was true that his personal leadership and popularity had been vital elements in its success. He had built up such a devoted personal following among California voters that they would keep him in the Senate until his death in 1945. But in doing everything he could to discredit Stephens, his successor as governor, he further weakened what remained of California progressivism.

Along with these personal and factional quarrels, larger and deeper forces were also contributing to the decline of the progressive movement. Among these were the coming of the war, the consequent resurgence of conservatism, the strong antagonism toward the IWW, and the feeling of many progressives that political and moral reform, the essentials of their program, had already been accomplished. There had been little economic reform, beyond the minimum wage for women. The legislature had established a state conservation commission in 1911, but it was only a fact-finding body. Two years later, an act drafted by Francis J. Heney and ex-Governor Pardee had created a state water commission, but it had accomplished very little. A state health insurance plan put forward by Rowell and favored by Johnson was defeated in 1917. Conservatives branded all such measures as dangerously radical, and many business progressives agreed.

SELECTED BIBLIOGRAPHY

Mowry's *California Progressives,* Olin's *California's Prodigal Sons,* Everett's "Chester Rowell," cited in Chap. 22, and the second volume of Franklin Hichborn's "California Politics," cited in Chap. 21, are also of value here. Hichborn's *Story of the California Legislature of 1911,* and its counterparts for 1913 and 1915, analyze bills and votes. Michael Rogin, "Progressivism and the California Electorate" and John L. Shover, "The Progressives and the Working Class Vote in California," chaps. 2 and 3 in Rogin and Shover, *Political Change in California* (1970), analyze public reactions. On direct government, see V. O. Key, Jr., and Winston W. Crouch, *The Initiative and Referendum in California* (1939) and Frederick L. Bird and Frances M. Ryan, *The Recall of Public Officers: A Study of the Operation of the Recall in California* (1930). On regulation of railroads, other public utilities, banks, and other businesses, see Mansel G. Blackford, *The Politics of Business in California, 1890–1920* (1976).

On woman suffrage see Ronald Schaffer, "The Problem of Consciousness in the Woman Suffrage Movement: A California Perspective," *Pacific Historical Review,* XLV (November 1976), pp. 469–494, and Donald W. Rodes, "The California Woman Suffrage Campaign of 1911," M.A. thesis, California State University, Hayward (1974).

Labor measures are treated in Alexander P. Saxton, "San Francisco Labor and the Populist and Progressive Insurgencies," *Pacific Historical Review,* XXXIV (November 1965), pp. 421–438; Gerald D. Nash, "The Influence of Labor on State Policy, 1860–1920," *California Historical Society Quarterly,* XLII (September 1963), pp. 241–257; Norris C. Hundley, Jr., "Katherine Philips Edson and the Fight for the California Minimum Wage, 1912–1923," *Pacific Historical Review,* XXIX (August 1960), pp. 271–286; and two Ph.D. theses, University of California, Berkeley: Earl C. Crockett, "The History of California Labor Legislation, 1910–1930" (1931) and Samuel E. Wood, "The California State Commission of Immigration and Housing" (1942).

Accounts of the anti-Japanese agitation include Roger Daniels, *The Politics of Prejudice: the Anti-Japanese Movement in California and the Struggle for Japanese Exclusion* (1962); Herbert P. LePore, "Prelude to Prejudice: Hiram Johnson, Woodrow Wilson, and the California Alien Land Law Controversy of 1913," *Southern California Quarterly,* LXI (Spring 1979), pp. 99–110; Madelon Berkowitz, "The California Progressives and Anti-Japanese Agitation," M.A. thesis, University of California, Berkeley (1966); Thomas A. Bailey, "California, Japan, and the Alien Land Legislation of 1913," *Pacific Historical Review,* I (March 1932), pp. 36–59; and Robert E. Hennings, "James D. Phelan and the Woodrow Wilson Anti-Oriental Statement of May 3, 1912," *California Historical Society Quarterly,* XLII (December 1963), pp. 291–300. See also Robert Higgs, "The Wealth of Japanese Tenant Farmers in California, 1909," *Agricultural History,* LIII (April 1979).

On state attempts at regulation of agriculture, see Grace H. Larsen, "A Progressive in Agriculture: Harris Weinstock," *Agricultural History,* XXXII (July 1958), pp. 187–193.

The confusion that progressivism brought to the two-party system is described in A. Lincoln, "Theodore Roosevelt, Hiram Johnson, and the Vice-Presidential Nomination of 1912," *Pacific Historical Review*, XXVIII (August 1959), pp. 267–284, and two Ph.D. theses, University of California, Berkeley: Robert E. Hennings, "James D. Phelan and the Wilson Progressives of California" (1961) and Joseph P. Giovinco, "The California Career of Anthony Caminetti, Italian-American Politician" (1973). The origins of cross-filing are discussed in Franklin Hichborn, "The Party, the Machine, and the Vote; the Story of Cross-Filing in California Politics," *California Historical Society Quarterly*, XXXVIII (December 1959), pp. 349–357 and XXXIX (March 1960), pp. 19–34; James C. Findley, "Cross-Filing and the Progressive Movement in California Politics," *Western Political Quarterly*, XXII (September 1959), pp. 699–711; and Robert E. Burke, "Cross-Filing in California Elections, 1914–1946," M.A. thesis, University of California, Berkeley (1947).

On the campaign of 1916, see Edward A. Dickson, "How Hughes Lost California in 1916," *Congressional Record*, Aug. 19, 1954, and F. M. Davenport, "Did Hughes Snub Johnson?" *American Political Science Review*, XLIII (April 1949), pp. 321–332.

THE TRIUMPH OF CONSERVATISM

RISE AND FALL OF THE SOCIALIST MOVEMENT

In California, as well as in the United States as a whole, socialism reached its highest point during the progressive era. This not only alarmed conservatives but also gave them an opportunity to attack and weaken progressivism by linking it with socialism.

The beginning of the organized socialist movement in the state went back to the 1880s, when Burnette G. Haskell preached a modified Marxism in San Francisco and Kaweah, and the eccentric millionaire H. Gaylord Wilshire developed a peculiarly American brand of socialism in Los Angeles.

Wilshire was an irrepressible and almost incredible figure in the history of southern California. The son of a Cincinnati capitalist, he inherited and lost one furtune and then made and lost a series of others in real estate, orange groves, banks, gold mines, billboards, and even a cure-all electric belt of his own invention. In the boom of the 1880s he developed and subdivided the "Wilshire Tract" west of Los Angeles's Westlake Park. Harrison Gray Otis and Edwin T. Earl bought large adjoining lots and built their mansions in this subdivision, through the center of which ran a thoroughfare 120 feet wide named Wilshire Boulevard. But with the collapse of the boom in 1888 Gaylord Wilshire became an avowed socialist, and in 1890 under the Bellamyite Nationalist label he was the first socialist in the United States to run for Congress. Next he founded *Wilshire's Magazine*, which became the country's most widely circulated socialist journal. Its motto was "Let the Nation Own the Trusts," an idea that would also play a central part in Jack London's novel, *The Iron Heel*. For a time in the 1890s Wilshire lived in England and was a friend of George Bernard Shaw and the Fabian socialists.

In later years Wilshire Boulevard would be to Los Angeles more or less what the Champs Elysees was to Paris, and more than 200 enterprises from a hotel and a country club to a cleaning and dyeing company would take the name of Wilshire because it signified impeccable commercial prestige. Few if any of the proprietors or patrons of these establishments knew the identity of the original bearer of the name.

In the 1890s the leadership of the California socialist movement passed from Wilshire to Job Harriman, a labor union lawyer who came to Los Angeles for his health. Running for governor on a socialist ticket in 1898, he drew only 5000 votes, but within a few years the extremely repressive tactics of Harrison Gray Otis and the Merchants' and Manufacturers' Association had driven so much of Los Angeles labor to socialism that Harriman repeatedly came close to being elected mayor of the city. He would almost certainly have been elected mayor in 1911 if he had not committed the socialist cause to the belief that the McNamara brothers were innocent victims of a capitalist frame-up and if the McNamaras had not shattered this faith by confessing their guilt a few days before the city election. (See Chapter 19.) Even after that great set-back Harriman came within 800 votes of being elected mayor 2 years later, but after this final defeat he turned from political activity to the management of a socialist cooperative experiment at Llano del Rio in the Mojave Desert region north of Los Angeles.

In the state election of 1910 more than 12 percent of the vote went to the Socialist candidate for governor, J. Stitt Wilson, a Berkeley Methodist minister who described himself as a "social evangelist." In 1911 Wilson was elected mayor of Berkeley, although in his 2 years in that office he neither attempted nor accomplished anything radical. In 1912 he ran as the Socialist candidate for Congress against Joseph R. Knowland, the impregnable Republican leader of Oakland and dean of the California congressional delegation; although Knowland won 54 percent of the votes, Wilson drew a remarkable 40 percent.

In 1912, Socialist congressional nominees in California won 18 percent of the votes, and Eugene V. Debs won nearly 12 percent of the vote for President. One Socialist assemblyman from Los Angeles was elected, and in several other districts the Socialists ran far ahead of the Democrats. The elections of 1914 produced two Socialist assemblymen and one state senator.

Though socialism called in theory for public ownership of all the means of production and distribution, the Socialists in the California Legislature pressed mainly for such limited measures as the 8-hour day. Most of the actual legislative proposals of the Socialists were so moderate that they were hardly distinguishable from those advocated by the more liberal of the progressives, but conservative forces formed a Sound Government League in order to fight them, and one of the league's bulletins denounced "creeping socialism," with which conservatives lumped most progressive measures.

The rising tide of socialism in the United States in the first 15 years of the century was a general humanitarian as well as working-class reaction to such prevailing conditions as poverty, long hours and low wages, and the abuse of child labor. The coming of World War I virtually shattered the socialist movement, not only by distracting the country's attention from these conditions but also by creating extreme disunity among the socialists themselves. In California such prominent Socialists as Stitt Wilson and Jack London favored the Allied cause and resigned from the Socialist party in 1916 when it opposed American intervention.

THE MOONEY CASE

In northern California the beginning of a long period of antilabor reaction coincided with the beginning of the war in Europe. In 1914, after several months of economic depression, an "army" of 1500 unemployed under "General" Charles T. Kelley was driven out of Sacramento by a force of deputized citizens armed with clubs. In Stockton, after a labor campaign for the closed shop, employers formed a merchants' and manufacturers' association in July 1914, imported professional strikebreakers and armed guards, and launched an open-shop drive that produced one of the bitterest labor wars in the state's history.

The San Francisco employers began their drive for the open shop in July 1916. Then, during a longshoremen's strike, the San Francisco Chamber of Commerce called a mass meeting of 2000 business people, who cheered an inflammatory address by Captain Robert Dollar and then voted to form a Law and Order Committee in a deliberate appeal to the city's vigilante tradition. In the summer of 1916, labor in general was opposing the military preparedness movement, while most employers favored that movement and seized the opportunity to discredit labor as unpatriotic. San Francisco business and patriotic organizations planned a great Preparedness Day parade on Market Street, in which no labor union participated. The parade was held on July 22. In the midst of it, at 2:06 in the afternoon, a bomb explosion at the corner of Stewart and Market killed 10 persons and wounded 40. Suspicion soon fell upon a radical labor agitator named Thomas J. Mooney.

For several years before the Preparedness Day bombing, Mooney had been active in San Francisco as a left-wing trade union socialist with an aggressive personality and a genius for antagonizing people. An iron molder by trade, he was not a union official. The description of him as a "labor leader" came from opponents of organized labor. He was interested in strike activity for the purposes of social revolution.

In 1913 the electrical workers' union had conducted a long strike against the Pacific Gas and Electric Company throughout northern California during which there were hundreds of depredations against the company's property, 18 of them by dynamite explosions. Warren K. Billings, a young friend of Mooney, had been arrested at Sacramento for the illegal transportation of a suitcase full of dynamite and sentenced to 2 years in prison. Later in 1913 Mooney was arrested for illegal possession of explosives and charged with planning to use them to destroy the transmission line across Carquinez Straits, an act which would have shut off the electric light and power of most of the Bay Area. He was tried at Martinez, but the evidence was flimsy and he was acquitted.

In the summer of 1916 Mooney tried to organize a union among employees of the United Railroads in San Francisco. The company had not permitted union organization since 1907. Mooney's plan was to start a wildcat strike by a few of the streetcar motormen and then to stampede the others into it, but the attempt to do this, on July 14, 1916, was a fiasco. The Preparedness Day explosion occurred 8 days later.

Within a few days after the explosion the police arrested Mooney, his wife Rena, and three of their associates, Warren Billings, Edward D. Nolan, and Israel Weinberg, a jitney driver. All five were arrested without evidence, warrants, or formal charges and were denied the right of legal counsel until after they were indicted. From the time of the arrests the police and the district attorney's office dropped all further search for evidence except that which could be made to point to the defendants' guilt. Billings was tried for murder in September, convicted, and sentenced to life imprisonment. Mooney was tried in January 1917, convicted, and sentenced to hang. Later in the year Rena Mooney and Israel Weinberg were acquitted. Edward Nolan was not brought to trial.

The main witnesses for the prosecution testified that they had seen Billings and the Mooneys at or near the scene of the crime and that Billings was carrying a suitcase presumably containing a time bomb. Overwhelming evidence indicates that these witnesses were perjuring themselves, and it is hard to escape the conclusion that District Attorney Charles M. Fickert was aware of their perjury and encouraged it. Fickert had originally been elected district attorney of San Francisco in 1909 on his tacit promise to end the graft prosecution. He was at best an incompetent lawyer who had always been accustomed to garble or invent facts to suit his purposes. In the Mooney case he did not prosecute the defendants in good faith but because they were widely hated as radicals and because he believed that to convict them would make him governor of California.

Again, as in the *Times* bombing a few years earlier, millions of people throughout the country believed what their social predilections made them wish to believe about the guilt or innocence of the accused. This time, however, many were afraid of being deceived by the cry of "frame-up" that had been so discredited before, and this made Fickert's work easier. The evidence against the McNamara brothers, so widely disbelieved and denounced, had turned out to be quite genuine. The evidence against Mooney and Billings, so readily believed, was fabricated.

It was apparent to many, however, that there had been an outrageous miscarriage of justice. The case took on international importance in April 1917, with a demonstration outside the American embassy in Petrograd against the execution of a political prisoner named "Muni." President Wilson, concerned both for the interests of justice and for the American image in a war to make the world safe for democracy, asked Governor William D. Stephens to consider a commutation. The California Supreme Court refused to order a new trial, largely for the technical reason that the main exposure of the perjuries had occurred after the time during which a motion for a retrial was allowed.

Tom Mooney, interviewed by a reporter in 1933. *(Courtesy of the Bancroft Library.)*

In November 1918 Governor Stephens commuted Mooney's sentence to life imprisonment. In the antiradical hysteria of the war and postwar periods, most Californians held to a fixed belief in Mooney's guilt.

THE CRIMINAL SYNDICALISM LAW

Throughout the war the IWW openly opposed America's participation in it and maintained that the only just war was a class war against capitalism. Long denounced as advocates of industrial sabotage, terrorism, and violence, the Wobblies were now also branded as antipatriotic and pro-German and often described as "Imperial Wilhelm's Warriors." They were actively involved in bitter wartime strikes, especially in the lumber industry. Late in 1918, 46 IWW members were arrested in Sacramento and tried in the federal courts as seditious conspirators. Most of them were convicted and sentenced to prison.

After the end of the war the wave of emotional antiradicalism became even greater, for the full force of public hatred was then turned upon "internal enemies." In February 1919 a 5-day general strike in Seattle, organized by militant locals of the AFL, was widely attributed to the IWW, and conservative newspapers in California cited it as proof of an imminent danger of Bolshevik revolution. In April 1919 the California Legislature passed a criminal syndicalism act, although the legislature of 1917 had rejected a similar measure.

This statute defined criminal syndicalism as "any doctrine or precept advocating ... unlawful acts of force and violence ... as a means of accomplishing a change in industrial ownership or control, or effecting any political change." Under this law several hundred persons were prosecuted in California during the next 5 years.

One of the first of these trials, and by far the most famous, was that of Charlotte Anita Whitney. Before her arrest in November 1919, when she was 52 years old, Miss Whitney's career had hardly been such as to suggest that she was a dangerous criminal. Rather, she was well known as a philanthropist, social worker, and suffragist. She could trace her descent from five Mayflower pilgrims, her father had been a state senator from Alameda County, and her uncle was United States Supreme Court Justice Stephen J. Field. After graduating from Wellesley College she had worked in a settlement house in New York and then served for many years as secretary of the Associated Charities of Oakland. She had joined the Socialist party in 1914, and during the war she was active in the pacifist movement and in the defense of Mooney and Billings.

In 1919 a number of left-wing Socialist split off to form the Communist Labor party, whose state organization was formed at a convention in Oakland. Miss Whitney, as a delegate from the Oakland Socialist local, worked for a resolution favoring only democratic and peaceful methods, but this resolution was voted down, and instead the convention ratified the national platform of the Communist Labor party. The American Communist party, which was also formed in 1919, had a platform so similar that the two organizations, were later merged.

Miss Whitney's trial began in January 1920, not long after United States Attorney General A. Mitchell Palmer, who hoped to be the next Democratic candidate for President, had launched a new program of raids against "Bolshevists, anarchists, and kindred radicals." The proceedings against Miss Whitney were conducted in an atmosphere of hysterical superpatriotism, and they set a pattern for many subsequent prosecutions in which mere membership in an organization advocating violence was interpreted as sufficient evidence of criminal syndicalism under the state law. She was convicted and sentenced to 1 to 14 years in the penitentiary.

Fremont Older, one of the leading critics of the prosecution in the Mooney case, also came vigorously to the defense of Miss Whitney and persuaded his former star reporter, John Francis Neylan, to take charge of her appeal. Neylan had studied law in his spare time, and after the end of his service as chairman of the state board of control had begun a highly successful law practice in San Francisco. William Randolph Hearst had employed him to negotiate the purchase of the *San Francisco Call*, had made him its publisher, and later made him general counsel of all the Hearst publications.

Neylan disagreed sharply with Miss Whitney's political views but believed that she had been unjustly convicted, and for 7 years, while she remained free on bail, he fought with all the legal and political resources he could muster to keep her out of prison. The United States Supreme Court finally rendered a decision in the case in May 1927. Unanimously it upheld the conviction, and also upheld the constitutionality of the California law as being within the state's police power. Neylan was more successful in his fight for a pardon, which Governor Clement C. Young finally granted in June 1927. In explaining his decision the governor made use of an argument which Neylan had also been careful to emphasize, that to imprison Miss Whitney would "revive the waning spirits of radicalism" by making her a martyr. Besides, Young concluded, she was a "lifelong friend of the unfortunate," rather than "in any true sense a 'criminal,'" and "to condemn her at 60 years of age to a felon's cell" was "absolutely unthinkable."

Upton Sinclair and others, observing sardonically that a number of obscure men had been imprisoned for offenses identical in principle with Miss Whitney's, charged that there was one law for the rich and another for the poor. Altogether, there had been 504 arrests and 264 trials under the California criminal syndicalism law, and 128 persons, mostly members of the IWW, had been sent to prison. Twenty-four states had adopted such laws, mostly in 1919, but in all these states except California they were dead letters after 1921. In California, active prosecutions continued until 1924, largely to discourage further attempts by the IWW to organize migratory farm workers.

DECLINE OF ORGANIZED LABOR

In the 1920s the business community had considerable success in branding labor unions as unpatriotic. A large segment of American public opinion believed that the unions had at best been lukewarm in their support of the war and that they had been inclined to defend seditious radicals instead of joining in the national condemnation of them. Adding these widely held beliefs to their arsenal of weapons, employer organizations resumed their prewar battles for the open shop, and this time succeeded in establishing it even in what had previously been the union stronghold of San Francisco.

In the summer of 1921, after an unpopular and unsuccessful strike by the building trades unions, the San Francisco Chamber of Commerce created a new Industrial Association to establish and enforce "the American plan." This expression had recently received the approval of the National Association of Manufacturers as the official name for the open shop. The drive made such remarkable headway in San Francisco that for the rest of the decade the open shop predominated even in the construction of municipal buildings. The Industrial Association maintained a "permit system" under which it withheld building materials from employers who continued to "discriminate against non-union men" by making closed-shop contracts with unions. An Impartial Wage Board, established by the association and headed by the Roman Catholic archbishop, E. J. Hanna, nearly replaced collective bargaining in the building industry. Under the philosophy of "welfare capitalism" the association also established free training schools for apprentices, employee group insurance plans, and a free employement bureau for nonunion workers. Representatives of the Industrial Association of San Francisco often argued that it was not a "union-busting" organization, because it forbade employers to discriminate against union members—provided they were willing to work with nonunion people.

In Los Angeles, however, employers were often more candidly eager to destroy unions entirely. The Better America Federation, a new auxiliary of the Merchants' and Manufacturers' Association, was organized in Los Angeles in May 1920 to conduct a lobbying and propaganda battle against organized labor and progressivism. Its drives for members and money made the sort of patriotic appeal that had been used to sell Liberty Bonds during the war, and indeed it made a particular effort to recruit as its publicists the people who had been the most successful bonds sellers. It lobbied against higher state taxes on banks and utilities and in favor of proposals to establish the open shop by law and to abolish all the state regulatory boards and commissions that the progressives had created. Its propaganda sought to associate with treason and subversion anyone who disagreed with its objectives.

Throughout the 1920s membership in labor unions steadily declined. In a period of prosperity and high employment, this was remarkable. The prestige of organized labor was low, and the prestige of employer organizations was correspondingly high. Many agreed with the Better America Federation in adopting as mottoes the slogan of President Warren Harding, "less government in business, more business in the government," and the aphorism of President Calvin Coolidge, "the business of America is business."

COLLAPSE OF THE DEMOCRATIC PARTY

During the last third of the nineteenth century the balance between the two major parties had been close in California, and Democratic candidates had won five gubernatorial elections to the Republicans' four. After 1900, however, a long series of defeats began to have a cumulative effect on the Democratic party's morale.

In the postwar decade the Republicans benefited from the general prosperity and from the wholesale migration to California of retired farmers and small businesspeople from the middle west. Throughout the 1920s the Democrats could win no more than 1 of California's 11 congressional seats; cross-filing Republicans repeatedly won the Democratic nominations for 6 of them and were thus elected in the primaries, in which, in several cases, no Democrat even bothered to file. In 1922, of the 80 seats in the state assembly, the Democrats won only 3. In 1924 the electors pledged to the Democratic candidate for President, John W. Davis, received only 8 percent of the California vote. Through most of the decade Republicans outnumbered Democrats in California by four to one in voter's registrations.

Democratic leadership was uninspiring. James D. Phelan, who had gone to the United States Senate in 1914 as the leader of the "Wilson progressives" of California, was defeated for reelection in 1920, and the only political ideas he continued to advocate with any consistency were the ban on Japanese immigration and a loosening of the prohibition laws to permit the manufacture of wine and beer. When William G. McAdoo transferred his residence from New York to California in 1922, the California Democrats hoped that this acquisition of a leading contender for the presidency of the United States would revive their strength. But McAdoo, who favored strong enforcement of prohibition, made his home in Los Angeles and assumed the leadership of the dry Democrats of southern California, thus deepening the split with the northern California wing of the party, which was decidedly wet. Early in 1924 the Los Angeles oil magnate Edward L. Doheny, under investigation for the bribery of Secretary of the Interior Albert B. Fall, let drop the fact that McAdoo was on his payroll as an attorney, and McAdoo's chances for the presidential nomination were instantly ruined even though he had no actual connection with the oil scandals. William Randolph Hearst remained a nominal Democrat through the early 1920s, but after a bitter quarrel with Alfred E. Smith, Hearst became a supporter and personal admirer of President Calvin Coolidge. Will Rogers, "cowboy humorist" and political commentator of the 1920s, remarked that "I am not a member of any organized political party. I'm a democrat."

THE CONTINUING DECLINE OF REPUBLICAN PROGRESSIVISM

Senator Hiram Johnson had abandoned the remnants of the Progressive party by 1918, and he campaigned for the Republican presidential nomination in 1920 on a platform of narrowly nationalistic and isolationist "Americanism." His irreconcilable opposition to the League of Nations so far overshadowed his interest in domestic issues that he supported the conservative lawyer Samuel M. Shortridge for the Republican nomination for United States Senator, against the distinguished progressive William Kent, largely because Shortridge opposed the League and Kent favored it.

Prohibition was another issue that confused the alignments among progressive and conservative Republicans, as well as among the Democrats. Many of the California progressives were "drys," and the disastrous failure of the prohibition experiment accelerated the general decline in the moral fervor of progressivism. Congress had submitted the Eighteenth Amendment to the states in December 1917, in the midst of the war, and California ratified it the spring of 1919, after the necessary 36 other states had already done so. It proved even less popular and less effective in California than in the rest of the country. Efforts to enforce it were concentrated against small cafés rather than against large distillers and bootleggers, and the Mexican border and long coastline made smuggling easy. The obvious breakdown of prohibition tended to weaken all respect for law and government. One jury had to be admonished for drinking up the liquor that was the chief evidence in the trial.

The continuing crusade against the Japanese, which had never had any genuine connection with progressivism, now became a part of the new wave of superheated patriotic antiforeignism that was aiding the conservative revival throughout the country. An initiative measure adopted by a vote of three to one in 1920 repealed the provision of the law of 1913 that had permitted Japanese aliens to lease land for 3 years. In the federal immigration act of 1924, California won its long fight for the complete exclusion of "aliens ineligible to citizenship." Without this clause, the quota system finally provided in the act would have permitted only 100 Japanese immigrants per year; nevertheless, Johnson and Shortridge demanded complete Japanese exclusion, and secured the support of the conservative Republican leader of the Senate, Henry Cabot Lodge. The United States had never before offered Japan so gratuitous an insult, but the Japanese ambassador's warning of "grave consequences" was interpreted in Congress as a threat, and for this reason it actually contributed to the passage of the exclusion clause.

The triumph of conservatism was most apparent in the election of Friend W. Richardson as governor in 1922. A former state treasurer and publisher of the *Berkeley Gazette*, Richardson promised and achieved a program of "sweeping retrenchment." His "economy budget" drastically reduced appropriations, particularly for regulatory boards, humanitarian agencies, and education. "The schools," he told the legislature, "must be put on a business basis. They must not only teach but practice thrift." As heads of the various regulatory commissions, he replaced the men appointed under Johnson and Stephens with conservatives, often representatives of the business interests that the commissions had been designed to regulate.

For the election of 1926, Chester Rowell, Rudolph Spreckels, Franklin Hichborn, and others formed a Progressive Voters' League and rallied behind the gubernatorial aspirations of Clement C. Young of Berkeley. Young, a developer of suburban real estate, had been speaker of the assembly during the progressive era and was now lieutenant governor. In his race for the governorship in 1926 he made his progressive followers uneasy by accepting the support of A. P. Giannini and his Bank of Italy.

Giannini's swiftly growing institution, soon to be renamed the Bank of America, was well on the way toward its goal of a system of branches to cover the whole of California. Under Governor Richardson the state authorities had yielded to the complaints of independent bankers and rival branch systems and had tried through administrative rulings to restrict the statewide growth of branch banking. Shortly before the primary of 1926 the Bank of Italy contributed generously to the Young campaign fund, and the employees of the bank's branches throughout the state gave generously of their services as volunteer campaigners. By a narrow margin, Young won the Republican nomination from Richardson. At a time when California was almost a one-party state, this assured Young of the governorship.

As Franklin Hichborn put it, he and his fellow progressives had marveled at such a "fortunate acquisition" of support, but when Young became governor they learned that "we were the acquisition." Early in 1927 Young's new superintendent of banks revoked the restrictions on branch banking. During the remainder of that year the branches of the Bank of Italy increased from 98 to 289.

Although Young's administration disappointed his most progressive supporters, he did reverse some of the most reactionary policies of Richardson. An act of 1929, with Young's support, made California the first state to require that every county provide old-age pensions. His most substantial achievement was a "businesslike reorganization" of the state government, which inaugurated the cabinet system in the executive branch and improved the budget system.

In the election of 1930, when the main contest was between Young and James Rolph, Jr., for the Republican nomination, Richardson had his revenge. Young was a dry and Rolph was a wet. Richardson encouraged the district attorney of Los Angeles to enter the race, and thus to divide the dry vote in southern California, so that Rolph narrowly defeated Young in the primary. With Rolph's election as governor, Republican progressivism in California went into an even further decline.

THE "FEDERAL PLAN" OF REAPPORTIONMENT

A new system of apportioning the state senate, adopted in 1926, played a little-understood but highly important part in the successful drive of conservative business interests to consolidate their influence upon the state government.

Representation in both houses of the legislature had previously been apportioned according to population, and reapportioned, with considerable gerrymandering, every 10 years. By the early 1920s, however, Los Angeles had grown so enormously that the legislators from San Francisco and Oakland joined with those from the rural northern California counties to block any reapportionment bill that would have given the southern metropolis its full representation.

In 1926 the voters were given a choice between two initiative constitutional amendments. One provided for reapportionment in both houses on the customary basis of population. This was officially called the "All Parties" proposal, but its main support was in Los Angeles County. Its opponents always called it "the Los Angeles Plan," and thus assured its unpopularity in every other county in the state. The alternative proposal, on the other hand, bore the disingenuous but effectively persuasive label of "the Federal Plan." Based on a misleading analogy with the equal representation of the states in the upper house of Congress, this scheme apportioned the seats in the state senate at not more than one to a county and at not more than three counties to a senatorial district.

This proposal was also advertised as coming from the "dirt farmers" of California, and the four largest agricultural organizations did support it with enthusiasm. Significantly, however, the major financial contribution in aid of its passage came from the San Francisco Chamber of Commerce, though this source was not revealed until after the election. As Franklin Hichborn observed, the plan was ideally suited to the interests of those special California farmers who labored in the tall buildings on Montgomery Street, the heart of the San Francisco financial district. Over the next several years the ingenuity of their plan became apparent in the membership of the state senate. Dirt farmers were not in evidence, and a remarkable proportion of the new senators from the rural districts turned out to be attorneys, insurance agents, and others who were local representatives of corporations with headquarters in San Francisco.

California agriculture itself was becoming steadily more industrialized and its interest more and more identified with those of the business community. The new California senate would often be described as "rural dominated." To put the matter more accurately, it became a stronghold of business conservatism, rural and urban.

SELECTED BIBLIOGRAPHY

Ralph Hancock, *Fabulous Boulevard* (1949) includes a chapter on the "Man Named Wilshire." Howard Quint, "Gaylord Wilshire and Socialism's First Congressional Campaign," *Pacific Historical Review*, XXVI (November 1957), pp. 327–340, describes the election of 1890. On the career of Job Harriman, see Grace H. Stimson, *Rise of the Labor Movement in Los Angeles* (1955) and Robert V. Hine, *California's Utopian Colonies* (1953). J. Stitt Wilson, and the socialist movement in general, are treated in Ralph E. Shaffer, "A History of the Socialist Party of California," M.A. thesis, University of California, Berkeley (1955). See also Ira B. Cross, "Socialism in California Municipalities," *National Municipal Review*, I (1912), pp. 611–619.

Richard H. Frost, *The Mooney Case* (1968) is by far the best account. Others are in Fremont .lder, *My Own Story* (1926); Curt Gentry, *Frame-Up* (1967); and the chapter on "Preparedness Day, 1916" in R. L. Duffus, *The Tower of Jewels* (1960). On newspaper opinion of the war in Europe and the preparedness movement see Richard B. Rice, "The California Press and American Neutrality, 1914 to 1917," Ph.D. thesis, University of California, Berkeley (1957); consult also Thomas G. Paterson, "California Progressives and Foreign Policy," *California Historical Society Quarterly*, XLVII (December 1968), pp. 329–342.

Woodrow C. Whitten, *Criminal Syndicalism and the Law in Calfornia, 1919–1927* (1969) and his "The Trial of Charlotte Anita Whitney," *Pacific Historical Review*, XV (September 1946), pp. 286–294, are objective studies of a wave of antiradical emotions. See also Ralph E. Shaffer, "Formation of the California Communist Labor Party," *Pacific Historical Review*, XXXVI (February 1967), pp. 59–78, and "Communism in California, 1919–1924," *Science and Society*, XXXIV (Winter 1970); Al Richmond, *Native Daughter: The Story of Anita Whitney* (1942); and Howard A. DeWitt, *Images of Ethnic and Radical Violence in California Politics, 1917–1930* (1975).

The crusade for the open shop in the 1920s is described in "The American Plan," a series of articles in *Pacific Industries*, I (February 1922), pp. 15–24; David Warren Ryder, "The 'American Plan' in San Francisco," *Review of Reviews*, LXV (February 1923), pp. 187–190, and "San Francisco's Fight for Industrial Freedom," *ibid.*, LXXVII (January 1927), pp. 82–85; and Edwin Layton, "The Better America Federation: A Case Study of Superpatriotics," *Pacific Historical Review*, XXX (May 1961), pp. 137–148.

On the Democratic debacle, consult H. Brett Melendy, "California's Cross-Filing Nightmare: The 1918 Gubernatorial Election," *Pacific Historical Review*, XXXIII (August

1964), pp. 317–330; Robert E. Hennings, "California Democratic Politics in the Period of Republican Ascendancy," *Pacific Historical Review*, XXXI (August 1962), pp. 267–280; and Daniel P. Melcher, "The Challenge to Normalcy: The 1924 Election in California," *Southern California Quarterly*, LX (Summer 1978), pp. 155–182.

On Hiram Johnson's drift away from progressivism, see Richard D. Batman, "The Road to the Presidency: Hoover, Johnson, and the California Republican Party, 1920–1924," Ph.D. thesis, University of Southern California (1965), and Richard Lower, "Hiram Johnson and the Progressive Denouement, 1910–1920," Ph.D. thesis, University of California, Berkeley (1969).

Political issues of the 1920s are also discussed in the third and fourth volumes of Franklin Hichborn, *California Politics, 1891–1939*; Gilman M. Ostrander, *The Prohibition Movement in California, 1848–1933* (1957); Wendell E. Harmon, "The Bootlegger Era in Southern California," *Southern California Quarterly*, XXXVII (1955), pp. 335–346; Roger Daniels, *The Politics of Prejudice* (1962); Gladys H. Waldron, "Antiforeign Movements in California, 1919–1929," Ph.D. thesis, University of California, Berkeley (1956); Russell M. Posner, "The Progressive Voters' League, 1923–1926," *California Historical Society Quarterly*, XXXVI (September 1957), pp. 251–261, and the same writer's "State Politics and the Bank of America, 1920–1934," Ph.D. thesis, University of California, Berkeley (1956); Marquis James and Bessie R. James, *Biography of a Bank; the Story of Bank of America* (1954); and Jackson K. Putnam, "The Persistence of Progressivism in the 1920s: The Case of California," *Pacific Historical Review*, XXXV (November 1966), pp. 395–411.

On the adoption of the "Federal Plan," see George W. Bemis, "Sectionalism and Representation in the California State Legislature, 1911–1931," Ph.D. thesis, University of California, Berkeley (1935) and Thomas S. Barclay, "Reapportionment in California," *Pacific Historical Review*, V (June 1936), pp. 93–129.

OIL, AUTOMOBILES, AND MOVIES

ORIGINS OF THE OIL INDUSTRY

Though the "black gold" of California was far more valuable than the yellow gold, its rise to historical importance followed a very different trajectory. Gold production reached its height in the fifth year after it began and then settled down for the next 80 years at about a third of the peak output of 1852. California's oil industry, on the other hand, had its first boom in the 1860s but did not begin to reach major proportions until the 1890s, and its great modern expansion came in the twentieth century.

For thousands of years oil had been taken from shallow pits and used for lamp fuel, caulking, internal and external medication, and a luxuriant variety of other purposes. In Mexican California, *brea*, or tar, was used for the roofs of adobe houses and sometimes mixed with earth for the floors.

The world's first commercial oil well opened near Titusville, Pennsylvania, in 1859, after Benjamin Silliman, Jr., professor of chemistry at Yale, reported that an oil sample from it could be refined into high-grade kerosene. California's first oil well was drilled 2 years later, a few miles south of Eureka. Although it produced no oil, there were 40 other wells in Humboldt County by 1865, mostly in the Mattole River region, where a village was overoptimistically named Petrolia. The total output of this "field," however, was so small that it was measured in gallons rather than barrels. The more significant developments of the 1860s took place in Ventura County (part of Santa Barbara County until 1872). George S. Gilbert, a whale oil merchant, built a small refinery on the Ojai Ranch north of Ventura in 1861. From seepage oil, Gilbert manufactured small quantities of kerosene. In 1864 Thomas A. Scott, vice president of the Pennsylvania Railroad, sent Silliman to evaluate some western mineral properties. In the course of the same trip Silliman investigated the oil resources of the Ventura region.

After absorbing the glib optimism of Gilbert, Silliman wrote a number of rosy reports. "California," he predicted, "will be found to have more oil in its soil than all the whales in the Pacific Ocean." In the Ojai region "the oil is struggling to the surface at every available point and is running away down the river for miles." The first 10 wells drilled on the Ojai property, he estimated, would yield an annual profit of more than $1 million.

Scott placed full faith in Silliman's judgment for he had already made a large profit by purchasing and developing oil land near Titusville. Convinced that California's oil would far exceed Pennsylvania's, Scott headed a group of investors who bought the Ojai and several neighboring ranches and sent out the best drilling machinery then in existence. As manager of his California properties Scott chose Thomas R. Bard, a young man from Pennsylvania. In the summer of 1865 Bard began drilling a series of wells, but none of them produced oil in commercial quantities.

Silliman's California reports were quite true, and even understated, as a kind of mystical vision of the ultimate future, but as conclusions from the evidence actually before him they were fantastically exaggerated, and based on a slipshod investigation. He was unaware that California's geology, with its characteristically tilted and folded strata, would make both the finding and the extracting of oil more difficult than in Pennsylvania. Moreover the crude oil found in California in the early years was extremely heavy, asphaltic, and gummy. It made inferior lubricant, and California kerosene, when burned for illuminating purposes, flickered, smoked, and smelled. Scott refused to finance any further search for oil on his California properties, and the state's first oil boom was over by the end of 1867.

Prospecting continued, however, notably in Pico Canyon, which was still public land and in which oil ventures were conducted under a system of mining claims patterned after those of the mother lode country. Pico Number One, opened in 1875, became the first commercial well in California.

Gradually, deeper drilling began to yield larger quantities and better grades. In 1890 Thomas R. Bard joined with two small operators in organizing the Union Oil Company of California. Bard had turned from oil prospecting to land management in Ventura County and had built a fortune by subdividing Thomas A. Scott's vast lands for ranching purposes, buying lands of his own, and separately leasing the ranches and the oil rights. Bard served as the first president of Union, though he soon relinquished this office and withdrew from active participation in the company's affairs after his election to the United States Senate in 1900.

THE BLACK BONANZA

Silliman's vision began to become a reality in the early 1890s. The Union Oil Company made several substantial discoveries that laid the foundations of its future career as one of the giants of the California industry, and in 1892 Edward L. Doheny made his sensational discovery of a major oil field within the city of Los Angeles. Doheny was a prospector and lawyer who had made and lost small fortunes in gold and silver mining in New Mexico. He had never hunted oil and had never even seen a derrick, but one day in Los Angeles, when he saw a wagonload of tarry, greasy brown dirt being hauled from an excavation to be burned as a substitute for coal in a small manufacturing plant, he realized that a mother pool of oil was feeding the pits, the oil thickening to tar as it reached the surface.

In November 1892 Doheny and his partner Charles A. Canfield leased a vacant lot near West Second Street and Glendale Boulevard and dug a shaft with pick and shovel, lifting out the dirt with a hand windlass. At a depth of 155 feet oil began to flow into the shaft, enabling them to hire a drilling rig. The flow increased rapidly, and the Los Angeles oil boom was on. Hundreds of oil wells mushroomed in front yards and back yards. For the year 1895 the total flow was more than 700,000 barrels, mostly from a strip of land about 600 feet wide and 2 miles long which overlay a pool of great richness and depth.

Finding a market for this outpouring was an urgent problem. The answer was the substitution of oil for coal. California had produced a little low-grade coal, mainly in the Mount Diablo area, but had imported most of its coal supply at great expense. Now it suddenly had a surplus of a better and much cheaper fuel. Oil burners for locomotives were quickly developed, and by the turn of the century the railroads of the whole southwestern United States were converting to oil. The saving in cost was matched by the relief of the passengers, for western locomotives had burned soft coal that produced enormous quantities of smoke and cinders. The conversion of the railroads was a turning point, showing the way to the use of oil for powering ships as well as all sorts of stationary engines and ensuring California's future as a major industrial state.

In the years after Doheny's discovery of the Los Angeles City field, other important producing areas were developed in the southern California coastal region, notably the Santa Maria and Summerland fields in Santa Barbara County and the Fullerton, Whittier, Coyote, and Montebello fields in the Los Angeles basin. But the larger discoveries in the period between 1895 and 1920 came in the San Joaquin Valley. Great new fields were brought into production on the Kern River east of Bakersfield, and at Coalinga, McKittrick, and Midway-Sunset.

On March 15, 1910, a Union subsidiary company drilling north of Maricopa brought in one of the world's greatest gushers, Lakeview Number One. The driller, a certain "Dry Hole Charlie" Woods, was instantly renamed "Gusher Charlie." So tremendous was the blast that the derrick disappeared into the crater. Not for several weeks was the gusher brought under control, and then only by building a huge earthen dam around it, high enough to smother it in a lake of its own oil. For the next 18 months the flow varied between 15,000 and 68,000 barrels a day, a total of nearly 10 million barrels from one well. At last the casing wore out, the hole caved in, and the great gusher was dead, but the surrounding field grew into an oil empire, with its capital in the new town of Taft, named for the incumbent President.

The near monopoly that Standard Oil had established throughout the nation in the last third of the nineteenth century was broken in the early twentieth. As the petroleum industry entered its modern period of enormous growth and passed from its "age of illumination" to its "age of energy," it became highly competitive, although the most important competition was among great corporations.

From the late 1870s to the middle 1890s Standard had dominated the market in California with oil products imported by rail from its eastern fields and refineries. The major part of this market had been for illuminant kerosene, for which California crude was relatively worthless; however, the use of kerosene declined with the advance of gas, electricity, and fuel oil. Enormous new areas of crude oil production were opening in California and in the midcontinent and gulf regions, larger than the Standard-dominated fields of Pennsylvania, Ohio, and Indiana.

Standard moved into producing and refining operations in the far west in 1900 when it purchased control of the Pacific Coast Oil Company. This concern had been organized in 1878 by United States Senator Charles N. Felton and Lloyd Tevis, two of San Francisco's leading venture capitalists. In 1906 it was renamed the Standard Oil Company (California). In 1911 the antitrust decision of the United States Supreme Court forced the dissolution of the Standard network into its constituent companies, but Standard of California had already become by far the largest refiner on the Pacific coast.

Another California giant was the Associated Oil Company, originally formed by a number of small producers in the San Joaquin Valley in 1901. The Southern Pacific Railroad purchased control of Associated in 1909, mainly in order to develop its own burgeoning oil interests in the western San Joaquin Valley.

In 1919 the Southern Pacific Land Company owned more than 19 percent of all the proved oil land in California, and through its controlling interest in the Associated Oil Company the railroad produced about 18 percent of the state's oil. During the next several years, however, the Southern Pacific gradually divested itself of its direct interests in oil production and refining, and by 1928 the control of Associated had passed to the Tidewater Oil Company of New Jersey. Later it passed to Phillips 66.

In addition to Standard, Associated, and Union, the major California operators in this period included Shell, Richfield, the General Petroleum Corporation, which was purchased by the Standard Oil Company of New York, later called the Mobil Oil Corporation, the Texas Company, and Edward L. Doheny's Pan-American Petroleum Company.

THE OIL BOOM OF THE TWENTIES

Three tremendous discoveries in the early 1920s, all in the Los Angeles basin area, surpassed all the earlier developments and launched a boom that put oil in the forefront of California's headlong economic expansion in the "prosperity decade." Standard opened the massive new field at Huntington Beach in 1920. The next year, Union brought in the great Santa Fe Springs field south of Whittier, and Shell tapped the still greater bonanza of Signal Hill at Long Beach—richest of all the world's oil deposits in terms of barrels per acre. In 1923, these three fields together produced more than 183 million barrels of oil, out of California's total production of 263 million barrels. The value of the California crude oil produced in the decade of the 1920s was more than $2½ billion. This figure compares very strikingly with the value of all the gold ever mined in the state—about $2 billion. California ranked first among the states in crude oil production for several years in the 1920s, though it has ranked second to Texas in total cumulative output.

In 1919 about two-thirds of California's oil came from the San Joaquin Valley, and the major refineries were concentrated in the San Francisco Bay area, but in the 1920s the predominance in all aspects of the oil industry quickly passed to the Los Angeles region. Exports of oil from Los Angeles harbor made it the largest oil port in the world. Petroleum refining became the state's largest manufacturing industry. In 1925 the value of oil refinery products was more than $369 million. This was twice the value of the output of California's second-largest branch of manufacturing, the canning and preserving of fruits and vegetables, and it was 15 percent of the entire value of all manufactured goods produced in the state.

The most infamous episode in the history of California's great oil boom of the postwar decade was the involvement of Edward L. Doheny in the scandal of the Elk Hills naval oil reserve. Doheny and other oilmen persuaded the federal government that the best way to conserve the oil on western public lands, against the possibility of a future war in the Pacific, was to extract the oil and store it in tanks. With Secretary of the Interior Albert B. Fall, an old friend and a former fellow prospector in New Mexico, Doheny arranged to lease and develop the federal oil lands in the Elk Hills field in western Kern County. A large part of the oil was to be stored in tanks which Doheny agreed to build for the government on the west coast and at Pearl Harbor.

Fall received a payment of $100,000 in cash, which Doheny's son brought to him in a satchel. Later Fall was convicted of taking this money as a bribe, but Doheny was acquitted of having bribed him with it. Doheny insisted that in his own view the payment had been simply a loan to an old friend to help him save his ranch from foreclosure, a loan that he would have made whether the leases were granted or not. To Fall $100,000 was a large sum but it was a trifling amount to Doheny, whose fortune exceeded $100 million. In spite of the legal determination that Doheny was innocent of criminal intent while Fall was guilty of it, the government in a civil suit won a cancellation of Doheny's leases on the ground that they had been obtained through a bribe.

By another irony, the whole Elk Hills affair was regarded at the time as less important than the scandal of the Teapot Dome reserve in Wyoming. For a similar leasing arrangement of the midcontinent oil, operator Harry F. Sinclair paid Fall $300,000, presumably reflecting Teapot Dome's greater richness. But that field proved to be relatively unimportant, while Elk Hills proved to be the second-largest field in the nation, exceeded only by the later discoveries on the north slope of Alaska. After the return of the federal lands at Elk Hills to the status of a naval reserve, the government adopted a policy of taking out only enough oil to keep the wells in condition, but in 1976 the Elk Hills field was ordered into full-scale development; the Navy was to retain jurisdiction and sell the oil to commercial companies.

THE AUTOMOBILE REVOLUTION

The vast, deep pools of oil that were discovered in the Los Angeles basin in the early 1920s proved extraordinarily rich in gasoline. Thus huge quantities of this great source of motive power became available at the very time and in the very region where the use of the automobile was spreading more rapidly than in any other time or place in history. In the early decades of the oil industry, gasoline had been a worse-than-useless by-product of the refineries, important only because of the difficult and dangerous problem of getting rid of it. But in the automobile age, gasoline became the most valuable ingredient in a barrel of oil, and the refineries were completely redesigned to extract as much of it as possible.

At the turn of the century there were only about 4000 horseless carriages in America, and they were toys of the rich, but a major turning point came when Henry Ford introduced his Model T in 1908 and when one of these remarkable cars set a new record for automobile travel a year later by crossing the continent in a mere 22 days, arriving in San Francisco with New York air still in its two front tires. This achievement proved that an inexpensive car could be a good one and that long-distance travel would soon be practical. At the same time, the reports of the primitive road conditions that the Ford had encountered dramatized the need for highways that would "get the country out of the mud."

In nineteenth century America the counties were responsible for the building and maintenance of roads, but they had notoriously failed to perform this function either efficiently or honestly. In California the Southern Pacific used its control of county government to concentrate road building almost exclusively on feeders for its railroad lines. Some improvement came in the 1880s and 1890s, when bicycling became the rage and when the League of American Wheelmen became important as a better-roads lobby. Demands of farmers for passable roads increased with the establishment of rural free delivery of mail in 1894. Denunciations of glaring waste and corruption on the part of county road overseers led to the creation of a California state bureau of highways in 1895, but it had only research and advisory powers.

Two private organizations of motorists, the Automobile Club of Southern California with headquarters in Los Angeles and the California State Automobile Association with headquarters in San Francisco, were formed in 1900, and with many wealthy and influential people among the auto enthusiasts on their boards of directors they soon became major forces in the battle for good roads. In 1909 the California Legislature authorized a bond issue of $18 million for the beginning of a system of paved state highways, and the voters approved the bonds in the general election the next year.

Financial support from the national government began with the federal Highway Aid Act of 1916, with dollar-matching grants to the states. Another major source of money was the state gasoline tax. First discovered by the Oregon Legislature in 1919, this form of revenue had several outstanding advantages. With obvious fairness, it apportioned the cost of highways among the users of them, service station records provided an accurate measure of use as well as a sure and inexpensive method of collection, and the tax was relatively painless because it was paid in driblets and as a part of the price of the commodity. With funds for highways thus assured, the age of motorization was ready to come into full flower.

Mass motorization transformed California, and most of all, southern California, where climate, scenery, and boosterism combined with low gasoline prices and increasingly good roads to make the region a motorist's paradise. From 1920 to 1930 the population of Los Angeles County more than doubled, from less than a million to 2,208,492. The number of registered private automobiles quintupled, rising to 806,264. By 1925 the city of Los Angeles had one automobile for every three persons—more than twice the national average. Los Angeles became the most thoroughly motorized and motor-conscious city in the world.

It was also the first American metropolis whose major expansion occurred entirely within the automobile era, and the automobile intensified a process that Henry Huntington's Pacific Electric had begun—the freeing of the people of Los Angeles from the urban centralization that the limitations of the streetcar had enforced upon other great American cities. With their own cars people could live at a considerable distance from their work, and could own their homes, with lawns, flowers, and shrubbery. With the coming of the great construction boom of the 1920s Los Angeles soon had a larger ratio of single-family residences and a lower population density than any other large city in the United States. The modern supermarket, designed for customers who could provide their own transportation for large quantities of groceries, was born in Los Angeles. And Realtor A. W. Ross's "Miracle Mile," on a part of Wilshire Boulevard that had been uninhabited shortly before, was probably the first large business district in the world to be created especially for the automobile age.

Tourism increased enormously in a great new wave of the American westward movement, and "auto camps" and "tourist cabins" sprang up. Service stations became a major new institution. The first of them has been credited to Earl B. Gilmore, whose father had bought land for a dairy farm on a part of the Hancock family's domain, once the Rancho La Brea. A substantial oil field had been opened there in 1901, near the famous pits that had held the bones of prehistoric animals mired in the tar. When Wilshire Boulevard was extended from Los Angeles to the beach at Santa Monica in 1909, Earl Gilmore was just out of Stanford. He put a tank on a farm wagon, painted it red and

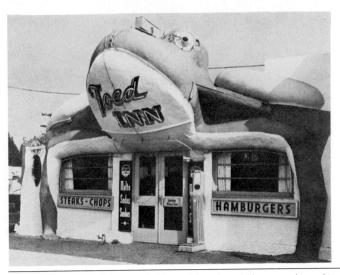

The automobile spawned a remarkable tradition of roadside vernacular architecture. Shown here is an early drive-in restaurant in Santa Monica Canyon featuring "service in your car." (Courtesy of American Stock Photos, Los Angeles.)

yellow, parked it at the corner of Wilshire Boulevard and La Brea Avenue, and sold gasoline from his father's nearby refinery—at 10 cents a gallon.

"Our forefathers," said the *Los Angeles Times* in 1926, "in their immortal independence creed set forth 'the pursuit of happiness' as an inalienable right of mankind. And how can one pursue happiness by any swifter and surer means . . . than by the use of the automobile?" Such was the spirit that dominated the prosperous twenties for better and sometimes for worse. The motorcar contributed heavily, for example, to the deterioration of personal morals in the era of jazz, hip flasks, and flappers, for an automobile was a reasonable facsimile of a private room, readily transportable beyond the reach of chaperonage.

Quite as revolutionary as the effects of the internal combustion engine on the cities were its effects on agriculture and on rural life. The automobile put an end to the isolation of rural areas and reduced the differences in outlook between the farmer and the city dweller, the truck brought much greater flexibility to agricultural marketing, and the tractor was one of the most crucial laborsaving devices ever invented. Tractor factories had been greatly expanded during their temporary wartime conversion to military purposes, after the British government had placed huge orders with California's Holt Manufacturing Company for certain vehicles. In a successful effort to surprise the Germans on the western front, the British had circulated the information that the Holt contracts were merely for "tanks" to carry water for British troops in the deserts of Mesopotamia. In fact, of course, these "tanks" were armored artillery vehicles with caterpillar treads.

Even during the great depression of the 1930s the use of the automobile continued to increase, particularly in California. Both the city workers and the agricultural migratory laborers kept their cars, even when they were unemployed and on relief.

THE MOVIES DISCOVER CALIFORNIA

Of the machines that changed American life in the first half of the twentieth century, the movie camera was as important as the internal combustion engine in the degree of its influence. To comparable degrees, also, the history of the movies and the history of the automobile were especially intertwined with the history of California.

At the turn of the century and for several years afterward most American films were made in New York or New Jersey. The first substantial American narrative film was *The Great Train Robbery*, an 8-minute western made by Edwin E. Porter for Thomas A. Edison's film company, in the New Jersey countryside in 1903. This thrilling production told of a mail train holdup, the formation of a posse, and the pursuit and killing of the desperadoes. By taking the camera outdoors "on location" and by joining together bits of film shot in different places and at different times, Porter pioneered the whole technique of film editing that made possible the development of the motion picture as a truly distinctive art.

At this time, Edison and a few others controlled the American patents on cameras and projectors, but a number of "outlaw" film producers sprang up, and a bitter struggle developed. William Selig, who began to make movies in Chicago, was among the many "independents" who were harrassed by Edison's lawyers. It occurred to Selig that if he made his pictures in a more remote part of the country, it would be harder for Edison's subpoena servers to interfere with his operations. Late in 1907 a director and a cameraman in the employ of Selig arrived in southern California to make the outdoor scenes of a one-reel production of *The Count of Monte Cristo*, and early in 1908 they set up a studio on Main Street in downtown Los Angeles.

Another Chicago producer, George K. Spoor, had recently organized the Essanay Film Manufacturing Company, in partnership with Gilbert M. Anderson (the "A" in Essanay). Anderson, born Max Aronson in Little Rock, Arkansas, was a young ex-vaudevillian who had become famous as the star of *The Great Train Robbery*, and was known as Bronco Billy. Essanay was devoted largely to westerns, for which there was now an insatiable demand, and it obviously made more sense to produce westerns in the far west than in Chicago—not to mention the relatively greater freedom from legal harrassment. In 1908 Anderson experimented with various sites in the San Francisco Bay region and finally the canyon and ranch area near Niles, a short distance southeast of Oakland. There, during the next 6 years, Essanay ground out 375 one-reel westerns, one a week—all featuring the rugged, valiant, kindly cowboy Bronco Billy. This studio also produced some of the first great comedies of Charles Chaplin.

In 1909 Edison led seven American film companies and two French ones in pooling their patent claims and forming a group that would often be denounced as "the movie trust" because it claimed the right to deny "licenses" for filmmaking to all other companies. For several years, until the trust itself was prosecuted and dissolved as a conspiracy in restraint of trade in violation of the Sherman Act, the industry produced almost as many lawsuits as movies. Selig and Essanay, having become members of the trust, were no longer harried by legal charges of patent infringements. But a number of other companies, left outside the favored group and finding themselves more harried than ever, discovered that the Los Angeles suburb of Hollywood offered a very special advantage as a location for independent producers: It was fairly close to the international boundary. When process servers and confiscators of cameras appeared, the precious equipment and film stocks could be hastily packed into automobiles and rushed to safety across the Mexican border.

The environs of Los Angeles also had other and more permanent advantages for moviemaking, and these appealed to members of the trust as well as to independents. Movie cameras had not yet been developed to the point where they functioned reliably with artificial light alone; thus "indoor" scenes often had to be filmed in sets that were at least partially open to natural light, and there were fewer rainy days in Hollywood than in New York or Chicago. As for outdoor settings, within a few miles of the Hollywood studios were scenes that would substitute for any locale a plot might call for—from the Sahara Desert to the French Riviera, or the battlefield of Gettysburg. Early in 1910 D. W. Griffith brought a company of Biograph players to Los Angeles, where he used San Gabriel Mission for scenes in *The Thread of Destiny: A Story of the Old Southwest*, and a few weeks later he achieved striking new camera effects by photographing the southern California countryside from great distances in a production of *Ramona*.

Eventually the phrase "a Hollywood production" became an even more familiar and valuable asset in the advertising of movies than was the brand name "Sunkist" in the advertising of oranges. Even more than the orange groves, the movies increased southern California's romantic appeal and became a major factor in its burgeoning growth.

RISE OF "THE INDUSTRY"

A long strike of vaudeville actors in 1900 had led the theater managers, for the first time, to show programs consisting solely of movies. The rental of a series of short films cost less than the wages of a series of vaudeville actors, and the theater owners discovered not only that they could make a profit with an admission charge of only 5 cents, but that a vast audience, especially of immigrants in the large cities, would flock to see even the crudest films at that modest price. Soon there were thousands of new movie houses called "nickelodeons"—a charming word formed by combining the price of admission and the Greek work for theater.

Thus when the movies first came into mass production, they were the poor person's entertainment. Not only the audiences but also the distributors and producers of the early films were drawn very largely from the ranks of people who were struggling to rise from poverty. "Respectable" business people and financiers shunned the infant movie industry as a possible investment. As Leo Rosten has put it, "The men who built the motion picture industry . . . were not drawn from the supposedly farsighted ranks of American business," but from "the marginal and shabby zones of enterprise, from vaudeville, nickelodeon parlors, theatrical agencies, flea circuses, petty trade." William Fox, born in Hungary, worked as a cloth sponger in New York before he opened a penny arcade and then a nickelodeon in Brooklyn. Jesse L. Lasky began his working life as a vaudeville cornet player in San Francisco. His brother-in-law, Samuel Goldwyn, was born Samuel Goldfish in Poland, ran away from home in Warsaw, arrived in New York alone as a steerage passenger at 13, and began work as a glove salesman. Louis B. Mayer, born in Russia, spent part of his boyhood as a rag collector in Saint John, New Brunswick. Marcus Loew and Adolph Zukor were small fur dealers before they became partners in the theater business.

All these men were deeply sensitive about their origins. Only one member of the group, Lewis J. Selznick, took public pride in his humble beginnings. Hearing of the abdication of the Czar in March 1917, he sent him a famous and fascinating cablegram: "WHEN I WAS POOR BOY IN KIEV YOUR POLICEMEN WERE NOT KIND TO ME STOP I CAME TO AMERICA AND PROSPERED STOP NOW HEAR WITH REGRET YOU ARE OUT OF JOB OVER THERE STOP FEEL NO ILL WILL . . . SO IF YOU WILL COME NEW YORK CAN GIVE YOU FINE POSITION ACTING IN PICTURES STOP SALARY NO OBJECT STOP . . . SELZNICK."

In the early years the moviemakers, especially the members of the trust, were afraid that their mass audience was not intelligent enough to sit through any one picture longer than one reel (about 12 minutes) and too poor to afford the cost of longer and better pictures. But in 1913 the independent producer Jesse L. Lasky and his director Cecil B. deMille made the first American feature-length movie, *The Squaw Man,* in five reels and proved that longer films could be highly profitable.

Movie patrons had begun to favor certain players by 1910, but the companies in the trust would not advertise the names of actors and actresses lest they demand higher salaries. It was the independents who discovered the star system, through which they could achieve an unbroken succession of hits by featuring personalities so consistently attractive that the patrons would line up at the box office no matter what the quality of the films. Within a few years salaries of featured players leaped from a maximum of $15 a day to an average of $1500 a week. To the movie audiences the stars were figures of personified desire or symbols of the great moving forces of comedy or tragedy. Gladys Smith from Canada became better known as Mary Pickford, or America's Sweetheart, in which capacity she received $500,000 a year by 1915.

Movie audiences, centering their attention on the stars, have never developed an appreciation of the role of directors, but within the industry the vital importance of their function soon came to be recognized. Directors fuse the script, the performers, the camera operators, and the technicians into a single pattern, a motion picture. Ultimately their conception determines what the story is, what it means, and how it is told.

David Wark Griffith was the first great American director, and his film *The Birth of a Nation* was a remarkable motion picture, especially in such technological achievements as its filming of Civil War battle scenes. But it was also a racist distortion of American history, and because it was more widely shown and left a deeper emotional imprint on its audiences than almost any other film before or since, it stands as a classic example of both the enormous potential power of the art of the cinema and the possibilities for misuse of that power. Griffith was the son of a brigadier general in the Confederate Army, and his film, based on Thomas Dixon's novel *The Clansman*, glorified the role of the Ku Klux Klan in the reconstruction of the south and portrayed black people as an inferior race.

After a special showing of the film at the White House, President Wilson was reported to have said that "it is like writing history with lightning, and my one regret is that it is all so terribly true." Wilson was himself a southerner by birth and early education, and it was during his presidency that lunchrooms, drinking fountains, and lavatories in government buildings in the District of Columbia were racially segregated for the first time since the Civil War. But if President Wilson could see nothing wrong with *The Birth of a Nation*, there were many Americans who could; in the face of a great outcry from critics of the film, Wilson publicly disavowed his endorsement of it. The denunciations, however, merely gave it additional advertising. By 1930 more than 100 million people had seen *The Birth of a Nation*, and by 1948 it had grossed nearly $50 million. It did more to fasten racial stereotypes on the American mind than anything since *Uncle Tom's Cabin*, and it was partly responsible for the great revival of the Ku Klux Klan that reached its height in the 1920s.

A film of special significance in the cultural history of California was *Greed* (1923), based on Frank Norris's novel *McTeague, a Story of San Francisco* and directed by Erich von Stroheim. It was extravagantly produced and became a financial disaster that led to the decline of its director's career. The novel so fascinated von Stroheim that he filmed it not merely chapter by chapter but line by line, and not on artificial sets but in actual rooms and streets in San Francisco and actual places in Death Valley. After he had spent 6 months in reducing its enormous bulk, the film was still more than 4 hours long. When he refused to edit it further, the Metro-Goldwyn-Mayer executives took it out of his hands and turned it over to a cutter, who reduced it from 24 reels to 11. Von Stroheim refused to look at it again, though even in this mutilated form it was one of the greatest of all motion pictures.

Gradually the movies escaped from their earlier status as an essentially lower-class form of entertainment and began to make a very successful appeal to the middle classes. In the 1920s—the golden, or rather the most heavily gilded, age of the motion picture—theater owners in all the larger cities erected huge movie palaces, with lavish ornamentation and regiments of uniformed ushers.

The movies both reflected and accelerated the prevailing trends toward the urbanization of American attitudes and mores. Before 1917 more than half the films made in the United States had portrayed rural scenes and praised the simple values of rural life, but a survey made in the 1920s revealed that even rural audiences had begun to react unfavorably to films with rustic themes and characters, a trend that the theatrical trade paper *Variety* reported under the famous headline "STIX NIX HIX PIX."

Cecil B. deMille, the leading director for Paramount Pictures, both anticipated and helped to create the shift in moral attitudes that occurred in the war and postwar years. Between 1918 and 1921, in such pictures as *Forbidden Fruit, Male and Female, Why Change Your Wife?* and *For Better or For Worse,* deMille showed movie audiences in intimate detail the things that they should not do, and though these films came around to defending the institution of marriage in the final scenes, they also portrayed human weakness very sympathetically.

Some of Hollywood's most famous stars began to set unfortunate examples of flamboyant misconduct in their personal lives, notably Roscoe ("Fatty") Arbuckle, Mary Miles Minter, Mabel Normand, and Wallace Reid. In the face

Typical of the opulent "movie palaces" of the 1920s was Grauman's Chinese Theatre in Hollywood, here being readied for its first film, the 1927 premiere of Cecil B. DeMille's *The King of Kings. (Courtesy of Bison Archives, Beverly Hills.)*

of much criticism the leaders of the industry persuaded Will H. Hays of Indiana to leave his position of postmaster general in President Harding's cabinet and become the "czar of the movies," with power to draw up a new moral code. The plan of movie self-censorship that emanated from the "Hays Office" decreed that evil must never be made attractive and that it must always be punished. The chief result was a series of films that were ostensibly exhortations to repentance and reform, but still managed to include a great deal of sex and violence. DeMille, in particular, was highly successful in adapting to the Hays Office format in his productions of *The Ten Commandments* (1923) and *The King of Kings* (1927).

As the movies became big business, five major and three lesser companies emerged to dominate the film-producing industry. The "big five" were Loew's (including Metro-Goldwyn-Mayer as its production subsidiary), Warner Brothers, Paramount, Radio-Keith-Orpheum (RKO), and 20th Century-Fox. The "little three" were Columbia, Universal, and United Artists.

In the 1930s Louis B. Mayer became the highest-salaried business executive in America and the most powerful man in Hollywood. Mayer and the other "money men" who became the rulers of the industry were always intensely aware that they were engaged in the business of manufacturing commercial entertainment rather than in the creation of art.

The introduction of the "talkies" had pulled the industry out of a temporary slump in 1927, and throughout the great depression of the 1930s it remained more prosperous than most other industries because the public craving for its chief product—escape—was greater than ever. In 1941 there were more moving-picture theaters than banks in the United States. Attendance reached an all-time peak in 1945, but the great period of the movies ended soon after World War II, with the beginning of the rise of television. If the automobile had done much to break up the American family, the television set did just as much to bring it together again, though on a very passive basis.

SELECTED BIBLIOGRAPHY

Gerald T. White, *Formative Years in the Far West; a History of Standard Oil Company of California and Predecessors through* 1919 (1962) includes excellent material on the background of the California industry as a whole. See also his *Scientists in Conflict: The Beginnings of the Oil Industry in California* (1968). Thomas R. Bard's career is the subject of W. H. Hutchinson, *Oil, Land and Politics* (two volumes, 1965). A good chapter on petroleum, and valuable production tables, are in Robert G. Cleland and Osgood Hardy, *The March of Industry* (1929). Gerald T. White, "California's Other Mineral," *Pacific Historical Review,* XXXIX (May 1970), pp. 135–154, is one of the several articles in an issue on "The Petroleum Industry."

Highway development is described in Felix Riesenberg, Jr., *The Golden Road* (1962); *California Highways* (1920), by Ben Blow, manager of the Good Roads Bureau of the California State Automobile Association; and Phil T. Hanna, "The Wheel and the Bell; the Story of the First Fifty Years of the Automobile Club of Southern California," *Westways,* XLII (December 1950), pp. 41–56.

On various economic and social aspects, see R. M. Fogelson, *The Fragmented Metropolis: Los Angeles, 1850–1930* (1967); Ashleigh E. Brilliant, "Social Effects of the Automobile in Southern California during the Nineteen-Twenties," Ph.D. thesis, University of California, Berkeley (1964); the same writer's article on "Some Aspects of Mass Motorization in Southern California, 1919–1929," *Southern California Quarterly*, XLVII (June 1965), pp. 191–208; Earl S. Pomeroy, *In Search of the Golden West: The Tourist in Western America* (1957); and Ernest McGaffey, "Living in the Age of Motorization," *Southern California Business*, VII (March 1928), pp. 20–21, 34–35.

Hundreds of articles on motoring in California are cited in Anna Marie Hager and Everett G. Hager, *Cumulative Index—Westways, Touring Topics, 1909–1959* (1961).

Major contributions to the general history of motion pictures include Terry Ramsaye, *A Million and One Nights: A History of the Motion Picture through* 1925 (two volumes, 1926); Benjamin B. Hampton, *A History of the Movies* (1931); Lewis Jacobs, *The Rise of the American Film, a Critical History* (1939); Richard Griffith and Arthur Mayer, *The Movies; the Sixty-Year Story of the World of Hollywood and Its Effect on America, from Pre-nickelodeon Days to the Present* (1957, 1971); Arthur Knight, *The Liveliest Art* (1957); and A. R. Fulton, *Motion Pictures: The Development of an Art from Silent Films to the Age of Television* (1960).

Leo C. Rosten, *Hollywood; the Movie Colony; the Movie Makers* (1939) is a survey of the industry as it was in the late 1930s, written with the aid of a team of social scientists. Hortense Powdermaker, *Hollywood, the Dream Factory* (1950) is an anthropologist's view. See also Molly Haskell, *From Reverence to Rape; the Treatment of Women in the Movies* (1973).

On censorship, see Raymond Moley, *The Hays Office* (1945) and Ruth A. Inglis, *Freedom of the Movies* (1947).

In the 1960s and 1970s almost every major studio, producer, director, and star in the history of Hollywood became the subject of one or more books of widely varying value.

CONSERVATION, WATER, POWER, AND POLITICS

Nineteenth-century Americans had regarded their country's natural resources as inexhaustible and had exploited them with the greatest recklessness. In the progressive era, however, interest in conservation greatly increased. California's natural resources were so spectacular and the controversies over their use and development were so complicated and intense that the issues and problems of conservation inevitably became a major theme in the state's history.

THE YOSEMITE AND JOHN MUIR

One of the many tributes to the incomparable beauty of the Yosemite Valley was the fact that it was the first area in the United States to be designated by the federal government as a park. This action was also one of the first historical landmarks in the growth of the modern sense of public responsibility for conservation in America.

One of the early advocates of a Yosemite Park was California state geologist Josiah D. Whitney, for whom Mt. Whitney was named. But the strongest impetus for the park project came from the country's leading landscape architect, Frederick Law Olmsted, who came to California during an interval between his periods of service in the development of Central Park in New York City and who became entranced with the Yosemite while temporarily engaged in the management of Frémont's Mariposa estate. In 1864, largely as a result of Olmsted's urging, Congress passed and President Lincoln signed an act granting the Yosemite Valley and the Mariposa Grove of Big Trees to the state of California. Olmsted was then appointed by the governor as the first chairman of the Yosemite State Park Commission. There was no precedent for the idea of a *national* park, but federal grants of land to the states for an assortment of other purposes were so frequent that the proposal for a park met little opposition. Yellowstone became the first park administered by the national government, in 1872, mainly because Wyoming and Montana were not yet states.

Almost as important in the history of the conservation idea as the Yosemite Park itself, and closely interrelated with it, was the personality of John Muir, who first came to the valley as a young man in 1868 and was never again entirely happy anywhere else. The valley and the mountains around it inspired him to a lifetime of writings and crusades which proclaimed his gospel of humanity's rebirth through the enjoyment of nature's beauty and of humanity's obligation to preserve that beauty as a sacred trust.

Muir had been born in Scotland—"with heather in him," as he said—and had spent his boyhood on a wilderness farm in Wisconsin. Almost from infancy his father forced him to a regimen of memorizing great parts of the Bible, an influence that was very apparent in his later thinking and writing. A good example was his famous description of the Sierra as he first saw it after he had landed at San Francisco and walked southward from Oakland to Gilroy and thence to the summit of Pacheco Pass. Across the Central Valley on a clear morning the great range "seemed not clothed with light but wholly composed of it, like the wall of some celestial city. . . . It seemed to me that the Sierra should be called, not the Nevada or Snowy Range, but the Range of Light."

After a short time in the Yosemite region, Muir wrote in his diary that "John the Baptist was not more eager to get all of his fellow sinners into the Jordan than I to baptize all of mine in the beauty of God's mountains." "Climb the mountains and get their good tidings," he wrote in his first book, *The Mountains of California.* "Nature's peace will flow into you as sunshine flows into trees. The winds will blow their freshness into you and the storms their energy, while cares will drop off like autumn leaves."

In similar language Muir sent Ralph Waldo Emerson an invitation "to join me in a month's worship with Nature in the high temples of the great Sierra Crown beyond our holy Yosemite." When Emerson accepted and came to the valley in May 1872, it was one of the supreme moments of Muir's life, though he was somewhat disappointed when the great transcendentalist, at 67, regretfully declined to join him on a camping trip, and kept to the hotels and trails.

Although Muir had studied geology and botany at the University of Wisconsin, he was not a scientist but rather a brilliant amateur naturalist. Yet it was he, rather than Whitney and other professional geologists of the time, who first proved that a glacier had carved the Yosemite.

Muir's essentially religious approach to nature was a blend of theism and pantheism. God, he felt, was "ensouled as a Principle in all forms of matter." Believing that evolution was not mere chance and survival of the fittest, Muir insisted that humanity, like nature in general, evolved by cooperation rather than competition. Thus Muir offered a philosophy of society as well as a philosophy of nature. As his biographer Linnie Marsh Wolfe has pointed out, his remedy for human miseries was in some respects more radical than Henry George's. Brought into their true relationship with the wilderness, humanity would see that they were not a separate entity but an integral part of a harmonious whole. Human beings had no right to subdue their fellow creatures or to appropriate and destroy their common heritage; to do so brought unbalance in nature and loss and poverty for all.

In 1889 Muir gained an important ally in Robert Underwood Johnson, one of the editors of the *Century* magazine. On a tour of the central Sierra, Muir convinced Johnson that the Yosemite was being poorly protected under state control and pointed out the devastation which sheep—those "hoofed locusts"—were being allowed to inflict on the mountain valleys of the region. Johnson urged Muir to carry his appeal to the people of the whole nation through articles in the *Century*.

For the next 15 years the California Legislature resisted the demands of Muir and his admirers that the state return the Yosemite Valley to the federal government, but in 1890 the eloquent writings of "great Nature's priest," as Johnson called Muir, aroused so much national emotion that Congress set aside a large area surrounding the valley as a national forest reserve administered by the secretary of the interior, who designated it as "Yosemite National Park." At the same time Congress created the Sequoia National Park and the General Grant, which was later incorporated in Kings Canyon. The creation of Sequoia incidentally ensured the final eviction of Burnette Haskell's socialistic Kaweah colony, and the biggest *Sequoia gigantea*, which the Kaweahns had named the "Karl Marx tree," was hastily renamed the "General Sherman."

In 1892 Muir founded the Sierra Club, an organization as enthusiastically devoted to conservationist lobbying as it was to mountaineering, and at last, after many years of such pressure, the California Legislature finally approved the recession of the Yosemite Valley in 1905. A year later Congress approved the merging of the valley with the surrounding national park.

PINCHOT AND ROOSEVELT

In the eyes of John Muir and his followers, the most important of all natural resources was beauty, and the true object of the conservation movement was to preserve the beauty of the wilderness in its natural state. This school of thought came to be known as "aesthetic conservationism," or "preservationism." Sometimes allied with it, but often in sharp opposition, was "utilitarian" conservationism, which took form in the 1890s around the ideas of Gifford Pinchot, the pioneer of scientific forestry in America. Pinchot achieved spectacular success in convincing large lumber companies that they could greatly increase their long-range profits by selective logging and various other "sustained-yield" techniques of scientific forest management. In 1898 these companies enthusiastically supported his appointment as chief of the Division (later the Bureau) of Forestry in the United States Department of Agriculture.

With Theodore Roosevelt's accession to the presidency in September 1901, conservation gained a powerful impetus. Indeed Roosevelt was soon identifying the whole conservation movement as "my policy," and several years after he had left the White House he described conservation as the most important of all his domestic policies and his greatest contribution to reform. As a young man Roosevelt had found physical and emotional regeneration in "the strenuous life" of a ranch on the Montana-Dakota border, and his love of the outdoors was as deep and personal as that of John Muir.

Roosevelt was not, however, a preservationist, and his philosophy of conservation was much closer to Gifford Pinchot's than to Muir's. In May 1903, at Roosevelt's request, Muir served as his personal guide on a 4-day pack trip in the Yosemite region. Muir made the mistake of giving him a blunt lecture on the need to outgrow "the boyishness of killing things," to which Roosevelt, an incurable big-game hunter, made an abashed and evasive reply.

Roosevelt's own experiences in the semiarid west had given him a first-hand knowledge of its vital need for water, and another of his early policies as President was to support the passage of the Newlands Reclamation Act of 1902. Representative (later Senator) Francis G. Newlands of Nevada was a brilliant lawyer, educated at Yale and Columbia. He had become a resident of Nevada when he went there to manage the properties he inherited from his father-in-law, Senator William Sharon. The reclamation law that he drafted provided for the use of federal funds to build irrigation projects. Public lands within the area of these projects were to be open to entry only as homesteads of no more than 160 acres, in order to prevent speculation either by land companies or by the settlers themselves. Family farms, and not corporations, Newlands argued, should benefit from federal irrigation.

Though Newlands was a Democrat, the theory of his law was based not on democratic political convictions but rather on his belief that the best hope for the economic development of Nevada and other parts of the mountain west lay in the growth of a family-farm population, and that a farm of 160 acres, or even less, was quite large enough for irrigated agriculture.

THE HETCH HETCHY CONTROVERSY AND SAN FRANCISCO'S WATER SUPPLY

The city dweller, as well as the farmer, naturally attached great importance to an assured supply of water. San Francisco was worried by its dependence on the limited nearby resources of the Spring Valley Water Company. In 1900 a new city charter authorized a larger and municipally owned water system. The city engineer reported that the Hetch Hetchy Valley on the Tuolumne River in Yosemite National Park was the ideal site, superior to any of the possible alternatives.[1] Mayor James D. Phelan applied to the secretary of the interior for permission to convert the Hetch Hetchy Valley into a reservoir, but the moment John Muir heard of the plan, he mobilized his forces for battle, and they fought so valiantly that the federal government delayed its final approval of the project for 13 years.

---

[1]"Hetch Hetchy" was the Miwok name of a plant; "Yosemite" was a sonorous corruption of an Indian word meaning a grizzly bear.

Hetch Hetchy was about 20 miles northwest of its "sister valley," the Yosemite. Though only about half as long and half as wide as its much more famous neighbor, it bore a striking and charming resemblance to it and was sometimes called a "Yosemite in miniature." But Hetch Hetchy was so nearly inaccessible that very few people except Muir and some other members of the Sierra Club had ever seen it. Muir called it "the Tuolumne Yosemite" and stressed the comparison with the "other Yosemite" on the Merced. Many people thought that Yosemite National Park and Yosemite Valley were the same and telegraphed their representatives under the impression that the San Francisco proposal would "destroy the Yosemite Valley." Muir called the flooding of Hetch Hetchy as great a sacrilege as the destruction of a cathedral and denounced the proponents of it in the strongest terms he could think of.

James D. Phelan, an outstanding patron of the arts, was outraged at the accusation that he was callously indifferent to beauty. He denounced Muir in return and stoutly asserted that a lake, as well as a valley, could be beautiful.

Phelan and his supporters also argued that while the use of Hetch Hetchy would be granted free of charge, the possible alternative sites were not only inferior and inadequate but were all controlled by private interests who wished to sell them to the city at exorbitant prices. Considerable weight was given to this argument by sensational revelations concerning the designs of the Bay Cities Water Company. This corporation, of which the San Francisco capitalist William S. Tevis was the president and main stockholder, had acquired options on certain land and water rights near Lake Tahoe and on forks of the American and Consumnes rivers. It proposed to construct a water system which it would sell to the city for $10.5 million, and in 1906 the Union Labor board of supervisors actually voted approval of the project. But this action was hastily reversed in the following year when the confessions of Boss Ruef and the supervisors revealed that the total estimated cost of the project was only $7.5 million; that of the $3 million of estimated profit, the company had promised $1 million as a fee to Ruef; and that Ruef had promised to divide half of this money among the supervisors in return for their votes. This project, if it had been consummated, would have been by far the largest of all Ruef's corrupt transactions.

The federal government, sure of being denounced by someone for any action it might take in the Hetch Hetchy matter, vacillated and temporized. The settlement of the long struggle came at last in 1913, essentially because it happened that President Wilson's choice for secretary of the interior was Franklin K. Lane, who had been city attorney of San Francisco under Mayor Phelan and had written many of the city's briefs in the fight. With the weight of the new secretary thrown into the scales, Congress gave the final permission in an act drafted by Representative John E. Raker of California. John Muir, defeated by this shift in the sands of politics, was brokenhearted and died a few months later.

Construction of the new water system was a vast and expensive undertaking. Not until 1934 was the system in full operation, with 155 miles of aqueduct including a 25-mile tunnel under the coast range, the longest tunnel in the world at the time of its completion.

THE OWENS VALLEY-LOS ANGELES AQUEDUCT

San Francisco's chief source of water, the Tuolumne River, begins its flow at the foot of a glacier on Mt. Lyell. Only 15 miles eastward across the Sierra divide are the headwaters of the Owens River, the stream to which Los Angeles reached out for the first of the great and distant new sources of water that its phenomenal twentieth-century growth would require. The story of the Owens Valley–Los Angeles Aqueduct involved controversies even more bitter than the struggle over Hetch Hetchy.

The man who conceived the Owens Valley Aqueduct project was Fred Eaton, city engineer of Los Angeles in the 1890s and its mayor from 1899 to 1901. Born in Los Angeles, Eaton had achieved his first success by working his way up to the superintendency of the city's water system when it was a mere network of open ditches from the Los Angeles River, operated by a private company. For many years Eaton spent his vacations in prospecting for a new water supply. Choosing the Owens River, he recognized that the vital unit in its development would be a storage reservoir near its upper end, in Long Valley, above the main Owens Valley. Hoping for personal enrichment as the just reward of his concern for his native city, he quietly bought the land and the water rights in Long Valley and planned as a private enterprise to sell some of the Owens River water to farmers in Owens Valley and to sell the rest to the city of Los Angeles.

Between 1900 and 1905 the population of that city grew from 102,479 to more than 250,000. Moreover, the rainfall in these years was even less than usual, and in July 1904 Los Angeles came close to the stark terror of an actual water famine. The city engineer, William Mulholland, was a former protégé of Eaton's. For years he had responded with friendly ridicule to Eaton's confidential efforts to interest him in the remote Owens Valley. Now, however, Mulholland urgently begged Eaton to "show me this water supply."

In the meantime the United States Reclamation Service had formed a plan to irrigate the Owens Valley under the terms of the Newlands Act. When the federal agency refused to cooperate with Eaton as a private speculator and developer, he agreed to sell his interests to the city of Los Angeles. He also agreed to act as the city's confidential agent in purchasing further lands in Owens Valley necessary for an aqueduct. This he proceeded to do under the guise of buying lands for ranching purposes. The real purpose was to be kept secret as long as possible in order to prevent speculative increases in the price of the land.

The first public knowledge of the aqueduct project came in a long, detailed, and enthusiastic article in the *Los Angeles Times* on July 19, 1905. Not long afterward the *Los Angeles Examiner*, outraged that the *Times* had been permitted to scoop its rivals, published sensational charges of collusion and conspiracy.

Two years before, a syndicate including Harrison Gray Otis, Edwin T. Earl, Henry E. Huntington, William G. Kerckhoff, and others had acquired options to buy extensive lands in the San Fernando Valley. Under the Owens Valley Aqueduct plan, now revealed, a reservoir just north of Los Angeles would be adjacent to these lands and would provide water for their irrigation as well as for the city's domestic supply. The whole aqueduct project, the *Examiner* charged, had been conceived by the members of this San Fernando land syndicate for their own speculative profit.

This charge, though periodically revived ever since, was based on an erroneous conclusion. The evidence is clear that in 1903 when this group of wealthy men had acquired the San Fernando land options, Eaton's dream of an aqueduct, if they had yet heard of it at all, was not the basis of their plan. Rather, they were acting on inside information from Henry E. Huntington that he was about to build a new line of the Pacific Electric into the San Fernando Valley. The same men were employing this highly profitable technique of group investment in several other prospective suburbs of Los Angeles at this same time.

In a special election in September 1905 the voters of the city overwhelmingly approved an issue of bonds for the beginning of the Owens Valley project. At the end of still another summer of frightening water shortage, the citizens of Los Angeles were in no mood to vote against a plan that promised them an adequate water supply.

The farmers and townspeople of the Owens Valley now began a bitter campaign of denunciation which they would continue for decades, charging that the aqueduct was a corrupt scheme to enrich a few of the leading capitalists of Los Angeles by seizing the water that would be needed for the agricultural development of the Owens Valley and using it to irrigate the San Fernando Valley instead. The federal government sided with the city. President Roosevelt and Chief Forester Pinchot were persuaded that the whole future growth of Los Angeles was more important than the interests of "a few settlers in Owens Valley." In 1908, to prevent homestead entries in the path of the proposed aqueduct, Roosevelt ordered the extension of the Sierra National Forest eastward to include the prospective right-of-way, even though the only trees in the region were those planted by the settlers themselves.

Under the direction of City Engineer Mulholland the construction of the 233-mile aqueduct began in 1908 and ended 5 years later, at a cost within his estimate of $25 million. Unfortunately the aqueduct took its water directly out of the lower Owens River. If a year-to-year storage reservoir in Long Valley had been built when the aqueduct was constructed, or soon afterward, enough water could have been provided to meet the needs of Owens Valley, along with those of the city, for some time to come, and much bitterness could have been avoided. But Fred Eaton had demanded a price of at least $1 million for his Long Valley land, and Mulholland, breaking his old friendship with Eaton, had denounced the price as too high and advised the city not to pay it.

Unidentified saboteurs dynamited the Owens Valley-Los Angeles Aqueduct 14 times in 1927. *(Courtesy of the Bancroft Library.)*

In the early 1920s a new cycle of dry years and the continuing rapid growth of Los Angeles's population led the city to siphon off virtually the entire flow of the river, and in 1924 some residents of Owens Valley began to dramatize their protests with a campaign of sabotage which later culminated in the dynamiting of several sections of the aqueduct.

Mulholland later succeeded in negotiating a compromise price for Long Valley, and a personal reconciliation, with Fred Eaton. In 1941, several years after the deaths of Eaton and Mulholland, the dam in Long Valley was completed at last. The volume of water in the Owens River was also increased by extending a long tunnel northward to tap the streams flowing into the Mono basin.

ORIGINS OF THE BOULDER CANYON PROJECT

George Chaffey's Imperial Canal and Willaim Mulholland's Owens Valley Aqueduct were temporary and inadequate answers to southern California's insatiable thirst. Seeking flood control and increased irrigation for the Imperial Valley and water for the coastal cities, southern California turned its attention to a vast project for the development of the Colorado River.

That remarkable stream, in the agelong process of carving the world's most spectacular canyons, becomes loaded with reddish silt and thus takes on the color that led the Spaniards to name it the *Rio Colorado,* or Red River. The distinguished geologist John Wesley Powell was the first to explore the whole length of the main river, in 1869, as leader of an expedition that managed to survive a trip through the rapids in large rowboats.

In 1904 Powell's nephew Arthur Powell Davis, an engineer for the United States Reclamation Service, conceived a broad proposal for the development of the lower Colorado under the unified control of the federal government, with a great dam to store the floods and to serve as the heart of the project. The first strong public support for this plan came from the people of the Imperial Valley, who lived in terror of floods. They had not forgotten the catastrophe that began in 1905 when the river burst into the Imperial Canal and created the Salton Sea before it was finally checked in 1907.

The settlers of the valley had many reasons to be dissatisfied with the Imperial Canal, particularly with the fact that its source and the first 50 miles of its flow were in Mexican territory. The Mexican government, instead of contributing to the efforts at flood control, levied duties on the American materials imported for that purpose. It also required that half the canal's water be reserved for the irrigation of Mexican lands, and it held down the price of the water used south of the border, so that a much higher price had to be charged on the American side.

The Imperial Canal, in the meantime, had been acquired by the Southern Pacific at a receiver's sale. In 1911 the voters of the Imperial Valley formed the Imperial Irrigation District—the largest of its kind—and approved a bond issue to buy the canal from the railroad. Soon afterward they began to agitate for an all-American canal, to be built north of the border.

Early in 1922, Secretary of the Interior Fall joined with Arthur Powell Davis, now director of the Reclamation Service, in recommending an extensive plan. Soon afterward the proposals in the Fall-Davis report were introduced in Congress in the form of the Swing-Johnson bill. Phil Swing, who had served for several years as chief counsel of the Imperial Irrigation District and had then been elected to Congress, sponsored the bill in the House, and Hiram Johnson gave it his powerful support in the Senate. Six years later it was finally approved as the Boulder Canyon Project Act, but only after a long and bitter struggle in both houses.

Under this plan the federal government was to construct a dam in or near Boulder Canyon, a plant for generating hydroelectric power, and an all-American canal just north of the Mexican border from the river to the Imperial Valley. Leasing of the power to public and private agencies in the region would repay the government for the cost of building the dam, and the Imperial Irrigation District would ultimately repay the cost of building the canal.

The city of Los Angeles soon joined with the Imperial Valley in ardent support of the Boulder Canyon project. William Mulholland warned Los Angeles that its growth was outstripping its supply of water from the Owens Valley, and he called for the building of a much larger aqueduct as soon as possible, with the Colorado River as its source. Federal construction of the proposed high dam between Nevada and Arizona would greatly increase the feasibility and greatly lower the cost of a municipal aqueduct reservoir farther downstream.

On the other hand, the federal project aroused tremendous opposition. The first difficulty to be surmounted was a wrangle among the seven states in the Colorado River area. The upper-basin states of Wyoming, Colorado, Utah, and New Mexico complained that all the benefits would go to the lower-basin states, Arizona, Nevada, and California, whose development would be so stimulated that they would gain an unfair share of the water under the laws of prior appropriation. In November 1922 Secretary of Commerce Herbert Hoover persuaded representatives of all seven states to agree to the Colorado River Compact, assuring the upper basin of a permanent claim to about half the flow of the river. Six of the state legislatures ratified the compact, but Arizona balked and began an opposition to the Boulder Canyon project that continued for years and a quarrel with California that continued for decades.

Further opposition came from the American owners of irrigated lands in Mexico, of whom the most notable was Harry Chandler, the son-in-law, heir, and successor of Harrison Gray Otis. Chandler headed a syndicate that owned 862,000 acres of land in Lower California, mainly in the region of the Imperial Canal. Not surprisingly, he and his *Los Angeles Times* denounced the Swing-Johnson bill as a socialistic menace to free American enterprise, but as Phil Swing remarked, Chandler was "building Boulder Dam by his opposition to it." The project was very popular in southern California, and Chandler's motives were very obvious, as William Randolph Hearst's *Los Angeles Examiner* often pointed out.

PUBLIC OR PRIVATE POWER?

Of all the sources of opposition to the Boulder Canyon project, however, the most formidable were the private power companies, not only in the southwest but throughout the country. The struggle of private power and light interests against federal development of the lower Colorado can be understood only in connection with their simultaneous battle to keep the government from "entering the power business" in the Tennessee Valley. During the first World War the government had constructed a dam on the Tennessee River in northern Alabama to provide power for wartime nitrate production. In the 1920s the Senate passed a bill to create a public corporation that would expand the government's existing facilities to develop and sell power and light, in competition with the private utility companies in the region. In 1928 President Coolidge vetoed the bill as socialistic. President Hoover opposed it on the same ground, and the creation of the Tennessee Valley Authority had to await the coming of the New Deal.

For the Boulder Canyon project, on the other hand, the Swing-Johnson bill offered a compromise under which the federal government would not act as the distributor of the power, but would lease it to private or municipal corporations, which would build their own transmission lines. Nevertheless the private companies fought the measure, largely for two reasons. The huge project would reduce the price of power in the southwest by increasing the supply of it, and much of the power would go to the municipally owned electric system of the city of Los Angeles, thus encouraging its growth at the expense of private companies, and giving aid and comfort to the "public power movement" in general.

That public ownership and distribution of electric power had come into existence in Los Angeles, a city as passionately committed to private enterprise as any community in the United States, is one of the many striking paradoxes of California history. It was even more remarkable in view of the fact that in northern California the private Pacific Gas and Electric Company (PG&E) achieved an almost complete monopoly over the distribution of power and light. In 1925, after a long controversy, the San Francisco board of supervisors turned over the power from Hetch Hetchy to PG&E. This arrangement was carried out even though Congress in a section of the Raker Act of 1913 had flatly forbidden the city to dispose of the power to any private company. Moreover, San Francisco made an almost incredibly bad bargain. PG&E paid the city $2.4 million a year for the Hetch Hetchy power, and then retailed the same power for $9 million a year. Nevertheless, in a long series of elections San Francisco's voters perennially failed to provide the necessary majorities for the bonds that would have financed a city-owned electrical distribution system.

In sharp contrast, the City of Los Angeles Bureau of Power and Light gradually crowded out and bought out the distribution systems of the Southern California Edison Company, Henry E. Huntington's Pacific Light and Power Company, and the Los Angeles Gas and Electric Corporation, in a process that those companies regarded as not merely creeping, but galloping, socialism.

"Socialized" ownership and distribution of electricity in Los Angeles had its origin in the Owens Valley water project. Chief Engineer Mulholland had pointed out that in order to ensure its ability to pay for the Owens Valley Aqueduct, the city would have to sell not only the water but also the highly valuable byproduct, power. He had also believed that the city must sell directly to the consumer, because it could not afford to share the revenues with private companies. The bond election of 1910 provided for the building of a municipally owned generating system, and in 1914 the voters authorized the city to buy the private distribution systems. When some of the private companies resisted for a time and others announced that they would hold out to the bitter end, the city built its own competing distribution system and ultimately forced them all to sell. By the late 1930s, with a great new supply of power from the Colorado added to the supply obtained from Owens Valley, Los Angeles had a single, complete, integrated, municipal power and light system, furnishing cheap electricity to every consumer in the city.

Oddly enough, Job Harriman and his socialist followers had opposed the entire Owens Valley project on the theory that it was a plot for the further enrichment of a syndicate of land speculators. Thus for a time the socialists of Los Angeles had found themselves in a strange alliance with the private power companies against a public enterprise. In any case it was not socialistic doctrine that induced Los Angeles to adopt public power. The reasons were pragmatic, not dogmatic. Arid Los Angeles desperately needed water, which had to be brought from great distances at great cost. The sale of power would help to pay the enormous cost of the water.

The liveliest of the congressional debates on the Swing-Johnson bill took place in February 1927, when it came so near to passage in the Senate that its opponents resorted to a filibuster. Senator Lawrence C. Phipps of Colorado, who had interests in several electric companies, joined with the Arizona senators and others in keeping the bill from coming to a vote. But the filibuster also served to focus national attention on the issue, and Senator Hiram Johnson countered the power companies' arguments against the project with oratory as vigorous and colorful as any he had ever directed against the Southern Pacific.

Secretary of Commerce Herbert Hoover, as a Californian and a rival of Hiram Johnson for leadership of the Republican party both in California and in national politics, could hardly have opposed the Boulder Canyon project, and although he was deeply troubled by the charge that in building a great power plant the federal government would be dealing a heavy blow to a leading American private industry, he could see no other way to pay for the dam. Hoover's election to the presidency, and the knowledge that he favored the project, finally ended the long battle over its adoption, and the Swing-Johnson bill became law on December 21, 1928.

HOOVER DAM

In its final form the Boulder Canyon Project Act of 1928 provided that the principal dam might be built either in Boulder Canyon or a few miles downstream in Black Canyon. The government's engineers chose Black Canyon. Thus the name of "Boulder Dam," unofficially used during the years of debate on the project, became inaccurate. The official choice of a name for a federal dam was a time-honored prerogative of the secretary of the interior. Dr. Ray Lyman Wilbur, who held that office under President Hoover, chose the name that seemed to him in every way most eminently suitable—Hoover Dam.

However, Harold L. Ickes succeeded Dr. Wilbur when the mighty structure was about half finished, and to the confusion of cartographers and the fury of Republicans the self-styled Old Curmudgeon of the New Deal was determined "to give Boulder dam its original and proper name, which my predecessor in office attempted feloniously to take from it." It was as "Boulder Dam" that President Franklin D. Roosevelt officially dedicated the structure, on September 30, 1935. In 1947 the Republican Eightieth Congress passed a bill to restore the name of "Hoover Dam," and President Truman signed the bill into law. Nevertheless, usage has sometimes continued to vary with partisan preference—or merely with confused recollection.

When it was finished, and for many years afterward, the dam was the highest and largest in the world. The project was so great that neither the government nor any one private contractor was willing to undertake its construction alone. The successful bid came from several western engineering firms newly allied for the purpose. Felix Kahn of San Francisco suggested the name of the new group, "Six Companies, Inc.," after "the famous tribunal to

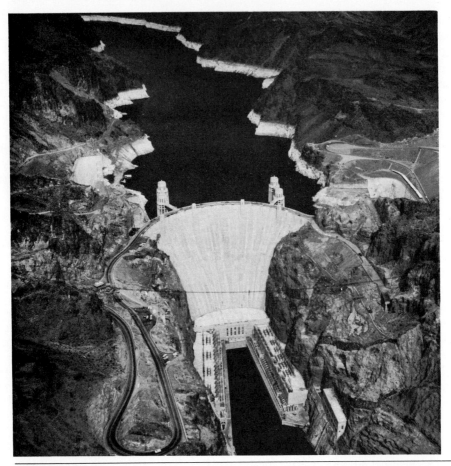

Hoover Dam. *(Photograph by E. E. Hertzog. Courtesy of the United States Bureau of Reclamation.)*

which the Chinese tongs in San Francisco had submitted their differences in preference to warring with hatchet-men." Henry J. Kaiser was made chairman of the board of directors, and Frank Crowe was general superintendent of construction.

One of the participants, Frank Waters, was a man with a talent for writing as well as for engineering, and in his book on *The Colorado* he described some of the problems the Six Companies faced: " . . . sheer canyon walls so high that they distorted perspective; the lack of even a sand bar for initial footage; the desert on each side without housing or transportation facilities; and greatest of all, the terrific current of the silt-choked river." When bonding companies at first refused to touch the project because they considered the working conditions unendurable, a fully air-conditioned model city was built to house 5000 workers. To divert the river from the construction site, four bypass tunnels had to be built through the canyon walls, two on each side. Each of these tunnels was a mile long and 50 feet in diameter with a 3-foot concrete lining.

Before any concrete could be poured for the foundation of the dam, the riverbed had to be cleaned down to the bare rock. Then it had to be kept clean and dry during the whole period of construction.

When the dam first began to rise, it did not resemble a dam at all, but a jumble of wooden boxes. If the concrete had been poured into a single block, the structure would have taken 125 years to cool and the expansion would have split it apart. An ammonia refrigeration plant had to be built, and 662 miles of tubing, carrying water just above the freezing point, had to be run between and through the huge concrete blocks.

As the dam neared completion, it was still honeycombed with narrow galleries. Workers walked a quarter of a mile through the base of it. To its crest, they rode a small elevator to the height of a 60-story building. As Waters recalled, it was "a labyrinth of cold passages; the dark interior of a great pyramid; the heart of a stone mountain; the depths of a mine. . . . Then the tubing was removed, the corridors were pumped full of concrete, and the dam was sealed."

At the base of the dam was the world's largest powerhouse to date, containing the world's largest turbines and generators. They began to operate on September 11, 1936, when President Roosevelt pushed a golden key. Behind the dam was the world's largest reservoir, Lake Mead; its capacity was 30 million acre-feet, or nearly 10 trillion gallons. Vast as the reservoir was, engineers soberly pointed out that it was doomed to impermanence. They warned that the Colorado, often described as "a little too thick to drink and a little too thin to plow," would fill Lake Mead with silt within 300 years and that over the next 30 centuries the whole process would have to be repeated 10 times, at each of the 10 other possible sites.

THE COLORADO RIVER AQUEDUCT

In 1923 Los Angeles and several neighboring communities had begun to plan the formation of a metropolitan water district for the purpose of building the world's longest and largest domestic water supply line from the Colorado River to the coastal basin. In the discussion of water projects in southern California it had become impossible to avoid the constant repetition of the phrase "the world's largest."

The Metropolitan Water District of Southern California, officially organized in 1928, originally included Los Angeles and 10 nearby cities. Many others later joined. Los Angeles itself had already grown from its original pueblo area of 4 square leagues, or 28 square miles, to an area of more than 400 square miles, through many piecemeal annexations in which the need for water and the success of Los Angeles in acquiring it had been the prime factors.

The $220 million bond issue for the great aqueduct came before the district's voters on September 29, 1931. Though the concern of most of the voters was with water for domestic use, its role in the region's industrial development was equally vital. In 1919, for example, the Goodyear Tire and Rubber Company had become the first major industrial concern to locate a branch plant in Los Angeles because the city could promise the 8 million gallons of water a day that the plant would need. The company had rejected both San Francisco and San Diego because of the slower development of their water projects. In the crucial petroleum industry, 77,000 gallons of water were needed to refine 100 barrels of oil. Later improvements in equipment would enable refineries to recover much of the water and use it repeatedly, but in 1930 the Union Oil Company plant at Long Beach was still using more water than all the rest of the city.

With such compelling arguments in its favor, the huge bond issue passed by more than five to one, even though the market for municipal bonds had been steadily declining since the great crash of 1929. The Reconstruction Finance Corporation, created by Congress in 1932, came to the rescue of the project and ultimately bought almost the entire issue. The dam was finished on schedule in 1938, and in 1941 the aqueduct began to deliver water to the coastal cities.

San Diego remained outside the Metropolitan Water District for several years, partly because it hoped to get water from a branch of the All-American Canal. The city had often shown desperate ingenuity in its long struggle with its water problem. In December 1915 in the midst of a particularly serious drought it had even signed a contract with a professional rainmaker, Charles M. Hatfield. Promising to fill the Morena reservoir for a fee of $10,000, Hatfield built a number of "evaporating tanks," presumably to send up fumes from some combination of chemicals that remained his professional secret. A few weeks later a cloudburst overflowed the reservoir, washed out a smaller dam below it, and flooded a part of the town. The city council refused to pay Hatfield his fee; they pointed out that he had contracted to fill the reservoir, not to flood the community.

The growth of San Diego during World War II finally compelled the city and its neighbors to form a subgroup of the Metropolitan Water District of Southern California, and in 1945 construction work began on the first of two branch lines from the Colorado River Aqueduct to the San Diego region.

THE CENTRAL VALLEY PROJECT

Proposals for a large government project to aid the advance of irrigation in the great Central Valley were made as early as the 1870s. Strong support for the idea began to crystallize in 1920 when Col. Robert Bradford Marshall, chief geographer of the United States Geological Survey but acting in a private capacity, offered the state of California a broad and challenging plan. In its largest features, this was a proposal "to turn the Sacramento River into the San Joaquin Valley" through great canals and to regulate the flow of the upper Sacramento with a high dam near Redding.

On the subject of electric power, the "Marshall plan" was vague; it said only that "the sale of . . . power at fair rates" would repay much of the cost of the water developments. Many progressives urged that the state government should undertake the public distribution of the power produced by the state-financed water projects, but PG&E was able to block every one of a long series of bills and initiative propositions in the 1920s that would have put the state into the power business. PG&E was a consolidation of more than 400 smaller corporations; it had annexed virtually all the power and light companies of northern and central California. To defeat the proposals for state distribution of water and power PG&E spent enormous sums through such dummy organizations as the Greater California League. The Greater California League was Eustace Cullinan, a San Francisco attorney for PG&E. South of the Tehachapis the Southern California Edison Company spent freely through a similar front called the People's Economy League.

PG&E also used various "community relations" techniques in its battles against public power. One was a "practical incentive" plan designed to gain the "friendship and cooperation" of local bankers. According to a letter from its president, A. F. Hockenbeamer, to an eastern utility executive who wished to know the secrets of PG&E's political success, the company had "accounts with 230 country banks scattered all over our territory," and while this policy kept "an average of around a million and a half dollars tied up in balances in these country depositories, we believe it is well worth while. . . . Incidentally, we require no interest on these deposits."

In 1933 the legislature adopted the California Central Valley Project Act. The clinching argument was that California's economy lay prostrate in the grip of the depression and that the Central Valley Project could act as an emergency rescue measure. The state at that time had no real hope of being able to pay for the project, and the only hope lay in persuading the federal government to assume the cost. In 1935 the Federal Bureau of Reclamation assumed the responsibility. Construction began in 1937.

The original Central Valley Project, authorized in the 1930s and regarded as the first phase of a much larger program, came into operation as a coordinated system in the 1950s. Its main features were three dams, five canals, and two power transmission lines. The most impressive unit was Shasta Dam, impounding the waters of the Sacramento, McCloud, and Pit rivers in Shasta Lake. Keswick Dam, 9 miles downstream on the Sacramento, was designed to serve both as a regulating afterbay and for the generation of additional power. Friant Dam was built on the San Joaquin River, 20 miles northeast of Fresno.

From a point just below Friant Dam the Friant-Kern Canal extended 160 miles southeastward to the region of Bakersfield. The Madera Canal ran 37 miles northwestward from Friant Dam. On the west side of the valley the Delta-Mendota Canal carried Sacramento River water 120 miles south to the Mendota pool at the great bend of the San Joaquin River, to replace water formerly taken from the San Joaquin. The Contra Costa Canal, 58 miles long, brought fresh water from the delta to agricultural, industrial, and urban users

MAJOR CALIFORNIA WATER PROJECTS
1900-1980

·················· = municipal

————————— = federal

- - - - - - - = state

+·+·+·+·+· = Central Valley
Project power lines

⌒ = dams

▨ = Metropolitan Water
District of Southern
California

Shasta Lake
Shasta Dam
Keswick Dam

Tehama-Colusa Canal (1971)

Oroville

Putah South Canal (1959)

Lake Tahoe

Sacramento

Contra Costa Canal (1940)

Mokelumne Aq. (1929)

San Francisco

(1962)

Tracy

Mono Lake

Hetch Hetchy Aqueduct (1934)

Kings

Madera Canal (1944)

Delta-Mendota Canal (1951)

Friant Dam

Mono Extension (1940)

Owens River

California Aqueduct (1968)

Friant-Kern Canal (1949)

Los Angeles Aqueduct (1913)

California Aq. (1971)

Bakersfield

Lake Mead
Hoover Dam

Davis Dam

California Aq. (1973)

Lake Havasu
Parker Dam

Los Angeles

Colorado River Aq.

(1941)

Coachella Canal (1949)

First San Diego Aq. (1947)

Salton Sea

Second San Diego Aq. (1960)

San Diego

Imperial Dam

All-American Canal (1941)

between Antioch and Martinez, and the Delta Cross Channel carried Sacramento River water to the intake of the Delta-Mendota Canal.

Through all the years when the dams and canals were being built, PG&E managed to block every congressional appropriation for government-owned transmission lines. When the generating plant at Shasta Dam began to produce power in 1944, Secretary of the Interior Ickes had no choice but to negotiate a 5-year agreement for the sale of all of this power to PG&E. Repeatedly the company's officials asserted before congressional committees that the Bureau of Reclamation had a "grandiose scheme" for "the socialization of the power industry in northern and central California." As the Southern Pacific had done a few decades earlier, PG&E denounced government infringement on free enterprise, although in both cases it was really monopoly, not free enterprise, which the corporation was fighting to preserve.

At last, through a series of agreements beginning in 1951, PG&E and the federal authorities solved the problem by entering into an uneasy partnership. The Bureau of Reclamation continued to sell power to PG&E; the company agreed, for the first time, to permit the use of its lines for the delivery of federal power from Shasta Dam to the Sacramento Municipal Utility District; and the Bureau of Reclamation was finally able to build its two long-projected transmission lines from Shasta and Keswick dams to its own plant at Tracy for use in pumping water through the Delta-Mendota and Contra Costa canals.

Even more controversial than the power question was another issue that involved the federal reclamation laws. Ever since the Newlands Act of 1902 it had been the government's policy to limit the amount of water that any one owner of land could obtain from a federal reclamation project. The maximum was enough water to irrigate 160 acres, or 320 acres in the case of a married couple.

In California, very little was said publicly about this limitation until 1944, and the large landowners indulged in much wishful thinking to the effect that it would never actually be applied to the Central Valley Project. Then, however, the secretary of the interior began to comply with the federal laws that required him to negotiate contracts with irrigation districts, and to include the 160-acre limit in these contracts.

The large landowners of California, including many powerful corporations, now launched a campaign to have the acreage limit set aside. They formed a political coalition with PG&E, supporting that company on power issues in return for its support of their viewpoint on the acreage matter, and this formidable alliance mounted a concerted attack on the Bureau of Reclamation and the Department of the Interior.

In the years of intense debate that followed, much confusion resulted from popular misconceptions, sometimes deliberately fostered. One of these was the widespread and entirely erroneous notion that the 160-acre limit restricted "the amount of land a man could own." What the federal laws actually did was to restrict the amount of federally subsidized water that any one landowner could buy. In 1951, for example, the average price of the best grade of irrigation water from the Central Valley Project was about $2.50 per acre-foot, while the average price for the same grade of water from other sources was $6.77 per acre-foot.

Another misconception was that the owners of land in excess of 160 acres could receive no "project water" at all unless they contracted to sell the "excess" land. The truth was that the larger owners were free to buy cheap federal water for a 160-acre *portion* of their land. They could irrigate the rest of it with "commercial" or "non-project" water. Or they *could* buy federal water for the larger acreage. It was only if they chose the latter alternative that they were required to sign a contract to sell the "excess" acres within a certain period of years, at prices that would not allow them an unfair profit from the increase in land values resulting from the federal project.

Congress repeatedly declined to repeal the 160-acre limitation, and the large Central Valley landholders sought relief in the courts. In 1957 the supreme court of California ruled in their favor by a majority of four to three in the test case of the Ivanhoe Irrigation District. The acreage provision in the federal reclamation laws, in the opinion of the majority of the California justices, was unconstitutional. "It is an unlawful discrimination," they argued, "to limit the extent of the right of an owner of real property to the use and enjoyment of his property right, including the water right which may be attached thereto, on the sole basis of the amount of property he owns."

But in 1958 the United States Supreme Court unanimously reversed this judgment. The claim of discrimination, said the highest court, "overlooks the purpose for which the project was designed." That purpose was "to benefit people, not land," and to distribute the benefits "in accordance with the greatest good of the greatest number of individuals. The limitation ensures that this enormous expenditure will not go in disproportionate share to a few individuals with large land holdings. Moreover, it prevents the use of the federal reclamation service for speculative purposes. In short, the excess acreage provision acts as a ceiling, imposed equally upon all participants, on the federal subsidy that is being bestowed." The most significant effect of this decision was to convince most of the political leaders of California that the massive water projects of the 1960s and after must be built with state rather than federal funds, so that the larger units of land could obtain cheap, publicly subsidized water.

SELECTED BIBLIOGRAPHY

Linnie March Wolfe, *Son of the Wilderness; the life of John Muir* (1945) is an excellent biography. On conservation as a national movement in this period see Samuel P. Hays, *Conservation and the Gospel of Efficiency: The Progressive Conservation Movement, 1890–1920* (1959) and Elmo R. Richardson, *The Politics of Conservation; Crusades and Controversies, 1897–1913* (1963).

On the Hetch Hetchy problem, see Kendrick A. Clements, "Politics and the Park: San Francisco's Fight for Hetch Hetchy, 1908–1913," *Pacific Historical Review*, XLVII

(May 1979), pp. 185–216, and "Engineers and Conservationists in the Progressive Era," *California History*, LVIII (Winter 1979–1980), pp. 282–303; Elmo R. Richardson, "The Struggle for the Valley; California's Hetch Hetchy Controversy," *California Historical Society Quarterly*, XXXVIII (September 1959), pp. 249–258; and Holway R. Jones, *John Muir and the Sierra Club: The Battle for Yosemite* (1965).

The best treatments of the Owens Valley–Los Angeles Aqueduct are in Abraham Hoffman, *Vision or Villainy: Origins of the Owens Valley–Los Angeles Water Controversy* (1981); Remi A. Nadeau, *The Water Seekers* (1950); Vincent Ostrom, *Water & Politics: A Study of Water Policies and Administration in the Development of Los Angeles* (1953); and William L. Kahrl, "The Politics of California Water: Owens Valley and the Los Angeles Aqueduct, 1900–1927," *California Historical Quarterly*, LV (Spring and Summer 1976), pp. 2–25. Willie A. Chalfant, *The Story of Inyo* (1933); Morrow Mayo, in the chapter called "The Rape of Owens Valley" in his *Los Angeles* (1933); and Carey McWilliams, *Southern California Country* (1946) revived the syndicate conspiracy version of the Owens Valley project. W. W. Robinson disagreed in "Myth Making in the Los Angeles Area," *Southern California Quarterly*, XLV (March 1963), pp. 83–94.

Paul L. Kleinsorge, *The Boulder Canyon Project; Historical and Legal Aspects* (1941) is a thorough study by an economist. Norris Hundley, *Water in the West: The Colorado River Compact and the Politics of Water* (1975); Beverly B. Moeller, *Phil Swing and Boulder Dam* (1971); and Donald C. Swain, *Federal Conservation Policy, 1921–1933* (1963) discuss the national political problems. Also useful are Norris Hundley, *Dividing the Waters: A Century of Controversy between the United States and Mexico* (1966); John U. Terrell, *War for the Colorado River* (two volumes, 1965); and Erwin Cooper, *Aqueduct Empire* (1968). Frank Waters, *The Colorado* (1946) is particularly notable for its vivid descriptions of the building of what was then the world's largest dam.

Vincent Ostrom, *Water & Politics: A Study of Water Policies and Administration in the Development of Los Angeles* (1953) and Nelson S. Van Valen, "A Neglected Aspect of the Owens River Aqueduct Story: The Inception of the Los Angeles Municipal Electric System," *Southern California Quarterly*, LIX (Spring 1977), pp. 85–109, deal with the city's adoption of public power as well as with the development of the Metropolitan Water District and the building of the Colorado River Aqueduct. On the rejection of public power in San Francisco, see Florence R. Monroy, "Water and Power in San Francisco since 1900; a Study in Municipal Government," M.A. thesis, University of California, Berkeley (1944). John W. Noble, *Its Name was M.U.D.* (1970) is a history of the East Bay Municipal Utility District.

Useful works on the Central Valley Project are Marion Clawson, *The Effect of the Central Valley Project on the Agricultural and Industrial Economy and on the Social Character of California* (1945); Mary Montgomery and Marion Clawson, *History of Legislation and Policy Formation of the Central Valley Project* (1946); Robert de Roos, *The Thirsty Land* (1948); "The Central Valley Project and Related Problems," an edition of the *California Law Review*, XXXVIII (October 1950); Hugh G. Hansen, *Central Valley Project: Federal or State?* (1955); Clair Engle, *Central Valley Project Documents* (two parts, 1956); and three Ph.D. theses, University of California, Berkeley: Jack T. Casey, "Legislative History of the Central Valley Project" (1949); Alten B. Davis, "The Excess Law in the Central Valley of California" (1962); and Charles E. Coate, "Water, Power, and Politics in the Central Valley Project" (1969).

Charles M. Coleman, *P.G. and E. of California; the Centennial Story of Pacific Gas and Electric Company, 1852–1952* (1952) refers to the company's political activities only in very general and favorable terms. More detailed information, and a more critical view of the political methods of PG&E and other private utility corporations, may be found in Carl D. Thompson, *Confessions of the Power Trust* (1932), based on the hearings of the Federal Trade Commission.

Most of the arguments against the 160-acre limit were collected and elaborated in Sheridan Downey, *They Would Rule the Valley* (1947), "they" being the United States Bureau of Reclamation. The opposite viewpoint is well summarized in Paul S. Taylor, "Excess Land Law: Pressure versus Principle," *California Law Review*, XLVII (August 1959), pp. 499–541, and "Excess Land Law: Calculated Circumvention," same journal, LII (December 1964), pp. 978–1014. See also Clayton R. Koppes, "Public Water, Private Land: Origins of the Acreage Limitation Controversy, 1933–1953," *Pacific Historical Review*, XLVII (November 1978), pp. 607–636.

THE GREAT DEPRESSION AND POLITICS

The prosperity of the 1920s was not well distributed. Proportionally, too much of the national income was in profits and too little in wages, and therefore America's capacity to produce exceeded its capacity to consume. During the 1920s American individualism had too often degenerated into irresponsibility and greed. One manifestation of this trend was the urge to get rich quickly and easily by gambling in the stock market. As banks, investment trusts, and millions of individual speculators crowded into the market with borrowed money, they bid up the prices of corporation stocks to levels that were further and further beyond any meaningful relation to the value of the companies' properties or to their actual profits from the production of goods and services. The result was the great crash of October 1929, which marked the beginning of the worst and longest depression in American history.

In California, the number of freight-car loadings in 1933 was less than half of what it had been in 1928, and the number of building permits was less than one-ninth of the peak figure of 1925. The depression spread from Wall Street to San Francisco's Montgomery Street and then to many a small town's Main Street. California farm income sank in 1932 to scarcely more than half of what it had been in 1929, and there were thousands of mortgage foreclosures. With the spread of mass unemployment in both city and country, the number of Californians dependent upon public relief in 1934 was more than 1,250,000—about one-fifth of the whole population of the state. But no mere statistics can convey the real meaning of the great depression. Its meaning was in the suffering, anxiety, and grief of the millions whose lives it blighted.

In California politics, reaction to this disaster came slowly at first. Then it became extreme and frantic. But through the whole decade of depression that followed the crash, politics and government in California remained confused, demoralized, and ineffectual.

"SUNNY JIM"

The choice of a governor in 1930, the first year of the depression, represented politics as worse than usual. James Rolph, Jr., had been mayor of San Francisco for 19 years, since his first election in 1911. His early career as mayor was quite creditable, but in 1918 he lost the fortune that he had made in the shipping business, and his health and efficiency began to decline. During the 1920s he still commanded great popular affection, mainly because of the convivial folksiness of his innumerable appearances as the city's official host, greeter, and master of ceremonies. More and more often he was in a state of cheerful insobriety. In that "era of wonderful nonsense" he seemed a highly successful large-city mayor, but as governor, he was unable to cope with an emergency on the scale of the great depression.

Rolph's most important policy as governor was his opposition to tax reform. His views on taxation were those of the most conservative wing of the business community, and he was heavily in debt to one of San Francisco's leading bankers, who was also one of his closest political advisers.

The legislature of 1933 adopted a sales tax, with Rolph's approval, in order to provide state support for the public schools, which were in a financial crisis because of the shrinkage of local tax revenues. But when the legislature also passed an income tax measure, Rolph vetoed it. The burden of the sales tax fell heavily on the poor, and the inclusion of food among the items subject to the tax was especially resented. Corner grocers, ringing up small sales, bitterly reminded their customers that they must add "a penny for Jimmy."

In a desperate and deluded attempt to regain his popularity, Rolph made the worst mistake of his career. He openly abetted and defended a lynching.

There had been more lynchings in California than in any state outside the south, and more lynchings of white men than in any state whatever. Most of the California cases occurred in the early decades of the American period, but 59 men were lynched in California between 1875 and 1934—an average of one a year. Fifty of these were white, six were Indians, and three were Chinese; in contrast with the situation in the south, the California lynching victims were generally white men accused of murder rather than black people accused of sexual assault.

Throughout the country in the early 1930s there was a wave of kidnappings, including that of the Lindbergh baby in 1932. At San Jose, on November 26, 1933, two men who had confessed the kidnapping and murder of the son of a wealthy local merchant were being held in the county jail. When there was talk of mob action, Governor Rolph made a public "promise" that he would never call out the National Guard "to protect those two fellows." A few hours later, with this open incitement from the governor, a mob broke into the jail, beat the sheriff unconscious, and hanged the two prisoners to trees in a nearby park.

Rolph then asserted in another public statement that "This is the best lesson California has ever given the country." He promised to pardon anyone who might be arrested for "the good job," and added that he would like to release all convicted kidnappers from the state prisons into the hands of "those fine, patriotic San Jose citizens who know how to handle such a situation." The lynchers, Rolph theorized, were men with "pioneer blood in their veins," who "were probably reminded of the metage of justice by the vigilantes in the early days of San Francisco's history." As the *New York Times* remarked in a scathing editorial, Judge Lynch had always been a shadowy, unidentified figure. Now there was an actual and visible Governor Lynch.

In 1934 Rolph began another of his picturesque election campaigns. In burnished leather boots and a red sash he inaugurated every fiesta, parade, and rodeo. But he collapsed during a precampaign tour and died on June 2. Lieutenant Governor Frank Merriam, a Long Beach real estate agent, succeeded him as governor.

SOCIAL MESSIAHS

Californians in the early 1930s were desperately searching for new leadership. It was increasingly clear that they could expect no help from the administrations of President Hoover and Governor Rolph, and the depression was growing steadily worse.

The sufferings of old people were especially severe. Thousands of them had come from other parts of the country to retire in Los Angeles or its suburbs. In the 1920s when they had been able to live fairly comfortably, before they lost their savings in the depression, most of them had been conservative in their economic and political ideas, and their interest in colorful leaders had been directed mainly toward religious evangelists. One of these was Sister Aimee Semple McPherson, who preached the "Four Square Gospel" with spectacular theatricality at her Angelus Temple and over her own radio station. Another was the Reverend Robert P. Shuler, who operated a rival station. In 1926 the Reverend Mr. Shuler had led the outcry against Sister Aimee when that somewhat tarnished angel was accused of having spent an illicit vacation in Carmel with her choir director during the time when she claimed to have been kidnapped and held for ransom in Mexico.

During the early 1930s Sister Aimee's following declined, not merely because of her personal indiscretions but because interest was shifting from religious to economic and political evangelism. "Bob" Shuler, who had been an active force in Los Angeles politics for years, maintained his influence by announcing the formation of the Commonwealth party, a new political movement under his leadership.

Technocracy, which advocated a new society based on scientific management, aroused so much enthusiasm in Los Angeles that chief technocrat Howard Scott moved his headquarters there from the east. In 1933 a group of unemployed businesspeople broke off from the technocratic persuasion to establish the Utopian Society. The utopians drew an overflow crowd for a pageant in the Hollywood Bowl, a spectacle that resembled some of Mrs. McPherson's productions at Angelus Temple except that it dramatized the triumph not of Good over Evil but of Abundance over Scarcity.

The founder of a much larger and more enduring new movement was Dr. Francis E. Townsend, an unemployed physician of Long Beach. Unsuccessful in private practice, he had been saved from poverty during the first 3 years of the depression by a job with the city health department. But in 1933 the city discontinued its health services program, and at the age of 66, having worked hard all his life, he was facing destitution. During the next few months he formulated the Townsend Plan and backed it with an organization called Old Age Revolving Pensions, Ltd. All Americans over 60 were to receive pensions of $200 a month, all of which they must spend within 30 days. The money would come from a federal sales tax. This plan, according to Dr. Townsend and his followers, would not only provide a decent living for old people but would also bring general prosperity by restoring "the proper circulation of money."

Though the heart of the movement remained in southern California, Townsend Clubs sprang up all over the nation and soon had a membership of about one and a half million "senior citizens." Their delegates assembled in regional and later in national conventions, where they sang "Onward Townsend Soldiers." To hundreds of thousands of old people the Townsend Clubs brought new hope, new friendships, and a renewed interest in life. The movement quickly became a powerful force in both state and national politics.

LABOR STRIFE

In the agonies of the depression California's long tradition of social violence was reborn in new and bitter struggles between labor and employers.

California labor problems had always been at their worst in agriculture, partly because the growers had always been able to block the development of collective bargaining. When the depression turned most of the farm regions into economic disaster areas, labor relations became worse than ever before. Agricultural workers, ill-fed or unfed, had to suffer the peculiar misery of watching food crops rot because they could not be sold for enough to pay the costs of harvesting and marketing.

Again, as in the days of the IWW, the wretched conditions of the migratory agricultural workers and the complete absence of conventional labor unions opened the door to the most extreme radicals, and the radicals played into the hands of the employers. The Cannery and Agricultural Workers' Industrial Union, which became active in 1933, was avowedly an arm of the Communist party and was openly eager to hasten the disintegration of the capitalist system in agriculture. It provided the leadership for the strikes of the grape pickers at Lodi and the cotton pickers in the southern San Joaquin Valley in 1933 and the vegetable pickers in the Imperial Valley in 1934.

Employer vigilante groups, sometimes deputized by county sheriffs, did not hesitate to use violence in crushing these strikes, and the "union" was dissolved when its Communist leaders were arrested and convicted under the state criminal syndicalism law.

The National Industrial Recovery Act of 1933, in its famous section 7a, recognized the right of employees "to organize and bargain collectively through representatives of their own choosing." In the San Francisco Bay region, where organized labor had once been strong, the unions took courage from the new federal law and set out to regain the power they had lost in the 1920s. When the employers resisted, the struggle became even more violent than in the agricultural regions. Class conflict went to such extremes that police and the National Guard were used to break a strike on the San Francisco waterfront, and in retaliation nearly all the unions in the bay region joined in a general strike in sympathy with the demands of the maritime workers.

The employers in the San Francisco shipping industry had destroyed the power of the International Longshoremen's Association (ILA) in the Bay Area by breaking its strike in 1919. They had used the presence of IWWs and other radicals in several maritime unions as an excuse to destroy unionism itself. From 1919 until 1934 the only longshoremen's union in the San Francisco Bay area was the employer-controlled "Blue Book" union. Hiring was done under the "shape-up" system. The men gathered on the docks each day, and an employer-controlled hiring boss chose the ones who would get the day's work. The system was riddled with bribery, favoritism, and blacklisting.

A new local of the International Longshoremen's Association was formed in San Francisco in the summer of 1933 and soon won practically all the workers away from the employer-controlled union. Within the new local of the ILA a working longshoreman named Harry R. Bridges led a militant group that persuaded the union to adopt its demands. These included union-controlled hiring halls, better wages and working conditions with extra pay for overtime, and coastwide bargaining so that the facilities on one port could not be used to break a strike in another and so that companies in other ports could not undercut the San Francisco wage level.

To a group of employers who had enjoyed virtual freedom from any union demands at all for more than a decade, this program seemed "revolutionary." The employers charged that Bridges was a Communist.

Bridges had been born in Australia and as a youthful member of a seamen's union had participated in the Australian general strike of 1917. He often said that his ideas were those of militant trade unionism and that he had held these opinions before the Communist party came into existence. He did believe in cooperation between the trade unions and the Communists, especially in labor disputes. In later years the United States government would make long and elaborate efforts to deport Bridges on the ground that he was a Communist, but he always denied the charge, and the government never proved it.

The dock workers in all the Pacific coast ports went on strike on May 9,

1934, and several seafaring unions struck soon afterward. The San Francisco Chamber of Commerce and the San Francisco Industrial Association held a joint meeting and made plans to support the Waterfront Employers' Union in an attempt to open the port with strikebreakers, on the ground that the long-shoremen's union was "in the hands of a group of Communists." The business community was confident that it could again break the longshore strike and destroy the union on the radicalism issue, as it had done in 1919.

On the morning of "bloody Thursday," July 5, 1934, 1000 San Francisco police officers tried to clear 5000 pickets from the Embarcadero, the main waterfront street, to enable strikebreakers to work. Pistols were fired on both sides. Sixty-four people were injured (thirty-one of them shot), and two strik-ers were killed. Governor Frank F. Merriam sent in the National Guard although Mayor Angelo Rossi had not asked for it. Seventeen hundred National Guard soldiers with fixed bayonets occupied the waterfront.

To this all-out attempt at "opening the port," organized labor responded by closing down most of the economic activity of most of the bay region. Vir-tually every union in San Francisco and Alameda counties joined in the gen-eral strike which began in the morning of Monday, July 16.

William Randolph Hearst, who was in England, sent instructions to John Francis Neylan, his chief counsel, to form a committee of the major Bay Area newspaper publishers and to unite them in a strategy of denouncing the gen-eral strike as Communist-inspired. News reports, as well as headlines and edi-torials, gave the impression that the strike was a part of the same Communist conspiracy that had caused all the recent troubles in agriculture. Bands of vig-ilantes, with explicit encouragement from the newspapers and from Governor Merriam, and with no interference from the police, broke into several Com-munist party offices in San Francisco and Oakland, smashed the furniture, and beat up anyone they found on the premises.

The general strike was called off at the end of its fourth day, Thursday, July 19. It had alienated majority public opinion to such a degree that Ameri-can labor has never attempted a repetition of it. But if the general strike was largely a failure, so was the intransigent effort of the San Francisco employers to retain the open shop. Federal officials, including President Franklin D. Roo-sevelt, were now determined to settle the basic issues by a federal arbitration that would compel the employers to accept the full meaning and spirit of sec-tion 7a. John Francis Neylan, though jubilant over the success of his role in the breaking of the general strike, had always believed in collective bargain-ing and now used his influence in persuading the waterfront employers to accept unconditional arbitration. The federal board's ruling, announced on October 12, provided for hiring halls and gave the longshore union virtually complete control of them. This was the demand that Bridges had emphasized most, and the ruling so increased his prestige that he was later made the head of the whole Pacific coast district of the ILA. For years afterward the maritime employers were bitter at what they regarded as a triumph for radicalism, accomplished through federal intervention.

UPTON SINCLAIR AND EPIC

At the beginning of the state political campaigns of 1934 it seemed highly probable that California would elect its first Democratic governor in the twentieth century. The blame for the depression had fallen heavily on the Republicans. In the presidential election of 1932 President Hoover had lost not only his home state of California but even his home county of Santa Clara, and Democrat William G. McAdoo had been elected United States Senator from California in the Roosevelt avalanche.

Nevertheless except for the uninspiring McAdoo the California Democrats were virtually leaderless. George Creel, whom President Roosevelt appointed as the San Francisco regional director of the National Recovery Administration (NRA) in the summer of 1933, emerged as the leading spokesman of the New Deal in California. Creel did not particularly want to run for governor, but several northern California Democrats persuaded him to enter the race. Some southern California Democrats were grooming Culbert L. Olson, a liberal Los Angeles attorney. Creel, Olson, or almost any other reasonably presentable New Dealer could probably have been elected governor of California in 1934, but Upton Sinclair, who had been the Socialist candidate for the governorship in 1926 and 1930, threw the whole campaign into a turmoil by announcing in September 1933 that he was changing his party registration and would run for governor as a Democrat.

Sinclair had been the county's best-known pamphleteer and propaganda novelist since 1906 when he had published *The Jungle,* a melodramatic story of the heartbreaking conditions of life among the immigrant packinghouse workers of Chicago. Sinclair moved to California in 1915 and made his home in Pasadena, northeast of Los Angeles. In the middle of the waterfront strike at San Pedro in 1923 he was arrested for trying to read the Constitution of the United States to a meeting of strikers on a vacant lot, and this episode led him to found the southern California branch of the American Civil Liberties Union.

By 1933 he had written 47 books (about half of his ultimate output), and there was hardly an aspect of capitalistic society in America that had not received unfavorable attention in one or another of his writings. On the other hand, he regarded Marx as a rigid doctrinaire. His own brand of socialism was of the romantic, Americanized sort that had produced the nineteenth-century utopian colonies.

It was characteristic of Sinclair that when he decided to run for governor as a Democrat, he began his campaign by writing a utopian novel about it. *I, Governor of California, and How I Ended Poverty: A True Story of the Future* (1933) was an imaginative history of California from 1933 to 1938. In lively fiction it told how Sinclair was elected governor after a campaign of unprecedented bitterness and how he then put all the unemployed to work in state-aided cooperative enterprises.

Through this catchy, quasi-literary device Sinclair set forth his program to End Poverty in California (EPIC). If the voters should decide to let him make his novel come true, a California Authority for Land (CAL) would purchase all the farms that were sold for taxes and establish cooperative agricultural colonies on them, with cooperative stores for the members. A California Authority for Production (CAP) would acquire thousands of factories that had been idle or only partially in use, and a California Authority for Money (CAM) would issue bonds to finance the purchases of the lands and factories and scrip to serve as the medium of exchange among the members of the cooperatives.

Instead of the New Deal policy of curtailing production in order to raise prices, Sinclair advocated "production for use." As for the effects of EPIC on the parts of the economy that would remain in private ownership, Sinclair vacillated in different passages in his book and in various statements during his subsequent campaign. Sometimes he described EPIC as "production for use under capitalism" and the cooperatives as merely an autonomous economic system within the capitalistic order. But at other times his enthusiastic belief in the superiority of socialism showed through. "Private industry began to crumble," he wrote in *I, Governor*, "and as quickly as any productive enterprise failed, it was made over into a public institution."

The Communist party denounced Sinclair as a "social fascist"—its current term for anyone who advocated compromise with capitalism. The Socialist party of California also repudiated him in somewhat milder language, but he was, in fact, a Socialist who was temporarily doing his best to turn himself into a left-wing liberal Democrat because he would have a serious chance of election under the Democratic label.

The national Democratic administration regarded Sinclair's candidacy as extremely unfortunate and unwelcome. The goal of the New Deal was not to undermine the capitalist system but to save that system by reforming it. In California, however, the Democrats had never recovered from the temporary success of the Republican progressives in making themselves the party of reform. After many years of disastrous weakness the Democrats of California had no candidate strong enough to stop a Socialist pamphleteer from capturing their party. Not even a statement from President Roosevelt opposing Sinclair could have prevented him from defeating Creel for the Democratic nomination. Under these circumstances the President adopted a policy of making no public comment whatever about the campaign in California.

The depression was still raging, and thousands of people still lived in terror of being unable to provide food for their families. Wherever Sinclair went, these people crowded around him to wring his hand and promise him their support. In August 1934 he won the nomination with the highest vote that a Democratic candidate for governor had ever received in a California primary. More than two-thirds of his total vote came from southern California. Fifty-four percent of it came from Los Angeles County, where unemployment and other forms of economic hardship were even worse than in the state as a whole.

In the Republican primary the extremely conservative Governor Merriam won by a plurality over three relatively progressive candidates. As George

'On to California!'

Typical of the ridicule heaped on Upton Sinclair during his 1934 gubernatorial campaign was this political cartoon by Fred Korburg in the *San Francisco Call-Bulletin.* (Courtesy of the San Francisco Examiner.)

Creel remarked, this left the voters of California with "a choice between epilepsy and catalepsy. Sinclair has a fantastic, impossible plan, and Merriam is as modern as the dinosaur age."

The California Republicans, now thoroughly frightened, organized an attack against Sinclair on a scale so elaborate and intensive that it marked the beginning of a whole new era in the history of American political campaign techniques. Louis B. Mayer, head of Metro-Goldwyn-Mayer studios and chairman of the Republican state central committee, mobilized the resources of the public relations, advertising, and movie industries.

Sinclair's own writings over the previous 30 years provided his opponents with much of their ammunition. He had denounced and antagonized a remarkable number of groups and institutions: the clergy, in his book *The Profits of Religion;* American colleges and universities and their governing boards, presidents, and professors, in *The Goose Step;* public schools and schoolteachers, in *The Goslings;* and the press, in *The Brass Check.* But his opponents did not content themselves with reprinting passages from the most abrasive parts of these works; they also indulged in outright fabrications and distortions, suggesting falsely that Sinclair was an athiest, a Communist, and a believer in free love. In a faked newsreel a group of "tramps," who were actually movie extras made up for the part, were shown debarking from a freight train and telling an interviewer that they were the first of an army of hoboes from the east who were on their way to California because they had heard that as soon as Sinclair was elected there would be a general sharing of the wealth.

Sinclair lost the support of Dr. Townsend and his followers by criticizing the Old Age Revolving Pensions plan as "a mere money scheme" and by proposing pensions of $50 a month instead of the Townsend plan's $200. Merriam, on the other hand, won an endorsement from Townsend by promising to recommend his plan to the national Congress. Merriam also made a strong bid for Democratic votes by declaring that he was "heartily in accord with President Roosevelt's policies."

In the November election Merriam won with a vote of 1,138,620 to 879,557 for Sinclair. A vote of 302,519 went to Raymond L. Haight, a Los Angeles Republican lawyer and state corporation commissioner who had won the nominations of the Commonwealth and Progressive parties.

FROM MERRIAM TO OLSON

Governor Merriam realized and acknowledged that he could not have been elected without the support of many relatively conservative New Deal Democrats, and in 1935 he signed a number of bills that brought the state into conformity with some of the New Deal's policies and measures. The most active Democratic leader in the legislature was Culbert L. Olson, who had been elected state senator from Los Angeles County as a supporter of Sinclair. Though the senate was still predominantly conservative, Olson secured its approval of new laws which repealed the sales tax on food and established a moderate state income tax. Another measure slightly increased the provisions for assistance to the indigent aged, reflecting the provisions of new federal social security legislation.

In the New Deal's Social Security Act of 1935, and in the corresponding Old Age Security program which California adopted in the same year, the use of the word "security" was a gross exaggeration of the benefits actually provided for old people. For state-sponsored old age pensions the federal government contributed four-fifths of the first $25 per month and half of any further amount up to $55. California set its maximum figure at $35, which was higher than in many other states, but to receive this maximum pension old people had to be not only without income but without relatives who could contribute to their support.

These provisions were not only inadequate, but they required humiliating investigations of personal finances and family relationships. At the same time, hopes for the Townsend Plan were waning because Congress had rejected it in favor of the Social Security Act. The way was open for a new pension scheme for the state of California alone, and the result was the aberration known as "Ham 'n Eggs."

Robert Noble, a Los Angeles radio commentator, formed an organization called California Revolving Pensions and summarized its plan with the slogan "twenty-five dollars every Monday morning." Noble entrusted some of his advertising to an agency operated by the brothers Willis and Lawrence Allen, whose chief client up to that time had been the manufacturer of Grey-Gone, a hair tonic. The Allen brothers then formed their own pension organization, excluding Noble. They shifted his slogan to "thirty dollars every Thursday," and one of their campaign orators hit upon the motto "Ham 'n Eggs for California," by which the plan came to be commonly known.

In the California elections of 1938, pensions were the most important single issue. William G. McAdoo's denunciation of the Ham 'n Eggs movement cost him his seat in the United States Senate, when Sheridan Downey, who had won an endorsement from the Allen brothers by enthusiastically endorsing their plan, defeated McAdoo in the Democratic primary. Downey, a Sacramento lawyer, had been the EPIC candidate for lieutenant governor as Upton Sinclair's running mate in 1934 (opponents had disparaged the ticket as "Uppey and Downey").

If Governor Merriam had flirted with the Ham 'n Eggers in 1938 as he had flirted with the Townsendites in 1934, he would probably have been reelected. But he openly opposed Ham 'n Eggs, while Culbert L. Olson won the Democratic nomination and the governorship largely by avoiding a clear stand on the issue. As Initiative Proposition Number 25, the Ham 'n Eggs scheme was defeated by about 255,000 votes. But the vote in its favor, more than 1,143,000, was shockingly large, and it might have passed had it not been for the exposure, during the last days of the campaign, of some of the corrupt practices and unconscionable profits of the Allen brothers, its cynical and irresponsible promoters.

One of Olson's first acts as governor was to carry out his campaign pledge of a pardon for Tom Mooney. Warren K. Billings, Mooney's codefendant, had also been convicted on perjured evidence, but because Billings had previously been convicted of a felony, his pardon would have required a recommendation by the state supreme court. The court recommended only a commutation of sentence to time served, and this Olson granted. Billings would ultimately receive his full pardon from another Democratic governor, Edmund G. Brown, in 1961.

At the end of his first week in office Governor Olson collapsed from exhaustion, and a month passed before he was able to resume his duties. This left the new administration without leadership at the most crucial time, and it never fully recovered from this demoralizing blow. But Olson could have accomplished little at best. Conservative Republicans still controlled the state senate, and although the Democrats had a small majority in the assembly, they were split into factions. Olson had almost no previous experience as an administrator. Tactless and quick-tempered, he often antagonized people whose support would have been essential to his success. The main accomplishments of his governorship were a few modest reforms in the state's penal system and in its provisions for the care of the mentally ill.

Throughout the country the reformist enthusiasm of the New Deal was waning. The number of the liberal Democrats in Congress was sharply reduced in the 1938 elections, and as the war clouds gathered in Europe and Asia, President Roosevelt turned most of his attention to the problems of foreign affairs and national defense. Olson's chance of bringing a New Deal to California was both too little and too late.

SELECTED BIBLIOGRAPHY

Frank L. Kidner, *California Business Cycles* (1946) and California Emergency Relief Administration, *Economic Trends in California, 1929–1934* (1935) describe the economic effects of the depression.

On the careers and administrations of Rolph, Merriam, and Olson, see H. Brett Melendy and Benjamin F. Gilbert, *The Governors of California* (1965). Several theses written at the University of California, Berkeley, deal with the politics of the period. Robert Pitchell, "Twentieth Century California Voting Behavior," Ph.D. (1955), analyzes the interrelations between social and economic factors and politics. Royce D. Delmatier, "The Rebirth of the Democratic Party in California, 1928–1938," Ph.D. (1955), stresses the overwhelming votes for Roosevelt in 1932 and 1936, rather than the failure of the Democrats to unite the voters into an effective organization in the politics of the state. Ronald E. Chinn, "Democratic Party Politics in California, 1920–1956," Ph.D. (1958), is a broader study. Warren F. Webb, "History of Lynching in California since 1875," M.A. (1935), throws light on the historical background of the San Jose tragedy, while Brian McGinty, "Shadows in St. James Park," *California History*, LVII (Winter 1978–1979), pp. 290–307, describes the event itself. Herman G. Goldbeck, "The Political Career of James Rolph, Jr.," M.A. (1936), concentrates on Rolph's earlier and happier years, as does Morley Segal, "James Rolph, Jr., and the Early Days of the San Francisco Municipal Railway," *California Historical Society Quarterly*, XLIII (March 1964), pp. 3–18. See also Delmatier et al., *The Rumble of California Politics* (1970) and John L. Shover, "The Resurgence of the Democratic Party in California," Chapter 5 in Rogin and Shover, *Political Change in California* (1970).

Arthur M. Schlesinger, Jr., *The Politics of Upheaval* (1960) includes excellent accounts of some of the major political developments in California in 1933 and 1934. Luther Whiteman and Samuel L. Lewis, *Glory Roads; the Psychological State of California* (1936) describe technocracy, the Utopian Society, and other proposed roads to the millennium. William E. Akin, *Technocracy and the American Dream, 1900–1941* (1977) is a thorough analysis. Biographies of Aimee Semple McPherson are Nancy Barr Mavity, *Sister Aimee* (1931) and Lately Thomas, *The Vanishing Evangelist* (1959) and *Storming Heaven* (1970). On the Townsend Plan, see Francis E. Townsend, *New Horizons: An Autobiography* (1943); Abraham Holtzman, *The Townsend Movement: A Political Study* (1963); and J. D. Gaydowski, "The Genesis of the Townsend Plan," *Southern California Quarterly*, LII (December 1970), pp. 365–382.

On the agricultural labor strikes, see Clarke A. Chambers, *California Farm Organizations . . . 1929–1941* (1952); on the general strike, David W. Mabon, "The West Coast Maritime and Sympathy Strikes of 1934," Ph.D. thesis, University of California, Berkeley (1965); Paul S. Taylor and Norman L. Gold, "San Francisco and the General Strike," *Survey Graphic*, XXIII (September 1934), pp. 405–411; on Bridges, Harvey Schwartz, "Harry Bridges and the Scholars: Looking at History's Verdict," *California History*, LIX (Spring 1980), pp. 66–79; and Charles P. Larrowe, *Harry Bridges: The Rise and Fall of Radical Labor in the United States* (1972). See also Gerald A. Rose, "The March Inland: The Stockton Cannery Strike of 1937," *Southern California Quarterly*, LIV (1972), pp. 67–82, 155–176, 255–275; and Harvey Schwartz, *The March Inland: Origins of the ILWU Warehouse Division, 1934–1938* (1978).

Sinclair's temporary capture of the Democratic party is described in Charles E. Larsen, "The Epic Campaign of 1934," *Pacific Historical Review*, XXVII (May 1958), pp. 127–148; Clarence F. McIntosh, "Upton Sinclair and the EPIC Movement, 1933–1936," Ph.D.

thesis, Stanford University (1955); Leon Harris, *Upton Sinclair, American Rebel* (1975); *The Autobiography of Upton Sinclair* (1962); and George Creel, *Rebel at Large* (1947). Martin Zanger, "Politics of Confrontation: Upton Sinclair and the Launching of the ACLU in Southern California," *Pacific Historical Review*, XXXVIII (November 1969), describes a significant episode. See also Leonard Leader, "Upton Sinclair's EPIC Switch: A Dilemma for American Socialists," *Southern California Quarterly*, LXII (Winter 1980), pp. 361–385; Judson A. Grenier, "Upton Sinclair: A Remembrance," *California Historical Society Quarterly*, XLVIII (June 1969), pp. 165–169; and Walton Bean, "Ideas of Reform in California," in George H. Knoles (ed.) *Essays and Assays: California History Reappraised* (1973), pp. 13–26.

An informal history of the rise of the Ham 'n Eggs movement is Winston Moore and Marian Moore, *Out of the Frying Pan* (1939). See also Carey McWilliams, "Pension Politics in California," in David Farrelly and Ivan Hinderaker (eds.), *The Politics of California* (1951) and Frank A. Pinner, Paul Jacobs, and Philip Selznick, *Old Age and Political Behavior* (1959). Jackson K. Putnam, *Old-Age Politics in California: From Richardson to Reagan* (1970) is a major contribution.

An excellent study of the Olson administration is Robert E. Burke, *Olson's New Deal for California* (1953).

CULTURAL TRENDS

The cultural history of California during the early decades of the twentieth century was distinguished by several writers of great scope and power. As a cultural region, California was fast becoming one of the most dynamic and promising of any area in the United States.

ROBINSON JEFFERS

California's grestest poet was born in 1887 in Pittsburgh, Pennsylvania, where his father, William Hamilton Jeffers, was a distinguished professor of biblical literature in a Presbyterian theological seminary. At the age of 5 Robinson Jeffers began to learn Greek and Hebrew. His father was a liberal theologian who taught him to read the Bible as oriental literature rather than divine revelation.

When the boy was 16, the family moved to Pasadena. He attended Occidental College and then began graduate work at the University of Southern California, where he fell in love with Una Call Kuster, a student who was 2 years older than he, and who was the wife of another man. Eight years later Una Kuster finally obtained a divorce, and she and Jeffers were married. The outbreak of the First World War made their plans to live in Europe impractical; besides, they chanced to discover Carmel.

Jeffers immediately recognized the place where he would do his life's work. In the mountains of the Carmel coast he saw "people living amid magnificent unspoiled scenery essentially as they did in the Idyls or the Sagas, or in Homer's Ithaca. Here was life purged of its ephemeral accretions. Men were riding after cattle, or plowing the headland, hovered by white sea-gulls, as they have done for thousands of years."

On the point of land between the lovely little bay and the mouth of the river, with granite carried up from the beach with his own hands, he built Tor House and Hawk Tower, a separate study.

In 1916 he published *Californians*, a volume of poems written in conventional poetic forms, but soon afterward, instead of rhyme and meter, Jeffers developed forms directly imitating nature. Also unconventional were the starkly tragic themes of the long narrative poems that began with *Tamar* (1924) and *Roan Stallion* (1925). Tamar Cauldwell, daughter of a rancher at Point Lobos, commits incest with her brother, and the whole family perishes when an insane aunt sets fire to the house. In *Roan Stallion* a part-Indian woman named California transfers her affections from her white husband to her horse, and when her husband is being trampled by the stallion in the corral, though she could save his life by killing the horse with a rifle, she deliberately holds her fire until after her husband is dead.

Tamar and California resemble personifications of nonhuman forces of nature, rather than individual human beings, and their stories were inspired in large part by Greek myths, which had vital importance in Jeffers's poetry and thought. The third of his long narratives, *The Tower beyond Tragedy* (1925), takes place in ancient Mycenae and retells the myth of the murder of King Agamemnon by his queen Clytemnestra and of her murder, in turn, by their children Electra and Orestes.

With the publication of these poems in the middle of 1920s, the work of Jeffers immediately found a place in the upper levels of American literary reputation. *The Women at Point Sur* (1927) was much less enthusiastically received, for its theme was even more shocking to most readers than the themes of the earlier narratives, though its story was told with equally compelling power and beauty of poetic form and metaphor. Barclay, a minister, after losing his son in the world war, denounces his church, becomes insane, goes to live as a boarder on an isolated ranch, and founds a new religion in which he is God. Then he rapes his own daughter. In addition, the plot includes episodes of child murder and suicide.

Jeffers rejected formal religions, not religion as such. "The Answer," published in *Such Counsels You Gave to Me* (1937), was one of many of his poems which made it clear that his God was in nature.

Jeffers described his own philosophy as "Inhumanism," though he used the term in his own very special sense. He rejected humanism because it overemphasized the rational, the urbane, and the civilized and because it attached too much importance to human consciousness—the characteristic of human beings that seemed to set them apart from nature. Jeffers's poems sought to explore the unconscious, the realm of humanity's "felt nature." But though he read Freud and Jung, Jeffers never sought the aid of a psychotherapist for himself, and both the poet and his wife denied that the circumstances of their own lives had anything to do with his choice of tragic themes.

It seemed, indeed, that no man could have asked more of fortune than to live with a beautiful, talented, and devoted wife in a place that looked north on Carmel Bay and south on Point Lobos, and there to write some of the most unforgettable of modern poetry. But if Jeffers had no conscious feeling of self-blame for loving the wife of another man and taking her to live in these isolated and beautiful surroundings, the subconscious fear of punishment was there nevertheless. It seems clear that the "imagined victims" in his poems suffered horrible punishments so that Jeffers and his wife need not suffer them.

In the 1920s, as Radcliffe Squires has suggested, Jeffers's poetry "castigated a society whose feelings of guilt demanded the castigation," but "the whip seemed excessive when an economic depression descended." People felt more than sufficiently punished by their economic sufferings, and in the 1930s Jeffers's popularity and reputation sharply declined. The themes of his long poems continued to be unrelentingly harsh—his trilogy of narratives, *Cawdor* (1928), *Thurso's Landing* (1932), and *Give Your Heart to the Hawks* (1933), dealt with adultery, murder, madness, and suicide. Jeffers had no sympathy with the complaint that his poems were full of tragedy and violence. These were the themes of Sophocles and Shakespeare, he pointed out, and they were not out of place in a century in which two world wars had killed 100 million people, and a third threatened to exterminate all the rest.

Jeffers was a poet of the atomic age. Always deeply interested in science, he made several visits to Lick Observatory near San Jose, where his younger brother Hamilton was a member of the staff. Astronomy had an important influence on his conception of nature, and in the 1920s when T. S. Eliot supposed that the world would end not with a bang but a whimper, Jeffers was already aware that the opposite might be the case. While physicists moved toward the splitting of the atom, Jeffers conceived a vital analogy between the atomic scientist and the tragic poet. In *Roan Stallion* in 1925 he wrote that "humanity is the atom to be split," and one of the central conceptions of his own poetry became the idea that the violent shattering of the individual human personalities of his characters, though it might be destructive, would also lead to new discoveries and to the release of tremendous new energy.

He was well aware of the risks. "The Inquisitors," published in *The Double Axe and Other Poems* (1948), described three hills in the coast range, squatting like giant Indians to examine the pitiful remnants of human beings after an atomic holocaust.

Jeffers died in 1962, at 75. He has not had, and is not likely to have, any successful imitators.

JOHN STEINBECK

As clearly as Robinson Jeffers was California's most important poet, John Steinbeck might be said to be its most important novelist. Steinbeck's early writing had as distinctive a relation to the Salinas Valley and Monterey as did Jeffers's poems to the Carmel coast. Indeed Steinbeck portrayed the Salinas Valley with a thoroughness not given to any other American region in modern fiction, except perhaps William Faulkner's Mississippi.

Steinbeck was born in Salinas in 1902, the year Frank Norris died. He graduated from Salinas High School in 1919 and studied at Stanford University, but, like Norris at Berkeley, he never completed the requirements for a degree.

His first novel, *Cup of Gold* (1929), was an allegorical romance about Sir Henry Morgan, the pirate-governor of Jamaica. From this, Steinbeck turned to the California scene, which would provide the locales for most of his best writing. *The Pastures of Heaven* (1932) was set in a lovely, secluded, fictional valley somewhere near the Salinas Valley. Its unifying theme was the Munroe family, their thoughtless, vicious mediocrity, and the series of episodes in which they ruined the lives of their neighbors by trying to force them into conformity with the Munroes' notions of what was proper and respectable.

Steinbeck's satirizing of pretentious middle-class values was also apparent in *Tortilla Flat* (1935), which won him the beginnings of financial success and critical notice. Though several publishers had rejected this droll account of some Mexican-American idlers in Monterey on the ground that it was too frivolous for the hard times of the depression, the book sold quite well to readers who enjoyed its supposed praise of a group of irresponsible people who were living on next to nothing. Steinbeck himself had been getting along on very little. His earlier novels had brought him only a few hundred dollars in royalties, and when he was writing *Tortilla Flat*, he would have been destitute if his father, who had been for several years the treasurer of Monterey·County, had not provided him with a small house in Pacific Grove and an allowance of $25 a month. But the real theme of *Tortilla Flat* was satirical and tragic, and not a mere glorification of anarchic escapism. Steinbeck explained in a letter to the publisher that the story was based on the Malory version of the Arthurian legends. He also recorded that the first book he had owned, at the age of 9, was the Caxton edition of Thomas Malory's *Morte d'Arthur* and that it had had more effect on him than any book except the King James version of the Bible. Allegories based on the Arthurian myths were clearly present in several of his early novels, but in *Tortilla Flat* he burlesqued the Arthurian legends, and did it more effectively though less obviously than Mark Twain did in *A Connecticut Yankee in King Arthur's Court*.

In Dubious Battle, published early in 1936, took its title from a line in Milton's *Paradise Lost* but dealt with the intensely contemporary and controversial theme of a strike of migratory agricultural laborers organized and led by Communists. The episodes were largely drawn from an actual strike in the cotton fields of the San Joaquin Valley 2 years earlier, though the "Torgas Valley" of the novel was a composite locale. It resembled the Pajaro Valley, north of Salinas, but there had been no strike there, and the crop in the novel was apples rather than cotton.

The main characters were also composites, partly drawn, like all of Steinbeck's characters, from persons he had known, including in this case two actual Communists. But the widespread charge that *In Dubious Battle* was communistic propaganda ignored the fact that its picture of the leading Communist organizer of the strike is extremely critical. Mac cares nothing for the fate of the workers and wishes only to use them for the destruction of private ownership. Steinbeck had as deep a dislike for communism as he had for any system that subordinated the spirit and dignity of the individual to a "Cause."

The strike is not yet over at the end of the novel, but it is obviously doomed, and the battle is "dubious" not in its outcome but in the merits of both sides. Steinbeck was equally critical of the radical leadership of the strike and the ruthlessness of the growers and their vigilante supporters. His most extreme contempt was reserved for the vigilantes. For once he was in full agreement with Mac: "They're the dirtiest guys in any town. . . . They like to hurt people, and they always give it a nice name, patriotism or protecting the constitution." In "The Vigilante," one of the stories collected in Steinbeck's volume *The Long Valley* (1938), he stressed the relation between mob sadism and sexuality.

Steinbeck made an intensive personal investigation of migratory labor conditions in the middle 1930s and summarized his conclusions in a series of articles in the *San Francisco News* in October 1936, later reprinted as a pamphlet under the title *Their Blood Is Strong*. As background he sketched the history of California's importation of foreign labor, which he called "a disgraceful picture of greed and cruelty." Then he described the new agricultural labor supply, the impoverished native American migrants from the "dust bowl" area. For the solution of the desperate and dangerous problem he recommended that a new state agricultural labor board help to allot labor and determine fair wages and that the workers be helped to form union organizations and to acquire small subsistence farms where they could live when there was no call for migratory labor. Finally, he insisted that vigilantism be drastically punished. It was, Steinbeck wrote, "a system of terrorism that would be unusual in the Fascist nations of the world," and its methods were being "more powerfully and more openly practiced in California than in any other place in the United States."

Of Mice and Men (1938) was a touching allegory of the life of California ranch hands. Made into a successful motion picture, it further increased Steinbeck's reputation. His masterpiece, however, was *The Grapes of Wrath*, published the following year and narrating the experiences of the Joad family, who were evicted from their farm in the Oklahoma dust bowl, journeyed to California in an ancient automobile, and suffered the miseries of migratory laborers in the San Joaquin Valley. It was "a crime . . . that goes beyond denunciation," Steinbeck wrote, that children were being allowed to die of starvation in the midst of rotting plenty.

The Kern County Board of Supervisors banned *The Grapes of Wrath* from the public schools and libraries under its jurisdiction, and the Associated Farmers launched an unsuccessful campaign to extend the ban to other counties, but the novel won the Pulitzer Prize and was a runaway best seller. During the next 15 years it was reprinted nearly 50 times in 16 editions in English and translated into a dozen other languages. Darryl Zanuck of Twentieth Century-Fox made it into a film while it was still at the top of the national best seller list. He had taken the precaution of sending private detectives to deter-

Migrant Mother. Dorothea Lange took this famous photograph in 1936 at Nipomo, on Highway 101, south of San Luis Obispo. The family of Dust Bowl refugees had just sold the tires from its car to buy food. *(Courtesy of the Library of Congress.)*

mine the accuracy of the novel, and they had reported that actual conditions were even worse than the ones Steinbeck described.

The financial success of *The Grapes of Wrath* enabled Steinbeck to take an extended vacation, which also served as the basis for his next book. He accompanied his friend Edward F. Ricketts, the proprietor of a laboratory of marine biology at Monterey, on an expedition to collect biological specimens in the Gulf of California and described this experience in *The Sea of Cortez* (1941). The mysteries of biology had always fascinated Steinbeck and had given him a deep reverence for the unity of all life. He regarded human beings as essentially animals—but this view was in no sense derogatory either to the human beings or to the animals. It was a love and respect for life in all its forms. Steinbeck immortalized Ed Ricketts, who deeply shared this feeling, in the character of Doc, the hero of *Cannery Row* (1945).

East of Eden (1952) was a powerful novel on which Steinbeck worked with intense labor for 4 years. He began it in order to record for the two small sons of his second marriage the story of his maternal ancestors, the Hamiltons, following their migration to the Salinas Valley after the Civil War. But the fictional family of Adam Trask entered the story and ultimately dominated it. As the final title suggests, the novel became an allegorical reworking of the story of Cain and Abel.

In 1962 Steinbeck's name was added to those of Sinclair Lewis, Ernest Hemingway, and William Faulkner among the very small group of American novelists to win the Nobel Prize for Literature. He died 6 years later.

WILLIAM SAROYAN AND OTHER WRITERS

Like Steinbeck's Salinas, William Saroyan's native town of Fresno provided much of the best material for his writing career. When Saroyan was 3 years old, his Armenian-born father died, leaving the family in poverty. From the age of 7 Saroyan sold newspapers on the streets of Fresno and later worked as a telegraph messenger and grape picker. He left school at 15, never received a high school diploma, and never went to college.

His first book, *The Daring Young Man on the Flying Trapeze*, consisted of 26 short stories, written at the rate of one a day in a furnished room in San Francisco in January 1934, when he was 25 years old. The title story describes the thoughts and fantasies of a young writer on a day when he has nothing to eat and is completely destitute except for one penny that he finds on the sidewalk.

To Saroyan the vital ingredient in literary style was creative spontaneity, and he worked to establish what he called a "tradition of carelessness," or a "jump in the river and start swimming immediately" style of writing. For many years he was in almost continuous production of hundreds of short stories, often with such engaging titles as "The Celebrated Jumping State of California" and "Love, Here Is My Hat."

His most famous novel, and probably his best, was *The Human Comedy* (1943). It dealt mostly with the alternately touching and delightful experiences of two boys who were called Ulysses and Homer Macauley, but were obviously William Saroyan and his older brother, in a town that was called Ithaca, California, but was obviously Fresno.

He wrote several plays, including *My Heart's in the Highlands, The Time of Your Life*, and *Love's Old Sweet Song*, all produced in 1939, and *The Beautiful People*, produced in 1941. The theme of *My Heart's in the Highlands* was that aspiration is all-important and success quite unimportant. In *The Time of Your Life*, the characters are the habitués of a San Francisco waterfront bar, who are enabled to find their inherent virtue when a wealthy drunk gives them money to pursue their aspirations. This play won a Pulitzer Prize in 1940, but Saroyan declined to accept the $1000 award because he believed that "any material or official patronage . . . vitiates and embarrasses art at its source."

Louis B. Mayer brought Saroyan to Hollywood, but Saroyan detested Mayer and he disliked Hollywood, especially as a place to work and especially in comparison with San Francisco. Nevertheless *The Human Comedy* and *The Time of Your Life* were made into successful films in 1943 and 1948. Following World War II Saroyan shunned the public limelight, saying that creativity required isolation. He divided his later years between Paris and Fresno and died in his hometown in 1981.

Saroyan was only one of several major novelists and playwrights who were attracted, however briefly, to southern California in the late 1930s and 1940s by the film industry. Two of the most important of these writers were Nathanael West, a native of New York who came to Hollywood as an aspiring scriptwriter, and the English novelist Aldous Huxley, who moved to Los Angeles in 1937. Both West and Huxley were powerfully struck by the contrast between the grim reality of depression-era southern California and the fanciful image of the region presented in the movies.

The Los Angeles of Nathanael West was a city built of illusion and artifice. In *The Day of the Locust* (1939), West describes the desperate quest of people who have been attracted by the California dream of opportunity and romance, but who find themselves impoverished and defeated. The dream becomes a nightmare, and in their desperation the people turn to violence. West's novel ends with an apocalyptic vision of Los Angeles in flames. Huxley shared West's distaste for southern California, regarding Los Angeles as a symbol for corrupt values and deception. In *After Many a Summer Dies the Swan* (1939) Huxley satirized the excesses of southern California's architecture and its religious and scientific cults. The major focus of the novel is on a California tycoon, modeled on William Randolph Hearst, whose opulent mansion became for Huxley a bizarre Los Angeles in miniature.

WILLIAM RANDOLPH HEARST AND OTHER JOURNALISTS

Until his death in 1951, at 88, William Randolph Hearst continued to exert a powerful influence in California journalism and in several other aspects of California society and culture. His publishing empire, at its peak in 1932, included 26 newspapers in cities from Boston to Seattle and from Baltimore to Los Angeles. Their Sunday editions had 22.5 percent of the total national circulation. In California, he owned and controlled the *San Francisco Examiner* and *Call-Bulletin*, the *Los Angeles Examiner* and *Herald-Express*, and the *Oakland Post-Enquirer*. In total circulation of California newspapers in 1932, Hearst papers ranked first, second, third, and fifth, with Harry Chandler's *Los Angeles Times* ranking fourth. Thus a fantastic amount of power and influence was attached to the whims of one man who had never entirely ceased to be a spoiled child.

Hearst had been one of a pair of twins. The other infant had died at birth, and Phoebe Apperson Hearst had been advised that it would be dangerous to have more children. She and her husband then ceased to live as husband and wife, and she lavished her affections on her only son. In later years she remarked that "every time Willie feels badly, he goes out and buys something." When his candidate lost the New York gubernatorial election in 1926, he bought a tenth-century Spanish cloister. He had it dismantled stone by stone, crated, and shipped to California.

Among many other things, Hearst also bought a motion-picture company in order to advance the career of his constant companion, the actress Marion Davies. Later he formed an alliance with the much larger Metro-Goldwyn-Mayer studio, for the same reason.

In 1919 Hearst had begun the building of his "castle" at San Simeon, which ultimately cost at least $30 million and was the most expensive and lavish residence, either private or royal, in the world. On one of the largest of his father's ranches was a 2000-foot eminence overlooking the Pacific. There, during family camping trips and picnics in his childhood, Hearst had experienced the happiest moments of his life. He called it *La Cuesta Encantada*, The Enchanted Hill, and on its summit, with the aid of his mother's favorite architect Julia Morgan of Berkeley, he built three palatial guest houses and a fourth and much larger structure called *La Casa Grande.*

This central castle was never entirely finished because unaccustomed financial stringencies forced him to stop its construction after 1935. Even so, there were 100 rooms in the castle, many of them transported from Europe with all their paneling, ceilings, and furniture. The rooms were filled with art objects and antiques, and the gardens and terraces with statuary. A huge, rocky hillside was planted with hundreds of full-grown trees at enormous expense because Hearst found its bareness unpleasant. The grounds were stocked with his own private zoo.

In his will Hearst expressed the wish that his castle should go to the University of California as a memorial to his mother, but the university felt that it lacked the funds to maintain the castle. Hearst's sons then persuaded the state of California to accept it as a gift in 1957. The fears that it would prove a

Hearst Castle. *(Courtesy of the California Department of Transportation.)*

massive and costly white elephant were not borne out. Half a million people visited it within the first 2 years after its opening as a state monument. Among the attractions of the place, along with its art treasures, was the chance to participate vicariously in the life of a man who had made such a determined attempt to have everything in the world that he wanted.

Even before his death, however, Hearst's newspaper chain had entered a gradual but steady decline, and by 1965 sales and consolidations had reduced the number of Hearst papers to about a third of what it had once been. In California's two principal cities the Hearst *Examiners*, after years of losing money, were forced to surrender the entire daily morning field to the *Los Angeles Times* and the *San Francisco Chronicle*.

For newspapers, as well as for nations, hereditary monarchy has always been a notoriously risky method of choosing top management personnel. Hearst's sons did not approach the journalistic pace that their father had set. The *Times* and the *Chronicle* were also family concerns. Their founders had no sons, but they were able to pass on their power effectively through the female line.

Harry Chandler, who succeeded his father-in-law Harrison Gray Otis as publisher of the *Times* in 1917, was even more energetic than Otis himself. Harry's son Norman, who became the publisher in 1945, improved the quality of the paper in some respects. And Norman's son Otis Chandler, who succeeded his father in 1960, improved it considerably more.

The *San Francisco Chronicle* passed from M. H. de Young to his son-in-law George T. Cameron in 1925, and to de Young's grandson Charles de Young Thieriot 30 years later. Under Cameron and his general manager Paul C. Smith the *Chronicle* made a valiant though generally thankless effort to be a west coast *New York Times*. But under Thieriot the *Chronicle* launched a much more successful drive to out-Hearst the *Examiner* in entertainment.

The Hearst papers finally gave up the long and debilitating circulation wars with the *Times* and the *Chronicle*. The *Los Angeles Examiner*, in 1962, and the *San Francisco Examiner*, in 1965, ceased publication as morning dailies and were merged with the Hearst evening papers in both cities. In the Sunday field, a new and strange alliance produced the *San Francisco Sunday Examiner & Chronicle*, with sections independently edited by the *Examiner* and by the *Chronicle*. Several nationwide trends had combined to force such consolidations. From 1945 to 1965, the cost of newspaper production in large cities increased twice as fast as the income from advertising. At the same time there was an enormous increase in the number of suburban dailies. Both circulation and advertising followed the bulk of the population increase into the suburbs. Still further competition came from television advertising and newscasting.

THE ARTS

San Francisco maintained its reputation as the cultural capital of California without effective challenge until World War II, after which Los Angeles became a serious rival for cultural leadership.

For many years after its founding in the middle 1920s, the M. H. de Young Memorial Museum in San Francisco's Golden Gate Park remained the principal art gallery on the Pacific coast. By 1960 its attendance exceeded 1 million persons a year, and on Sundays it often had more visitors than even the Metropolitan Museum of Art in New York City. The California Palace of the Legion of Honor was established in 1924 as a memorial to the California soldiers who died in World War I. Located in Lincoln Park overlooking the Golden Gate, it attracted almost as large an attendance as the de Young. These two museums, though they occasionally sponsored exhibitions of contemporary art, were heavily committed to the time-tested and accepted art of the past. The San Francisco Museum of Art, on the other hand, attempted the more difficult role of educating the public in the appreciation of contemporary painting and sculpture.

During the early decades of the twentieth century several public and private institutions for the promotion of the arts were established in southern California, laying the ground for the eventual preeminence of Los Angeles as a cultural center. In 1917 the Otis Art Institute was founded in the former home of Harrison Gray Otis, and 4 years later the Chouinard Art Institute, a school of art and design, was established by Nelbert Chouinard. The richly endowed Henry E. Huntington Library and Art Gallery in San Marino continued to expand its collection; in 1922 it purchased Gainsborough's *Blue Boy* for $620,000.

In the field of music, California's chief distinction was the rise of the San Francisco Opera Company. Founded in 1923, it was the second-oldest continuous opera group in the United States, after New York's Metropolitan. In quality, it became one of the three outstanding American companies, ranking with the Metropolitan and with Chicago's Lyric.

Grand opera, ideally produced, is the most spectacular and multisensuous of the performing arts, but also the most expensive. William H. Crocker had proposed the building of a San Francisco opera house in 1913, under a plan in which the Crockers and other wealthy families would make subscriptions in return for the right to have boxes reserved for themselves and their heirs in perpetuity. But the project would have required municipal funds also, and Mayor Rolph felt compelled to veto an appropriation of public money because labor leaders denounced the aristocratic pretensions in Crocker's plan.

Gaetano Merola, a Neapolitan conductor, had visited San Francisco many times, had fallen in love with the city, and had wondered why it had no permanent opera company of its own. His enthusiasm and leadership were catalysts in the establishment of the company in 1923. Nine years later its history entered a second major phase with the opening of the War Memorial Opera House—the first municipally owned opera house in the nation.

Among the state's symphony orchestras there was no serious attempt to rival the leadership of the San Francisco Symphony until 1919, when William Andrews Clark, Jr., who had made his fortune in mining in Montana, became the first outstanding patron of music in southern California by endowing the Los Angeles Philharmonic. In 1922 this orchestra began to present its famous summer concerts under the stars in the new Hollywood Bowl. With 22,000 seats, the Bowl was the world's largest natural amphitheater.

ARCHITECTURE

At several periods in the twentieth century, California produced or attracted some of the most-talented architects in America. Of these, Willis Polk, Bernard Maybeck, and John Galen Howard in the San Francisco Bay area, the Greene brothers in Pasadena, and Irving Gill in San Diego and Los Angeles had begun their work before the turn of the century, though their most notable achievements came after 1900.

Willis Polk, the son of a San Francisco architect, was trained in the offices of A. Page Brown in San Francisco and Daniel Hudson Burnham in Chicago. Polk collaborated with Brown in the design of San Francisco's Ferry Building in 1896 and assisted Burnham in 1903 in drafting the elaborate and ill-fated San Francisco master plan, of which the idea of the Civic Center was the only major feature actually adopted.

After the earthquake and fire, Polk became known as "the man who rebuilt San Francisco," an exaggerated description which he himself did not hesitate to endorse. The Chronicle Building, the Mills Building, the Pacific Union Club, and the restoration of Mission Dolores, as well as many of the finest residences in the city, were among his more famous assignments.

Most of Polk's downtown commercial buildings were of a monumental and conservative style, with much neoclassical ornamentation, but in 1918 he produced the world's first "glass skyscraper." This was the Hallidie Building on Sutter near Montgomery, appropriately named for another local pioneer, the inventor of the cable car. Polk could not entirely forgo the use of decoration, in the form of lacy ironwork that contrasted oddly with the great glass facade, but his Hallidie Building was the first really outstanding architectural innovation ever attempted in San Francisco. Polk was a diminutive person, of considerable vanity along with his considerable genius. Late in his career when someone unearthed the fact that he had never had an architect's license, he replied that he was no mere architect but "a master builder."

Bernard Maybeck, too, had his own special genius for the new as well as for the old in architecture. To Maybeck all ages were the present. He was equally interested in the industrial environment of the twentieth century and in the Romanesque and gothic structures he had admired as a student in Paris, and these interests combined to produce a remarkably freewheeling eclecticism.

In 1896, when Phoebe Apperson Hearst visited the campus of the University of California with an offer to endow a mining building as a memorial to her late husband, Maybeck was a young man holding a bread-and-butter job as a teacher of descriptive geometry. He was also the university's nearest approach to a professor of architecture, and as such he was delegated to encourage Mrs. Hearst's tentative interest in providing future buildings for the campus. To his own amazement he succeeded in persuading her to endow a lavish international architectural competition for a master plan. Emile Benard of Paris, who won the prize, refused to come to Berkeley in order to put his own plan into practice. Instead John Galen Howard of New York was brought to Berkeley in 1901 to supervise the plan's execution. The Benard plan for the campus gradually became the Howard plan. Howard became professor of architecture and Maybeck was out of a job.

During the next few years Maybeck designed many residences in Berkeley and San Francisco, most of them immediately recognizable as "Maybecks" because of his distinctive blend of gothic revival with Bay region redwood shingle. His most striking design, however, was that of the Christian Science Church on Dwight Way in Berkeley, built in 1910. When a group of women asked him to build them a church with materials "that are what they claim to be, not imitations," he was reminded of the sincere faith of the people who had built the early Romanesque churches in southern France. They would, he was sure, have used the most modern materials obtainable. From the industrial architecture of his own time, Maybeck took asbestos panels and steel factory sash for the windows. Cast concrete and local redwood completed the list of materials. Supporting the exterior were square fluted columns of concrete. Atop each column was a large trellis of redwood beams to carry wisteria vines. With complete confidence and amazing success Maybeck intermingled Romanesque columns with the timberwork of a Japanese shrine, with gothic tracery, and with Byzantine decoration.

His most famous building was the Palace of Fine Arts, with its delightful lagoon, designed for the Panama Pacific International Exposition of 1915. Originally the architectural committee had excluded Maybeck from the planning of the fair on the ground that he had never before designed a large structure. The committee had assigned the Palace of Fine Arts to Willis Polk, who found himself too busy with other phases of the exposition. Polk employed Maybeck as a drafter and paid him by the hour. The resulting structure became such a beloved part of the San Francisco landscape that when its temporary materials eventually crumbled, it was rebuilt in permanent form.

In Pasadena the brothers Charles and Henry Greene created the California bungalow style, which not only dominated residential architecture in southern California in the early twentieth century but also was widely imitated in other states. "Bungalow" was originally a British-Indian corruption of the word "Bengali," and referred to a single-storied house or cottage designed for English civil servants during short terms of residence. Pasadena attracted many wealthy people who also wanted fairly simple dwellings for part-time occupancy.

In 1903 the Greene brothers designed for Arturo Bandini a bungalow modeled on the plan of the early California adobes, though built of redwood. The rooms were grouped around three sides of a patio or central court, enclosed on the fourth side by a wooden, flower-covered pergola. The patio was an outdoor living room, and there was great freedom of movement between the indoor and outdoor parts of the house.

Postcard view of an early twentieth-century bungalow in Los Angeles. *(Courtesy of the California State Library, Sacramento.)*

The Greenes acquired so many wealthy clients that virtually all of their later houses were large and expensive, but their many imitators designed thousands of modest bungalows that were pleasant, practical, and enormously popular as homes, though they lacked the quality of the Greene brothers' fine woodcrafting.

The first California architect to be deeply committed to modernism was Irving Gill. Like Frank Lloyd Wright, Gill was trained as a drafter under Louis H. Sullivan in Chicago. Sullivan's motto was that "form follows function," and chronologically, at least, he was the father of architectural modernism. Poor health brought Gill to San Diego in 1893, and there he developed a highly original style, using plaster-coated reinforced concrete walls, flat roofs, and simple windows, all with an austere complete absence of ornament.

When planning began for San Diego's Panama Pacific Exposition to be held in 1915, Gill was the city's best-known architect, but the local authorities entrusted the control of the building plans for the fair to Bertram Goodhue of New York, who had written a book on Spanish colonial architecture in Mexico. Goodhue, in his California Building and other permanent structures for the San Diego exposition, revived the extravagant and sometimes capricious ornamentation that José Churriguera had made the dominant style of architecture in Spain and Mexico in the late seventeenth and early eighteenth centuries. For many years after the San Diego fair there was a great vogue for the Churrigueraesque in California, with the towers of Hearst's castle at San Simeon as a notable example.

Nothing could have been in more extreme contrast with the work of Irving Gill. The San Diego exposition and its revival of Churrigueraesque disheartened Gill and set back the public acceptance of his ideas in much the same way that the Chicago fair and its classical revival had shattered the promising career of Louis Sullivan and stunted the progress of his work. Gill gave up his practice in San Diego and moved his office to Los Angeles, where he received only a few commissions.

When modernism finally began to achieve genuine acceptance in California, it was largely through the work of Richard Neutra, an Austrian architect who settled in Los Angeles in 1926. Neutra was one of the small international group, including Adolf Loos and Frank Lloyd Wright, who achieved an early realization that the machine was at the base of the new architecture, and not an evil spirit to be feared and exorcised.

Neutra and other architects of the "international" style made use of many of the new materials and methods that machine production made possible. Examples were their uses of plate glass or prefabricated structural parts and of reinforced concrete as a self-supporting slab. Employing such modern materials and taking particular advantage of the mild climate to make the fullest use of sliding glass doors (or rather walls), Neutra designed some of the most delightful and beautiful homes, schools, and commercial buildings in southern California. A contemporary of Neutra's, also from Vienna, was R. M. Schindler, a master of hillside planning and of new designs for small houses, to which he gave an informal dignity that did much to bring residential architecture in Los Angeles out of a long period of provincialism.

SELECTED BIBLIOGRAPHY

Robinson Jeffers had the unique honor of becoming, within less than 10 years after the publication of his first major volume of poems, the subject of an important biographical and critical study and of a full volume of bibliography. These were Lawrence Clark Powell, *Robinson Jeffers; the Man and His Work* (1932, new editions in 1934 and 1940) and S. S. Alberts, *Bibliography of the Works of Robinson Jeffers* (1933). Later studies include Radcliffe Squires, *The Loyalties of Robinson Jeffers* (1956) and Frederic I. Carpenter, *Robinson Jeffers* (1962). Melba Berry Bennett, *The Stone Mason of Tor House; the Life and Times of Robinson Jeffers* (1966) is the first full-length biography. See also *The Selected Poetry of Robinson Jeffers* (1938); George Sterling, *Robinson Jeffers, the Man and the Artist* (1926); and David Brower (ed.), *Not Man Apart; Lines from Robinson Jeffers; Photographs of the Big Sur Coast* (1965).

Important treatments of Steinbeck are in E. W. Tedlock, Jr., and C. V. Wicker (eds.), *Steinbeck and His Critics, a Record of Twenty-five Years; an Anthology with Introduction and Notes* (1957); Peter Lisca, *The Wide World of John Steinbeck* (1958); Warren French, *John Steinbeck* (1961) and *A Companion to* The Grapes of Wrath (1963); Joseph Fontenrose, *John Steinbeck: An Introduction and Interpretation* (1964); and Jackson J. Benson and Anne Loftis, "John Steinbeck and Farm Labor Unionization: The Background of *In Dubious Battle*," *American Literature*, LII (May 1980), pp. 194–223.

Valuable commentaries on California writers are Edmund Wilson, *The Boys in the Back Room* (1941); Frederick Bracher, "California's Literary Regionalism," *American Quarterly*, VII (Fall 1955), pp. 275–284; Lawrence C. Powell, *Land of Fiction; 32 Novels and Stories about Southern California from Ramona to The Loved One* (1952); and Powell's *California Classics; the Creative Literature of the Golden State* (1971).

General anthologies of California literature include John and LaRee Caughey (eds.), *California Heritage* (1971) and Robert Pearsall and Ursula S. Erickson (eds.), *The Californians: Writings of Their Past and Present* (two volumes, 1960). Several hundred novels about California are listed and briefly described in Alice K. Melton, *California in Fiction* (1961). See also Newton D. Baird and Robert Greenwood, *An Annotated Bibliography of California Fiction, 1664–1970* (1971).

W. A. Swanberg, *Citizen Hearst* (1961) is the best biography. Several of the other works previously cited in the bibliography of Chapter 20 for the earlier part of Hearst's long career are relevant for the later part of it as well. See also Rodney P. Carlisle, "The Political Ideas and Influence of William Randolph Hearst, 1928–1936," Ph.D. thesis, University of California, Berkeley (1965), and Oscar Lewis, *Fabulous San Simeon, a History of the Hearst Castle* (1958). Robert Gottlieb and Irene Wolt, *Thinking Big: The Story of the Los Angeles Times, Its Publishers and Their Influence on Southern California* (1977) covers nearly 100 years. Robert A. Rosenstone, "Manchester Boddy and the L. A. Daily News," *California Historical Society Quarterly*, XLIX (December 1970), pp. 291–307, describes the only major liberal newspaper in Los Angeles from 1926 to 1952. William Rivers and David Rubin, *A Region's Press: Anatomy of Newspapers in the San Francisco Bay Area* (1971) is a critical analysis from a liberal viewpoint. Paul C. Smith, *Personal File* (1964) is a good memoir.

The Arts in California (1966), the first general report of the California Arts Commission, surveys the cultural and artistic resources of the state in 1965. Howard Swan, *History of Music in the Southwest, 1825–1950* (1952) is a social history with music as its central thread. Consult also Arthur Bloomfield, *The San Francisco Opera, 1923–1961* (1961); Ronald L. Davis, *A History of Opera in the American West* (1965); Isabel M. Jones, *Hollywood Bowl* (1936); José Rodríguez (ed.), *Music and Dance in California* (1940); and Richard D. Saunders (ed.), *Music and Dance in California and the West* (1948).

Studies of individual architects include Kenneth H. Cardwell, *Bernard Maybeck: Artisan, Architect, Artist* (1977); Randell L. Makinson, *Greene and Greene: Architecture as Fine Art* (1977); Helen M. Ferris, "Irving John Gill," *Journal of San Diego History*, XVII (Fall 1971); and W. Boesiger (ed.), *Richard Neutra, Buildings and Projects* (1951). Esther McCoy, *Five California Architects* (1960) describes the careers of Maybeck, the Greene brothers, Gill, and Schindler. An excellent sequel is the same author's study of *Richard Neutra* (1960). See also Judd Kahn, *Imperial San Francisco: Politics and Planning in an American City, 1897–1906* (1979); Reyner Banham, *Los Angeles: The Architecture of Four Ecologies* (1971); Frank Harris (ed.), *A Guide to Contemporary Architecture in Southern California* (1951); and Douglas Honnold, *Southern California Architecture, 1769–1956* (1956).

WARTIME GROWTH AND PROBLEMS

From 1919 to 1941 the strongest feeling of the majority of Americans toward world affairs was their determination that the United States must never be involved in another world war. Senator Hiram Johnson of California was in the forefront of those who were called "isolationists" in this sense. But the raid on Pearl Harbor on December 7, 1941, left the American people no further choice. The Japanese attack, which came without warning and destroyed or crippled most of the American Pacific fleet with bombs and aerial torpedoes, immediately produced more support for an all-out military and industrial effort than Americans had shown in any previous war.

THE IMPACT OF FEDERAL SPENDING

In the period including the fiscal years from 1940 to 1946 the federal government spent $360 billion within the continental United States. Of this sum, it spent about $35 billion in the state of California. It would be almost impossible to exaggerate and it is difficult even to comprehend the full effects of these unprecedented expenditures in stimulating economic expansion. Every previous element in the state's economic history was dwarfed in comparison.

In the fiscal year ending June 30, 1930, the federal government's total expenditures had been less than $3 billion, of which it had spent only $191 million in California. In fiscal 1940, federal spending in the state had risen to $728 million, much of it for relief and old-age pensions. But in the single wartime fiscal year 1945 the federal government spent more than $8.5 billion in California.

When the Nazis began the war with their invasion of Poland in September 1939, neither California nor the rest of the country had fully recovered from the depression that had begun with the crash nearly 10 full years before. The state's population had increased 21.7 percent during the depressed 1930s (the lowest percentage increase recorded for any decade since American acquisition). But the total personal income of California in 1939 barely exceeded the 1930 figure of $5 billion, and this meant that per capita income in 1939 had not yet climbed back to the level of 1930.

In 1945, however, the personal income of Californians was $15 billion. In other words, the war and the increase in federal spending raised total personal income in California to more than *three times* its prewar figure. This meant an enormous increase in per capita wealth, even allowing for a 30 percent inflation and for a state population growth of 30 percent between 1940 and 1945. Federal expenditures in California during World War II were 45 percent of the total personal income of California residents.

Federally financed activities took many forms, of which the most obvious were new or expanded military installations and new defense industries. In 1930 there had been only a handful of military installations in California, including the San Francisco Presidio, Fort Ord, the Mare Island Naval Shipyard, some naval facilities at San Diego, and March Field. By the end of the war all of these had been enormously expanded, and the list had grown to include camps Beale, Cooke, Pendleton, Roberts, and Stoneman; the Oakland Army Base and the Oakland Naval Supply Center; the Alameda Naval Air Station, the San Francisco Naval Shipyard, and the Treasure Island Naval Station; and several major Air Force bases—Castle, McClellan, Parks, and Travis.

Government money poured out through wage and salary payments to civilian and military personnel, investments in public and private facilities, purchases of supplies, and payments in the form of grants, subsidies, and interest. California received a disproportionate share of all these federal expenditures at a time when they had grown enormously.

The most apparent effect on California's economy, apart from the general increase in its size, was the wartime expansion of manufacturing. Under government contracts American private industry produced a great variety of the sinews of war. In California, almost overnight, ships and airplanes became the most important of all the state's products.

WARTIME SHIPYARDS

With the government providing the bulk of the capital, Henry J. Kaiser of Oakland became the chief private entrepreneur of California's wartime shipbuilding industry. Kaiser's reputation as an engineering and industrial genius had begun with the construction of Hoover and Parker dams and had continued to grow with his major role in the building of the San Francisco Bay Bridge and the dams at Bonneville and Grand Coulee. In order to produce his own cement, Kaiser had built Permanente, the largest cement plant in the world. Before the United States entered the war, he had projected the first steel mill on the Pacific coast, at Fontana 50 miles east of Los Angeles.

New shipyards sprang up in 1942 at Richmond, Oakland, Sausalito, Vallejo, and San Pedro. In full operation for 24 hours a day in three shifts, they were soon building "liberty ships" in 25 days, and in 1943 a new freighter was launched every 10 hours at one or another of the Kaiser shipyards.

At the peak of production in July 1943, civilian employment in the shipbuilding industry in California was nearly 300,000. Instead of the mass unemployment of the 1930s there was now a desperate shortage of labor. To one sign that said "Help Wanted!!! Male or Female, Young or Old, Experienced or Inexperienced," someone added "Dead or Alive!!!" Kaiser advertised for workers in every part of the country, and in addition to the climate he offered such inducements as high wages, on-the-job training, a subsidized plan for group medical care, and exemption from the draft by virtue of employment in an essential war industry.

Since the shipyards could not afford to exclude anyone from their desperately short supply of labor, they offered extraordinary opportunities for women, members of minority races, and other groups whose previous chance for good pay in skilled occupations had been limited. But the disunity within American life was painfully evident in the intense prejudices of male shipyard workers against women, of whites against nonwhites, and of all groups against blacks.

The mushroom growth of the shipyards put heavy strains on the surrounding communities, and every facility from schools to sewers was stretched to the breaking point or beyond it. Thousands of families lived in "temporary" wartime housing projects that would remain as slums for decades afterward. The most severe growing pains were probably those of the cities of Richmond and Vallejo. In each, the population increased from about 20,000 in 1940 to more than 100,000 in 1945, and the nonwhite population rose from less than 2 percent to nearly 14 percent.

Throughout California, and indeed the nation, wartime prosperity also brought strains and inconveniences. Things that had been regarded as necessities, even in the depression, were now luxuries. Meat and gasoline, for example, were tightly rationed. Civilian travel was discouraged, and signs in buses and railway cars sternly asked: "Is This Trip Necessary?"

RISE OF THE AIRCRAFT INDUSTRY

The importance of shipbuilding was doomed to end with the war, but the wartime expansion in the manufacturing of aircraft and in the industries closely related to it became a much more enduring and ultimately a much larger factor in California's growth.

Before the 1930s, aircraft manufacturing in the United States was a small industry in which skilled artisans engaged in the leisurely production of custom-built planes. The more substantial factories were then in the east. Glenn L. Martin, who had established one of the first airplane factories in America in 1909, built some of his early planes in southern California, but he later moved his operations to Cleveland and then to Baltimore. In 1916 the brothers

Allen and Malcolm Loughead set up a shop in Santa Barbara in association with John K. Northrop. During World War I they got a contract to build seaplanes for the Navy, but the war ended before they could begin production. Refusing to be discouraged, the three men moved their little factory to Burbank and dispelled the previously hopeless confusion over the pronunciation of "Loughead" by adopting "Lockheed" as their company name.

In 1920 young Donald Douglas left a job as chief engineer and vice president of Glenn L. Martin's company in Cleveland to go into business for himself in southern California. With an initial capital of $600 Douglas set up his drafting room in the rear half of a barber shop on Pico Boulevard in Los Angeles. No banker would lend him a cent, but Bill Henry, a Los Angeles sportswriter, happened into the barber shop for a haircut, met Douglas, and insisted that he present his case to Harry Chandler, publisher of the *Times* and perpetual booster of new industry for the Los Angeles area. On the strength of an order for three Navy torpedo planes, Chandler and nine other southern California businesspeople lent Douglas a total of $15,000, enabling him to establish a factory in an abandoned motion-picture studio in Santa Monica. That factory succeeded so well that in 1924 two Douglas-built Army planes made the first flight around the world, though they took several months to complete it.

T. Claude Ryan, a former Army flyer, established the first daily scheduled airline passenger service in the United States in 1922 between San Diego and Los Angeles, and the next year he began to manufacture planes at San Diego. There, his small company achieved a national reputation by building the *Spirit of St. Louis,* in which Charles A. Lindbergh made his spectacular flight from New York to Paris in 1927.

The depression was particularly hard on the aircraft industry. In 1932 Douglas went for 4 months without an order and kept his workers employed at gardening and plant maintenance, while the Lockheed company, whose general manager had mortgaged his house and car to meet a payroll during the previous Christmas week, went into bankruptcy. A small eastern group headed by Robert E. Gross then bought Lockheed from a federal receivership for $40,000.

Even in the period between the two world wars, more than half the country's airplane production was done under government contract, and no company survived without a share of military orders. Nevertheless, the military air forces of the United States in the late 1930s were alarmingly unprepared for war. As late as 1939, the entire output of the American aircraft industry was less than 6000 planes of all types—the full capacity of the factories then in existence, but in May 1940, when the Nazis flanked the Maginot Line and swept through Belgium into northern France, President Roosevelt called for an output of 50,000 planes a year, and although this figure was then regarded as shocking and impossible, actual production would more than double it by 1944.

The wartime expansion of aircraft manufacturing compressed 40 years of normal industrial progress into 40 months. In 1933, all of the airframe factories in southern California together employed only about 1000 people. In November 1943 they employed 280,300. Airframe plants, which made up the bulk of the aircraft industry in California, were only a part of the total process of aircraft production, but they were the largest part. They built the fuselage, wings, and tail, while the engines, propellers, and other equipment were made in separate factories. During the war much of the automobile industry in Detroit was converted to making aircraft engines, but it was the airframe plants that not only manufactured the shell of the aircraft but also assembled all the parts into the finished plane.

Aircraft accounted for nearly 60 percent of the money that the federal government spent under prime contracts for goods manufactured in California during World War II, but the profits of the aircraft companies were small. The great bulk of the expansion was accomplished with federal funds, through contracts under which the government guaranteed the entire cost and the companies received only a fixed fee in addition.

Four of the country's leading aircraft producers, Douglas, Lockheed, North American, and Northrop, had their main plants in the Los Angeles area, and two, Consolidated Vultee (or Convair) and Ryan, were in San Diego. Because clear, mild, and consistent weather offered great advantages for the production, testing, storage, and delivery of aircraft, climate became one of the principal factors in the location of airframe plants, and southern California therefore received a large share of the industry's wartime expansion. That share would have been even larger than it was had it not been for the memory of Pearl Harbor and the fear that Japanese carrier-based bombers might attack the Pacific coast. The gigantic Douglas factory at Santa Monica was hidden under a camouflage cover, with dummy houses, streets, and trees, so that from the air and even from the ground it was almost impossible to distinguish the plant from its suburban residential surroundings.

THE "RELOCATION" OF THE JAPANESE AMERICANS

The elaborate and expensive camouflaging of southern California aircraft factories, though it proved unnecessary, did no great harm, but the fear of Japanese attack also led the government of the United States into a massive, tragic, and needless blunder. This was the evacuation from the west coast of all persons of Japanese ancestry and the imprisonment of most of them, citizens and aliens alike, without trial, behind barbed wire, under armed guard, in "relocation" camps in desert areas in the interior.

The attack on Pearl Harbor and false rumors of sabotage and other treasonable acts by Japanese Americans reactivated all the stereotyped racist delusions that had long formed the beliefs of many Californians about the Japanese. Since the early years of the century a number of the state's most influential newspapers, politicians, and organizations had frequently portrayed all persons of Japanese extraction as sly, sinister, ruthless, and incapable of loyalty to any country but Japan.

For the more effective dissemination of such ideas, Valentine S. McClatchy, publisher of the *Sacramento Bee,* had formed the California Joint Immigration Committee in 1921. This body coordinated the propaganda activities of four previous anti-Japanese and antioriental organizations. Its members also included the secretary-treasurer of the state Federation of Labor, the master of the state Grange, the grand president of the Native Sons of the Golden West, the deputy adjutant of the California Department of the American Legion, and the attorney general of California. Attorney General Ulysses S. Webb, one of the principal authors of the state's alien land legislation, was often active in the work of the Joint Immigration Committee, and he often asserted in public speeches that persons of Japanese origin had inherent racial traits that rendered them unassimilable and untrustworthy as Americans. Earl Warren, when he succeeded Webb as attorney general of California in 1939, held similar views.

Immediately after the raid on Pearl Harbor, rumors of treacherous acts by Japanese Americans in Hawaii began to circulate both in the islands and on the mainland. Rumormongers claimed to know on the best authority that Japanese vegetable trucks had blocked roads, or that one truck had rushed across Hickham Field and knocked the tails off a line of fighter planes, or that a huge arrow cut in a field of sugarcane the night before the raid had guided the Japanese bombers to this or that important target.

Secretary of the Navy Frank Knox, after returning from a hasty personal inspection of the disaster, held a tense press conference in Washington on December 15, 1941, in which he made the unfortunately phrased remark that "the most effective fifth-column work of the entire war was done in Hawaii, with the possible exception of Norway." What Knox apparently meant was that the Japanese consulate in Honolulu had been the center of a highly efficient professional espionage network, and this was true, but many reporters and newspaper readers assumed from Knox's remark that Japanese American residents of Hawaii had participated in espionage and sabotage—and this was false.

For the first several weeks after the Pearl Harbor raid the gradually increasing demands for some sort of mass action against the Japanese Americans on the west coast received little support from Lt. Gen. John L. DeWitt, head of the Western Defense Command. On December 26 DeWitt telephoned from his headquarters at the San Francisco Presidio to the provost marshal general in Washington to report that he had just received a visit from a representative of the Los Angeles Chamber of Commerce who demanded the internment of all the "Japanese" in Los Angeles area, regardless of whether they were citizens of the United States. DeWitt was opposed. "I'm very doubtful that it would be a commonsense procedure," he told the provost marshal general. It would be "likely to alienate the loyal Japanese," and "an American citizen, after all, is an American citizen."

A month later, however, General DeWitt changed his mind, largely as a result of the sensational publicity given to the report of the Pearl Harbor investigating commission under Supreme Court Justice Owen J. Roberts. That report, published on January 25, 1942, laid the blame for the disaster mainly on the Army and Navy commanders in Hawaii, Lt. Gen. Walter C. Short and Adm. Husband E. Kimmel, respectively, and charged these two officers with "dereliction of duty" in having failed to take adequate precautions for the defense of the islands. Short and Kimmel had already been removed from their commands, but several congressional leaders now demanded that they suffer the further disgrace of being court-martialed.

The Roberts Report also asserted that the "Japanese spies on the Island of Oahu" had included not only "consular agents" but "persons having no open relations with the Japanese Foreign Service." Many Americans interpreted this statement as new and official evidence of widespread Japanese American disloyalty.

The truth was that there was not a scrap of valid evidence to connect any Japanese-American resident of Hawaii with any act of espionage or sabotage. But this would not be widely known until after the war, and the Roberts Report, at the time it was published, had an enormous and inflammatory effect on public opinion, especially in California. Moreover, no one found it more alarming than did General DeWitt, the officer most directly responsible for the defense of the west coast.

On January 27 DeWitt had a long conference with Governor Culbert L. Olson. A few weeks before, Olson had pleaded for tolerance of the Japanese Americans and for confidence in their loyalty, but now, DeWitt informed the War Department, the governor had joined those who were "bringing pressure to move all the Japanese out." Attorney General Earl Warren, Mayor Fletcher Bowron of Los Angeles, and many others were making this demand, DeWitt reported, and the agitation for it came not merely from "people who are not thinking" but from "the best people of California. Since the publication of the Roberts Report they feel that they are living in the midst of a lot of enemies." In a conference a few days later DeWitt remarked with intense emotion that "I am not going to be a second General Short."

DeWitt was now in a state of suppressed terror, brought on by fear of the disgrace that had befallen Short and Kimmel, and it was in this state of mind that he prepared a report headed "Final Recommendation . . . to the Secretary of War . . . Subject: Evacuation of Japanese and other Subversive Persons from the Pacific Coast." Among other remarkable statements, this document asserted that "the Japanese race is an enemy race" and that "along the vital Pacific Coast over 112,000 potential enemies, of Japanese extraction, are at large today. There are indications that these are organized and ready for concerted action at a favorable opportunity. The very fact that no sabotage has taken place to date is a disturbing and confirming indication that such action will be taken."

This fantastic line of reasoning was very widely accepted. Walter Lippmann lent the great prestige of his column to it on February 12 and added that the Pacific coast "is in imminent danger of a combined attack from within and without . . . It may at any moment be a battlefield. Nobody's constitutional rights include the right to reside and do business on a battlefield." Lippmann wrote this column at San Francisco, after discussions with Attorney General Earl Warren and with the district attorney of Santa Barbara County. The day after it was published, the whole west coast congressional delegation sent a letter to President Roosevelt demanding the "immediate evacuation of all persons of Japanese lineage . . . aliens and citizens alike" from "the entire strategic area" of California, Oregon, and Washington.

Secretary of War Henry L. Stimson and Assistant Secretary John J. McCloy, in a conference with President Roosevelt at the White House on February 11, had already asked the President for authorization to move Japanese-American citizens as well as aliens from "restricted areas" on the west coast. There would "probably be repercussions," Roosevelt replied, but they must act from their judgment of military necessity. McCloy informed DeWitt by telephone that the President had given the War Department "carte blanche."

Attorney General Francis Biddle and his assistants in the Department of Justice had prepared a battery of arguments opposing the mass evacuation of American citizens as unconstitutional and the evacuation of the enemy aliens as unnecessary and unwise, but before they could present these arguments, the President informed Biddle that the question would be decided entirely on military grounds.

On February 19 President Roosevelt signed a most extraordinary document. This was Executive Order 9066, authorizing the secretary of war "whenever he or any designated Commander deems such action necessary or desirable, to prescribe military areas . . . from which any or all persons may be excluded."

On March 2, the Western Defense Command issued its Public Proclamation No. 1. All persons of Japanese ancestry were, in effect, *ordered* to migrate *voluntarily* from "Military Area No. 1"—the western halves of California, Oregon, and Washington and the southern half of Arizona. But this led to bitter protests from communities and states in the interior against being "used as a dumping ground" for the presumably disloyal and dangerous Japanese, and on March 27 another proclamation ordered the coast Japanese to cease voluntary migration and instead to await controlled evacuation and internment. Soon afterward this order was extended to include Military Area No. 2—the other halves of the west coast states and Arizona.

There were then more than 93,000 Japanese Americans in California, 14,000 in Washington, and 4000 in Oregon, or a total of about 112,000 in the three coastal states. Of these more than 71,000 were *Nisei* and about 41,000 *Issei*. Nisei were American-born citizens, of whom only a few hundred were more than 35 years old, while a large majority were under 21. Issei were Japanese immigrants, nearly all of whom were adults, since Japanese immigration had virtually ceased when Congress banned it in 1924. Because the Issei were Asians, they had never been eligible for naturalization, and their legal status was now that of enemy aliens. But in any case, the proclamations of the Western Defense Command generally used the word "Japanese" without making a distinction in the matter of citizenship.

During the spring of 1942, under Army supervision, nearly all the west

A former landscape gardener from southern California demonstrated his skill and ingenuity by creating a rock garden alongside his tar paper-covered barracks at the Manzanar relocation center in 1942. *(Photograph by Dorothea Lange. Courtesy of the Bancroft Library.)*

coast Japanese Americans were confined in improvised "assembly centers" at racetracks, fairgrounds, or livestock exhibition halls. During the summer and fall they were evacuated to more permanent relocation camps. There were 10 of these, located in some of the bleakest parts of the continent. Two were in California—at Manzanar in the Owens Valley and at Tule Lake, between the lava beds region and the Oregon border. Two were in Arkansas. The rest were in Arizona, Utah, Colorado, Wyoming, and Idaho. All but the Arkansas camps were in desert regions, intensely hot in summer and bitterly cold in winter. The buildings were made of wood frame and tar paper.

These barracks cities were called relocation centers rather than concentration camps, and they were under the control of a civilian agency, the War Relocation Authority (WRA). The administrators of the WRA were carefully chosen, mostly from the permanent staffs of the federal departments of Agriculture and the Interior, and in general they were able and understanding persons who wished to allow the internees the maximum of self-government that was possible under the circumstances. But the camps were essentially prisons, surrounded by tall barbed wire fences and guarded by soldiers.

The evacuation was based upon the argument of "military necessity," but this argument was never tenable. The evidence that the Japanese contemplated an attack on the west coast was trifling and ludicrous. In the evening of February 23, 1942, a lone Japanese submarine fired a few shells from its deck gun at an oil field near Santa Barbara and did minor damage to a wooden pier. Thirty hours later, at about 2:30 A.M. on February 25, Army antiaircraft guns along the beach at Santa Monica fired several thousand rounds of ammunition at an object in the sky. It was later established that this was only a lost American weather balloon and that there were no Japanese aircraft carriers within range of the coast. Secretary Knox assured the press that the whole thing was "a false alarm" touched off by "jittery nerves."

The Japanese never contemplated an invasion of the mainland of the United States, and moreover neither General DeWitt nor any other commander ever maintained that such a landing might be attempted. As for the possibility of air raids, the Japanese lost one of their carriers in the Battle of the Coral Sea, May 4–8, 1942; in the Battle of Midway, June 4–6, they lost four more—all the carriers they could have committed to any further action in the central Pacific, let alone in the eastern Pacific. Any possibility of an air attack on the American mainland ended with the Battle of Midway. Yet the movement of Japanese-American internees from the local assembly centers on the west coast to the relocation centers in the interior took place *after* that battle.

The logic behind the claim of military necessity becomes even more puzzling when the evacuation from the west coast is contrasted with the government's policy toward the Japanese Americans in the Hawaiian Islands. Numbering about 160,000—nearly one-third more than the number on the mainland—persons of Japanese ancestry constituted 38.5 percent of the population of Hawaii, as against 0.1 percent of the population of the continental United States, and 1.3 percent of the population of California. Not only did thousands of them live in close proximity to military and naval installations on Oahu, but they actually worked in them. Furthermore they continued to do so after Pearl Harbor, simply because they formed the bulk of the skilled labor on the island and could not have been replaced for months. All major "Japanese relocation" plans for Hawaii were thus abandoned. As an Army spokesman explained to the Honolulu press, "The shipping situation and the labor shortage make it a *military necessity* to keep most of the people of Japanese blood on the island." [The italics are inserted.]

It was not only the labor force of Hawaii that was dependent on the Japanese Americans at the outbreak of the war. The two Hawaiian National Guard regiments that shared in the task of guarding the islands included many men of Japanese descent. They were not withdrawn from the Guard regiments until May 1942, when sufficient replacements had finally arrived from the west coast. Then they were formed into the 100th Infantry Battalion. Later, mainland Japanese Americans recruited from relocation camps were enlisted in the all-Nisei 442d Regimental Combat Team. Their units distinguished themselves and suffered heavy losses in the invasion of Italy in the autumn of 1943. The 442d became the most-decorated regiment in the annals of the American Army.

In the words of the official history of *The United States Army in World War II*, "little support for the argument that military necessity required a mass evacuation of the Japanese can be found in contemporary evidence." Instead, in defense of the Army, its official history makes the remarkable suggestion that "the cooperation of the white population of the Pacific states in the national defense effort could not have been ... assured" if the government and the military had not bowed to "formidable pressure" from west coast civilians for Japanese-American removal.

On the other hand, the United States Supreme Court in upholding the evacuation maintained that the Army had acted from military necessity and that in time of war it was not the prerogative of any civilians, even the members of that Court itself, to attempt to evaluate the decisions of the military on military matters. With remarkable inconsistency, the Court neglected to recall the judgments that Justice Roberts had pronounced upon the actions of General Short and Admiral Kimmel.

In the Hirabayashi case in 1943 and the Korematsu and Endo cases in 1944, the Supreme Court drastically weakened the constitutional rights of all Americans in wartime by condoning a massive injustice that had been inflicted on a particular group of Americans because of their race. As Justice Frank Murphy put it in his dissent in the case of Korematsu, the majority of the Court upheld the government and the military in an action that went "over the ... brink of constitutional power and ... into the ugly abyss of racism."

Justice Roberts, also dissenting, said that while a temporary or emergency exclusion from the west coast might have been justified, the imprisonment of the Japanese in concentration camps, solely because of their ancestry and "without evidence or inquiry" as to their "loyalty and good disposition towards theUnited States," was clearly unconstitutional. And Justice Robert H. Jackson, in his separate dissent, pointed out that the principle approved by the majority decision would thereafter lie about "like a loaded weapon ready for the hand of any authority that can bring forward a plausible claim of an urgent need."

Most of the evacuees were held in the relocation camps for more than 2 years until after the War Department revoked the west coast exclusion orders in December 1944. About half of them returned to the west coast during 1945 and 1946. In many cases their return was greeted with threats and acts of terrorism, but strong voices were also raised in their behalf. Gen. Joseph W. Stilwell, in particular, denounced the terrorists as "barfly commandos." Mary Masuda, a young woman who had spent 2½ years at the Gila River relocation center, received threats of violence from a group of vigilantes when she returned to her home at Talbert, near Santa Ana. Her brother, a war hero who had been killed in Italy, was posthumously awarded the Distinguished Service Cross. On December 8, 1945, General Stilwell presented Sergeant Masuda's medal to his sister in her home at Talbert, and this sobering incident received wide publicity.

In the postwar years many Californians gradually came to realize the enormity of the mistake that had been made. Many could accept the view of the War Relocation Authority in its final report (1946): "Since we are continually striving, with the better part of our minds, to be a united people, it becomes important for us to understand and evaluate what we did, both officially and unofficially, to this particular racial segment of our population in time of global war."

SELECTED BIBLIOGRAPHY

Sterling L. Brubaker, "The Impact of Federal Government Activities on California's Economic Growth, 1930–1956," Ph.D. thesis, University of California, Berkeley (1959), clarifies the significance of the enormous expansion in federal spending after 1940.

On the development of California manufacturing in general, see Victor R. Fuchs, *Changes in the Location of Manufacturing in the United States since 1929* (1962); Forest G. Hill, "The Shaping of California's Industrial Pattern," *Proceedings of the Thirteenth Annual Conference of the Western Economic Association* (1955); and James J. Parsons, "California Manufacturing," *Geographical Review*, XXXIX (April 1949), pp. 229–241.

On the relationship between urban development and defense planning before World War II see Roger W. Lotchin, "The City and the Sword: San Francisco and the Rise of the Metropolitan Military Complex, 1919–1941," *Journal of American History*, LXV (March 1979), pp. 996–1020; "The Metropolitan-Military Complex in Comparative Perspective: San Francisco, Los Angeles, and San Diego, 1919–1941," *Journal of the West*, XVII (July 1979); and "The Darwinian City: The Politics of Urbanization in San Francisco between the World Wars," *Pacific Historical Review*, XLVIII (August 1979), pp. 357–382.

Wartime Employment, Production and Conditions of Work in Shipyards, Bureau of Labor Statistics Bulletin 824 (1945) charts the expansion of shipbuilding from 1940 to 1944. Katherine Archibald, *Wartime Shipyard: A Study in Social Disunity* (1947) is a perceptive record of the problems of group prejudice. "Richmond Took a Beating," *Fortune*, XXXI (February 1945), pp. 262–269, is one of several articles in an issue on west coast wartime developments. See also U.S. Congress House of Representatives Select Committee to Investigate National Defense Migration, *Hearings* (1941, 1942).

John B. Rae, *Climb to Greatness: The American Aircraft Industry, 1920–1960* (1968) is the standard short account. Others are Kenneth M. Johnson, *Aerial California* (1961), on the years before 1917; Arlene Elliott, "The Rise of Aeronautics in California, 1849–1940," *Southern California Quarterly*, LII (March 1970), pp. 1–32; Frank J. Taylor and Lawton Wright, *Democracy's Air Arsenal* (1947); William G. Cunningham, *The Aircraft Industry, a Study in Industrial Location* (1951); *Fortune*, XXIII (March 1941), *passim*; Arthur P. Allen and Betty V. H. Schneider, *Industrial Relations in the California Aircraft Industry* (1956); and Leonard G. Levenson, "Wartime Development of the Aircraft Industry," *Monthly Labor Review*, LIX (November 1944), pp. 909–910.

On other wartime economic developments see Wytze Gorter and George H. Hildebrand, *The Pacific Coast Maritime Shipping Industry, 1930–1948* (two volumes, 1952–1954); Ewald T. Grether, *The Steel and Steel-using Industries of California* (1946); and Nedra B. Belloc, *Wages in California; War and Postwar Changes* (1948).

Jacobus tenBroek, Edward N. Barnhart, and Floyd W. Matson, *Prejudice, War, and the Constitution* (1954); U.S. Department of the Interior, War Relocation Authority, *WRA; a Story of Human Conservation* (1946); Allan R. Bosworth, *America's Concentration Camps* (1967); Roger Daniels, *Concentration Camps USA: Japanese Americans and World War II* (1971); and Dillon S. Myer, *Uprooted Americans* (1971) are general accounts of the causes, events, and historical and legal significance of the Japanese-American evacuation.

The status of the California Japanese before relocation is the subject of John Modell, *The Economics and Politics of Racial Accommodation: The Japanese of Los Angeles, 1900–1942* (1977) and Donald H. Estes, "Before the War: The Japanese in San Diego," *Journal of San Diego History*, XXIV (Fall 1978), pp. 425–426.

Morton Grodzins, *Americans Betrayed; Politics and the Japanese Evacuation* (1949), stresses the influence of California pressure groups and politicians on the making of the decision. U.S. Army, Western Defense Command, *Final Report; Japanese Evacuation from the West Coast, 1942* (1943) is a distressingly unreliable and misleading apologia, written largely by Col. Karl R. Bendetsen and submitted over the signature of General DeWitt. U.S. Department of the Army, Office of Military History, *Command Decisions* (1959), edited by Kent R. Greenfield, includes a chapter by Stetson Conn on "The Decision to Evacuate the Japanese from the Pacific Coast." This adds much material drawn from the files of the War Department. An essentially similar chapter, revised in several important details, is in Conn et al., *Guarding the United States and Its Outposts* (1964), a volume in the official history of *The United States Army in World War II*. Michi Weglyn, *Years of Infamy: The Untold Story of America's Concentration Camps* (1976) emphasizes the strategic importance of building up a hostage and reprisal reserve.

On the Supreme Court decisions, in addition to the work by tenBroek, Barnhart, and Matson cited above, see Edward S. Corwin, *Total War and the Constitution* (1947); Eugene V. Rostow, "The Japanese American Cases—a Disaster," *Yale Law Journal*, LIV (June 1945), pp. 489–553; and Sidney Fine, "Mr. Justice Murphy and the Hirabayashi Case," *Pacific Historical Review*, XXXIII (May 1964), pp. 195–210.

Alexander H. Leighton, *The Governing of Men; General Principles and Recommendations Based on Experiences at a Japanese Relocation Camp* (1945), is a psychological study. On the sociological aspects, see Dorothy S. Thomas et al., *The Spoilage* (1946) and *The Salvage* (1952); Leonard Broom and Ruth Riemer, *Removal and Return; the Socioeconomic Effects of the War on Japanese Americans* (1949), which concentrates on Los Angeles County; Mine Okubo, *Citizen 13660* (1946), an enlightening memoir; *Impounded People: Japanese Americans in the Relocation Centers*, written by Edward H. Spicer et al. for the War Relocation Authority in 1946 and published in 1969; Harry H. L. Kitano, *Japanese Americans: The Evolution of a Subculture* (1969); Bill Hosokawa, *Nisei: The Quiet Americans* (1969); Audrie Girdner and Anne Loftis, *The Great Betrayal: The Evacuation of the Japanese Americans during World War II* (1969); Edison Uno, *Japanese Americans: The Untold Story* (1971); and Maisie and Richard Conrat, *Executive Order 9066* (1972), with photographs by Dorothea Lange and others.

REPUBLICAN ASCENDANCY AND DEMOCRATIC REVIVAL

The rolls of registered voters show that the great depression of the 1930s had converted California from an overwhelmingly Republican to a heavily Democratic state. In 1930 the number of Californians registered as Democrats had been only 22 percent of the two-party registration. In 1936 it had risen to 60 percent, and this three to two superiority of Democratic over Republican voters continued with little variation for decades afterward. Yet from 1942 until 1958 the preponderantly Democratic voters of California elected heavy majorities of Republicans to state offices.

"NONPARTISANSHIP" FAVORS THE REPUBLICANS

More than ever before, the political conditions of the depressed 1930s had identified the Republicans as the party of the "haves" and the Democrats as the party of the "have-nots." A large majority of the business community continued to be Republican. So did a substantial proportion of white Anglo-Saxon protestants. The Democrats, on the other hand, drew the bulk of their following from labor, the unemployed, and ethnic and religious minority groups. Most of the huge increase in Democratic registration in the early 1930s was made up of citizens who had never taken the trouble to register before and who did so now out of a desire to vote for a government that would take a greater interest in the less advantaged members of society.

All this meant, however, that most Democratic voters were less educated and less informed than most Republican voters. In this situation California's peculiar cross-filing law tended to keep Republican incumbents in office. Under that law the party affiliations of candidates did not appear on the primary election ballot, but a candidate running for reelection was listed first and identified as "Incumbent." Hundreds of thousands of Democratic voters were quite unaware that the incumbent whose name appeared on the Democratic primary ballot could be and in fact usually was a Republican. Under this system, three-fourths of the election to state offices were won in the primaries by incumbents who won the nominations of both major parties. In the legislative session of 1945, for example, 36 of the 40 state senators were elected in the primaries, and most of them were Republican incumbents.

In other respects, also, the Republicans were in a much better position than the Democrats to cope with the "nonpartisan" system (or rather the anti-party system), which the Republican progressives under Hiram Johnson had introduced. The Republicans not only had most of the experienced and successful candidates; they also had far more money for political campaigning, and they had the support of a great majority of the newspapers, including the three most influential ones, the *Los Angeles Times*, the *San Francisco Chronicle*, and the *Oakland Tribune*.

A newspaper is ordinarily a business enterprise, dependent for the bulk of its income on the advertising of other business enterprises. Consequently most newspaper publishers preferred the Republican party, with its orientation toward business interests, low taxes, and a minimum of governmental control. Remembering the preponderance of Democratic voters, however, California newspapers tended to support Republican candidates as individuals without overstressing their party affiliation.

THE GOVERNORSHIP OF EARL WARREN

The California Republicans also found a leader who was ideally qualified to turn the state's nonpartisan tradition to Republican advantage. Earl Warren did this so successfully that when he was elected to his second term as governor in 1946, he won the Democratic as well as the Republican nomination and became the only California governor ever elected in the primary.

Warren was born in Los Angeles in 1891 and grew up in Kern City, a railroad town near Bakersfield. His father, who had come from Norway, was a master car repairman for the Southern Pacific and later a real estate broker.

Like Hiram Johnson, his political hero, Warren studied at the University of California in Berkeley and made his early political reputation as a public prosecutor. But the personalities of the two men were very different. Johnson was emotional and volatile; Warren was calm and almost stolid. Johnson's courtroom manner, when he served as the deputy prosecutor in the trial of Abe Ruef, had been flamboyant. Warren, as district attorney of Alameda County in the 1920s and 1930s, was equally effective but more judicious, and more concerned for the legal rights of the accused.

After a term as state attorney general, Warren easily defeated Culbert L. Olson for the governorship in 1942. During the war years when California enjoyed the unprecedented blessing of a large surplus of revenue from the wartime boom, Warren became a very popular governor. He sponsored reductions in taxes and still was able to preserve a surplus in the treasury for the postwar expansion of such services as highways and public higher education to keep up with the state's tremendous growth.

In 1945 Warren alarmed his conservative supporters by recommending a state compulsory health insurance law. He carried a private medical and hospital insurance policy for himself, his wife, and their six children, but he also felt great concern for the tragedy that major illness could bring to less fortunate families, and he recalled from childhood his father's moving account of the loss of an uncle who had died because there was no money to pay for a doctor. Some of the more advanced Republican progressives, led by Chester Rowell, had advocated state health insurance as early as 1916, but this, along with many other social reforms, had been a casualty of World War I. Governor Olson had revived the proposal, but the opposition of the California Medical Association and the private insurance companies, in alliance with conservative interests in general, had always defeated it. The same alliance now defeated Warren's proposals also, and the experience did much to disillusion him with the conservative elements in the Republican party.

The oil and trucking lobbies disillusioned him further by their resistance to an increase in the gasoline tax, which Warren requested in 1947 in order to pay for a great expansion of state highways and freeways. Sam Collins, speaker of the assembly, permitted an oil lobbyist to use the speaker's office as a command post for the battle against the tax bill, though a compromise increase was finally agreed upon. As Warren pointed out, the oil and trucking interests were remarkably shortsighted in their opposition to the measure, since it made possible a new statewide network of freeways that increased the sale of gasoline and greatly aided the growth of the trucking industry.

In his election to an unprecedented third term as governor of California in 1950, Warren did not quite repeat his triumph of 1946 by winning the Democratic as well as the Republican nomination in the primary, but in the general election in November he received a million votes more than the Democratic nominee, Congressman James Roosevelt of Los Angeles.

Democrats often complained that Warren represented himself as nonpartisan whenever he ran for governor, but that in presidential years he was strictly a Republican. As temporary chairman and keynote speaker of the Republican national convention in 1944 he delivered an intensely partisan address. In 1948—the only election he ever lost—he was the Republican nominee for Vice President, as the running made of Governor Thomas E. Dewey of New York. In 1952 Warren was an important contender for the Republican presidential nomination, which he would probably have received as the compromise candidate if the convention had not managed to break the deadlock between Senator Robert A. Taft and Gen. Dwight D. Eisenhower.

In September 1953, after the death of Chief Justice Frederick M. Vinson, President Eisenhower appointed Governor Warren as Chief Justice of the United States.

THE POWER OF SPECIAL INTERESTS

Cross-filing and other antiparty laws had been designed to destroy the power of corrupt "political machines" in California, but in weakening the power and responsibility of the party organization, these laws opened the way for an extraordinary development of the interest-group machine, which filled the power vacuum. Arthur H. Samish, a lobbyist for a coalition of liquor, oil, bus, trucking, mining, banking, billboard, theatrical, racetrack, and other interests, came to have almost as much power in the 1930s and 1940s as William F. Herrin had exercised at the turn of the century.

Lobbying has often been known as "the fourth branch of government" or as "the third house" of a legislature. In fact, the lawmaking process in any democratic government would be crippled if the legislative body tried to operate without the constant flow of information from representatives of interested groups. But the corrupt use of power and especially the power of money to influence legislation and the elections of legislators has always been a menace to democracy. The California constitution of 1879 stated that "Any person who seeks to influence the vote of a member of the Legislature by bribery, promise of reward, intimidation, or any other dishonest means, shall be guilty of lobbying, which is hereby declared a felony." But no penalty was specified, and no one was ever convicted under this provision. The line between good and bad lobbying proved very hard to draw.

Arthur H. Samish, king of the California lobbyists, organized the state's brewers, distillers, and tavernkeepers into a kind of prosaloon league, and in 1935 he made a contract with the California State Brewers' Association providing an assessment of 5 cents on every barrel of beer for a political fund to be dispensed by Samish with no accounting. In later years he often reminded his clients in the liquor industry that as a result of his efforts California had the lowest liquor taxes in the nation. He also reminded the oil companies which retained him as a lobbyist that oil severance taxes in Louisiana and Texas were about 100 times as high as in California.

In 1938 the Sacramento grand jury employed a private detective named Howard R. Philbrick to investigate charges of attempts to bribe members of the state senate. Philbrick reported finding "ample evidence that corruption, direct and indirect, has influenced the course of legislation." Samish, Philbrick discovered, had received or controlled about $500,000 during the previous 3 years, and "some of his clients undoubtedly paid more in fees to Mr. Samish than they paid in state taxes for the support of all legitimate functions of state government." The basis of Samish's method was "to acquire influence with a group of Legislators through campaign contributions or other favors and then to sell that influence to industries concerned with legislation."

Ten years later, on August 13 and 20, 1949, *Collier's* magazine published an exposé called "The Secret Boss of California." Forgetting, for once, the importance of secrecy in his operations, and giving way to the most arrogant braggadocio, Samish posed for a color photograph in his hotel suite at the state capital. On his knee he held a ventriloquist's dummy which he addressed as "Mr. Legislature." The appearance of such an article and especially of such a picture in a national magazine finally compelled the California Legislature to take some sort of action.

Governor Warren asked for new restrictions on lobbying in a special session in December 1949, but the legislature would pass only a compromise bill

Arthur H. Samish and "Mr. Legislature." Taking pictures for *Collier's*, photographer Fred Lyon caught Samish in this remarkable pose in his suite at the Senator Hotel in Sacramento. *(Courtesy of United Press International.)*

that he considered inadequate. This law required lobbyists to register and to file monthly financial statements, but these statements usually proved to be so vague that they were meaningless. The downfall of Samish resulted from his failure to report his income and expenditures to the federal government. In 1953 he was convicted of income tax evasion, and later served 2 years in a federal penitentiary. The state assembly reorganized its committee system in 1953 to eliminate Samish's influence. The next year one former speaker of the assembly was convicted of bribery in liquor license transactions and another was indicted, but released after two hung juries.

In addition to lobbying, which gained such a dangerous degree of influence over the California Legislature, special interests also found another powerful weapon in the professional campaign-management firm—a distinctive contribution of California to American politics. The publicity for American political campaigns had previously been handled, as Carey McWilliams put it, by "broken down politicians and alcoholic camp followers," but in the 1930s an organization called Campaigns, Inc., a remarkable partnership of two Californians, Clem Whitaker and Leone Baxter, revolutionized political campaigning by making carefully planned use of mass media and of the commercial techniques of the advertising industry. It was natural that the first full-fledged professional campaign-management firm in the United States should have developed in California because of the state's lack of party organization, its constant influx of new voters, and its extraordinarily frequent use of the initiative and the referendum.

Clem Whitaker was a reporter in Sacramento at the age of 17. Within a few years he was operating his own Capitol News Bureau, furnishing syndicated news on state politics to more than 80 California papers. In 1933 he met Leone Baxter, an articulate young widow who worked for the Redding Chamber of Commerce in opposition to the Pacific Gas and Electric Company's referendum campaign against the state's Central Valley Project law. Joining forces, Whitaker and Baxter organized the countercampaign that defeated the referendum by a narrow margin. In 1934 Whitaker and Baxter managed the Republican campaign against Upton Sinclair, and though they later expressed regret at some of the shabbier devices they felt compelled to use against him, it was this campaign that firmly established their reputation. The partners were married in 1938.

For the next 20 years their support decided many of the key issues of California politics. They usually managed the campaigns for or against five or six initiative or referendum propositions in every state election. They opposed Ham 'n Eggs and reapportionment of the state senate and worked for higher salaries for teachers, for state aid to public schools, and for the state employees' retirement system. They managed Earl Warren's first campaign for governor, teaching him to smile and to take full advantage of the photogenic qualities of his large and happy family. But they turned against him in 1945 by taking over the campaign of the California Medical Association to brand his state health plan as "socialized medicine"; their success led the American Medical Association (AMA) to employ them in 1949 for its drive to block President Harry S. Truman's federal health insurance proposals.

Whitaker and Baxter would accept no campaign that was not in accord with their own political views, and as their financial success increased, their views became more and more conservative. The purposes of their clients, Baxter wrote, must be consistent with "individual initiative and personal responsibility; the free operation of our economic society; reasonable freedom from government control and direction." For the campaign against "medicare" they set up offices in Chicago and for many years administered a multimillion-dollar fund drawn largely from special compulsory assessments upon the doctor members of the AMA. This was the largest cause that Whitaker and Baxter had ever served, but it was not the most meritorious. Their tactics, and those of the AMA created so much resentment that they ultimately did almost as much to advance as to retard the movement toward nationwide health insurance, which finally went into effect in 1966 in spite of their efforts.

THE SPURIOUS ISSUE OF "LOYALTY"

The years after World War II saw the beginning of a "cold war" between the United States and the Soviet Union and also of a period of reaction in American domestic politics. From the defeat of Germany and Japan, Russia secured an enormous expansion of its military power, and of communist influence, in eastern Europe and eastern Asia. In the United States the Republican party had considerable success in blaming these menacing developments on the policies of the Democratic national administration. By charging that the liberal Democratic leadership was "soft on Communism," the Republicans had their revenge for all the years when they had been branded unfairly but effectively as the party of depression: They now branded the Democrats unfairly but effectively as the party of treason.

In the congressional elections of 1946 the Republicans gained control of both houses of Congress, and in California seven Democratic incumbents lost their seats in the house to Republicans. One of the victorious Republicans was Richard M. Nixon of Whittier, a political newcomer who defeated Jerry Voorhis, the liberal Democrat who had represented the district for 10 years and had been one of the most effective supporters of the New Deal.

Richard Nixon would later become the first native son of California to win the presidency of the United States. He was born in 1913 to Quaker parents at Yorba Linda in Orange County. In 1922 the family acquired a general store and gasoline station in Whittier, and there Richard and his brothers worked long hours after school. He worked his way through Whittier College, won a scholarship that enabled him to attend and graduate with honors from the law school of Duke University, practiced law in his hometown, and served during the war as a Naval Reserve officer.

In his campaign against Voorhis in 1946 Nixon followed a strategy of innuendo which the Republican National Committee had recommended to the party's candidates. He accused his Democratic opponent of disloyalty to America, not directly but through guilt by association. He charged that Voorhis was "one of those who front for un-American elements, wittingly or otherwise, by advocating increased federal controls over the lives of the people"; that Voorhis had the endorsement of the CIO Political Action Committee; and that the CIO-PAC was Communist-infiltrated. "Of course I knew that Jerry Voorhis wasn't a Communist," Nixon remarked afterward, "but I had to win. . . . Nice guys and sissies don't win many elections." Adlai Stevenson, a later victim of similar attacks, would describe them more harshly: "Nixonland, a land of slander and scare, of sly innuendo, of a poison pen, the anonymous phone call, and hustling, pushing, shoving—the land of smash and grab and anything to win."

As a member of the House Committee on Un-American Activities during his first term in Congress, Nixon rendered a service of enormous practical value to his party. He discovered convincing evidence that Alger Hiss, a Democrat who had served in the State Department during the war, had been a secret Communist during the 1930s, when he had engaged in an espionage scheme to transmit government documents to the Russians. Eventually, on January 21, 1950, Hiss was convicted of perjury for denying these charges.

Hiss had been a member, though a minor member, of the American delegation at Yalta. He had been secretary-general of the conference that had organized the United Nations at San Francisco in 1945. In 1948, when the accusations against him were made, he was president of the Carnegie Endowment for International Peace.

Republicans now argued that under the Democrats a one-time Communist spy had been able to infiltrate the upper levels of the federal government, even the Department of State, and that therefore the Democratic party in general must be tainted with communism. This reasoning ignored the fact that John Foster Dulles, the Republican party's principal adviser on foreign affairs and later secretary of state, was chairman of the board of the Carnegie Endowment for International Peace when that board had carefully screened Hiss's record before selecting him as president. But this fact received little publicity.

It was a time of intense fear of world communism, a fear that was increased by the explosion of the first Russian atomic bomb in 1949 and the outbreak of the Korean war in 1950. In this period many Americans were even willing to credit the wild charges of Senator Joseph R. McCarthy of Wisconsin, who made a series of speeches in which he "held in his hand a list" alleged to contain the names of "card-carrying Communists now employed in the State Department." McCarthy never uncovered a single person who was or ever had been a Communist in the government service. Nixon, on the other hand, had actually uncovered one such person, according to the verdict of a jury.

In 1950 Nixon won election to the United States Senate over the Democratic nominee Congresswoman Helen Gahagan Douglas, a former Broadway actress and the wife of the actor Melvyn Douglas. Nixon's most effective campaign weapon against Mrs. Douglas was the charge that her voting record in the House of Representatives corresponded with the Communist party line.

Nixon had chanced upon the most rapid political escalator that the times provided. In 1951, after his election as senator, and again in 1953 after his further elevation to the vice presidency, nearly every Republican member of the House of Representatives applied for a seat on the committee on un-American activities. That institution, originally founded in 1938 under the chairmanship of the conservative Democratic Representative Martin Dies of Texas, had been imitated in a number of states. The California Legislature established a joint "Fact-Finding Committee on Un-American Activities" in 1941, with Jack B. Tenney of Los Angeles as chairman. Tenney was a piano player and songwriter whose first widely known achievement was the composing of a popular song called "Mexicali Rose." During the 1930s Tenney was a left-wing Democrat, but in 1939 his views shifted from the left to the far right after his defeat for reelection as president of the Los Angeles local of the musicians' union, which he blamed upon communist elements in the union organization. He later changed his party registration to Republican.

As chairman of California's "little Dies Committee," Tenney followed the worst practices of such investigations. He set himself up as prosecutor, judge, and jury. He bullied witnesses and denied them the rights of due process that they would have had in a normal legal proceeding. He bracketed the innocent with the guilty, convicted by accusation, punished by publicity, and tried to silence criticism by directing these methods against every critic.

The reports of the Tenney committee often included charges of communist influence in the University of California. Early in 1949 Tenney introduced a proposal for a state constitutional amendment to take from the regents and give to the legislature the power to ensure the loyalty of the university's employees. The university's lobbyist and comptroller, James H. Corley, considered this a dangerous political interference in university affairs. He persuaded Tenney not to push his constitutional amendment in return for a promise that the university itself would take some sort of action. This led to the adoption of the famous "loyalty oath," which embroiled the University of California in the bitterest controversy in the history of American higher education up to that time. The new oath required the professor or other university employee to swear that he or she did "not believe in," was "not a member of," and did not "support any party or organization that believes in, advocates, or teaches the overthrow of the United States Government, by force or by any illegal or unconstitutional methods." The faculty rebelled. Many distinguished scholars whose loyalty was beyond question refused to sign, and the university was thrown into an uproar that continued for nearly 3 years.

Ironically, the state supreme court eventually ruled that Tenney's proposed constitutional amandment would have been meaningless because the legislature had always had, and the regents had never had, the authority to ensure the loyalty of university employees. Another irony was that shortly after the proposed university oath was made public, Tenney was discredited and deprived of all his power in the legislature. In June 1949 he was forced to resign the chairmanship of the un-American activities committee because he had begun to accuse fellow members of the legislature of being Communist sympathizers.

In the face of the faculty rebellion against the special oath, President Sproul reversed himself and asked the regents to repeal it. But Regent John Francis Neylan led a majority of the board in refusing to do so, and in clinging to the refusal during a year of bitter debate. This was the same Neylan who had once accepted the case of Charlotte Anita Whitney and appealed her conviction for criminal syndicalism all the way to the United States Supreme Court. But during his close association with William Randolph Hearst in the 1930s, Neylan had drifted steadily to the right, and in 1950 this fighting liberal of earlier years was still fighting but no longer liberal. He was, in fact, a strong admirer of Senator McCarthy.

Governor Warren, as an ex officio member of the board of regents, favored repeal of the special oath. It was, he argued, not only harmful to the university and to academic freedom; it was also completely worthless. A Communist, he pointed out, "would take the oath and laugh." No one who was plotting to commit treason would cavil at mere perjury. But these arguments did not prevail. Regent Lawrence Mario Giannini, son and successor of the founder of the Bank of America, said that if the board rescinded the oath, "flags would fly in the Kremlin" in celebration and he himself would feel compelled to "organize twentieth-century vigilantes" against the subsequent wave of communism in California. Other regents argued that "insubordination" not "disloyalty" was the issue. In August 1950, by a vote of 12 to 10 the board voted to dismiss 32 nonsigning professors. In September the academic senate at Berkeley voted to "condemn" this action of "a bare majority" of the regents. Thus for the first time in history an American university faculty adopted a formal resolution of censure against a university governing board.

Professor Edward C. Tolman, previously chairman of the Berkeley psychology department, led the nonsigners in bringing suit against the board as represented by its secretary and treasurer, Robert M. Underhill, and in 1951 a state district court of appeals ruled that the special oath violated the state constitutional provision protecting the freedom of the university against political influence. The state supreme court disagreed with this interpretation in its final ruling in *Tolman v. Underhill* in 1952, but it also invalidated the oath and ordered the professors reinstated, on the narrower ground that the requirement of a loyalty oath was within the power of the legislature and not of the regents. The legislature, in a special session called after the beginning of the Korean war in 1950, had adopted the Levering Act requiring an elaborate nondisloyalty oath of all state employees, including those of the university, and the state supreme court upheld this requirement. In doing so it was following the current doctrines of the United States Supreme Court; however, under Warren as Chief Justice that body became more liberal. In the 1960s, it struck down similar oath laws in several other states and thus enabled the supreme court of California to declare the Levering oath unconstitutional in 1967, largely on the ground that mere membership in an organization was not evidence of disloyalty. The case was *Vogel v. County of Los Angeles;* Robert Vogel was a taxpayer who sued to stop the spending of tax money on the administration of an unconstitutional requirement. A few months later, in 1968, the California criminal syndicalism act of 1919 was invalidated when the federal district court in Los Angeles in *Harris v. Younger* ruled the act unconstitutionally vague and overbroad and a violation of the guarantee of freedom of speech under the First Amendment.

The state committee on un-American activities went out of existence in 1971, after the senate's new president pro tem, James R. Mills, a liberal Democrat from San Diego, discovered that it had established "subversive" files on several senators because they had voted against its appropriations.

THE GOVERNORSHIP OF GOODWIN J. KNIGHT

In October 1953, when Earl Warren left the governorship for higher office, his successor was Lieutenant Governor Goodwin J. Knight, a Republican from Los Angeles. An affable man with a husky physique, an impressive appearance, and a sonorous voice, Knight had campaigned vigorously for Governor Frank Merriam in 1934, and the next year Merriam appointed him to a superior court judgeship in Los Angeles. He served in this office for 11 years, and was elected lieutenant governor with the aid of Whitaker and Baxter in 1946.

Though he strenuously opposed the liberal policies of Governor Warren on such issues as state health insurance and loyalty oaths, Knight recognized that Warren's remarkable successes in gaining reelection as a Republican governor were based on his ability to capture Democratic votes, and particularly labor votes. Therefore Knight made and kept a promise that as governor he would veto all antilabor measures. Thus he received the formal endorsement of the California Federation of Labor, and in his campaign in 1954 he easily defeated his Democratic opponent, who had little political experience and was virtually unknown to most of the voters.

Knight's decision to imitate the basic strategy of Governor Warren might have given him still another term in Sacramento if William F. Knowland, his staunchly conservative rival for the leadership of the California Republicans, had not shattered the party by deciding to leave the United States Senate and run for governor in 1958 on a platform openly antagonistic to organized labor. In 1952 the Republicans had held five of the six statewide executive offices that were filled by partisan elections, both of the United States senatorships, nearly two-thirds of the seats in the House of Representatives, and more than two-thirds of the seats in the state legislature. After 1958 these proportions were almost exactly reversed. Through a combination of Democratic efforts and Republican blunders, the latent Democratic majority was at last able to assert itself.

RISE OF INFORMAL PARTY ORGANIZATIONS

A major turning point was the formation in 1953 of the California Democratic Council (CDC), a federation of local clubs made up of "amateur Democrats." The Republicans had formed such a body, the California Republican Assembly (CRA), at a low point in their party's fortunes in 1933, but the Democrats had been unable to follow suit because of the lack of comparable dedication and enthusiasm among their grass roots volunteer workers. In 1952, however, Adlai E. Stevenson became a kind of patron saint for liberal Democrats, and hundreds of new Democratic clubs sprang up in support of his presidential candidacy. Intense disappointment at his defeat played a part in bringing these clubs together in a statewide federation the next year.

State conventions of the unofficial California Republican Assembly had contributed heavily to Republican successes by making preprimary endorsements of candidates. On the other hand, extreme confusion and division had continued to weaken the Democratic aspirants in the primaries until their party acquired its own informal nominating machinery in the state conventions of the California Democratic Council. For some years after this system was established, few candidates of either party could win nomination without the endorsement of the CRA or the CDC. Some protested that these endorsements defeated the whole purpose of the direct primary and virtually returned the nominating function to the party convention system, but the informal organizations were much more democratic and less subject to boss control than the old party conventions had been, and to the degree that they could unite each party behind one candidate, they reduced the costs of preprimary campaigning and the excessive role of money in elections.

THE DEMOCRATIC TRIUMPH OF 1958

When Senator William F. Knowland first decided to run for governor of California, it seemed highly probable that he would win. In 1952 he had been reelected to the United States Senate in the primaries, having won the Democratic as well as the Republican nomination, an honor that no other candidate except Hiram Johnson had ever received.

Knowland had been in the Senate since 1945, when Governor Earl Warren had taken the opportunity to reward an old friend and staunch supporter, Joseph R. Knowland, publisher of the *Oakland Tribune,* by appointing his able and promising son to the seat that Hiram Johnson's death had left vacant. Robert A. Taft was so impressed with Knowland that he made him his own successor as the leader of the Republicans in the Senate.

Knowland's strategy in running for governor in 1958 had several aspects. As governor he could head the large California delegation to the Republican national convention of 1960. Thus he might secure the presidential nomination for himself, or at least deny it to Vice President Richard M. Nixon, with whom he was not on friendly terms. Another objective was to reverse Governor Knight's prolabor policies by securing the passage of a state right-to-work law in California. Thus Knowland would consolidate his right to succeed his mentor, Senator Taft, as the recognized leader of the forces of conservatism in American politics. Taft's most famous achievement, the Taft-Hartley labor relations act of 1947, had permitted the states to adopt laws forbidding union shop contracts, and during the next 10 years several nonindustrial states had passed such measures. Among the advocates of these laws the phrase "right to work," based on the idea that a worker should not have to join a union in order to hold a job, had replaced the earlier open shop slogan, "the American plan."

Knowland anticipated that he would defeat Knight in the gubernatorial primary, in which the labor vote would be so divided between Knight and the most likely Democratic candidate, Edmund G. Brown, that Knowland might even win both nominations. But this strategy collapsed when the *Los Angeles Times* joined with President Eisenhower and Vice President Nixon in urging Knight to run for Knowland's seat in the Senate instead of fighting him for the governorship. Eisenhower was persuaded that this was necessary for party harmony. Nixon was delighted because both of his two chief rivals in his home state were about to be eliminated as serious political contenders.

Knowland succeeded in winning the Republican nomination for governor, while Edmund G. Brown emerged as the victor in the Democratic primary. Voters in the November election were thus faced with a sharp choice between candidates and philosophies. Knowland endorsed a right-to-work ballot proposal, Initiative Proposition 18, and Brown campaigned against it.

In the campaign of 1958 organized labor achieved the greatest degree of unity that it had shown in the whole history of California politics, in support of Brown and in opposition to Knowland and the open shop. There were about 1.5 million union members in California, and with their close relatives they constituted more than a third of the eligible voters. Many union leaders discovered that more than half of their members had not registered to vote and that an even larger proportion of them were uninformed on political issues. Labor organizations now united in persuading an unprecedented number of union members to register and to vote. Against Proposition 18, labor collected a campaign fund in excess of $2.5 million, more than twice the total funds contributed in the proposition's favor. Labor also sponsored a huge campaign of billboard, television, and newspaper advertising, stressing the argument that the "so-called right to work means the right to work for less and less and less."

In the election of November 1958 Brown won nearly 60 percent of the votes, and Proposition 18 lost by almost exactly the same percentage. The vote for Brown was 3,140,176; for Knowland, 2,110,911. Brown carried 54 of the state's 58 counties. The Democrats won margins of 27 seats to 13 in the state senate and 47 to 33 in the assembly.

BROWN'S LEGISLATIVE PROGRAM

Edmund G. Brown, who now emerged as the leader of the California Democrats, was a native San Franciscan, born in 1905. When he was in the seventh grade at Fremont Grammar School, a ringing patriotic speech for the sale of liberty bonds had earned him the nickname of "Patrick Henry" Brown, and he continued to be known as Pat throughout his later career. He graduated from the San Francisco College of Law, became district attorney of San Francisco in 1944, and was elected state attorney general in 1950.

When Brown was inaugurated as governor in January 1959, the Democrats were in control of both houses of the California Legislature for the first time in 80 years. In his inaugural address, Governor Brown promised to follow "the path of responsible liberalism . . ., in the giant footsteps of such memorable governors as Hughes and Roosevelt in New York, Wilson in New Jersey, La Follette in Wisconsin, Altgeld and Stevenson in Illinois, and Johnson and Warren in California."

Brown proposed a number of liberal measures, and the legislature enacted most of them. He recommended a law against racial discrimination by employers and labor unions, and the legislature responded with a fair employment-practices act. Maximum payments for unemployment insurance, disability, and workers' compensation were substantially increased. For the protection of consumers, a state office of consumer's counsel was created, with authority to act against false or misleading practices in labeling and packaging and deceptive carrying charges on installment credit purchases. A state economic development agency was established to attract new industries and aid long-range planning.

Tax increases were adopted to meet a deficit left over from the previous year and to enable the state government to keep up with the swift growth of the state's population by expanding its programs of highways, aid to local school districts, and crime control. At the governor's urging the legislature authorized studies that led to a master plan for higher education and to plans for the reorganization of many state offices under centralized departments. Cross-filing in elections was abolished.

Only a few of Governor Brown's proposals failed of enactment in 1959, most notably his request for a minimum wage of $1.25 an hour for workers not covered by federal law. Abolition of capital punishment, which he urged in 1960, was also rejected.

THE CALIFORNIA WATER PLAN

Probably Brown's greatest single achievement as governor was the adoption of the huge bond issue that enabled the state to proceed with its master plan for water development.

Most of California's water was in the northern half of the state, while most of the need for water was in the southern half. The Los Angeles basin, for example, had only 0.06 percent of California's natural stream flow of water. Under Governor Earl Warren, the legislature had authorized studies for a statewide water program that would ultimately be much larger than the federal Central Valley Project, but organized labor, conservative bankers, and majority opinion in northern California were strongly opposed to the state plan. Labor leaders argued that because the state program would not come under the federal limitation of 160 acres on the size of farms eligible to receive publicly subsidized water, the plan would result in the "unjust enrichment" of huge landowning corporations that were already too rich and too powerful. Major beneficiaries, labor pointed out, would include the Southern Pacific, Standard Oil, the Kern County Land Company, the Los Angeles Times Corporation, and other groups that held vast tracts in the southwestern San Joaquin Valley.

In the face of this opposition Governor Knight refused to become involved in the battle, but Governor Brown believed that the water plan was indispensable for California's future growth, and he threw all his political weight behind it. In 1959, at his insistence, the legislature authorized the submission to the voters of a bond issue of $1.75 billion. This was the largest issue of bonds ever adopted by any state for any purpose. Most of the money would be used for the Feather River Project, the first phase of a much larger long-range plan. The voters of California approved "Brown's water bonds" in November 1960 after he had urged them to do so in speeches throughout the state.

Republicans later protested against Brown's receiving so much of the credit. They pointed out that many of the details of the plan had been worked out during the administrations of Warren and Knight. But it was Brown who was willing to stake his political career on the controversial proposal, and it was he who persuaded the legislature and the voters to adopt it.

The heart of the Feather River Project was Oroville Dam, 735 feet high, the tallest in the United States, storing a trillion gallons or 3.5 million acre-feet, and assuring a controlled flow of water to the San Joaquin delta region. From the delta, as Brown said at the groundbreaking ceremonies in October 1961, "we are going to build a river 500 miles long" in order "to correct an accident of people and geography." He was referring to the aqueduct that would carry water along the western side of the San Joaquin Valley and into southern California.

EXTREMISTS, RIGHT AND LEFT

One of the key factors in California politics in the 1960s was the emergence of vividly colorful but startlingly eccentric new varieties of fanaticism at both ends of the political spectrum. On the far right, the John Birch Society became a ludicrous parody of the conservatism of the Republicans, and thus contributed substantially to their defeats in the state election of 1962 and the national election of 1964. At the other extreme, an anarchistic student wing of the "new left," in coalition with the "hippies," parodied the liberalism of the Democrats and contributed to the defeat of Governor Brown in the election of 1966.

The tendency to polarization in philosophical and political opinions has always characterized the discussion of human affairs. Medieval philosophers asserted that every human being was born either a Platonist or an Aristotelian. Environment is a more probable explanation than heredity, though Gilbert and Sullivan, in the context of English party politics in the nineteenth century, maintained that

> Every boy and every gal
> That's born into the world alive
> Is either a little Liberal
> Or else a little Conservative.

In twentieth-century American politics, especially after the 1930s, liberalism was the belief that government should take positive actions in the interests of the greater welfare and greater liberties of the whole people and that it should also take negative, regulatory actions to protect the public from abuses of freedom by private business. Most American conservatives, during the same period, regarded their doctrine as an alternative and superior theory of progress. They argued not merely for the need to conserve what was good in the past, but also for the related belief that the best way to ensure the continued progress and improvement of American society was to leave the fullest possible freedom to the operations of private enterprise. The mainstream of American politics was a constant process of compromise between these two philosophies. But to the extremists of both the radical right and the radical left, compromise was unendurable.

The John Birch Society, founded in December 1958, was named in honor of a young man who had been a Baptist missionary in China before World War II and who was killed by Chinese Communists in August 1945 while serving as a captain in the American Army. The founder of the Birch Society was Robert Welch, a retired candy manufacturer who had been defeated for the Republican nomination for lieutenant governor of Massachusetts and who suspected that communist infiltration of the Republican party had been responsible for his defeat. Welch and many of his followers believed that the graduated income tax, social security, the United Nations, and racial integration in the public schools were communist plots; that the fluoridation of water was a communist conspiracy to weaken the American people by slow poison; that all mental health work was a plot to brainwash Americans into communism; and that President Harry S. Truman, President Dwight D. Eisenhower, Secretary of State John Foster Dulles, and Chief Justice Earl Warren were communist agents.

Most Birchers concealed their membership, and the general public first became aware of the society's existence in January 1961, when Thomas M. Storke, veteran publisher of the *Santa Barbara News-Press*, exposed some of its activities in his newspaper. An ostensibly student-sponsored "Freedom Club" at the University of California at Santa Barbara had been offering prizes for essays advocating the impeachment of Chief Justice Earl Warren. The *News-Press* revealed that an outsider, a Birch organizer, was directing the club and using outside funds. In 1962, Storke received a Pulitzer Prize for distinguished achievement in journalism "for calling public attention to the efforts of the semisecret John Birch Society to wage a campaign of hate and vilification."

The *Los Angeles Times* published its own attack on the Birchers in March 1961. Nevertheless, the organization continued to grow in several parts of the country, and most of all in southern California. Wealthy business people and retired military officers joined it in considerable numbers. Two Republican members of the House of Representatives from southern California, John Rousselot and Edgar Hiestand, avowed their membership in the Birch Society.

To Richard M. Nixon, who was planning to run for governor of California in 1962, the fantastic doctrines of Robert Welch and his followers were a serious embarrassment. Nixon felt that the Birch Society was "the monkey on the elephant's back" and that if he accepted its support, the result would be the best-financed but most disastrous campaign in the state's political history. Therefore he publicly repudiated the Birchers and stated that there was no place in the Republican party for anyone who charged that Dwight D. Eisenhower and John Foster Dulles were communists. Nixon could hardly have done otherwise. He was indebted to Eisenhower for two terms as Vice President and for the Republican presidential nomination in 1960. In that year, with Eisenhower's support, Nixon had received a total popular vote that was only a tiny fraction less than John F. Kennedy's, and he had won the electoral vote of California, though by a narrow margin. Having attempted to dissociate himself from right-wing extremism, and having thus lost some of his right-wing support, Nixon made a desperate effort to use his old issue of left-wing extremism against Governor Edmund G. Brown. But his campaign charge that Brown, a Roman Catholic, was "soft on communism," was absurdly unconvincing.

Another discreditable tactic backfired when Leone Baxter concocted a scheme, approved by Nixon and his campaign manager H. R. Haldeman, for a postcard poll pretending to come from an actually nonexistent group of Democrats and condemning the California Democratic Council as pro-Communist. Democratic leaders discovered and denounced this fraud, and 10 years later would recall it as a "warm-up for Watergate."

Throughout the 1962 campaign Nixon gave an irritating impression of arrogance and overconfidence that disenchanted many who had once voted for him. Many also disliked his apparent intention to serve only 2 years as governor and then use the office as a stepping-stone to the presidency in 1964. In the election on November 6, 1962, Brown defeated Nixon by nearly 300,000 votes, although Senator Thomas H. Kuchel, a liberal Republican, was reelected by a margin of 700,000. On the morning after the election, Nixon appeared at a press conference, unshaven and distraught, and delivered a rambling attack on the press, blaming his defeat on unfair reporting of his campaign. A few weeks later he announced that he would leave California to become a partner in a law firm in New York City.

The split between the moderates and the right-wing extremists continued to bedevil the Republicans in 1964. In the California presidential primary the ultraconservative Senator Barry Goldwater of Arizona, who opposed medicare and social security, defeated the moderate Governor Nelson Rockefeller of New York, and at the Republican national convention in San Francisco the large California delegation, headed by ex-Senator William F. Knowland, clinched the nomination for Goldwater.

It was widely reported that at least a hundred of Goldwater's delegates were Birchers. When Rockefeller proposed a platform amendment condemning "the Ku Klux Klan, the Communist Party, and the Birch Society," he was shouted down. On the other hand, Goldwater included in his acceptance speech a statement that "extremism in the defense of liberty is no vice" and that "moderation in the pursuit of justice is not a virtue." His supporters at the convention cheered widly, but the words had an opposite effect on millions of voters in the television audience, and the next day Rockefeller spoke for many moderate Republicans when he called the statement "dangerous, irresponsible, and frightening." In the election in November, President Lyndon B. Johnson defeated Goldwater, both in California and in the nation, by the widest margins given to a presidential candidate since 1936.

Thus in 1964 the Democrats seemed firmly entrenched both in Washington and in Sacramento, but the political sands were soon to shift again. Lyndon Johnson was about to ruin his presidency with a disastrous war. And the screen and television actor Ronald Reagan had attracted considerable interest with a widely televised fund-raising address that was the highlight of the campaign for Goldwater.

SELECTED BIBLIOGRAPHY

Eugene C. Lee, *California Votes* (1963) is a review and analysis of registration and voting from 1928 to 1962. William Buchanan, *Legislative Partisanship: The Deviant Case of California* (1963) includes a perceptive account of legislative politics from 1935 to 1960.

On the effects of cross-filing, in addition to the words cited for Chapter 27, see Dean E. McHenry, "Cross Filing of Political Candidates in California," *Annals of the American Academy of Political and Social Science*, CCXLVIII (November 1946), pp. 226–231; Robert J. Pitchell, "The Electoral System and Voting Behavior: The Case of California's Cross-Filing," *Western Political Quarterly*, XII (June 1959), pp. 459–484; and Dean R. Cresap, *Party Politics in the Golden State* (1954).

Earl Warren and his governorship are discussed in Leo Katcher, *Earl Warren: A Political Biography* (1967); Richard B. Harvey, *Earl Warren: Governor of California* (1969); Lloyd R. Henderson, "Earl Warren and California Politics," Ph.D. thesis, University of California, Berkeley (1965); James R. Bell, "The Executive Office of the California Governor under Earl Warren, 1943–1953," Ph.D. thesis, University of California, Berkeley (1956); Irving Stone, *Earl Warren: A Great American Story* (1948), a campaign biography; Raymond Moley, *27 Masters of Politics* (1949); Thomas S. Barclay, "Earl Warren, So-Called Nonpartisan," in J. T. Salter (ed.), *Public Men in and out of Office* (1946); and John D. Weaver, *Warren: The Man, the Court, the Era* (1967). See also *The Memoirs of Earl Warren* (1977).

The most-detailed treatment of lobbying activities is Elmer R. Rusco, "Machine Politics, California Model: Arthur H. Samish and the Alcoholic Beverage Industry," Ph.D. thesis, University of California, Berkeley (1960). For the principal exposés, see Howard R. Philbrick, *Legislative Investigative Report* (1939) and Lester Velie, "The Secret Boss of California," *Collier's*, CXXIV (Aug. 13, 1949), pp. 11–13, 71–73, and (Aug. 20, 1949), pp. 12–13, 60, 62–63. Parts of the Philbrick and Velie accounts are reprinted in David Farrelly and Ivan Hinderaker (eds.), *The Politics of California* (1951). Sarah J. Conwill, "Regulation of Lobbying in California," M.A. thesis, University of California, Berkeley (1959), and Edgar Lane, *Lobbying and the Law* (1964) emphasize the difficulty and ineffectiveness of state legal regulation. Arthur H. Samish and Bob Thomas, *The Secret Boss of California* (1971) is a lively memoir.

Important accounts of the rise of campaign management firms are Carey McWilliams, "Government by Whitaker and Baxter," *The Nation*, CLXXII (Apr. 14 and 21 and May 5, 1951), and Robert J. Pitchell, "The Influence of Professional Campaign Management Firms in Partisan Elections in California," *Western Political Quarterly*, XI (June 1958), pp. 278–300. On the use of money in elections see Leonard C. Rowe and William Buchanan, "Campaign Funds in California: What the Records Reveal," *California Historical Society Quarterly*, XLI (September 1962), pp. 195–210.

The congressional career of Jerry Voorhis from 1936 to 1946, and that of Richard Nixon from 1946 to 1952, illustrated the decline of support for New Deal viewpoints and the rising popularity of conservative Republican ones in the postwar years. On Voorhis see Paul Bullock, *Jerry Voorhis: The Idealist as Politician* (1978); the chapter by Claudius O. Johnson in J. T. Salter, *Public Men*, pp. 322–343; and Jerry Voorhis, *Confes-*

sions of a Congressman (1947). Paul Bullock, "Richard Nixon's 1946 Campaign against Jerry Voorhis," *Southern California Quarterly*, LV (Fall 1973), pp. 319–359, and Ingrid W. Scobie, "Helen Gahagan Douglas and her 1950 Senate Race with Richard M. Nixon," same journal, LVIII (Spring 1976), pp. 113–126, are revealing. Earl Mazo, *Richard Nixon: A Political and Personal Portrait* (1959, 1960) is moderately favorable. William Costello, *The Facts about Nixon; an Unauthorized Biography* (1960) is moderately critical. See also Richard M. Nixon, *Six Crises* (1962).

On the loyalty issue in California, consult Ingrid W. Scobie, "Jack B. Tenney: Molder of Anti-communist Legislation in California, 1940–49," Ph.D. thesis, University of Wisconsin (1970); Edward L. Barrett, Jr., *The Tenney Committee* (1951); David P. Gardner, *The California Oath Controversy* (1967); George R. Stewart, *The Year of the Oath* (1950); John W. Caughey, "A University in Jeopardy," *Harper's Magazine*, CCI (November 1950), pp. 68–73, and "Farewell to California's 'Loyalty' Oath," *Pacific Historical Review*, XXXVIII (May 1969), pp. 123–128; and R. L. Pritchard, "California Un-American Activities Investigations," *California Historical Society Quarterly*, XLIX (December 1970), pp. 309–327.

Accounts of the political career of Governor Goodwin J. Knight are in H. Brett Melendy and Benjamin F. Gilbert, *The Governors of California* (1965) and Frank J. Taylor, "How to Run for Office," *Saturday Evening Post*, CCXXVIII (Oct. 29, 1955), 34ff.

The rise of informal party organizations is described in Leonard C. Rowe, *Pre-primary Endorsements in California Politics* (1962); Markell C. Baer, *Story of the California Republican Assembly* (1955); Francis Carney, *The Rise of the Democratic Clubs in California* (1958); and James Q. Wilson, *The Amateur Democrat* (1962), a discussion of club politics in New York, Chicago, and Los Angeles.

On the sweeping Democratic victory of 1958, see Totton J. Anderson, "The 1958 Election in California," *Western Political Quarterly*, XII (March 1959), pp. 276–300. Melendy and Gilbert, *The Governors of California* includes a summary of Brown's governorship through 1964.

California Water Resources Board Bulletin No. 3, *The California Water Plan* (1957) is the basic description of the 60-year project. Harvey P. Grody, "From North to South: The Feather River Project and Other Legislative Water Struggles in the 1950s," *Southern California Quarterly*, LX (Fall 1978), pp. 287–326 and Sydney Kossen, "California's $2 Billion Thirst," *Harper's Magazine*, CCXXII (March 1961), pp. 94–102, describe the Feather River Project. William L. Kahrl (compiler), *The California Water Atlas* (1979) contains the best short history of the state's water use and development.

Thomas M. Storke describes his exposure of the Birch Society in *I Write for Freedom* (1963). On Brown's victory over Nixon, see Totton J. Anderson and Eugene C. Lee, "The 1962 Election in California," *Western Political Quarterly*, XVI (June 1963), pp. 396–420.

INDUSTRIALIZED AGRICULTURE AND DISORGANIZED LABOR

GREEN GOLD

Though the processes of urbanization were continuing and accelerating, agriculture was still California's largest single industry. The value of the state's farm products exceeded the value of the output of any branch of manufacturing in the state—or rather of any *other* branch of "manufacturing." California farms themselves, in the words of Carey McWilliams, had long been "factories in the field."

The structure of agriculture in California was not only extraordinarily complex in itself; it was also closely interrelated with other industries, especially the canning, packing, processing, transportation, and marketing of food and kindred products. One in every five jobs in the state was directly related to agriculture.

Among the states, California had ranked first in farm income since the 1930s, and its lead was steadily widening. Several of its climates permitted year-round growing and favored the production of fruit and truck crops for luxury markets at seasons when other states could offer little or no competition. California's unmatched level of farm capitalization permitted the greatest use of scientific techniques and resulted in the nation's highest level of farm productivity. One-fourth of the nation's irrigated land was in California; two-thirds of the state's cultivated land was irrigated.

California's agriculture was not only the most prosperous in the country, but far and away the most diversified. Because of the variety of its soils and climates it had 118 different types of farms, according to the United States census classification, while Pennsylvania, which ranked second in this respect, had only 25 types. Thanks in part to the genius of Luther Burbank of Santa Rosa, nearly 300 different agricultural commodities were produced in California, including all of the nation's commercial supply of almonds, artichokes, figs, nectarines, and olives; practically all of the walnuts, dates, and lemons; a third of the nation's fruit, including most of the apricots, grapes, pears, plums, and prunes; and more than a fourth of the nation's vegetables, including most of the asparagus, broccoli, carrots, celery, and lettuce. California also ranked first in beef cattle, beet sugar, strawberries, tomatoes, and turkeys. It was second in cotton and third in the production of milk.

Although California agriculture as a whole was remarkably diversified, the great majority of the farms were extremely specialized. Specialization even within a crop was common. For example, many farms produced peaches exclusively for canning or for drying, and many produced grapes only for the table or for raisins or for wine.

While total farm income in California was going steadily up, the number of farm units was going steadily down. From 1940 to 1960 the number of farms in the state decreased from 133,000 to less than 100,000, while their average size increased from 230 acres to 372 acres. By 1980 there were 62,000 farms in California, and their average size had risen to 538 acres.

More than 70 percent of California farm income went to less than 15 percent of the farms, and most of the large farm units, which produced the bulk of the total output, were owned by large corporations. There were still thousands of commercial family farms, but in the general trend to consolidation, mechanization, and constantly increasing capitalization many small farmers were squeezed out. The proportion of farm residents in California dropped from 9.7 percent of the state's population in 1940 to 5.8 percent in 1950, and 2.7 percent in 1960.

Although the cultivated acreage in California was only 3 percent of the national total in 1980, it produced about 10 percent of the dollar value of the nation's harvested crops. The income of commercial family farms in California for years was more than twice the national average, and the margin in favor of the large corporation farms was even larger. These facts provided, in themselves, an eloquent commentary on the claims of California growers that they could not afford to pay higher wages to their workers than did farmers in other parts of the United States.

THE EMPIRE OF AGRIBUSINESS

Successful farming was becoming a business organized in larger and larger units. This was occurring not only through "horizontal integration," or the merging of farm units into larger ones, but also through the still more revolutionary process of "vertical integration," in which a large company operated at every level from the field to the supermarket. The men who had pioneered in the formation of these vertically integrated agricultural corporations and had set the pattern for them were two Italian immigrants, Mark J. Fontana and Joseph Di Giorgio.

Fontana had created the California Fruit Canner's Association in 1899 and in 1916 had been instrumental in merging four large packing concerns into the California Packing Corporation (CalPac), which became the world's largest canner of fruits and vegetables. CalPac was the grower as well as the packer of many of the goods that were sold under its Del Monte label. In 1965 it owned 24,000 acres of cultivated land and leased 74,000. It also contracted with hundreds of smaller growers for their crops, often before they were harvested and sometimes before they were planted. It owned 44 canneries, and its 50 warehouses were spread throughout the United States and Canada. Its sales were nearly $400 million a year. Joseph Di Giorgio had become a large grower in the southern San Joaquin Valley early in the century and had bought the marketing and shipping interests of the Earl Fruit Company in 1910. The canned goods produced by the Di Giorgio Corporation were known to consumers through its S&W label.

Another integrated "farmer" was Schenley Industries, which raised many of the grapes that went into its wines. Among the many other large owners of farm lands were the Bank of America, the Southern Pacific and Santa Fe railroads, the Kern County Land Company, the Los Angeles Times Corporation, and the Irvine Corporation. Hunt Foods and Industries, headed by Norton Simon, did not operate as a grower but was important as the world's largest processor and distributor of tomato products and as a major producer of salad and cooking oils.

The backing of such large aggregations of capital facilitated the constant development of new technological advances in all of the complex operations of agribusiness. An indispensable ally in this process was the University of California's college of agriculture, an outgrowth of the Morrill Land Grant College Act, adopted a century earlier for the purpose of aiding the country's millions of small farmers. The federal and state funds that supported the college's tremendously successful research program were augmented by the funds of the Giannini Foundation of Agricultural Economics. Amadeo Peter Giannini, founder of the Bank of America, was also a regent of the university. His son, Lawrence Mario Giannini, succeeded him both as a regent and as head of the bank.

The impact of science and technology on California agriculture was astounding. In 1961 university agricultural engineers devised a mechanical tomato picker so efficient and gentle that when they ran a fresh egg through it, the egg was deposited in the box uncracked. Soon afterward they developed a mechanical thumb that could press down on the top of each head of lettuce, decide electronically whether it was ready to be picked, and signal another part of the machine to pick it. Nine-tenths of California's cotton was being picked by machinery before the rate reached one-tenth in the southern states. Agricultural scientists developed mechanical tree shakers for fruits and nuts. For the more delicate fruits there were machines that could lift a human picker into the branches of the tree and swing him or her rapidly among them.

A major factor encouraging the further advance of a mechanized, highly capitalized agriculture, concentrated in high-income-per-acre crops, was the continuing growth of the income of the average American family. With this increase came ever-greater demand for fruits, vegetables, dairy products, poultry, and eggs—all California specialties. Another pressure for crops that used

Cotton harvesting in the San Joaquin Valley. The plants had been defoliated by aerial spraying. *(Courtesy of Agricultural Publications, University of California, Berkeley.)*

land intensively was the rapidly rising value of land itself. Of California's slightly less than 100 million acres, only about 17.5 million were suitable for cultivation, and more than 13 million were being cultivated in 1965. Cities, factories, freeways, and other nonfarm uses occupied more than 3 million acres. Inconveniently, the land that was most valuable for agriculture was often the land that lay directly in the paths of urban growth. Los Angeles County, for example, had been for many years the richest agricultural county in the nation, but as its suburbs spread over what had once been prime irrigated cropland, its agricultural output rapidly fell behind that of such counties as Fresno and San Joaquin.

"FARM FASCISM" IN THE 1930s

California growers had discovered very early that the cost of labor was the only cost of production that they could usually keep down, and they had kept it down, with all the economic and political power at their command.

Since the early American period farmland values in California had been capitalized on the basis of the availability of cheap, unorganized migratory labor, much of it alien and nonwhite—Chinese, then Japanese, and later Mexican and Filipino. Thus the historic cheap-labor surplus, by helping to keep land prices high and farm mortgages heavy, had kept the small farmers' return on their own labor to a low level, while at the same time it had maintained the profits of the large farms that employed the bulk of the hired workers.

In 1933 and 1934, when the Communist party organized a series of agricultural strikes and made a determined effort to unionize migratory farm labor, the forces of agribusiness launched an all-out countercampaign through a new organization called the Associated Farmers of California. The funds for its support came largely from the California Packing Corporation; the Southern Pacific Railroad; the Industrial Association of San Francisco; Southern Californians, Inc., a group of industrial employers; the Holly Sugar Corporation;

and the Spreckels Investment Company. The Pacific Gas and Electric Company also made common cause with the large growers because their needs for power to pump irrigation water made them some of its best customers. Most of these big-business concerns tried to keep their contributions to the Associated Farmers confidential in order to maintain the image of a "farmers' organization."

Throughout the state, units of the Associated Farmers worked in intimate cooperation with local law enforcement officials. Most county sheriffs were allied with agribusiness interests. In some counties, migratory workers could not be employed unless they were registered with the sheriff's office, and the Associated Farmers provided the sheriff with lists of "agitators" and "dangerous radicals," including all persons known to have been members of unions. Such people were not only denied employment but were often ordered out of the county.

When a strike threatened, growers or their managerial employees were often made special deputies, though they did not always wait for this legal authorization and often acted simply as armed vigilantes. In the strike of the AFL lettuce packers' union at Salinas in 1936, agribusiness groups recruited a "general staff" which supplanted the sheriff and the chief of police. Col. Henry Sanborn, an Army Reserve officer and publisher of an anti-Communist journal, was employed as "coordinator" of all antistrike forces, including the local law enforcement officers as well as a "citizens' army" armed with shotguns and pick handles. The chief of the state highway patrol and a representative of the state attorney general's office gave their approval to this arrangement.

The Associated Farmers also aided in many prosecutions not only of Communists but of almost any other agricultural strike leaders under the state criminal syndicalism law.

Among the justifications used by the embattled "farmers" in their extreme resistance to any form of labor unionism were two arguments that had some color of validity during the darkest years of the great depression in 1933 and 1934. At that time it was often true that growers could not have paid higher wages without raising the cost of production above the prices that the crops could be sold for; it was also true that the main attempts to organize migratory farm laborers were then in the hands of the Communist party. But agribusiness interests continued to repeat these arguments in later years when prices and profits had risen greatly and when radical influence was no longer substantially involved.

In the middle and later years of the 1930s, dispossessed families from the Dust Bowl region came into California at the rate of more than 100,000 persons a year, most of them to swell the supply of migratory farm labor. People of Anglo-American stock, working in family groups, now made up the bulk of the state's migratory labor force for the first time, and as a result, the public interest in the plight of farm laborers increased somewhat, though only temporarily. Carey McWilliams's *Factories in the Field* and John Steinbeck's *The Grapes of Wrath*, both published in 1939, helped to stimulate this interest.

McWilliams's book included a chapter on the activities of the Associated Farmers and their allies entitled "The Rise of Farm Fascism."

In the administration of Governor Culbert L. Olson, McWilliams was chief of the state division of immigration and housing, and in that capacity he made himself a thorn in the flesh of agribusiness by inspecting private farm-labor camps and denouncing their vile conditions. The annual convention of the Associated Farmers passed a resolution describing McWilliams as "California's Agricultural Pest Number One, outranking pear blight and the boll weevil." The state legislature, under agribusiness influence, passed a bill to abolish McWilliams's position, but Governor Olson pocket-vetoed this proposed "anti-McWilliams act."

In 1939 and 1940 the La Follette committee, a subcommittee of the United States Senate Committee on Education and Labor under the chairmanship of Senator Robert M. La Follette, Jr., of Wisconsin, held extensive hearings in California to investigate "violations of free speech and rights of labor." But most of its recommendations for reform, introduced in 1942, produced no action in Congress. With the coming of World War II the "Okies" flocked to the shipyards; Mexicans and Mexican Americans again became the majority of the California farm labor force; and the public lost what interest it had had in the whole matter. The Dies committee was attracting more attention than the La Follette committee, and in 1946, as the reactionary cycle swung still further, La Follette lost the Wisconsin Republican senatorial nomination to Joseph R. McCarthy.

THE RISE AND FALL OF THE BRACERO PROGRAM

The demands of World War II produced a sudden, genuine, and desperate shortage of farm labor, and the California growers called for large numbers of workers from Mexico. In 1942, under an act of Congress and an agreement with Mexico, the United States Department of Agriculture assumed the responsibility for recruiting, contracting, transporting, housing, and feeding these temporary immigrant farm workers. In a formal sense, this was the beginning of the "bracero program." The meaning of the Spanish word *braceros* ("the strong-armed ones") bore a striking resemblance to the meaning of the Tamil word *kuli*.

There had been an informal bracero program 25 years earlier during World War I, when private labor contractors had supplied California growers with seasonal workers from Mexico. Thousands of peons had been eager for the opportunity, since the Mexican revolution had turned hordes of them into displaced persons, much as the Taiping Rebellion had nudged thousands of destitute Chinese toward California in the 1850s.

The growers were able to persuade Congress not to include Mexico in the postwar quota system of immigration restrictions, and the surge of Mexicans into California had continued through the 1920s, but it had slowed in the depression years, and the Mexican government had then found itself forced to pay the costs of repatriating many of its impoverished nationals who could no longer obtain work in California and who were not eligible for relief there. In 1942 the Mexican government feared that this experience would be repeated, and it therefore demanded that the United States government, rather than private labor contractors, must take responsibility for the immigrant workers.

After World War II the bracero program continued in force with the enthusiastic support of California growers, though President Truman, to their irritation, removed the program from the grower-oriented Department of Agriculture and assigned it to the Department of Labor by executive order in 1948.

More numerous than the braceros in the years after the end of World War II were the illegal "wetbacks." While their exact numbers could not be known, it was estimated that more than half a million of these illegal immigrants crossed and recrossed the international boundary each year, most of them to work in the fields of California and other states in the southwest.

In 1951 Congress adopted the famous Public Law 78 and also gave special legislative recognition to a new agreement with Mexico. Together these measures provided the most elaborate plan of importing contract workers in which the United States had ever engaged, and although the plan was approved as a "Korean war emergency" measure, it ultimately provided the basis for continuing the bracero program until 1964, 11 years after the Korean war had ended.

Under this system, Mexican officials assembled the braceros, and the United States Department of Labor provided for their transportation to reception centers north of the border. There they were turned over to labor contractors representing the growers' associations. At the insistence of the Mexican government, there were standard contracts covering wages, hours, transportation, housing, and working conditions. The American government guaranteed the provision of emergency medical care, workmen's compensation, disability and death benefits, and burial expenses. Though such provisions were minimal, they were far superior to the benefits available to American farm laborers, who enjoyed no legal protection at all.

In 1957, the peak year, California imported 192,438 braceros. In 1960 about 100,000 of them were at work in the state at the peak season in early September, and they formed about a quarter of the seasonal farm labor force. Most of them worked on the larger farms; about 5.2 percent of the farms in California employed 60 percent of the total number of seasonal hired workers—including more than 80 percent of the braceros.

As Congress continued to grant extensions of the program, it became increasingly hard to disguise the fact that the bracero system perpetuated the tragic poverty of the American migratory laborers. It depressed wages, destroyed the bargaining power of the domestic worker, and drove away local labor. There were many incidents in which braceros were used as strikebreakers with the connivance of government officials. Ostensibly, P.L. 78 allowed the importation of braceros only when it would "not adversely affect the wages and working conditions of domestic argicultural workers," when "sufficient domestic workers . . . [were] not available," and when "reasonable efforts [had] been made to attract domestic workers at wages . . . comparable to those offered foreign workers." This last provision would have tended to freeze farm wages at the wretched levels of the early 1950s, even if the rest of the provisions of P.L. 78 had been effectively enforced—which they were not. In effect, the system encouraged the growers to offer the lowest possible wages and the worst possible conditions to domestic workers, not merely because this practice saved money for the growers, as it always had, but also because it reduced the "availability" of domestic laborers and thus maximized the growers' legal eligibility to hire braceros.

To employers of seasonal farm workers, the braceros represented a supply of cheap, docile, and "dependable" labor—guaranteed to arrive and to vanish exactly when the employers wanted it to. California growers continued to rationalize such motives on the basis of race, as they had done for more than a century. Anglo-Americans, the growers constantly assured themselves and the public, simply could not perform stoop labor as well as nonwhites, who were equipped by racial heredity with stronger backs. There was no scientific basis for this assumption, and Californians who knew their state's history should not have had to be reminded that Anglo-Americans with gold pans had not only performed the most backbreaking form of stoop labor ever invented, but had also insisted that *only* whites were suited for it.

As agribusiness clung to the braceros, public criticism slowly intensified. Agriculture was in the untenable position of being the only private industry which maintained that the government was obligated to provide it with a labor supply, and a cheap one at that. At last, in 1963 Congress refused to approve the customary 2-year extension of the bracero program and instead ordered its termination at the end of the following year, with a few minor exceptions. The growers predicted disastrous shortages of harvest labor and warned consumers of food scarcities and drastic price increases. These predictions proved baseless; 1965 was another record year in California agricultural output, and food prices rose insignificantly or not at all. By offering better wages and working conditions, the growers were able to attract enough domestic labor and thus to refute their own perennial claims that it would be impossible to do so.

UNIONIZATION BREAKS THROUGH

Though the growers often denied that their desire for braceros was in any way related to their desire to block the organization of labor unions by domestic farm workers, the connection was inescapable and the growers used many of the same arguments for both purposes. Most of these arguments were variations on the traditional American political theme that "farming" was "different" from all other business enterprises.

Because the harvesting of perishable crops was intensely seasonal, one argument ran, growers required a "dependable" labor force and were uniquely vulnerable to strikes and therefore could never tolerate unions. This contention ignored a number of facts. Canning was equally seasonal, yet it had long been unionized with great advantage to the employers rather than any undue hardship to them. The marketing of perishable crops was as dependent on transportation workers as it was on harvest and cannery workers, yet the industries involved in the transportation of food had been entirely unionized for decades. Most of the employers in the canning, trucking, railroad, and shipping industries had long since tacitly conceded that union contracts were the best method of assuring a dependable labor supply. A contention of California growers was that like other "American farmers" they had always maintained a personal solicitude toward their hired hands and that this would be sacrificed in the "impersonal" process of union bargaining. Much of the public in California consisted of recent arrivals from the northcentral and northeastern parts of the nation, where this idea had once had some faint semblance of truth. Many remained unaware that it had never had any validity as applied to the typical employer-employee relationships in the agriculture of California, where wage rates were set by growers' associations and where hiring was usually done through labor contractors who performed the functions of company unions.

Growers also maintained that they believed in "collective bargaining," but only with persons who actually worked for them, not with labor union officials, whom they almost invariably described as "outside agitators." But this was the same claim that employers in virtually every other industry had used in earlier times in efforts to block the beginnings of unions. It ignored the fact that collective bargaining could not be genuine if workers were denied the right to choose experienced representatives as their bargaining agents. The growers wished to continue to hire such representatives of their own—the labor contractors—while continuing to deny any effective representation to the workers.

The most genuine objection of the growers to collective bargaining was that it was sure to raise costs. But not even this objection was valid, even on a strictly economic level. Higher wages would enable hundreds of thousands of American migrant-worker families to buy more food and at the same time would lower the costs of welfare and many other costs of poverty.

Extreme poverty and the disorganization that accompanied it had always been a major obstacle to organizing farm workers, who were generally regarded as too demoralized to be even potential union material. The AFL had repeatedly attempted the job and had repeatedly given it up. Clark Kerr, on the basis of his wide experience as a mediator of labor disputes, maintained as late as 1961 that "about the only time you ever get farm workers organized is when it is done by some group with an ideological inclination for more than a bona fide union purpose." He recommended wage boards to set minimum standards as the main hope of improvement. Varden Fuller, one of the ablest students of the problem, long believed that farm workers could never be unionized until some unprecedented awakening of public conscience impelled the federal government to bring farm labor under the laws guaranteeing the right of collective bargaining.

But the two largest national labor groups had merged in 1955, and 4 years later the organization thus formed, the AFL-CIO, returned to the offensive on the farm-labor front with a new Agricultural Workers Organizing Committee (AWOC). Soon afterward, Cesar Chavez left a secure and comfortable job as an official of a Mexican-American community service society to begin the hard and hazardous task of organizing a new and independent union called the National Farm Workers Association (NFWA), at a salary of $50 a week.

Chavez had been born near Yuma, Arizona, on a small homestead near the Colorado River. This family farm was lost through unpaid taxes in the depression of the 1930s. He had worked as a migrant farm laborer from early childhood and consequently had obtained his 8 years of formal education with difficulty in nearly 40 different California public schools.

Chavez conceived the new NFWA as a labor organization that would offer its members the benefits of a credit union and other services while it offered employers a stable and dependable work force made up of skillful and well-organized crews of NFWA members working with no-strike contracts. At that time he placed no hope in agricultural strikes, having seen too many disheartening examples of them, but in September 1965 AWOC members began a strike against 33 grape growers in the district around Delano in northern Kern County, and 2 weeks later Chavez's NFWA decided to join it. For the first several months there seemed to be no chance that the strike could win. So many strikebreakers were brought in that the grape harvest in the district was larger than in the previous year. Yet the strike continued until, in the spring and summer of 1966, it won a series of brilliant victories that set a precedent for ultimate unionization of at least the larger farms throughout California.

If the Delano strike had been attempted a few years earlier, it would have met the fate of every previous attempt to organize farm labor. But now a new force was at work—the strong and increasing sympathy of a part of the white public for the civil rights of ethnic minorities in general and farm workers in particular. Neither of the unions involved in the Delano strike was segregated, but the AWOC local, under Larry Itliong as regional director, consisted mainly of Filipino Americans, while most of the members of Chavez's NFWA were Mexican Americans. The brief flicker of public sympathy for migrant workers in the late 1930s had arisen mainly because, for the first time, they were then predominantly "Nordic." In the 1960s, however, new and different manifestations of public conscience were emerging.

The NFWA had been awarded a substantial grant as a part of the federal "war on poverty" program. Payments under this grant were deferred during the strike, with the approval and indeed at the insistence of Chavez, who often remarked that "the only way to fight poverty is with a union contract." But gifts of money and food for the strikers poured into Delano from several other labor unions, from church groups throughout California, and from many other sympathizers with the civil rights movement.

The dock workers in the San Francisco Bay area refused to load grapes from the struck vineyards, of which the largest were owned by Schenley Industries and the Di Giorgio Corporation. Nationwide boycotts were launched against Schenley wines and liquors, against Di Giorgio's S&W canned goods, and against stores that sold them. In the spring of 1966, executives of Schenley concluded that the adverse publicity was counteracting the effects of the large sums the company spent to advertise its products. In this light, the much smaller amounts the company saved by refusing to raise wages in its vineyards were obviously a poor economy. On April 6, 1966, Schenley Industries made the historic announcement that it had agreed to recognize the National Farm Workers' Association as the sole bargaining representative for its field-workers—the first recognition of a farm worker's union by a major California grower.

The next day the Di Giorgio Corporation announced that it would permit its workers to decide by ballot whether they wished to be represented by a union, and if so, what union. The victorious allies, Itliong's AWOC and Chavez's NFWA, merged to form the United Farm Workers Organizing Committee. In the election in August 1966, although the Di Giorgio Corporation had always insisted that its employees did not want to be unionized, its field-workers voted 530 for UFWOC, 331 for the Teamsters, and 12 for no union.

Several northern California growers of wine grapes then signed contracts with the United Farm Workers (UFW), but the great majority of California producers of table grapes held out. They were encouraged by the election of Ronald Reagan, a vigorous opponent of farm unions, to the governorship in 1966. In August 1967 Chavez called for a boycott against the Giumarra vineyards, the nation's largest table grape producers, and in 1968 the UFW launched a national boycott of all California table grapes. This move captured the attention of the whole country and became a burning social issue. Although Governor Reagan, Senator George Murphy, and presidential candidate Richard Nixon condemned the boycott, the mayors of San Francisco, New York, Chicago, Cleveland, Honolulu, and several other large cities announced their approval of it, and it became so effective that the growers were threatened with ruin. At last, in July 1970, Giumarra and most of the other large California table grape growers agreed to union contracts with the United Farm Workers.

Chavez's next move was against the lettuce growers of the Salinas Valley, but as soon as those growers learned that the grape producers were about to surrender, they hurriedly negotiated contracts with the Teamsters Union in order to forestall the UFW drive. One maverick Salinas lettuce grower, Bud Antle, had included his field-workers in his contracts with the Teamsters since 1961. Now there was a rush to imitate him because, said a Salinas growers' representative, "the Teamsters are a trade union; Chavez's union is a civil rights movement." Chavez denounced the Teamsters' agreements as "sweetheart contracts."

In March 1977, after several years of struggle and periodic negotiation, Chavez and the Teamster executives signed a 5-year jurisdictional agreement.

The UFW was to represent all field-workers in future contracts with the growers, leaving all cannery workers and some truck drivers to the Teamsters.

"THE EQUAL PROTECTION OF THE LAWS"

Until 1966 agricultural labor was specifically excluded from the provisions of virtually every federal and state law that protected the rights of other workers. Minimum wages, unemployment insurance, social security, collective bargaining—all were guaranteed to others and specifically denied to farm labor. The rationalization for this was always that "farmers had special problems." The truth was that they had special political power. Agricultural employers were heavily overrepresented in Congress and in almost every state legislature, while the interests of farm workers were almost totally unrepresented until the 1960s.

The ending of the bracero program had been an important preliminary to reform, but only a negative one. At long last, in 1964, Congress made its first positive moves toward correcting a shameful set of conditions. The Economic Opportunity Act of 1964 included grants to agencies aiding migrant workers, and an amendment to the National Housing Act provided direct loans for construction of farm-labor housing. In September 1966, Congress took the historic step of extending the protection of a new federal minimum wage law to farm workers. This was only a token beginning. While the minimum wage for most other workers was raised to $1.60 an hour, effective in 1968, the national minimum for farm labor was set at only $1, and not even this would apply to small employers.

These new federal laws were merely an entering wedge. More subsidies to help provide decent housing for migrant workers were essential in order to eradicate the rural slums that were far worse than anything in the cities. For migrant workers and their families the conditions of recruitment, transportation, health, sanitation, workers' compensation, child labor, education, and civil and political rights were disgracefully and incredibly substandard.

Of central importance was the right of collective bargaining and the guarantee of this right through extension to agriculture of laws governing union representation elections. At the federal level, attempts to extend the provisions of the National Labor Relations Act (NLRA) to farm workers remained deadlocked, partly because Chavez did not wish to give up the weapon of the secondary boycott, which was illegal for workers covered by the NLRA.

But in California the replacement of Governor Ronald Reagan by Edmund G. Brown, Jr., made possible a landmark law providing for state-supervised secret-ballot elections in which California's 250,000 farm workers could pick a union to represent them, or reject unionization. Brown personally hammered out the compromise that was adopted in May 1975. The new law created a state agricultural relations board with quasi-judicial powers to oversee elections. The act allowed harvest-time strikes and permitted secondary boycotts in some limited circumstances. For California's agricultural workers, a new era had begun.

SELECTED BIBLIOGRAPHY

James H. Shideler (ed.), *Agriculture in the Development of the Far West* (1975), is a valuable symposium. Good sources of statistics are the *California Statistical Abstract* and U.S. Department of Agriculture, *Agricultural Statistics*, both annual publications.

Several theses at the University of California, Berkeley, contribute to California's agricultural history. On some of the effects of mechanization, see John W. Mamer, "The Generation and Proliferation of Agricultural Handlabor-saving Technology; a Case Study of Sugar Beets," Ph.D. (1958) and Francis J. Smith, "The Impact of Technological Change on the Marketing of Salinas Lettuce," Ph.D. (1961). On particular crops, see Colin C. Archibald, "History of Cotton Production in California," M.A. (1950); Rolf W. Ordal, "History of the California Walnut Industry," Ph.D. (1952); Elizabeth M. Riley, "History of the Almond Industry in California," M.A. (1948). Lawrence J. Jelinek, *Harvest Empire: A History of California Agriculture* (1979) contains an analysis of the development of large-scale farming and the role of government's expanding agricultural subsidies. See also Charles C. Cooley, "The California Date Growing Industry, 1890–1939," *Southern California Quarterly*, XLIX (March and June 1967), pp. 47–64, 167–192; Joseph Giovinco, "Democracy in Banking: The Bank of Italy and California's Italians," *California Historical Society Quarterly*, XLVII (September 1968), pp. 195–218; Hans C. Palmer, "Italian Immigration and the Development of California Agriculture," Ph.D. thesis, University of California, Berkeley (1965); and Richard J. Orsi (compiler), *A List of References for the History of Agriculture in California* (1974).

Walter Goldschmidt, *As You Sow* (1947), analyzed the social structure of Arvin, a community based on corporate agriculture and compared it unfavorably with the social structure of Dinuba, a town in a district of family farms. Some of the subsequent attacks on the methods and conclusions of Goldschmidt's study are described in Richard S. Kirkendall, "Social Science in the Central Valley of California: An Episode," *California Historical Society Quarterly*, XLIII (September 1964), pp. 195–218.

Varden Fuller, "The Supply of Agricultural Labor as a Factor in the Evolution of Farm Organization in California," Ph.D. thesis, University of California, Berkeley (1939), was published in United States Senate Committee on Education and Labor, *Violations of Free Speech and Rights of Labor. Hearings before a Subcommittee . . .* , part 54 (1940), pp. 19777–19898. The other parts of these hearings before the La Follette subcommittee (published 1940–1943), and also many of the parts of the subcommittee's *Report* (1942–1943), are indispensable sources for the troubled agricultural history of the 1930s. See also the *Hearings* (1940–1941) and *Reports* (1941) of the House of Representatives Select Committee to Investigate Interstate Migration of Destitute Citizens, chaired by Congressman John H. Tolan of Oakland; and Walter J. Stein, *California and the Dust Bowl Migration* (1973).

Other important works dealing with the state's peculiar farm-labor problems are Carey McWilliams, *Factories in the Field; the Story of Migratory Farm Labor in California* (1939) and *Ill Fares the Land; Migratory Labor in the United States* (1942); Dorothea Lange and Paul S. Taylor, *An American Exodus: A Record of Human Erosion* (1939); and Lloyd S. Fisher, *The Harvest Labor Market in California* (1953).

On the use of Mexican and other immigrant labor, see George C. Kiser and Martha

Woody Kiser, *Mexican Workers in the United States: Historical and Political Perspectives* (1979); Peter N. Kirstein, *Anglo Over Bracero: A History of the Mexican Worker in the United States from Roosevelt to Nixon* (1977); Mark Reisler, *By the Sweat of Their Brow: Mexican Immigrant Labor in the United States, 1900–1940* (1976); Paul S. Taylor, *Mexican Labor in the United States: Imperial Valley, California* (1928); John R. Martinez, "Mexican Immigration to the United States, 1910–1930," Ph.D. thesis, University of California, Berkeley (1957); John C. Elac, "The Employment of Mexican Workers in U.S. Agriculture, 1900–1960," Ph.D. thesis, University of California, Los Angeles (1961); Charles Wollenberg, "*Huelga*, 1928 Style: The Imperial Valley Cantaloupe Workers' Strike," *Pacific Historical Review*, XXXVIII (February 1969), pp. 45–58; James F. Rooney, "The Effects of Imported Mexican Farm Labor in a California County," *American Journal of Economics and Sociology*, XX (October 1961), pp. 513–521, a study conducted in San Joaquin County in 1957; Leo Grebler, *Mexican Immigration to the United States—The Record and Its Implications* (1966); R. K. Das, *Hindustani Workers on the Pacific Coast* (1923); and Bruno Lasker, *Filipino Immigration to the United States* (1931).

Important studies of the bracero program are Henry P. Anderson, *The Bracero Program in California* (1976); Ernesto Galarza, *Merchants of Labor: The Mexican Bracero Story* (1964); Otey M. Scruggs, "The Evolution of the Mexican Farm Labor Agreement of 1942," *Agricultural History*, XXXIV (July 1960), pp. 140–149; Ellis W. Hawley, "The Politics of the Mexican Labor Issue, 1950–1965," ibid., XL (July 1966), pp. 157–176; N. Ray Gilmore and Gladys Gilmore, "The Bracero in California," *Pacific Historical Review*, XXXII (August 1963), pp. 265–282; and Truman E. Moore, *The Slaves We Rent* (1965). U.S. Department of Labor, *Year of Transition: Seasonal Farm Labor, 1965* (1966) is an incisive report by Secretary of Labor W. Willard Wirtz on the results of the termination of the bracero program and on the needs for reform in the conditions of domestic farm labor.

On the background of the farm labor union question, see Ernesto Galarza, *Farm Workers and Agri-Business in California, 1947–1960* (1977); Stuart M. Jamieson, *Labor Unionism in American Agriculture*, U.S. Bureau of Labor Statistics Bulletin 836 (1945); Alexander Morin, *The Organizability of Farm Labor in the United States* (1952); and Varden Fuller, *Labor Relations in Agriculture* (1955).

On the movement led by Cesar Chavez, see Peter Matthiessen, *Sal Si Puedes: Cesar Chavez and the New American Revolution* (1969); John G. Dunne, *Delano: The Story of the California Grape Strike* (1967, 1971); Joan London and Henry Anderson, *So Shall Ye Reap* (1970); and Ronald B. Taylor, *Chavez and the Farm Workers* (1975).

DIVERSITY AND CONFLICT

One of the most deplorable aspects of the history of California has been the persistence of discrimination directed against the state's diverse ethnic and racial groups. During the twentieth century, progress was made in overcoming the burden of past discrimination, but the legacy of hostility and conflict remained.

CALIFORNIA INDIANS

All the nonwhite minorities in American California suffered from various kinds of unjust discrimination, but the mistreatment of the Indians began earliest and was by far the worst. In California, as in other parts of the United States, the history of American treatment of the Indians in the nineteenth century was too often a sickening record of racist murder and sanctimonious fraud.

The problems of the Indians in California were different from those of most other American Indian tribes in that only a minority of the California Indians were ever placed on reservations. The treaties of the early 1850s, providing for large reservations in California, were never ratified, and most of the attempts to provide small reservations were unsuccessful. The California Indians were left to survive as best they might on the fringes of white settlement; most of them did not survive. Of those who did, the majority became agricultural laborers.

Several idealistic individuals tried to improve the situation. In the early 1880s the New England author Helen Hunt Jackson sent copies of her critique of American Indian policy, *A Century of Dishonor* (1881), to all members of Congress. At Jackson's request Congress then made her a member of a special commission to report on the Indians of southern California. Although the commission's report had little effect on federal policy, Jackson's research for it aided the writing of *Ramona* (1884), a novel she intended to be the *Uncle Tom's*

Cabin of Indian reform. *Ramona* powerfully portrayed the destitution of the homeless Indians of southern California and also, quite unintentionally, created a collection of regional myths that stimulated the tourist trade.

In 1901 Charles F. Lummis organized the Sequoya League with the aid of Thomas R. Bard, David Starr Jordan, and others. Its main object was better treatment of the Indians, and its main accomplishment was an act of Congress that provided money to purchase a tract of land near Pala for the Cupeño Indians who were evicted from Warner's Ranch in San Diego County.

During World War I a number of Indians served in the armed forces, and in 1924, partly in recognition of that service, Congress gave American Indians the rights of citizenship in the United States and in the states of their residence. Congress also recognized that an injustice had been done to the California Indians, in particular, by the failure to ratify the reservation treaties of the early 1850s, which had promised them more than 7 million acres of land. In 1928 Congress authorized the attorney general of California to bring suit against the United States on behalf of the California Indians to determine what financial compensation should be made to them. A special census provided by the act of 1928 enumerated 23,585 persons as living descendants of California Indians, and thus entitled to compensation. But the case dragged on until 1944, and when the federal court of claims finally made its award, it was only for a little more than $5 million, or about $200 per person.

In the special case of the survivors of the Cahuilla tribe, also known as the Palm Springs Indians, the results of litigation were startlingly different. In the 1870s the federal government had granted the odd-numbered sections of desert land in the Palm Springs area to the Southern Pacific Railroad and the even-numbered sections, checkerboard-fashion, to the Cahuilla Indians. When Palm Springs became a booming resort town in the 1920s, the surviving Cahuilla, numbering about 100, tried to persuade the federal government to permit the leasing of some of their lands to the eager hotel promoters, but the government refused. Lee Arenas, one of the Cahuilla, managed to interest a former justice of the California Supreme Court, John W. Preston, in taking the case to the Supreme Court of the United States. In 1944 the Court ruled that each of the Cahuilla should receive the rental from $350,000 worth of individually allotted tribal land, as well as a share of the income from 30,000 acres of communal tribal land.

The contrast between the ridiculously inadequate award by the federal court of claims to the California Indians in 1944 and the lucrative award by the Supreme Court to the Palm Springs Indians in the same year was so striking that it helped persuade Congress to pass the Indian Claims Commission Act of 1946. This law entitled American Indians to payments from the federal government equivalent to the original value of the lands their ancestors had once occupied. The determination of the amounts was a fantastically complex matter, but in 1965, after many years of hearings, the descendants of the California Indians finally received and voted to accept an award of a little more than $29 million. This was about 45 cents an acre for 64 million acres of land, nearly two-thirds of the total area of California.

The long and tragic decline in Indian population was reversed in the twentieth century, and the number of persons of Indian ancestry in the state began to rise steadily. The growth in population was due to natural increase and to migration to California of Indians from other states, who were aided by job training and relocation programs of the federal government. In 1965 the number of Indians living in California had risen to 75,000, less than 10 percent of whom were living on the 82 federal reservations. Only three reservations, at Hoopa Valley, Fort Yuma, and Bishop, had more than 500 residents, and only 18 reservations had more than 100. During the 1970s the Indian population in the state more than doubled, and in 1981 the Census Bureau reported that California, with more than 198,000 Indians, had the largest Indian population of any state in the nation.

Throughout the twentieth century both the United States and the state of California demonstrated awakenings of conscience in their treatment of Indian people. California abolished all legal distinctions between persons of Indian ancestry and other citizens and led the states in making Indians fully eligible to receive the benefits of the public schools, welfare assistance, old-age and survivors payments, and other public services. In spite of these gains, the Indians of California remained the state's most economically depressed minority group. The rate of unemployment among California Indians was more than three times as high as the rate for whites and somewhat above the rate for blacks. The California State Advisory Commission on Indian Affairs reported in 1966 that the median annual income for reservation Indians was $2268 per family. More than 40 percent of all rural and reservation Indians in the state had not gone beyond the eighth grade, and the school dropout rate for Indians was three times that of the general population.

During the 1960s California Indians increased their level of political involvement and established several pantribal organizations. The American Indian Historical Society, organized in 1964 by Cahuilla tribal chairman Rupert Costo, established an active publication program and called for the revision of textbooks which contained negative stereotypes of Indians. In 1967 concern over the inadequacy of primary and secondary education for Indian youth led to the formation of the California Indian Education Association, and on many college campuses Native American Studies departments were formed.

The occupation of Alcatraz Island in San Francisco Bay by a group called Indians of All Tribes in 1969 to 1971 ushered in a period of increased activism among California Indians. In northeastern California, members of the Achumawi tribe engaged in sit-ins and took legal action to regain forest lands acquired by the Pacific Gas and Electric Company. In the northwestern part of the state, Yurok Indian fishermen clashed with law enforcement officers over fishing rights along the Klamath River. In 1978 and 1979 Indians in the Santa Barbara area occupied the site of a proposed supertanker terminal to protest the destruction of what they regarded as sacred land.

In recent years California Indians also have demonstrated a growing interest in the preservation and revival of their native cultures. This resurgence of interest has produced some remarkable results. In 1974 the Cupeño, whose plight had spurred the Sequoya League to action in 1901, dedicated the Cupa Cultural Center at the Pala reservation and offered classes in Cupeño language, culture, and history. In neighboring Riverside County the Cahuilla founded the Malki Museum, offering native language classes and establishing a repository for Cahuilla artifacts and ethnographic information.

ASIANS

If the worst racial persecutions in American history were those inflicted on the Indians before 1900, the most obvious and flagrant racist abuse in the United States in the twentieth century was that which the Japanese Americans suffered when they were deprived of their liberty and placed in concentration camps during World War II. But that abuse was a temporary one, and the very extremity of the blundering injustice of it ultimately helped enable the people of the United States and the people of California to learn a lesson from it.

Even during the war itself some Californians had opposed the anti-Japanese hysteria. The Pacific Coast Committee on American Principles and Fair Play, organized in December 1941 with President Robert Gordon Sproul and several members of the faculty of the University of California among its leaders, carried on a valiant campaign in defense of the rights of the Japanese Americans. The heroism of Nisei soldiers was a reproach to anti-Japanese racism, and after the end of the war the memory of Hiroshima and Nagasaki neutralized the memory of Pearl Harbor.

As the War Relocation Authority pointed out in the concluding sentence of its final report in 1946, "Although there is undoubtedly a marked xenophobic tendency in the United States, there is also a strong and stubborn potential for fair-mindedness among the American people—a potential which should be carefully studied, fostered, and brought to the highest degree of assertiveness in the interest of greater racial tolerance and a richer realization of democratic values."

Congress recognized in 1948 that the Japanese Americans were entitled to financial compensation. Families had sold their homes and businesses in frantic haste. Some had lost everything they had, and many had lost most of what they had. Claims totaling $400 million were filed by 44,000 Japanese Americans, who ultimately received settlements totaling $38 million, less than 10 cents on every dollar of estimated loss in real and personal property. Congress also provided for the return of confiscated bank deposits, though the legal process was difficult and the recovery was slow and incomplete.

In 1952, after California's alien land law had been in effect for 39 years, the state supreme court struck it down as unconstitutional. At about the same time, Congress entirely abandoned the racial definition of "aliens ineligible for citizenship." Very few nations had ever withheld the privilege of naturalization on racial grounds, and in doing so the United States had been in the company of Nazi Germany and the Union of South Africa. In 1952 the

McCarran-Walter Immigration and Nationality Act provided that "the right of a person to become a naturalized citizen of the United States shall not be denied or abridged because of race."

An important factor in turning the tide of public feeling in favor of the Japanese Americans was that they reacted to mistreatment in an extraordinary way—by establishing an unrivaled record of good citizenship. They ranked higher in education and lower in crime and juvenile delinquency than any other ethnic group in the United States, including the native whites. In 1960 they averaged 12 years of schooling, as against 11 for whites and 8.6 for blacks. By the 1970s the difference in educational attainment among the three groups had narrowed considerably, but the Japanese Americans retained a slight edge over the others. In impressive numbers they obtained advanced degrees and jobs in such professional fields as business administration, engineering, and optometry; by 1970 their median family income was $3000 higher than the national median. Their record of physical and mental health was almost incredible. The average longevity of Japanese Americans was 74.5 years for men and 81.2 years for women—nearly 7 years above the figures for California whites and well above the record of any other group in human history. Three Japanese traditions, the strength of the family, the belief in the value of education, and the belief in the virtue of hard work, did most to account for this unparalleled triumph over adversity.

S. I. Hayakawa, the controversial president of San Francisco State University, became in 1976 the first Californian of Japanese ancestry to be elected to the United States Senate. He became embroiled in a dispute with other Japanese-American leaders over a proposal that Congress provide additional reparations to Japanese Americans interned in the wartime relocation camps. Hayakawa, who was born in Canada and remained a Canadian citizen during World War II, denounced the idea of reparations as "ridiculous." In testimony before the United States Commission on Wartime Relocation and Internment of Civilians, Hayakawa described relocation as a "vacation" for many Japanese Americans.

The decline of anti-Japanese sentiment after World War II was foreshadowed during the war years by the federal government's removal of legal discrimination against the Chinese. Congress repealed the Chinese Exclusion Act in 1943 in order, as President Roosevelt put it, to "correct a historic mistake and silence the distorted Japanese propaganda." The results were more important in principle, however, than in practice. Although China was now permitted to have an immigration quota, it was so low that only about 10,000 Chinese were admitted under it in the next 20 years. In 1965, however, Congress abolished the national-origins quota system. Under the new law, total annual immigration remained about the same, but admission was on the basis of skills or family relationships. This permitted a substantial increase in Chinese immigration, much of it from Hong Kong to California.

Chinese Americans in the postwar period established a high rate of achievement grounded in traditional values similar to those underlying the success of the Japanese Americans. By the 1970s their average length of school attendance, for instance, surpassed that of whites but did not quite equal the record of the Japanese. For the Chinese Americans the educational picture was one of extremes: a very high proportion of them had gone to college, but also many had not gone beyond the eighth grade. The wartime shortages of engineers, scientists, doctors, and nurses opened thousands of professional jobs to educated Chinese Americans; this began to occur before the end of World War II, rather than after it, as in the case of the Japanese.

As with other minorities, Chinese Americans in recent years also have increased their political activity. In 1974 March Fong Eu was elected California's secretary of state, becoming the first person of Chinese ancestry to hold statewide office in California. She carried every county except San Diego in 1974 and received the largest vote of any constitutional officer in 1978 when she was reelected. By 1980 five Chinese Americans held elective office in San Francisco, whereas a decade earlier there had been none.

Filipino Americans in the years after World War II became one of the fastest-growing minority groups in the state. During the early decades of the twentieth century most Filipinos drawn to California were farm laborers, but under the 1965 immigration law the majority of Filipino immigrants were accountants, nurses, and other skilled professionals. State certification regulations often made it difficult for Filipino immigrants to practice their professions, and many were forced to take low-skilled and low-paying jobs. To escape chronic underemployment, Filipino-American professionals took legal action to reform the state certification process. A similar upsurge was also seen in the number of Korean Americans, especially in southern California. By 1980 there were some 200,000 Koreans in the Los Angeles area alone, a 500 percent increase since 1976.

Following the American withdrawal from Vietnam in the early 1970s, the escalating turmoil in southeast Asia led to a mass exodus of refugees. In desperation tens of thousands of Vietnamese, Laotians, and Cambodians fled to the sea, and eventually many of these "boat people" were resettled in the United States.

California received about 40 percent of the nation's total Indo-Chinese refugee population, and state officials petitioned the federal government for additional aid in handling the influx. By 1981 an estimated 145,000 refugees were in the state, more than 92,000 of whom were on public welfare. Volunteer agencies, including many church-related organizations, assisted in the resettlement effort by sponsoring individual refugee families.

BLACKS

Of all the racial minorities, black people attracted the largest share of public attention in the decades after the end of World War II. They became more active than other groups in openly protesting against racial discrimination, and their protests, both peaceful and violent, received wide coverage in the national news media.

Blacks formed about 11 percent of the total population of the United States in 1940. Their major migration to California began in 1942 with the sudden demand for labor in the shipyards and other war industries, and thereafter the percentage of blacks in the state's population, which had been only 1.8 in 1940, rose to 4.3 in 1950 and 7.7 in 1980. But their presence was even more apparent because most of them became concentrated in all-black neighborhoods in the cities of Los Angeles, San Francisco, Oakland, Berkeley, and Richmond.

As Gunnar Myrdal pointed out in *An American Dilemma* (1944), a tragic "conflict between equalitarian ideals and discriminatory practice" had long characterized American treatment of black people, and as a result "their situation is pathological. . . . The masses of American Negroes are destitute."

The family, which was so great a source of strength for the Asian Americans, was tragically weaker among American blacks. For two centuries, under the system of slavery, the law had not recognized marriages between black slaves, and during that period the outrages committed by whites against black family life had had shattering psychological effects. In later years the ability of the black husband and father to protect his family and to provide for its support remained limited, and as a consequence the proportion of black men who deserted their families was far higher than in any other group. Also underlying the plight of black Americans was the lack of education. In 1960 more than 40 percent of California blacks had not gone beyond the eighth grade, and this became increasingly disastrous as mechanization and automation eliminated more and more unskilled jobs. The level of educational attainment of blacks rose steadily over the next two decades, but by the late 1970s only 58 percent of black teenagers were functionally literate as compared with 92 percent of white youth. The proportional difference between blacks and whites who were college students was actually greater in 1980 than it was in 1950.

In the long struggle for equality, major obstacles had to be overcome in three closely related areas: housing, employment, and education.

California was the first state to attempt a legal sanction promoting segregated housing when the constitution of 1879 authorized cities and towns to restrict the occupancy of Chinese and even to forbid their residence within the city limits. In 1890 the United States Supreme Court struck down this provision in the case of a San Francisco ordinance purporting to define the "boundaries" of Chinatown. In the twentieth century, real estate interests, wishing to maintain the racial integrity of all-white neighborhoods, often relied upon the right of contract. Deeds for the sale of residential property included "restrictive covenants" in which the buyer promised not to sell to anyone other than Caucasions. But in 1948, in *Shelley v. Kraemer,* the Supreme Court refused to permit the continued enforcement of these contracts by the courts, on the ground that such enforcement by agencies of state government violated the Fourteenth Amendment guarantee of the equal protection of the laws. The Los Angeles Board of Realtors and the California Real Estate Association launched a campaign to reverse the Court's ruling, but this project failed.

In 1959 the heavily Democratic California Legislature adopted the Unruh Civil Rights Act, named for Jesse Unruh, the speaker of the assembly. This law forbade racial discrimination by anyone engaged in business (including real estate brokers) and permitted anyone who suffered such discrimination to recover damages in the courts. In 1963 the legislature passed the Rumford Act, named for black Assemblyman W. Byron Rumford of Berkeley, which declared racial discrimination in housing to be against public policy and forbade owners of residential property including more than four units, or owners of any publicly assisted residential property, to engage in racial discrimination in its rental or sale. Enforcement was in the hands of a state commission empowered to investigate complaints, conciliate disputes, and if necessary issue cease-and-desist orders.

Not long after the passage of the Rumford "fair housing" or "open occupancy" law, the California Real Estate Association began a campaign not only against this particular act but against every form of what the association denounced as "forced housing." This led to the drafting of Initiative Proposition 14, a state constitutional amendment incorporating what the realtors' organization called "the right to sell." That remarkable document proposed to invalidate every past or future state law or local ordinance that limited the right of any person to refuse "to sell, lease, or rent any part or all of his real property ... to such person or persons as he in his absolute discretion chooses."

In November 1964 the voters of California approved Proposition 14 by more than two to one, and thus most of the white voters demonstrated that they were bitterly opposed to residential desegregation and deeply frightened by it. They feared a loss of social status if nonwhites moved into their neighborhoods. They feared decline of property values, though several studies had shown that this did not necessarily occur and that when it did, the neighborhoods were usually those where property values had already been deteriorating. Part of this white backlash was essentially irrational—the cancerous terror that came with the mass delusional neurosis of racism.

The passage of Proposition 14 was among the many grievances that contributed to the massive and tragic Watts riot in Los Angeles in 1965. The number of blacks in Los Angeles County had grown from about 25,000 before World War II to nearly 650,000 in 1965, and most of them were crowded into the southcentral part of the city, including the Watts district. Housing in Los Angeles, as the county commission on human relations pointed out, was more strictly segregated than in any city in the southern states. The riot in the "palm tree ghetto" of Watts began on the sweltering and smoggy evening of August 11, 1965, following the arrest of a young black man for drunken driving and the spread of a rumor that two black women had been victims of police brutality. The ensuing riot lasted for several days and was brought under control only by the intervention of the National Guard. At least 34 persons were killed, 31 of them blacks. In terms of loss of life this did not equal the record of the East St. Louis riot of 1917, but in terms of property losses, amounting to more than $40 million, the Los Angeles riot was the most destructive in American history. More than 600 buildings were damaged, including more than 200 completely destroyed by fire.

In May 1966 the state supreme court struck down Proposition 14 as an unconstitutional denial of the equal protection of the laws. There were many protests that the court had "violated the will of the people," but the following year the United States Supreme Court confirmed the unconstitutionality of the initiative.

Decisions by state and federal courts also played a central role in the movement to achieve equality of educational opportunity. The most important of these decisions was *Brown v. Board of Education of Topeka* in 1954, in which the Supreme Court forbade racial segregation in the public schools. It was written by Chief Justice Earl Warren for a unanimous court. Reversing the decision of the Court in *Plessy v. Ferguson* in 1896, which had permitted so-called separate but equal facilities, the Court now ruled that public school segregation was a denial of the equal protection of the laws. To segregate black children solely on the grounds of their race, said Chief Justice Warren, "generates a feeling of inferiority as to their status in the community that may affect their hearts and minds in a way unlikely ever to be undone." Warren had learned a great deal about racism from his own mistake in advocating Japanese evacuation.

Formal segregation of pupils by race had been abolished in most of the public school districts of California for many years, and the state law which had permitted local districts to continue the practice had been repealed in 1946. Yet *de facto* school segregation continued and even increased mainly because of continued residential segregation.

During the 1960s several communities in the state, most notably Riverside and Berkeley, began voluntarily to end segregation of their schools. More typical, however, was the case of Los Angeles in which the school board began the task of desegregation only when under direct court order to do so. The sprawling Los Angeles Unified School District was the nation's second-largest school system. By 1970 about one-quarter of the district's 700,000 students were black, 90 percent of whom attended predominantly black schools, and another 23 percent were of Mexican ancestry, two-thirds of whom attended schools predominantly Mexican. In 1970 Superior Court Judge Alfred Gitelson ruled that the district was guilty of unconstitutional segregation and ordered the school board to implement a desegregation plan. Governor Ronald Reagan labeled the ruling "utterly ridiculous," and the school board took no action pending an appeal of the desegregation order. Judge Gitelson was defeated for reelection, but the state supreme court in 1976 upheld his ruling and ordered the board to prepare a desegregation plan. The following year the board designed a plan which included several voluntary programs and the mandatory busing of some 40,000 students in the fourth through eighth grades. The plan went into effect in the fall of 1978 with considerable confusion, but few disruptive incidents.

In ordering the desegregation of Los Angeles schools, the state supreme court went beyond existing federal desegregation decisions. The federal courts had held that mandatory busing was required only in cases of intentional or *de jure* segregation, where it could be shown that a school district had deliberately segregated its schools in the past. The state court, however, ruled that busing was also a proper remedy for *de facto* or unintentional segregation, where segregated schools were the result of established residential patterns.

The antibusing forces in Los Angeles swiftly moved on the offensive. In 1979 the school board president, who supported mandatory busing, was recalled and replaced by an antibusing leader; in the November election an antibusing constitutional amendment limiting busing to cases of *de jure* segregation won statewide approval by a vote of more than two to one. In the spring of 1981 the state supreme court effectively upheld the constitutionality of the antibusing amendment, and the Los Angeles school board immediately announced the abandonment of the mandatory busing portion of its desegregation plan.

The greatest threat to the success of school desegregation in Los Angeles, as in cities around the country, was the decline of white enrollment. In the first year of court-ordered busing one-third of the white students assigned to new schools under the desegregation plan left the Los Angeles school district. Although the rate of "white flight" slowed the following year, the proportion of white students in the district declined from 56 percent in 1966 to 24 percent by 1980. The decline of white enrollment was part of a nationwide population shift from the central cities to the suburbs, a movement caused only partly by the controversy over desegregation. Nevertheless, the prospects for effective desegregation were considerably dimmed by the abandonment of the city schools by white students. As one school integration specialist commented, "There are simply not enough white children to go around."

At least as important as the political and social resistance to black penetration of white neighborhoods and schools was the economic discrimination that kept blacks in menial jobs, or kept them from getting any jobs at all. In California, as in most other states, nearly all labor unions in fields involving skilled workers had excluded blacks entirely until World War II. As the number of blacks in the California work force increased dramatically during the war, many unions established all-black "auxiliaries." Black workers in the auxiliaries were required to pay full union dues but were barred from voting in union elections and received unequal union benefits. In January 1945 the California Supreme Court ruled, in *James v. Marinship,* that the auxiliary practice was "contrary to public policy." This ruling produced important changes in union membership practices, but few blacks actually benefited from the decision. As the war ended, the number of blacks in the skilled work force began to decline rapidly. In San Francisco 75 percent of black heads of households had been skilled industrial workers during the war; by 1948 only 25 percent still held skilled jobs, and the black unemployment rate was nearly three times that for all persons.

Thirty years after the end of World War II the unemployment rate for blacks in the state was about twice that for the general population, and unemployment among black youths averaged nearly 40 percent. Almost a quarter of all black families in California lived in poverty in 1975, compared with less than 8 percent of whites. By 1980 the income of the typical black family was still less than 60 percent that of the average white family.

Although blacks continued to experience discrimination in many areas, during the 1970s and early1980s the number of blacks elected to political office steadily increased. Wilson Riles in 1970 was elected superintendent of public instruction over the archconservative Max Rafferty, becoming the first black to win statewide office. Three years later former police officer and city councilman Thomas Bradley was elected mayor of Los Angeles, receiving the largest white vote for a black candidate in any American city. Also, by 1973 California had three black representatives in Congress, Yvonne Brathwaite Burke, Ronald V. Dellums, and Augustus Hawkins, and the following year black state senator Mervyn Dymally was elected lieutenant governor. In 1978 Dymally failed to win reelection, and Burke was defeated in the race for attorney general by veteran Republican state senator George Deukmejian. By 1980 two black senators and six black assembly members, including Assembly Speaker Willie L. Brown, Jr., of San Francisco, were serving in the state legislature. Probably the most popular black official holding partisan office was Los Angeles Mayor Bradley. He won reelection in 1977 and 4 years later was elected to a third term with 64 percent of the vote. In 1982 Bradley won the Democratic nomination for governor.

MEXICAN AMERICANS

By far the largest ethnic minority in California in recent years has been the group that the 1980 census listed as of "Spanish origin," most of whom, in California, were Mexican Americans. In 1980 more than 4.5 million Hispanics lived in California, and they formed more than 19 percent of the state's population, as compared with 7.7 percent blacks, and 5.3 percent Asians and Pacific Islanders.

In 1910, the census had enumerated only 51,000 persons of Mexican ancestry in California, but the Mexican revolution of 1910–1920 combined with World War I to begin a long process of mass immigration from Mexico to the American southwest. By 1945, only Mexico City had a larger Mexican population than Los Angeles. The result, however, was what George I. Sánchez has called "cultural indigestion." Most of the immigrants were laborers. Barriers of prejudice and of language blocked their economic advancement and their social assimilation. In Los Angeles, they were concentrated in the eastern part of the city almost to the degree that blacks were concentrated in the southern part of it. World War II brought some limited progress. Paradoxically, some of this resulted from uneasy afterthoughts about two flagrant war-time episodes of Anglo-American bigotry—the "Sleepy Lagoon" murder trial and the "zoot suit" riots.

On August 2, 1942, on the east side of Los Angeles, the body of a Mexican-American boy with a fractured skull was found beside a germ-infested old reservoir used as a swimming hole, which the newspapers dubbed the "Sleepy Lagoon." There had been some scuffling the night before between two juvenile gangs, but there was no direct evidence of murder, and no witness. Nevertheless, 300 young Mexican Americans were arrested, 23 indicted, and 17 convicted. The defendants were brutally treated while in jail, and racial prejudice was apparent throughout the proceedings. In a pseudoscientific report to the grand jury, a police lieutenant explained violent crime by Mexicans as a racial characteristic, and the chief of police and the sheriff endorsed the report. The bias in the trial was so blatant and so clearly symptomatic of a larger social injustice that it ultimately led to some improvement in public attitudes. This came in part from the work of a defense committee headed by Carey McWilliams and in part from the verdict of the appellate court, which threw out all the convictions and strongly rebuked the trial judge.

During this period, some young Mexican Americans were wearing the "zoot suit," originally as the proper costume for jitterbug dancing but later to attract attention, to show their emanicipation from their elders, and to express their group solidarity. Much of the public believed that not only all zoot-suiters but virtually all young Mexican Americans were *pachucos,* or juvenile hoodlums. On June 3, 1943, mobs of white sailors, soldiers, and civilians in downtown Los Angeles began to beat up zoot-suiters and tear off their clothes, and these race riots continued for 6 days until the Navy declared Los Angeles off limits.

The war and postwar periods brought a degree of occupational and geographical mobility that considerably weakened barriers against intermarriage, equality of employment, and housing opportunities. Mexican Americans were not segregated in the armed forces, and many acquired a new experience of integrated living. They volunteered in greater numbers and won more Congressional Medals of Honor, proportionately, than any other ethnic group. After the war many improved their status by education under the "G.I. bill."

By the 1960s, Mexican Americans in California were more heterogeneous and much more urbanized than was commonly supposed. More than 85 percent of them lived in cities; less than 15 percent of those employed were agricultural laborers. During the 1960s many younger Mexican Americans joined a militant new crusade in search of ethnic identity. Reviving the belief of Mexican philosopher José Vasconcelos that people of mixed race would inherit the earth, many Mexican Americans began to call themselves *La Raza*—"the race" or "the people." Another appellation, also embraced with defiant pride, was *Chicano,* a shortened form of *Mexicano* with the first syllable dropped and the "x" pronounced as "ch" in the fashion of Mexico's Chihuahua Indians. The term "Chicano" was often used to embrace all Spanish-speaking people in the state, although a substantial portion of the Hispanic population was derived from places other than Mexico. In Los Angeles, for instance, 20 percent of all Hispanics were descendant from Cuba, Puerto Rico, and Central and South America.

California's Spanish-speaking population was a deeply disadvantaged minority, caught in a vicious cycle of undereducation and underemployment. Of the Mexican Americans employed in California, about half were semi-skilled or skilled workers, including those in the entrepreneurial and professional fields, but within almost every occupational group the earnings of the Mexican Americans were much lower than the average. In 1976 their median annual income was slightly more than $10,000, compared with nearly $15,000 for Anglo-Americans. The percentage of families with annual incomes below the official poverty level was nearly twice the percentage for families in general. The school dropout rate for Hispanic students was twice that of Anglo students, and more than half of all Hispanics in the job market lacked a high school diploma. Many children had grown up in households where only Spanish was spoken. In 1976 the state legislature adopted the most ambitious bilingual education program in the nation to help schools begin to deal more effectively with the language problem. By 1980 about 330,000 students were enrolled in special bilingual and bicultural classes.

Although Hispanics outnumbered blacks in the state by more than two to one, Mexican Americans had great difficulty in gaining political representation. The election of Edward R. Roybal to the Los Angeles city council in 1949 broke a long tradition of Anglo exclusiveness, but during the two decades following his election to Congress in 1962 no other Mexican American served on the council. No Hispanic served as mayor of a major California city in modern history, and no Hispanic was elected to statewide office. During the administration of Edmund G. Brown, Jr., Hispanics were appointed in record numbers to the courts and state agencies, but by 1980 representation in the state legislature was limited to three senators and three members of the assembly.

Several factors contributed to the relative political weakness of the state's largest minority. Geographical diffusion of the Hispanic population drained off political strength, and in areas where their numbers were greatest, gerrymandering of election districts often prevented Hispanics from exerting what strength they had. Anti-Hispanic prejudice remained a barrier. A disproportionate number of Hispanic judges, for instance, failed to win confirmation at the polls. Internal disunity, with too many ambitious individuals unwilling to withdraw from campaigns in favor of electable candidates, and a lack of ideological cohesion also cut Hispanic strength. Perhaps the biggest factor, however, was low voter participation by the Hispanic community. In Los Angeles, where Hispanics constituted about 20 percent of the voting-age population, they accounted for only about 5 percent of the voter turnout in most citywide elections.

Illegal immigration of "undocumented workers" from Mexico continued to swell the Hispanic population in California and remained an unsolved problem for state and federal officials. By crossing the border, Mexican immigrants could instantly increase their earning power ten times or more. In the face of this powerful motive, all efforts to curb the flow of illegal immigrants proved ineffective. Estimates of the size of the illegal immigrant population in the state, in 1980, ranged from 750,000 to 1.5 million. Their impact on the state also remained unclear. Some studies indicated that the illegal aliens cost the state and federal government millions of dollars through their use of public services, while other observers maintained that they contributed revenues far in excess of the cost of services they received. About 4 percent of the illegal aliens made claims on the welfare system in 1980, while nearly 75 percent paid income and social security taxes, and all paid sales taxes.

WOMEN

California has an ambiguous record in the history of thought, writing, and action relating to the place of women in society. The late-nineteenth-century feminist movement was well-represented in California by such energetic advocates of women's rights as Charlotte Perkins Gilman, author of *Women and Economics* (1898), and Laura De Force Gordon, the pioneer California journalist, lawyer, and suffragist. Following Gordon's successful campaign for the admission of women lawyers to the California bar, the state constitutional convention in 1879 approved the text she drafted for Article XX, section 18 of the new state constitution: "No person shall, on account of sex, be disqualified from entering upon or pursuing any lawful business, vocation or profession." Gordon's views were shared by San Francisco novelist Gertrude Atherton who, both in her personal life and in her writing, was in constant rebellion against domesticity and the subjection to the male that she believed it involved.

In the next generation, however, the novelist Kathleen Norris, 23 years younger than Atherton, held opposite views about the social role of women and had far greater influence in spreading her views. Norris considered motherhood and the family the heart of any successful and happy woman's life, and this was the message of most of her nearly 80 books of phenomenally popular fiction, beginning in 1911 with *Mother,* an instant best-seller. In the 1930s her novels and short stories made her the highest-paid woman in the world. Her own success was implicit evidence that a woman could have both a career and a family, but she once wrote that "The whole basis of my entire life is Family. I don't care about anything else."

Although California had been one of the early states to grant women the vote, in 1911, California women were rarely successful in obtaining elective office. At first it appeared that it would be otherwise, for in 1918 four women were elected to the state assembly. Yet during the next 50 years only 10 other women were elected to the lower house, and none to the state senate. Women in the California congressional delegation usually numbered only one or two. Representative Florence Kahn was elected in 1925 to her late husband's seat in the House, where she continued to represent San Francisco and to maintain his vigorous advocacy of military preparedness until 1936, and Representative

Helen Gahagan Douglas served in Congress from 1945 until her defeat by Richard Nixon in the senatorial election of 1950. As late as 1975 California ranked 48th among the states in the percentage of state elective offices held by women.

The nationwide women's movement of the 1960s and 1970s finally made itself felt in California state elections in 1976, when the number of women in the legislature doubled from three to six, including Rose A. Vuich of Dinuba, the first woman ever elected to the California Senate. By 1981 11 of the legislature's 120 members were women, the highest number in state history, but Secretary of State March Fong Eu remained the only woman holding statewide office, and only 1 woman, antibusing leader Bobbi Fiedler of Los Angeles, was serving in the state's congressional delegation.

On the local level, the number of women elected to public office increased remarkably beginning in the 1970s. Dianne Feinstein was president of the San Francisco Board of Supervisors in 1978 when Mayor George Moscone and Supervisor Harvey Milk were assassinated in their city hall offices. Feinstein was selected by her fellow supervisors to serve out the term of the slain mayor, and in 1979 she became the first woman to be elected the city's chief executive. The election attracted national attention because of the role of San Francisco's large homosexual population, estimated to constitute 20 percent of the city's electorate. Feinstein successfully appealed for support from homosexual voters, and the support they gave her was an important factor in her victory. Earlier in 1974, San Jose city councilwoman Janet Gray Hayes became the first woman elected mayor of the state's fourth-largest city. Perhaps of even greater significance, by 1981 a majority of the members of the San Jose City Council and the San Francisco Board of Supervisors were women. The California League of Cities reported that the number of women mayors in the state had risen to 64 in 1981, more than double the number 7 years earlier.

The number of women who have served in high appointive positions in state government has been nearly as meager as that of women who have held elective office. Katherine Philips Edson served as the first executive officer of the Industrial Welfare Commission under Governor Hiram Johnson, and Kate Richards O'Hare Cunningham, a nationally known crusader for prison reform, was appointed assistant director of the department of penology by Governor Culbert L. Olson in 1939. Phoebe Apperson Hearst became the first woman on the Board of Regents of the University of California in 1897 and served until her death in 1919. Others on the board included Dorothy Buffum Chandler, wife of Los Angeles Times publisher Norman Chandler, who served from 1954 to 1968 and was elected by her colleagues as vice chairwoman; Catherine Campbell Hearst, a regent from 1956 until her resignation in 1976; and Vilma S. Martinez, a founder and president of the Mexican-American Legal Defense and Educational Fund, who was appointed to the board in 1976.

It was in the administration of Governor Edmund G. Brown, Jr., that women for the first time were appointed to top positions of power throughout state government. In his two terms in office Brown appointed more than 1600 women to various boards and commissions and named women as directors of the departments of agriculture, finance, transportation, veterans affairs, motor vehicles, conservation, and corrections. In February 1977 Rose Elizabeth Bird became the first woman ever appointed to the California Supreme Court—and Governor Brown made her not only a justice but the *chief* justice. The following year Bird won confirmation at the polls by an extremely close margin.

Employment opportunities for women gradually expanded in the twentieth century, and an increasing proportion of women sought employment outside the home. World War II was a catalyst for change in the status of California women, just as it was for the state's racial minorities. Government and military officials and leaders of industry exhorted women to take jobs in factories and offices. "Rosie the Riveter" was the epitome of a woman doing her patriotic duty. About half the women who went to work in the wartime shipyards and aircraft plants had already been in the labor force, usually at lower-skilled and lower-paying jobs. At war's end most of the women workers wanted to continue in the work they were doing, but as male workers returned from the armed forces and as wartime industries cut back production, many women were displaced from their jobs. Nevertheless, the number of women in the work force continued to increase. In 1950, 30 percent of all California women were working outside the home; by 1977 a majority of California women were in the labor force. Overwhelmingly women sought employment for economic reasons. Working was a necessity for the many widowed, divorced, and separated women who comprised a major part of the female labor force. For other women, work was necessary to support their families or to provide better education or health care for their children. In the years following the war relatively few California women sought employment merely for personal fulfillment.

Women assembly workers rivet a gusset to a wing rib at the Long Beach plant of the Douglas Aircraft Company in October 1943. *(Courtesy of Clarity Educational Productions, Incorporated.)*

Although women made inroads into a few occupations with high status and high earnings—by 1978 about one-tenth of all lawyers, doctors, and industrial engineers in California were women—the majority of women continued to be employed as clerks and service workers. As more women moved into the labor force, the discrepancy between their wages and those of men actually increased in some fields. Overall the median income for full-time women workers in 1975 was still less than 60 percent of the median for males. Most women in the work force remained concentrated at the lower end of the pay scale, earning considerably less money than their male coworkers.

In the early 1970s the National Organization for Women and other women's rights groups conducted a strong campaign for the equal rights amendment (ERA): "Equality of rights under the law shall not be denied or abridged by the United States or by any state on account of sex." The ERA had first been introduced in Congress in 1923, but for nearly 40 years it had received little support. Many feminists had opposed it because they feared it would nullify the "protective laws," hard-won state legislation that had given women a minimum wage and other forms of special protection. There were also widespread fears that the ERA would deprive women of their femininity, or men of their masculinity, or both; that it would end the obligation of husbands to support their wives and children; and that it would require the drafting of women for military combat. By 1970, to the satisfaction of most careful students of the subject, these fears were generally shown to be groundless. Congress approved the ERA by overwhelming votes in both houses in March 1972 and set a 7-year deadline for ratification of the amendment by three-fourths of the nation's state legislatures. In California the assembly approved the ERA less than a month after Congress had officially proposed it, and, following considerable debate, the state senate joined in ratifying it in November 1972.

In the states as a whole, however, after an initial spurt of ratifications, strong opposition developed and stalled the process for several years. By the fall of 1978, 35 states had ratified the ERA, three short of the needed three-fourths majority. After a vigorous campaign by the amendment's supporters, Congress extended the deadline to June 30, 1982, but even with this extension the ERA did not win the additional ratifications and thus failed to become the Twenty-Seventh Amendment.

SELECTED BIBLIOGRAPHY

Several articles in Robert F. Heizer (ed.), *California* (1978) provide information on California Indians in the twentieth century. See also George H. Phillips, *The Enduring Struggle: Indians in California History* (1981); Jack D. Forbes, *Native Americans of California and Nevada* (1969); and Frank Quinn, *Indians of California, Past and Present* (1956). On population trends, see Sherburne F. Cook, *The Population of the California Indians, 1769–1970* (1976). Kenneth M. Johnson's monograph, *K-344, or The Indians of California vs. the United States* (1966), also includes information on the broader history of California Indian problems. Heizer (ed.), *The California Indians vs. The United States of America* (1978) contains documents from the 1959 Indian Claims Commission ruling. See also Ferdinand

F. Fernandez, "Except a California Indian: A Study in Legal Discrimination," *Southern California Quarterly*, L (June 1968), pp. 161–175. Steve Talbot, "Free Alcatraz: The Culture of Native American Liberation," *Journal of Ethnic Studies*, VI (Fall 1978), is an account of the upsurge of Indian activism.

"The Asian American" was the subject of an issue of the *Pacific Historical Review*, XLIII (November 1974). On the improvement of attitudes toward the Japanese Americans, see William Petersen, "Success Story, Japanese-American Style," *New York Times Magazine* (Jan. 9, 1966), 20ff; but see also the warnings in John Modell, *The Economics and Politics of Racial Accommodation* (1977). Good general studies are Robert A. Wilson and Bill Hosokawa, *East to America: A History of the Japanese in the United States* (1980); Stanford W. Lyman, *The Asian in North America* (1977); and Yamato Ichihashi, *Japanese in the United States* (1932). Works on the Chinese Americans include Shien Woo Kung, *Chinese in American Life; Some Aspects of Their History, Status, Problems, and Contributions* (1962); Rose Hum Lee, *The Chinese in the United States of America* (1960); Fred W. Riggs, *Pressures on Congress: A Study of the Repeal of Chinese Exclusion* (1950); Kian Moon Kwan, "Assimilation of the Chinese in the United States: An Exploratory Study in California," Ph.D. thesis, University of California, Berkeley (1958); Kwang-Ching Liu, *Americans and Chinese* (1963); and Betty Lee Sung, *Mountain of Gold* (1967), reprinted as *The Story of the Chinese in America* (1971). See also H. Brett Melendy, *Asians in America: Filipinos, Koreans, and East Indians* (1977). Lorraine J. Crouchett, "Third-Wave Filipino Immigration," *Migration Today* (June 1979), pp. 17–22, describes the immigration of Filipino professionals to California.

For historical background on the wartime and postwar black migration, see Douglas Henry Daniels, *Pioneer Urbanites: A Social and Cultural History of Black San Francisco* (1980) and Lawrence B. de Graaf, "The City of Black Angels: Emergence of the Los Angeles Ghetto, 1890–1930," *Pacific Historical Review*, XXXIX (August 1970), pp. 323–352. On the migration and its problems see Edward E. France, "Some Aspects of the Migration of the Negro to the San Francisco Bay Area since 1940," Ph.D. thesis, University of California, Berkeley (1962); de Graaf, "Negro Migration to Los Angeles, 1930–1950," Ph.D. thesis, University of California, Los Angeles (1962); Charles Wollenberg, "Black vs. Navy Blue: The Mare Island Mutiny Court-Martial," *California History*, LVIII (Spring 1979), pp. 62–75 and "*James vs. Marinship*: Trouble on the New Black Frontier," *California History*, LX (Fall 1981), pp. 262–279; John H. Denton (ed.), *Race and Property* (1964), a symposium; Thomas W. Casstevens, *Politics, Housing, and Race Relations: California's Rumford Act and Proposition 14* (1967); Raymond E. Wolfinger and Fred E. Greenstein, "The Repeal of Fair Housing in California: An Analysis of Referendum Voting," *American Political Science Review*, LXII (September 1968), pp. 753–769; and Ray Marshall, *The Negro and Organized Labor* (1965).

Charles Wollenberg, *All Deliberate Speed: Segregation and Exclusion in California Schools, 1855–1975* (1976); Irving G. Hendrick, *The Education of Non-whites in California, 1849–1970* (1977); and Lillian Rubin, *Busing and Backlash: White Against White in an Urban California School District* (1972) describe the controversy over school integration.

On the Watts riot, see John A. McCone et al., *Violence in the City—An End or a Beginning? A Report of the Governor's Commission on the Los Angeles Riots* (Dec. 2, 1965); Robert Conot, *Rivers of Blood, Years of Darkness* (1967); and Nathan Cohen (ed.), *The Los Angeles Riots: A Socio-Psychological Study* (1970).

On the Mexican Americans, a useful bibliography is the *Guide to Materials Relating to Persons of Mexican Heritage in the United States* (1969), compiled by the United States Inter-agency Committee on Mexican-American Affairs. An extensive general study is Leo Grebler, Joan W. Moore, Ralph C. Guzmán, et al., *The Mexican-American People; the*

Nation's Second Largest Minority (1970). Other valuable works in the order of their appearance include *Mexicans in California* (1930), the report of Gov. C. C. Young's Mexican Fact-Finding Committee; Manuel Gamio, *Mexican Immigration to the United States* (1930) and *The Mexican Immigrant, His Life Story: Autobiographic Documents* (1931); Emory S. Bogardus, *The Mexican in the United States* (1934); Carey McWilliams, *North From Mexico* (1949); Beatrice W. Griffith, *American Me* (1948); Fernando Penalosa, "The Changing Mexican American in Southern California," *Sociology and Social Research,* LI (July 1967), pp. 405–417; Matt S. Meier and Feliciano Rivera, *The Chicanos: A History of Mexican Americans* (1972); Norris Hundley, Jr. (ed.), *The Chicano* (1975); Ricardo Romo, "Work and Restlessness: Occupational and Spatial Mobility among Mexicanos in Los Angeles, 1918–1928," *Pacific Historical Review,* XLVI (May 1977), pp. 157–180; Albert Camarillo, *Chicanos in a Changing Society: From Mexican Pueblos to American Barrios* (1979); and Richard Griswold del Castillo, *The Los Angeles Barrio, 1850–1890: A Social History* (1980). See also the writings of Paul S. Taylor, Mark Reisler, John R. Martinez, and others, cited for Chapter 31.

Wayne A. Cornelius, *Building the Cactus Curtain: Mexican Migration and U.S. Responses from Wilson to Carter* (1980) offers an analysis of the major policy alternatives for dealing with illegal immigration from Mexico. See also Paul R. Ehrlich, *Golden Door: International Migration, Mexico and the United States* (1979).

Anthologies on racial problems in California are Roger Daniels and Spencer C. Olin, Jr., (eds.), *Racism in California: A Reader on the History of Oppression* (1972); George E. Frakes and Curtis B. Solberg (eds.), *Minorities in California History* (1971); an issue of the *California Historical Quarterly,* L (September 1971), also reprinted as *Neither Separate nor Equal* (1971); and Charles Wollenberg (ed.), *Ethnic Conflict in California History* (1970).

Among the many biographies of California women see Mary A. Hill, *Charlotte Perkins Gilman: The Making of a Radical Feminist, 1860–1896* (1980) and Charlotte S. McClure, *Gertrude Atherton* (1976). On early political activity see Jean M. Smith, "The Voting Women of San Diego, 1920," *Journal of San Diego History,* XXVI (Spring 1980), pp. 133–154. On the status of women workers see *Women at Work in California* (1978), compiled by the California Employment Development Department; see also the United States Department of Labor report, *The Earnings Gap Between Women and Men* (1979). The battle over the ERA is described in Margaret I. Miller and Helene Linker, "Equal Rights Campaigns in California and Utah," *Society,* VI (May/June 1974), pp. 40–53. *California Women* is a monthly bulletin published by the California Commission on the Status of Women.

THE MOST
POPULOUS STATE

The social history of California in the 1960s is a study in contrasts. In the prosperous early years of the decade California became the most populous state in the union, culminating more than a century of phenomenal growth. The ability of the state to provide such basic services as transportation, housing, and education for its burgeoning population was sorely tested.

The 1960s were also years of unprecedented social ferment. Beginning at Berkeley in 1964, college campuses around the state were rocked by a series of student strikes and protest demonstrations. Many young people, alienated from a society they regarded as corrupt and decadent, turned to drugs and adopted unconventional styles of dress and behavior. The unpopular Vietnam war added immensely to the sense of youthful alienation and became the focus of a nationwide antiwar movement. The Watts riot of 1965 was evidence of another kind of discontent, and the following year the radical Black Panther party was organized in Oakland.

By the decade's end the population growth of California had sharply declined. Changed economic conditions, as well as a kind of malaise which affected the state and its image, contributed to a dramatic slowdown of migration to the state. In the 1970s the historic pattern of growth reasserted itself, but even then the rate of growth remained below that of previous decades.

THE GROWTH RATE: PEAK AND SLOWDOWN

Through the first half of the 1960s, economic opportunity continued to combine with the amenities of mild climate, scenic beauty, and California's romantic reputation to attract new residents from other states at the rate of almost 1000 a day. These newcomers made up nearly two-thirds of a total annual population increase of 600,000 at the peak in 1963. When California passed New York and became the most populous state late in 1962, Gov. Edmund G. Brown proclaimed a 4-day celebration—"California First Days"—and called for "the biggest party the state has ever seen." Communities across the state staged local celebrations, and at Truckee an official delegation ceremoniously welcomed the latest carload of newcomers as they crossed the state line. Not everyone viewed California's rise to preeminence as an occasion for celebration. Californian Earl Warren, then United States Chief Justice, warned: "I would not celebrate with fireworks or dancing in the streets. Mere numbers do not mean happiness."

The growth of California's population was urban—or rather *suburban*—and was greatest in the southern part of the state. By the mid 1970s more than 90 percent of the people of California lived in the 17 areas that the Census Bureau listed as "metropolitan," and thus California was the nation's most urbanized as well as most populous state. Los Angeles–Long Beach had about 33 percent of the state's population, San Francisco–Oakland about 15 percent, and San Diego 8 percent. Los Angeles County was the most populous county in the nation, and the city of Los Angeles was second only to New York as a center of industrial employment. Orange and San Diego counties grew phenomenally, and part of the migration to them came from Los Angeles. The population of San Francisco declined slightly but steadily, and in the Bay Area, as in southern California, the growth came in the surrounding communities rather than in the central city. San Francisco remained a major financial center, as the permanent site of the Federal Reserve bank of the district, but the increasing ratio of population in favor of southern California—more than two-thirds of the state's people lived south of the Tehachipis—led to the shift of such agencies as the regional headquarters of the Securities and Exchange Commission and the region's stock exchange from San Francisco to Los Angeles.

An important element in the growth of population and wealth in California in the 1950s and 1960s was the tremendous expansion of the aerospace industry, mostly financed by the federal government. Large numbers of immigrants from Mexico and poor blacks from the rural south continued to arrive in California during these years, but far more attention was paid to the coming of thousands of highly skilled and highly paid aerospace engineers and scientists. In 1965 nearly 500,000 Californians—about one-third of the total number employed in manufacturing—were employed in the various branches of the aerospace industry, including the production of aircraft, missiles, electronic equipment, and related instruments.

The United States in the 1960s was engaged in a race with the Soviet Union to be the first nation to place a person on the moon and a race to acquire a supply of missiles great enough to guarantee its "security." California received more than 40 percent of the billions of dollars spent by the federal government under research contracts in the aerospace field. Southern California became the nation's leading center of aerodynamic research in guided missiles, jet propulsion, and supersonic flight, partly because a large part of the aircraft industry had already been concentrated there, and partly because the empty spaces of the Mojave Desert to the north and east of Los Angeles were ideal for aerospace testing and experimentation. Another factor was the concentration of scientific talent at the California Institute of Technology in Pasadena. In northern California, there were similar concentrations at Stanford and the University of California at Berkeley, and this played a part in the growth of vast new aerospace research and manufacturing facilities, especially at Sunnyvale and other points between San Jose and San Francisco.

Beginning in 1969, however, federal spending on aerospace was drastically cut, and this coincided with the onset of a long period of economic slowdown, including a major nationwide recession in 1969 to 1970 and an even worse one in 1973 to 1975. Moreover, this period of relative depression in the economy had a cruelly unfamiliar and unwelcome aspect—it was simultaneously a period of severe and continuous inflation.

This strange combination was largely a result of the peculiar economic policies of the federal government during the Vietnam war. The social and psychological consequences of that conflict, as well as its economic consequences, were very different from those of World War II. Pearl Harbor had united the nation, but the war in southeast Asia became one of the most bitterly divisive issues in American history. In the years before America was plunged into World War II the country had gone to great lengths to try to avoid an inevitable involvement; in the case of Vietnam many felt that the United States had gone far out of its way to engage in a futile conflict of which the necessity and even the morality were doubtful at best, and the costs tragic and apparently wasted. At the beginning of World War II, the American economy was still in the depression and still operating at a fraction of its productive capacity; it badly needed the injection of huge government expenditures, made psychologically and politically acceptable by unquestioned military demands. During World War II, federal price and wage controls and huge wartime taxes kept some brakes on inflation. At the beginning of major involvement in southeast Asia, on the other hand, the American economy was already operating close to capacity, and during the great buildup of American forces in Vietnam between 1965 and 1968, involving vast expenditures for the undeclared war, the federal government failed to apply wartime economic controls, and avoided substantial increases in taxes. The result was a massive inflation and overheating of the economy, with dangerously high percentage rates of price increases, compounded from year to year.

In an attempt to halt the inflation process the Nixon administration in 1969 began drastic cuts in federal spending for the armed forces and for the space program, and the Federal Reserve Board made a series of increases in interest rates. These actions, though they failed to stop the inflation, led to the first recession in 10 years, and the worst and longest one in 30 years. The stock market fell 300 points. Unemployment rose sharply throughout the nation, but California suffered more than the rest of the country because so much of its manufacturing depended on federal spending for the aerospace industry. Aerospace employment in California fell by 40 percent.

The first landing of American astronauts on the moon in July 1969 was a dazzling and historic event, breathlessly watched on television by millions, but public interest in the space program did not remain high enough to keep the expenditures for the National Aeronautics and Space Administration from being cut in half between 1968 and 1971.

The remarkable economic expansion and population growth of the early 1960s was reversed by the end of the decade. Though the state's population reached 20 million in 1970, giving it five more seats in Congress, the increase during that year was less than 1 percent. This was the lowest annual percentage increase on record, and for the first time in its entire history the state's population grew at a slower rate than did that of the nation as a whole. Natural increase, which had almost always formed the smaller part of the state's growth, had suddenly become by far the largest part. Net migration in 1970 was only 27,000 compared with 356,000 in 1963, the peak year of the previous decade. These were the official figures of the state department of finance. Some unofficial estimates maintained that 25,000 more persons actually *left* the state in 1970 than came into it.

The abrupt slowdown in California's growth rate was caused in part by depressed economic conditions, the product of continuing inflation and recession, and also by a fundamental deterioration of the popular image of the state. The traditional picture of California as the land of opportunity, sunshine, and romance was overshadowed by images of a state beset by high unemployment, crowded suburbs, a polluted atmosphere, and campus and racial unrest. A rash of books and articles, with such titles as *How to Kill a Golden State, Anti-California*, and *California: The Vanishing Dream*, either mourned or celebrated the alleged demise of the California dream. Although these popular commentaries often suggested corrective measures, they did little to attract newcomers to the state.

TRANSPORTATION

Transportation was one of the many fields in which California's broader economic and population trends were reflected. The state's "love affair with the automobile" continued. There were three registered automobiles in California for every four persons of driving age, by far the largest ratio in the world. A vast network of freeways spread over the length and breadth of the state, and most communities welcomed their coming, though the engineers of the division of highways sometimes showed limited imagination in their design. But in San Francisco a major "freeway revolt" began in 1959 when the new Embarcadero Freeway cut off the view of the lower half of the Ferry Building as seen from Market Street. The public outcry forced the state engineers to leave the freeway half finished, instead of carrying out their plan to extend it all the way around the Embarcadero and the Marina. In 1964, when the state authorities proposed a freeway through a part of Golden Gate Park, the revolt flared again, after folksinger Malvina Reynolds composed a stirring protest song called "The Cement Octopus." Such intransigence made San Francisco the despair of both state and federal highway planners, who called the city the worst highway bottleneck in America.

The absence of another form of modernization, that of the port facilities of San Francisco, was more clearly disastrous for the city. In 1960 San Francisco still handled all the foreign imports of the Bay Area. By 1975 it had lost most of its seagoing traffic, largely to the port of Oakland, where the voters had approved bonds to build the massive cranes required for loading and unloading "containers." These were steel or aluminum boxes the size of a truck, lifted from a ship directly onto a truck chassis or railroad flatcar.

The railroads continued to prosper from the hauling of freight, but their passenger traffic steadily declined. They often begged the state public utilities commission to approve the discontinuance or drastic reduction of their passenger service, but the commission turned down most of these requests. The railroads were often accused of making their passenger trains and schedules as unattractive and inconvenient as possible, in the hope that they would eventually be permitted to discontinue entirely the unprofitable business of carrying passengers in competition with automobiles, buses, and airplanes. California's air transportation industry meanwhile doubled its volume in the 1960s, and the air lane between Los Angeles and San Francisco became the most-traveled in the world.

While San Francisco was rebelling against freeways, it took the lead in planning an electrified rapid transit system that would have the great advantage of reducing not only traffic congestion but also air pollution from motor vehicle exhausts. In 1962 the voters of San Francisco, Alameda, and Contra Costa counties approved the formation of the Bay Area Rapid Transit (BART) District and the building of a rail network that would connect the cities and suburbs of the East Bay with the stations of a subway under Market Street in downtown San Francisco. BART carried its first passengers in 1972 using an automated, computerized operating system, no conductors, and only a single attendant on each train. It was the first all-new transit system to be built in the United States in 60 years, and in spite of many technical difficulties it was ultimately rated as one of the best.

In Los Angeles, on the other hand, most of the voters and taxpayers showed their determination to cling to the privilege of doing all their traveling throughout the sprawling metropolis in their private automobiles. Los Angeles had 1000 miles of freeways and 10,000 miles of cars. On an average day more than 350,000 cars and trucks passed one point near the civic center, at the junction of six freeways, where the interchange resembled the mechanism of a giant watch. Except for the very poor nearly everyone between the ages of 15 and 85 had an automobile. The affluent majority repeatedly refused to subsidize a public rapid transit system, but it often showed considerable enthusiasm for elaborate transit studies and reports. The latest of these was of a proposed "people mover," or automated sidewalk for downtown Los Angeles. A Southern California Rapid Transit District did come into existence, on paper, but for years it could do no more than operate a fleet of traffic-bound buses. It was not until 1980 that Los Angeles voters approved a sales tax increase to finance construction and operation of a new rail rapid transit system.

REAPPORTIONMENT

The population boom of the 1950s and early 1960s also led to increased demands for reform of the state's system of political representation. With the continued growth of the suburban parts of the metropolitan areas, especially those in southern California, the archaic "federal" system of representation in the California State Senate became more and more obviously inequitable. Los Angeles County, with a population of 6,036,771 in the 1960 census, was the most populous legislative district in the United States, yet it had the same number of votes in the state senate as the Alpine-Mono-Inyo district, with 14,294 people: one vote. A resident of Alpine, Mono, or Inyo County cast a vote worth 422 times as much as the vote of a resident of Los Angeles County. This was by far the widest disparity in any state. One-quarter of the population elected three-quarters of the California state senators. A majority of the senators could be elected by 10.7 percent of the California voters.

Initiative proposals to modify the "little federal" system and reapportion the California Senate were rejected at the polls in 1928, 1948, 1960, and 1962. Most voters clung to the hazy and misleading idea that what was appropriate for the federal government must be appropriate for the states. But the United States Supreme Court ruled in *Reynolds v. Sims*, on June 15, 1964, that one person's vote must be worth as much as another's in the election of state legislators. The equal protection clause of the Fourteenth Amendment, said the Court, required that seats in both houses of a state legislature be apportioned on a population basis. The so-called federal analogy was discarded as fallacious and inapplicable. Counties, the Court pointed out, were merely political subdivisions created by the state governments, not sovereign entities like the states themselves. Chief Justice Earl Warren was one of the prime movers in the adoption of this "one man, one vote" doctrine, even though as governor of California he had been one of those who had opposed reapportionment of its state senate. The northern members of the California senate, many of whom would lose their seats, engaged in a series of desperate maneuvers in the attempt to escape reapportionment. Senator Joseph A. Rattigan of Santa Rosa asked whether a proposal for armed insurrection would be in order, but in 1965 the legislature approved a new apportionment law that included no deviations of more than 15 percent in the populations of the new senatorial districts. Consequently in the election of 1966, under the new plan of apportionment, the control of the state senate passed to southern California, which had elected a majority of the assembly members since the 1930s.

In 1965, the last year under the federal system, a large group of state senators from northern California revived a proposal that had been made periodically since the 1850s. This was a plan to divide the state at the Tehachapi Mountains, and this latest version of it would have included the counties of Santa Barbara and Kern within the northern state, giving only seven counties to the southern one. But polls showed that more than two-thirds of the voters, even in the north, were opposed to any plan for state division.

EDUCATION

In the years of headlong growth and general prosperity that followed World War II, California's public schools remained impoverished. The state spent more than 40 percent of its budget for education, and its per capita expenditures for public schools were among the highest in the country—but these figures were grossly misleading because California's school-age population grew twice as fast as its general population. Between 1950 and 1960, while the total number of people in the state was increasing by roughly 50 percent, public school enrollment grew by more than 100 percent. An unprecedentedly large proportion of the people who were migrating to California were young married couples, able and inclined to produce numerous children. The schools were chronically short of money, of classroom space, of teachers—of everything, in fact, except pupils.

The annual tidal waves of postwar babies that flooded into the public schools in the 1950s began to inundate the colleges and universities in the following decade, and the state responded by greatly expanding its system of public higher education.

California's state college system traced its origin to 1862, when a 2-year normal school was established in San Francisco. This was moved to San Jose in 1870. Other such schools were later established in various parts of the state. After their programs had been lengthened to 4 years, they were promoted to the rank of "teachers' colleges" in 1921, and designated as general "state colleges" in 1935. After adding graduate instruction, most of them were renamed "state universities" in 1971.

The beginnings of 2-year junior colleges stemmed from the passage of a state law in 1907 authorizing the governing boards of city, district, or county high schools to establish post-high school courses. Fresno established the first public junior college in the United States in 1910, and California has since led all the states in the establishment and support of such instutitions. By midcentury they had begun to be called "city colleges" or "community colleges," though state policy prevented them from expanding their programs to 4 years. They numbered more than 100 by 1980.

The general campuses of the University of California increased to eight. At Los Angeles, a "normal school" had become the University of California, Southern Branch, in 1919. This had become UCLA in 1931, and by the 1960s its student body was larger than the one at Berkeley. Santa Barbara State College became the University of California, Santa Barbara, in 1944. In the late 1940s, colleges of letters and science were established at Davis and at Riverside in connection with what had originally been branches of the universitywide college of agriculture. After 1960, under a state master plan, new general campuses of the university were established at Santa Cruz, Irvine, and San Diego.

By the early 1970s it was clear that higher education had overexpanded. The postwar baby boom continued through the 1950s, but the decline in birthrate following the introduction of oral contraceptives in 1960 and the decline in migration to the state in the late 1960s undercut earlier projections of growth in college enrollment. The master plan had estimated that the University of California would enroll 250,000 students in 1985 and that the new campuses at Santa Cruz, Irvine, and San Diego would have 27,500 each, but by 1971 the official predictions were that the three newest campuses would have less than half that many.

Funds for public education were slashed at all levels. California dropped from sixth in the nation in per-pupil expenditure for public education to twenty-first by 1981. Many school districts, faced with reduced budgets as well as declining enrollment, sold excess school buildings and other properties. The "state universities and colleges" system and the community colleges were able to balance their budgets only by assigning a scandalously large share of their teaching loads to part-time teachers, to whom they paid low hourly wages. There was a surplus of trained teachers, as well as of many other people with college and university training, who suddenly found themselves over-qualified and underemployed.

CAMPUS TURMOIL

American college students of the 1950s had been called "the silent generation." Those who reached college age in the 1950s had been born in the 1930s, and when these "depression babies" became young adults, they were too driven by anxiety about material success to be interested in any form of political or social dissent. Students took virtually no part, for example, in the University of California loyalty oath controversy.

The college students of the middle and later 1960s, on the other hand, were part of the great wave of postwar babies, born and reared in relative affluence, but in such numbers that they badly overcrowded the public schools and the colleges, and were often discontented with the crowding. Some of them discovered that their massive numbers could be a form of power.

Stirrings of student unrest in California had appeared as early as May 1960 when a crowd of college students, protesting their exclusion from a hearing of the House Un-American Activities Committee in the San Francisco city hall, jammed the rotunda by sitting down in the balcony. The police washed them down the stairs with fire hoses and drove them from the building with clubs. At about the same time, black college students in the southern states began to attack the racial segregation of lunch counters with the tactic of the sit-in. This tactic had been used for a short time in 1937, in a different context, by some of the relatively radical new CIO unions, in the form of the "sit-down strike" in which striking workers occupied the property of the employer, but organized labor had soon abandoned the sit-down, not only because it was ruled illegal but also because it alienated the public. In the early 1960s, however, the federal courts ruled that the racial segregation of lunch counters was unconstitutional and therefore that those who had participated in the lunch counter sit-ins were merely demanding their constitutional rights and could not be validly arrested.

Several students from the University of California at Berkeley had spent their summers in civil rights activities in the deep south, and when they returned to the campus in the fall of 1964, they organized sit-ins and other demonstrations to protest racial discrimination by Bay Area businesses. In September the university administration announced that a sidewalk area at the southern entrance to the campus—an area previously thought to belong to the city of Berkeley and thus to be beyond university control—was university property and ordered all student groups to stop using the area for setting up tables, recruiting members, or otherwise organizing for off-campus political activity. The groups affected by the university's order included student civil rights organizations, as well as groups ranging in their political philosophy from the far left to the far right. When the administration attempted to enforce its new order, students organized the Free Speech movement (FSM), called a student strike, and used the civil rights tactics of mass civil disobedience against the university.

The university charter law of 1868 and the state constitution of 1879 (Article IX, section 9) had sought to keep the state university free from "political or sectarian influence," and the regents had long chosen to interpret that phrase as forbidding any political advocacy on a university campus. This had never been the true meaning of the provision. The full sentence forbade "political or sectarian influence *in the appointment of* [*the university's*] *regents and the administration of its affairs* [italics inserted]." Every governor of California with the possible exception of Earl Warren had flatly violated this provision by appointing regents for political reasons. But the regents, like the governors, preferred to ignore this aspect of the matter. Apparently they also chose to ignore the advice of their own attorney that their rules against political speech and advocacy on campus were in violation of the United States Supreme Court's decision in *Edwards v. South Carolina* in 1963. This ruling stated that "student speakers may even advocate violations of the law provided such advocacy does not constitute a clear and present danger. . ." and that "much of the conduct that the public finds objectionable is constitutionally protected."

Thus the student rebellion at Berkeley in its beginnings was truly a free speech movement against unconstitutional restrictions, and in this particular sense it was successful. Following the disciplining of several students who defied the administration's order restricting political activity, crowds of students occupied the campus administration building. In December 1964 the largest sit-in occurred at Sproul Hall, and Governor Brown ordered state and local police to intervene. In the largest mass arrest in the state's history more than 700 persons, mostly students, were dragged or carried from the building. Later, in a mass trial, 578 of them were found guilty of trespassing, and many of resisting arrest. Less than a week after the Sproul Hall arrests, the Berkeley faculty passed resolutions that the university should not regulate the content of political advocacy, but should regulate only the time, place, and manner of it in order to prevent interference with normal university functions, and the unversity administration agreed to liberalize its rules governing student political activity.

At first the Berkeley student rebels relied on methods that were nonviolent, even though they did involve a kind of mass force, but the young radical leaders of the movement became overconfident. In a speech from the steps of Sproul Hall, FSM leader Mario Savio promised his followers that he could protect them from going to jail or from any other form of punishment. The apparent success of the tactics of sitting-in and going limp when arrested made the students feel invincible and invulnerable. The courts soon ruled, however, that occupying a university building was merely a form of illegal trespass and that going limp was merely a form of resisting arrest. When hundreds of students were sentenced to jail after their mass trial in Berkeley in 1965, many became disenchanted and embittered. The sense of newness and magic began to go out of the movement, and a sense of frustration and desperation took its place. The idea of nonviolence was soon lost in a welter of confrontation and disruption, and a drift toward violence and vandalism set in. Some student rebels made a mockery of the name of the Free Speech movement and began to deny the right of free speech to anyone but themselves by shouting down any speaker who disagreed with them. This was a tragedy, not only for the young people themselves but for a society that cried out for improvement and that badly needed the freshness of youthful idealism.

The Free Speech movement of 1964 gave Berkeley a considerable reputation as the cradle of student revolt in America, and in the subsequent years this reputation attracted many young radicals, some of them students and others former students, to the university campus and to parts of Berkeley and Oakland to the south of it. Protest against the escalation of the war in Vietnam and a continuing crusade against racism at home were now the major channels of youthful rebellion.

In October 1967 a major draft riot occurred after a crowd of antiwar demonstrators, trying to shut down the Oakland induction center, were routed by police who sprayed them with a temporarily blinding chemical known as Mace. The new vogue of student power spread across the country. In April 1968 hundreds of students staged a sit-in at Columbia University, and when it was broken up by police, many violently resisted arrest. In August, during the Democratic national convention in Chicago, there was a violent confrontation between police and the mass of young militants who had gathered in an effort to pressure the convention into taking a stand against the Vietnam war and into nominating Senator Eugene McCarthy. Prominent among the leaders of the Chicago demonstrations were two Californians: Tom Hayden, a leader of the radical Students for a Democratic Society, and Jerry Rubin, once a graduate student in sociology at Berkeley but now a full-time "revolutionary." Combining his political activities with the use of drugs, which he advocated as an aid to revolution, Rubin was addicted to the politics of absurdity. Earlier he had confronted the House Un-American Activities Committee dressed in a rented Revolutionary War uniform, and had made outrageous statements urging junior high school students to prepare to kill their parents and burn their school libraries.

Late in 1968 radical students at San Francisco State College demanded the creation of a black studies department run exclusively by blacks. This was the most important of a series of "non-negotiable demands," some of which had been drafted by a "Third World Liberation Front" including Latin-American and Asian-American radical students. To gain acceptance of their demands, the student leaders began a long strike characterized by Maoist rhetoric, violent disruption of classes, vandalism, and personal assault. The large tactical squad of the San Francisco police, specially trained for campus riot duty, finally broke the strike with mass maneuvers and arrests.

Before this uprising was over, a similar movement was launched at Berkeley, early in 1969, with a strike to demand an autonomous "third world college." Though this demand was not granted, the campus did establish a department of ethnic studies. Next came the disastrous affair of the "People's Park," in May 1969. This began when Berkeley's radical young "street people" tried to appropriate a block of university-owned land near Telegraph Avenue as a park for their own use. When the university fenced the block, a mob gathered to try to destroy the fence, and there was a riot in which sheriff's deputies responded to the throwing of rocks by firing shotguns. One young bystander, watching from a rooftop on Telegraph Avenue, was killed and another was blinded. This tragedy frightened, enraged, and "radicalized" thousands of young people throughout the region and produced such a massive movement to "take the park" that a force of the National Guard was sent to protect it. A National Guard helicopter broke up a disorderly crowd on the campus by

Helmeted members of the National Guard and the police stand guard before the ivy-covered walls of the chancellor's residence on the Berkeley campus during the 1969 "People's Park" controversy. (Photograph by Lou de la Torre.)

spraying the whole area with tear gas, which drifted into dozens of classrooms and even into the campus hospital.

By this time, Berkeley was only one of many American university towns with large groups of rebellious and violence-prone young people. There was repeated violence and arson at Stanford. The University of California at Santa Barbara had long been thought of as a quietly conservative campus, but in February 1970 its student residential community of Isla Vista exploded in a series of riots in which the branch of the Bank of America was burned and a student was killed when a deputy's gun discharged accidentally. Student rebellion reached a nationwide climax in May 1970 after a detachment of the Ohio National Guard shot and killed four young people on the campus of Kent State University, following the burning of the ROTC building in protest against the spreading of the war in southeast Asia to Cambodia. For the rest of the spring term many American campuses experienced various degrees of disruption. At Berkeley, thousands of students and a few faculty members tried to "reconstitute" the campus as a center for public argumentation against the war and tried to stop all other campus activity until the war was ended.

THE HIPPIE MOVEMENT

The college student radicalism of the 1960s was at first quite separate from the hippie movement, but gradually the two phenomena became interrelated. The word "hip" has been defined as "to be in the know, particularly about the drug underworld." The word "hippie" was derived from Norman Mailer's term "hipster." The appeal of the hippie mystique to young people in the 1960s had many aspects, including social protest and normal feelings of rebellion characteristic of adolescence. But many young adherents of the hippie movement were motivated by deep personal maladjustment and alienation. Craving love, joy, and self-realization many of them believed that such needs could be satisfied by certain drugs, especially when taken in the company of other young people with similar feelings. They often described their movement as a "subculture" or "counterculture," and sometimes quite candidly as a "drug culture." Its culture included electronically amplified rock music, psychedelic art, the doctrines of astrology and Krishna consciousness, and communal social relationships analogous with those of gypsies or of certain American Indian tribes.

An essential factor in the spread of the hippie movement was the popularization of the new drug lysergic acid diethylamide, or LSD. This drug was first synthesized by a Swiss chemist in 1938. In the early 1960s Dr. Timothy Leary, a lecturer on clinical psychology at Harvard and the holder of a Ph.D. in psychology from the University of California at Berkeley, was one of a group engaged in experiments with several drugs, including LSD, which they described as "psychedelic" or "consciousness-expanding." Their critics insisted that LSD was more accurately described as mind-distorting and hallucinogenic and that its effects on different individuals were dangerously unpredictable, a kind of "chemical Russian roulette." Colors intensified and changed, shape and spatial relations were distorted, and inanimate objects seemed to pulsate and to assume great emotional significance. To some the experience was deeply moving, exhilarating, and "self-revealing"—an experience of "cosmic oneness" or an "exploration of inner space." But to others it brought panic, bizarre and suicidal behavior, and temporary or even permanent psychosis. The frequency of the hippies' use of LSD varied considerably, but many of them used marijuana almost every day when they could obtain it.

In 1966 the news media began to give the hippies massive publicity and often described them as "flower children" or "the love generation." In 1967 when the movement reached its peak, there were probably about 200,000 hippies in the nation, and millions of other Americans, young and old, were sympathetic to the movement. The largest colony was in the Haight-Ashbury district of San Francisco, scene of the nationally publicized "summer of love" in 1967. Other large concentrations of hippies could be found in the Telegraph Avenue area south of the university campus in Berkeley; in Los Angeles on the Sunset Strip and along Fairfax Avenue in West Hollywood; and in Greenwich Village in New York. Smaller enclaves sprang up in almost every major American city, and there were various rural communes, notably in California, New Mexico, and Colorado.

Hippie leaders maintained that they were seeking to establish a new communal freedom from individual anxieties and to remove themselves from a decadent society full of war and oppression into a utopia of peace and love. It was more than coincidental that the years in which the hippie movement attracted its greatest following were also the years of the great expansion of American armed forces in Vietnam. Many young Americans believed that their country's participation in the war in southeast Asia was morally indefensible, and their hatred of the war was a major factor in their feelings of alienation from the whole prevailing system of society.

BLACK RADICALISM

About the time when student radicals had shifted their main attention to opposing the Vietnam war, and away from the black civil rights movement, that movement itself had taken a new and radical turn. In 1966, Stokley Carmichael became the new head of the Student Nonviolent Coordinating Committee. He soon turned it into a movement of violent nonstudents, ordered all whites to get out of it, and raised the cry of "black power." In the autumn of 1966, the Black Panther Party for Self-Defense was founded in Oakland by two young black militants, Huey P. Newton and Bobby G. Seale. They had met as students at the old Grove Street campus of Merritt College, a public junior college drawing many of its students from predominantly black areas in west and north Oakland. Newton and Seale were influenced by the writings of Malcolm X and Frantz Fanon, and later by those of Marx, Lenin, Mao Tse-tung,

Ho Chi Minh, and Che Guevara. But their strongest feeling, growing out of their personal experience, was a hatred of the frequently prejudiced and cruel treatment of black people by white police. The black panther was originally the ballot emblem of a black civil rights party organized in Alabama in 1965. Newton liked the name and adopted it because, he said, the panther was reputed never to make an unprovoked attack, but to defend itself ferociously. Newton and Seale established a system of patrol cars; carrying law books and guns, they trailed police cars through the Oakland slums to protect the constitutional rights of black people.

One of the new party's first and most important converts was Eldridge Cleaver, a vigorously articulate black man who had twice been in prison. His first term, beginning when he was 18, had been spent in the California state prison at Soledad for possession of marijuana. After his release, according to his widely read memoir, *Soul On Ice,* he was burning with resentment and had turned to the raping of white women as a symbolic act of "insurrection," intended "to send waves of consternation throughout the white race." This brought him another and longer term in prison, during which he came to repudiate the act of rape and to regard his own resort to it as a symptom of the "dehumanization" that he had suffered; however, he resolved to fight by more effective means against the social system that he felt had brutalized and degraded black people like himself.

In prison Cleaver had become an admirer of the Black Muslim leader Malcolm X, who was assassinated in 1965. Early in 1967, the widow of Malcolm X made a visit to San Francisco, and Cleaver, recently released on parole, wanted to meet her. A squad of Black Panthers appeared at the airport and acted as her bodyguards while she was in the city. They wore paramilitary black uniforms and black berets and carried guns. The sight of them was an exhilarating experience for Cleaver, and he threw himself into the cause of the new party. He became its "minister of information." Seale was "chairman," and Newton was "minister of defense" and later "supreme commander."

Intense fear and hostility between police and Panthers soon led to many tragic shooting affrays. On October 28, 1967, gunfire erupted after an Oakland police car stopped an automobile driven by Huey Newton. One officer was killed; another policeman and Newton were wounded. On April 6, 1968, also in Oakland, there was more shooting in which two policemen were wounded, a young Panther was killed, and Eldridge Cleaver was wounded and arrested. Newton was tried in the summer of 1968 and convicted of manslaughter, but the conviction was reversed on appeal, and two later trials ended in hung juries. Cleaver was released on bail, became the candidate of the Peace and Freedom party for the presidency of the United States, and chose Jerry Rubin as his running mate. Shortly afterward, a higher court ordered Cleaver's parole revoked, and rather than return to prison he jumped bail and fled to Algeria.

Though their beliefs and tactics were radical, the Panthers did not share the extreme separatism of the black "cultural nationalist" groups and ridiculed their advocacy of wearing African styles of dress and studying Swahili and other aspects of African culture. In January 1969, during an argument over such issues at a meeting of the Black Students Union at UCLA, two young leaders of the Black Panther movement in Los Angeles were shot and killed by members of a cultural nationalist faction, in a dispute partly fomented by undercover agents of the FBI. Black radicalism was further divided and weakened when a bitter quarrel developed between Cleaver, who issued periodic calls for revolutionist guerrilla warfare from his exile in Algeria, and Newton, who favored much more moderate tactics including free breakfasts for children, a free medical clinic, and free bus transportation for relatives of prisoners on visiting days.

THE DECLINE OF RADICALISM

By the fall of 1970 the volcano of student rebellion had become dormant, if not extinct. By 1971 even radical students at Berkeley began to speak of "the old New Left of the 1960s" and to debate "why the movement died." Foremost among the reasons for the decline in student radicalism was the gradual winding down of the Vietnam war. Other factors were the extreme political reaction of taxpaying voters against the disruptive tactics of the student demonstrators, the dampening effects of the economic recession, the coming of the 18-year-old vote, and the growth of interest among young people in the possibilities of "working within the system." Mass disruption on the campus was an idea whose time had come and gone.

Throughout the 1970s the mood on college campuses in California and across the nation grew steadily more conservative. A survey of students entering Berkeley in 1980 revealed a marked contrast to the attitudes of students polled 8 years earlier. The proportion of students who described themselves as "middle-of-the-road" politically increased from 33 to 45 percent, while those who said they were "conservative" rose from 10 to 17 percent. Those who identified themselves as "liberal" declined from 50 to 37 percent, and those who said they were "far left" dropped from 7 to 2 percent. Faced with greater economic uncertainty after graduation, a growing number of students in the 1970s chose majors in business and engineering rather than in the social sciences or liberal arts, and when asked about the most important objective in their life, they responded "to be well-off financially." The resumption of draft registration in 1980 led to a flurry of antidraft rallies on campuses throughout the state, but some observers speculated that the new antidraft movement was related more to the rise of "careerism" on campus than to any widespread political or moral opposition to military service. Today's college students, cynics charged, were opposed to the draft because it would delay their entry into the job market.

A few of the leaders of the radical movement were still in the news during the 1970s but were no longer very radical. Eldridge Cleaver returned from exile in 1976 to surrender himself for trial, explaining that he had acquired a new and more favorable view of the United States after several years of unpleasant experiences elsewhere. Jerry Rubin complained that reporters, who occasionally still interviewed him, treated him "like a museum piece"; by 1980 he had become a research analyst for a New York investment firm. Bobby Seale and Tom Hayden became unsuccessful though quite conventional political candidates for mayor of Oakland and United States senator, respectively. Moreover, John Tunney's Senate seat was lost in 1976 not to Tom Hayden in the Democratic primary but rather to the Republican nominee, S. I. Hayakawa, who had become an outstanding symbol of resistance to student radicalism when he was president of San Francisco State University.

Although the radical era ended in public rejection, it left some positive and permanent aftereffects. The decade of protest had generated a greater awareness of the rights of racial minorities, and the liberalization of public attitudes had resulted in some legislative reforms. Possession of small amounts of marijuana, for example, had been reduced from a felony to a misdemeanor comparable to a traffic citation, and state laws forbidding various sexual activities between consenting adults were repealed. Tom Hayden rebounded from his 1976 defeat to found a grass roots political organization, the Campaign for Economic Democracy, which won passage of rent control ordinances and elected progressive candidates in cities across the state. Furthermore, many young people who had been part of "the movement" in the 1960s carried their earlier values with them as they entered the professions, assumed greater responsibilities, and began the task of rearing a new generation of Californians.

SELECTED BIBLIOGRAPHY

Economic and population trends may be followed in the *California Statistical Abstract* and in the *Economic Report of the Governor* prepared by the state department of finance, both annual publications. On developments up to the 1950s, see Margaret S. Gordon, *Employment Expansion and Population Growth, the California Experience, 1900–1950* (1954); Davis McEntire, *The Labor Force in California . . . 1900–1950* (1952); Warren S. Thompson, *Growth and Changes in California's Population* (1955); and Edward L. Ullman, "Amenities as a Factor in Regional Growth," *Geographical Review*, XL (January 1954), pp. 119–132. James J. Rawls, "Visions and Revisions," *The Wilson Quarterly*, IV (Summer 1980), pp. 57–65, describes the deterioration of the popular image of California in the late 1960s and early 1970s.

Los Angeles and its Environs in the Twentieth Century: A Bibliography of a Metropolis (1973), edited by Doyce B. Nunis, Jr., is a valuable guide to materials. See also John Halpern, *Los Angeles: Improbable City* (1979); John Caughey and LaRee Caughey (eds.), *Los Angeles: Biography of a City* (1977); John Anson Ford, *Thirty Explosive Years in Los Angeles County* (1961), on the 1930s through the 1950s; Christopher Rand, *Los Angeles, the Ultimate City* (1967); and Francis Carney, "The Decentralized Politics of Los Angeles," *Annals of the American Academy of Political and Social Science* (May 1964), pp. 107–121. Other metropolitan areas are treated in James E. Vance, Jr., *Geography and Urban Evolution in the San Francisco Bay Area* (1964); Frederick M. Wirt, *Power in the City: Decision Making in San Francisco* (1974); Lawrence Kinnaird, *History of the Greater San Francisco Bay*

Region (three volumes, 1967); Richard F. Pouarde, *City of the Dream: The History of San Diego* (1977); and Christian L. Larsen, *Growth and Government in Sacramento* (1966). On reapportionment, see Don A. Allen, Sr., *Legislative Sourcebook; The California Legislature and Reapportionment, 1849–1965* (1965).

Material on the history and problems of the public schools may be found in Irving G. Hendrick, *California Education: A Brief History* (1980); Roy W. Cloud, *Education in California; Leaders, Organizations, and Accomplishments of the First Hundred Years* (1952); and Merton E. Hill, *The Junior College Movement in California, 1907–1948* (1949). The best of the institutional histories are Edith R. Mirrielees, *Stanford: The Story of a University* (1959) and Verne A. Stadtman, *The University of California, 1868–1968* (1970).

Landon Y. Jones, *Great Expectations: America and the Baby Boom Generation* (1980) is a portrait of the generation which reached maturity in the 1960s. On campus radicalism, see Seymour M. Lipset and Sheldon S. Wolin (eds.), *The Berkeley Student Revolt: Facts and Interpretations* (1965); Michael V. Miller and Susan Gilmore (eds.), *Revolution at Berkeley* (1965); and Irwin Unger, *The Movement: A History of the American New Left, 1959–1972* (1974). On the hippie phenomenon, see Gene Anthony, *The Summer of Love: Haight-Ashbury at Its Highest* (1980); Theodore Roszak, *The Making of a Counter Culture* (1969); and Lewis Yablonsky, *The Hippie Trip* (1968), a sociological study.

Important works on black radicalism include Eldridge Cleaver, *Soul on Ice* (1968); Bobby Seale, *Seize the Time: The Story of the Black Panther Party and Huey P. Newton* (1970); and Philip S. Foner (ed.), *The Black Panthers Speak* (1970).

CONTEMPORARY CALIFORNIA CULTURE

In the years after World War II California emerged as a leading cultural region of the United States. Hollywood remained the nation's movie capital and soon became a center for the production of films, serials, and commercials for television. Works by California writers and artists, architects, and musicians achieved widespread recognition and often expressed values and attitudes distinctly Californian.

LITERATURE

A remarkable group of poets gathered in San Francisco in the late 1940s. Several of them, notably Robert Duncan and William Everson, had been conscientious objectors during the war and were attracted to San Francisco by the circle of pacifists and philosophical anarchists that formed there. The opposition of these poets to all government, and particularly to war, which they regarded as government at its worst, had an important influence on the intellectual atmosphere of the San Francisco Bay area for many years to come. Their poetry often manifested what Everson called "the repudiation of received forms," a conscious rejection of established literary standards of composition. In several articles in national magazines, the older poet Kenneth Rexroth did much to publicize "the San Francisco Renaissance" as a name for this regional movement of innovative and experimental poetry.

In the mid 1950s the cultural libertarianism of San Francisco attracted another group of writers, particularly from the New York area. Self-styled the "beat generation," they began to achieve notoriety in 1956 with the publication of Jack Kerouac's exuberant and formless novel *On the Road* and Allen Ginsberg's startling *Howl and Other Poems*. The beat writers were a somewhat different group from the poets of the San Francisco Renaissance, though they were often lumped together. They were even more extreme in rebelling against the prevailing norms of society and government and also against the established poetic and literary forms. Kerouac announced in a television interview that "beat," a word of his own coinage, meant "beatific." In its rhythmic sense "beat" also implied a connection between the writers of the 1950s and modern jazz, and in its meaning of being tired or "beaten down" it aptly characterized the response of the beat writers to modern life. When the Russians put the first Sputnik into orbit, the San Francisco columnist Herb Caen dubbed the beat generation the "beatniks," and the derisive nickname stuck.

Ginsberg's poems were first published in England, and much of their original fame resulted from their seizure by the San Francisco customs office on the ground that they were obscene. They were then published in San Francisco by Lawrence Ferlinghetti, poet and proprietor of the City Lights Bookshop, a center for many writers and artists. Ferlinghetti was tried and acquitted on a charge of publishing an obscene book, and the publicity of this trial did much to ensure popular interest in the beats and their writings. Kerouac's novels and Ferlinghetti's poems were relatively gentle and benevolent, but Ginsberg's poetry, though it had a kind of Whitmanesque power, was intensely morbid. His *Howl* consisted of one continuous sentence nearly 2000 words long and was filled with references to drugs, tragically unhappy sexual encounters, madness and suicide, all blamed upon the corruption of the existing form of society. In many poems and speeches Ginsberg inveighed against materialism, technology, the war machine—"all the forces that have assaulted the individual human spirit."

In the 1960s a new generation of California writers established themselves as major figures in contemporary American literature. In some ways their work was an extension of the literary style and concerns of the beat generation, but it also reflected the turbulence of their own times. The impulse toward experimentalism, evident earlier in the poetry of Ginsberg and the runaway prose of Kerouac, was manifest in the complex layering of voices in the novels of Ken Kesey and the surreal imagery of Richard Brautigan. Kesey, born in Colorado in 1935, studied creative writing at Stanford University and worked briefly in the Veteran's Hospital at nearby Menlo Park. His comic, macabre first novel, *One Flew Over the Cuckoo's Nest* (1962), is set in a mental ward and powerfully portrays the struggle of the individual against the overwhelming forces of conformity in modern society. Kesey adopted a lifestyle as unconventional as his prose, becoming a cult hero in the 1960s as he toured the country with a busload of followers known as the Merry Pranksters. Richard Brautigan moved to the San Francisco Bay area in the 1950s from his native Washington and first received widespread attention with his unorthodox and disturbing book *Trout Fishing in America* (1967). Like some modern-day Leatherstocking, the narrator of *Trout Fishing* longs for the restoration of frontier innocence and agrarian simplicity, but finds that such qualities are beyond recall in the age of technology and commerce. In one memorable scene the narrator visits a wrecking yard in San Francisco and encounters, among the inventory of used doors and toilets, a "used trout stream," stacked in piles of various lengths and ready for sale.

Since the beginnings of the state's literature, serious California writers have provided a counterpoint to the prevailing myth of California as the land of boundless opportunity, success, and romance. The failure of this myth became a major preoccupation for the writers of the 1930s, finding its most powerful expression in the works of Nathanael West and John Steinbeck. The later generations of California writers also used the California dream as a background or a foil for their fiction. Much of the appeal of their work, as James D. Houston has pointed out, derived "from the fact that the dream is always there—if only to be betrayed—the ongoing western promise of the Big Romance, the Second Chance, which is a given in the environment, as potent and as insistent as the coastline."

The most important figure among the new California writers, and the one who most profoundly invoked the California mythos, was novelist-essayist Joan Didion. Born and reared in Sacramento, Didion was graduated from the University of California at Berkeley in 1956 and worked for the next 8 years in New York as a writer and editor. In 1963 she published her first novel, *Run River*, an evocative story of a rancher's daughter in California who, under the accumulation of a multitude of small pressures, goes insane. The novel is suffused with a pervasive sense of loss, the decline of a "certain pride," and the disappearance of old, familiar ways in the author's native Sacramento Valley. During the next several years Didion wrote a series of essays, collected as *Slouching Towards Bethlehem* (1968), which expanded her vision of California in decline. In "Notes from a Native Daughter," Didion described the dramatic early history of Sacramento and its gradual evolution into the comfortable, rich farm town she knew as a girl. "In that gentle sleep Sacramento dreamed until perhaps 1950," she wrote, "when something happened. What happened was that Sacramento woke to the fact that the outside world was moving in, fast and hard. At the moment of its waking Sacramento lost, for better or for worse, its character. . . ." Didion made plain that she was talking about more than just her hometown, "for Sacramento *is* California, and California is a place in which a boom mentality and a sense of Chekhovian loss meet in uneasy suspension; in which the mind is troubled by some buried but ineradicable suspicion that things had better work here, because here, beneath that immense bleached sky, is where we run out of continent."

Didion also wrote about those who had come from "the outside world" to California, seeking and often not finding that which had eluded them somewhere else. In "Some Dreamers of the Golden Dream" she told the pathetic story of a desperate woman, convicted of the murder of her husband, who lived in the San Bernardino Valley. "Of course she came from somewhere else, came off the prairie in search of something she had seen in a movie or heard on the radio, for this is a Southern California story." In the title essay, "Slouching Towards Bethlehem," Didion provided a first-hand look at the Haight-Ashbury district of San Francisco in the spring of 1967. With an ear finely tuned to the rhetoric of the drug culture, she described with precision the sense of anomie and rootlessness of the young people drifting into San Francisco for the much heralded "summer of love."

Joan Didion in the living room of her Malibu home in 1977. *(Photograph by Mary Lloyd Estrin. Courtesy of Simon & Schuster.)*

In *Play It As It Lays* (1970), Didion's second novel, the heroine is a former Los Angeles model and actress who, somewhat like the central character in *Run River,* is poised on the brink of psychic collapse. On the surface the novel was about the callous and corrupt world of Hollywood, but its analysis extended much deeper. As in her earlier writing, Didion's concern was with portraying a sense of loss, of disintegration, not just in California but in all of contemporary society. The novel was filled with images of alienation and desolation, of failed dreams and moral collapse. Following its publication a reviewer in the *New York Times* observed, "There hasn't been another American writer of Joan Didion's quality since Nathanael West." Throughout the 1970s Didion published essays on such diverse California topics as the grisly Charles Manson murders, the J. Paul Getty museum near Pacific Palisades, the cult of motorcycle gangs, and Mrs. Nancy Reagan. These and other essays were collected and published in 1979 as *The White Album.*

Didion's third novel, *A Book of Common Prayer* (1977), provided a more personal metaphor for dissolution and collapse. The central character, a San Francisco matron named Charlotte Douglas, slowly disintegrates under the shock of learning from the FBI that her teenage daughter has set off a pipe bomb in the Transamerica Building, hijacked a plane, and sent back a tape recording filled with revolutionary rhetoric. Inspired perhaps by the bizarre kidnapping and radical "conversion" of Patricia Hearst in 1974, *A Book of Common Prayer* explored further the effects of the breakdown which Didion had witnessed 10 years earlier in the Haight-Ashbury. Like all of Didion's heroines, Charlotte Douglas is emptied of faith, and feeling, and the ability to cope.

The new generation of California writers included several black, Hispanic, and Asian-American authors whose work added a richness and distinctive texture to the recent literature of the state. In the early 1970s black novelists Al Young and Ishmael Reed began publishing in Berkeley the *Yardbird*

Reader, a journal dedicated to the promotion of a diverse, multicultural American literature. Reed, a native of Tennessee, regarded California as the natural place for such an enterprise because here was America's first "truly world state," a state which had produced "a colorful gumbo culture." Reed called his own writing "neo-hoodooism," a blend of black magic, African imagery, and contemporary Afro-American life. The complex, unrestrained style of his novels placed Reed squarely in the tradition of California's experimental literature. As the central character in Reed's *Yellow Back Radio Broke-Down* (1969) observes, "No one says a novel has to be one thing. It can be anything it wants to be, a vaudeville show, the six o'clock news, the mumblings of wild men saddled by demons." Like many other writings of his generation, Reed's work was a response to the dissension and chaos of recent California history. In *The Last Days of Louisiana Red* (1974), a novel set in Berkeley in the 1960s, Reed offered a thinly veiled parody of the Black Panther party and the once-fashionable rhetoric and violence of such organizations.

In 1959 José Antonio Villareal published *Pocho,* the first novel about Mexican-American life written by a Mexican American. Son of immigrant parents, Villareal was born in the Imperial Valley and worked as a youth in California's orchards and fields. *Pocho* chronicled the hardships of Mexican immigrants who came to the United States following the revolution of 1910. It focused on the disintegration of the Rubio family in the Santa Clara Valley and on the dilemma of young Richard Rubio, torn between the traditional Mexican values of his parents and the new way of life he finds in California. The most important figure in the emergence of a Mexican-American literature was Luis Valdez, a playwright and director born in Delano in 1940. After graduation from San Jose State College, Valdez returned to Delano in 1965 and founded *El Teatro Campesino.* Combining ancient Mexican myths, bilingual dialogue, and a concern for contemporary political issues, *El Teatro* toured the state's agricultural labor camps and became the dramatic voice of the farm worker movement. The highly imaginative and inventive plays of Valdez had an appeal far beyond the farm workers for whom they were originally written. In 1976 *El Teatro Campesino* made its first European tour as an official event of the American bicentennial, and in subsequent years it enjoyed several other highly successful tours abroad. In 1978 Valdez's most ambitious work, *Zoot Suit,* premiered in Los Angeles and later made a brief run on Broadway. The play centered on the Los Angeles "Sleepy Lagoon" murder case of 1942 and introduced theatergoers to *calo,* the slang dialect of Mexican-American youth in the 1940s. Although Valdez took great care to depict the *pachucos* as neither heroes nor innocents, some critics denounced the play for its projection of racial stereotypes.

Reflecting the constant movement of people into California, a recurring theme in the state's literature has been the interplay of a character's present with a past lived somewhere else. This theme, evident in the work of the new Mexican-American writers, was also a major concern of Maxine Hong Kingston, daughter of immigrants from China who came to the United States in the 1930s. Kingston was born in Stockton in 1940 and grew up with a keen interest in the stories and legends of her family's life in China. In *The Woman Warrior* (1976), a book subtitled *Memoirs of a Girlhood among Ghosts*, Kingston explained: "Those of us in the first American generations have had to figure out how the invisible world the emigrants built around our childhoods fit in solid America." Kingston's narrative explored both her childhood memories of growing up in the family laundry in Stockton and the customs, traditions, and fables of village life in China. In *China Men* (1980) Kingston took this exploration even farther, contemplating the nature of exile and the effects of discrimination on earlier generations of Chinese immigrants.

Similar concerns distinguished the work of Japanese-American writers during this period. A common source of dramatic tension in their work was the contrast between contemporary California and a remembered or imagined life in Japan. Among the many books to deal with the experience of "relocation" during World War II, the most successful was *Farewell to Manzanar* (1973), written by Jeanne Wakatsuki Houston and her husband James D. Houston. *Farewell to Manzanar* tells the story of the Wakatsukis, an industrious southern California family resettled in 1942 at the Manzanar relocation camp in Owens Valley. The Wakatsukis face their hardships with dignity and resourcefulness, but disintegrate as a family unit. "I felt the miserable sense of loss," Jeanne Wakatsuki Houston recalled, "that comes when the center has collapsed and everything seems to be flying apart around you." The tension between acculturation and tradition, evident in Villareal's *Pocho* and Kingston's *Woman Warrior*, was thus heightened for Japanese Americans by the tragedy of relocation.

California has always been a fertile ground for the imagination. The latest generation of California writers, continuing in the tradition of Frank Norris and John Steinbeck, have created from California's recent past a literature redolent of the region but whose power and diversity are part of the larger American culture.

PAINTING AND SCULPTURE

Two of the most significant art movements in California since the end of World War II were abstract expressionism in the San Francisco Bay area in the late 1940s and the "L.A. look" of southern California in the 1960s. These two movements were part of larger currents in the development of modern art, but were also shaped by the distinct artistic sensibilities of northern and southern California. Their order of occurrence was evidence of the growing importance of Los Angeles in the state's cultural history.

In the early 1930s the California art scene was vitalized by the visit of the German-born painter Hans Hofmann, often called the dean of abstract expressionism. Hofmann, whose abstract paintings exhibited bold thrusts of vibrant color, was a visiting instructor at the University of California at Berkeley and the Chouinard Art Institute in Los Angeles. His influence was especially strong in the Bay Area where in the late 1940s the California School of Fine

Arts (later renamed the San Francisco Art Institute) invited Clyfford Still and Mark Rothko, two of the nation's leading abstract expressionists, to join the faculty. Still's paintings were characterized by large, ragged patches of dissonant color, while Rothko produced forceful rectangular shapes, blurred at the edges, painted in a more limited color range. The work of Still, Rothko, and the generation of artists they influenced—Richard Diebenkorn, Sam Francis, Hassel Smith, and Frank Lobdell—marked the "golden age" of San Francisco painting.

By the middle 1950s abstract expressionism in the Bay Area had begun to decline. Many of the students of Clyfford Still followed him to New York where abstract expressionism was gaining acceptance, and the work of those left behind became increasingly imitative. Out of this decline came a movement away from total abstraction and back to a style of painting which represented figures or elements of the landscape. The most important of the so-called Bay Area figurative painters were David Park and Richard Diebenkorn, both of whom taught at the California School of Fine Arts. Park led the movement to representation with his richly colored paintings emphasizing the human form, while Diebenkorn remained essentially an abstract expressionist until 1955, after which he turned slowly to landscapes, figures, and still life. In his later work Diebenkorn attempted to incorporate the brushwork of abstract expressionism into the recognizable forms of representational art. His colors, as one critic observed, were "essentially tonal, rooted in the California landscape."

It was also in the 1950s that the California beat generation made a distinct contribution to the evolution of modern art, the assemblage. The art of assemblage, a kind of sculpture created from bits of cast-off materials from everyday life, was a reaction against "high brow" art just as the writing of Kerouac and Ginsberg represented a rejection of established literary standards. Constructed from old furniture, clothing, tin cans, license plates, store mannequins, wire and string, the completed three-dimensional assemblages were often a statement of horror or anguish at the materialism and corruption of modern industrial society.

Out of the assemblage tradition came what was known as "funk art," a hybrid of painting and sculpture constructed from such materials as leather, clay, steel, and vinyl. The term "funk" apparently was borrowed from the vocabulary of jazz or blues musicians where "funky" meant a heavy beat, an earthy, sensual sound. Correspondingly, the constructions of such funk artists as Robert Arneson often were biomorphic forms with ribald or scatological connotations. In the tradition of Bay Area nonconformity, several northern California artists in the 1970s were identified with what came to be called "bad" painting, art which deliberately rejected the classic standards of good taste and the conventions of fine art. The paintings of San Francisco native Joan Brown, a professor at the University of California at Berkeley, combined "a solemnity about art with a total rejection of standard art attitudes," while Oakland painter James Albertson produced highly imaginative works which were jarringly "ugly" and parodied traditional art values with an incisive wit.

It was clear by the 1960s that the momentum in California art had shifted south. Abstract expressionism continued to be the dominant style of painting in Los Angeles in the 1950s, but by the end of the decade a distinctive regional variation had emerged. Among the paintings of Los Angeles artist Craig Kauffman in 1957 and 1958 were several works in which forms appeared sharply outlined in silhouette. The impresssion of these paintings was of a "clean" composition, freed from the ragged or blurred edges characteristic of the work of such Bay Area artists as Still and Rothko. A contemporary of Kauffman, Los Angeles painter Billy Al Bengston, commented that Kauffman "was the first southern California artist *ever* to paint an original painting." In 1959 the Los Angeles County Museum opened an exhibition of four California painters whose work emphasized an austere form of composition marked by geometric forms clearly, distinctly delineated. A Los Angeles critic christened the new style "hard edge," a term which accurately suggested the abrupt boundaries between shapes and colors in the new paintings. The exhibit at the county museum traveled to London, and hard edge abstraction provided Los Angeles with its first international success as a center for modern art.

One of the chief concerns of the hard edge painters was to achieve an immaculate finish to their work. By an extraordinarily even application of paint and by limiting their colors to two or three saturated hues, the hard edge abstractionists were able to create paintings with a remarkable optical shimmer. Critic Peter Plagens saw in these qualities a reflection of the esthetic climate of Los Angeles. "Hard Edge arose out of Los Angeles's desert air, youthful cleanliness, spatial expanse, architectural tradition . . . and, most vaguely and most importantly, out of optimism."

In the middle 1960s a group of Los Angeles artists and sculptors, most notably Ed Ruscha, Billy Al Bengston, John McCracken, and Larry Bell, carried the concern for precision and impeccability of surface to an extreme. Their work achieved international recognition as the California finish fetish or, more commonly, the L.A. look. The objects they created were as lustrous as the glossy surface of a highly polished automobile or a new fiberglass surfboard. Among such sculptors the preferred materials were polyester resin or other new forms of plastic, neon, and stainless steel. Larry Bell, a sculptor born in Chicago in 1939 and educated at the Chouinard Art Institute, mastered the complicated procedures and expensive technology necessary to work the new materials and produced in the 1960s a series of mirrorlike cubes of chrome and glass. Bell graded the surfaces of his glass cubes between total transparency and total reflectivity so that while approaching the object, the viewer's image would appear and disappear. The inspiration for the cubes of Larry Bell seemed to be the "glass box" office buildings of downtown Los Angeles. Their materials were drawn from the local aerospace industry, and their concern with the surface of things, the facade, mirrored the influence of Hollywood. Even more than hard edge abstraction, the L.A. look was a product of the peculiar atmosphere of southern California.

One of the major international art movements of the 1960s was "pop art," a movement which both ridiculed and celebrated the affluent consumer society. Pop art flourished in southern California and, like abstract expressionism in the previous decade, took on there a distinctive regional quality. Los Angeles pop artists regarded impeccable craftmanship as crucial to their work, and they took great pains to produce art of a highly polished, finished quality. Pop art in Los Angeles, in other words, had the characteristic L.A. look. It was also distinguished by a mildness, subtlety, and benevolence that was lacking in the more strident pop art produced elsewhere.

Typical of the easygoing, nonmilitant pop artists working in southern California in the 1960s was Edward Ruscha. Born in Omaha in 1937 and reared in Oklahoma City, Ruscha moved to Los Angeles and attended Chouinard from 1956 to 1960. Ruscha's work began with a series of brittle word-paintings and soon evolved to the creation of whole environments for words. His *Large Trademark with Eight Spotlights* (1962) was a monumental painting of the familiar logo "20th Century-Fox." In the late 1960s he produced several silk-screen prints of Standard Oil Company gasoline stations, each rendered in stylized detail and a variety of hues. One of Ruscha's best-known works was *Hollywood* (1968), a series of prints depicting the large sheet-metal letters in the Hollywood hills. In addition to his paintings and prints, Ruscha also produced books such as *Twenty-Six Gasoline Stations* (1962), containing snapshots of gas stations between Los Angeles and Oklahoma City, and *Thirty-Four Parking Lots* (1967), photographs of Los Angeles parking lots shot from a helicopter.

The popular culture of Los Angeles obviously was a major inspiration for the work of Ruscha, although his attitude toward that culture was ambiguous. "I've been influenced by everything about L.A.," he once commented. "I remember that when I first came here, the things that impressed me the most were the flat, horizontal character of the city, the palm trees, and the whole car culture—especially hot rods. Actually, what really got me was the hot rods *next to* the palm trees." One critic saw in the work of Ruscha a "mock worship of California's earthly paradise," and indeed Ruscha's approach to the symbols of California's film industry and automobile culture was often sardonic. There was also, however, in his work a kind of affectionate regard for Los Angeles and its environs. It remained for the viewer to decide whether the pastel sky

Hollywood. A silk-screen print by Edward Ruscha. *(Gift of the Phoenix Collection of Graphic Art, San Francisco. Courtesy of the University Art Museum, University of California, Berkeley.)*

of *Hollywood,* created by Ruscha out of Pepto-Bismol and caviar, was a tribute to the beauty of a Los Angeles sunset or a reminder of the unpleasant effects of smog.

California art in the 1970s came to be dominated more by institutions than individuals. At the beginning of the decade two architecturally distinguished museums had just been completed in the San Francisco Bay area. In 1968 the University Art Museum in Berkeley opened its new $3 million building, designed by Mario J. Ciampi, which included a special gallery for the large Hans Hofmann collection recently donated to the university by the artist. The following year the Oakland Museum opened its extraordinary new complex, a museum dedicated exclusively to the history, art, and natural history of California. Its art gallery included a retrospective of California art from the watercolors of visiting artists during the Spanish period, through the landscapes of William Keith and Albert Bierstadt, to the reflective cubes of Larry Bell.

Meanwhile in southern California the Los Angeles County Museum of Art in 1965 was installed in magnificent new quarters on Wilshire Boulevard, adjacent to the La Brea tar bed, and in its first year it attracted a larger attendance than any other museum in the west. In 1971 it opened a massive exhibition called "Art and Technology," the culmination of a 5-year project by the museum to foster collaboration between local artists and local industry. The director of the museum had been impressed by the "futuristic character of Los Angeles, especially as it is manifested in its advanced technology," and the exhibition included luminous gas-filled tubes, kinetic sculptures, and elaborate constructions of materials from the southern California aerospace industry. Also in 1971 the California Institute of the Arts, known popularly as Cal Arts, opened its new campus in the San Fernando Valley. Incorporating the Chouinard Art Institute and the Los Angeles Conservatory of Music, Cal Arts became a major educational institution for the visual and performing arts. Its new campus was in large part a monument to the generosity of the family of Walt Disney who contributed some $30 million to the institute.

Two other wealthy southern Californians made important contributions to the arts in the 1970s. In 1974 the Pasadena Art Museum, whose new buildings had opened in 1969 as a showcase for contemporary art, became the Norton Simon Museum. Simon, a business executive with headquarters in Los Angeles, had created one of the largest collections of paintings and sculpture assembled by an individual in modern times. His collection included masterpieces by Rembrandt and Degas and became the permanent collection of the new Pasadena museum. The same year the J. Paul Getty Museum opened its new quarters near Pacific Palisades. The museum, modeled on a Roman villa, drew mixed reviews, for it included reproductions as well as authentic art among its displays of Greek and Roman antiquities, paintings, sculpture, and furniture. When Getty died in 1976, he left the bulk of his estate, valued at more than $1 billion, to the museum, making it the richest museum in the United States.

The 1970s were also a time of renewed interest in art history, an interest much less apparent in the avant-garde days of the previous decade. In 1976 the San Francisco Asian Art Museum hosted "The Chinese Exhibition," which drew record crowds to view ancient treasures from the Peoples' Republic of China. In 1978 an even greater number queued up to see the "Treasures of Tutankhamen" at the Los Angèles County Museum and at San Francisco's De Young, while "The Splendors of Dresden" exhibit at the California Palace of the Legion of Honor also drew record crowds.

ARCHITECTURE

The suburban growth of California's population following World War II spawned several distinctive forms of commercial and domestic architecture. At the center of the new suburban communities, dispersed widely by the spreading freeway system, were "shopping centers," clusters of stores designed exclusively for the automobile-borne shopper. The orientation of these stores toward their expansive parking lots, rather than toward the main street, was a major break with past traditions of commercial architecture. By the 1960s shopping centers had been transformed into "shopping malls," large self-contained units which centered on an enclosed mall and contained an array of small shops and one or more major department stores.

The houses which filled the new suburban tracts in the late 1940s and 1950s were almost all variations of a single style, the California ranch house. The roots of this ubiquitous style lay in the California bungalow of the early twentieth century, and like the bungalow the new ranch-style homes typically were single-floor dwellings, low in profile, with an informal arrangement of living spaces. Both styles were distinctly Californian in their emphasis on the close relation between indoor and outdoor living. The ranch-style homes were characterized by picture windows, sliding glass doors, terraces, patios, and, in the wealthier suburbs, swimming pools. Like the California bungalow, the "California ranch" was widely copied and came to be accepted as an important regional contribution to American domestic architecture.

Along the wind-swept cliffs of the Sonoma County coastline, a planned community of homes and condominiums known as Sea Ranch initiated in the 1960s yet another California style. Architects Charles Moore and William Turnbull in effect turned the California ranch house on end to create an elongated vertical box, sheathed in wooden siding and covered by a shedlike roof. Because the coastal winds were so strong, the Sea Ranch buildings were designed without overhanging eaves. The resulting "vertical shed-roof box" became the latest California export. As the cost of single-family homes rose to unbelievable heights, clusters of shed-roofed box apartments and condominiums began to dot the landscape from coast to coast. Roof gardens, balconies, and hot tubs succeeded terraces, patios, and pools, and the California ideal of the indoor-outdoor house lived on.

While the suburbs of California proved to be centers of major architectural innovation in the twentieth century, California cities tended to follow rather than initiate trends in architectural design. The dominant style for commercial and institutional buildings since the end of World War II was the "international style," in which the structural skeleton of a building was often enclosed by a "curtain wall" of nonsupporting glass and metal panels. The impression of the typical international-style building was one of machinelike precision and anonymity, and skylines of cities across the state in the 1950s and 1960s came to be dominated by monuments to the high-rise esthetic of internationalism.

Inevitably a reaction set in to the boring, unbearable monotony of the new buildings. California architects began to design structures such as Wurster Hall (1965) on the university campus at Berkeley and the civic center (1969) in Fremont which conformed to the tenets of "brutalism," bluntly exposing the building's concrete or steel frame as well as such "innards" as water pipes and air ducts. Also in the 1960s California shared in a movement known as the new formalism which reintroduced classical symmetry and such traditional materials as marble and granite. The Los Angeles Music Center (1964–69) designed by Welton Becket, including the Dorothy Chandler Pavilion and the colonnade-enclosed Mark Taper Auditorium, was a striking example of the new style.

Most of the new commercial and institutional buildings in California cities were designed with an apparent disregard for their California setting. They could have been built anywhere. Architectural historian David Gebhard, however, has suggested that a distinctive "lack of intellectual intent" among California architects has given their work "a lightness and at times tinselly quality of make-believe which has more to do with Disneyland and Magic Mountain than it does with the traditional values of Modern architecture." Gebhard found a remarkable playfulness in the California architects' arbitrary use of such geometric shapes as circles, cones, and pyramids. San Francisco's Transamerica Pyramid (1972), designed by Los Angeles architect William Pereira, was a monumental and often unappreciated example of this whimsical quality of California design.

The resurgent interest in art history during the 1970s was paralleled in California architecture by a strong movement of historicism. In some parts of the state the earlier mission revival and Spanish colonial revival had never really ended. Since the mid 1920s new buildings in central Santa Barbara, by tradition and city ordinance, were Spanish in design. Thus in the mid 1970s new "Spanish-style" parking garages and overpasses for a crosstown freeway were proposed. In Sacramento a major effort to restore and rebuild the "old town" section of the city neared completion and more than $67 million was approved by the state legislature for renovation of the 1869 state capitol. In communities around the state a rash of "Tudor" condominiums, "Norman" restaurants, and "medieval" motels suggested the breadth of interest in earlier styles. The most impressive manifestation of the new historicism was the J. Paul Getty Museum (1972–73), modeled after the first-century Roman villa at Herculaneum.

The popularity of art history and revival architecture in the 1970s constituted a fairly predictable, conservative response to the preceding years of innovation and experiment. The familiar standards of the old masters and earlier styles of architectural design provided a sense of tradition and security, two qualities in short supply during the cultural and social upheavals of the 1960s.

MUSIC

By midcentury California had become a world center for the composition and performance of the most advanced forms of contemporary music. In large measure the musical prominence of California was a product of the immigration to the state of leading European composers during the years before World War II.

The first and probably most influential of the Europeans to settle in California was Arnold Schoenberg, developer of the revolutionary twelve-tone technique of composition. Schoenberg had been a professor of music in Berlin until deposed by the Nazis because of his unconventional music and Jewish origins. In 1933 he immigrated to the United States and decided to settle permanently in Los Angeles, where he was appointed to the faculty of the University of Southern California in 1935 and later became a professor at UCLA. In 1940 Schoenberg was joined in southern California by Igor Stravinsky, the most important composer of the twentieth century. Stravinsky's music, like that of Schoenberg, was highly controversial and represented a radical departure from traditional forms of composition. He remained in Hollywood until 1969 and composed there major works for orchestra and chorus. Meanwhile in northern California Darius Milhaud, the foremost French composer since Ravel, joined the faculty of Mills College in Oakland after fleeing Nazi-occupied France. Following the war, Milhaud remained at Mills and also served as a professor of composition at the Paris Conservatory.

Schoenberg and Milhaud, through their teaching, directly influenced a generation of California composers and musicians. Most prominent among the twentieth-century composers born and educated in California was Los Angeles native John Cage. Like many of his contemporaries, Cage believed that the music of the western world was at a dead end and that composers henceforth must seek new sounds, new media, and indeed a new "language" of musical expression. In search of such a language, Cage studied composition under Schoenberg but soon moved beyond the twelve-tone technique to the use of electronic equipment, tape recordings, noisemakers, and assorted unconventional percussion instruments. His "Third Construction in Metal" (1941) was scored for rattles, drums, tin cans, cowbells, and a lion's roar.

The performance of contemporary music, often subject to skepticism and even hostility from concertgoers, was encouraged in California by several key individuals and institutions. In 1945 a group of young composers around

Roger Sessions, then a professor of music at Berkeley, organized the Composers' Forum which for years sponsored a concert series featuring the work of Stravinsky, Schoenberg, and other contemporary composers. Under the direction of Pierre Monteux the San Francisco Symphony Orchestra in the 1940s also became a major force in popularizing the music of modern composers.

The San Francisco symphony continued to flourish under the leadership of the noted Austrian conductor Josef Krips during the 1960s and Seiji Ozawa in the early 1970s. Ozawa, born in China of Japanese parents, invariably conducted the classics as well as the most advanced contemporary music from memory—a remarkable feat. Replacing Ozawa in 1977 was the Dutch conductor Edo de Waart, under whose direction the San Francisco orchestra moved to its new quarters at the $31 million Louise M. Davies Symphony Hall in 1980. Davies Hall, together with the accompanying addition to the War Memorial Opera House and construction of the Zellerbach rehearsal hall, brought to completion the San Francisco Performing Arts Center begun nearly 50 years earlier. Meanwhile the San Francisco Opera company, led by Kurt Herbert Adler, ventured extensively into modern opera, performing works by Stravinsky, Janáček, and Shostakovich. In the 1960s Adler established two smaller auxiliary companies, the Spring Opera and the Western Opera Theater, to promote further innovation in repertory and to provide training for younger singers.

Across the bay, the Oakland Symphony Orchestra made great progress under the direction of Gerhard Samuel and won recognition as an orchestra of great merit and interest. Samuel resigned in 1970 and was succeeded by Harold Farberman and Calvin Simmons. In 1973 the orchestra occupied its new home amidst the splendor of the refurbished Paramount Theater in downtown Oakland.

As in all things cultural, the recent history of California music also reflected the rise of southern California. The traditional dominance of San Francisco had first been challenged by the creation of the Los Angeles Philharmonic Orchestra in 1919 which, under the direction of conductor Otto Klemperer in the 1930s, rose to first rank. From 1961 to 1978 the Los Angeles Philharmonic was under the direction of Zubin Mehta, a brilliant and glamorous conductor born in Bombay in 1936. During Mehta's tenure the Philharmonic finally obtained a permanent year-round home. Since the 1920s the summer concerts of the Los Angeles orchestra had been performed in the spectacular Hollywood Bowl, but the winter concerts were confined to an unsatisfactory leased auditorium. Los Angeles voters repeatedly had rejected bond issues for a municipally owned center for the performing arts. Dorothy Buffum Chandler worked almost single-handed to secure enough private contributions to make possible a new complex of buildings for music and drama at the civic center. The largest of these structures, the Dorothy Chandler Pavilion, opened in 1964.

In the years following World War II California also played a major role in the development of American popular music. In the 1940s much of the impetus for "traditionalist" jazz came from the state, and in the 1950s California was the center of the so-called west coast jazz movement. The band of Stan Kenton, a native of Kansas reared near Los Angeles, served as an important training ground for other California musicians. Pianist and composer Dave Brubeck organized a quartet in northern California which quickly rose to the top among modern jazz bands in the United States. Born in Concord in 1920, Brubeck had studied composition under Milhaud and Schoenberg.

If California can be said to have an indigenous music in the twentieth century, it would have to be rock. Although regarded by musicologists as being of little or no musical importance, rock music nevertheless was an important part of recent California history. During the 1960s California groups initiated several new rock styles and had an enormous impact on national and international popular music. Rock also was a galvanizing force for the "youth movement" of the 1960s, shaping and recording the social history of the period. Furthermore the new music from California often reinforced long-held popular conceptions about life in the Golden State and had a significant economic impact on the California economy. The recording industry generated thousands of new jobs and millions of dollars of income for Californians.

The emergence of rock in the late 1950s coincided with the onset of adolescence among the first wave of the postwar baby boom, the bulge in the American population caused by returning fathers at the end of World War II. The popularity of rock music and the strong sense of generational identity in the 1960s were rooted in this basic demographic fact. The so-called hard rock of the late 1950s was true teenage music, based on simple chords any adolescent could master on the guitar and celebrating in its lyrics the passions of teenage romance. By the end of the decade it appeared that rock music had exhausted its limited repertory.

California in the 1960s made three distinct contributions to popular music which revitalized rock. The "California sound" first appeared in the music of a group appropriately styled the Beach Boys, formed in 1961 in the suburbs of Los Angeles. Through their energetic melodies and cheerful repetitions, the Beach Boys effectively captured the bright simplicity of life on the southern California beaches in the early 1960s. The California sound not only reinvigorated American popular music, it also created a kind of modern legendry for California. Wholesome, tanned, and vigorous, the Beach Boys appeared in concert to be the very embodiment of California outdoor living; their lyrics were paeans to the climate of southern California. "Surfin' Safari" and "California Girls" insisted that life among the dunes and surf was carefree and that romantic opportunity was bountiful. A sense of easy mobility and love of speed was reflected in a score of recordings such as "Little Deuce Coupe" and "This Car of Mine."

Beginning in 1964 American young people were introduced to more sophisticated musical technique and melodic intricacy by a series of English rock bands. First, of course, came the Beatles, followed closely by Mick Jagger and the Rolling Stones. The first indications of an American response to the English invasion of popular music came from California. The new "Los Angeles sound," pioneered by a southern California group known as the Byrds, was essentially a combination of folk and rock music. The mix appealed to earlier devotees of hard rock and folk music and had the advantage of an American twang of country harmony. The popularity of Los Angeles folk rock was soon overshadowed by the appearance in San Francisco of the startling and highly controversial "acid rock." Originally intended to reproduce the distorted hearing of a person under the influence of LSD, acid rock was characterized by hyperamplification, bizarre electronic effects, and exotic imagery in its lyrics. When acid rock was performed at one of the city's auditoriums, such as the Fillmore or Avalon ballrooms, the illusion of an LSD experience was further heightened by "light shows" designed to reproduce the visual distortion induced by the drug.

The proliferation of rock bands in San Francisco in 1966 and 1967 was a measure of the tremendous influx of young people into the city. Some of the bands, such as the Quicksilver Messenger Service and the Grateful Dead, were immensely popular among residents of the Haight-Ashbury district, but did not achieve immediate commercial success. The first San Francisco band to establish a national following was the Jefferson Airplane, whose music was a blend of jazz, folk, blues, and "surrealistic tinkering." With the recording of such hits as "Embryonic Journey" and "White Rabbit," the band became a national sensation. Radio stations across the country broadcast the intonations of lead vocalist Grace Slick that "one pill makes you larger, and one pill makes you small."

In rapid succession California had spawned surf rock, folk rock, and acid rock. California was the center of the youth movement of the 1960s, and the music of the decade reflected this preeminence. It was appropriate, therefore, that a California musical event should become a symbol for the end of the decade and for the demise of "the movement." At the conclusion of their 1969 American tour, the Rolling Stones sought to hold a free concert in San Francisco's Golden Gate Park. The city refused to grant permission, and the concert was rescheduled for the Altamont Raceway in Alameda County. There, on December 6, 1969, more than 300,000 young people attended the performance, an event marred by violence. The Rolling Stones had recruited members of the Hell's Angels motorcycle gang to provide "security" for the band, and in the process the gang administered numerous beatings and stabbed one boy to death as he tried to reach the stage.

Altamont, combined with the death by drug overdose of rock superstars Jimi Hendrix and Janis Joplin the following year triggered a change in the attitude of many young people toward drugs and signaled a sobering reevaluation of the future of the now-aging youth movement. One of the most popular rock lyrics of the early 1960s had celebrated the decade as "the dawning of the age of Aquarius," and one observer now remarked that the age of Aquarius had ended with the flash of a knife at Altamont. The student newspaper at the University of California at Berkeley described the tragedy of Altamont as "the end of a decade of dreams; the beginning of a decade of facing the realities of the human condition."

SELECTED BIBLIOGRAPHY

Anthologies of recent California literature include Gerald Haslam and James D. Houston (eds.), *California Heartland: Writing from the Great Central Valley* (1979); Houston (ed.), *West Coast Fiction* (1979); and Ishmael Reed (ed.), *Calafia: The California Poetry* (1979). Lawrence Ferlinghetti, *Literary California* (1980) is a lively survey by a central figure in the beat generation. See also William Everson, *Archetype West: The Pacific Coast as a Literary Region* (1976); Thomas Parkinson (ed.), *A Casebook on the Beats* (1961); and Dennis McNally, *Desolate Angel: Jack Kerouac, the Beat Generation, and America* (1980). Mark Royden Winchell, *Joan Didion* (1980) is an analysis of the author's major works.

The best survey of modern California painting and sculpture is Peter Plagens, *Sunshine Muse: Contemporary Art on the West Coast* (1974). The northern California scene is described in Lawrence Ferlinghetti, "Bay Region Painting and Sculpture," *Art Digest* (August 1955), 26 ff., and Mary Fuller McChesney, *A Period of Exploration: San Francisco, 1945–50* (1973), a catalog from an exhibition at the Oakland Museum. On specific movements see Peter Selz, *Funk* (1967) and Marcia Tucker, *"Bad" Painting* (1978), a catalog from the New Museum of New York. The emergence of Los Angeles is described in Barbara Rose, "Los Angeles: The Second City," *Art in America*, LIV (January 1966), pp. 110–115, and Nan R. Piene, "L.A. Trip," *Art in America*, LVIII (March 1970), pp. 138–141. Marcia R. McGrath, *Edward Ruscha, Books, Prints* (1972) is a catalog from an exhibition at the University of California, Santa Cruz.

The indispensable guides to contemporary California architecture are David Gebhard et al., *A Guide to Architecture in San Francisco and Northern California* (1973) and Gebhard and Robert Winter, *A Guide to Architecture in Los Angeles and Southern California* (1977). Important interpretations include Gebhard and Susan King, *A View of California Architecture: 1960–1976* (1976) and Reyner Banham, *Los Angeles: The Architecture of Four Ecologies* (1971). Sally B. Woodbridge, "The California House," *The Wilson Quarterly*, IV (Summer 1980), pp. 83–91, traces the evolution of California domestic architecture.

A valuable resource for the history of California music is Philip S. Boone's oral history, *The San Francisco Symphony, 1940–1972* (1978). On southern California see P. Yates, "Los Angeles, the Demi-Wasteland: Music in Southern California," *High Fidelity* XII (1962), pp. 38, 110, and A. Goldberg, "The Music Center," *Los Angeles Times*, Dec. 6, 1964. Useful guides to recent popular music include Leonard Feather, *The Encyclopedia of Jazz* (1960); Lillian Roxon, *Rock Encyclopedia* (1969); and Jim Miller (ed.), *The Rolling Stone Illustrated History of Rock and Roll* (1976; rev. ed., 1980). Barbara Rowes, *Grace Slick: The Biography* (1980) contains a portrait of San Francisco rock bands in the 1960s and Anthony Fawcett, *California Rock, California Sound* (1979) surveys the major groups in southern California in the 1970s. Richard Aquila, "Images of the American West in Rock Music," *Western Historical Quarterly*, XI (October 1980), pp. 415–432, includes an analysis of California imagery.

POLITICS IN THE REAGAN YEARS

The most visible political result of the turmoil of the 1960s was a new wave of political conservatism in state and national affairs. The man who most benefited from that conservative resurgence was Ronald Reagan.

THE EMERGENCE OF REAGAN

Reagan was a convert to conservatism. As a student at a small college in Illinois, the state of his birth, he had been one of the leaders of a strike against a drastic cut in the college's budget, a strike so successful that it forced the resignation of the president who had proposed the cut. After his graduation Reagan spent 5 years as a radio sportscaster in Des Moines before he came to Hollywood in 1937 at the age of 26. In his interests in politics and in the affairs of the Screen Actors Guild, of which he later became president, his views in these early years were those of a liberal Democrat. His name was once omitted from a list of supporters of Helen Gahagan Douglas because he was considered too far left. But later he became a Democrat for Eisenhower and a Democrat for Nixon, and finally changed his registration to Republican in 1962.

Reagan acquired a 305-acre ranch in the Malibu hills for the breeding of thoroughbred horses. The rise in the value of the land, and a series of large increases in the taxes on it, coincided with a change in Reagan's political philosophy. He became strongly hostile toward taxation and toward the growth of governmental activities that required tax support. During the same period, in the 1950s and early 1960s, the General Electric Company employed him to appear regularly on the television programs it sponsored and also to make speeches to its employees and to civic groups. These addresses lauded private enterprise and were increasingly critical of government.

During the presidential campaign of 1964, Reagan delivered a nationwide television speech in support of Barry Goldwater. Although the speech could not save Goldwater's doomed candidacy, it demonstrated beyond doubt the effectiveness of Reagan as a political campaigner. Following the Republican debacle in the November election, some conservatives expressed the wish that Reagan had been the candidate instead of Goldwater.

Among those attracted to Reagan were a group of wealthy southern California Republicans who formed the nucleus of a movement to make him the next governor of California, and who later became members of Reagan's unofficial "kitchen cabinet" of political advisers. The group included Henry Salvatori, chairman of a petroleum exploration company; A. C. Rubel, former head of Union Oil Company; Justin Dart, president of a huge southern California consumer products company; and Holmes Tuttle, one of the largest automobile distributors in Los Angeles. In 1965 Reagan met with members of this group, and, after expressing some reluctance to become a candidate, he agreed to enter the Republican primary the following year. Reagan won the Republican nomination with considerable ease and faced in the general election Edmund G. Brown, the Democratic incumbent, who was seeking a third term.

In the gubernatorial campaign of 1966 Reagan was remarkably successful in restoring a degree of unity among the California Republicans. He followed a policy laid down by the chairman of the party's state central committee, Dr. Gaylord Parkinson, a southern California obstetrician. This policy was sometimes known as "Parkinson's law," or "the Eleventh Commandment": "Thou shalt not speak ill of any other Republican." When some advisers urged Reagan to repudiate the John Birch Society, as Nixon had done in 1962 and as even Goldwater finally did in 1966, Reagan replied that he would not "blanket-indict" any group, and that "if a man votes for me, it means that he's buying my philosophy, not that I'm buying his."

The Birchers on the far right and the campus radicals on the far left seemed equally repellent to most voters, but the disorderly demonstrations at Berkeley and elsewhere were now receiving far greater attention from the news media. Although Governor Brown had taken a hard line in dealing with the Free Speech movement, Reagan now used to his own advantage the issue of campus unrest and pledged that if elected he would clean up the "mess at Berkeley."

Undoubtedly, however, the most decisive single factor in the California gubernatorial campaign of 1966 was the white backlash against black demands for residential desegregation and job equality. These issues shattered the coalition between organized labor and racial minority groups that had been essential to Brown's victories in 1958 and 1962. Brown had approved passage of the open-housing Rumford Act in 1963 and had denounced opponents of the law as "the shock troops of bigotry." But the next year the voters overwhelmingly approved Proposition 14, rejecting the new open-housing legislation. The Watts riot of 1965 intensified further the white reaction against the civil rights movement in general and residential integration in particular.

Reagan, in his campaign speeches, repeatedly expressed his opposition to the Rumford Act but insisted that in doing so he was defending the right of private property, not indulging in racial bigotry. This stand won him the votes of many white Democrats, including many labor union members and their families. Precinct by precinct, all over the state, the vote for Reagan in 1966 was almost identical with the vote for Proposition 14 in 1964.

Reagan's attacks on the rising costs of government also won some defectors from the Democratic ranks. Brown favored monthly withholding of state income taxes, which had been adopted in most other states. Reagan opposed this measure on the ground that "people should hurt when they pay taxes," and withholding would make the payments less painful. Many members of labor unions, and of the lower and middle classes in general, had been enjoying rising incomes and were experiencing a new resentment against taxation.

In the election on November 8, 1966, Reagan defeated Brown by 3,742,913 to 2,749,174, a margin just short of a million votes. But the Democrats retained small majorities in both houses of the legislature, and under the leadership of Speaker Jesse Unruh they were in a position to make Reagan's administration extremely difficult.

"THE CREATIVE SOCIETY"

The governorship of Ronald Reagan began on January 2, 1967, and he chose to take the oath of office within the first few minutes after midnight, in the capitol rotunda. His first public utterance as governor, recorded on television, was a quip to Senator George Murphy: "Well, George, here we are on the late show again." The customary procedure would have been to combine the swearing-in with the delivery of the inaugural address 3 days later on the capitol mall. In another departure from custom, Reagan chose to receive the oath from an associate justice of the supreme court who was a conservative, rather than from the chief justice who was a liberal. The outgoing governor was also excluded from the proceedings.

The reasons for the extraordinary timing of the oath were never clearly explained, but there was no mystery about the central idea of the new administration, as stated in the inaugural address on January 5: "The cost of California's government is too high. It adversely affects our business climate. . . . We are going to squeeze and cut and trim until we reduce the cost of government." Speaking as a self-styled "citizen-politician" who had never before held a public office, Reagan thus made a powerful appeal to the popular mood of hostility toward government and taxation. For many years, he said, "you and I have been shushed like children and told there are no simple answers to complex problems which are beyond our comprehension. Well, the truth is, there are simple answers—there are just not easy ones. . . . The time has come to run a check to see if all the services government provides were in answer to demands or were just goodies dreamed up for our supposed betterment."

"This does not mean," he said, that "there is no part for government to play. Government has a legitimate role . . . in taking the lead in mobilizing

Governor Ronald Reagan is sworn in by California Supreme Court Justice Marshall F. McComb in the specially decorated capitol rotunda shortly after midnight, Jan. 2, 1967. Reagan's left hand is on the Bible of Father Junipero Serra, which is held by California Senate Chaplain Wilbur Choy. In the background are statues of Queen Isabella and Christopher Columbus. *(Courtesy of United Press International.)*

the full and voluntary resources of the people. In California we call this part-nership between the people and government the 'creative society.'"

Reagan's conservative philosophy was not, he insisted, "a retreat into the past." Yet it had an intensely nostalgic quality. Reagan described his constit-uency as "the forgotten American . . . that fellow . . . working 60 hours a week to provide the advantages for his family, but being taxed heavily to take care of some other people's problems." This was remarkably reminiscent of the "forgotten man," a phrase first used as the title of a public lecture by the con-servative economist William Graham Sumner in 1883 and referring to "the self-supporting and self-respecting person who has to bear the cost of all the political bungling and social quackery. There is always somebody who pays," said Sumner, "and it is always the sober, honest, industrious, economical men or women."

Reagan's political and social philosophy was a stunning reversal of the ideas of such governors as Earl Warren and Edmund G. Brown, who had believed that government services should have a great, direct, and positive role in the state's development. The weakest aspect of Reagan's philosophy was its fixed idea that as forces in American society, democratic government and its agencies, including public education, were not as "creative" as private or corporate enterprise.

An actual reduction in the total budget of a huge and growing state, in a period of inflation, was an impossibility. Most of the state government's annual expenditures were mandated by law. The largest of the state services whose budgets could be reduced at the governor's discretion were in the fields of state higher education and mental health, and in these sensitive and vulnerable areas Reagan made drastic cuts. He decided to reduce state funds for the University of California by nearly 30 percent of what the regents had asked for the coming year, although enrollments and costs were increasing, and he decreed a similar reduction in funds for the state college system. To make up part of the difference, Reagan proposed that the university and the state colleges institute substantial tuition charges. These, he said at a press conference, "would help get rid of undesirables. Those there to agitate and not to study might think twice before they pay tuition." Reagan himself had worked to earn his way through a private college, with a substantial tuition only partly covered by an athletic scholarship. His views on tuition were in interesting contrast with those of Edmund G. Brown, who had been unable to afford to go to college at all except for night law school, but who believed all the more deeply in California's long-established policy of tuition-free public higher education.

In one of his campaign speeches, Reagan had said that he was "sick at what has happened at Berkeley. Sick at the sit-ins, the teach-ins, the walkouts. When I am elected governor I will organize a throw-out, and Clark Kerr will head that list." Reagan was not, however, solely responsible for the dismissal of President Kerr, although it occurred at the first regents' meeting that he attended as governor, early in 1967. Most of the regents had been dissatisfied with Kerr's handling of student disruptions since the Sproul Hall sit-in of December 1964, when Governor Brown had sent the state police into the building at the request of Berkeley Chancellor Edward W. Strong, and against Kerr's advice; Kerr had proposed instead that he and the governor should enter the building together and attempt personal negotiations with the students. The regents might have dismissed him in 1965 if Brown had not interceded to prevent it, and Reagan's accession merely tipped the balance. But the dismissal of Kerr sent shock waves throughout the national academic community, where it was angrily denounced as an anti-intellectual assault on academic freedom. Brown wrote in 1970 that he was "shocked by Reagan's attack on higher education in the state. He had done about everything destructive possible except to invite commercial lumber interests to log the beautiful groves of trees off the university campuses."

However, most of the voters of California approved of Reagan's education policies, and he did not modify them as the years passed. This was not true of his assault on the budget of the state department of mental hygiene, which became generally regarded as the greatest mistake of his first year in office and which even Reagan later tacitly recognized as an error, to be partially rectified in future budgets. In March 1967, on the basis of misleading statistics and wishful thinking, Reagan announced that a decrease in the number of patients in the state hospitals would permit a reduction of 3700 in the department's staff and a saving to the state of more than $17 million. The result was a major setback in the state's progress toward adequate care of the mentally ill. The state had already established as its objective a new policy of treating such patients in expanded facilities in their own communities, rather than in the large, old, and isolated state hospitals. Reagan agreed with this policy, but saw it primarily as a way to save money for the state; he opposed the increases in state subsidies to the local communities that would have been necessary to provide adequate new facilities.

In spite of such widely publicized "economies," Reagan was forced in July 1967 to sign a record budget of more than $5 billion, and tax increases of nearly $1 billion, although he was able to claim that he had cut the rate of annual increase in the state budget from 16 percent to 8 percent.

Reagan's inaugural address had also promised to "support a bipartisan effort" to lift the "archaic" 160-acre limit on irrigation water from federal projects. He appointed a governor's task force headed by Burnham Enerson, water attorney for the Kern County Land Company, to organize the attack on the limitation. The task force recommended that the limit be raised to 640 acres and that water for larger units be made available at a higher price in order to "remove the subsidy," according to a formula long proposed by the late Democratic Senator Clair Engle. Senator George Murphy introduced a bill to this effect, but it failed to win approval in Congress.

REAGAN, NIXON, AND 1968

Ever since Henry Salvatori and the other wealthy conservative Republicans had formed the "Friends of Ronald Reagan" in 1965, they had made little or no secret of the fact that they were grooming him not only for the governorship of California but also for the presidency of the United States. The phrase "the creative society," though it represented a political philosophy quite opposite to that of "the great society" and the "war on poverty" of the national Democratic administration, was also intended to suggest a presidential program. On the night of his election as governor, Reagan announced that he would head a slate of delegates pledged to him as California's favorite-son candidate for President in the Republican national convention in 1968. This was necessary, he said, to protect the party unity of California Republicans from the effects of another struggle like the Goldwater-Rockefeller contest that had divided them so bitterly in the California Republican primary of 1964.

Though Reagan insisted that he had no real presidential ambitions and would be fully concerned with his duties as governor, he was actually a very serious presidential candidate. He was much in demand as a speaker at Republican fund-raising dinners throughout the country, particularly in the southern states. The party had been growing rapidly there, and it was expected that the south would hold the balance of power in the next election. Though Reagan was as conservative as Goldwater, the country was in a more conservative mood than it had been in 1964, thanks largely to hostile public reaction against the riotous behavior of radicals, whom Reagan never ceased to denounce. And although his ideas and policies as governor were often criticized as simplistic and negativistic, few observers could still question his appeal and effectiveness as a political campaigner. Television had created a whole new world of political campaigning, and Reagan was a master of that medium. Most of the critics who tried to write him off as a second-rate actor who got into politics because his acting career had declined were now forced to recognize him as a highly skilled politician who had by accident spent several years as an actor.

Richard Nixon, until his strength emerged in the 1968 presidential primaries, was widely assumed to be disqualified by the stigma of his defeat for the governorship of his own state of California in 1962. Reagan had now defeated Brown, who had defeated Nixon. On the day after the 1962 election, many newspapers reported that the voters of California had "removed Richard Nixon from politics," but the reports of his political death were greatly exaggerated. For the next several years, while building up a fortune as a partner with John Mitchell in a leading law firm in New York, Nixon also worked loyally and patiently for Republican candidates and party treasuries throughout the nation, and in the process maintained his contacts with party leaders. He worked hard for Goldwater in 1964, and in the end, 4 years later, Goldwater threw his support to Nixon even though his ideological preference was for Reagan.

Reagan was substantially to the right of Nixon on virtually all issues, foreign and domestic. On the war in Vietnam, Nixon had been in a sense "the original hawk" when as Vice President in the mid-1950s he had advocated American military intervention many years before it became a reality. But in 1968, recognizing the mounting disillusionment with the stalemated conflict, Nixon took a very cautious stand, claiming to have a plan for bringing the war to an early end, a plan that he would reveal after he was elected. Reagan, on the other hand, did not waver from his ultrahawkish position. He deplored the restraints placed on American military action by the fear that China might intervene in Vietnam as it had in Korea. "The Viet Cong," said Reagan, "should go to bed every night afraid we might use atomic weapons." *Los Angeles Times* cartoonist Paul Conrad responded with a cartoon captioned: "Americans should go to bed every night afraid Reagan might become President." Conrad's cartoons criticized Reagan more consistently than did the *Times* editorials; in this and other respects he was sometimes described as "ahead of the *Times*."

On racial issues, also, Nixon was more successful than Reagan in avoiding dangerously unambiguous stands. Reagan refused to avow any disagreement with the political views of George Wallace of Alabama, the third-party candidate who was a serious rival of both Nixon and Reagan for the support of the south.

"Americans should go to bed every night afraid Reagan might become President." Cartoon by Paul Conrad in the *Los Angeles Times,* July 5, 1967. *(Courtesy of The Register and Tribune Syndicate.)*

When the Republican national convention was about to assemble at Miami Beach, Goldwater advised Reagan to release the California delegates to Nixon as soon as possible, but Reagan persisted to the last moment in the belief that he might actually be nominated himself. Some Republicans still cherished a fantastic hope that Rockefeller and Reagan might join as running mates on a "dream ticket" uniting the party's moderate and conservative wings. But Nixon could not be stopped.

The Democrats in 1968 were more badly divided than the Republicans. President Johnson's smashing victory over Senator Goldwater in 1964 had been in considerable part a result of Goldwater's open advocacy of an escalation of the war in Vietnam, but Johnson himself had since followed the tragic course of enormous military involvement. Victory proved unattainable, however, and under tremendous criticism Johnson announced in March 1968 that he would not run for reelection. He hoped to be succeeded by Hubert Humphrey, who as Vice President had supported him on Vietnam. In the California Democratic primary, the principal contenders were Senators Robert Kennedy and Eugene McCarthy, both strong critics of the administration's war policies. Kennedy won with a slate of delegates headed by Jesse Unruh, but on the night of his California primary victory Kennedy was assassinated in Los Angeles. Humphrey won the nomination in the stormy convention at Chicago, but Unruh gave him almost no support in the subsequent campaign, and in November Nixon won the electoral votes of California by a narrow margin, as he had done in 1960. Nixon's nationwide popular vote margin over Humphrey was only 0.71 of 1 percent, but it was enough for victory, and thus Nixon became the first native-born Californian to be elected to the presidency. He soon transferred his state citizenship from New York back to California and his personal residence to a coastal mansion that would serve as the "western White House" at San Clemente in his native Orange County.

REAGAN AND THE ELECTIONS OF 1970

Governor Reagan enjoyed very little success with his legislative programs during his first term. The Democrats had narrowly retained control of both the senate and the assembly in the elections of 1966, and although the Republicans won both houses by equally narrow margins in 1968, their majorities were not solid enough to ensure passage of the governor's measures. In 1970 he campaigned vigorously for Republican candidates in many legislative districts, hoping to carry them into office on his political coattails, but although his personal charisma was strong enough to win his own reelection over the Democratic challenger, Assembly Speaker Jesse Unruh, his efforts to purge Democratic legislators failed dismally, and the Democrats regained both houses. Unruh could console himself with the boast that "we cut off his coattails right up to the lapels."

There were few clear issues in the 1970 gubernatorial election. The question of the responsibility for the absence of any substantial tax reform was so complex that the blame seemed to be about equally divided. As for the continuation of campus disorders through the spring of 1970, Unruh tried to blame Governor Reagan, as Reagan had blamed Governor Brown 4 years earlier, but the voters doubted Unruh's claim that he could have dealt with unruly students more effectively. The hostile reaction of most California voters to the radicalism of the student new left contributed heavily to Reagan's reelection. Public opinion polls showed that many of his supporters were disappointed because state taxes had been raised in spite of his promises to reduce them, but showed that the most widely supported of all his policies was the firmness with which he had dealt with "campus rioters." When the votes for governor were counted, Reagan had 3,439,664 to Unruh's 2,938,607. The margin of 501,057 was only half as large as Reagan's margin of nearly a million votes over Brown in 1966, but it was still an impressive victory.

On the other hand, the elections for United States senator and for the legislature were heavy setbacks for the Republicans. Early in 1970, it was revealed that during his senatorship George Murphy had secretly received a large salary and other perquisites from the Technicolor Corporation, and although he denied that this had compromised his integrity, many felt that it had. President Nixon considered it vital that Murphy's seat in the Senate, from Nixon's own state, should not go to the Democrats, especially since the other seat had been lost to the liberal Democrat Alan Cranston in 1968. Shortly before the election, Nixon appeared with Murphy and Reagan at San Jose to speak for them and for other Republican candidates. A crowd of antiwar demonstrators had gathered, and it was widely reported, though also denied, that they threw rocks and other missiles that struck the President's car. There was evidence that Nixon, Murphy, and Reagan deliberately baited the demonstrators in the hope of gaining greater political advantage from their discreditable behavior. Reporters quoted Reagan as saying, "We gave them the peace sign back. That always infuriates them." Murphy's campaign managers ran a full-page newspaper advertisement headed "ANARCHY," in which they falsely accused his Democratic opponent, Congressman John Tunney, of sympathizing with such disorders and of failing to support "law and order" in general. But such desperate tactics failed, and Tunney defeated Murphy overwhelmingly.

In 1971 the Democrats, again in control of the state legislature, passed a decennial reapportionment bill that favored their party. Reagan therefore vetoed it, and this standoff continued for 2 years until the state supreme court appointed a panel of three "special masters" who finally drew the new legislative and congressional district boundaries.

WELFARE AND TAXATION

Early in his second term Governor Reagan renewed and intensified his calls for "reform" of the welfare system, which to him meant primarily reduction of its cost. He called it "a cancer eating at our vitals" and pointed out that California, with 10 percent of the country's population, had 16 percent of the total number of persons on welfare. The economic recession intensified the cost problem by enlarging the welfare rolls while it decreased the state's revenues from income and sales taxes. Early in 1971, nearly 10 percent of the people of California were receiving public assistance, compared with less than 7 percent for the nation as a whole; 14 percent of the people of San Francisco were on relief, and 12.7 percent of the people of Los Angeles County. Leaders of the Democratic majority in the legislature were skeptical that massive cuts in welfare could be achieved. They pointed out that Reagan's hopes of removing many people from the welfare rolls by requiring them to work would be limited by the fact that only about 1 percent of the recipients were able-bodied adult males, whereas the mass of them were mothers, children, the blind, the disabled, or the aged. In August 1971 Reagan and the Democratic speaker of the assembly, Robert Moretti, worked out a compromise that was intended to bring reductions of about $200 million in California's total costs, mainly through tightened eligibility standards, better control of frauds, and lower maximum grants.

A companion measure, the result of a similar partisan compromise, sought to reduce the costs and tighten the administration of the state program of payments for the "medically indigent." After Congress had created the federal system of "Medicare" for the elderly in 1965, it had also provided federal matching grants to the states to help them pay for medical care for those too poor to afford it, whether they were on welfare or not. Nationally this system was known as "Medicaid"; California's subsidiary system, known as "MediCal," went into effect in 1966. Since his first year in office, Governor Reagan had repeatedly tried to cut MediCal payments by administrative orders, which were often ruled illegal by the courts.

When Reagan submitted his annual budget in January 1971, he insisted that the state's expenses for the next fiscal year could be met without increasing taxes, if welfare and MediCal costs were reduced, cost-of-living increases denied to state employees, and various other state expenses cut to the barest minimum. President Charles J. Hitch of the University of California complained that the governor had cut the university's budget "not merely to the bone but to the marrow." Yet in spite of these austerities Reagan was forced in December 1971 to sign a bill increasing state taxes by $500 million, largely because of declining revenues in another year of recession. The bulk of the new revenues came in the form of an income withholding tax, effective on January 1, 1972. Of the 38 states with income taxes, California had been the only one that did not provide for withholding; Reagan had long promised never to approve it, and after signing the bill he told reporters that he had had to be "dragged kicking and screaming" to the desk where he did so. In the following year it was discovered that more than 1 million Californians had been escaping the payment of any state income taxes prior to the institution of a payroll deduction system. Another blow to Reagan's prestige among tax-conscious voters came when it was revealed that he had paid no state taxes on his own income for 1969 and 1970, mainly, he explained, because he had made some investments in buying a ranch in Riverside County and stocking it with cattle, which had involved large outlays and no immediate profits.

County and city governments and local school districts were in even worse financial condition than was the state, even though property taxes had been tremendously increased. Both Republicans and Democrats had promised tax relief for local governments and for the homeowners, but this was slow in coming, partly because of the deadlock between the conservative Republican governor and the Democratic legislature over how it should be accomplished. The problem became even more complex in September 1971 when the California Supreme Court ruled in *Serrano v. Ivy Baker Priest* (who was the state treasurer) that the entire system of financing public schools through local property taxes was unconstitutional because it violated the equal-protection clause of the Fourteenth Amendment. The court pointed out that the wealthy school district of Beverly Hills spent $1231 for each pupil while the poor district of Baldwin Park spent only $577. For years afterward California tried and failed to find satisfactory solutions to the problems of public school financing and of taxation in general.

In 1973 Reagan sought to embody the essence of his conservative philosophy in a sweeping tax reduction measure. Reagan's proposal would have forced the gradual reduction of state spending over a period of years from the existing level of 8.3 percent of the total personal income of Californians to 7 percent. It would also have required a two-thirds vote rather than a simple majority of the legislature to adopt a new tax or increase an existing one. The legislature rejected the scheme; then, for the first time on record, a governor called a special election to place before the public an initiative proposition sponsored by the governor himself. Drafted by one of Reagan's special task forces, a team of conservative economists and business executives, the measure was 5000 words long, very complex, and full of obfuscating phraseology. In an unguarded moment Reagan confessed to a reporter that he himself did not fully understand the language of it. Legislative auditor A. Alan Post, a fiscal conservative though a more moderate one, opposed the proposition on the grounds that it would dangerously reduce state services and shift the burden to local taxpayers. The plan went to the voters as Proposition 1 in November 1973, when except for a few local elections it was the only thing on the ballot. As expected, the turnout was light. In such circumstances Republicans were more likely to vote than were Democrats, but even with this advantage, on which Reagan had counted heavily, the measure was decisively rejected, and the voters thus handed the Governor a stinging personal defeat.

All Reagan's promises of massive tax reductions proved impossible to carry out. The state budgets he signed increased every year, from $5 billion for 1967–1968 to $10.2 billion for 1974–1975.

NIXON AND WATERGATE

During the 1972 presidential campaign five men hired by agents of the Committee to Reelect the President (CREEP) were arrested while burglarizing and wiretapping the national headquarters of the Democratic party in the Watergate building in Washington, D.C. There is no evidence that President Nixon had any prior knowledge of this clumsy and ridiculous crime. When he first heard of it, he was violently angry at its perpetrators. If he had pressed for an immediate, full, and honest investigation and had promptly dismissed all those responsible, the affair might have done him little permanent harm. But he soon learned that those responsible included John Mitchell, his close friend, former law partner and attorney general, and present chairman of the campaign committee. Nixon then chose the low road of cover-up, and on June 23, 6 days after the arrests, he ordered that the Central Intelligence Agency (CIA) on the pretext of national security ask the FBI not to investigate the source and transmission of the money used to hire the burglars. The cover-up was so successful in November 1972 that the Democratic candidate George

McGovern could carry only Massachusetts and the District of Columbia against the overwhelmingly popular and trusted President.

Nixon's cover-up scheme was the worst kind of obstruction of justice. The President of the United States had committed a felony, although for more than 2 years, until the final revelation of his guilt compelled him to resign in disgrace in August 1974 to escape impeachment and removal, he issued a series of denials, constantly lying to the American people, the Congress, the courts, his own lawyers, and even to his own family. Meanwhile Nixon's Vice President, Spiro T. Agnew, had resigned in the face of evidence that he had taken bribes, and Nixon had appointed Representative Gerald R. Ford to the vice presidency. Ford then succeeded Nixon as President and a few weeks later granted him a full pardon for any crimes he might have committed, though Nixon never acknowledged that he had committed any.

Some have theorized that special conditions of California politics were responsible for the habitually underhanded methods and the flawed personality and character of Richard Nixon, but there had been no parallel or precedent among other outstanding California political leaders. Whatever one may think of the varying political ideas and actions of Earl Warren, William Knowland, Pat Brown, or Ronald Reagan, one does not reasonably think of them as doing things dishonestly, but Nixon seemed incapable of doing or saying anything that was entirely honest, or without some convoluted subterfuge. The politics of suburbia did have some influence on Nixon, who was first elected in the suburbs of Los Angeles, but no more than on Spiro Agnew, first elected in the suburbs of Baltimore. The explanation may lie more in the early history of Nixon's personal life than in his early political environment. For example, Theodore H. White has stressed the extreme poverty of Nixon's family during his childhood. Bruce Mazlish has suggested that Nixon's father was a quick-tempered man who often whipped his sons, and that Richard learned as a boy how to speak to his father so that someone else got the whipping. But psychohistory still has a long way to go to explain Richard Nixon.

PRESIDENTIAL POLITICS, 1976

In 1976 Ronald Reagan launched an all-out campaign for the Republican nomination for President. As Hiram Johnson had once dreamed of "Californianizing the nation" by taking to Washington the progressive program that he felt he had created in California, so Reagan hoped to take his conservative crusade all the way to the White House. The odds against him were heavy. Though he still seemed full of youthful energy, he was 65 years old. Several of his campaign statements were extreme and inept. He asserted that the Panama Canal Zone was as much sovereign territory of the United States as Texas or Alaska, which was simply not true. He proposed a $90 billion reduction of the federal budget, mainly by shifting various expenditures for welfare, Medicaid, education, and other items to the states, and he proposed investing the funds of the Social Security system in the stock market.

Only about 20 percent of the nation's registered voters in 1976 were Republicans while nearly twice as many were Democrats (though a still-larger number, the largest in history, declined to state an affiliation with either party). Most of the Republicans were a solid core of conservative true believers, and Reagan would have been overwhelmingly their first choice for President had Ford not been the incumbent. Otherwise, as pollster George Gallup pointed out, Ford would not have been even their tenth choice. Ford's record as minority leader of the House and as President was almost as conservative as Reagan's record, but he lacked Reagan's charisma. On the other hand, polls suggested that although neither Ford nor Reagan would defeat the Democratic nominee, former Governor Jimmy Carter of Georgia, Ford would have a better chance to do so. With the Republican convention in this dilemma, Reagan came within about 100 delegate votes of winning the nomination away from an incumbent President who was seeking it—something that had not happened since 1884 when Chester A. Arthur lost to James G. Blaine.

Many observers now concluded that Reagan's career in major public office was over, but Reagan and his advisers began at once laying the ground for yet another campaign for the presidency. More than $1 million in leftover campaign funds from the 1976 race was transferred to a new political action committee, Citizens for the Republic, organized to advance Reagan's future candidacy by supporting conservative Republicans for office at all levels of government across the country. Top Reagan aides formed the steering committee of the new organization, and its newsletter was mailed to former Reagan contributors and campaign workers. Reagan also kept in the public eye through a widely syndicated newspaper column, a radio program, and speeches before groups of bankers, business people, physicians, and others. His message was the same as it had been 20 years earlier—cut taxes and government spending, balance the budget, eliminate welfare fraud, and reduce government regulation of business.

SELECTED BIBLIOGRAPHY

The careers of Pat Brown and Ronald Reagan are analyzed in Melvin H. Bernstein, "Political Leadership in California," Ph.D. thesis, University of California, Los Angeles (1970). Totton J. Anderson and Eugene C. Lee, "The 1966 Election in California," *Western Political Quarterly*, XX (June 1967), pp. 535–554, deals with Reagan's election. Ronald Reagan, *Where's the Rest of Me?* (1965) is an autobiography as told to Richard Hubler. Reagan, *The Creative Society* (1968) is a collection of speeches. Dissenting views may be found in Edmund G. Brown, Sr., *Reagan and Reality: The Two Californias* (1970) and *Ronald Reagan, the Political Chameleon* (1976). Biographical studies include Bill Boyarsky, *The Rise of Ronald Reagan* (1968); Joseph Lewis, *What Makes Reagan Run?* (1968); and Lou Cannon, *Ronnie and Jesse: A Political Odyssey* (1969), on Reagan and Unruh.

See also Gladwin Hill, *Dancing Bear: An Inside Look at California Politics* (1968); Royce D. Delmatier et al., *The Rumble of California Politics* (1970), chap. XIII, "California and National Politics"; Frank H. Jonas and John L. Harmer, "The 1968 Election in California," *Western Political Quarterly*, XXII (September 1969), pp. 468–474; Totton J. Anderson and Charles G. Bell, "The 1970 Election in California," *ibid.*, XXIV (June 1971), pp. 252–273; Eleanor Fowle, *Cranston, the Senator from California* (1980); James Q. Wilson, "The Political Culture of Southern California," *Commentary* (May 1967); and Raymond E. Wolfinger and Fred I. Greenstein, "Comparing Political Regions: The Case of California," *American Political Science Review*, LXIII (March 1969), pp. 74–85.

The roots of Richard Nixon are described in Renee K. Schulte, *The Young Nixon: An Oral Inquiry* (1978), a collection of interviews with early Nixon acquaintances in California. For an analysis see Fawn Brodie, *Richard Nixon: The Shaping of His Character* (1981) and Bruce Mazlish, *In Search of Nixon: A Psychohistorical Inquiry* (1972). Jules Witcover, *The Resurrection of Richard Nixon* (1970), and Gary Wills, *Nixon Agonistes* (1970), deal with Nixon's attainment of the Presidency. The many books on his fall from it include Theodore H. White, *Breach of Faith* (1975); Carl Bernstein and Bob Woodward, *All the President's Men* (1974), and *The Final Days* (1976); Dan Rather and Gary Paul Gates, *The Palace Guard* (1974); and Paul J. Halpern, editor, *Why Watergate?* (1975).

Concerning welfare policies, historical background material may be found in James Leiby, "State Welfare Administration in California, 1879–1929," *Pacific Historical Review*, XLI (May 1972), pp. 189–206; Jacobus tenBroek, "California's Welfare Law—Origins and Development," *California Law Review*, XLV (July 1957), pp. 241–303; and Jackson K. Putnam, *Old-Age Politics in California from Richardson to Reagan* (1970). The *California Journal*, beginning in January 1970, is a useful monthly digest of state government and politics.

THE ERA
OF LIMITS

As the United States prepared to celebrate its bicentennial in 1976, California Gov. Edmund G. Brown, Jr., announced, "We are entering an era of limits. In place of a manifest economic destiny, we face a sobering reassessment of new economic realities, and we have all got to get used to it." Convinced that public problems could not be solved "simply by throwing money at them," Brown advised Californians to "lower their expectations" of what government could do. These pronouncements by the 37-year-old governor, and the austere state budgets which he presented to the legislature, disappointed Brown's liberal supporters but reflected accurately the conservative mood of many Californians. Beset by rapid increases in the cost of living, voters had become increasingly restive under the burden of taxation and resentful of the growth of government.

THE RISE OF JERRY BROWN

Any analysis of the career of Jerry Brown must begin with the fact that he was the son of Edmund G. Brown, Sr. Known from youth as "Jerry," the younger Brown at first rejected his political inheritance and entered a Jesuit seminary to prepare for the priesthood. After 4 years he left the seminary, enrolled at the University of California at Berkeley, where he majored in Latin and Greek, and was graduated from Yale Law School in 1964. Moving to southern California, Brown launched his political career in 1969 with a successful campaign for a seat on the Los Angeles Community College District Board of Trustees. There were no incumbents in the race and more than 100 candidates filed for the election. Brown's easy victory made plain the enormous political asset he possessed in his, or rather his father's, name.

The following year, when Ronald Reagan was running for reelection, Brown announced his candidacy for the office of secretary of state. The incumbent secretary chose not to run, and Brown's Republican opponent was a political unknown. Jerry Brown won the election in 1970 and achieved the enviable position of being the only Democrat to hold statewide office during Reagan's second term. As secretary of state Brown vigorously enforced campaign disclosure laws which had been ignored for decades and advocated stronger controls over campaign practices. In 1974 Brown became one of the principal sponsors of an initiative, known as the Political Reform Act, which called for imposition of tight limits on campaign contributions and spending, establishment of stricter disclosure requirements, and creation of a Fair Political Practices Commission.

Reagan's effective use of the third-term issue in 1966 against Pat Brown made it practically impossible for Reagan himself to seek a third term in 1974. For the first time since 1958 the incumbent governor chose not to run for reelection, and the wide-open contest attracted 29 candidates, 18 in the Democratic primary alone, each of whom strove to achieve greater "name recognition." In this crowded field the Democrat whose name already had the highest statewide recognition was Edmund G. Brown, Jr. And furthermore, with the Watergate scandal dominating headlines, Brown's name was linked with the most popular issue of the day, political reform. Brown won the Democratic primary, and the Political Reform Act was overwhelmingly approved by the voters. (The new act was the most stringent campaign finance law in American history; many of its provisions were later ruled unconstitutional.) Meanwhile in the Republican primary, Reagan's heir apparent, Lt. Gov. Ed Reinecke, was indicted for perjury by the Watergate grand jury and was defeated by State Controller Houston Flournoy.

Brown entered the general election campaign against Flournoy with a commanding lead in public opinion polls. He denounced his Republican opponent as "a recycled Reagan," although Flournoy's conservatism actually was a moderate variety. As state controller, Flournoy had opposed Reagan's famous Proposition 1 in 1973. Brown's campaign strategy was to avoid controversy, make the contest with Flournoy as dull as possible, *reduce* media coverage, and rest on his early lead. He and Flournoy entered an unprecedented "campaign contract" which limited spending on advertising and restricted media coverage of a series of debates between the two candidates. As Brown's campaign manager later explained, "It was our feeling that the less coverage the better. . . . The duller the race the better." Brown's strategy nearly backfired. He defeated Flournoy on November 5, 1974, by 3,131,648 to 2,952,954, but his margin of victory, less than 3 percentage points, made the race the closest in California since 1920.

Once in office, Brown soon restored his popularity. Through largely symbolic actions he appealed to the strain of antigovernment sentiment still potent among voters in the aftermath of Watergate. He canceled the inaugural ball. He denounced the new governor's mansion, built for Reagan with gifts of money from his wealthy supporters, as "that Taj Mahal" and chose instead to live in a modest apartment. In contrast to Reagan's official Cadillac, Brown went about in a blue Plymouth sedan. On a more substantial level, Brown adopted the policy of appointing "public members" to state licensing boards. His appointees were often denounced by the regulated professions, but won for Brown widespread public support. More than any other governor in California history, Brown opened up top administrative and judicial posts to women and minorities. His policies toward government spending and taxation were consistently conservative. At the beginning of his first term Brown pledged that he would approve no new taxes or general tax increases, and he recommended reducing proposed increases in state funds for higher education and social welfare programs. "The first test of all of us," Brown counseled the legislature, "is to live within realistic limits."

The most important accomplishment of Brown's first term was enactment of the landmark Agricultural Relations Act of 1975. The new law, which created the Agricultural Labor Relations Board (ALRB) to oversee union elections by the state's farm workers, was a personal triumph for the governor and his secretary of agriculture, Rose Elizabeth Bird. Representatives from the state's agricultural districts became angered when Brown appointed a majority of labor-oriented members to the ALRB and the board adopted policies which the growers opposed. Opposition became so strong that operating funds for the board were withheld by the legislature. Cesar Chavez mounted an initiative campaign, endorsed by Governor Brown, to change the law further in favor of the farm workers. The legislature subsequently restored funds for the ALRB, but Chavez's initiative was defeated in the November 1976 election by a margin of about two to one.

The 1976 presidential election presented Brown with a familiar opportunity. The Democratic nomination was being sought by no less than 15 contenders, none of whom had a clear early advantage. Brown hesitated, however, to enter the race, and when he did begin his campaign, Georgia Gov. Jimmy Carter already had established a substantial lead. Brown nevertheless beat Carter in three of the six state primaries he entered, and in California he received an impressive 59 percent of the vote to Carter's 21 percent. Brown's name was placed in nomination before the Democratic convention in New York by longtime ally Cesar Chavez. Only after the first roll call vote, which gave the nomination to Carter, did Brown concede defeat.

In late 1976 and early 1977 Brown's popularity encountered some setbacks. California public school finance was in serious difficulty, and there was shocking new evidence of scandalous conditions in several of the state's mental hospitals. It was unrealistic to maintain that these problems could be solved unless considerable amounts of state money were "thrown at" them, or that this could be done without some kind of state tax increase. At Brown's press conferences, when several reporters pressed him on these points, they found his answers disingenuous and evasive and they virtually told him so. His relations with the press and other media reporters degenerated to a level that almost rivaled Richard Nixon's famous "last press conference" in November 1962.

Brown came under powerful attack from business and labor groups which charged that he had created an "adverse business climate." Through his appointments to such agencies as the Air Resources Board and Energy Commission, Brown oversaw vigorous enforcement of environmental protection standards and withheld licensing of large-scale power plant facilities. In 1977 the Dow Chemical Company, complaining of excessive regulation and bureaucratic red tape, canceled its plans to build a major petrochemical plant on the Sacramento River, and the Fantus Company, a subsidiary of Dun & Bradstreet, ranked California as 47th among the 48 contiguous states as a favorable place to locate new industry. Business leaders charged Brown was stifling economic development, and labor leaders complained of the loss of jobs.

The latest attacks on Brown were not entirely fair. Brown alone was not responsible for the pullout by Dow, and many of the statistics used in the Fantus report were compiled from the Reagan years. Nevertheless Brown launched a counteroffensive. Stung by criticism that the "era of limits" was antibusiness, Brown began speaking of the "era of possibilities." He created an Office of Business Development to lure new industries to the state, traveled to Japan to encourage location of an automobile assembly plant in California, and supported legislation to streamline the regulatory process permitting new industrial construction.

Brown's close identification with Cesar Chavez and his support for the 1976 farm worker initiative had convinced California farmers that Brown was unsympathetic to their interests. As he approached the end of his first term, Brown took several steps to try to win farm support. Amid charges that his appointments to the ALRB and other state agencies were stacked in favor of farm workers, Brown appointed a farmer as director of the department of agriculture. In 1977 the Carter administration announced its intention to require users of federally subsidized water to sell land held in excess of acreage limitations established in the 1902 Newlands Reclamation Act. Large landowners in California, who had fought for decades to have the acreage limit set aside, reacted angrily. For more than a year Governor Brown had been a strident supporter of tough enforcement of the acreage limitation provisions, yet shortly after the federal government announced its intentions, Brown's new agricultural secretary denounced them. When pressed by reporters to clarify the matter, Brown responded that his agricultural secretary spoke for the administration.

Brown's reelection prospects, and his hopes for higher office, depended upon his ability to conciliate such broad interests as business and agriculture. His reversals of policy on questions such as the acreage limitation issue, however, opened Brown to charges of inconsistency and political opportunism.

The one very evident problem which Brown—and the legislature—had failed to solve was the need for tax reform. The overriding issue in the 1978 elections proved to be an initiative to reduce property taxes written by Howard Jarvis and Paul Gann and which appeared on the June primary ballot as Proposition 13. Brown campaigned vigorously against the initiative, while his chief Republican rival, Atty. Gen. Evelle Younger, supported it. In the June election voters approved Proposition 13 by a landslide margin of nearly 2 million votes, and Brown and Younger each won a party nomination for governor. Brown entered the general election campaign in serious trouble. For all his careful maneuvering to build support among major constituencies in the state, he had badly miscalculated the enormous popularity of the tax-cutting initiative. In June, he and Younger were about even in public opinion polls, while one Los Angeles survey showed Brown trailing his opponent by 4 percentage points. Brown clearly had a choice. He could continue to oppose Proposition 13 and probably lose the election, or he could reverse his position and win.

Brown quickly became an enthusiastic supporter of the initiative. He imposed a freeze on all state hiring, banned pay raises for state employees, cut cost-of-living increases for welfare recipients, and worked with the legislature to distribute surplus state funds to local governments. "I've been talking about limits since I got here," Brown proudly announced, "and now Jarvis has given me new tools." Brown's enthusiasm following Proposition 13's passage was sufficient to convince voters that it was he, and not Younger, who would best be able to implement it. Younger's lackluster campaign, which began with an ill-advised vacation in Hawaii, was marked by considerable ineptitude. In November 1978 Brown defeated Younger by more than 1.3 million votes. Typical of the lack of party discipline in the state, Brown's lieutenant governor, Mervyn Dymally, was defeated by the Republican candidate, recording executive Mike Curb.

Brown began his second term in office with a call for further retrenchment in state government. He proposed a reduction of 5000 employees in the state work force, a tax rebate of more than $1 billion, and an overall budget increase well below the rate of inflation. Brown defended his conservative economic policies by reminding the legislature that his proposed budget "reflects the clear mandate of the voters for a leaner government." His inaugural address in January was so reminiscent of that of Reagan in 1967—"We are going to squeeze and cut and trim until we reduce the cost of government"—that one political commentator saw it as the beginning of "Ronald Reagan's Third Term." Brown's inaugural message also signaled his intention to challenge Carter for the presidency in 1980 by mounting a campaign to cut federal taxes and government spending. Brown called for a constitutional amendment, through the convening of a national constitutional convention if necessary, to require a balanced federal budget.

BROWN, REAGAN, AND THE ELECTION OF 1980

Brown's presidential campaign got off to a bad start. His proposal for a constitutional convention was regarded by many as a threat to the integrity of the Constitution and a needless endangering of the Bill of Rights. The California Legislature soundly defeated the proposal. When Brown traveled to New Hampshire—months in advance of that state's presidential primary—he was humiliated by being prevented from testifying before a legislative committee in support of his proposed constitutional amendment. Brown also faced further embarrassment at home by the actions of his Republican lieutenant governor. Mike Curb began to take advantage of Brown's frequent absences from the state by employing the full powers of the governor, making judicial appointments and signing executive orders. Brown challenged Curb's right to take such actions, but the state supreme court ruled that the lieutenant governor was acting within his constitutional powers. (The court decision had little effect on Brown's campaign travels: during the first 16 months of his second term he was absent from the state 173 days.) Brown's campaign was also beset by financial problems. While other candidates were whisked about in chartered jets, Brown was forced to travel by chartered bus or on a commercial airliner. Singer Linda Ronstadt and such rock groups as the Eagles held benefit concerts for the beleaguered candidate from California.

Brown's record in the 1980 presidential primaries was one of dismal failure. He began his formal campaign in November 1979 with only 5 percent of the national electorate expressing a preference for his candidacy. Having encountered strong opposition to his call for a constitutional convention, Brown attempted to capitalize on the Three Mile Island nuclear plant accident by emphasizing his opposition to nuclear power. He failed to win a single delegate in the early New England primaries and counted on a victory in Wisconsin to restore his credibility as a candidate. To accompany an election-eve television broadcast to the Wisconsin voters, Brown staged an extravaganza of special effects produced by San Francisco film director Francis Ford Coppola. Typical of his entire campaign effort, the broadcast was botched, and Brown emerged from the primary in third place.

Declaring that "voters do not think I am ready to be President," Brown withdrew from the race and returned to California where he faced the formidable task of rebuilding his sagging popularity. Brown's approval rating in the latest California poll was the lowest of any governor in nearly two decades. His relations with the legislature had reached crisis proportions. By the time he withdrew from the presidential campaign, he had had more vetoes overridden by the legislature than had all other governors since 1942 combined.

Brown's failure in 1980 was due in part to factors beyond his control. Massachusetts Senator Edward Kennedy entered the race earlier than Brown had expected, and Kennedy won the support of dissident Democrats whom Brown had hoped to attract. The crises in Iran and Afghanistan strengthened President Carter's hand in dealing with both Kennedy and Brown and were a major factor in Carter's renomination victory. Brown's failure was also due to his image in the national media as a "flake"—a man impulsive, eccentric, and wholly inconsistent. Garry Trudeau, creator of the syndicated cartoon strip *Doonesbury*, lampooned Brown mercilessly throughout the campaign. Brown contributed to this negative image by his rapid and frequent changes in political positions. His reversal on Proposition 13 was a necessity in his campaign for reelection as governor, but proved to be a formidable obstacle in his quest

Cartoon by Garry Trudeau during the 1980 presidential campaign of Jerry Brown. *(Courtesy of Universal Press Syndicate.)*

for the presidency. Brown's controversial tour of Africa with Linda Ronstadt raised questions about his judgment, while his advocacy of the colonization of outer space struck many listeners as bizarre.

The main cause of Brown's failure, however, was his startling lack of basic skills in the art of politics. His campaign, always short of funds, suffered from disorganization, patchwork scheduling, and a lack of coherence. His preference for extemporaneous speaking rendered his campaign oratory meandering and ineffective. Brown had not made a sustained effort to build upon his success in the 1976 primaries by establishing a network of supporters and campaign contributors. Brown saw himself as a man of issues, not organization, and he openly showed disdain for conventional party politics. In short, Brown failed ever to establish a national constituency. The main body of Democrats alienated from Carter were liberals, and even if Kennedy had not entered the race, Brown would have had difficulty attracting them to his brand of fiscal conservatism. What loyal supporters Brown did have—the farm workers, the antinuclear forces, and various so-called new age and futuristic groups—were not an adequate base for a presidential campaign.

On the day Jimmy Carter accepted the Democratic party's renomination for the presidency, Brown announced he was launching a national newsletter to spread his views around the country. Brown was following in the footsteps of Ronald Reagan who, after losing the presidential nomination in 1976, had also established a new political organization with a newsletter to build support for his 1980 campaign. Brown appeared to have learned quickly the lessons of his own defeat. At the Democratic convention his behind-the-scenes meetings with labor leaders and party regulars signaled his desire to move into the mainstream of Democratic party politics. Brown had begun his governorship speaking of an era of limits and the need for Californians to lower their expectations. There seemed to be no limit, however, to the expectations of Jerry Brown.

In comparison with Brown's disastrous 1980 campaign for the presidency, Ronald Reagan's was a model of efficiency. His national network of campaign headquarters was staffed by a well-trained corps of veteran political organizers and highly motivated volunteers. His success as a fund-raiser enabled him to travel in relative comfort and style. While Brown was never able to get his campaign off the ground, Reagan scored a landslide victory in the pivotal New Hampshire primary and eventually forced all other contenders for the Republican nomination to drop from the race. Although Reagan and Brown held opposite views on many environmental and social issues, there were areas of agreement between the two Californians. Both candidates proposed closer ties with energy-rich Mexico and Canada to form a North American "common market." On the critical issue of economic policy, Brown's budget-balancing rhetoric went far beyond that of Jimmy Carter and placed him in essential agreement with Reagan's more conservative views.

At the Democratic national convention President Carter launched a scathing attack on Reagan as an advocate of a "fantasy world" of "tinsel and make-believe . . . where some politicians shoot first and ask questions later." Carter's determination to depict Reagan as a dangerous reactionary was reminiscent of Lyndon Johnson's successful attack on Barry Goldwater in 1964. Carter's strategy had considerable merit, but it failed to convince a majority of voters. Reagan's campaign emphasized his own conservative record as governor of California, claiming success in his battle to reform the welfare system, slash taxes, and reduce the size of government. Reagan provoked considerable controversy during the campaign by casting doubts on Darwinian evolution, embracing the war in Vietnam as "a noble cause," and proposing a naval blockade of Cuba to induce the Soviets to withdraw from Afghanistan. Following his pronouncement that air pollution in the United States had been "substantially controlled," Reagan arrived in Los Angeles to find the city beset by one of the worst sieges of smog in its history. Reagan easily overcame these occasional political gaffes through his mastery of the medium of television. He announced his candidacy over a network of independent television stations in 90 cities. Repeated endlessly during the campaign was a television commercial that summarized his accomplishments as California governor, presenting an image of Reagan as a reliable, experienced government executive.

The size of the Republican victory in the November 1980 election was a surprise to most observers. Reagan won 489 electoral votes to Carter's 49, and for the first time in 26 years a Republican majority was elected to the United States Senate. Reagan defeated the incumbent president in California by more than 1.4 million votes.

In personnel and policy the new Reagan administration bore many similarities to Reagan's years as California governor. His chief of staff in Sacramento and top campaign strategist, Edwin Meese, III, was appointed counselor to the President and remained Reagan's most trusted adviser. Meese, a former Alameda County deputy district attorney, had first come to the attention of Reagan following Meese's successful prosecution of students arrested during the 1964 Free Speech movement in Berkeley. Lyn Nofziger, Reagan's Sacramento press secretary and later head of the Citizens for the Republic, became Reagan's chief White House adviser on political affairs. One of Reagan's longtime political backers from southern California, William French Smith, was appointed attorney general. Smith had been Reagan's personal attorney since the mid-1960s and had guided many of Reagan's investments. Caspar Weinberger, Reagan's budget-slashing finance director in Sacramento, became secretary of defense, and William Clark, a veteran Reagan aide and former California supreme court justice, was named national security adviser in 1982.

Reagan's efforts to reduce the state budget and cut taxes in California were duplicated on the national level when he won congressional approval in 1981 of his "program for economic recovery." This sweeping program, which included the largest reduction in individual and business taxes ever enacted by Congress, called for a cut in personal income taxes of nearly 25 percent over the next 3 years. At the center of the Reagan program was a major reduction in virtually every area of the federal budget except defense. Reminiscent of Reagan's budgets in California, the heaviest cuts in federal spending were reserved for such areas as food stamps, Medicare, unemployment benefits, and student aid. Reagan also called for the reform or elimination of many federal regulations of business. Just as Reagan's philosophy as California governor had stood in sharp contrast to that of his predecessor, his federal economic policy marked a dramatic reversal of nearly half a century of expanding government involvement in the nation's social welfare.

THE TAX REVOLT

The reputation of a president or a governor is often defined in crisis. The nearest thing to a crisis during Jerry Brown's first term as governor was the onset of two winters of extraordinarily warm and dry weather in 1976 and 1977, when California faced the greatest danger of drought since the dry winters of the 1860s had wiped out the state's early cattle industry. Fortunately the rains returned and the crisis passed. The victory of Proposition 13 in the June 1978 primary marked the beginning of a different sort of drought, a massive reduction in government revenues, and presented Governor Brown, the legislature, and the people of California with a crisis of major proportions.

The roots of the tax revolt lay in several separate but related developments. First, inflation had deeply eroded the real income of California taxpayers. In the decade prior to the passage of Proposition 13 the cost of living in California had risen 79 percent. The cost of government was the one price that consumers had the power to vote down. Second, because state and local taxes were steadily increasing at rates greater than the general inflation rate, taxes were absorbing an increasing share of personal income. Property taxes in the decade before 1978 had increased nearly twice as much as the cost of living. Third, although the cost of government was steadily rising, the level of satisfaction with government services was declining. Dissatisfaction was especially strong among middle-income taxpayers who believed that in recent years government spending had shifted from programs that directly benefited them, such as those for streets and highways, to programs such as welfare that benefited only a few. Voters had become convinced that there was "fat" in state and local government—inefficiency, waste, unwanted services, high salaries and fringe benefits for government workers—which could be cut without reducing such essential services as police and fire protection.

The sponsors of Proposition 13, Howard Jarvis and Paul Gann, needed about half a million signatures to qualify their measure for the June 1978 ballot. They soon gathered more than 1.2 million. Jarvis, director of the Apart-

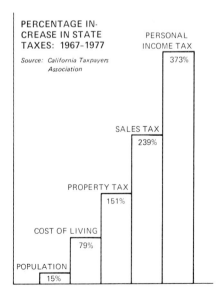

PERCENTAGE IN-
CREASE IN STATE
TAXES: 1967-1977

Source: California Taxpayers
Association

PERSONAL
INCOME TAX
373%

SALES TAX
239%

PROPERTY TAX
151%

COST OF LIVING
79%

POPULATION
15%

ment Owners Association of Los Angeles, had for years been a minor figure in California politics. He had come to California from his native Utah in the 1930s and established a small chemical plant and factory that produced latex pads for heavy machinery. During World War II the federal government appropriated Jarvis's latex, shutting down his factory and triggering a lifelong resentment of government. Gann, a grade school dropout from Arkansas, had also been driven west by the depression. In California he had worked for years as a car salesman and realtor before teaming with Jarvis to found the United Organizations of Taxpayers in 1977.

The Jarvis-Gann constitutional amendment provided that property taxes should be limited to 1 percent of a property's assessed value. This meant an average reduction in property taxes of about 57 percent and a reduction in annual property tax revenues for cities, counties, school districts, and other units of local government of about $7 billion. The assessed value of all property would be rolled back to its 1975 level and could rise from that figure by only 2 percent per year. Property would be reassessed only when sold or improved. Furthermore, state and local governments were forbidden from increasing property taxes. The legislature or local voters could raise other taxes, but only by a two-thirds vote rather than by the previous simple majority.

The essence of Proposition 13, the restriction of property taxes to 1 percent of value, had appeared on the ballot in 1968 and again in 1972 but had been soundly defeated. By the latter half of the 1970s, however, property values in California were rising about 2 percent *per month*. Because several years often intervened between reassessments of a property's value, increases in property taxes of 40 or 50 percent were common and in some areas taxes had increased 90 percent between assessments. Property owners were outraged, and many homeowners wondered whether the increased tax burden would force them to sell their homes. Throughout the state, homeowners expressed their anger at outdoor rallies, at appearances before county boards of supervisors, and by signing the petitions of Jarvis and Gann.

The anger of California taxpayers was also fueled by the growth of a surplus in the state treasury, labeled "obscene" by Howard Jarvis. In 1976 the state reported a surplus of $486 million. By June of 1978 it had grown to at least $3.5 billion and possibly much larger. The surplus had been generated in part by real economic growth, which increased revenues from such levies as bank and corporation taxes, and by inflation. As workers received annual cost-of-living wage increases to keep up with inflation, they found themselves in higher income tax brackets where the state claimed a larger percentage of their income. In the decade prior to the passage of Proposition 13, revenue from the state's personal income tax more than tripled. While the state was thus collecting ever-greater amounts of revenue, the budgets of Governor Brown increased state spending only modestly.

In the spring of 1978 Brown was joined by virtually the entire state political establishment in opposing the Jarvis-Gann amendment. Opponents argued that the tax-cutting measure would produce chaos on all levels of government, reduce vital services, and cause the layoff of hundreds of thousands of government workers. Supporters of the initiative countered that it would reduce waste and inefficiency in government and stimulate the economy to further growth. The proposition passed with 65 percent of the vote. It received majority support in all but 3 of the state's 58 counties.

In the aftermath of the victory of Proposition 13 the legislature passed an emergency measure to bail out local governments by providing them with financial aid from the state surplus. Cities, counties, schools, and other local districts supported by property taxes thus were cushioned from the full impact of Proposition 13 and escaped during the first year after its passage with their budgets reduced only slightly or, in some cases, not at all. In 1979 the legislature adopted a new bail-out formula, allocating local governments additional funds from the surplus and providing for modest annual increases in state aid.

The second blow of the tax revolt was struck in November 1979 when California voters approved an initiative to limit state and local government spending. The measure, promoted by an organization called the "Spirit of 13" and headed by Paul Gann, appeared on the ballot as Proposition 4. The measure limited annual increases in spending by all units of government in the state to a rate no greater than the rate of inflation and the percentage increase in population growth. Proposition 4 also directed state and local governments to return excess revenues to the taxpayers, presumably through tax cuts or rebates, and limited the imposition of new fees for government services.

The Gann initiative was similar to Ronald Reagan's ill-fated Proposition 1 of 1973 which also had proposed a limit on state spending. Unlike the Reagan initiative, however, Proposition 4 aroused almost no statewide opposition. The Spirit of 13 organization collected more than $1.5 million in contributions, virtually all of it coming from corporations or business groups such as the California Chamber of Commerce. The massive media campaign in favor of the measure claimed that Proposition 4 offered voters "a chance to govern our lives again." Few state politicians dared oppose the measure; Governor Brown belatedly announced his endorsement a week before the election. Whereas Reagan's initiative had received only 46 percent of the vote, Proposition 4 won approval by nearly three to one.

In less than 2 years Californians had cut their property taxes by more than half and imposed a mandatory limit on all government spending. The state captured national attention as the birthplace of the modern tax revolt. "There's a west wind blowing out of California," Paul Gann told his supporters in Los Angeles, "and, best we can tell, it's heading for Washington, D.C."

In 1980 Howard Jarvis presented California voters with yet another opportunity to reduce taxes. The taxation initiative, known as Jarvis II or among its opponents as Jaws II, appeared on the November ballot as Proposition 9 and proposed cutting state income tax rates by half. The initiative would reduce state revenues by nearly $5 billion, an amount greater than that which the state was currently spending for *all* state operations—colleges, universities, prisons, mental hospitals, and parks. Jarvis relied on the services of a professional campaign management firm to obtain signatures for the initiative through direct-mail solicitation, and for the first time in California history a proposition qualified for the ballot without face-to-face contact between a petition carrier and a petition signer.

More than $3 million was spent by Jarvis's supporters to get their message to the voters, about 90 percent for television commercials. When questioned why so little was being spent for printed campaign literature or newspaper advertisements, Jarvis blandly replied, "People who decide elections don't read." The main strategy of the opposition campaign was to identify and mobilize voters, such as public employees, senior citizens, and educators, who would be adversely affected by the measure. University of California President David S. Saxon wrote the university's 130,000 students to inform them that if the initiative passed, tuition might be charged for the first time in the university's 112-year history.

In the June 1980 election Proposition 9 carried only one county and received statewide only 39 percent of the vote. The majority of Californians apparently had been convinced that an additional cut in revenues, coming at a time when the state surplus was nearing depletion, would indeed have an adverse effect on schools, libraries, and other government services. Jarvis himself also became an issue in the Proposition 9 battle and contributed to its defeat. "Howard Jarvis is the best friend we have," commented the director of the opposition campaign. At an appearance on the California State University campus in Sacramento, Jarvis called one student questioner "stupid," another a "dumbhead," and a third a "slob." His often crude and intemperate remarks alienated even some of his former supporters.

THE IMPACT OF PROPOSITION 13

In the first years after its adoption, the Jarvis-Gann initiative fulfilled neither the worst fears of its opponents nor the most optimistic hopes of its supporters. Employment in the public sector declined, but not nearly as much as had been feared. Libraries, parks, and recreation departments reduced services, and most school districts eliminated summer school programs. On the other hand, California's per capita tax burden fell from one of the nation's highest to about average among the states, and California's economy continued to prosper. It was uncertain, however, what effect Proposition 13 had had on that prosperity.

Homeowners in the state were gratified that their property taxes had been more than cut in half. Some were disturbed, however, at the growing disparity in taxation of identical properties. Because Proposition 13 permitted reassessments of a property when it was sold, the new purchaser of a home often found that the newly assessed taxes were much greater than those of the previous owner or those of neighbors living in homes of comparable value. When the state supreme court confirmed the constitutionality of the Jarvis-Gann initiative, Chief Justice Rose Elizabeth Bird argued in a minority opinion that such inequity violated the equal-protection clause of the United States Constitution. "As the years go by," Bird predicted, "the skewed nature of the tax world created by Proposition 13 will become even more pronounced."

Homeowners, like everyone else, also faced new or increased "users' fees" for services provided by local governments. School districts began charging school bus fares ranging from 15 cents to $1 a day, while many communities increased fees for using public swimming pools, museums, and zoos. Some of the largest fee increases were aimed at restricting the construction of new residential developments. Local governments found that the reduced property tax revenues available under Proposition 13 were not sufficient to meet the cost of providing new residents with roads, schools, and police and fire protection. The San Diego suburb of La Mesa raised the cost of a sewer connection by 1200 percent, while other communities imposed builders' fees of up to $5000 for each unit of new construction. Such measures aggravated an already severe housing shortage in the state and encouraged the process known as "gentrification," the rehabilitation of older residences in urban areas by middle-income homeowners who in earlier years would have moved to the suburbs. As UCLA economist David Shulman observed, one of the unforeseen effects of Proposition 13 was "a historic reversal of California's trend towards urban sprawl."

The greatest beneficiaries of Proposition 13 were the owners of large business properties in the state. A few corporations, including several public utilities, passed their windfall property tax savings on to their customers or donated them to charities. Most businesses treated the income as profit. *The Wall Street Journal* estimated that in the first year after its passage Proposition 13 saved Southern Pacific $20 million in taxes and Standard Oil of California about $47 million. Apartment owners and other landlords doubly benefited because the measure contained no requirement that they pass on any property tax savings to their tenants. Before the election Howard Jarvis offered disingenuous assurances that landlords would voluntarily share their savings with tenants. In fact few landlords moved to lower rents after the election while some actually increased them. Rent control measures soon appeared on the ballot in communities around the state, and city councils adopted ordinances to roll back or freeze rents.

Homeowners had supported Proposition 13 as a means to reduce their property taxes, yet in every year after its adoption homeowners came to bear an ever-greater share of the total property tax burden. Because residential properties tended to change hands more often than business properties and because under Proposition 13 property could be reassessed only when it was sold, property taxes on residences increased at rates greater than those on businesses. In Santa Clara County, for instance, business and residential taxpayers had paid approximately equal shares of the total tax bill before Proposition 13. Within a year of its passage, homeowners were providing 57 percent of the total, and businesses only 43 percent. The county tax assessor predicted that within 5 years the ratio would shift to 70 and 30 percent, respectively. Similar trends elsewhere in the state led to increased pressure for a change in the Jarvis-Gann initiative restoring the tax balance between the two sectors.

Among those who lost the most from Proposition 13 were the state's public employees. Prior to its enactment many state and local government workers had enjoyed regular increases in salary and benefits and had just been granted collective-bargaining rights. Under Proposition 13 they faced layoffs, increased workloads, reduced opportunities for upward mobility, and pay increases often less than the rise in the cost of living. Governor Brown denied state and local workers any pay increases in fiscal year 1978–1979, but the state supreme court later ruled his action unconstitutional. Demoralization among the ranks of public employees increased, and many workers left for jobs in the private sector. Militancy among public employee unions also increased, and strikes by sanitation workers, transit drivers, and public school teachers became more common. Ed Salzman, editor of the *California Journal*, predicted that the 1980s would be remembered as "the decade of economic warfare between the California public and its employees."

Minorities and the poor also lost ground under Proposition 13. Layoffs of public employees affected a disproportionate number of minority workers because they were commonly the last hired and were, thus, forced by civil service laws to be the first fired. Freezes on government hiring made affirmative action programs meaningless. Cutbacks in funds for public libraries, adult education, health care, and park and recreation programs hurt the poor more than they did the affluent, as did increased fees for access to public facilities.

As state and local governments were forced to cut back on spending, budgets for the maintenance and repair of roads, bridges, sewers, water mains, and public buildings were often deferred or severely reduced. In Oakland the schedule for routine street resurfacing was extended from once every 30 years to once every 200 years. Reductions in force also crippled the ability of police and fire departments to respond to emergencies. The Los Angeles Police Department suffered a 10 percent reduction in personnel, and the ranks of the fire department were thinned by 300. Following a devastating fire in Laurel Canyon in 1980, the Los Angeles fire chief said more homes might have been saved had his fire companies not been operating with personnel cutbacks brought about by Proposition 13.

The Jarvis-Gann initiative also produced a redistribution of revenue and power among the levels of government. Within the state there was a fundamental centralization of power, one of the most far-reaching structural changes in any governmental system in the United States since the New Deal. Units of local government—cities, counties, school districts, community colleges—became dependent upon the state for a larger proportion of their operating budget and thus came under increased state control. The bail-out legislation, distributing state funds to local governments, permitted state intrusion into areas which previously had been local domain. Meanwhile, the federal government increased its annual income tax collection from California by about $2 billion, for California taxpayers had experienced a decline in their federal income tax deductions equal to the amount of their Proposition 13 tax savings.

The distribution of bail-out funds from the surplus in the state treasury delayed for several years the full impact of Proposition 13. After its enactment the state began spending annually about a billion dollars more than it collected in tax revenues, and the surplus was steadily depleted. Finally, in 1981, Governor Brown made the fateful announcement: "The surplus is gone. The cupboard is bare." The governor ordered immediate cuts in the budgets of most state departments, including the colleges and universities, and warned that California cities and counties would have "to tighten their belts in the face of a new fiscal austerity." With the surplus exhausted, California governments at last faced the awful dilemma of sharply reducing existing programs or raising new taxes.

Economists disagreed over the ultimate effects of Proposition 13. Conservatives welcomed the prospects of drastic cuts in the size and power of government—in effect the dismantling of the welfare state—and predicted renewed prosperity and economic progress. University of Southern California economist Arthur Laffer argued that the reduction in taxes would leave workers with more of their earnings to invest or to purchase goods, thus stimulating more production, jobs, and economic expansion. According to the theory known as the "Laffer curve," tax cuts actually benefited government because as more jobs were created in the private sector, they generated new taxes to support government services. Liberal economists, on the other hand, viewed the future with alarm and warned of increases in unemployment, recession, and social unrest. Cutbacks in government services, they argued, would lead to a dangerous buildup of social and political pressures among those groups most affected. Speaking at Berkeley in 1980, Harvard economist John Kenneth Galbraith denounced the tax revolt as a crusade "against the least fortunate of our citizens." To discard social welfare programs, which for decades had softened the harsh edges of American capitalism, was to invite disaster. "Perhaps the disadvantaged are now too few to make a revolution," Galbraith concluded. "But they could make life uncomfortable for all."

Although California was not the first state in the nation to limit taxes or government spending, it had made an important contribution to the national movement for tax reform. By 1981 half the states in the union had imposed some sort of limit on local taxes or on state revenues or expenditures, and Ronald Reagan had been elected President on a pledge to reduce federal taxes and government spending. California long had been regarded as the land of the future. In 1962 Richard Armour wrote:

> So leap with joy, be blithe and gay,
> Or weep my friends with sorrow.
> What California is today,
> The rest will be tomorrow.

For good or ill, Proposition 13 tended to confirm this view. The "era of limits," defined as an era of reduced taxes and scaled-down government, had come to encompass a territory far larger than California.

SELECTED BIBLIOGRAPHY

Jerry Brown has been the subject of several books: Ed Salzman, *Jerry Brown: High Priest and Low Politician* (1976); John C. Bollens and G. Robert Williams, *Jerry Brown in a Plain Brown Wrapper* (1978); J. D. Lorenz, *Jerry Brown: The Man on the White Horse* (1978); Robert Pack, *Jerry Brown: The Philosopher Prince* (1978); and Orville Schell, *Brown* (1978).

Mary Ellen Leary, *Phantom Politics: Campaigning in California* (1977), is an analysis of the 1974 gubernatorial election and the role of television in California politics. Richard Reeves, *Convention* (1977) contains some revealing glimpses of Brown's 1976 presidential campaign. For a survey of Brown's first term see Jackson K. Putnam, *Modern California Politics, 1917–1980* (1980), pp. 72–88, and Ed Salzman, "The Latest Jerry Brown," *California Journal*, VIII (June 1977), pp. 187–190, and "The Brown Record," *California Journal*, IX (June 1978), pp. 173–176. For a generally positive appraisal of Brown's 1980 presidential campaign see Alexander Cockburn and James Ridgeway, "The Not-So-Flaky Candidate: Tracking the 'New' Jerry Brown," *San Francisco Bay Guardian*, Jan. 10, 1980. An analysis of the failure of that campaign is offered by Leo Rennert in "Does Jerry Brown Have a Future?" *California Journal*, XI (May 1980), p. 211.

Two of the more perceptive analyses by journalists of Brown's personality and political career are T. D. Allman, "Jerry Brown: Nothing to Everyone," *Harper's*, CCLIX (July 1979), pp. 13–20, and Jamie Wolf, "Looking for Jerry," *New West*, VI (April 1981), pp. 88–93, 149–151.

On the rise of Ronald Reagan and the early part of his presidency, see Hedrick Smith et al., *Reagan: The Man, the President* (1980) and William Boyarsky, *Ronald Reagan: His Life and Rise to the Presidency* (1981).

The *Tax Revolt Digest*, published monthly by the *California Journal* from November 1978 to October 1979, contains a wealth of information on the tax revolt in California and elsewhere. Terry J. Dean and Ronald J. Heckart (compilers), *Proposition 13 in the 1978 California Primary* (1979) and Ed Duensing, *Tax Reform and Municipal Finance: With Emphasis on Proposition 13* (1979) are useful bibliographies. For a view from the inside see Howard Jarvis, with Robert Pack, *I'm Mad as Hell: The Exclusive Story of the Tax Revolt and Its Leader* (1979).

The public policy issues of government finance reform are examined in Frank M. Bowen and Eugene C. Lee, *Limiting State Spending: The Legislature or the Electorate* (1979) and Thomas Fletcher et al., *Allocating the One Percent Local Property Tax in California* (1979). Among the many publications which assess the impact of Proposition 13 see especially John J. Kirlin and Jeffrey I. Chapman, *California State Finance and Proposition 13* (1979); Kirlin, *The Impacts of Proposition 13 upon California Governments* (1979); and Selma J. Muskin (ed.), *Proposition 13 and Its Consequences for Public Management* (1979), the proceedings of a conference sponsored by the Council for Applied Social Research. Maureen S. Fitzgerald, "California's Future under Proposition 13," *California Journal*, XI (November 1980), pp. 425–428, is a brief summary of the effects of the tax revolt on state and local government.

THE ENVIRONMENT AND ENERGY

One of the major themes in California history since at least the progressive era has been controversy over the use and preservation of the state's natural resources. In recent years new groups have joined forces with older conservation organizations such as the Sierra Club to lobby for the protection of California's land, air, and water. Throughout the late 1960s and 1970s the environmental protection movement scored a series of impressive victories, both in the state legislature and through the initiative process. The opponents of the environmentalists, however, marshaled their forces and began an effective counterattack. California business interests, allied often with organized labor, argued that environmental legislation retarded economic development, caused unemployment, and contributed to inflation. The struggle between the forces of economic development and environmental protection was waged on many fronts.

REGIONAL PROTECTION

The first important victory for the environmental protection movement came in 1965 with the establishment by the state legislature of the San Francisco Bay Conservation and Development Commission (BCDC). Uncontrolled filling of the bay during the previous century had reduced its size by 40 percent, and conservationists warned that without effective controls the bay would eventually become little more than a river. The new BCDC regulated all developments in a 100-foot-wide band around the bay shoreline and virtually halted any further filling of the bay. Under its supervision water quality improved, and the bay wildlife population increased. The BCDC also provided a model for the creation of other regional agencies to control development elsewhere in the state.

More emotional fuel was added to the environmental movement early in 1969 when an offshore well of the Union Oil Company sprang a leak in the Santa Barbara Channel and smeared hundreds of square miles of ocean and 30 miles of beaches with oil. In 1970 the state legislature, acting partly in response to the Santa Barbara oil spill, passed the California Environmental Quality Act which required that an environmental impact report be submitted to appropriate public agencies for approval prior to the commencement of any project "which could have a significant effect on the environment." Under terms of the act, environmentalists brought suit to halt or modify scores of environmentally damaging projects. The California Chamber of Commerce denounced the act as harmful to the state's economy, and the executive secretary of the California Labor Federation suggested that every new measure of environmental regulation ought to require an "economic impact report."

Californians in growing numbers were becoming convinced that the scenic regions of the state needed special protection from private development. In 1972 voters approved an initiative creating for 4 years a Coastal Zone Conservation Commission to govern development of California's coastline and to preserve reasonable public access to it. The legislature in 1976 established a permanent California Coastal Commission which became the final arbiter for the issuance of permits to build or develop property along the coast. By 1981 it had processed over 50,000 applications, approving more than 90 percent. The commission often required substantial modifications in the proposals it approved and denied permits for several large commercial developments. The California Council on Economic and Environmental Balance, a prodevelopment group, charged that the commission was guilty of "bureaucratic and environmental zeal" and supported legislation to curtail its powers.

The Tahoe Regional Planning Agency, jointly operated by California and Nevada and authorized by Congress in 1967, tried to combat both the pollution of Lake Tahoe's pure, blue waters by sewage and the threatened destruction of the beauty of its surroundings by excessive and hasty construction, but for years the agency was unable to prevent the building of new gambling casinos on the Nevada shores. The problem lay with a "dual majority" provision in the bistate compact, which allowed disputed projects to be built even though a majority of the agency board opposed them. In 1980 President Carter signed legislation which eliminated this controversial provision, thus effectively banning further construction of new casinos and hotels in the Tahoe basin. Carter also established a federal coordinating council to ensure that federal agencies did nothing to stimulate further growth in the basin area. The council was abolished by President Ronald Reagan in 1981.

Environmentalists also supported measures to increase California parklands. In 1962 the National Park Service began to acquire land for the Point Reyes National Seashore, an area which would ultimately include the 10-mile Point Reyes Beach and the land around Drake's Bay. Congress created the Redwood National Park in northwestern California in 1968 and the Golden Gate National Recreation Area in Marin and San Francisco counties in 1972. In spite of these developments and many additions to the state's own park system,

California parklands remained crowded and inadequate. Between 1950 and 1980 California parks doubled in size, but the number of annual visitors increased twentyfold. To the dismay of environmentalists, President Reagan's interior secretary James Watt announced in 1981 a halt to new parkland acquisitions. Watt declared that the national park system was already too large and that some of its lands—including part of the Golden Gate National Recreation Area—were "not worthy" of federal protection.

Among the most spectacular lands in the national park system was California's Yosemite Valley, which by the late 1970s was being visited by 2.5 million people a year. On summer weekends the valley, only a mile wide and 7 miles long, became the retreat for as many as 18,000 visitors. The National Park Service came under conflicting pressure from environmental organizations to "deurbanize" the valley and from the Yosemite Park and Curry Company, the park concessionaire owned by the powerful Music Corporation of America, to maintain adequate services and conveniences for visitors. In 1980 the park service unveiled a master plan to remove most employee housing and offices to outlying areas of the park, to reduce overnight accommodations, and to restrict the number of visitors admitted to the valley. The following year, however, Interior Secretary Watt proposed that the role of private concessionaires in the national parks be enlarged. Environmentalists feared that the new policy would lead to further overcrowding and commercial development in Yosemite and in other national parks.

GROWTH CONTROL

The environmental movement, although its roots lay deep in California history, represented a radical reversal of traditional values. Throughout the state's history, growth had been thought of as the greatest good, but the environmentalists denounced unrestricted growth as a menace to the quality of life.

Beginning with a Petaluma ordinance in 1973 limiting construction of new residential units within the city to 500 per year, communities across the state took steps to limit their population growth. Builders criticized the Petaluma measure as a "no-growth" plan and challenged its constitutionality, but in 1976 the United States Supreme Court upheld the ordinance. San Jose in the 1960s had the distinction of being the fastest-growing city in the nation—its 1950 population had increased nearly fivefold by 1970—and local politics were dominated by a progrowth coalition of developers, construction unions, and local merchants. In 1973 San Jose voters adopted a measure to control growth, and the following year Janet Gray Hayes, who campaigned on a slogan of "making San Jose better before making it bigger," defeated for mayor the candidate favored by builders.

The growth-control movement was under constant attack from prodevelopment forces. Critics charged the movement was "elitist," dominated by wealthy residents who wanted to protect their own property values by stopping further housing construction. Developers succeeded in defeating growth-control measures in Tuolomne County and Novato and in recalling local antigrowth officials elsewhere. Proposition 13, however, added new strength to the movement. In the first 2 years after its adoption, 19 California cities and counties—including the cities of Stockton, Belmont, Saratoga, and Santa Cruz—passed ordinances controlling growth, and growth-control candidates were elected in San Diego and Orange counties.

After the abrupt slowdown of statewide population growth in the late 1960s, California's overall growth resumed at a modest annual rate in the mid-1970s. The Census Bureau reported that the state's 1980 population was 23,668,562, an increase of 18.5 percent since 1970. The census report set off another round in the state's decennial reapportionment debate, and it also contained some surprises in the pattern of population growth. The largest numerical growth continued to occur in the state's major metropolitan areas, with San Diego and Orange counties leading the way, but for the first time in modern history the state's rural areas grew at a faster rate than its urban ones.

	County	1970 Population	1980 Population	Percent Increase		County	1970 Population	1980 Population	Percent Increase
1	Alpine	484	1,097	126.7	30	Sierra	2,365	3,073	29.9
2	Mono	4,016	8,577	113.6	31	Lassen	16,796	21,661	29.0
3	Nevada	26,346	51,645	96.0	32	Merced	104,629	134,560	28.6
4	El Dorado	43,833	85,812	95.8	33	Napa	79,140	99,199	25.3
5	Lake	19,548	36,366	86.0	34	Del Norte	14,580	18,217	24.9
6	Mariposa	6,015	11,108	84.7	35	Fresno	413,329	515,013	24.6
7	Amador	11,821	19,314	63.4	36	Sutter	41,935	52,246	24.6
8	Trinity	7,615	11,858	55.7	37	Imperial	74,492	92,110	23.7
9	Toulumne	22,169	33,920	53.0	38	Sacramento	634,373	783,381	23.5
10	Calaveras	13,585	20,170	52.4	39	Yolo	91,788	113,374	23.5
11	Madera	41,519	63,116	52.0	40	Kern	330,234	403,089	22.1
12	Santa Cruz	123,790	188,141	52.0	41	Glenn	17,521	21,350	21.9
13	Placer	77,632	117,247	51.0	42	Santa Clara	1,066,313	1,295,071	21.6
14	Shasta	77,640	115,715	49.0	43	Siskiyou	33,225	39,732	19.6
15	Plumas	11,707	17,340	48.1	44	San Joaquin	291,073	347,342	19.3
16	San Luis Obispo	105,690	155,345	47.0	45	Contra Costa	556,116	657,252	18.2
17	Sonoma	204,885	299,827	46.3	46	Monterey	247,450	290,444	17.4
18	Riverside	456,916	663,923	45.3	47	Modoc	7,469	8,610	15.3
19	Butte	101,969	143,851	41.1	48	Inyo	15,571	17,895	14.9
20	Ventura	378,497	529,899	40.0	49	Santa Barbara	264,324	298,660	13.0
21	San Benito	18,226	25,005	37.2	50	Yuba	44,736	49,733	11.2
22	San Diego	1,357,854	1,861,846	37.1	51	Kings	66,717	73,738	10.5
23	Solano	171,989	235,203	36.8	52	Humboldt	99,692	108,024	8.4
24	Stanislaus	194,506	265,902	36.7	53	Marin	208,652	222,952	6.9
25	Orange	1,421,233	1,931,570	35.9	54	Los Angeles	7,041,980	7,477,657	6.2
26	Tehama	29,517	38,888	31.7	55	San Mateo	557,361	588,164	5.5
27	San Bernardino	682,233	893,157	30.9	56	Alameda	1,071,446	1,105,379	3.2
28	Mendocino	51,101	66,738	30.6	57	Colusa	12,430	12,791	2.9
29	Tulare	188,322	245,751	30.5	58	San Francisco	715,674	678,974	-5.1
						TOTAL	19,971,069	23,668,562	18.5

California Population Change. Percentage Growth by County, 1970 to 1980. (Copyright 1981, *Los Angeles Times*. Reprinted by permission.)

The highest rate of growth occurred in the counties from Plumas south to Mariposa, and within these counties unincorporated communities grew faster than incorporated cities. Much of the growth came from highly educated, middle-aged professionals who were moving from urban or suburban areas, willing to accept a reduction in income and job status in exchange for the imagined blessings of rural life. By the early 1980s growth control had become a prime issue in rural areas throughout the state.

AIR POLLUTION

Air pollution was the most obvious menace to the quality of the environment. "Smog" began to produce a sharp decrease in visibility and painful irritations of nose and eyes in Los Angeles in 1943, and by the 1960s this condition had become so chronic that on bad days the city vanished. When, as often happened, the air in and over the Los Angeles basin became stagnant and a temperature inversion occurred, the rays of the sun reacted photochemically with various waste products in the air to produce new and still more dangerous pollutants. The result was not merely a blight on the beauty of the region and a cause of sharp discomfort, but also a menace to health and a source of costly damage to several crops. The growing of leafy vegetables in the Los Angeles basin virtually ceased.

The San Francisco Bay area, like the Los Angeles basin, had a bowl-like shape, and smog began to be a severe problem in the bay region also. Los Angeles created an air pollution control district in 1947, and the San Francisco Bay counties formed a similar district in 1955. These agencies had some success in persuading or compelling industrial plants to reduce the emission of noxious wastes, often by installing expensive equipment. Yet the smog grew steadily worse. It became apparent that the chief offender was the automobile, with its output of hydrocarbons, oxides of nitrogen, and toxic carbon monoxide.

As the number of motor vehicles steadily increased, smog began to form in the interior valleys and threatened ultimately to spread over most of the state. Even in the San Bernardino Mountains, at altitudes up to 7000 feet, pine trees began to show signs of damage.

The state legislature in 1960 passed the first automobile antismog law in the nation, requiring the installation of various smog-control devices in motor vehicle engines. Action by the federal government came 10 years later when Congress created the Environmental Protection Agency (EPA) and, in the Clean Air Act of 1970, provided that by 1976 new cars must be equipped with devices to reduce emissions of hydrocarbons, carbon monoxide, and nitrogen oxide by 90 percent. The automakers failed to come anywhere near this goal, however, and Congress had to relax the provisions and extend the deadline.

In 1977 Congress adopted a "get tough" attitude and amended the Clean Air Act to provide economic sanctions against states which did not meet federal air quality standards. States such as California, where automobiles were significant sources of pollution, were required to establish an annual vehicle

inspection program. The EPA estimated that annual inspections would produce half of the reduction in hydrocarbons needed to meet federal standards
and one-fourth of the reduction in nitrogen oxides. The state legislature established a limited inspection plan requiring cars to be inspected for smog-con-
ducive emissions when they changed ownership, but balked at requiring
annual testing of all vehicles. Many legislators feared that annual inspections,
which would cost motorists about $20 per vehicle, would be unpopular among
their constituents. The American Automobile Association and the United
States Chamber of Commerce, as part of a national campaign to force Congress
to rewrite the Clean Air Act and relax its pollution standards, urged the defeat
of bills requiring annual inspections.

Meanwhile eye-searing, throat-burning smog continued to smother large
parts of the state. In the late summer of 1979 Los Angeles experienced severe
smog alerts for 7 consecutive days, its worst bout of air pollution in 24 years.

In August 1979 the EPA imposed a ban on further construction in California of industrial plants which could become major sources of pollution and
warned of further penalties unless California adopted an annual inspection
program. The legislature failed to act, and in December 1980 the EPA placed
restrictions on $850 million in federal funds for highway and sewage treat-
ment projects in the state. Following the election of Ronald Reagan, the Cham-

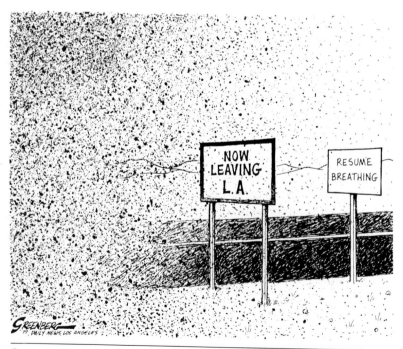

Cartoon by Steve Greenberg in the *Daily News,* Los Angeles, Sept. 16, 1979. The cartoon appeared
following a prolonged bout of first- and second-stage smog alerts in the Los Angeles basin. *(Courtesy of
the* Daily News, *Los Angeles.)*

ber of Commerce and other business organizations intensified their efforts to win relaxation of federal air quality standards. They argued that existing standards "erred on the side of health safety." In 1982 the EPA announced that it was dropping its requirement for annual vehicle inspections in California, accepting biennial or "periodic" inspections instead.

WATER RESOURCES

The long-standing controversy over the use and distribution of the state's water resources was renewed in the late 1970s as the legislature considered authorization of the Peripheral Canal, a 43-mile-long, 400-foot-wide channel around the periphery of San Francisco Bay which would connect the Sacramento River directly with the existing California Aqueduct. By being drawn from the Sacramento, rather than from the southern end of the Sacramento–San Joaquin delta, the annual supply of water delivered by the aqueduct to southern California could be increased by at least 700,000 acre-feet.

Support for the Peripheral Canal was virtually unanimous throughout southern California. The Metropolitan Water District (MWD) and the Kern County Water District, which together absorbed more than three-fourths of the supplies provided by the California Water Project, lobbied vigorously in support of the canal. The MWD, called "the General Motors of waterdom" by the *New York Times,* supplied more than 11 million residential and industrial customers in southern California and estimated that the population of its service area would grow to 14 million by the year 2000. Meanwhile, in accordance with a United States Supreme Court decision, the MWD was scheduled to lose a substantial amount of its water entitlement from the Colorado River when the Central Arizona Project was completed in the mid-1980s. Placed in the double bind of increasing demand and decreasing supply, the MWD insisted that expansion of the state water project was essential. The Kern County District served vast agricultural developments in the San Joaquin Valley. Among the largest holders of agricultural land which would benefit from increased supplies of state water were Shell Oil Company, Getty Oil, Chevron, Tenneco, and the Southern Pacific.

Opposition to the canal was led by environmental groups such as the Planning and Conservation League and others in northern California who believed that the massive diversion of fresh water supplies from the delta would harm San Francisco Bay and delta water quality. Opponents contended that without periodic flushing with fresh water from the Sacramento the bay would become "a stinking sink of dead fish" and salt water intrusion would destroy rich farmlands in the delta. The Peripheral Canal would have more than a dozen gates along its side to release fresh water into the delta, but northern Californians feared that during dry years a southern majority would order the gates closed to protect the flow of water south no matter what damage it might do to the delta. Environmentalists also feared that the canal would discourage water conservation and generate pressures for additional supplies from the remaining undammed rivers of the north. David Abelson, executive director of the Planning and Conservation League, said the Peripheral Canal would be "a loaded gun pointed at the North Coast Rivers." Critics questioned as well the need for any further expansion of the state water project. They charged that the MWD overestimated its future needs for water and that through conservation and reclamation efforts it could compensate for the reduction in supply from the Colorado. If farmers—who used more than 85 percent of all developed water in the state—could achieve a mere 5 percent reduction in demand through conservation and improved groundwater management, they would save more water than would be provided by the canal.

As legislation authorizing the canal neared approval, opposition in northern California became strident. The *San Francisco Chronicle* denounced it as a "ruthless water grab," and one Bay Area assemblyman warned: "Please, southerners, don't think you can rob our water and destroy our ecosystem, because there will be a civil war in this state if you do. The aqueduct will be blown up. National guardsmen will be shot."

In 1980, however, the legislature passed a bill which authorized construction of the Peripheral Canal and related facilities, and outlined environmental protections for the delta. This action by the legislature represented the most important addition to the state water project since its inception in 1959. In an attempt to allay the fears of northern Californians and environmentalists, the legislature approved an amendment which would place in the state constitution minimum water quality standards for the delta and make it more difficult to dam the "wild and scenic" rivers of the north coast. The amendment, supported by the MWD, was opposed by the California Farm Bureau and San Joaquin Valley agricultural interests. The farmers succeeded in defeating a companion bill to require water conservation and groundwater management programs.

In signing the water project expansion bill, Governor Brown offered assurances to northern Californians that the Peripheral Canal and related projects would not harm the environment. "This bill marks the end of an era," Brown said, "an era of growth without strict conservation." Edmund G. Brown, Sr., who had been largely responsible for the measure financing initial construction of the state project, said the latest legislation was "the fulfillment of my dreams."

A coalition of environmentalists, northern California public officials, and others remained opposed to the canal, however, and placed on the ballot a referendum to block its construction. In a remarkable development, the California Farm Bureau threw its support behind the challenge, hoping to win later passage of new legislation authorizing the canal but free of any environmental restrictions. If the referendum were defeated, the 1980 amendment protecting the northern rivers would also be nullified. Even more startling was the attempt by Governor Brown to straddle the growing controversy over the canal. When questioned about his stand on the referendum, Brown declared, "I may not inject myself into the bitter controversy I see about to unleash itself on this state." When the referendum finally appeared on the ballot, in June 1982, the canal was rejected statewide by a vote of 62 percent. In southern California the canal was supported somewhat less enthusiastically than expected, largely due to rising concerns over the cost of the project, and in the northern counties the margin of defeat was a resounding nine to one.

Meanwhile environmentalists suffered setbacks in two other battles involving water resources: the campaigns to preserve Mono Lake and to stop the filling of the New Melones Reservoir on the Stanislaus River. The battle over Mono Lake pitted the National Audubon Society and a host of environmental groups against the city of Los Angeles. Described by Mark Twain as "one of the strangest freaks of nature to be found in any land," Mono Lake was the primary breeding ground for 90 percent of the California gull population and an important stopover for millions of migratory birds. Since the early 1940s Los Angeles had been tapping the streams flowing into Mono Lake, but in 1970 the city was granted the right to appropriate the entire flow from four of Mono's five tributaries. As the water level in the lake began dropping more rapidly, an island which had served as a protected breeding and nesting ground became a peninsula vulnerable to predators, and the chemical content of the lake began to change dramatically, thus reducing the supply of brine shrimp necessary for the survival of the nesting gulls and their chicks. In 1979 an interagency task force recommended that Los Angeles reduce its diversions of Mono Lake water by 85 percent and institute a program of urban water conservation to make up the loss. Implementation of the recommendation, supported by virtually every environmental organization in the state, was blocked by Los Angeles public officials who predicted that the cost of replacing lost water and hydroelectric power would be enormous. A University of California biologist reported in 1981 that nearly all the California gulls hatched at Mono Lake that year had died before reaching maturity.

A similar battle was waged over the preservation of the free-flowing waters of the Stanislaus River. If filled to capacity the reservoir behind the New Melones Dam, part of the federal Central Valley Project, would contain 2.4 million acre-feet of water for flood control, hydroelectric power generation, and downstream irrigation for farmers in the San Joaquin Valley. The reservoir would also inundate a scenic limestone canyon on the upper Stanislaus and destroy a nine-mile stretch of white water rapids. Support for filling the reservoir came from agricultural interests and the Pacific Gas and Electric Company, while the Sierra Club, Friends of the River, and other environmental groups argued that filling the reservoir to capacity was both unnecessary and unwise. Friends of the River sponsored an unsuccessful statewide ballot initiative in 1974, endorsed by Governor Brown, to stop the filling of the reservoir, and in 1979 one environmentalist chained himself to a rock near the water's edge to protest inundation of the canyon. The failure of Congress to designate the Stanislaus as a protected "wild and scenic" river cleared the way for the filling of the reservoir, but the ultimate fate of the project remained to be decided by the federal courts.

PESTICIDES AND TOXIC WASTES

The use of pesticides and the disposal of toxic wastes in California became matters of intense controversy in the late 1970s. The state's $14 billion agricultural industry was using more than 300 million pounds of pesticides each year to increase the yield and enhance the appearance of California farm produce. Because residues from the pesticides posed a danger to human health, state and federal agencies established minimum levels of tolerance and began a residue inspection program. Environmentalists charged these steps were inadequate, and in 1978 the Brown administration instituted new regulations which subjected pesticides to stricter health and environmental tests, required manufacturers to provide more information on possible hazards, and established new requirements for the issuance of pesticide permits.

In June 1980 Mediterranean fruit flies, a pest capable of destroying more than 50 commercially grown crops in California, were discovered in the Santa Clara Valley. Leaders of the state's agricultural industry called for the aerial application of pesticides in the infested area. Residents of the area, however, strenuously objected, and Governor Brown approved instead an "integrated pest management" program which included fruit stripping, ground spraying, and the release of millions of sterile flies. Unfortunately, the following spring more fertile medflies were discovered. The California Farm Bureau and the governor's own medfly advisory committee unanimously recommended immediate aerial spraying. Brown continued to object, asserting that aerial pesticide spraying posed an unacceptable health risk to residents of the area. Only after the Reagan administration threatened to impose a federal quarantine on all California produce did Brown reverse himself and order aerial spraying of the pesticide malathion. Critics of Brown's leadership in the crisis contended that his belated approval of aerial spraying had needlessly endangered California's agricultural future. State officials, however, hoped to proclaim the medfly eradicated by the fall of 1982.

For decades the dumping of toxic substances from industrial and chemical plants in California and elsewhere went uncontrolled and largely unnoticed. As the wastes began to leach into the surrounding soil and water supply and to release noxious fumes into the atmosphere, they became serious health hazards. One such dump in Fullerton, site of a newly completed housing project, was found to be emitting toxic vapors from chemicals capable of causing cancer and damaging the liver, respiratory tract, and central nervous system. In 1972 the legislature passed the Hazardous Waste Control Act, establishing regulations governing the handling, processing, and disposal of dangerous wastes.

Governor Brown in 1980 labeled the control of toxic wastes "the number one environmental issue of the decade" and signed legislation to regulate further the use and disposal of dangerous chemicals and other toxic substances. In signing the bill Brown described it as "the boldest action program to control toxic waste anywhere in the country." The following year, however, a report of the state auditor general charged that the state's hazardous waste control program was largely a failure, characterized by inefficiency, lack of direction, and virtually no enforcement of toxic-waste laws.

THE ENERGY CRISIS

The Arab oil embargo and the rapid quadrupling of the price of oil in the winter of 1973–1974 confronted California and the nation with a startling new crisis. Within the space of a few weeks the Organization of Petroleum Exporting Countries (OPEC) increased the price of a barrel of crude oil from $2.41 to $10.95, and over the next decade continued to push the price steadily higher. By the fall of 1981 OPEC's price for a barrel of crude had risen to $34.

During the middle decades of the twentieth century Americans had enjoyed the luxury of an abundant supply of cheap oil, primarily from domestic sources. Cheap gasoline fueled the legions of California's automobiles and spurred construction of its freeways and suburbs. Petroleum-based plastics, synthetic fibers, and fertilizers became essential parts of the California economy. In 1970, however, domestic oil production peaked, and the nation began to rely on ever-greater supplies of foreign oil. By 1980 the United States was importing about half of the oil it consumed, whereas a decade earlier only a quarter of its supplies came from abroad. The cost of imported oil had increased twentyfold, from $3 billion a year to $60 billion.

The increased dependence on foreign oil and the drastic rise in oil prices had an enormous impact on the nation and the state. California depended upon petroleum for about 60 percent of its total energy supply; by 1981 the state was consuming 1.9 million barrels of oil per day. The most visible register of rising oil prices was at the gasoline pump, where the average price of a gallon of regular rose from 68 cents in 1978 to a peak of $1.35 three years later. Since the largest share of California's electricity was generated at oil- and gas-fired power plants, utility bills also grew at an alarming rate. The soaring price of petroleum contributed to two economic recessions and helped propel inflation to the highest sustained levels in the peacetime history of the nation.

The energy crisis was not a crisis of diminishing energy sources, it was a crisis of diminishing supplies of cheap foreign oil. The solution to the crisis lay in the development of new sources of energy. Such development, however, became a matter of controversy when it threatened newly gained environmental safeguards. In an effort to increase domestic supplies of petroleum, Interior Secretary James Watt proposed in 1981 the opening of four basins off the northern California coast to oil drilling. He encountered stiff opposition to his proposal from environmentalists, representatives of the state's tourism and fishing industries, and local and state government officials. Opponents feared that an oil spill from an offshore rig would devastate the north coast, just as the 1969 spill had fouled the beaches of Santa Barbara. When the state's Republican leadership also warned Watt that his unpopular proposal would hurt the chances of Republican candidates in the 1982 state elections, Watt announced that the four basins would be exempted from drilling in the foreseeable future. Later Watt opened virtually the entire central and northern California coast to potential oil and gas exploration.

Controversy also erupted over a plan to ship additional supplies of natural gas to California. By the late 1970s California was using natural gas to meet about 30 percent of its total energy needs, but utility officials warned that unless new supplies were developed, the state would soon face a critical natural gas shortage. The Southern California Gas Company and PG&E joined forces in a multibillion dollar project to import liquefied natural gas (LNG) from Indonesia and Alaska to a terminal on a remote stretch of coastline near Point Conception.

The Point Conception terminal was opposed by a diverse group of environmentalists, local property owners, the Air Force, and a contingent of California Indians. Critics contended that frequent poor weather conditions at the site would make the docking of LNG-laden supertankers a hazardous proposition and that a vapor cloud from an LNG spill could travel inland several miles and ignite in an enormous fireball. Several earthquake faults in the vicinity posed additional hazards. The Air Force feared that debris from missiles launched at its nearby Vandenburg test center could rain down on tanks holding the volatile gas. (The Air Force eventually dropped its opposition when the utilities agreed to assume all financial risks in the event an accident was caused by missile debris.) Indian groups pressed legal action and briefly occupied the proposed terminal site, arguing that construction of the terminal would desecrate land which, according to Chumash tradition, was the "Western Gate" through which new life entered the world and the dead departed. By 1981 federal and state agencies had overruled most of these objections and were prepared to approve the site, with the proviso that the terminal be built to strict seismic safety standards.

NUCLEAR POWER

In the early 1960s energy planners blithely predicted that by the end of the century nuclear power would be able to supply half of the nation's energy needs and would be "too cheap to meter." Twenty years later that prospect had dimmed considerably.

The nation's first licensed commercial nuclear reactor began operations in 1957 at Vallecitos in Alameda County. Six years later PG&E activated a second California reactor at Humboldt Bay, a plant plagued by malfunctions and frequent shutdowns after it was found to be releasing excessive amounts of radioactive vapors. The first large-scale nuclear facility in California, the San Onofre plant located halfway between Los Angeles and San Diego, began operations in 1968 and by 1980 was providing Southern California Edison with 4 percent of its energy supply. In northern California the Rancho Seco plant near Sacramento went "on line" in 1975, but a series of breakdowns kept it from operating at full capacity.

Opposition to nuclear power arose out of concern for the safe disposal of radioactive wastes produced by the plants, which remain potentially lethal for thousands of years. Opponents also feared the disastrous consequences of an accident at a nuclear plant. As early as 1957 the Atomic Energy Commission had estimated that an accident at a small reactor would cause 3400 deaths, 43,000 cases of acute illness, and $7 billion in property damage. The likelihood of such an accident was small, but its effects would be devastating.

In 1976 environmental groups placed on the ballot an initiative, Proposition 15, calling for a system of safeguards against possible catastrophes at nuclear plants and against the danger of faulty disposal of radioactive wastes. Almost every major corporation in the energy industry denounced the measure, arguing that it would effectively block all future development of nuclear power in the state. The voters defeated Proposition 15 by two to one, but in the meantime the vigorous campaign in favor of it had aroused the legislature to adopt a plan of less extreme but quite substantial increases in nuclear safeguards. The new plan prohibited the California Energy Commission, formed in 1975, from authorizing construction of any further nuclear plants until the federal government had approved "a documented technology for the disposal of high-level nuclear waste." Acting under this mandate the Energy Commission denied permission to the San Diego Gas and Electric Company to construct its proposed $3 billion Sundesert nuclear reactor in Riverside County.

The nuclear power industry suffered a crippling blow in March 1979 when the Three Mile Island plant near Harrisburg, Pennsylvania, experienced a near meltdown of its nuclear core, the most catastrophic of possible accidents. Further development of nuclear power in the United States came to a virtual standstill.

Perhaps the biggest victim of the Three Mile Island accident was the massive 2200-megawatt nuclear plant built for PG&E at Diablo Canyon near San Luis Obispo. (One megawatt equals 1000 kilowatts, enough power to supply the electricity needs of about 1000 residential customers.) Construction of the Diablo Canyon plant began in 1969 and was nearly complete when PG&E reported the discovery of a major offshore earthquake fault. After extensive new buttresses and other safeguards were added, the federal Nuclear Regulatory Commission was on the verge of granting the plant an operating license in 1979 when the Three Mile Island accident raised new questions about safety and stalled further the licensing process.

In 1981 a coalition of environmental and antinuclear organizations known as the Abalone Alliance attempted to blockade the entrances to the plant. The demonstration was nonviolent and 1600 protesters were arrested. Finally, in September 1981, the Nuclear Regulatory Commission announced it was granting PG&E a permit to load fuel and begin low-power testing of the plant. Within days of the announcement, however, it was discovered that wrong diagrams had been used to design and build seismic safety supports in the reactor containment building. Additional design errors were uncovered in subsequent reviews, the testing permit was revoked, and the opening of the plant was further delayed.

The Diablo Canyon nuclear power plant. *(Courtesy of Pacific Gas and Electric Company.)*

Supporters of Diablo Canyon discounted the importance of the design errors and pointed to the need to get the plant on line as soon as possible. Power generated by the plant would offset the burning of 20 million barrels of oil a year. PG&E estimated that the $2.3 billion plant would add almost 20 percent to the company's total generating capacity and help provide the power necessary to meet future energy needs.

ALTERNATIVE SOURCES

Governor Jerry Brown believed that the long-term solution to the energy crisis lay in the more efficient use of traditional energy supplies and the development of a variety of "alternative sources" such as solar and wind power.

Brown's emphasis on energy efficiency took practical form in a series of orders and tax credits which, taken together, amounted to the most sweeping program of energy conservation in the nation. The California Department of Transportation (CalTrans) promoted a variety of projects—ride sharing, park-and-ride lots, exclusive bus and carpool lanes—to increase the energy efficiency of the state highway system. The California Energy Commission set maximum energy consumption limits for new household appliances sold in the state and established the nation's most stringent energy conservation standards for new residential and commercial buildings. In 1980 the legislature authorized a 40 percent income tax credit to homeowners for installation of energy-saving devices such as weather stripping and timer thermostats. Perhaps most promising of all, the state Public Utilities Commission (PUC) in 1981 authorized utility companies to provide interest-free loans to their residential customers for energy conservation measures. Under the "Zero Interest

Plan," homeowners could obtain financing for such things as thermal windows or insulation and repay the loan through their monthly utility bills.

California also led the nation in the development of alternative sources of energy. With an average of 270 days of sunshine a year, the state had more than 40 percent of the total United States solar collector capacity. The winds off the Pacific coastline represented an enormous energy potential, and the volatile geology of the state provided California with the nation's largest geothermal resources. In 1981 renewable and alternative energy sources met less than 5 percent of California's total energy needs, but the Energy Commission estimated that by the year 2000 these sources could be providing more than 20 percent of California's energy supply. According to Energy Commission projections, the expansion of conservation efforts coupled with accelerated development of alternative energy sources could eliminate the need for foreign oil imports in California during most of the 1990s.

The technology for converting sunlight into electricity, through photovoltaic cells, was still in the experimental stage, but the use of solar energy for water and space heating was a relatively simple matter. The PUC calculated that if 80 percent of all residential water heaters in the state were fitted with solar systems, the energy savings would be equivalent to more than 21 million barrels of oil per year. To encourage homeowners to switch to solar power the state authorized a 55 percent income tax credit, the highest in the nation, for solar installation. On the local level San Diego, Santa Barbara, and Santa Clara counties became the first in the country to require solar water heating in new residential construction. Altogether there were over 70,000 solar installations in California between 1976 and 1981. In spite of these gains, the widespread acceptance of solar energy still faced such barriers as initial high installation costs, financing, and consumer confidence.

The motion of wind and water presented California with additional renewable, nonpolluting sources of energy. By the late 1970s virtually all the high-quality hydroelectric sites in the state were exhausted, but Governor Brown in 1980 called for the construction of several hundred small hydroelectric generating plants at existing dams and canals throughout the state. In 1978 the legislature passed a wind energy bill which set a goal of meeting 10 percent of California's projected electricity needs with wind power by the year 2000. Southern California Edison inaugurated the state's first commercial wind turbine generator in 1980. This monster windmill, located just northwest of Palm Springs, stood nearly 200 feet high and had a generating capacity of 3000 kilowatts. The following year PG&E announced plans for the world's largest wind energy project. The "wind farm" of 146 windmills in the rolling hills of Solano County was designed to supply enough electricity for 150,000 homes when completed in 1989.

In 1960 the nation's first commercial geothermal power plant began operations at The Geysers in Sonoma County, where superheated steam released at the earth's surface was fed to turbines to generate electricity. By 1981 PG&E had 15 geothermal plants in operation with a total output of more than 900 megawatts of power, representing enough electricity to meet the needs of a

Resembling a propeller from a giant aircraft, Southern California Edison's wind turbine generator began commercial operation in 1980. *(Courtesy of Southern California Edison Company.)*

city nearly the size of San Francisco. Geothermal resources elsewhere in California—notably in the Imperial Valley, along the eastern Sierra, and in the northeastern part of the state—boosted the total geothermal energy potential of the state to 15,000 megawatts. Another important alternative source of energy was cogeneration, the use of waste heat, steam, or gases from an industrial plant for the generation of electricity. Used in Europe for decades, cogeneration only recently attracted much attention in the United States. In 1979 cogeneration represented only about 1 percent of the state's electric power production. The PUC, however, adopted an aggressive policy and ordered the state's utilities to offer incentives to their large industrial customers so that they could profitably produce their own electricity.

One of the major points of contention between the proponents of conservation and alternative sources and those who favored construction of large central power plants was the size of future energy demand in the state. Throughout the 1970s the major utilities predicted a high rate of growth and frequently asserted that unless new plants were constructed, California would face serious energy shortages. Typical of this attitude was the remark of one utility official that, "If people believe that conservation is going to eliminate the need for new power plants, they are just deluding themselves." On the other hand, environmentalists and many state planners argued that energy demand in California would grow only slightly and that increased conservation and development of renewable energy sources would make unnecessary the construction of any more large power plants in the state.

By the early 1980s several developments had worked together to change the attitude of the utilities. The policies of the Energy Commission and PUC, combining penalties and incentives to win compliance, began to have some effect. Central power plants also grew so expensive and needed such a long time to complete that they came to entail unacceptable financial risks for the utilities. The cost of constructing a major oil-fired power plant in 1980 was more than five times what it had been in 1970. The cost of a typical nuclear power plant climbed to well over $1 billion, and its average construction time increased to more than 12 years.

The most remarkable development affecting the utilities was a fundamental reduction in the growth of energy demand. The consumption of electricity in California grew regularly at an annual rate of 7 or 8 percent before the Arab oil embargo of 1973 but averaged only about 3 percent afterward. Higher prices and lower demand also produced, in the early 1980s, a nationwide glut of natural gas. Likewise, gasoline consumption was reduced by the introduction of more fuel-efficient vehicles and by a reduction in the number of miles driven by the typical California motorist.

The effect of these combined developments was readily apparent on the state's utilities. In 1980 PG&E withdrew its financial support from major components of the Point Conception LNG project and, citing lower-than-expected demand and staggering new costs, announced it was dropping or postponing the construction of several large electric generating plants. In announcing these changes in policy, a utility official observed that conservation measures had proved so successful that "we now consider conservation as another energy resource." Southern California Edison also postponed construction of two major plants it had expected to build, and in 1980 it became the first major utility in the nation to commit itself to large-scale development of alternative energy sources. The utility projected that by 1990 it would meet about 30 percent of its additional electricity needs from energy supplied by such sources as wind, solar, and geothermal power and by cogeneration. "It is the policy of Edison," said William R. Gould, chief executive of the utility, "to devote our corporate resources to the accelerated development of a wide variety of future electric power sources which are renewable rather than finite."

The energy crisis had wrought fundamental changes in the lives of many Californians and in the California economy. As petroleum prices escalated, Californians reduced their consumption of energy and developed alternative sources. Having entered the era of limits, Californians found that their own resolve and imagination were two resources in unlimited supply.

SELECTED BIBLIOGRAPHY

Ann Ehrlich, Paul Ehrlich, and John Holdren, *Ecoscience* (1977), is a useful introduction to a wide range of environmental problems. Ed Salzman (ed.), *California Environment and Energy* (1980) contains a collection of articles from the *California Journal* on contemporary California issues. For historical background see Raymond F. Dasmann, *The Destruction of California* (1965), *California's Changing Environment* (1981), and "Environmental History," an edition of the *Pacific Historical Review*, XLI (August 1972). The environmentalist viewpoint is represented in such periodicals as *Cry California, Not Man Apart,* and the Sierra Club's *National News Report.* For a critique of the environmental movement see Bernard J. Frieden, *The Environmental Hustle* (1979).

The coastal issue is examined in Stanley Scott, *Governing California's Coast* (1975), and Scott (ed.), *Coastal Conservation: Essays on Experiments in Governance* (1981). On the issues of land use and conservation see Robert C. Fellmeth et al., *Power and Land in California* (1971), condensed as *Politics of Land* (1973), produced by Ralph Nader's organization. Ted K. Bradshaw and Edward J. Blakely, *The Rural Community in the Advanced Industrial Society* (1980) examines in depth California's changing rural communities as they are affected by new population growth.

The California Water Atlas (1980) is a monumental collection of maps and text illustrating the development of state water resources. For background on the Peripheral Canal issue see W. Turrentine Jackson and Alan M. Patterson, *The Sacramento-San Joaquin Delta: The Evolution and Implementation of Water Policy* (1977) and Elizabeth Johnson, "The Delta Canal, Anything but a Peripheral Issue," *California Journal*, XI (October 1980), pp. 376-378. See also W. Turrentine Jackson and Stephen D. Mikesell, *The Stanislaus River Drainage Basin and the New Melones Dam: Historical Evolution of Water Use Priorities* (1979).

State and federal efforts to reduce smog may be followed in James E. Krier and Edmund Ursin, *Pollution and Policy: A Case Essay on California and Federal Experience with Motor Vehicle Air Pollution, 1940-1975* (1977).

Raymond Vernon, *The Oil Crisis* (1976), contains a discussion of the national and international aspects of the escalation of OPEC prices. On the controversy over nuclear power, see Hal Rubin, "Guide to Nuclear Power in California," *California Journal*, X (June 1979), pp. 200-207; John W. Gofman and Arthur Tamplin, *Poisoned Power* (1971); Joseph Castrovinci, "Nuclear Power: Arguments for the Defense," *San Francisco Business*, XIV (April 1979), pp. 12-14; and *The Three Mile Island Nuclear Power Plant Accident and Its Implications for California* (1979), a report by the Assembly Committee on Resources, Land Use, and Energy. The energy potential of conservation and alternative renewal resources is described in Robert Stobaugh and Daniel Yergin (eds.), *Energy Future* (1979); Jennifer K. Hollon, *Solar Energy for California's Residential Sector: Progress, Problems, and Prospects* (1980); Hal Rubin, "Woodchips and Windmills," *California Journal*, VII (June 1978), pp. 187-189; and Mary Ellen Leary, "Conserving Energy, California Style," *California Journal*, XI (June 1980), pp. 219-223. For a full assessment of public policy affecting California energy use, see *Energy Tomorrow: Challenges and Opportunities for California* (1981), the biennial report of the California Energy Commission.

INDEX

Abalone Alliance, 507
Abstract expressionism, 451–453
Adams & Company, failure of, 160
Adler, Kurt Herbert, 459
Admission as a state, 98, 99, 102, 105–106
Aerospace industry, 430–432, 453–455
AFL (American Federation of Labor), 212, 219, 404–405
Agnew, Spiro T., 475
Agricultural labor, 54, 142, 220–223, 399–408, 410, 450
Agricultural Labor Relations Board (ALRB), 407–408, 480
Agricultural Relations Act (1975), 407–408, 480
Agricultural Workers Organizing Committee, 405–408
Agriculture, 3, 5, 162–163, 199–208, 396–408, 504
Ahmanson, Howard S., 468
Air pollution, 455, 485, 499–501
Aircraft industry, 359–361
Albertson, James, 452
Alcatraz Island, Indian occupation of (1969–1971), 412
Alemany, Joseph S., 155, 242
Alien Land Law (1913), 279–281, 413
All-American Canal, 332, 328
Allen, Lawrence, 344–345
Allen, Willis, 344–345
Alta California (newspaper), 117, 146, 152
Altamont, rock concert at (1969), 461
Alvarado, Juan Bautista, 46, 49, 51–53, 65, 66
American Civil Liberties Union (ACLU), 341
American Express Company, 160
American Federation of Labor (AFL), 212, 219, 404–405
American Indian Historical Society, 412
American Legion, 369
American Medical Association (AMA), 382

American party, 107, 121
"American Plan" for open shop, 292
Ames, John J., 148
Anderson, Gilbert M., 307
Anti-Saloon League, 275
Antle, Bud, 406
Anza, Juan Bautista de, 28–32
Arbuckle, Roscoe ("Fatty"), 311
Architecture, 64, 238–239, 359–362, 456–458
Arenas, Lee, 411
Argonaut (magazine), 228
Argüello, Concepción, 41
Armour, Richard, 493
Aronson, Max, 307–308
Art, 235–238, 357–358, 451–456
Associated Farmers of California, 351–352, 400–401
Associated Oil Company, 302
Atherton, Gertrude, 228, 423
Atomic Energy Commission, 507
Austin, Mary, 228
Australian ballot, 254
Automobile Club of Southern California, 304
Automobiles and "automobile culture," 304–307, 312, 432, 454, 499–500
Avery, Russ, 264
Avila, José María, 49
Ayala, Juan Miguel de, 30
Ayres, Thomas B., 236

"Bad" painting, 452
Baker, Edward D., 109–111, 121
Baldwin, Elias Jackson ("Lucky"), 186
Bancroft, George, 71, 75, 78
Bancroft, Hubert Howe, 95, 102, 114, 131, 232–234, 236
Bandini, Juan, 46
Bandini, Maria, 63

Bank of America (formerly Bank of Italy), 295, 398
Bank of California, 184–186
Banking, regulation of, 252, 272, 295
Banning, Phineas, 163
Barclay, John S., 119–120
Bard, Thomas R., 300, 411
Barstow, David P., 119
BART (Bay Area Rapid Transit) District, 433
Bartleson, John, 65–66
Bartlett, Washington Allon, 86
Bassett, J. M., 248
Baxter, Leone, 381–382, 393
Bay Area figurative painters, 452
Bay Area Rapid Transit (BART) District, 433
Bay Cities Water Company, 318
Beach Boys, 460
Beale, Edward F., 88, 138–140
Bean, J. H., 119
Bear Flag Revolt (1846), 76–78
"Beatniks," 447
Becket, Welton, 457
Beerstecher, Charles J., 196
Bell, Larry, 453, 455
Bell, Theodore A., 266, 268
Bellamy, Edward, 255, 286
Bengston, Billy Al, 453
Benton, Thomas Hart, 71, 73, 74, 81
Berdue, Thomas, 116
Berkeley, George, 240
Better America Federation, Los Angeles, 293
Biddle, Francis, 371
Bidwell, John, 65–66
Bierce, Ambrose, 227–229
Bierstadt, Albert, 236, 455
"Big Four," 164–174, 177–180, 245–253
Bigelow, Harden, 128
Bigler, John, 107, 149
Billings, Warren K., 288–289, 345
Biograph (film company), 308
Bird, Rose Elizabeth, 480, 490–491
Birth of a Nation (film), 310
Black, Jeremiah, 130–131
Black Panther Party, 429, 441–443, 450
Blacks:
    constitution of 1849 and, 101–102, 105
    literature by, 449–450
    oppression of, 142–143
    among original settlers, 33
    in the twentieth century, 366, 415–420, 441–443
    (See also names of individuals)
"Bloody Thursday" (1934), 340
Bonneville, Benjamin, 62, 74
Booth, Newton, 254
Borica, Diego de, 39–40, 54
Bouchard, Hippolyte de, 43, 62
Boulder Canyon Project, 321–325
Boundaries, state, 102–103
Braceros, 401–403
Bradley, Thomas, 420

Branciforte, Villa de, 39
Brannan, Samuel, 85–88, 115–118, 203
Brautigan, Richard, 447
Bridges, Harry R., 339–340
Broderick, David C., 106–109, 120
Brooklyn (ship), 86
Brown, Edmund G. "Pat," 388–393, 429, 437, 464–466, 475, 478, 502
Brown, Edmund G., Jr., "Jerry":
    background, 478–479
    governor, 407, 422, 424–425, 478–482, 486–488, 492–493, 502–504, 508, 509
    presidential candidate, 480, 482–485
Brown, Joan, 452
Brown, Willie L., Jr., 420
Brown v. Board of Education of Topeka (1954) (school integration), 418
Browne, J. Ross, 142
Brubeck, Dave, 460
Bryan, William Jennings, 280
Bryant and Sturgis, 58
Bryce, James, 245, 257
Bucareli, Antonio de, 29–32
Buchanan, James, 72
Buckley, Chris, "Blind Boss," 255
Budd, James H., 251, 255
Buffum, E. Gould, 115
"Bull Moose" party, 273–274, 281–283
Burbank, Luther, 396
Bureau of Reclamation, U.S., 329, 331
Burke, Yvonne Brathwaite, 420
Burlingame, Anson, 184, 188
Burlingame Treaty (1868), 177, 188
Burnett, Peter H., 104, 137, 140, 142
Burnham, Daniel Hudson, 359
Burns, William J., 218, 261
Burr, Aaron, 257
Butler, Anthony, 70
Butterfield, John, 164

Cabrillo, Juan Rodríguez, 12–13
Caen, Herb, 447
Cage, John, 458
Cahuenga Pass, battles of, 49, 52
Calhoun, Patrick, 261–262
California and the Civil War, 110–111
California Coastal Commission, 496
California Colored Convention, 168
California Council on Economic and Environmental Balance, 496
California Democratic Council, 387, 393
California Department of Transportation (CalTrans), 508
California dream (popular image of the state), 355, 448
California Energy Commission, 481, 508–509, 511
California Environmental Quality Act (1970), 496
California Farm Bureau, 502, 504

California Fruit Growers' Exchange, 202–203
California Indian Education Association, 412
California Institute of the Arts (Cal Arts), 455
California Institute of Technology (Cal Tech), 431
California Journal, 492
California Labor Federation, 496
California Medical Association, 379, 382
California Packing Corporation (CalPac), 397–398
"California ranch" style of architecture, 456
California Real Estate Association, 416–417
California Republican Assembly, 387
California School of Fine Arts, 451–452
"California sound" (popular music style), 460–461
California Star, 85, 87–88, 146
California Steam Navigation Company, 171, 179
Californian, 87, 146
Cameron, George C., 357
Caminetti, Anthony J., 206, 277, 280
Campaign for Economic Democracy, 444
Campaign management firms, 381–382, 386
Canby, E. R. S., 141
Canfield, Charles A., 301
Cannery and Agricultural Workers' Industrial Union, 338–339
Capital punishment, 390
Carmichael, Stokely, 441
Carpentier, Horace W., 177
Carrillo, José Antonio, 46, 49, 52, 100
Carrillo, Josefa, 63
Carson, James H., 87
Carson, Kit, 75, 80
Carter, Jimmy, 476, 480–486, 496
Casey, James P., 120–121
Castro, José, 46, 51, 52, 73, 75, 76, 79
Central Pacific Railroad, 166–174, 177–179
Central Valley Project, 328–332, 503
Century (magazine), 316
Chabot, Anthony J., 158
Chaffey, George, 207–208, 321
Chandler, Dorothy Buffum, 424, 457, 459
Chandler, Harry, 323, 357, 367
Chandler, Norman, 357, 424
Chandler, Otis, 357
Chaney, William H., 231
Chaplin, Charles, 307
Chapman, Joseph, 62
Chapman (ship), 110
Chavez, Cesar, 405–408, 480, 481
Chicanos (*see* Mexicans and Mexican Americans)
Chico, Mariano, 51
Chinese and Chinese Americans:
    discrimination against in gold rush, 134–136
    exclusion of, 197, 414
    immigration of, 177, 188–190
    literature by, 450–451

Chinese and Chinese Americans (*Cont.*):
    political movements against, 188–190, 195, 278
    railroad construction workers, 172–174
    in twentieth century, 414–415
    (*See also names of individuals*)
Chouinard, Nelbert, 358
Chouinard Art Institute, 358, 453, 455
Churriguera, José, 361
Ciampi, Mario J., 455
Citizens for the Republic, 476, 486
Civil War, California and, 110–111
Clapp, Louise Amelia Knapp Smith ("Dame Shirley"), 147–148
Clark, George T., 252
Clark, William, 486
Clark, Williams Andrews, Jr., 358
Clean Air Act (1970), 499–500
Cleaver, Eldridge, 442–444
Clemens, Samuel L., 151
Cleveland, Richard, 58
Clipper ships, 90
Coal, 163, 301
Coalinga oil field, 301
Cogeneration of electricity, 510
Coleman, William Tell, 117, 118, 121–122, 163, 191
Colleges and universities, 154–155, 239–242, 435–440
    (*See also specific colleges and universities*)
Collins, Sam, 379
Coloma, gold discovery at, 84–85
Colorado River Aqueduct, 327–328
Colorado River Compact, 321–323
Colton, David D., 246–247, 249, 254
Colton, Ellen M., 246–247
Colton, Walter, 87, 99, 100, 146
Colton letters, 246–247, 249
Columbia Pictures, 312
Commission of Immigration and Housing, 278
Communism, 291, 338, 339, 351, 383–385, 393
Communist Labor Party, 291
Comstock, Henry Tompkins Paige, 161
Comstock lode, 151, 157, 160–162, 184–186, 190
Cone, Joseph S., 196
Conrad, Paul, 469–470
Conservation and use of natural resources, 314–317, 495–505
Consolidated Virginia mine, 185–186, 190
Consolidated Vultee (Convair), 368
Consolidation Act, San Francisco, 124
Constitutions:
    1849, 99–105
    1879, 191–196, 226, 252, 423, 437
Contra Costa Canal, 329–331
Contract and Finance Company, 174, 178
Cook, James, 38
Coolbrith, Ina, 154
Coolidge, Calvin, 294, 323

Cooper, John, 63
Coppola, Francis Ford, 483
Cora, Charles, 121–122
Corley, James H., 385
Cortés, Hernan, 11–12
Costansó, Miguel, 23, 24
Costo, Rupert, 412
Cranston, Alan, 472
Crédit Mobilier, 174
Creel, George, 341, 343
Crespi, Juan, 22–26
Criminal Syndicalism Law (1919), 290–292, 339
Crocker, Charles, 168, 171–173, 192
Crocker, Edwin B., 171, 236
Crocker, William H., 282–283, 358
Crocker Art Gallery, 236
Croix, Teodoro de, 34
Cross-filing, 273, 378, 379, 390
Crow, Walter J., 183
Cullinan, Eustace, 329
Cunningham, Kate Richards O'Hare, 424
Curb, Mike, 482, 483

Daggett, Rollin M., 147
"Dame Shirley," 147–148
Dana, Richard Henry, 54, 59, 63, 214
Dana, William Goodwin, 62–63
Darrow, Clarence, 219
Dart, Justin, 464
Darwin, Charles, 226, 231
Davenport, Homer, 250
Davenport, J. R., 264
Davies, Louise M., Symphony Hall, 459
Davies, Marion, 356
Davis, Arthur Powell, 322
Davis, John W., 293
Day, Mollie, 228
"Dear Pard" letters, 246, 248
Debs, Eugene V., 287
Deidesheimer, Philip, 161
Delano, Alonzo ("Old Block"), 148
Dellums, Ronald V., 420
Delta-Mendota Canal, 329–331
deMille, Cecil B., 309–311
De Quille, Dan, 151–152
Derby, George H. ("John Phoenix"), 148
Deukmejian, George, 420
Dewey Thomas E., 379
DeWitt, John L., 369–371, 373
de Young, Charles, 196, 234
de Young, M. H., 234, 252, 357
    Memorial Museum, 358, 456
Diablo Canyon nuclear power plant, 507–508
Dickerson, G. D., 160
Dickson, Edward A., 264, 266, 267, 283
Didion, Joan, 448–449
Diebenkorn, Richard, 452
Dies, Martin, 384
Di Giorgio Corporation, 406

Direct Legislation League, 263–264
Direct primary, 266, 267
Disney, Walt, 455
Disneyland, 457
Dixon, Thomas, 310
Dodge, Grenville M., 174
Doheny, Edward L., 294, 300, 303
Dollar, Robert, 288
Donner party, 67
Dorr, Ebenezer, 57–58
Douglas, Donald, 367–368
Douglas, Helen Gahagan, 384, 424, 463
Dow Chemical Company, 481
Downey, Sheridan, 345
Drake, Francis, 13–16
Duels, 104, 108–109
Dulles, John Foster, 384, 392
Duncan, Robert, 446
Durán, Narcisco, 51, 61
Durst, Ralph, 222–223, 277
Dust bowl migration, 352–353, 400–401
Dwinelle, John W., 240
Dymally, Mervyn, 420, 482

E Clampus Vitus, 96
Earl, Edwin T., 264, 283, 286, 320
Eaton, Fred, 319–320
Echeandía, José Maria, 48, 49, 60, 61
Edison, Thomas A., and movies, 307–308
Edson, Katherine Philips, 275, 277, 424
Education:
    and campus turmoil, 436–440
    constitution of 1849 and, 103
    before 1846, 54–55
    since 1900, 435–436
    to 1900, 154–155, 239–242
    segregation in, 278, 418–419
    student attitudes toward, 443
    (See also Colleges and universities)
Edwards v. South Carolina (1963) (free speech on college campus), 437
Eisenhower, Dwight D., 379, 388, 392, 463
Electric railways in Los Angeles, 209–210
Electricity, cogeneration of, 510
Eliot, T. S., 350
Elk Hills naval oil reserve, 303–304
Emerson, Ralph Waldo, 315
End Poverty in California (EPIC), 341–344
Endo v. United States (1944) (Japanese "relocation"), 374
Energy crisis, 505–511
Enerson, Burnham, 468
Englehardt, Zephyrin, 37
Environment, concern for, 314–317, 495–505
Environmental Protection Agency (EPA), 499–501
Equal rights amendment (ERA), 426
Eshleman, John M., 271, 282, 283
Essanay Film Manufacturing Company, 307–308

Estanislao (Miwok leader), 48
Eu, March Fong, 415, 424
Everson, William, 446
"Excess land law" (*see* Newlands, Francis G., and Reclamation Act of 1902)

Fages, Pedro, 23, 26, 28, 40
Fair Political Practices Commission, 479
Fall, Albert B., 294, 303
Fantus Company, 481
Faulkner, William, 350, 354
Feather River Project, 390–391
"Federal Plan" of reapportionment (1926), 296–297
Feinstein, Dianne, 424
Felton, Charles N., 302
Fennimore, James, 161
Ferlinghetti, Lawrence, 447
Fickert, Charles M., 262, 289
Fiedler, Bobbi, 424
Field, Stephen J., 189, 252, 253, 291
Figueroa, José, 48–51, 54–55
Filipinos, 415
Fitzpatrick, Thomas ("Broken Hand"), 66
Flag of California, 77
Flint, Timothy, 62
Flood, James C., 185, 186
Flores, José Maria, 79, 80
Flournoy, Houston, 479
Flying Cloud (ship), 90
Foltz, Clara Shortridge, 274
Fontana, Mark J., 397
Forbes, Alexander, 71
Ford, Gerald R., 475, 476
Ford, Henry, 304
Ford, Richard ("Blackie"), 223
Ford, Tirey L., 261
Foreign miners' license tax, 133–134
Foster, Stephen C. (mayor of Los Angeles), 119
Fox, William, 309
Francis, Sam, 452
Free speech movements, 222–223
   at Berkeley (1964), 437–438, 464, 467, 486
Frémont, Jessie Benton, 73, 74, 81–82, 128, 150
Frémont, John Charles, 60, 67, 73–82, 128, 130
Fresno Morning Republican, 266
Friant Dam and Friant-Kern Canal, 329–331
Friends of the River, 503
Fuller, Varden, 404
Funding bill, 249–251
"Funk art," 452
Furuseth, Andrew, 215

Galbraith, John Kenneth, 493
Gale, William A., 58
Gálvez, José de, 19–21, 22, 34
Gann, Paul, 481, 487–489

Garcés, Francisco, 21, 35
Gayley, Charles Mills, 241
Gebhard, David, 457
General Electric Company, 463
General strike, San Francisco (1934), 339–340
George, Henry, 131, 225–227
Geothermal power, 509–510
Getty, J. Paul, Museum, 449, 455, 457
Getty Oil Company, 501
Giannini, Amadeo Peter, 295, 398
Giannini, Lawrence Mario, 385, 398
Gilbert, George S., 299
Gill, Irving, 361–362
Gillespie, Archibald, 75, 77, 79
Gillett, James N., 265
Gilman, Charlotte Perkins, 423
Gilman, Daniel Coit, 240–241
Gilmore, Earl B., 305
Gilroy, John, 62
Ginsberg, Allen, 446–447, 452
Gitelson, Alfred, 418
Glenn, Hugh J., 199–200
Godoy, Manuel, 42
Gold discovery:
   at Coloma, 84–85
   Placerita Creek (1842), 84
Golden Era (literary magazine), 147, 150
Golden Gate National Recreation Area, 496
Goldwater, Barry, 393–394, 463–464, 468–470, 485
Goldwyn, Samuel, 309
Gompers, Samuel, 219
Good Government League, Los Angeles, 262–264, 277
Goodhue, Bertram, 361
Goodyear Tire and Rubber Company, 328
Gordon, Laura De Force, 274, 423
Gould, William R., 511
Graft prosecution in San Francisco, 259–262, 265
Graham, Isaac, 51, 66
Granger movement, 194–196, 254
Greed (movie), 310
Green, Duff, 72
Green, Thomas Jefferson, 101, 105, 133
Greenback Labor Party, 230
Greene, Charles, 360–361
Greene, Henry, 360–361
Griffith, David Wark, 308, 310
Grigsby, John, 67, 76
Grosh, Ethan Allen, 161
Grosh, Hoseah Bellow, 161
Guadaloupe Hidalgo, Treaty of, 82, 131
Gutiérrez, Nicolas, 51
Gwin, William M., 100–104, 106–109, 129, 138, 160

Haight, Raymond L., 344
Haight-Ashbury district, San Francisco, 441, 448, 449, 461

Haldeman, H. R., 393
Hale, Edward Everett, 11–12
Halleck, Henry W., 102, 103, 128
Hallidie, Andrew L., 209
"Ham 'n Eggs" (pension plan), 344–345
Hanna, E. J., 292
Haraszthy, Agoston, 201
Harding, Warren G., 293
Harpending, Asbury, 110
Harriman, Edward H., 209–219, 262, 267
Harriman, Job, 287, 324
Harris v. Younger (1968) (criminal syndicalism law), 386
Hart, Mills D., 183
Harte, Bret, 42, 147, 149–151
Hartnell, William E. P., 52, 55, 58
Haskell, Burnette G., 213–215, 286, 316
Hastings, Lansford W., 67, 91
Hatfield, Charles M., 328
Hawkins, Augustus, 420
Hayakawa, S. I., 414, 444
Hayden, Tom, 438, 444
Hayes, Janet Gray, 424, 497
Haynes, John Randolph, 263–264, 266
Hays, Will H., 312
Hazardous Waste Control Act (1972), 504
Health insurance, 284
Hearst, Catherine Campbell, 424
Hearst, George, 234, 255
Hearst, Patricia, 449
Hearst, Phoebe Apperson, 355, 359
Hearst, William Randolph, 218, 228, 234, 265–266, 291, 340, 355–357
Helper, Hinton R., 96
Hendrix, Jimi, 461
Heney, Francis J., 260–262, 267, 280, 282, 284
Henshaw, Frederick W., 265
Herrin, William F., 253–254, 262, 265, 268, 271, 380
Hetch Hetchy controversy and San Francisco's water supply, 317–319, 324
Hichborn, Franklin, 295
Hidalgo, Miguel de, 43
Híjar, José Maria, 50
Hilgard, Eugene W., 240–241
Hill, Sarah Althea, 253
Hill, Thomas, 236–237
Hippie movement, 440–441
Hiss, Alger, 383–384
Hitch, Charles J., 473
Hittell, John S., 130, 159, 234
Hittell, Theodore H., 106, 234
Hockenbeamer, A. F., and letter on tactics against public power, 329
Hofmann, Hans, 451, 455
Hollywood, 308–312, 354, 454–455
Holmes, Rachel Hobson, 63
Holt, Benjamin, 200
Holt Manufacturing Company, 306
Homestead Act (1862), 181
Hoover, Herbert, 241, 323, 325, 341
Hoover Dam, 325–327

Hopkins, Mark, 168, 169, 172, 246
Hopkins, Sterling A., 123
Hounds, 115–116
House Un-American Activities Committee, 383–384, 436, 438
Housing, racial discrimination in, 195, 416–417, 464–465
Houston, James D., 448, 451
Houston, Jeanne Wakatsuki, 451
Houston, Sam, 69, 101
Howard, John Galen, 360
Howard, Volney E., 123
Howard, William A., 117
Hughes, Charles Evans, 282, 283
Humphrey, Hubert, 470–471
Humphrey, Issac, 92
Hunt, Timothy Dwight, 154
Huntington, Collis P., 168, 169, 171, 179, 183, 209, 246, 248–251, 254
Huntington, Henry E., 209–210, 320, 324
Huntington Beach oil field, 302
Huntington Library and Art Gallery, 210, 358
Huxley, Aldous, 355
Hydroelectric power, 323–325, 331–332, 509

Ickes, Harold L., 325
Ide, William B., 67, 76–77
Imperial Canal, 208, 321, 322
Imperial Irrigation District, 322
Independence League (1906), 266
Independent Taxpayers party, 254
Indian Claims Commission Act (1946), 411
Indians:
    aboriginal, 3–10
    impact of missions on, 35–38
    insurrections of, 20, 29, 34–35, 48
    oppression of, 140–142
    population of, 5–6, 38, 142
    reservations for, 137–140
    Spain's policies toward, 17–19, 40
    in the twentieth century, 410–413, 506
    (See also names of individuals)
Indo-Chinese refugees, 415
Industrial Accident Board, 276
Industrial Association of San Francisco, 292
Industrial Welfare Commission, 277
Industrial Workers of the World (IWW), 221–223, 290, 292, 338
Initiative, 264, 266, 272
International Longshoremen's Association, 339–340
Irvine Corporation, 398
Irving, Washington, 74
Ishi, 141
Ivanhoe Irrigation District, case of, and 160-acre limitation, 332

Jackson, Andrew, 69, 71
Jackson, Helen Hunt, 410–411
Jackson, Robert H., 374

James v. Marinship Corporation (1945) (blacks in labor unions), 419
Jansen, C. J., 116
Japanese and Japanese Americans:
agitation and legislation against, 278–281
literature by, 451
"relocation" of, 368–374, 413
removal of restrictions against, 413–414
(*See also names of individuals*)
Jarvis, Howard, 481, 487–491
Jayme, Luís, 30
Jazz movement, West Coast, 459–460
Jeffers, Robinson, 348–350
Jefferson Airplane, 461
Jenkins, John, 117–118
John Birch Society, 391–393, 464
Johnson, Grove L., 267, 278
Johnson, Hiram Warren:
prosecutor, 267–268, 378
governor, 223, 248, 267–268
senator, 282–283, 295, 322, 325, 364
Johnson, J. Neely, 107–108, 121–123
Johnson, Lyndon B., 393, 470, 485
Johnson, Robert Underwood, and Yosemite National Park, 316
Jones, Thomas ap Catesby, 70
Jones, William Carey, 128–129
Joplin, Janis, 461
Jordan, David Starr, 204, 241, 411
Journalism, 145–147, 234–235, 252, 355–357
Juanita (lynched at Downieville), 119
Judah, Theodore D., 166–172, 236

Kahn, Felix, 325
Kahn, Florence Prag, 423
Kaiser, Henry J., 326, 365–366
Kalloch, Isaac S., 196
Kauffman, Craig, 453
Kaweah colony, 214, 286, 316
Kearney, Denis, 191–194, 212
Kearny, Stephen W., 80–81
Keesling, Francis V., 282
Keith, William, 237–238, 455
Kelley, "General" Charles T., 288
Kemble, Edward C., 87, 146
Kennedy, Edward M., 483, 485
Kennedy, John F., 393
Kennedy, Robert F., 471
Kent, Elizabeth Thacker, 275
Kent, William, 275, 294
Kent State University, 440
Kenton, Stan, 460
Kerckhoff, William G., 320
Kern County Land Company, 398, 468
Kern County Water District, 501
Kerouac, Jack, 446–447, 452
Kerr, Clark, 404, 467
Kesey, Ken, 447
Key System, 209
Kientepoos ("Captain Jack") (Modoc leader), 141

Kimmel, Husband E., 370
King, T. Butler, 100, 102
King, Thomas Starr, 111
King of William, James, 120–122
Kings Canyon National Park, 316
Kingston, Maxine Hong, 450–451
Kino, Eusebio, 19
Kittredge, Charmian, 232
Klemperer, Otto, 459
Knight, Goodwin J., 386–388
Knight, William, 76
Knights of Labor, 213
Knowland, Joseph R., 265, 282, 287, 388
Knowland, William F., 387–389, 393, 475
Know-Nothing movement, 106, 108, 121
Knox, Frank, 369, 373
Koreans, 415
Korematsu v. United States (1944) (Japanese "relocation"), 374
Kroeber, Alfred L., 141
Ku Klux Klan, 310, 393
Kuchel, Thomas H., 393
Kuster, Una Call, 348, 349

"L.A. look" (art movement), 451, 453–455
Laffer, Arthur, and "Laffer curve," 493
La Follette, Robert M., Jr., 401
Land grants:
Mexican, 53–55, 126–131
to railroads, 170, 177–178, 180–183
to states, 103, 181
Land ownership:
Japanese denied right to, 279–281
monopoly in, 180–183
single tax proposed for, 225–227
Lane, Franklin K., 265, 318
Langdon, William H., 267
Lange, Dorothea (photographer), 353, 372
La Pérouse, Comte Jean François de, 36
Larkin, Thomas O., 62, 63, 67, 72, 75, 238
Lasky, Jesse L., 309
Lassen, Peter, 91
Lasuén, Fermín Francisco de, 35
League of Nations, 294
Leary, Timothy, 440
Le Conte, Joseph, 240
Lee, Archy, case of (1858), 143
Leese, Jacob P., 73, 76, 86
Lelia Byrd (ship), 58
Levering Act (1950) (loyalty oath), 386
Lewis, Sinclair, 354
Lincoln, Abraham, 109–111, 170
Lincoln-Roosevelt Republican League, 264–268, 270, 275, 277
Lindbergh, Charles A., 367
Lippmann, Walter, 370–371
Liquified natural gas (LNG), 506, 511
Lissner, Meyer, 264, 266
Literature, 145–154, 225–234, 348–355, 446–451
Llano del Rio (utopian colony), 287

LNG terminal site at Point Conception, 506, 511
Lobdell, Frank, 452
"Lockheed" Aircraft Company, 367, 368
Loeser, Lucien, 88
Loew, Marcus, 309
Loew's (film company), 312
London, Jack, 154, 231–232, 286–288
Lonergan, Thomas, 261
Long Valley, reservoir in, 320–321
Los Angeles:
　air pollution in, 485–486, 499
　aircraft industry in, 366–368
　architecture of, 362
　art and music in, 358–359, 453–455, 457–461
　automobiles in, 305–306
　busing controversy in, 418–419
　electric railways in, 209–210
　founding of, 33–34
　freeways in, 433
　good government movement in, 262–264, 277
　harbor fight in, 248–249
　labor in, 216–220
　land grant controversy in, 131
　Mexican Americans in, 421
　movie industry in, 308–312
　oil discoveries in, 300–303
　population growth of, 430, 498
　rail connection in, 178
　water supplies of, 319–323, 327–328
　Watts riot in, 417–418, 429, 464
Los Angeles Better American Federation, 293
Los Angeles Board of Realtors, 416
Los Angeles Bureau of Power and Light, 324
Los Angeles Conservatory of Music, 455
Los Angeles County Museum, 453, 455
Los Angeles Examiner, 218, 319–320, 323, 355–357
Los Angeles Express, 264
Los Angeles Merchants' and Manufacturers' Association, 217, 287, 293
Los Angeles Music Center, 457
Los Angeles Philharmonic Orchestra, 459
Los Angeles Police Department, 492
Los Angeles Record, 217
"Los Angeles sound" (popular music style), 460–461
Los Angeles Times, 216–220, 248, 263, 282, 319–320, 323, 357, 392, 424, 469
Los Angeles Unified School District and busing controversy, 418–419
Loughead, Allen, 367, 368
Loughead, Malcolm, 367, 368
Love, Harry, 149
Loyalty oaths, 382–386, 436
Lubin, David, 278
Lubin, Simon, 278
Lummis, Charles F., 204, 411
Lux, Charles, 182, 207
Lux v. Haggin (1886) (riparian rights), 207

Lynching (see Vigilance committees)
Lyon, Fred (photographer), 381
Lysergic acid diethylamide (LSD), 440–441, 461

McAdoo, William G., 294, 341, 345
McCarran-Walter Immigration and Nationality Act (1952), 414
McCarthy, Eugene, 438, 471
McCarthy, Joseph R., 384, 385, 401
McCarthy, Patrick Henry, 262
McCarver, M. M., 101
McCauley, Hamilton, 119
McClatchy, Charles ("C. K."), 238
McClatchy, James, 128, 235
McClatchy, Valentine S., 369
McCloy, John L., 371
McClure, S. S., 230, 231, 261
McComb, Marshall F., 466
McCracken, John, 453
McCulloch, Hugh, 58
McDougal, John, 104, 109, 119, 122–123, 137
McDougall, James A., 169–170
McGovern, George, 474–475
McKay, Donald, 90
MacKay, John W., 185, 186
McKenzie, Robert, 118
McKinney, Joseph, 128
McKittrick oil field, 301
McLaughlin, Patrick, 161
McManigal, Ortie, 218–219
McNamara, Eugene, 71–72
McNamara, James B., 219–220, 287, 289
McNamara, John J., 219–220, 287, 289
McPherson, Aimee Semple, 337–338
McWilliams, Carey, 381, 396, 400–401
Maddern, Bessie, 232
Malaspina, Alejandro, 36–37
Maloney, J. R., 123
Manifest destiny, 70
Manila galleon, 15–16
Manrique, Miguel, 29–30
Manson, Charles, 449
Manzanar relocation camp, 372, 451
Market Street Railway Company, 249–250
Marriott, Frederick, 228
Marsh, John, 64, 66–67
Marshall, James Wilson, 84–85
Marshall, Robert Bradford, and plan for Central Valley Project, 328
Martin, Glenn L., 367
Martinez, Vilma S., 424
Marx, Karl, 213
Mason, Richard B., 85, 87, 88
Masuda, Mary, 374
Matteson, Edward E., 158
Maybeck, Bernard, 359, 360
Mayer, Louis B., 309, 312, 343, 354
MediCal, 473
Mediterranean fruit fly (medfly), 504

Meese, Edwin, III, 486
Mehta, Zubin, 459
Menken, Adah Isaacs, 154, 162
Merchants' and Manufacturers' Association
    of Los Angeles, 217, 287, 293
Merchants' and Manufacturers' Association
    of Stockton, 288
Merola, Gaetano, 358
Merriam, Frank, 337, 340, 344–345
Merritt, Ezekial, 76
Metcalf, Victor H., 278
Metro-Goldwyn-Mayer, 309, 310, 312, 343
Metropolitan Water District (MWD), of
    Southern California 327–328, 501–502
Mexican War, 73, 78–82
Mexicans and Mexican Americans, 45–55
    farm laborers, 401–408
    during gold rush, 133–134
    land grant controversy and, 53–55, 126–131
    literature by, 450–451
    after 1940, 420–423
    (See also names of individuals)
Micheltorena, Manuel, 52, 70, 72, 128, 131
Midway, Battle of (1942), 373
Midway-Sunset oil field, 301
"Migrant Mother" (photograph), 353
Migration, dust bowl, 352–353, 400–401
Milhaud, Darius, 458, 460
Militia, 105, 121–123, 137, 140–141
Miller, Henry, 181–182, 207
Miller, Joaquin, 153–154
Mills, Cyrus T., 242
Mills, James R., 386
Minimum wage, 266, 277
Minter, Mary Miles, 311
Missions, 17–43, 47–51
Mitchell, John, 469, 474
Mobil Oil Corporation, 302
Modoc War (1872–1873), 141
Mofras, Eugène Duflot de, 171
Mono Lake, 503
Montalvo, Garcí Ordoñez de, 11–12
Monterey:
    constitutional convention of 1849, 99–104
    discovery of, 16–17
    founding of, 23–26
"Monterey style" of architecture, 64, 238–239
Monteux, Pierre, 459
Mooney, Rena, 289
Mooney, Thomas J., 288–290, 345
Moore, B. F., 101
Moore, Charles, 456
Moraga, Gabriel, 41
Moraga, José, 32, 41
Moretti, Robert, 472
Morgan, Julia, 356
Mormons, 85–87, 103
Morrill Land Grant College Act (1862), 240
Moscone, George, assassination of, 424
Mother lode, 91–92
Moulder, Andrew Jackson, 155

Movies, 307–312, 446, 454
Mowry, George E., 280
Muir, John, 314–318
Mulholland, William, 319–322, 324
Mulligan, William, 123
Murieta, Joaquín, 149, 153
Murphy, Frank, 374
Murphy, George, 465, 468, 472
Murray, Hugh C., 136
Music, 238, 358–359, 458–461
Music Corporation of America, 497
Mussel Slough, battle of (1880), 182–183, 230
Myrdal, Gunnar, 426

Nahl, Charles Christian, 55, 235–236
National Aeronautics and Space Administra-
    tion (NASA), 432
National Association of Manufacturers, 292
National Farm Workers Association, 405–407
National Industrial Recovery Act, 339
National Organization for Women (NOW),
    426
National Recovery Administration (NRA),
    341
Nationalist party, 255, 286
Native Sons of the Golden West, 369
Natural resources, conservation and use of,
    314–317, 495–505
Neagle, David, 253
Negroes (see Blacks)
Nemos, William, 233
Neutra, Richard, 362
Neve, Felipe de, 32–34, 47
New Deal, 268, 323, 339, 341, 344–345
New left movement, 436–444
New Melones Dam, 503
Newlands, Francis G., and Reclamation Act
    of 1902, 317, 319, 331–332, 468, 481
Newton, Huey P., 441–443
Neylan, John Francis, 271, 291–292, 340, 385
Nixon, Richard M.:
    congressman, 383–384
    senator, 384, 424
    Vice President, 388, 392
    presidential candidate, 392–393, 463, 469–471
    gubernatorial candidate, 392–393, 464, 469,
      480
    President, 431, 471–472
    Watergate crisis, 474–475
Nofziger, Lyn, 486
Nolan, Edward D., 289
Normand, Mabel, 311
Norris, Frank, 229–230, 310, 451
Norris, Kathleen Thompson, 423
North, J. W., 201
Northrop, John K., 367, 368
NOW (National Organization for Women),
    426
NRA (National Recovery Administration),
    341

Nuclear power, 483, 506–508
Nuclear Regulatory Commission (NRC), 507

Oak, Henry L., 232–234
Oakland:
    antiwar demonstrations in, 438
    black radicalism in, 441
    founding of, 131
    impact of Proposition 13 on, 492
    port facilities of, 433
    waterfront monopoly in, 177
Oakland Museum, 455
Oakland Symphony Orchestra, 459
Oakland Transcript, 226
Oakland Tribune, 378, 388
Oakland Waterfront Company, 177
O'Brien, William S., 185, 186
Occidental and Oriental Steamship Company, 179
O'Donnell, Charles C., 195
O'Hare, Kate Richards, 424
Oil embargo (1973), 505
Oil industry, 299–304, 505
"Old Block" (Alonzo Delano), 148
Older, Fremont, 260–262, 291
Olmsted, Frederick Law, 314
Olson, Culbert L., 341, 344–345, 370, 378, 401, 424
OPEC (Organization of Petroleum Exporting Countries), 505
Open shop, "American Plan" for, 292
Ophir mine, 186
O'Riley, Peter, 161
Oroville Dam, 391
Otis, Harrison Gray, 216–220, 222, 248, 252, 263–264, 282, 286, 287, 320, 357, 358
Otis Art Institute, 358
Otter (ship), 57
Overland Monthly, 150–151, 154, 231
Owens Valley–Los Angeles Aqueduct, 319–321, 324
Oxnard, Henry, 200
Oxnard, Robert, 200
Ozawa, Seiji, 459

Pacheco, Romualdo, 49
Pacific Coast Oil Company, 302
Pacific Electric Railway Company, 209–210, 320
Pacific Gas and Electric Company (PG&E), 259, 288, 324, 329–331, 382, 400, 412, 503, 506–511
Pacific Light and Power Company, 324
Pacific Mail Steamship Company, 171, 179
Pacific Railroad Act, 170
Padrés, José María, 49, 50
Palace of Fine Arts, San Francisco, 358
Palace Hotel, 185
Palmer, A. Mitchell, 291

Palóu, Francisco, 22, 23, 26, 35
Panama Pacific Exposition, San Diego (1915), 361–362
Panama Pacific International Exposition, San Francisco (1913), 280, 360
Panama Star, 89
Pan-American Petroleum Company, 302
Paramount Pictures, 311, 312
Pardee, George C., 265, 284
Park, David, 452
Parker, Walter, 265
Parkinson, Gaylord, 464
Pasadena Art Museum, 455
Pattie, James Ohio, 61–62
Pattie, Sylvester, 61
Payne-Aldrich Tariff (1909), 268
People v. Hall (1854) (exclusion of Chinese testimony), 136
People's Park controversy, Berkeley (1969), 439–440
People's party, San Francisco, 124
People's (Populist) party, 255
"People's Railroad," 245
Peralta, Luis, 131
Peralta, Vicente, 131
Pereira, William, 457
Pérouse (see La Pérouse)
Pesticides, 504
Petaluma growth-control ordinance (1973), 497
Peripheral Canal, 501–503
Phelan, James D., 245, 260, 282
    mayor of San Francisco, 258, 317, 318
    senator, 282, 293–294
Philbrick, Howard R., 380
Phillips 66 (oil company), 302
Phipps, Lawrence C., and public power, 325
"Phoenix, John" (George H. Derby), 148–149
"Pick handle brigade" (1877), 191
Pickford, Mary, 309
Pico, Andrés, 80–81, 109, 111
Pico, Pío, 46, 52, 72, 79, 128, 131
Pinchot, Gifford, 316–317, 320
Placerita Creek gold discovery (1842), 84
Plagens, Peter, 453
Planning and Conservation League, 501, 502
Plessy v. Ferguson (1896) (racial segregation), 418
Point Conception, LNG terminal site at, 506, 511
Political Reform Act (1974), 479
Polk, James K., 71–73, 75, 78, 81, 88
Polk, Willis, 359–360
Pony Express, 164
Poole, Alonzo W., 183
"Pop art," 453–455
Populist movement, 255
Porter, Edwin E. (film producer), 307
Portolá, Gaspar de, 19, 23–26
Post, A. Alan, 474
Powell, John Wesley, 321

Power:
  geothermal, 509–510
  hydroelectric, 323–325, 331–332, 509
  nuclear, 483, 506–508
  wind, 508–510
Prat, Pedro, 23, 24
Pre-emption Act of 1841, 181
Preparedness Day parade and bombing, San Francisco (1916), 288–290
Preston, John W., 411
Progressive party, 273, 282–283
Prohibition, 275–276, 294
Proposition 1 (1973) (Reagan tax initiative), 474, 479
Proposition 4 (1979) (government spending limitation), 489, 493
Proposition 9 (1980) (income tax reduction), 489–490
Proposition 13 (1978) (property tax reduction), 481, 482, 486–493, 498
Proposition 14 (1964) (rejection of Rumford Act), 417, 464–465
Proposition 15 (1976) (nuclear plant regulation), 507
Prudon, Victor, 113–114
Public Utilities Commission (PUC), 271, 508–511

Racial discrimination in housing, 195, 416–417, 464–465
Radio-Keith-Orpheum (RKO), 312
Rafferty, Max, 420
Railroad regulation, 196, 271
Raker, John E., and Raker Act concerning Hetch Hetchy, 318, 324
Ralston, William Chapman, 184–186
Rancho Seco nuclear power plant, 506
Rattigan, Joseph A., 434
Reagan, Nancy, 449
Reagan, Ronald:
  background, 394, 463–465
  governor, 406, 407, 418, 465–468, 471–475, 478, 479, 489
  presidential candidate, 468–471, 475–476, 485–486
  President, 486, 493, 496, 497, 500, 504
Reapportionment of state legislature, 296–297, 434, 472, 498
Recall, 264, 266, 272, 273
Reclamation Act of 1902, 317, 319, 331–332, 468, 481
Reconstruction Finance Corporation, 328
Red Light Abatement Act (1913), 276
Redwood National Park, 496
Reed, Ishmael, 449–450
Referendum, 264, 266, 272
Refugees:
  Indo-Chinese, 415
  Vietnamese, 415
Reid, Hugo, 37

Reid, Wallace, 311
Reinecke, Ed, 479
Relocation camps:
  Manzanar, 372, 451
  Tule Lake, 372
Reservations for Indians, 137–140
Rexroth, Kenneth, 446
Reyes, Inocencia, 79–80
Reynolds, Malvina, 432
Reynolds v. Sims (1964) ("one man, one vote"), 434
Rezanov, Nikolai Petrovich, 41–42
Richardson, Friend W., 295–296
Richardson, William A., 86
Richardson, William H., 121
Richfield Oil Corporation, 302
Ricketts, Edward F., 353
Ridge, John Rollin ("Yellow Bird"), 149
"Right to work," 216–220, 287, 388–389
Riles, Wilson, 420
Riley, Bennet, 99, 101
Rivera y Moncada, Fernando, 23–24, 30–32, 34–35
RKO (Radio-Keith-Orpheum), 312
Roberts, Owen J., and report on Pearl Harbor, 369–370
Robinson, Alfred, 62, 67–68
Rockefeller, Nelson, 393, 468, 470
Rogers, Harrison G., 60
Rogers, Will, 294
Rolling Stones, 460, 461
Rolph, James, Jr., 296, 336–337
Roman, Anton, 150
Roney, Frank, 213
Ronstadt, Linda, 483, 484
Roosevelt, Franklin D., 325, 327, 341, 371, 414
Roosevelt, James, 379
Roosevelt, Theodore, 260
  and California progressives, 266–267, 271, 273, 278–279, 281–282
  and conservation, 316–317, 320
  and Japan, 278–279
Ross, A. W., 305
Rossi, Angelo, 340
Rosten, Leo, 309
Rothko, Mark, 452, 453
Rousselot, John, 392
Rowell, Chester H., 222, 266, 279, 284, 379
Rowland, John, 67
Roybal, Edward R., 422
Royce, Josiah, 46, 102, 114, 124, 234
Rubel, A. C., 464
Rubin, Jerry, 438–439, 444
Ruef, Abraham, 216, 257–262, 265, 267, 275, 318
Rumford Act (1963) (open housing law), 417, 464
Ruscha, Edward, 453–455
Ryan, Arabella ("Belle Cora"), 121–122
Ryan, T. Claude, 367

Sacramento Bee, 235
Sacramento Municipal Utilities District, 331
Sacramento Valley Railroad, 166–167
Salvatori, Henry, 464, 468
Salzman, Ed, 492
Samish, Arthur H., 380–381
San Diego:
    aircraft industry in, 368
    discovery of, 12–13
    labor relations in, 222
    native cultures of, 7
    nuclear power for, 506, 507
    population growth in, 430, 498
    solar water heating requirement for, 509
San Diego Gas and Electric Company, 507
San Francisco:
    air pollution in, 499
    culture of, 145–147, 357–358
    discovery of, 25
    earthquake and fire (1906) in, 259–260
    founding of, 28–32
    "freeway revolt" of, 432
    "golden age" of painting in, 451–452
    graft prosecution in, 259–262, 267
    Haight-Ashbury district, 441, 448, 449, 461
    labor in, 190–197, 213, 288–289, 339–340
    population growth in, 430, 498
    United Railroads of (*see* United Railroads of
        San Francisco)
    vigilance committees in, 115–118, 120–124
    water supply of, 317–319, 324
    waterfront control in, 177–178
    Workingmen's party activities in, 190–194,
        196
San Francisco Art Institute, 452
San Francisco Asian Art Museum, 456
San Francisco Bay Conservation and Devel-
    opment Commission (BCDC), 495
San Francisco Bulletin, 120, 147, 178, 234, 222,
    260, 271
San Francisco Call, 147, 193, 257, 291
San Francisco Chronicle, 193, 196, 234, 357, 502
San Francisco Consolidation Act, 124
San Francisco Examiner, 234–235, 250, 355, 357
San Francisco Franchise League, 168
San Francisco General Strike (1934), 339–340
San Francisco Herald, 226
San Francisco Museum of Art, 358
San Francisco News, 352
San Francisco News Letter, 228
San Francisco Opera, 459
San Francisco Performing Arts Center, 459
"San Francisco Renaissance" (poetry move-
    ment), 446
San Francisco State College, 439
San Francisco Symphony Orchestra, 459
San José:
    founding of, 32–33
    lynching in, 336–337
    mayoral election of, 424
    population growth in, 497

San José State College, 450
San Onofre nuclear power plant, 506
San Pascual, battle of (1846), 80
San Simeon ("Hearst's castle"), 355–357, 361
Sanborn, Henry, 400
Sánchez, George I., 420
Sánchez, José Bernardo, 60
Santa Anna, Anotonio López de, 69
Santa Barbara:
    campus turmoil in, 440
    native cultures of, 6, 10
    oil spill (1969), 496, 505
Santa Barbara News-Press, 392
Santa Fe Railroad, 204, 245
Santa Fe Springs oil field, 302–303
Sargent, Aaron A., 169, 247, 274
Sargent, Ellen Clark, 247
Saroyan, William, 354–355
Savio, Mario, 438
Saxon, David S., 490
Scannell, David, 121
Schenley Industries, 398, 406
Schindler, R. M., 362
Schmitz, Eugene E., 258, 262, 278
Schoenberg, Arnold, 458–460
Scott, Howard, 337
Scott, Thomas A., 299–300
Scripps, Edward W., 217
SDS (Students for a Democratic Society), 438
Sea Ranch housing development, 456
Seal of the state, 103–104
Seale, Bobby G., 441–442, 444
Secularization of missions, 19, 47–51
Securities and Exchange Commission, 430
Segregation in education, 278, 418–419
Selig, William (film producer), 307–308
Selznick, Lewis J., 309
Semple, Robert, 76, 102–103, 146
Sequoia National Park, 214, 316
Sequoya League, 411
Serra, Junípero, 21–35
Serrano v. Ivy Baker Priest (1971) (public school
    finance), 473
Shaler, William, 58, 59
Shannon, William E., 101
Sharon, William, 184–186, 253
Shasta Dam, 329–331
Shaw, George Bernard, 286
Shell Oil Company, 302, 501
Shelley v. Kraemer (1948) (fair housing), 416
Sherman, William Tecumseh, 121–123
Shima, George, 279
Shipbuilding industry, 365–366
"Shirley letters," 147–149
Short, Walter C., 370
Shortridge, Samuel M., 294
Shuler, Robert P., 337
Shulman, David, 491
Sierra Club, 316, 495, 503
Sierra National Forest, 320
Signal Hill oil field, 303

Silliman, Benjamin, Jr., 299–300
Simon, Norton, 398, 455
Simpson, George, 71
Sinclair, Harry F., 303
Sinclair, Upton, 292, 341–344, 382
Single tax, 225–227
Six Companies, Chinese, 189–190
"Six Companies, Inc." (engineering and construction firms), 325–326
"Sleepy Lagoon" murder trial (1942), 421, 450
Slick, Grace, 461
Slidell, John, 72, 78
Sloat, John D., 78–79
Smith, Alfred E., 294
Smith, Francis Marion ("Borax"), 209
Smith, Gladys (Mary Pickford), 309
Smith, Hassel, 452
Smith, Jedediah Strong, 60–61
Smith, Paul C., 357
Smith, Persifor F., 89
Smith, William French, 486
Smog, 455, 485, 499–501
Social Security Act (1935), 344
Socialism, 213–215, 255, 262, 324
    rise and fall of movement, 286–288, 290–292
    of Upton Sinclair, 341–344
Solá, Pablo Vicente de, 54
Solar energy, 508–509, 511
Southern California Edison Company, 324, 506, 509–511
Southern California Gas Company, 506
Southern California Rapid Transit District, 433
Southern Pacific Land Company, 302, 501
Southern Pacific Railroad, 177–178, 182–183, 204–205, 245–255, 264, 266, 268, 271, 302, 411, 491
Speer, William, 154
Spencer, Herbert, 226, 231
Spoor, George K., 307
Spreckles, Claus, 163, 200, 245
Spreckles, John D., 222, 245, 252
Spreckles, Rudolph, 260, 295
Spring Valley Water Company, San Francisco, 317
Sproul, Robert Gordon, 413
Sproul Hall, student demonstration at (1964), 437, 467
Squires, Radcliffe, 350
Stackpole, Ralph, 238
Standard Oil Company, 245, 301–302, 454
    of California, 302, 491
Stanford, Leland, 108, 110, 111, 168, 169, 171, 172, 174, 177, 179, 183, 236, 241, 247–248
Stanford University, 241, 431, 440, 447
Stearns, Abel, 62–63, 73, 203
Steffens, Lincoln, 219–220, 261–262, 264, 266
Steinbeck, John, 350–354, 400, 448, 451
Stephens, Henry Morse, 241
Stephens, William D., 283, 289–290

Stevenson, Adlai E., 383, 387
Stevenson, J. D., 99, 115
Still, Clyfford, 452, 453
Stilwell, Joseph W., 374
Stimson, Henry L., 371
Stimson, Marshall, 264
Stockton, Robert F., 79–81
Stoneman, George B., 196
Storke, Thomas M., 392
Stravinsky, Igor, 458, 459
Strobridge, J. H., 172
Stroheim, Erich von, 310
Strong, Daniel W., 167
Strong, Edward W., 467
Stuart, James ("English Jim"), 116, 118
Studebaker, John, 163
Student attitudes toward education, 443
Students for a Democratic Society (SDS), 438
Suhr, Herman, 223
Sullivan, Louis H., 361, 362
Sumner, William Graham, 466
Sundesert proposed nuclear reactor, 507
Sunkist Growers, Inc., 202–203
Sutro, Adolph, 185, 186, 245, 249–250
Sutter, John A., 64–65, 76, 84–85
Swett, John, 155
Swing, Phil, and Boulder Canyon Project, 322, 323

Taft, Robert A., 379, 388
Tahoe Regional Planning Agency, 496
Taney, Roger B., 130
Taxation, 109, 225–227, 305, 336, 471–474, 481–482, 486–493
    foreign miners' license tax, 133–134
Taylor, Bayard, 145
Taylor, Zachary, 78, 99–100, 102
Teague, Charles C., 203
Teapot Dome naval oil reserve, 304
Technicolor Corporation, 472
Technocracy, 337
Television, 312, 446, 469, 486
Tenneco, 501
Tenney, Jack B., 384–385
Terry, David S., 108–109, 123, 253
Tevis, Lloyd, 302
Tevis, William S., 318
Texas Company, 302
Thieriot, Charles de Young, 357
Thompson, Waddy, 70
Three Mile Island nuclear plant accident (1979), 483, 507
Tidewater Oil Company of New Jersey, 302
Tolman v. Underhill (1952) (loyalty oath case), 386
Torre, Joaquín de la, 77
Townsend, Francis E., and Townsend Plan, 338, 344
Toxic wastes, 504–505
Treaty of Guadaloupe Hidalgo, 82, 131

Trudeau, Garry, 483–484
Truman, Harry S, 382, 392
Tule Lake relocation camp, 372
Tunney, John, 444, 472
Turnbull, William, 456
Turner, Frederick Jackson, 181
Tuttle, Holmes, 464
Twain, Mark, 149, 151–152, 503
Twentieth Century-Fox, 312, 352, 454
Tyler, John, 78

Union Iron Works, 163
Union Labor Party of San Francisco, 216, 257–262
Union Oil Company of California, 301, 302, 328, 496
Union Pacific Railroad, 170, 174
United Artists, 312
United Farm Workers, 416
United Railroads of San Francisco, 210, 259, 261, 275, 289
U.S. Bureau of Reclamation, 329, 331
Universal Pictures, 312
Unruh, Jesse, 417, 465, 471
Unruh Civil Rights Act (1959), 417
Utopian Society, 337–338

Valdez, Luis, 450
Vallecitos nuclear power plant, 506
Vallejo, Mariano Guadalupe, 46, 48–50, 52, 55, 65, 73, 76, 100, 104
Van Buren, Martin, 69
Vancouver, George, 39
Van Ness, James, 121
Vasconcelos, José, 421
Vasquez, José Tiburcio, 33
Victor, Frances Fuller, 233
Victoria, Manuel, 49, 63
Vietnam War, 415, 429, 431, 438, 441, 443, 469, 485
Vietnamese refugees, 415
Vigilance committees, 113–124, 222, 288, 336–337, 340, 352
Vignes, Jean Louis, 200
Villareal, José Antonio, 450, 451
Vinson, Frederick M., 379
Virginia City Territorial Enterprise, 151–152
Vizcaino, Sebastián, 16–17, 28
Vogel v. County of Los Angeles (1967) (loyalty oath case), 386
Voorhis, Jerry, 383
Vuich, Rose A., 424

Wage, minimum, 266, 277
Walker, Franklin, 145
Walker, Joseph Reddeford, 62
Wallace, A. J., 275
Wallace, George, 469

Wanzer, Lucy Maria Field, 274
War Relocation Authority, 372, 374, 413
Warner Brothers, 312
Warren, Earl:
  attorney general, 361, 371
  governor, 378–381, 385–387, 390, 475
  Chief Justice, 379, 386, 392, 418, 430, 434
Warren, James Lloyd La Fayaette, 163
Wasp (magazine), 180, 193, 228
Water supplies and projects, 206–208, 317–332, 390–391, 501–503
Watergate scandal, 393, 474–475, 479
Waterman, Thomas T., 141
Waters, Frank, and Hoover Dam, 326
Watt, James, 497, 505
Watts riot in Los Angeles (1965), 417–418, 429, 464
Webb, Ulysses S., 280, 369
Webster, Daniel, 70, 105
Weinberg, Israel, 289
Weinberger, Caspar, 486
Weinstock, Harris, 277
Welch, Robert, 392
Welfare, 472–473, 476, 486
Weller, John B., 119, 137, 138
Wells, Fargo & Company, 160, 171
West, Nathanael, 355, 448, 449
West Coast jazz movement, 459–460
Western Pacific Railroad, 245
Wheatland riot (1913), 222–223, 277
Whitaker, Clem, 381–382, 386
White, Stephen M., 248, 255
Whitney, Asa, 166
Whitney, Charlotte Anita, 291–292, 385
Whitney, Josiah D., 314, 315
Whittaker, Samuel, 118
Wiggin, Kate Douglas, 239
Wilbur, Ray Lyman, 325
Willard, Charles Dwight, 263
Wilmot Proviso, 99, 105
Wilshire, H. Gaylord, 286–287
Wilshire's Magazine, 286
Wilson, Benjamin D., 67
Wilson, J. Stitt, 268, 287, 288
Wilson, Woodrow, 280, 289, 293, 310, 318
Wind power, 508–510
Windred, William, 116
Wolfe, Linnie Marsh, 315
Wolfskill, William, 62, 200
Women:
  appointment of, 424–425
  constitution of 1849 and, 103
  electoral politics and, 423–424
  employment patterns of, 425–426
  equal rights amendment (ERA), 426
  equal suffrage, 266, 274–275
  minimum wage for, 266, 277
  in native cultures, 4, 6
  in Spanish and Mexican periods, 18, 35, 37, 54
  (See also names of individuals)

Women's Christian Temperance Union, 274
Woods, "Gusher Charlie," 301
Wool, John E., 123
Workingmen's party of California, 190–196, 212
Workmen, William, 67
Workmen's compensation, 266, 276, 407
Wozencraft, Oliver M., 138
Wright, Frank Lloyd, 361, 362
Wright, William ("Dan De Quille"), 151–152
Wright Irrigation Act (1887), 207

"Yellow Bird" (John Rollin Ridge), 149
Yerba Buena, 86
Yosemite National Park, 314–316, 318, 497

Yosemite Valley, discovery of, 62
Young, Al, 449
Young, Brigham, 86
Young, Clement C., 292, 295
Young, Ewing, 62
Younger, Evelle, 481–482
Yuma massacre (1781), 34–35

Zalvidea, José Maria, 38, 60
Zamorano, Agustín, 49
Zanuck, Darryl, 352
"Zero Interest Plan," 508–509
Zola, Emile, 229
"Zoot suit" riots (1943), 421, 450
Zukor, Adolph, 309

(*continued from front cover*)

GOVERNORS OF CALIFORNIA | EVENTS IN CALIFORNIA HISTORY

Governors of California	Events in California History	Year
Newton Booth, Rep.	Los Angeles anti-Chinese riot	1871
	Modoc Indian War	1873
Romualdo Pacheco, Rep.		1875
William Irwin, Dem.		
	Workingmen's Party formed	1877
	New constitution	1879
George C. Perkins, Rep.	Battle of Mussel Slough	1880
	Los Angeles Times founded	1881
George Stoneman, Dem.		1883
	Santa Fe Railroad to L.A.	1885
Washington Bartlett, Dem.		1887
Robert W. Waterman, Rep.		
		1889
Henry H. Markham, Rep.	Stanford University opened	1891
	Sierra Club founded	1892
		1893
James H. Budd, Dem.		1895
		1897
Henry T. Gage, Rep.		1899
	Ruef and Schmitz in power	1901
		1902
George C. Pardee, Rep.		1903
	San Francisco Graft Prosecution	1906
James N. Gillett, Rep.	Lincoln-Roosevelt League formed	1907
		1909
	Republican Progressives sweep the state elections	1910
Hiram W. Johnson, Rep.	Ishi "discovered"	1911
	Los Angeles Aqueduct	1913
Hiram W. Johnson (as Prog.)		1915
	Preparedness Parade bombing	1916
William D. Stephens, Rep.		1917
	Criminal Syndicalism Law	1919
		1921
Friend W. Richardson, Rep.		1923
Clement C. Young, Rep.		1927
	First Academy Awards	1929
James Rolph, Jr., Rep.		1931
	Central Valley Project Act	1933
Frank F. Merriam, Rep.	Merrian defeats Sinclair	1934
Culbert L. Olson, Dem.	*Grapes of Wrath* published	1939
		1941
	Japanese evacuation	1942
Earl Warren, Rep.		1943
		1945
		1950
Goodwin J. Knight, Rep.		1953
Edmund G. Brown, Dem.		1959
	California Water Bonds	1960
		1961
	Rumford Fair-Housing Act	1963
	Berkeley Free Speech Movement	1964
	Watts riot	1965
Ronald Reagan, Rep.		1967
	People's Park riot	1969
	BART opened	1972
		1973
		1974
Edmund G. Brown, Jr., Dem.	Agricultural Relations Act	1975
		1977
	Proposition 13	1978
	Medfly infestation	1981
	Peripheral Canal rejected	1982